LEARN HOW THIS BOOK CAN HELP YOU UNDERSTAND U.S. HISTORY

See pages xxii–xxvii.

Memorizing facts and dates for a history class won't get you very far. That's because history isn't just about "facts." This textbook is designed to help you focus on what's truly significant in U.S. history and to give you practice in thinking like a historian.

> Why did Congress object to Lincoln's wartime plan for reconstruction?

> How did the North respond to the passage of black codes in the southern states?

> How radical was congressional reconstruction?

> What brought the elements of the South's Republican coalition together?

> Why did reconstruction collapse?

> Conclusion: Was reconstruction "a revolution but half accomplished"?

The **chapter-opening questions** are also the questions that open each new section of the chapter and will be

Voting day, June 5, 1867. Black freedmen line up to vote in Washington, D.C. The Granger Collection, New York.

How to use this book to figure out what's really important

The **chapter title** tells you the subject of the chapter and identifies the time span that will be covered.

The **opening question** and **chapter introduction** identify the most important themes, events, and people that will be explored in the chapter.

16
RECONSTRUCTING A NATION
1863–1877

> What were the achievements and failures of reconstruction? Chapter 16 explores the era of reconstruction, in which the nation struggled to define the defeated South's status and the meaning of freedom for ex-slaves. Following the Civil War, the nation entered one of its most confused and violent periods as victorious

The Chapter Study Guide provides a process that will build your understanding and your historical skills.

> ## CHAPTER 16 STUDY GUIDE

STEP 1 Go online to complete the chapter's LearningCurve activity.

GET STARTED ONLINE

✓ LearningCurve • bedfordstmartins.com/roarkunderstanding
Now that you've read the chapter, make it stick by completing the LearningCurve activity.

STEP 2 Identify the key terms and explain their significance.

EXPLAIN WHY IT MATTERS

Put your reading into practice. Identify each term below, and then explain why it matters in U.S. history.

TERM	WHO OR WHAT & WHEN	WHY IT MATTERS
Freedmen's Bureau (p. 460)		
black codes (p. 463)		
Civil Rights Act of 1866 (p. 465)		
Fourteenth Amendment (p. 466)		
Military Reconstruction Act (p. 468)		
Fifteenth Amendment (p. 469)		
carpetbaggers (p. 472)		
scalawags (p. 472)		
Ku Klux Klan (p. 473)		
sharecropping (p. 474)		
Redeemers (p. 479)		
Compromise of 1877 (p. 482)		

STEP 3 Analyze differences and similarities among ideas, events, people, or societies discussed in the chapter.

MOVE BEYOND THE BASICS

To demonstrate a more advanced understanding, indicate below how each phase of reconstruction addressed the key issues involved.

Phase of reconstruction	Requirements for readmission	Role/rights of freedman	Achievements	Failures
Wartime reconstruction (Lincoln)				
Presidential reconstruction (Johnson)				
Congressional reconstruction				

484

"The pedagogical tools in *Understanding the American Promise* are superior."
—Tim Myers, Butler Community College

Understanding
the American Promise

A HISTORY

SECOND EDITION

Volume II
From 1865

James L. Roark
Emory University

Michael P. Johnson
Johns Hopkins University

Patricia Cline Cohen
*University of California,
Santa Barbara*

Sarah Stage
Arizona State University

Susan M. Hartmann
The Ohio State University

Bedford/St. Martin's
Boston • New York

For Bedford/St. Martin's

Publisher for History: Mary V. Dougherty
Executive Editor for History: William J. Lombardo
Director of Development for History: Jane Knetzger
Developmental Editor: Kathryn Abbott
Senior Production Editor: Karen S. Baart
Assistant Production Manager: Joe Ford
Executive Marketing Manager: Sandra McGuire
Associate Editors: Jack Cashman, Jennifer Jovin
Editorial Assistant: Emily DiPietro
Production Assistants: Elise Keller, Kim Lester
Copyeditor: Linda McLatchie
Indexer: Leoni Z. McVey, McVey & Associates, Inc.
Photo Researchers: Pembroke Herbert and Sandi Rygiel, Picture Research Consultants, Inc.
Senior Art Director: Anna Palchik
Text Designer: Cenveo Publisher Services
Cover Designer: Donna Lee Dennison
Cover Art: Yolanda Gonzalez, *La Familia.* Acrylic on canvas.
Cartography: Mapping Specialists, Limited
Composition: Cenveo Publisher Services
Printing and Binding: RR Donnelley and Sons

President, Bedford/St. Martin's: Denise B. Wydra
Director of Marketing: Karen R. Soeltz
Production Director: Susan W. Brown
Director of Rights and Permissions: Hilary Newman

Manufactured in the United States of America.

4 5 6   17 16 15

For information, write: Bedford/St. Martin's, 75 Arlington Street, Boston, MA 02116   (617-399-4000)

ISBN: 978–1–4576–3979–1 (Combined Edition)
ISBN: 978–1–4576–6414–4 (Loose-leaf Edition)
ISBN: 978–1–4576–3980–7 (Volume I)
ISBN: 978–1–4576–6415–1 (Loose-leaf Edition, Volume I)

ISBN: 978–1–4576–3982–1 (Volume II)
ISBN: 978–1–4576–6413–7 (Loose-leaf Edition, Volume II)
ISBN: 978–1–4576–6255–3 (High School Edition)

Acknowledgments

Page 553: From "Expulsion of the Immigrants" by Huang Zunxian, translated by J. D. Schmidt in *Waiting for the Unicorn: Poems and Lyrics of China's Last Dynasty, 1644–1911* by Irving Yucheng Lo and William Schultz. Copyright © 1986 by William Rudolph Schultz and Irving Yucheng Lo. Reprinted with permission of Indiana University Press.

Pages 704–05: "Pretty Boy Floyd." Lyrics and music by Woody Guthrie. Copyright © 1983 (Renewed 1991) WOODY GUTHRIE PUBLICATIONS (BMI)/Administration by BIG MUSIC. All Rights Reserved. Used by Permission. Reprinted by Permission of Hal Leonard Corporation.

PREFACE: Why This Book This Way

Understanding the American Promise grew out of many conversations over the last decade among ourselves and with others about the teaching and learning of history. We knew that instructors wanted a U.S. history text that introduced students to overarching trends and developments but at the same time gave voice to the diverse people who have made American history. We also knew that instructors wanted a text demonstrating that history is a discipline rooted in debate and inquiry. At the same time, we knew that even though many students dutifully read their survey texts, they often come away overwhelmed and confused about what is most important to know. Because of the difficulty many students have understanding the most important concepts when they read a traditional U.S. survey text, a growing number of instructors thought that their students needed a brief text that did not overwhelm them with detail. Instructors also wanted a text that would help students focus as they read, keep their interest in the material, and encourage them to learn historical thinking skills.

With these issues in mind, we took a hard look at the introductory course from a number of different directions. We reflected on the changes in our own classrooms, reviewed state-of-the-art scholarship on effective teaching, consulted learning experts and instructional designers, and talked to students and instructors about their needs. We talked to people who are teaching online and listened to instructors' wish lists for time-saving support materials. Understanding the American Promise is a textbook designed to address these wide-ranging concerns. With the second edition, we again combine an abridged narrative with an innovative design and unique pedagogy orchestrated to work together to aid students' understanding of the most important developments while also fostering students' ability to think historically. A number of revisions and additions make the second edition an even better tool for this textbook designed for understanding.

Because, like other instructors, we are eager to ensure students read and assimilate this rich material, we are excited to announce that the second edition of Understanding the American Promise comes with **LearningCurve**—an adaptive game-like online learning tool that helps students master content. The second edition also introduces **LaunchPad,** a new robust interactive e-book built into its own course space that makes customizing and assigning the book and its resources easy and efficient. To learn more about the benefits of LearningCurve and LaunchPad, see the "Versions and Supplements" section on page ix.

An Inquiry-based Model Designed for Understanding

By employing innovative pedagogy, we believe that Understanding the American Promise helps students not only understand the book's major developments but also begin to grasp the question-driven methodology that is at the heart of the historian's craft. Each chapter opens with a **NEW chapter-opening question** that drives students toward the overarching themes of the chapter, followed by a **brief chapter introduction** that identifies in simple, straightforward terms the most important events and people to be discussed. **Section-opening headings** expressed as questions and **section-ending quick review** questions further model the kinds of questions historians ask and help students engage in inquiry-based reading and understanding.

Chapter Study Guides Designed for Active Learning

At the core of *Understanding the American Promise*'s unique pedagogical features are the revised **Chapter Study Guides** that provide a carefully structured four-step process to help students build deep understanding of the chapter material. In **Step One,** students go online to complete the LearningCurve activity to ensure that they have a grasp of the basic content and concepts of the chapter. In **Step Two,** students not only identify the chapter's key terms but also explain why each matters. In **Step Three,** they begin to apply their understanding of the chapter material through activities that ask them to consider comparison, change-over-time, or cause and effect. In **Step Four,** analytical and synthetic questions require students to engage in higher-order historical thinking. And, finally, in an active recitation exercise, students **answer the chapter-opening question** to fully realize their understanding of the chapter.

Visual Learning Aids

Throughout each chapter, a wide range of visual material keeps students' attention and reinforces important concepts. Some narrative material has been moved into **figures and tables** to call out and organize certain concepts visually and provide an alternative mode of learning. Two **map activities** per chapter engage students in reading maps and making connections and thus enhance geographical literacy. In total, there are over 165 maps in the book. A **visual activity** in each chapter reinforces the role of images as historical evidence. Many of the 300-plus images in the book are historical artifacts that underscore the importance of material culture.

Additional Pedagogical Features

The second edition includes several other helpful learning tools. As mentioned earlier, the **NEW LearningCurve online adaptive activity** is designed to prepare students for class by reinforcing their work reading the textbooks. **Section-based chronologies** of historical developments help students keep events in context as they read. Because students often have difficulty seeing the forest for the trees, innovative **chapter locators** at the foot of the page remind students of where they are in the chapter's larger progression of events and concepts. **Key terms** highlighted in the text and then defined in the margins further remind students of what's most important to know.

Updated Scholarship

In our ongoing effort to offer a comprehensive text that braids all Americans into the national narrative and to frame that narrative in a more global perspective, we updated the second edition in many ways. We have paid particular attention to the most recent scholarship and, as always, appreciated and applied many suggestions from our users that keep the book fresh, accurate, and organized in a way that works best for students.

Volume I draws on exciting new scholarship on Native Americans, leading to enhanced coverage of Pontiac's Rebellion in chapter 6 and more attention to Indians and their roles in the conflict between the British and the colonists in chapter 7. Chapter 9 expands the coverage of American interactions with Indians in the Southwest, adding new material on Creek chief Alexander McGillivray. Chapter 10 greatly increases the coverage of Indians in the West, with a new section devoted to the Osage territory and the powerful Comanche empire known as Comanchería.

Volume II also includes expanded attention to Native Americans—particularly in Chapter 17, where we improved coverage of Indian schools, assimilation techniques used by whites, and Indian resistance strategies. For the second edition, we also provide more coverage of women, African Americans, and the global context of U.S. history. In the narrative, we consider the ways in which the GI Bill disproportionately benefited white men after World War II. Chapter 16 includes new coverage of the Colfax massacre, arguably the single worst incidence of brutality against African Americans during the Reconstruction era. Chapter 27 provides new coverage of civil rights activism in northern states.

Because students live in an increasingly global world and need help making connections with the world outside the United States, we have continued our efforts to incorporate the global context of American history throughout the second edition. This is particularly evident in Volume II, where we have expanded coverage of transnational issues in recent decades, such as the U.S. bombing campaign in Vietnam and U.S. involvement in Afghanistan.

In addition to the many changes noted above, in both volumes we have updated, revised, and improved this second edition in response to both new scholarship and requests from instructors. New and expanded coverage areas include, among others, taxation in the pre-Revolutionary period and the early Republic, the Newburgh Conspiracy of the 1780s, the overbuilding of railroads in the West during the Gilded Age, the 1918–1919 global influenza epidemic, finance reform in the 1930s, post–World War II considerations of universal health care, Latino activism, the economic downturn of the late 2000s, the most recent developments in the Middle East, and the Obama presidency.

Acknowledgments

We gratefully acknowledge all of the helpful suggestions from those who have read or taught from the previous edition of *Understanding the American Promise*, and we hope that our many classroom collaborators will be pleased to see their influence in the second edition. In particular, we wish to thank the talented scholars and teachers who gave generously of their time and knowledge to review this book: Brittany Adams, *Irvine Valley College*; John Bradford Bowers, *Pueblo Community College*; Vincent A. Clark, *Johnson County Community College*; Jane Dabel, *California State University–Long Beach*; Diane Duray, *Howard Community College*; Michael J. Engle, *Pueblo Community College*; Keith A. Erekson, *University of Texas–El Paso*; Josh Fulton, *Valley Community College*; Jessica Gerard, *Ozarks Technical Community College*; Geoffrey R. Hunt, *Community College of Aurora*; Josh Lieser, *MiraCosta College*; Steven Lurenz, *Mesa Community College*; Jeffrey J. Malanson, *Indiana University-Purdue University–Fort Wayne*; Tim

Myers, *Butler Community College*; Marjorie Moss Nash, *Alvin Community College*; Brian D. Page, *Edison State College*; Jessica Patton, *Tarrant County College*; Carmen Reys-Johnson, *Northeast Lakeview College*; Norman Rodriguez, *John Wood Community College*; Mark Roehrs, *Lincoln Land Community College*; Nancy E. Shockley, *Oakland Community College*; Allen N. Smith, Jr., *Ivy Tech Community College*; Adam M. Sowards, *University of Idaho*; Michael A. Sparks, *Ivy Tech Community College*; Danielle J. Swiontek, *Santa Barbara City College*; David Tegeder, *University of Florida*; Joseph Thurman, *Jefferson College*; Kirk Walton, *Black Hawk College*; Laura Westhoff, *University of Missouri–St. Louis*.

A project as complex as this requires the talents of many individuals. First, we would like to acknowledge our families for their support, forbearance, and toleration of our textbook responsibilities. Pembroke Herbert and Sandi Rygiel of Picture Research Consultants, Inc., contributed their unparalleled knowledge, soaring imagination, and diligent research to make possible the extraordinary illustration program.

We would also like to thank the many people at Bedford/St. Martin's who have been crucial to this project. Developmental editor Kathryn Abbott managed the entire revision and supplements program. Her skill, good judgment, and deep commitment to the project are obvious on every page. Thanks also go to associate editor Jack Cashman, who oversaw the development of the supplements, associate editor Jennifer Jovin who assisted in creating some of the reading and study tools, and editorial assistant Emily DiPietro for her help coordinating the pre-revision review and preparing the manuscript. We are also grateful to Jane Knetzger, director of development for history; William J. Lombardo, executive editor for history; and Mary Dougherty, publisher for history, for their support and guidance. For their imaginative and tireless efforts to promote the book, we want to thank John Hunger, Sean Blest, Sandra McGuire, and Alex Kaufman. With great skill and professionalism, senior production editor Karen Baart pulled together the many pieces related to copyediting, design, and composition with the guidance of associate production director Elise Kaiser. Assistant production supervisor Joe Ford oversaw the manufacturing of the book. Designer Carie Keller, copyeditor Linda McLatchie, and proofreaders Kathleen Lafferty and Angela Morrison attended to the myriad details that help make the book shine. Leoni McVey and Associates provided the index. The book's gorgeous covers were designed by Donna Lee Dennison. New media editors Kimberly Hampton and Marissa Zanetti and media producers Rebecca Merrill and Michelle Camisa made sure that *Understanding the American Promise* remains at the forefront of technological support for students and instructors. President of Bedford/St. Martin's Denise Wydra provided helpful advice throughout the course of the project. Finally, Charles H. Christensen, former president, took a personal interest in *The American Promise* from the start, and Joan E. Feinberg, co-president of Macmillan Higher Education, encouraged us through each edition.

James Roark
Michael Johnson
Patricia Cohen
Sarah Stage
Susan Hartmann

VERSIONS AND SUPPLEMENTS

Adopters of *Understanding the American Promise* and their students have access to abundant extra resources, including documents, presentation and testing materials, the acclaimed Bedford Series in History and Culture volumes, and much more. See below for more information, visit the book's catalog site at **bedfordstmartins.com/roarkunderstanding/catalog**, or contact your local Bedford/St. Martin's sales representative.

Get the Right Version for Your Class

To accommodate different course lengths and course budgets, *Understanding the American Promise* is available in several different formats, including three-hole-punched loose-leaf Budget Books versions and e-books, which are available at a substantial discount.

- **Combined edition** (Chapters 1–31)—available in paperback, loose-leaf, and e-book formats
- **Volume 1: To 1877** (Chapters 1–16)—available in paperback, loose-leaf, and e-book formats
- **Volume 2: From 1865** (Chapters 16–31)—available in paperback, loose-leaf, and e-book formats

Any of these volumes can be packaged with additional books for a discount. To get ISBNs for discount packages, see the online catalog at **bedfordstmartins.com/roarkunderstanding/catalog** or contact your Bedford/St. Martin's representative.

▶ **NEW Assign LaunchPad— the online, interactive e-book in a course space enriched with integrated assets.** The new standard in digital history, LaunchPad course tools are so intuitive to use that online, hybrid, and face-to-face courses can be set up in minutes. Even novices will find it's easy to create assignments, track students' work, and access a wealth of relevant learning and teaching resources. It is the ideal learning environment for students to work with the text, maps, documents, video, and assessment. LaunchPad is loaded with the full interactive e-book and the *Reading the American Past* documents collection—plus LearningCurve, additional primary sources, videos, guided reading exercises designed to help students read actively for key concepts, chapter summative quizzes, and more. LaunchPad can be used as is or customized, and it easily integrates with course management systems. And with fast ways to build assignments, rearrange chapters, and add new pages, sections, or links, it lets teachers build the course materials they need and hold students accountable.

▶ **Let students choose their e-book format.** In addition to the LaunchPad e-book, students can purchase the downloadable *Bedford e-Book to Go for Understanding* *the American Promise* from our Web site or find other PDF versions of the e-book at our publishing partners' sites: CourseSmart, Barnes & Noble NookStudy, Kno, CafeScribe, or Chegg.

NEW Assign LearningCurve So You Know What Your Students Know and They Come to Class Prepared

As described in the preface and on the inside front cover, students purchasing new books receive access to LearningCurve for *Understanding the American Promise*. Assigning LearningCurve in place of reading quizzes is easy for instructors, and the reporting features help instructors track overall class trends and spot topics that are giving students trouble so they can adjust their lectures and class activities. This online learning tool is popular with students because it was designed to help them rehearse content at their own pace in a non-threatening, game-like environment. The feedback for wrong answers provides instructional coaching and sends students back to the book for review. Students answer as many questions as necessary to reach a target score, with repeated chances to revisit material they haven't mastered. When LearningCurve is assigned, students come to class better prepared.

Send Students to Free Online Resources

The book's Student Site at **bedfordstmartins.com/roarkunderstanding** gives students a way to read, write, and study by providing plentiful quizzes and activities, study aids, and history research and writing help.

▶ **FREE Online Study Guide.** Available at the Student Site, this popular resource provides students with quizzes and activities for each chapter, including multiple-choice self-tests that focus on important concepts, flashcards that test students' knowledge of key terms, timeline activities that emphasize causal relationships, and map quizzes intended to strengthen students' geography skills. Instructors can monitor students' progress through an online Quiz Gradebook or receive e-mail updates.

▶ **FREE Research, Writing, and Anti-plagiarism Advice.** Available at the Student Site, Bedford's **History Research and Writing Help** includes the textbook authors' **Suggested References** organized by chapter; **History Research and Reference Sources,** with links to history-related databases, indexes, and journals; **Build a Bibliography,** a simple Web-based tool known as The Bedford Bibliographer that generates bibliographies in four commonly used documentation styles; and **Tips on Avoiding Plagiarism,** an online tutorial that reviews the consequences of plagiarism and features exercises to help students practice integrating sources and recognize acceptable summaries.

Take Advantage of Instructor Resources

Bedford/St. Martin's has developed a rich array of teaching resources for this book and for this course. They range from lecture and presentation materials and assessment tools to course management options. Most can be downloaded or ordered at **bedfordstmartins.com/roarkunderstanding/catalog.**

▶ **Instructor's Resource Manual.** The instructor's manual offers both experienced and first-time instructors tools for preparing lectures and running discussions. It includes chapter-review material, teaching strategies, and a guide to chapter-specific supplements available for the text, plus suggestions on how to get the most out of LearningCurve and a survival guide for first-time teaching assistants.

▶ **Guide to Changing Editions.** Designed to facilitate an instructor's transition from the previous edition of *Understanding the American Promise* to the current edition, this guide presents an overview of major changes as well as of changes in each chapter.

▶ **Computerized Test Bank.** The test bank includes a mix of fresh, carefully crafted multiple-choice, short-answer, and essay questions for each chapter. It also contains volume-wide essay questions. All questions appear in Microsoft Word format and in easy-to-use test bank software that allows instructors to add, edit, re-sequence, and print questions and answers. Instructors can also export questions into a variety of formats, including Blackboard, Desire2Learn, and Moodle.

▶ *The Bedford Lecture Kit:* **PowerPoint Maps, Images, Lecture Outlines, and i>clicker Content.** Look good and save time with *The Bedford Lecture Kit.* These presentation materials are downloadable individually from the Instructor Resources tab at **bedfordstmartins.com/roarkunderstanding/catalog** and are available on *The Bedford Lecture Kit* **Instructor's Resource CD-ROM.** They provide ready-made and fully customizable PowerPoint multimedia presentations that include lecture outlines with embedded maps, figures, and selected images from the textbook and extra background for instructors. Also available are maps and selected images in JPEG and PowerPoint formats; content for i>clicker, a classroom response system, in Microsoft Word and PowerPoint formats; the Instructor's Resource Manual in Microsoft Word format; and outline maps in PDF format for quizzing or handing out. All files are suitable for copying onto transparency acetates.

▶ *Reel Teaching: Film Clips for the U.S. History Survey.* This DVD provides a large collection of short video clips for classroom presentation. Designed as engaging "lecture launchers" varying in length from one to fifteen minutes or longer, the fifty-nine documentary clips were carefully chosen for use in both semesters of the U.S. survey course. The clips feature compelling images, archival footage, personal narratives, and commentary by noted historians.

▶ *America in Motion: Video Clips for U.S. History.* Set history in motion with *America in Motion,* an instructor DVD containing dozens of short digital movie files of events in twentieth-century American history. From the wreckage of the battleship *Maine* to FDR's fireside chats to Oliver North testifying before Congress, *America in Motion* engages students with dynamic scenes from key events and challenges them to think critically. All files are classroom-ready, edited for brevity, and easily integrated with PowerPoint or other presentation software for electronic lectures or assignments. An accompanying guide provides each clip's historical context, ideas for use, and suggested questions.

▶ **Videos and Multimedia.** A wide assortment of videos and multimedia CD-ROMs on various topics in U.S. history is available to qualified adopters through your Bedford/St. Martin's sales representative.

Package and Save Your Students Money

For information on free packages and discounts up to 50%, visit **bedfordstmartins .com/roarkunderstanding/catalog** or contact your local Bedford/St. Martin's sales representative. The products that follow all qualify for discount packaging.

▶ *Reading the American Past,* **Fifth Edition.** Edited by Michael P. Johnson, one of the authors of *The American Promise,* and designed to complement the textbook, *Reading the American Past* provides a broad selection of over 150 primary-source documents as well as editorial apparatus to help students understand the sources. Available free when packaged with the print text and included in the LaunchPad e-book. Also available on its own as a downloadable PDF e-book or with the main text's e-Book to Go.

▶ **NEW Bedford Digital Collections @ bedfordstmartins.com/bdc/catalog.** This source collection provides a flexible and affordable online repository of discovery-oriented primary-source projects and single primary sources that you can easily customize and link to from your course management system or Web site. Package discounts are available.

▶ **The Bedford Series in History and Culture.** More than 120 titles in this highly praised series combine first-rate scholarship, historical narrative, and important primary documents for undergraduate courses. Each book is brief, inexpensive, and focused on a specific topic or period. For a complete list of titles, visit **bedfordstmartins.com/history/series.** Package discounts are available.

▶ *Rand McNally Atlas of American History.* This collection of more than eighty full-color maps illustrates key events and eras from early exploration, settlement, expansion, and immigration to U.S. involvement in wars abroad and on U.S. soil. Introductory pages for each section include a brief overview, timelines, graphs, and photos to quickly establish a historical context. Available for $5.00 when packaged with the print text.

▶ *Maps in Context: A Workbook for American History.* Written by historical cartography expert Gerald A. Danzer (University of Illinois at Chicago), this skill-building workbook helps students comprehend essential connections between geographic literacy and historical understanding. Organized to correspond to the typical U.S. history survey course, *Maps in Context* presents a wealth of map-centered projects and convenient pop quizzes that give students hands-on experience working with maps. Available free when packaged with the print text.

▶ *The Bedford Glossary for U.S. History.* This handy supplement for the survey course gives students historically contextualized definitions for hundreds of terms—from *abolitionism* to *zoot suit*—that they will encounter in lectures, reading, and exams. Available free when packaged with the print text.

▶ *U.S. History Matters: A Student Guide to World History Online.* This resource, written by Alan Gevinson, Kelly Schrum, and the late Roy Rosenzweig (all of George Mason University), provides an illustrated and annotated guide to 250 of the most useful Web sites for student research in U.S. history as well as advice on evaluating and using Internet sources. This essential guide is based on the acclaimed "History Matters" Web site developed by the American Social History Project and the Center for History and New Media. Available free when packaged with the print text.

▶ **Trade Books.** Titles published by sister companies Hill and Wang; Farrar, Straus and Giroux; Henry Holt and Company; St. Martin's Press; Picador; and Palgrave Macmillan are available at a 50% discount when packaged with Bedford/St. Martin's textbooks. For more information, visit **bedfordstmartins.com/tradeup.**

▶ *A Pocket Guide to Writing in History.* This portable and affordable reference tool by Mary Lynn Rampolla provides reading, writing, and research advice useful to students in all history courses. Concise yet comprehensive advice on approaching typical history assignments, developing critical reading skills, writing effective history papers, conducting research, using and documenting sources, and avoiding plagiarism—enhanced with practical tips and examples throughout—have made this slim reference a best seller. Package discounts are available.

▶ *A Student's Guide to History.* This complete guide to success in any history course provides the practical help students need to be effective. In addition to introducing students to the nature of the discipline, author Jules Benjamin teaches a wide range of skills, from preparing for exams to approaching common writing assignments, and explains the research and documentation process with plentiful examples. Package discounts are available.

▶ *Going to the Source: The Bedford Reader in American History.* Developed by Victoria Bissell Brown and Timothy J. Shannon, this reader's strong pedagogical framework helps students learn how to ask fruitful questions in order to evaluate documents effectively and develop critical reading skills. The reader's wide variety of chapter topics that complement the survey course and its rich diversity of sources—from personal letters to political cartoons—provoke students' interest as it teaches them the skills they need to successfully interrogate historical sources. Package discounts are available.

▶ *America Firsthand.* With its distinctive focus on ordinary people, this primary documents reader, by Anthony Marcus, John M. Giggie, and David Burner, offers a remarkable range of perspectives on America's history from those who lived it. Popular Points of View sections expose students to different perspectives on a specific event or topic, and Visual Portfolios invite analysis of the visual record. Package discounts are available.

BRIEF CONTENTS

CONTENTS

16 RECONSTRUCTING A NATION

1863–1877   *456*

17 CONTESTING THE WEST

1865–1900   *486*

18

DEFINING THE GILDED AGE IN BUSINESS AND POLITICS

1865–1900 *516*

19

THE GROWTH OF AMERICA'S CITIES

1870–1900 *546*

20

DISSENT, DEPRESSION, AND WAR

1890–1900 *578*

☑ **LearningCurve**
bedfordstmartins.com/roarkunderstanding

☑ **LearningCurve**
bedfordstmartins.com/roarkunderstanding

☑ **LearningCurve**
bedfordstmartins.com/roarkunderstanding

21
PROGRESSIVISM FROM THE GRASS ROOTS UP
1890–1916 *610*

22
THE UNITED STATES AND WORLD WAR I
1914–1920 *644*

23
FROM NEW ERA TO GREAT DEPRESSION
1920–1932 *676*

30

THE CONSERVATIVE TURN

31

FACING THE PROMISES AND CHALLENGES OF GLOBALIZATION

✓ **LearningCurve**
bedfordstmartins.com/roarkunderstanding

✓ **LearningCurve**
bedfordstmartins.com/roarkunderstanding

MAPS, FIGURES, AND TABLES

How to use this book to figure out what's really important

The **chapter title** tells you the subject of the chapter and identifies the time span that will be covered.

The **opening question** and **chapter introduction** identify the most important themes, events, and people that will be explored in the chapter.

16
RECONSTRUCTING A NATION
1863–1877

> **What were the achievements and failures of reconstruction?** Chapter 16 explores the era of reconstruction, in which the nation struggled to define the defeated South's status and the meaning of freedom for ex-slaves. Following the Civil War, the nation entered one of its most confused and violent periods as victorious Northerners, defeated white Southerners, and newly freed African Americans battled to shape the postwar South.

☑ **LearningCurve**
bedfordstmartins.com/roarkunderstanding
After reading the chapter, use LearningCurve to retain what you've read.

456

Memorizing facts and dates for a history class won't get you very far. That's because history isn't just about "facts." This textbook is designed to help you focus on what's truly significant in U.S. history and to give you practice in thinking like a historian.

> Why did Congress object to Lincoln's wartime plan for reconstruction?

> How did the North respond to the passage of black codes in the southern states?

> How radical was congressional reconstruction?

> What brought the elements of the South's Republican coalition together?

> Why did reconstruction collapse?

> Conclusion: Was reconstruction "a revolution but half accomplished"?

The **chapter-opening questions** are also the questions that open each new section of the chapter and will be addressed in turn on the following pages. You should think about answers to these as you read.

Voting day, June 5, 1867. Black freedmen line up to vote in Washington, D.C. The Granger Collection, New York.

Each section has tools that help you focus on what's important.

The **question in red** asks about the specific topic being discussed in this section. Think about the answer to this question as you read the section.

> ## How did the North respond to the passage of black codes in the southern states?

The Black Codes

Titled "Selling a Freeman to Pay His Fine at Monticello, Florida," this 1867 drawing from a northern magazine equates black codes with the institution of slavery. The ascension of Andrew Johnson to the presidency emboldened many southern states to pass laws severely restricting blacks' freedom. *Granger Collection.*

ABRAHAM LINCOLN DIED on April 15, 1865, just hours after John Wilkes Booth shot him at a Washington, D.C., theater. Chief Justice Salmon P. Chase immediately administered the oath of office to Vice President Andrew Johnson of Tennessee. Congress had adjourned in March and would not reconvene until December. Throughout the summer and fall, Johnson drew up and executed a plan of reconstruction without congressional advice.

Congress returned to the capital in December to find that, as far as the president and former Confederates were concerned, reconstruction was completed. Most Republicans, however, thought Johnson's plan made far too few demands of ex-rebels. They claimed that Johnson's leniency had acted as midwife to the rebirth of the Old South, that he had achieved political reunification at the cost of black freedom. Republicans in Congress then proceeded to dismantle Johnson's program and substitute a program of their own.

Johnson's Program of Reconciliation

Born in 1808 in Raleigh, North Carolina, Andrew Johnson was the son of illiterate parents. Self-educated and ambitious, Johnson moved to Tennessee, where he built a career in politics championing the South's common white people and assailing its "illegitimate, swaggering, bastard, scrub aristocracy." The only senator from a Confederate state to remain loyal to the Union, Johnson held the planter class responsible for secession.

A Democrat all his life, Johnson occupied the White House only because the Republican Party in 1864 had needed a vice presidential candidate who would

CHAPTER LOCATOR | Why did Congress object to Lincoln's wartime plan for reconstruction? | **How did the North respond to the passage of black codes in the southern states?**

The **chapter locator** at the bottom of the page puts this section in the context of the chapter as a whole, so you can see how this section relates to what's coming next.

appeal to loyal, Union-supporting Democrats. Johnson vigorously defended states' rights (but not secession) and opposed Republican efforts to expand the power of the federal government. A steadfast supporter of slavery, Johnson had owned slaves until 1862, when Tennessee rebels, angry at his Unionism, confiscated them. When he grudgingly accepted emancipation, it was more because he hated planters than because he sympathized with slaves. "Damn the negroes," he said. "I am fighting those traitorous aristocrats, their masters." The new president harbored unshakable racist convictions. Africans, Johnson said, were "inferior to the white man in point of intellect — better calculated in physical structure to undergo drudgery and hardship."

Like Lincoln, Johnson stressed the rapid restoration of civil government in the South. Like Lincoln, he promised to pardon most, but not all, ex-rebels. Johnson recognized the state governments created by Lincoln but set out his own requirements for restoring the other rebel states to the Union.

Republican senator Lyman Trumbull of Illinois declared that the president's policy meant that an ex-slave would "be tyrannized over, abused, and virtually reenslaved without some legislation by the nation for his protection." Early in 1866, the moderates produced two bills that strengthened the federal shield. The first, the Freedmen's Bureau bill, prolonged the life of the agency established by the previous Congress. Arguing that the Constitution never contemplated a "system for the support of indigent persons," President Andrew Johnson vetoed the bill. Congress failed by a narrow margin to override the president's veto.

The moderates designed their second measure, what would become the **Civil Rights Act of 1866**, to nullify the black codes by affirming African Americans' rights to "full and equal benefit of all laws and proceedings for the security of person and property as is enjoyed by white citizens." The act required the end of racial discrimination in state laws and represented an extraordinary expansion of black rights and federal authority. The president argued that the civil rights bill amounted to "unconstitutional invasion of states' rights" and vetoed it.

In April 1866, an incensed Republican Party again pushed the civil rights bill through Congress and overrode the presidential veto. In July, it passed another Freedmen's Bureau bill and overrode Johnson's veto. For the first time in American history, Congress had overridden presidential vetoes of major legislation. As a worried South Carolinian observed, Johnson had succeeded in uniting the Republicans and probably touched off "a fight this fall such as has never been seen."

> CHRONOLOGY

1865
– Lincoln is assassinated; Andrew Johnson becomes president.
– Black codes are enacted.
– Thirteenth Amendment becomes part of Constitution.

1866
– Civil Rights Act.

Chronologies for each major section show the sequence of events and underlying developments in the section.

Civil Rights Act of 1866
▶ Legislation passed by Congress in 1866 that nullified the black codes and affirmed that black Americans should have equal benefit of the law. President Andrew Johnson vetoed this expansion of black rights and federal authority, but Congress later overrode his veto.

Key terms in the margins give you background on important ideas and events. Use these for reference while you read, but also think about which are emphasized and why they matter.

QUICK REVIEW ◄

When the southern states passed the black codes, how did the U.S. Congress respond?

The **quick review** helps you check your recall of the section before you resume reading.

| How radical was congressional reconstruction? | What brought the elements of the South's Republican coalition together? | Why did reconstruction collapse? | Conclusion: Was reconstruction "a revolution but half accomplished"? | LearningCurve Check what you know. bedfordstmartins.com /roarkunderstanding |

The Chapter Study Guide provides a process that will build your understanding and your historical skills.

> **CHAPTER 16 STUDY GUIDE**

STEP 1 Go online to complete the chapter's LearningCurve activity.

STEP 1

GET STARTED ONLINE

 LearningCurve ▪ bedfordstmartins.com/roarkunderstanding
Now that you've read the chapter, make it stick by completing the LearningCurve activity.

STEP 2 Identify the key terms and explain their significance.

STEP 2

EXPLAIN WHY IT MATTERS

Put your reading into practice. Identify each term below, and then explain why it matters in U.S. history.

TERM	WHO OR WHAT & WHEN	WHY IT MATTERS
Freedmen's Bureau (p. 460)		
black codes (p. 463)		
Civil Rights Act of 1866 (p. 465)		
Fourteenth Amendment (p. 466)		
Military Reconstruction Act (p. 468)		
Fifteenth Amendment (p. 469)		
carpetbaggers (p. 472)		
scalawags (p. 472)		
Ku Klux Klan (p. 472)		
sharecropping (p. 474)		
Redeemers (p. 479)		
Compromise of 1877 (p. 482)		

STEP 3 Analyze differences and similarities among ideas, events, people, or societies discussed in the chapter.

STEP 3

MOVE BEYOND THE BASICS

To demonstrate a more advanced understanding, indicate below how each phase of reconstruction addressed the key issues involved.

Phase of reconstruction	Requirements for readmission	Role/rights of freedmen	Achievements	Failures
Wartime reconstruction (Lincoln)				
Presidential reconstruction (Johnson)				
Congressional reconstruction				

STEP 4 | **PUT IT ALL TOGETHER** Now, take a step back and try to explain the big picture. Remember to use specific examples from the chapter in your answers.

PRESIDENTIAL AND CONGRESSIONAL RECONSTRUCTION

▶ What role did the black codes play in shaping the course of reconstruction?

▶ What steps did Congress take between 1865 and 1869 to assist ex-slaves in their lives as freedmen? How effective were these actions?

SOUTHERN RECONSTRUCTION IN ACTION

▶ How did white Southerners respond during reconstruction? Consider both Democrats and Republicans in your response.

▶ How did southern African Americans attempt to shape their own lives during reconstruction?

THE END OF RECONSTRUCTION

▶ How and why did the decline of northern support for reconstruction help southern Democrats "redeem" the South?

▶ Why did white supremacy become the foundation of southern politics in the 1870s?

LOOKING BACKWARD, LOOKING AHEAD

▶ How did long-held racial views among whites, in both the South and the North, shape reconstruction?

▶ What were the lasting accomplishments of reconstruction? What were its most important failures?

> **IN YOUR OWN WORDS**

Imagine that you must give an oral report to the class answering the following question: **What were the achievements and failures of reconstruction?** What would be the most important points to include and why?

 Do it online at the Student Site ■ bedfordstmartins.com/roarkunderstanding

STEP 4 Answer the big-picture questions using specific examples or evidence from the chapter.

ACTIVE RECITATION Explain how you would answer the chapter-opening question in your own words to make sure you have a firm grasp of the most important themes and events of the chapter.

Visit the FREE Student Site at **bedfordstmartins.com /roarkunderstanding** to do these steps online.

xxvii

Understanding
the American Promise

A HISTORY

16
RECONSTRUCTING A NATION

1863–1877

> **What were the achievements and failures of reconstruction?** Chapter 16 explores the era of reconstruction, in which the nation struggled to define the defeated South's status and the meaning of freedom for ex-slaves. Following the Civil War, the nation entered one of its most confused and violent periods as victorious Northerners, defeated white Southerners, and newly freed African Americans battled to shape the postwar South.

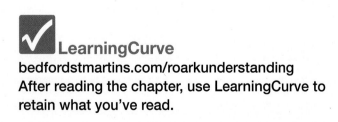

LearningCurve
bedfordstmartins.com/roarkunderstanding
After reading the chapter, use LearningCurve to
retain what you've read.

> Why did Congress object to Lincoln's wartime plan for reconstruction?

> How did the North respond to the passage of black codes in the southern states?

> How radical was congressional reconstruction?

> What brought the elements of the South's Republican coalition together?

> Why did reconstruction collapse?

> Conclusion: Was reconstruction "a revolution but half accomplished"?

Voting day, June 5, 1867. **Black freedmen line up to vote in Washington, D.C.** The Granger Collection, New York.

Why did Congress object to Lincoln's wartime plan for reconstruction?

Military Auction of Condemned Property, Beaufort, South Carolina, 1865

During the war, thousands of acres of land in the South came into federal hands as abandoned property or as a result of seizures because of nonpayment of taxes. The government authorized the sale of some of this land at public auction. This rare photograph shows expectant blacks (and a few whites) gathered in Beaufort, South Carolina, for a sale. The Huntington Library, San Marino, California.

RECONSTRUCTION DID NOT WAIT for the end of war. As the odds of a northern victory increased, thinking about reunification quickened. Immediately, a question arose: Who had authority to devise a plan for reconstructing the Union? President Abraham Lincoln firmly believed that reconstruction was a matter of executive responsibility. Congress just as firmly asserted its jurisdiction. Fueling the argument were significant differences about the terms of reconstruction. In their eagerness to formulate a plan for political reunification, neither Lincoln nor Congress gave much attention to the South's land and labor problem or to the aspirations of freedmen. But as the war rapidly eroded slavery and traditional plantation agriculture, Yankee military commanders in the Union-occupied areas of the Confederacy had no choice but to oversee the emergence of a new labor system.

"To Bind Up the Nation's Wounds"

As early as 1863, Lincoln began contemplating how "to bind up the nation's wounds" and achieve "a lasting peace." While deep compassion for the enemy guided his thinking about peace, his plan for reconstruction aimed primarily at shortening the war and ending slavery.

Lincoln's Proclamation of Amnesty and Reconstruction in December 1863 set out his terms. Lincoln's plan did not require ex-rebels to extend social or political rights to ex-slaves, nor did it anticipate a program of long-term federal assistance to freedmen. Clearly, the president looked forward to the rapid, forgiving restoration of the broken Union.

Lincoln's easy terms enraged abolitionists such as Wendell Phillips of Boston, who charged that the president "makes the negro's freedom a mere sham." He "is

> **CHRONOLOGY**

1863
– Proclamation of Amnesty and Reconstruction.

1864
– Lincoln refuses to sign Wade-Davis bill.

1865
– Freedmen's Bureau is established.

CHAPTER LOCATOR | **Why did Congress object to Lincoln's wartime plan for reconstruction?** | How did the North respond to the passage of black codes in the southern states?

458 CHAPTER 16 RECONSTRUCTING A NATION

- Lincoln offered a full pardon, restoring property (except slaves) and political rights, to most rebels willing to renounce secession and to accept emancipation.
- High-ranking Confederate military and political officers and a few other groups were to be excluded from this offer.
- When 10 percent of a state's voting population had taken an oath of allegiance, the state could organize a new government and be readmitted into the Union.

willing that the negro should be free but seeks nothing else for him." Phillips and other northern radicals called instead for a thorough overhaul of southern society. Their ideas proved to be too drastic for most Republicans during the war years, but Congress agreed that Lincoln's plan was inadequate.

In July 1864, Congressman Henry Winter Davis of Maryland and Senator Benjamin Wade of Ohio jointly sponsored their own less forgiving reconstruction bill. When Lincoln refused to sign the bill and let it die, Wade and Davis charged the president with usurpation of power.

> Wade-Davis Bill

- The bill demanded that at least half of the voters in a conquered rebel state take the oath of allegiance before reconstruction could begin.
- It banned almost all ex-Confederates from participating in the drafting of new state constitutions.
- It guaranteed the equality of freedmen before the law.

Undeterred, Lincoln continued to nurture the formation of loyal state governments under his own plan. Four states — Louisiana, Arkansas, Tennessee, and Virginia — fulfilled the president's requirements, but Congress refused to seat representatives from the "Lincoln states." In his last public address in April 1865, Lincoln defended his plan but for the first time publicly expressed his endorsement of suffrage for southern blacks, at least "the very intelligent, and . . . those who serve our cause as soldiers." The announcement demonstrated that Lincoln's thinking about reconstruction was still evolving. Four days later, he was dead.

Land and Labor

Of all the problems raised by the North's victory in the war, none proved more critical than the South's transition from slavery to free labor. As federal armies invaded and occupied the Confederacy, hundreds of thousands of slaves became free workers. In addition, Union armies controlled vast territories in the South where legal title to land had become unclear. The Confiscation Acts passed during the war punished "traitors" by taking away their property. The question of what to do with federally occupied land and how to organize labor on it engaged ex-slaves, ex-slaveholders, Union military commanders, and federal government officials long before the war ended.

In the Mississippi valley, occupying federal troops announced a new labor code. It required landholders to give up whipping, to sign contracts with ex-slaves, and to

| How radical was congressional reconstruction? | What brought the elements of the South's Republican coalition together? | Why did reconstruction collapse? | Conclusion: Was reconstruction "a revolution but half accomplished"? | ✔ LearningCurve Check what you know. bedfordstmartins.com /roarkunderstanding |

pay wages. The code required black laborers to enter into contracts, work diligently, and remain subordinate and obedient. Military leaders clearly had no intention of promoting a social or economic revolution. The effort resulted in a hybrid system that one contemporary called "compulsory free labor," something that satisfied no one.

Planters complained because the new system fell short of slavery. Blacks could not be "transformed by proclamation," a Louisiana sugar planter declared. Without the right to whip, he argued, the new labor system did not have a chance. Either Union soldiers must "compel the negroes to work," or the planters themselves must "be authorized and sustained in using force."

African Americans found the new regime too reminiscent of slavery to be called free labor. Its chief deficiency, they believed, was the failure to provide them with land of their own. Freedmen believed they had a moral right to land because they and their ancestors had worked it without compensation for more than two centuries. "What's the use of being free if you don't own land enough to be buried in?" one man asked. Several wartime developments led freedmen to believe that the federal government planned to undergird black freedom with landownership.

In January 1865, General William Tecumseh Sherman set aside part of the coast south of Charleston for black settlement. By June 1865, some 40,000 freedmen sat on 400,000 acres of "Sherman land." In addition, in March 1865, Congress passed a bill establishing the Bureau of Refugees, Freedmen, and Abandoned Lands. The **Freedmen's Bureau**, as it was called, distributed food and clothing to destitute Southerners and eased the transition of blacks from slaves to free persons. Congress also authorized the agency to divide abandoned and confiscated land into 40-acre plots, to rent them to freedmen, and eventually to sell them "with such title as the United States can convey." By June 1865, the Bureau had situated nearly 10,000 black families on half a million acres abandoned by fleeing planters. Other ex-slaves eagerly anticipated farms of their own.

Despite the flurry of activity, wartime reconstruction failed to produce agreement about whether the president or Congress had the authority to devise policy or what proper policy should be.

The African American Quest for Autonomy

Ex-slaves never had any doubt about what they wanted from freedom. They had only to contemplate what they had been denied as slaves. Slaves had to remain on their plantations; freedom allowed blacks to see what was on the other side of the hill. Slaves had to be at work in the fields by dawn; freedom permitted blacks to sleep through a sunrise. Freedmen also tested the etiquette of racial subordination. "Lizzie's maid passed me today when I was coming from church *without speaking to me*," huffed one plantation mistress.

To whites, emancipation looked like pure anarchy. Blacks, they said, had reverted to their natural condition: lazy, irresponsible, and wild. Actually, former slaves were experimenting with freedom, but they could not long afford to roam the countryside, neglect work, and casually provoke whites. Soon, most were back at work in whites' kitchens and fields.

But they continued to dream of land and economic independence. "The way we can best take care of ourselves is to have land," one former slave declared in

Freedmen's Bureau

▶ Government organization created in March 1865 to distribute food and clothing to destitute Southerners and to ease the transition of slaves to free persons. Early efforts by the Freedmen's Bureau to distribute land to the newly freed blacks were later overturned by President Andrew Johnson.

CHAPTER LOCATOR | Why did Congress object to Lincoln's wartime plan for reconstruction? | How did the North respond to the passage of black codes in the southern states?

CHAPTER 16
460 RECONSTRUCTING A NATION

Harry Stephens and Family, 1866 Dressed in their Sunday best, this Virginia family sits proudly for a photograph. Many black families were not as fortunate as the Stephens family and spent years seeking missing family members. The Metropolitan Museum of Art, Gilman Collection, Purchase, The Horace W. Goldsmith Foundation Gift, 2005 (2005.100.277)/Art Resource, NY.

1865, "and turn it and till it by our own labor." Freedmen also wanted to learn to read and write. "I wishes the Childern all in School," one black veteran asserted. "It is beter for them then to be their Surveing a mistes [mistress]."

The restoration of broken families was another persistent black aspiration. Thousands of freedmen took to the roads in 1865 to look for kin who had been sold away or to free those who were being held illegally as slaves. A black soldier from Missouri wrote his daughters that he was coming for them. "I will have you if it cost me my life," he declared. "Your Miss Kitty said that I tried to steal you," he told them. "But I'll let her know that god never intended for a man to steal his own flesh and blood." And he swore that "if she meets me with ten thousand soldiers, she [will] meet her enemy."

Independent worship was another continuing aspiration. African Americans greeted freedom with a mass exodus from white churches, where they had been required to worship when slaves. Some joined the newly established southern branches of all-black northern churches, such as the African Methodist Episcopal Church. Others formed black versions of the major southern denominations, Baptists and Methodists.

QUICK REVIEW

To what extent did Lincoln's wartime plan for reconstruction reflect the concerns of newly freed slaves?

How radical was congressional reconstruction?

What brought the elements of the South's Republican coalition together?

Why did reconstruction collapse?

Conclusion: Was reconstruction "a revolution but half accomplished"?

✓ **LearningCurve** Check what you know. bedfordstmartins.com /roarkunderstanding

How did the North respond to the passage of black codes in the southern states?

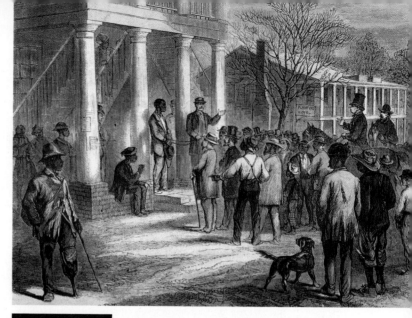

The Black Codes

Titled "Selling a Freeman to Pay His Fine at Monticello, Florida," this 1867 drawing from a northern magazine equates black codes with the institution of slavery. The ascension of Andrew Johnson to the presidency emboldened many southern states to pass laws severely restricting blacks' freedom. Granger Collection.

ABRAHAM LINCOLN DIED on April 15, 1865, just hours after John Wilkes Booth shot him at a Washington, D.C., theater. Chief Justice Salmon P. Chase immediately administered the oath of office to Vice President Andrew Johnson of Tennessee. Congress had adjourned in March and would not reconvene until December. Throughout the summer and fall, Johnson drew up and executed a plan of reconstruction without congressional advice.

Congress returned to the capital in December to find that, as far as the president and former Confederates were concerned, reconstruction was completed. Most Republicans, however, thought Johnson's plan made far too few demands of ex-rebels. They claimed that Johnson's leniency had acted as midwife to the rebirth of the Old South, that he had achieved political reunification at the cost of black freedom. Republicans in Congress then proceeded to dismantle Johnson's program and substitute a program of their own.

Johnson's Program of Reconciliation

Born in 1808 in Raleigh, North Carolina, Andrew Johnson was the son of illiterate parents. Self-educated and ambitious, Johnson moved to Tennessee, where he built a career in politics championing the South's common white people and assailing its "illegitimate, swaggering, bastard, scrub aristocracy." The only senator from a Confederate state to remain loyal to the Union, Johnson held the planter class responsible for secession.

A Democrat all his life, Johnson occupied the White House only because the Republican Party in 1864 had needed a vice presidential candidate who would

CHAPTER LOCATOR | Why did Congress object to Lincoln's wartime plan for reconstruction? | **How did the North respond to the passage of black codes in the southern states?**

462 CHAPTER 16 RECONSTRUCTING A NATION

appeal to loyal, Union-supporting Democrats. Johnson vigorously defended states' rights (but not secession) and opposed Republican efforts to expand the power of the federal government. A steadfast supporter of slavery, Johnson had owned slaves until 1862, when Tennessee rebels, angry at his Unionism, confiscated them. When he grudgingly accepted emancipation, it was more because he hated planters than because he sympathized with slaves. "Damn the negroes," he said. "I am fighting those traitorous aristocrats, their masters." The new president harbored unshakable racist convictions. Africans, Johnson said, were "inferior to the white man in point of intellect — better calculated in physical structure to undergo drudgery and hardship."

Like Lincoln, Johnson stressed the rapid restoration of civil government in the South. Like Lincoln, he promised to pardon most, but not all, ex-rebels. Johnson recognized the state governments created by Lincoln but set out his own requirements for restoring the other rebel states to the Union.

> CHRONOLOGY

1865
– Lincoln is assassinated; Andrew Johnson becomes president.
– Black codes are enacted.
– Thirteenth Amendment becomes part of Constitution.

1866
– Civil Rights Act.

> **Johnson's Plan to Restore Confederate States to the Union**

- Citizens of a state had to renounce the right of secession.
- They had to deny that the debts of the Confederacy were legal and binding.
- They had to ratify the Thirteenth Amendment abolishing slavery, which became part of the Constitution in December 1865.

Johnson also returned all confiscated and abandoned land to pardoned ex-Confederates, even if it was in the hands of freedmen. Reformers were shocked by Johnson's quick and easy plan of reconstruction. Instead of punishing treason and making planters pay as he had promised, Johnson canceled the promising beginnings made by General Sherman and the Freedmen's Bureau to settle blacks on land of their own. As one freedman observed, "Things was hurt by Mr. Lincoln getting killed."

White Southern Resistance and Black Codes

In the summer of 1865, delegates across the South gathered to draw up the new state constitutions required by Johnson's plan of reconstruction. They refused to accept even the president's mild requirements. Refusing to renounce secession, the South Carolina and Georgia conventions merely "repudiated" their secession ordinances, preserving in principle their right to secede. South Carolina and Mississippi refused to disown their Confederate war debts. Mississippi rejected the Thirteenth Amendment. Despite this defiance, Johnson did nothing. White Southerners began to think that by standing up for themselves they could shape the terms of reconstruction.

New state governments across the South adopted a series of laws known as **black codes**, which made a travesty of black freedom. The codes sought to keep ex-slaves subordinate to whites by subjecting them to every sort of discrimination. Several states made it illegal for blacks to own a gun. Mississippi made insulting gestures and language by blacks a criminal offense. The codes barred blacks from jury duty. Not a single southern state granted any black the right to vote.

black codes
▶ Laws passed by state governments in the South in 1865 that sought to keep ex-slaves subordinate to whites. At the core of the black codes lay the desire to force freedmen back to the plantations.

How radical was congressional reconstruction?

What brought the elements of the South's Republican coalition together?

Why did reconstruction collapse?

Conclusion: Was reconstruction "a revolution but half accomplished"?

☑ LearningCurve
Check what you know.
bedfordstmartins.com
/roarkunderstanding

463

At the core of the black codes, however, lay the matter of labor. Legislators sought to hustle freedmen back to the plantations. Whites were almost universally opposed to black landownership, and South Carolina attempted to limit blacks to either farmwork or domestic service by requiring them to pay annual taxes of $10 to $100 to work in any other occupation. Mississippi declared that blacks who did not possess written evidence of employment could be declared vagrants and be subject to involuntary plantation labor. Under so-called apprenticeship laws, courts bound thousands of black children — orphans and others whose parents were deemed unable to support them — to work for planter "guardians."

Johnson, a staunch defender of states' rights and white supremacy, refused to intervene. He also recognized that his do-nothing response offered him political advantage. A conservative Tennessee Democrat at the head of a northern Republican Party, he had begun to look southward for political allies. By pardoning powerful whites, by accepting governments even when they failed to satisfy his minimal demands, and by acquiescing in the black codes, Johnson won useful southern friends.

In the fall elections of 1865, white Southerners dramatically expressed their mood. To represent them in Congress, they chose former Confederates. Of the eighty senators and representatives they sent to Washington, fifteen had served in the Confederate army, ten of them as generals. Another sixteen had served in civil and judicial posts in the Confederacy. Nine others had served in the Confederate Congress. One — Alexander Stephens — had been vice president of the Confederacy. As one Georgian remarked, "It looked as though Richmond had moved to Washington."

Expansion of Federal Authority and Black Rights

Southerners had blundered monumentally. They had assumed that what Andrew Johnson was willing to accept, Republicans would accept as well. But southern intransigence compelled even moderates to conclude that ex-rebels were a "generation of vipers," still untrustworthy and dangerous. The black codes became a symbol of southern intentions to "restore all of slavery but its name." "We tell the white men of Mississippi," the *Chicago Tribune* roared, "that the men of the North will convert the State of Mississippi into a frog pond before they will allow such laws to disgrace one foot of the soil in which the bones of our soldiers sleep and over which the flag of freedom waves."

The moderate majority of the Republican Party wanted only assurance that slavery and treason were dead. They did not champion black equality, the confiscation of plantations, or black voting, as did the radical minority within the party. But southern obstinacy had succeeded in forging unity (at least temporarily) among Republican factions. In December 1865, Republicans refused to seat the southern representatives elected in the fall elections. Rather than accept Johnson's claim that the "work of restoration" was done, Congress challenged his executive power.

CHAPTER LOCATOR | Why did Congress object to Lincoln's wartime plan for reconstruction? | How did the North respond to the passage of black codes in the southern states?

CHAPTER 16
464 RECONSTRUCTING A NATION

This 1865 cartoon pokes fun at two Richmond ladies as they pass by a Union officer on their way to receive free government rations. One says sourly to the other, "Don't you think that Yankee must feel like shrinking into his boots before such high-toned Southern ladies as we?" Just a step behind is a smiling black woman, who obviously views the Yankee through different eyes. Miriam and Ira D. Wallach Division of Art, Prints, and Photographs, The New York Public Library. Astor, Lenox, and Tilden Foundations.

Republican senator Lyman Trumbull of Illinois declared that the president's policy meant that an ex-slave would "be tyrannized over, abused, and virtually reenslaved without some legislation by the nation for his protection." Early in 1866, the moderates produced two bills that strengthened the federal shield. The first, the Freedmen's Bureau bill, prolonged the life of the agency established by the previous Congress. Arguing that the Constitution never contemplated a "system for the support of indigent persons," President Andrew Johnson vetoed the bill. Congress failed by a narrow margin to override the president's veto.

The moderates designed their second measure, what would become the **Civil Rights Act of 1866**, to nullify the black codes by affirming African Americans' rights to "full and equal benefit of all laws and proceedings for the security of person and property as is enjoyed by white citizens." The act required the end of racial discrimination in state laws and represented an extraordinary expansion of black rights and federal authority. The president argued that the civil rights bill amounted to "unconstitutional invasion of states' rights" and vetoed it.

In April 1866, an incensed Republican Party again pushed the civil rights bill through Congress and overrode the presidential veto. In July, it passed another Freedmen's Bureau bill and overrode Johnson's veto. For the first time in American history, Congress had overridden presidential vetoes of major legislation. As a worried South Carolinian observed, Johnson had succeeded in uniting the Republicans and probably touched off "a fight this fall such as has never been seen."

Civil Rights Act of 1866
▶ Legislation passed by Congress in 1866 that nullified the black codes and affirmed that black Americans should have equal benefit of the law. President Andrew Johnson vetoed this expansion of black rights and federal authority, but Congress later overrode his veto.

QUICK REVIEW <

When the southern states passed the black codes, how did the U.S. Congress respond?

How radical was congressional reconstruction?

What brought the elements of the South's Republican coalition together?

Why did reconstruction collapse?

Conclusion: Was reconstruction "a revolution but half accomplished"?

☑ LearningCurve
Check what you know.
bedfordstmartins.com
/roarkunderstanding

465

How radical was congressional reconstruction?

State Convention at Richmond, Virginia

Between 1867 and 1869, every southern state except Tennessee held a convention to draft a new constitution. In Virginia, where blacks were more than 40 percent of the population, they made up about 20 percent of the convention. Richmond History Center.

BY THE SUMMER OF 1866, President Andrew Johnson and Congress had dropped their gloves and stood toe-to-toe in a bare-knuckle contest unprecedented in American history. Johnson made it clear that he would not budge on either constitutional issues or policy. Moderate Republicans responded by amending the Constitution. But the obstinacy of Johnson and white Southerners pushed Republican moderates ever closer to the radicals and to acceptance of additional federal intervention in the South. Congress also voted to impeach the president. In time, Congress debated whether to make voting rights color-blind, while women sought to make voting rights sex-blind as well.

The Fourteenth Amendment and Escalating Violence

Fourteenth Amendment
▶ Constitutional amendment passed in 1866 that made all native-born or naturalized persons U.S. citizens and prohibited states from abridging the rights of national citizens. The amendment aimed to provide a guarantee of equality before the law for black citizens.

In June 1866, Congress passed the **Fourteenth Amendment** to the Constitution, and two years later the states ratified it. The most important provisions of this complex amendment made all native-born or naturalized persons American citizens and prohibited states from abridging the "privileges and immunities" of citizens, depriving them of "life, liberty, or property without due process of law," and denying them "equal protection of the laws." By making blacks national citizens, the amendment provided a national guarantee of equality before the law. In essence, it protected blacks against violation by southern state governments.

CHAPTER LOCATOR | Why did Congress object to Lincoln's wartime plan for reconstruction? | How did the North respond to the passage of black codes in the southern states?

466 CHAPTER 16
RECONSTRUCTING A NATION

The Fourteenth Amendment also dealt with voting rights. It gave Congress the right to reduce the congressional representation of any state that withheld suffrage from some of its adult male population. In other words, white Southerners could either allow black men to vote or see their representation in Washington slashed.

The Fourteenth Amendment's suffrage provisions ignored the small band of women who had emerged from the war demanding "the ballot for the two disenfranchised classes, negroes and women." Founding the American Equal Rights Association in 1866, Susan B. Anthony and Elizabeth Cady Stanton lobbied for "a government by the people, and the whole people; for the people and the whole people." They felt betrayed when their old antislavery allies refused to work for their goals. "It was the Negro's hour," Frederick Douglass explained. Senator Charles Sumner suggested that woman suffrage could be "the great question of the future."

The Fourteenth Amendment provided for punishment of any state that excluded voters on the basis of race, but not on the basis of sex. The amendment also introduced the word *male* into the Constitution when it referred to a citizen's right to vote. Stanton predicted that "if that word 'male' be inserted, it will take us a century at least to get it out."

Tennessee approved the Fourteenth Amendment in July, and Congress promptly welcomed the state's representatives and senators back. Had President Johnson counseled other southern states to ratify this relatively mild amendment, they might have listened. Instead, Johnson advised Southerners to reject the Fourteenth Amendment and to rely on him to trounce the Republicans in the fall congressional elections.

Johnson had decided to make the Fourteenth Amendment the overriding issue of the 1866 elections and to gather its white opponents into a new conservative party, the National Union Party. The president's strategy suffered a setback when whites in several southern cities went on rampages against blacks. Mobs killed thirty-four blacks in New Orleans and forty-six blacks in Memphis. The slaughter shocked Northerners and renewed skepticism about Johnson's claim that southern whites could be trusted. "Who doubts that the Freedmen's Bureau ought to be abolished forthwith," a New Yorker observed sarcastically, "and the blacks remitted to the paternal care of their old masters, who 'understand the nigger, you know, a great deal better than the Yankees can.'"

The 1866 elections resulted in an overwhelming Republican victory. Johnson had bet that Northerners would not support federal protection of black rights and that a racist backlash would blast the Republican Party. But the war was still fresh in northern minds, and as one Republican explained, southern whites "with all their intelligence were traitors, the blacks with all their ignorance were loyal."

Radical Reconstruction and Military Rule

When Johnson continued to urge Southerners to reject the Fourteenth Amendment, every southern state except Tennessee voted it down. "The last one of the sinful ten," thundered Representative James A. Garfield of Ohio, "has flung back into our teeth the magnanimous offer of a generous nation." After the South rejected the moderates' program, the radicals seized the initiative.

Each act of defiance by southern whites had boosted the standing of the radicals within the Republican Party. Radicals such as Massachusetts senator Charles

> CHRONOLOGY

1866
– Congress approves Fourteenth Amendment.
– American Equal Rights Association is founded.

1767
– Military Reconstruction Act.
– Tenure of Office Act.

1868
– Impeachment trial of President Johnson.

1869
– Congress approves Fifteenth Amendment.

| How radical was congressional reconstruction? | What brought the elements of the South's Republican coalition together? | Why did reconstruction collapse? | Conclusion: Was reconstruction "a revolution but half accomplished"? | ✔ LearningCurve Check what you know. bedfordstmartins.com /roarkunderstanding |

467

Sumner and Pennsylvania representative Thaddeus Stevens united in demanding civil and political equality. Southern states were "like clay in the hands of the potter," Stevens declared in January 1867, and he called on Congress to begin reconstruction all over again.

In March 1867, Congress passed the **Military Reconstruction Act** and overturned the Johnson state governments and initiated military rule of the South.

Military Reconstruction Act

▶ Congressional act of March 1867 that initiated military rule of the South. Congressional reconstruction divided the ten unreconstructed Confederate states into five military districts, each under the direction of a Union general. It also established the procedure by which unreconstructed states could reenter the Union.

> **> Military Reconstruction Act**
>
> - The ten unreconstructed Confederate states were divided into five military districts.
> - Congress placed a Union general in charge of each district and instructed him to "suppress insurrection, disorder, and violence" and to begin political reform.
> - After the military had completed voter registration, which would include black men, voters in each state would elect delegates to conventions that would draw up new state constitutions.
> - Each constitution would guarantee black suffrage.
> - When the voters of each state had approved the constitution and the state legislature had ratified the Fourteenth Amendment, the state could submit its work to Congress.
> - If Congress approved the constitution, the state's senators and representatives could be seated, and political reunification would be accomplished.

Radicals proclaimed the provision for black suffrage "a prodigious triumph," for it extended far beyond the limited suffrage provisions of the Fourteenth Amendment. When combined with the disfranchisement of thousands of ex-rebels, it promised to cripple any neo-Confederate resurgence and guarantee Republican state governments in the South.

Despite its bold suffrage provision, the Military Reconstruction Act of 1867 disappointed those who also advocated the confiscation of southern plantations and their redistribution to ex-slaves. Thaddeus Stevens agreed with the freedman who said, "Give us our own land and we take care of ourselves, but without land, the old masters can hire us or starve us, as they please." But most Republicans believed they had provided blacks with what they needed: equal legal rights and the ballot. If blacks were to get land, they would have to gain it themselves.

Declaring that he would rather sever his right arm than sign such a formula for "anarchy and chaos," Andrew Johnson vetoed the Military Reconstruction Act, but Congress overrode his veto. With the passage of the Reconstruction Acts of 1867, congressional reconstruction was virtually completed. Congress left whites owning most of the South's land but, in a departure that justified the term "radical reconstruction," had given black men the ballot.

Reconstruction Military Districts, 1867

Impeaching a President

Despite his defeats, Andrew Johnson had no intention of yielding control of reconstruction. In a dozen ways, he sabotaged Congress's will and encouraged southern whites to resist. He issued a flood of pardons, waged war against the

CHAPTER LOCATOR | Why did Congress object to Lincoln's wartime plan for reconstruction? | How did the North respond to the passage of black codes in the southern states?

468 CHAPTER 16
RECONSTRUCTING A NATION

Freedmen's Bureau, and replaced Union generals eager to enforce Congress's Reconstruction Acts with conservative officers eager to defeat them. Johnson claimed that he was merely defending the "violated Constitution." At bottom, however, the president subverted congressional reconstruction to protect southern whites from what he considered the horrors of "Negro domination."

Radicals argued that Johnson's abuse of constitutional powers and his failure to fulfill constitutional obligations to enforce the law were impeachable offenses. According to the Constitution, the House of Representatives can impeach and the Senate can try any federal official for "treason, bribery, or other high crimes and misdemeanors." But moderates interpreted the Constitution to mean violation of criminal statutes. As long as Johnson refrained from breaking the law, impeachment (the process of formal charges of wrongdoing against the president or other federal official) remained stalled.

Then in August 1867, Johnson suspended Secretary of War Edwin M. Stanton from office. As required by the Tenure of Office Act, a law passed in March 1867 that demanded the approval of the Senate for the removal of any government official who had been appointed with Senate approval, the president requested the Senate to consent to Stanton's dismissal. When the Senate balked, Johnson removed Stanton anyway. "Is the President crazy, or only drunk?" asked a dumbfounded Republican moderate. "I'm afraid his doings will make us all favor impeachment."

News of Johnson's open defiance of the law convinced every Republican in the House to vote for a resolution impeaching the president. Supreme Court chief justice Salmon Chase presided over the Senate trial, which lasted from March until May 1868. When the vote came, thirty-five senators voted guilty and nineteen not guilty. The impeachment forces fell one vote short of the two-thirds needed to convict.

After his trial, Johnson called a truce, and for the remaining ten months of his term, congressional reconstruction proceeded unhindered by presidential interference. Without interference from Johnson, Congress revisited the suffrage issue.

The Fifteenth Amendment and Women's Demands

In February 1869, Republicans passed the **Fifteenth Amendment** to the Constitution, which prohibited states from depriving any citizen of the right to vote because of "race, color, or previous condition of servitude." The Reconstruction Acts of 1867 already required black suffrage in the South; the Fifteenth Amendment extended black voting nationwide.

Some Republicans, however, found the final wording of the Fifteenth Amendment "lame and halting." Rather than absolutely guaranteeing the right to vote, the amendment merely prohibited exclusion on grounds of race. The distinction would prove to be significant. In time, white Southerners would devise tests of literacy and property and other apparently nonracial measures that would effectively disfranchise blacks yet not violate the Fifteenth Amendment. But an amendment that fully guaranteed the right to vote courted defeat outside the South. Rising antiforeign sentiment — against the Chinese in California and

Fifteenth Amendment

▶ Constitutional amendment passed in February 1869 prohibiting states from depriving any citizen of the right to vote because of "race, color, or previous condition of servitude." It extended black suffrage nationwide. Woman suffrage advocates were disappointed that the amendment failed to extend voting rights to women.

| How radical was congressional reconstruction? | What brought the elements of the South's Republican coalition together? | Why did reconstruction collapse? | Conclusion: Was reconstruction "a revolution but half accomplished"? | ✓ LearningCurve Check what you know. bedfordstmartins.com /roarkunderstanding |

469

Outspoken suffragists Elizabeth Cady Stanton (left) and Susan B. Anthony (right) were veteran reformers who advocated, among other things, better working conditions for labor, married women's property rights, liberalization of divorce laws, and women's admission into colleges and trade schools. Their passion for other causes led some conservatives to oppose women's political rights because they equated the suffragist cause with radicalism in general. © Bettmann/Corbis.

European immigrants in the Northeast — caused states to resist giving up total control of suffrage requirements. In March 1870, after three-fourths of the states had ratified it, the Fifteenth Amendment became part of the Constitution.

Woman suffrage advocates, however, were sorely disappointed with the Fifteenth Amendment's failure to extend voting rights to women. Elizabeth Cady Stanton and Susan B. Anthony condemned the Republicans' "negro first" strategy and pointed out that women remained "the only class of citizens wholly unrepresented in the government." The Fifteenth Amendment severed the early feminist movement from its abolitionist roots. Over the next several decades, feminists established an independent suffrage crusade that drew millions of women into political life.

Republicans took enough satisfaction in the Fifteenth Amendment to promptly scratch the "Negro question" from the agenda of national politics. Even Wendell Phillips, a steadfast crusader for equality, concluded that the black man now held "sufficient shield in his own hands. . . . Whatever he suffers will be largely now, and in future, his own fault." Northerners had no idea of the violent struggles that lay ahead.

> **QUICK REVIEW**

Why did Congress impeach President Andrew Johnson?

CHAPTER LOCATOR | Why did Congress object to Lincoln's wartime plan for reconstruction? | How did the North respond to the passage of black codes in the southern states?

CHAPTER 16
470 RECONSTRUCTING A NATION

What brought the elements of the South's Republican coalition together?

Black Woman in a Cotton Field, Thomasville, Georgia

Few images of everyday black women during the Reconstruction era survive. This photograph was taken in 1895, but it nevertheless goes to the heart of the labor struggle after the Civil War. Before emancipation, black women worked in the fields; after emancipation, white landlords wanted them to continue working there. Freedom allowed some women to escape field labor, but not this Georgian, who probably worked to survive. Courtesy, Georgia Department of Archives and History, Atlanta, Georgia.

NORTHERNERS BELIEVED they had discharged their responsibilities with the Reconstruction Acts and the amendments to the Constitution, but Southerners knew that the battle had just begun. Black suffrage established the foundation for the rise of the Republican Party in the South. Gathering together outsiders and outcasts, southern Republicans won elections, wrote new state constitutions, and formed new state governments.

Challenging the established class for political control was dangerous business. Equally dangerous were the confrontations that took place on southern farms and plantations, where blacks sought to give fuller meaning to their newly won legal and political equality. Freedom remained contested territory, and Southerners fought pitched battles with one another to determine the contours of their new world.

Freedmen, Yankees, and Yeomen

African Americans made up the majority of southern Republicans. After gaining voting rights in 1867, nearly all eligible black men registered to vote as Republicans. "It is the hardest thing in the world to keep a negro away from the polls," observed an Alabama white man. Southern blacks did not all have identical political priorities, but they united in their desire for education and equal treatment before the law.

> CHRONOLOGY

1866
– Ku Klux Klan is founded.

1867
– Southern African Americans gain voting rights under the Military Reconstruction Act.
– Southern states hold elections for delegates to state conventions.

1875
– One-half of South Carolina's and Mississippi's children, the majority black, attend school.
– Sharecropping is the dominant labor system for rural southern blacks.

| How radical was congressional reconstruction? | **What brought the elements of the South's Republican coalition together?** | Why did reconstruction collapse? | Conclusion: Was reconstruction "a revolution but half accomplished"? | ☑ LearningCurve Check what you know. bedfordstmartins.com /roarkunderstanding |

carpetbaggers

▶ Southerners' pejorative term for northern migrants who sought opportunity in the South after the Civil War. Northern migrants formed an important part of the southern Republican Party.

scalawags

▶ A derogatory term that Southerners applied to southern white Republicans, who were seen as traitors to the South. Most were yeoman farmers.

Ku Klux Klan

▶ A social club of Confederate veterans that quickly developed into a paramilitary organization supporting Democrats. With too few Union troops in the South to control the region, the Klan went on a rampage of violence to defeat Republicans and restore white supremacy.

Northern whites who made the South their home after the war were a second element of the South's Republican Party. Conservative white Southerners called them **carpetbaggers**, opportunists who stuffed all their belongings in a single carpet-sided suitcase and headed south to "fatten on our misfortunes." But most Northerners who moved south were young men who looked upon the South as they did the West — as a promising place to make a living. Northerners in the southern Republican Party supported programs that encouraged vigorous economic development along the lines of the northern free-labor model.

Southern whites made up the third element of the South's Republican Party. Approximately one out of four white Southerners voted Republican. The other three condemned the one who did as a traitor to his region and his race and called him a **scalawag**, a term for runty horses and low-down, good-for-nothing rascals. Yeoman farmers accounted for the majority of southern white Republicans. Some were Unionists who emerged from the war with bitter memories of Confederate persecution. Others were small farmers who wanted to end state governments' favoritism toward plantation owners. Yeomen supported initiatives for public schools and for expanding economic opportunity in the South.

The South's Republican Party, then, was made up of freedmen, Yankees, and yeomen — an improbable coalition. The mix of races, regions, and classes inevitably meant friction as each group maneuvered to define the party. But Reconstruction represents an extraordinary moment in American politics: Blacks and whites joined together in the Republican Party to pursue political change. Formally, of course, only men participated in politics — casting ballots and holding offices — but white and black women also played a part in the political struggle by joining in parades and rallies, attending stump speeches, and even campaigning.

Most whites in the South condemned southern Republicans as illegitimate and felt justified in doing whatever they could to stamp them out. Violence against blacks — the "white terror" — took brutal institutional form in 1866 with the formation in Tennessee of the **Ku Klux Klan**, a social club of Confederate veterans that quickly developed into a paramilitary organization supporting Democrats. The Klan went on a rampage of violence to defeat Republicans and restore white supremacy. Rapid demobilization of the Union army after the war left only twenty thousand troops to patrol the entire South. Without effective military protection, southern Republicans had to take care of themselves.

Republican Rule

In the fall of 1867, southern states held elections for delegates to state constitutional conventions, as required by the Reconstruction Acts. About 40 percent of the white electorate stayed home because they had been disfranchised or because they had decided to boycott politics. Republicans won three-fourths of the seats. About 15 percent of the Republican delegates to the conventions were Northerners who had moved south, 25 percent were African Americans, and 60 percent were white Southerners. As a British visitor observed, the delegate elections reflected "the mighty revolution that had taken place in America."

The reconstruction constitutions introduced two broad categories of changes in the South: those that reduced aristocratic privilege and increased democratic equality and those that expanded the state's responsibility for the general welfare. In the first

CHAPTER LOCATOR | Why did Congress object to Lincoln's wartime plan for reconstruction? | How did the North respond to the passage of black codes in the southern states?

472 CHAPTER 16 RECONSTRUCTING A NATION

category, the constitutions adopted universal male suffrage, abolished property qualifications for holding office, and made more offices elective and fewer appointed. In the second category, they enacted prison reform; made the state responsible for caring for orphans, the insane, and the deaf and mute; and exempted debtors' homes from seizure.

To Democrats, however, these progressive constitutions looked like wild revolution. Democrats were blind to the fact that no constitution confiscated and redistributed land, as virtually every former slave wished, or disfranchised ex-rebels wholesale, as most southern Unionists advocated. And they were convinced that the new constitutions initiated "Negro domination." In fact, although 80 percent of Republican voters were black men, only 6 percent of Southerners in Congress during reconstruction were black (**Figure 16.1**). The sixteen black men in Congress included exceptional men, such as Representative James T. Rapier of Alabama. No state legislature experienced "Negro rule," despite black majorities in the populations of some states.

Southern voters ratified the new constitutions and swept Republicans into power. When the former Confederate states ratified the Fourteenth Amendment, Congress readmitted them. Southern Republicans then turned to a staggering array of problems. Wartime destruction littered the landscape. Making matters worse, racial harassment and reactionary violence dogged Southerners who sought reform. In this desperate context, Republicans struggled to rebuild and reform the region.

Activity focused on three areas — education, civil rights, and economic development. Every state inaugurated a system of public education. Before the Civil War, whites had deliberately kept slaves illiterate, and planter-dominated governments rarely spent tax money to educate the children of yeomen. By 1875, half of Mississippi's and South Carolina's eligible children were attending school. Although schools were underfunded, literacy rates rose sharply. Public schools were racially segregated, but education remained for many blacks a tangible, deeply satisfying benefit of freedom and Republican rule.

State legislatures also attacked racial discrimination and defended civil rights. Republicans especially resisted efforts to segregate blacks from whites in public transportation. Mississippi levied fines and jail terms for owners of railroads and steamboats that pushed blacks into "smoking cars" or to lower decks. But passing color-blind laws was far easier than enforcing them. A Mississippian complained: "Education amounts to nothing, good behavior counts for nothing, even money cannot buy for a colored man or woman decent treatment and the comforts that white people claim and can obtain." Despite the laws, segregation — later called Jim Crow — developed at white insistence and became a feature of southern life long before the end of the Reconstruction era.

Republican governments also launched ambitious programs of economic development. They envisioned a South of diversified agriculture, roaring factories, and booming towns. State legislatures chartered scores of banks and industrial companies, appropriated funds to fix ruined levees and drain swamps, and went on a railroad-building binge. These efforts fell far short of solving the South's economic troubles, however. Republican spending to stimulate economic growth also meant rising taxes and enormous debt that siphoned funds from schools and other programs.

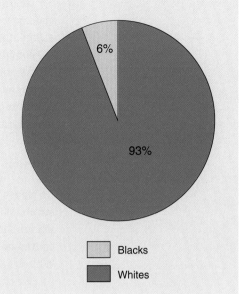

6%

93%

Blacks
Whites

FIGURE 16.1 ■ Southern Congressional Delegations, 1865–1877

The statistics contradict the myth of black domination of congressional representation during reconstruction.

How radical was congressional reconstruction?

What brought the elements of the South's Republican coalition together?

Why did reconstruction collapse?

Conclusion: Was reconstruction "a revolution but half accomplished"?

✓ LearningCurve
Check what you know.
bedfordstmartins.com
/roarkunderstanding

473

The southern Republicans' record, then, was mixed. To their credit, the bira-cial party adopted an ambitious agenda to change the South. But money was scarce, the Democrats continued their harassment, and factionalism threatened the Republican Party from within. Moreover, corruption infected Republican governments. Nonetheless, the Republican Party made headway in its efforts to purge the South of aristocratic privilege and racist oppression. Republican governments had less success in overthrowing the long-established white oppression of black farm laborers in the rural South.

White Landlords, Black Sharecroppers

Ex-slaves who wished to escape slave labor and ex-masters who wanted to rein-stitute old ways clashed repeatedly. Except for having to pay subsistence wages, planters had not been required to offer many concessions to emancipation. They continued to believe that African Americans would not work without coercion. Whites moved quickly to restore as much of slavery as they could get away with.

Ex-slaves resisted every effort to turn back the clock. They believed that land of their own would anchor their economic independence and end planters' inter-ference in their personal lives. They could then, for example, make their own deci-sions about whether women and children would labor in the fields. Indeed, within months after the war, perhaps one-third of black women abandoned field labor to work on chores in their own cabins just as poor white women did. Black women also negotiated about work ex-mistresses wanted done in the big house. Hundreds of thousands of black children enrolled in school. But without their own land, ex-slaves had little choice but to work on plantations.

Although forced to return to the planters' fields, they resisted efforts to restore slavelike conditions. Instead of working for wages, a South Carolinian observed, "the negroes all seem disposed to rent land," which increased their independence from whites. Out of this tug-of-war between white landlords and black laborers emerged a new system of southern agriculture.

Sharecropping was a compromise that offered something to both ex-masters and ex-slaves but satisfied neither. Under the new system, planters divided their cotton plantations into small farms that freedmen rented, paying with a share of each year's crop, usually half. Sharecropping gave blacks more freedom than the system of wages and labor gangs and released them from day-to-day supervision by whites. Black families abandoned the old slave quarters and built separate cabins for themselves on the patches of land they rented (**Map 16.1**). Still, most black fami-lies remained dependent on white landlords, who had the power to evict them at the end of each growing season. For planters, sharecropping offered a way to resume agricultural production, but it did not allow them to restore the old slave plantation.

Sharecropping introduced the country merchant into the agricultural equation. Landlords supplied sharecroppers with land, mules, seeds, and tools, but blacks also needed credit to obtain essential food and clothing before they harvested their crop. Under an arrangement called a crop lien, a merchant would advance goods to a sharecropper in exchange for a *lien*, or legal claim, on the farmer's future crop. Some merchants charged exorbitant rates of interest, as much as 60 percent, on the goods they sold. At the end of the growing season, after the landlord had taken half of the farmer's crop for rent, the merchant took most of the rest. Sometimes,

sharecropping

▶ Labor system that emerged in the South during reconstruction. Under this system, planters divided their plantations into small farms that freedmen rented, paying with a share of each year's crop. Sharecropping gave blacks some freedom, but they remained dependent on white landlords and country merchants.

CHAPTER LOCATOR | Why did Congress object to Lincoln's wartime plan for reconstruction? | How did the North respond to the passage of black codes in the southern states?

474   CHAPTER 16   RECONSTRUCTING A NATION

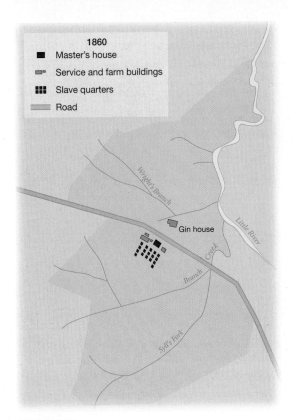

1860
- ■ Master's house
- ⬛ Service and farm buildings
- ⊞ Slave quarters
- ▬ Road

Wright's Branch

Little River

Creek

Gin house

Branch

Syll's Fork

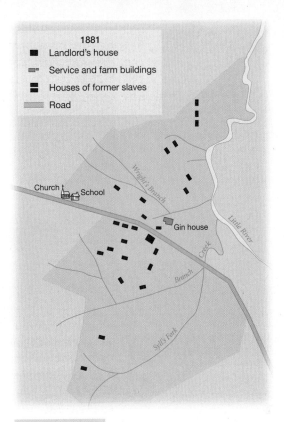

1881
- ■ Landlord's house
- ⬛ Service and farm buildings
- ▮ Houses of former slaves
- ▬ Road

Church · School

Wright's Branch

Little River

Gin house

Creek

Branch

Syll's Fork

MAP 16.1 ■ A Southern Plantation in 1860 and 1881

These maps of the Barrow plantation in Georgia illustrate some of the ways in which ex-slaves expressed their freedom. Freedmen and freedwomen deserted the clustered living quarters behind the master's house, scattered over the plantation, built family cabins, and farmed rented land. The former Barrow slaves also worked together to build a school and a church.

> **> MAP ACTIVITY**

READING THE MAP: Compare the number and size of the slave quarters in 1860 with the homes of the former slaves in 1881. How do they differ? Which buildings were prominently located along the road in 1860, and which could be found along the road in 1881?

CONNECTIONS: How might the former master feel about the new configuration of buildings on the plantation in 1881? In what ways did the new system of sharecropping replicate the old system of plantation agriculture? In what ways was it different?

the farmer did not earn enough to repay the debt to the merchant, and he would have to borrow more from the merchant and begin the cycle again.

An experiment at first, sharecropping soon dominated the cotton South. Lien merchants forced tenants to plant cotton, which was easy to sell, instead of food crops. The result was excessive production of cotton and falling cotton prices, developments that cost thousands of small white farmers their land and pushed them into the great army of sharecroppers. The new sharecropping system of agriculture took shape just as the political power of Republicans in the South began to buckle under Democratic pressure.

QUICK REVIEW ◀

How did politics and economic concerns shape reconstruction in the South?

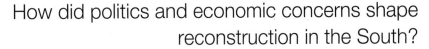

How radical was congressional reconstruction?

What brought the elements of the South's Republican coalition together?

Why did reconstruction collapse?

Conclusion: Was reconstruction "a revolution but half accomplished"?

✓ LearningCurve
Check what you know.
bedfordstmartins.com
/roarkunderstanding

> Why did reconstruction collapse?

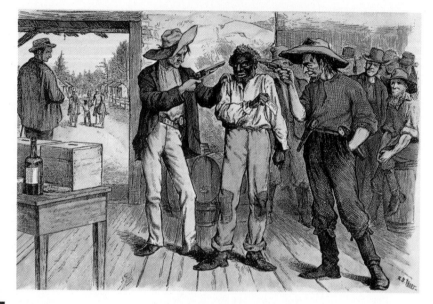

"Of Course He Wants to Vote the Democratic Ticket"

This Republican cartoon from the October 21, 1876, issue of *Harper's Weekly* comments sarcastically on the possibility of honest elections in the South. The caption reads, "You're free as air, ain't you? Say you are or I'll blow yer black head off." Granger Collection.

BY 1870, after a decade of war and reconstruction, Northerners wanted to put "the southern problem" behind them. Practical business-minded men came to dominate the Republican Party, replacing the band of reformers and idealists who had been prominent in the 1860s. Civil war hero Ulysses S. Grant succeeded Andrew Johnson as president in 1869 and quickly became an issue himself, proving that brilliance on the battlefield does not necessarily translate into competence in the White House. As northern commitment to defend black freedom eroded, southern commitment to white supremacy intensified. Without northern protection, southern Republicans were no match for the Democrats' economic coercion, political fraud, and bloody violence. One by one, Republican state governments fell in the South. The election of 1876 both confirmed and completed the collapse of reconstruction.

Candidate	Electoral Vote	Popular Vote	Percent of Popular Vote
Ulysses S. Grant (Republican)	214	3,012,833	52.7
Horatio Seymour (Democrat)	80	2,703,249	47.3
Nonvoting states (Reconstruction)			

MAP 16.2 ■ The Election of 1868

Grant's Troubled Presidency

In 1868, the Republican Party's presidential nomination went to Ulysses S. Grant, the North's favorite general. His Democratic opponent, Horatio Seymour of New York, ran on a platform that blasted reconstruction as "a flagrant usurpation of power . . . unconstitutional, revolutionary, and void." The

CHAPTER LOCATOR | Why did Congress object to Lincoln's wartime plan for reconstruction? | How did the North respond to the passage of black codes in the southern states?

Republicans answered by "waving the bloody shirt" — that is, they reminded voters that the Democrats were "the party of rebellion." Grant gained a narrow 309,000-vote margin in the popular vote and a substantial victory (214 votes to 80) in the electoral college (**Map 16.2**).

Grant was not as good a president as he was a general. The talents he had demonstrated on the battlefield — decisiveness, clarity, and resolution — were less obvious in the White House. Grant sought both justice for blacks and sectional reconciliation. But he surrounded himself with fumbling kinfolk and old friends from his army days and made a string of dubious appointments that led to a series of damaging scandals. Charges of corruption tainted his vice president, Schuyler Colfax, and brought down two of his cabinet officers. Though never personally implicated in any scandal, Grant was aggravatingly naive and blind to the rot that filled his administration.

In 1872, anti-Grant Republicans bolted and launched the Liberal Party. To clean up the graft and corruption, Liberals proposed ending the spoils system,

> CHRONOLOGY

1868
– Ulysses S. Grant is elected president.

1871
– Ku Klux Klan Act.

1872
– Liberal Party is formed.
– President Grant is reelected.

1873
– Economic depression sets in.
– *Slaughterhouse* cases.
– Colfax massacre.

1874
– Democrats win majority in House of Representatives.

1877
– In the disputed presidential election of 1876, Rutherford Hayes is declared the winner.

Grant and Scandal

This anti-Grant cartoon by Thomas Nast, the nation's most celebrated political cartoonist, shows the president falling headfirst into the barrel of fraud and corruption that tainted his administration. During Grant's eight years in the White House, many members of his administration failed him. Sometimes duped, sometimes merely loyal, Grant stubbornly defended wrongdoers, even to the point of perjuring himself to keep an aide out of jail. Library of Congress.

> VISUAL ACTIVITY

READING THE IMAGE: How does Thomas Nast portray President Grant's role in corruption? According to this cartoon, what caused the problems?

CONNECTIONS: How responsible was President Grant for the corruption that plagued his administration?

| How radical was congressional reconstruction? | What brought the elements of the South's Republican coalition together? | **Why did reconstruction collapse?** | Conclusion: Was reconstruction "a revolution but half accomplished"? |

✓ **LearningCurve**
Check what you know.
bedfordstmartins.com /roarkunderstanding

by which victorious parties rewarded loyal workers with public office, and replacing it with a nonpartisan civil service commission that would oversee competitive examinations for appointment to office. Liberals also demanded that the federal government remove its troops from the South and restore "home rule" (southern white control). Democrats liked the Liberals' southern policy and endorsed the Liberal presidential candidate, Horace Greeley, the longtime editor of the *New York Tribune*. The nation, however, still felt enormous affection for the man who had saved the Union and reelected Grant with 56 percent of the popular vote.

Northern Resolve Withers

Although Grant genuinely wanted to see blacks' civil and political rights protected, he understood that most Northerners had grown weary of reconstruction and were increasingly willing to let southern whites manage their own affairs. Citizens wanted to shift their attention to other issues, especially after the nation slipped into a devastating economic depression in 1873. More than eighteen thousand businesses collapsed, leaving more than a million workers on the streets. Northern businessmen wanted to invest in the South but believed that recurrent federal intrusion was itself a major cause of instability in the region. Republican leaders began to question the wisdom of their party's alliance with the South's lower classes — its small farmers and sharecroppers. One member of Grant's administration proposed allying with the "thinking and influential native southerners . . . the intelligent, well-to-do, and controlling class."

Congress, too, wanted to leave reconstruction behind, but southern Republicans made that difficult. When the South's Republicans begged for federal protection from increasing Klan violence, Congress enacted three laws in 1870 and 1871 that were intended to break the back of white terrorism. The severest of the three, the Ku Klux Klan Act (1871), made interference with voting rights a felony. Federal marshals arrested thousands of Klansmen and came close to destroying the Klan, but they did not end all terrorism against blacks. Congress also passed the Civil Rights Act of 1875, which boldly outlawed racial discrimination in transportation, public accommodations, and juries. But federal authorities never enforced the law aggressively, and segregated facilities remained the rule throughout the South.

By the early 1870s, the Republican Party had lost its leading champions of African American rights to death or defeat at the polls. Other Republicans concluded that the quest for black equality was mistaken or hopelessly naive. In May 1872, Congress restored the right of office holding to all but three hundred ex-rebels. Many Republicans had come to believe that traditional white leaders offered the best hope for honesty, order, and prosperity in the South.

Underlying the North's abandonment of reconstruction was unyielding racial prejudice. Northerners had learned to accept black freedom during the war, but deep-seated prejudice prevented many from accepting black equality. Even the actions they took on behalf of blacks often served partisan political advantage. Northerners generally supported Indiana senator Thomas A. Hendricks's harsh declaration that "this is a white man's Government, made by the white man for the white man."

CHAPTER LOCATOR | Why did Congress object to Lincoln's wartime plan for reconstruction? | How did the North respond to the passage of black codes in the southern states?

478   CHAPTER 16
RECONSTRUCTING A NATION

The U.S. Supreme Court also did its part to undermine reconstruction. The Court issued a series of decisions that significantly weakened the federal government's ability to protect black Southerners. In the *Slaughterhouse* cases (1873), the Court distinguished between national and state citizenship and ruled that the Fourteenth Amendment protected only those rights that stemmed from the federal government, such as voting in federal elections and interstate travel. Since the Court decided that most rights derived from the states, it sharply curtailed the federal government's authority to defend black citizens. Even more devastating, the *United States v. Cruikshank* ruling (1876) said that the reconstruction amendments gave Congress the power to legislate against discrimination only by states, not by individuals. The "suppression of ordinary crime," such as assault, remained a state responsibility. The Supreme Court did not declare reconstruction unconstitutional but eroded its legal foundation.

The mood of the North found political expression in the election of 1874, when for the first time in eighteen years the Democrats gained control of the House of Representatives. As one Republican observed, the people had grown tired of the "negro question, with all its complications, and the reconstruction of Southern States, with all its interminable embroilments." Reconstruction had come apart. Rather than defend reconstruction from its southern enemies, Northerners steadily backed away from the challenge. By the early 1870s, southern Republicans faced the forces of reaction largely on their own.

White Supremacy Triumphs

Reconstruction was a massive humiliation to most white Southerners. Republican rule meant intolerable insults: Black militiamen patrolled town streets, black laborers negotiated contracts with former masters, black maids stood up to former mistresses, black voters cast ballots, and black legislators such as James T. Rapier enacted laws. Republican governments in the South attracted more hatred than did any other political regimes in American history. The northern retreat from reconstruction permitted southern Democrats to set things right.

Taking the name **Redeemers**, Democrats in the South promised to replace "bayonet rule" (a few federal troops continued to be stationed in the South) with "home rule." They promised that honest, thrifty Democrats would supplant corrupt tax-and-spend Republicans. Above all, Redeemers swore to save southern civilization from a descent into "African barbarism." As one man put it, "We must render this either a white man's government, or convert the land into a Negro man's cemetery."

Southern Democrats adopted a multipronged strategy to overthrow Republican governments. First, they sought to polarize the parties around color. They went about gathering all the South's white voters into the Democratic Party, leaving the Republicans to depend on blacks, who made up a minority of the population in almost every southern state. To dislodge whites from the Republican Party, Democrats fanned the flames of racial prejudice. A South Carolina Democrat crowed that his party appealed to the "proud Caucasian race, whose sovereignty on earth God has proclaimed." Local newspapers published the names of whites who kept company with blacks, and neighbors ostracized offenders.

Redeemers

▶ Name taken by southern Democrats who harnessed white rage in order to overthrow Republican rule and black political power and thus, they believed, save southern civilization.

How radical was congressional reconstruction?

What brought the elements of the South's Republican coalition together?

Why did reconstruction collapse?

Conclusion: Was reconstruction "a revolution but half accomplished"?

☑ LearningCurve
Check what you know.
bedfordstmartins.com
/roarkunderstanding

479

This silk ribbon from the 1868 presidential campaign between Republican Ulysses S. Grant and his Democratic opponent, New York governor Horatio Seymour, openly declares the Democrats' goal of white supremacy. During the campaign, Democratic vice presidential nominee Francis P. Blair Jr. promised that a Seymour victory would restore "white people" to power by declaring the reconstruction governments in the South "null and void." Collection of Janice L. and David J. Frent.

Democrats also exploited the severe economic plight of small white farmers by blaming it on Republican financial policy. Government spending soared during reconstruction, and small farmers saw their tax burden skyrocket. "This is tax time," a South Carolinian reported. "We are nearly all on our head about them. They are so high & so little money to pay with" that farmers "[are] selling every egg and chicken they can get." In 1871, Mississippi reported that one-seventh of the state's land — 3.3 million acres — had been forfeited for nonpayment of taxes. The small farmers' economic distress had a racial dimension. Because few freedmen succeeded in acquiring land, they rarely paid taxes. In Georgia in 1874, blacks made up 45 percent of the population but paid only 2 percent of the taxes. From the perspective of a small white farmer, Republican rule meant that he was paying more taxes and paying them to aid blacks.

If racial pride, social isolation, and financial hardship proved insufficient to drive yeomen from the Republican Party, Democrats turned to terrorism. "Night riders" targeted white Republicans as well as blacks for murder and assassination. Whether white or black, a "dead Radical is very harmless," South Carolina Democratic leader Martin Gary told his followers.

But the primary victims of white violence were black Republicans. Violence escalated to an unprecedented ferocity on Easter Sunday in 1873 in tiny Colfax, Louisiana. The black majority in the area had made Colfax a Republican stronghold until 1872, when Democrats turned to intimidation and fraud to win the local election. Republicans refused to accept the result and eventually occupied the courthouse in the middle of the town. After three weeks, 165 white men attacked. They overran the Republicans' defenses and set the courthouse on fire. When the blacks tried to surrender, the whites murdered them. At least 81 black men were slaughtered that day. Although the federal government indicted the attackers, the Supreme Court ruled that it did not have the right to prosecute. And since local whites would not prosecute neighbors who killed blacks, the defendants in the Colfax massacre went free.

Even before adopting the all-out white supremacist tactics of the 1870s, Democrats had taken control of the governments of Virginia, Tennessee, and North Carolina. The new campaign brought fresh gains. The Redeemers retook Georgia in 1871, Texas in 1873, and Arkansas and Alabama in 1874. As Mississippi's election approached in 1876, Governor Adelbert Ames appealed to Washington for federal troops to control the violence, only to hear from the attorney general that the "whole public are tired of these annual autumnal outbreaks in the South." Abandoned, Mississippi Republicans succumbed to the Democratic onslaught in the fall elections. By 1876, only three Republican state governments survived in the South (**Map 16.3**).

CHAPTER LOCATOR | Why did Congress object to Lincoln's wartime plan for reconstruction? | How did the North respond to the passage of black codes in the southern states?

480 CHAPTER 16 RECONSTRUCTING A NATION

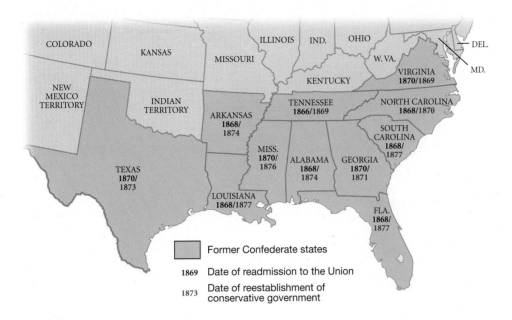

COLORADO | KANSAS | ILLINOIS | IND. | OHIO | DEL.
NEW MEXICO TERRITORY | INDIAN TERRITORY | MISSOURI | W. VA. | MD.
KENTUCKY | VIRGINIA 1870/1869
ARKANSAS 1868/1874 | TENNESSEE 1866/1869 | NORTH CAROLINA 1868/1870
TEXAS 1870/1873 | MISS. 1870/1876 | ALABAMA 1868/1874 | GEORGIA 1870/1871 | SOUTH CAROLINA 1868/1877
LOUISIANA 1868/1877 | FLA. 1868/1877

Former Confederate states

1869 Date of readmission to the Union

1873 Date of reestablishment of conservative government

MAP 16.3 ■ The Reconstruction of the South

Myth has it that Republican rule of the former Confederacy was not only harsh but long. In most states, however, conservative southern whites stormed back into power in months or just a few years. By the election of 1876, Republican governments could be found in only three states, and they soon fell.

> MAP ACTIVITY

READING THE MAP: List in chronological order the readmission of the former Confederate states to the Union. Which states reestablished conservative governments most quickly?

CONNECTIONS: What did the former Confederate states need to do in order to be readmitted to the Union? How did reestablished conservative governments react to reconstruction?

An Election and a Compromise

The year 1876 witnessed one of the most tumultuous elections in American history. The election took place in November, but not until March 2 of the following year did the nation know who would be inaugurated president on March 4. The Democrats nominated New York's governor, Samuel J. Tilden, who immediately targeted the corruption of the Grant administration and the "despotism" of Republican reconstruction. The Republicans put forward Rutherford B. Hayes, governor of Ohio. Privately, Hayes considered "bayonet rule" a mistake but concluded that waving the bloody shirt remained the Republicans' best political strategy.

On election day, Tilden tallied 4,288,590 votes to Hayes's 4,036,000. But in the all-important electoral college, Tilden fell one vote short of the majority required for victory. The electoral votes of three states — South Carolina, Louisiana, and Florida, the only remaining Republican governments in the South — remained in doubt because both Republicans and Democrats in those states claimed victory. To win, Tilden needed only one of the nineteen contested votes. Hayes had to have all of them.

Congress had to decide who had actually won the elections in the three southern states and thus who would be president. The Constitution provided no guidance for this situation. Moreover, Democrats controlled the House, and Republicans controlled the Senate. Congress created a special electoral

| How radical was congressional reconstruction? | What brought the elements of the South's Republican coalition together? | **Why did reconstruction collapse?** | Conclusion: Was reconstruction "a revolution but half accomplished"? | ✔ LearningCurve Check what you know. bedfordstmartins.com /roarkunderstanding |

MAP 16.4 ■ The Election of 1876

Candidate	Electoral Vote	Popular Vote	Percent of Popular Vote
Rutherford B. Hayes (Republican)	185*	4,036,298	47.9**
Samuel J. Tilden (Democrat)	184	4,288,590	51.0

*19 electoral votes were disputed.

**Percentages do not total 100 because some popular votes went to other parties.

commission to arbitrate the disputed returns. All of the commissioners voted their party affiliation, giving every state to the Republican Hayes and putting him over the top in electoral votes (**Map 16.4**).

Some outraged Democrats vowed to resist Hayes's victory. Rumors flew of an impending coup and renewed civil war. But the impasse was broken when negotiations behind the scenes resulted in an informal understanding known as the **Compromise of 1877**. In exchange for a Democratic promise not to block Hayes's inauguration and to deal fairly with the freedmen, Hayes vowed to refrain from using the army to uphold the remaining Republican regimes in the South and to provide the South with substantial federal subsidies for railroads.

Stubborn Tilden supporters bemoaned the "stolen election" and damned "His Fraudulency," Rutherford B. Hayes. Old-guard radicals such as William Lloyd Garrison denounced Hayes's bargain as a "policy of compromise, of credulity, of weakness, of subserviency, of surrender." But the nation as a whole celebrated, for the country had weathered a grave crisis. The last three Republican state governments in the South fell quickly once Hayes abandoned them and withdrew the U.S. Army. Reconstruction came to an end.

Compromise of 1877

▶ Informal agreement in which Democrats agreed not to block Rutherford Hayes's inauguration and to deal fairly with freedmen; in return, Hayes vowed not to use the army to uphold the remaining Republican regimes in the South and to provide the South with substantial federal subsidies for railroads. The compromise brought the Reconstruction era to an end.

> **QUICK REVIEW**

How did the Supreme Court undermine reconstruction?

CHAPTER LOCATOR | Why did Congress object to Lincoln's wartime plan for reconstruction? | How did the North respond to the passage of black codes in the southern states?

Conclusion: Was reconstruction "a revolution but half accomplished"?

IN 1865, when General Carl Schurz visited the South, he discovered "a revolution but half accomplished." White Southerners resisted the passage from slavery to free labor, from white racial despotism to equal justice, and from white political monopoly to biracial democracy. The old elite wanted to get "things back as near to slavery as possible," Schurz reported, while African Americans such as James T. Rapier and some whites were eager to exploit the revolutionary implications of defeat and emancipation.

Although the northern-dominated Republican Congress refused to provide for blacks' economic welfare, it employed constitutional amendments to require ex-Confederates to accept legal equality and share political power with black men. Conservative southern whites fought ferociously to recover their power and privilege. When Democrats regained control of politics, whites used both state power and private violence to wipe out many of the gains of Reconstruction, leading one observer to conclude that the North had won the war but the South had won the peace.

The Redeemer counterrevolution, however, did not mean a return to slavery. Northern victory in the Civil War ensured that ex-slaves no longer faced the auction block and could send their children to school, worship in their own churches, and work independently on their own rented farms. Sharecropping, with all its hardships, provided more autonomy and economic welfare than bondage had. It was limited freedom, to be sure, but it was not slavery.

The Civil War and emancipation set in motion the most profound upheaval in the nation's history. War destroyed the largest slave society in the New World and gave birth to a modern nation-state. Washington, D.C., increased its role in national affairs, and the victorious North set the nation's compass toward the expansion of industrial capitalism and the final conquest of the West.

Despite massive changes, however, the Civil War remained only a "half accomplished" revolution. By not fulfilling the promises the nation seemed to hold out to black Americans at war's end, Reconstruction represents a tragedy of enormous proportions. The failure to protect blacks and guarantee their rights had enduring consequences. It was the failure of the first reconstruction that made the modern civil rights movement necessary.

How radical was congressional reconstruction?

What brought the elements of the South's Republican coalition together?

Why did reconstruction collapse?

Conclusion: Was reconstruction "a revolution but half accomplished"?

✓ LearningCurve
Check what you know.
bedfordstmartins.com
/roarkunderstanding

CHAPTER 16 STUDY GUIDE

 STEP 1 **GET STARTED ONLINE**

✓ **LearningCurve** ■ bedfordstmartins.com/roarkunderstanding

Now that you've read the chapter, make it stick by completing the LearningCurve activity.

 STEP 2 **EXPLAIN WHY IT MATTERS**

Put your reading into practice. Identify each term below, and then explain why it matters in U.S. history.

TERM	WHO OR WHAT & WHEN	WHY IT MATTERS
Freedmen's Bureau (p. 460)		
black codes (p. 463)		
Civil Rights Act of 1866 (p. 465)		
Fourteenth Amendment (p. 466)		
Military Reconstruction Act (p. 468)		
Fifteenth Amendment (p. 469)		
carpetbaggers (p. 472)		
scalawags (p. 472)		
Ku Klux Klan (p. 472)		
sharecropping (p. 474)		
Redeemers (p. 479)		
Compromise of 1877 (p. 482)		

 STEP 3 **MOVE BEYOND THE BASICS**

To demonstrate a more advanced understanding, indicate below how each phase of reconstruction addressed the key issues involved.

Phase of reconstruction	Requirements for readmission	Role/rights of freedmen	Achievements	Failures
Wartime reconstruction (Lincoln)				
Presidential reconstruction (Johnson)				
Congressional reconstruction				

PUT IT ALL TOGETHER

Now, take a step back and try to explain the big picture. Remember to use specific examples from the chapter in your answers.

PRESIDENTIAL AND CONGRESSIONAL RECONSTRUCTION

▶ What role did the black codes play in shaping the course of reconstruction?

▶ What steps did Congress take between 1865 and 1869 to assist ex-slaves in their lives as freedmen? How effective were these actions?

SOUTHERN RECONSTRUCTION IN ACTION

▶ How did white Southerners respond during reconstruction? Consider both Democrats and Republicans in your response.

▶ How did southern African Americans attempt to shape their own lives during reconstruction?

THE END OF RECONSTRUCTION

▶ How and why did the decline of northern support for reconstruction help southern Democrats "redeem" the South?

▶ Why did white supremacy become the foundation of southern politics in the 1870s?

LOOKING BACKWARD, LOOKING AHEAD

▶ How did long-held racial views among whites, in both the South and the North, shape reconstruction?

▶ What were the lasting accomplishments of reconstruction? What were its most important failures?

> ## IN YOUR OWN WORDS

Imagine that you must give an oral report to the class answering the following question: **What were the achievements and failures of reconstruction?** What would be the most important points to include and why?

17
CONTESTING THE WEST

1865–1900

> **What was most significant about American expansion after the Civil War?** Chapter 17 explores the westward expansion of the United States in the late nineteenth century. It examines the impact of expansion on Native Americans, the role mining played in the creation of the American West, the cultural diversity of the West, and American settlement and exploitation of western lands.

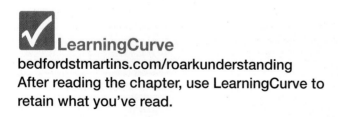

LearningCurve
bedfordstmartins.com/roarkunderstanding
After reading the chapter, use LearningCurve to retain what you've read.

> What did U.S. expansion mean for Native Americans?

> In what ways did different Indian groups defy and resist colonial rule?

> How did mining shape American expansion?

> How did the fight for land and resources in the West unfold?

> Conclusion: How did the West set the tone for the Gilded Age?

Cliffs of the Upper Colorado. When artist Thomas Moran arrived in Wyoming Territory in 1871, these towering buttes were his first sight. Smithsonian American Art Museum, Washington, D.C./Art Resource, NY.

What did U.S. expansion mean for Native Americans?

Crazy Horse at the Little Big Horn

This pictograph by Amos Bad Heart Bull, an Oglala Sioux from the Pine Ridge Reservation, pictures Crazy Horse at the center of the Battle of the Little Big Horn. Although the artist was only seven years old in 1876, he based his pictures on the recollections of his uncle and other Oglala elders. The Granger Collection, New York.

WHILE THE EUROPEAN POWERS expanded their authority and wealth through imperialism and colonialism in far-flung empires abroad, the United States focused its attention on the West. From the U.S. Army attack on the remainder of the Comanche empire to the conquest of the Black Hills, whites pushed Indians aside as they moved west. As posited by historian Frederick Jackson Turner in 1893, American exceptionalism derived from the ways in which the history of the United States differed from that of European nations, and he cited America's western frontier as a cause. In what has become known as Turner's "frontier thesis," the availability of land provided a "safety valve," releasing social tensions and providing opportunities for social mobility for Americans. Yet expansion in the trans-Mississippi West involved the conquest, displacement, and rule over native peoples — a process best understood in the global context of imperialism and colonialism.

The U.S. government, through trickery and conquest, pushed the Indians off their lands (**Map 17.1**) and onto designated Indian territories or reservations. The

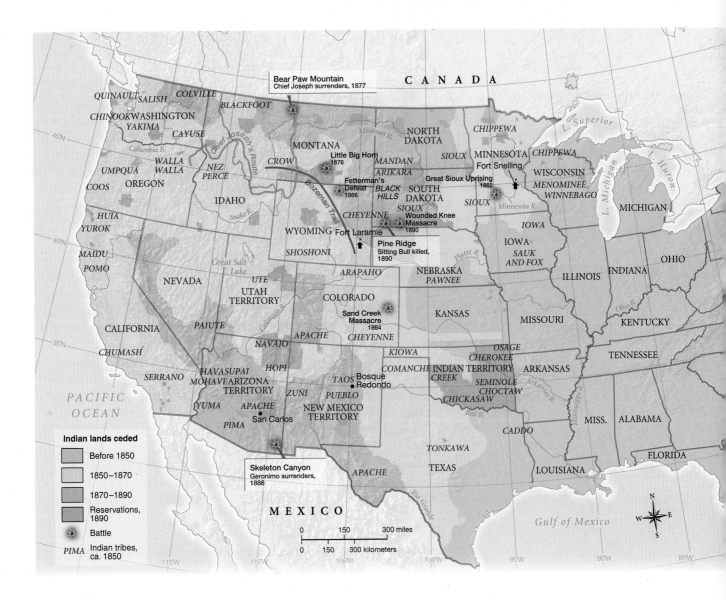

MAP 17.1 ■ The Loss of Indian Lands, 1850–1890

By 1890, western Indians were isolated on small, scattered reservations. Native Americans had struggled to retain their land in major battles, from the Santee Uprising in Minnesota in 1862 to the massacre at Wounded Knee, South Dakota, in 1890.

> MAP ACTIVITY

READING THE MAP: Where was the largest reservation located in 1890? Which states on this map show no reservations in 1890? Compare this map to Map 17.3 on page 509.
CONNECTIONS: Why did the federal government force Native Americans onto reservations? What developments prompted these changes?

Indian wars that followed the Civil War depleted the Native American population and handed the lion's share of Indian land over to white settlers. The decimation of the bison herds pushed the Plains Indians onto reservations, where they lived as wards of the state. Through the lens of colonialism, we can see how the United States, with its commitment to an imperialist, expansionist ideology, colonized the West.

| In what ways did different Indian groups defy and resist colonial rule? | How did mining shape American expansion? | How did the fight for land and resources in the West unfold? | Conclusion: How did the West set the tone for the Gilded Age? | ✓ LearningCurve Check what you know. bedfordstmartins.com /roarkunderstanding |

reservations

▶ Land given by the federal government to American Indians beginning in the 1860s in an attempt to reduce tensions between Indians and western settlers. On reservations, Indians subsisted on meager government rations and faced a life of poverty and starvation.

Indian Removal and the Reservation System

Manifest destiny — the belief that the United States had a "God-given" right to aggressively spread the values of white civilization and expand the nation from ocean to ocean — dictated U.S. policy toward Indians and other nations with claims in North America. In the name of manifest destiny, Americans forced the removal of the Five Civilized Tribes of the South (the Cherokee, Chocktaw, Chickasaw, Creek, and Seminole peoples) to Oklahoma in the 1830s; colonized Texas and won its independence from Mexico in 1836; conquered California, Arizona, New Mexico, and parts of Utah and Colorado in the Mexican-American War of 1846–1848; and invaded Oregon in the mid-1840s.

By midcentury, hordes of settlers crossed the Great Plains on their way to the goldfields of California or the rich farmland of Washington and Oregon. In their path stood a solid wall of Indian land, much of it in **reservations** granted by the U.S. government in its policy of Indian removal. In 1851, some ten thousand Plains Indians came together at Fort Laramie in Wyoming to negotiate a treaty that ceded a wide swath of their land to allow passage of wagon trains headed west. In return, the government promised that the remaining Indian land would remain inviolate.

The Indians who "touched the pen" to the 1851 Treaty of Fort Laramie hoped to preserve their land and culture in the face of the white onslaught. Settlers and miners cut down trees, polluted streams, and killed off the bison. Whites brought alcohol, guns, and something even more deadly — disease. Between 1780 and 1870, the population of the Plains tribes declined by half. "If I could see this thing, if I knew where it came from, I would go there and fight it," a Cheyenne warrior lamented. Disease also shifted the power from Woodland agrarian tribes to the Lakota (Western) Sioux, who fled the contagion by pursuing an equestrian nomadic existence that displaced weaker tribes in the western plains.

Poverty and starvation stalked the reservations. Confined by armed force, the Indians eked out an existence on stingy government rations. Styled as stepping-stones on the road to "civilization," Indian reservations closely resembled colonial societies where native populations, ruled by outside bureaucrats, saw their culture assaulted, their religious practices outlawed, their children sent away to school, and their way of life attacked in the name of progress and civilization.

To Americans raised on theories of racial superiority, the Indians constituted, in the words of one Colorado militia major, "an obstacle to civilization . . . [and] should be exterminated." This attitude pervaded the military. In November 1864 at the Sand Creek massacre in Colorado Territory, Colonel John M. Chivington and his Colorado militia descended on a village of Cheyenne, mostly women and children. Their leader, Black Kettle, raised a white flag and an American flag to signal surrender, but the charging cavalry ignored his signal and butchered 270 Indians. Chivington watched as his men scalped and mutilated their victims and later justified the killing of Indian children with the terse remark, "Nits make lice." The city of Denver treated Chivington and his men as heroes, but a congressional inquiry eventually castigated the soldiers for their "fiendish malignity" and condemned the "savage cruelty" of the massacre.

CHAPTER LOCATOR | What did U.S. expansion mean for Native Americans?

The Decimation of the Great Bison Herds

After the Civil War, the accelerating pace of industrial expansion brought about the near extinction of the American bison (buffalo). The development of larger, more accurate rifles combined with the growth of the nation's transcontinental rail system, which cut the range in two and divided the herds, hastened the bison's decline. For the Sioux and other nomadic tribes of the plains, the buffalo constituted a way of life — a source of food, fuel, and shelter and a central part of their religion and rituals. To the railroads, the buffalo were a nuisance, at best a cheap source of meat for their workers and a target for sport. "It will not be long before all the buffaloes are extinct near and between the railroads," Ohio senator John Sherman predicted in 1868.

The decimation of the great bison herds contributed to the army's conquest of the Plains Indians. General Philip Sheridan acknowledged as much when he applauded white hide hunters for "destroying the Indians' commissary." With their food supply gone, Indians had to choose between starvation and the reservation. "A cold wind blew across the prairie when the last buffalo fell," the great Sioux leader Sitting Bull lamented, "a death wind for my people."

On the southern plains in 1867, more than five thousand warring Comanches, Kiowas, and Southern Arapahos gathered at Medicine Lodge Creek in Kansas to negotiate the Treaty of Medicine Lodge. They sought to preserve limited land and hunting by moving the tribe to a reservation. Three years later, hide hunters poured into the region, and within a decade they had nearly exterminated the southern bison herds. Luther Standing Bear recounted the sight and stench: "I saw the bodies of hundreds of dead buffalo lying about, just wasting, and the odor was terrible. . . . They were letting our food lie on the plains to rot." With the buffalo gone, the Indians faced starvation and became dependent on the stingy allotments provided on the reservations.

Indian Wars and the Collapse of Comanchería

The Indian wars in the West marked the last resistance of a Native American population devastated by disease and demoralized by the reservation policy pursued by the federal government. The Dakota Sioux in Minnesota went to war in 1862. For years, under the leadership of Chief Little Crow, the Dakota — also known as the Santee — had pursued a policy of accommodation, ceding land in return for the promise of annuities. But with his people on the

"Slaughtered for the Hide"

In 1874, *Harper's Weekly* featured this illustration of a buffalo-hide hunter skinning a carcass on the southwestern plains. City father Colonel Richard Dodge wrote of the carnage, "The air was foul with sickening stench, and the vast plain which only a short twelve months before teemed with animal life, was a dead, solitary putrid desert." Library of Congress.

> **VISUAL ACTIVITY**

READING THE IMAGE: What virtues and stereotypes of the West does this magazine cover extol?
CONNECTIONS: How does the magazine's subtitle, "Journal of Civilization," fit the picture?

In what ways did different Indian groups defy and resist colonial rule?

How did mining shape American expansion?

How did the fight for land and resources in the West unfold?

Conclusion: How did the West set the tone for the Gilded Age?

verge of starvation (the local Indian agent told the hungry Dakota, "Go and eat grass"), Little Crow led his angry warriors in a desperate campaign against the intruders, killing more than 1,000 settlers. American troops quelled the Great Sioux Uprising (also called the Santee Uprising) and marched 1,700 Sioux to Fort Snelling, where 400 Indians were put on trial for murder and 38 died in the largest mass execution in American history.

Farther west, the great Indian empire of **Comanchería** had stretched from the Canadian plains to Mexico in the eighteenth century. By 1865, it numbered fewer than five thousand Comanche, ranging from west Texas north to Oklahoma. Through decades of dealings with the Spanish and the French, the Comanche had built a complex empire based on trade in horses, hides, guns, and captives. Expert riders, the Comanche waged war in the saddle, giving the U.S. Cavalry reason to hate and fear them.

After the Civil War, President Ulysses S. Grant faced the prospect of protracted Indian war on the Great Plains. Reluctant to spend more money and sacrifice more lives in battle, Grant adopted a "peace policy" designed to segregate and control the Indians while opening up land to white settlers. This policy won the support of both friends of the Indians and those who coveted the Indians' land. The army herded the Indians onto reservations (see Map 17.1), where the U.S. Bureau of Indian Affairs hired agents who, in the words of Paiute Sarah Winnemucca, did "nothing but fill their pockets." In 1871, Grant's peace policy in the West gave way to all-out warfare as the U.S. Army dispatched three thousand soldiers to wipe out the remains of Comanchería. Raiding parties of Comanche virtually obliterated white settlements in west Texas. To defeat the Indians, the army adopted the tactics of burning and destroying everything in their path using the tactics that General William Tecumseh Sherman had used in his march through Georgia during the Civil War. At the decisive battle of Palo Duro Canyon in 1874, only three Comanche warriors died in battle, but U.S. soldiers took the Indians' camp, burning more than two hundred tepees, hundreds of robes and blankets, and thousands of pounds of winter supplies and shooting more than a thousand horses. Coupled with the decimation of the bison, the army's scorched-earth policy led to the final collapse of the Comanche people. The surviving Indians of Comanchería, now numbering fewer than 1,500, reluctantly retreated to the reservation at Fort Sill.

The Fight for the Black Hills

On the northern plains, the fever for gold fueled the conflict between Indians and Euro-Americans. In 1866, the Cheyenne united with the Sioux in Wyoming to protect their hunting grounds in the Powder River valley, which were threatened by the construction of the Bozeman Trail connecting Fort Laramie with the goldfields in Montana. Captain William Fetterman, who had boasted that with eighty men he could ride through the Sioux nation, was killed along with all of his troops in an Indian attack. The Sioux's impressive victories led to the second Treaty of Fort Laramie in 1868, in which the United States agreed to abandon the Bozeman Trail and guaranteed the Indians control of the **Black Hills**, land sacred to the Lakota Sioux.

The government's fork-tongued promises induced some of the tribes to accept the treaty. The great Sioux chief Red Cloud led many of his people onto the reser-

Comanchería
► Indian empire based on trade in horses, hides, guns, and captives that stretched from the Canadian plains to Mexico in the eighteenth century. By 1865, fewer than five thousand Comanches lived in the empire, which ranged from west Texas north to Oklahoma.

Black Hills
► Mountains in western South Dakota and northeast Wyoming that are sacred to the Lakota Sioux. In the 1868 Treaty of Fort Laramie, the United States guaranteed Indians control of the Black Hills but broke its promise after gold was discovered there in 1874.

CHAPTER LOCATOR | What did U.S. expansion mean for Native Americans?

vation. Red Cloud soon regretted his decision. "Think of it!" he told a visitor to the Pine Ridge Reservation. "I, who used to own . . . country so extensive that I could not ride through it in a week . . . must tell Washington when I am hungry. I must beg for that which I own." Several Sioux chiefs, among them Crazy Horse and Sitting Bull, refused to sign the treaty. Crazy Horse said that he wanted no part of the "piecemeal penning" of his people.

In 1874, the discovery of gold in the Black Hills of the Dakotas led the government to break its promise to Red Cloud. Miners began pouring into the region, and the Northern Pacific Railroad made plans to lay track. Lieutenant Colonel George Armstrong Custer trumpeted news of the gold strike. At first, the government offered to purchase the Black Hills. But the Lakota Sioux refused to sell. The army responded by issuing an ultimatum ordering all Lakota Sioux and Northern Cheyenne bands onto the Pine Ridge Reservation and threatening to hunt down those who refused.

In the summer of 1876, the army launched a three-pronged attack led by Custer, General George Crook, and Colonel John Gibbon. Crazy Horse stopped Crook at the Battle of the Rosebud. Custer, leading the second prong of the army's offensive, divided his troops and ordered an attack. On June 25, he spotted signs of the Indians' camp. Crying "Hurrah Boys, we've got them," he led 265 men of the Seventh Cavalry into the largest gathering of Indians ever assembled on the Great Plains (more than 8,000) camped along the banks of the Greasy Grass River (whites called it the Little Big Horn). Indian warriors led by Sitting Bull and Crazy Horse set upon Custer and his men and quickly annihilated them. "It took us about as long as a hungry man to eat his dinner," the Cheyenne chief Two Moons recalled.

"Custer's Last Stand," as the **Battle of the Little Big Horn** was styled in myth, turned out to be the last stand for the Sioux. The nomadic bands that had massed at the Little Big Horn scattered, and the army hunted them down. "Wherever we went," wrote the Oglala holy man Black Elk, "the soldiers came to kill us." In 1877, Crazy Horse was captured and killed. Four years later, in 1881, Sitting Bull surrendered. The government took the Black Hills and confined the Lakota to the reservation. The Sioux never accepted the loss of the Black Hills. In 1923, they filed suit, demanding the return of the land illegally taken from them. After a protracted court battle lasting nearly sixty years, the U.S. Supreme Court ruled in 1980 that the government had illegally violated the Treaty of Fort Laramie and upheld an award of $122.5 million in compensation to the tribes. The Sioux refused the settlement and continue to press for the return of the Black Hills.

Battle of the Little Big Horn

▶ 1876 battle begun when American cavalry under George Armstrong Custer attacked an encampment of Indians who refused to remove to a reservation. Indian warriors led by Crazy Horse and Sitting Bull annihilated the American soldiers, but their victory was short-lived.

QUICK REVIEW ◀

How did the slaughter of the bison contribute to the Plains Indians' removal to reservations?

In what ways did different Indian groups defy and resist colonial rule?

How did mining shape American expansion?

How did the fight for land and resources in the West unfold?

Conclusion: How did the West set the tone for the Gilded Age?

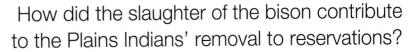

LearningCurve Check what you know. bedfordstmartins.com /roarkunderstanding

In what ways did different Indian groups defy and resist colonial rule?

Ghost Dancers Arapaho women at the Darlington Agency in Indian Territory (Oklahoma) participate in the Ghost Dance. Different tribes performed variations of the dance, but generally dancers formed a circle and danced until they reached the trancelike state shown here. Whites feared the dancers and demanded that the army dispatch troops to subdue them. The result was the killing of Sitting Bull and the massacre at Wounded Knee.

National Anthropological Archives, Smithsonian Institution, Washington, D.C. (#81-9626).

IMPERIALISTIC ATTITUDES of whites toward Indians continued to evolve in the late nineteenth century. To "civilize" the Indians, the U.S. government sought to force assimilation on their children. Reservations became increasingly unpopular among whites who coveted Indian land. A new policy of allotment gained favor. It promised to put Indians on parcels of land, forcing them into farming, and then to redistribute the rest of the land to settlers. In the face of this ongoing assault on their way of life, Indians actively resisted, contested, and adapted to colonial rule.

Indian Schools and the War on Indian Culture

Indian schools constituted the cultural battleground of the Indian wars in the West, their avowed purpose being "to destroy the Indian . . . and save the man." In 1877,

CHAPTER LOCATOR | What did U.S. expansion mean for Native Americans?

Congress appropriated funds for Indian education, reasoning that it was less expensive to educate Indians than to kill them. Virginia's Hampton Institute, created in 1868 to school newly freed slaves, accepted its first Indian students in 1878. Although many Indian schools operated on the reservations, authorities much preferred boarding facilities that isolated students from the "contamination" of tribal values.

Many Native American parents resisted sending their children away. When all else failed, the military kidnapped the children and sent them off to school. An agent at the Mescalero Apache Agency in Arizona Territory reported in 1886 that "it became necessary to visit the camps unexpectedly with a detachment of police, and seize such children as were proper and take them away to school, willing or unwilling." The parents put up a struggle. "Some hurried their children off to the mountains or hid them away in camp, and the police had to chase and capture them like so many wild rabbits," the agent observed. "This unusual proceeding created quite an outcry. The men were sullen and muttering, the women loud in their lamentations and the children almost out of their wits with fright."

Once at school, the children were stripped and scrubbed, their clothing and belongings confiscated, and their hair hacked off and doused with kerosene to kill lice. Issued stiff new uniforms, shoes, and what one boy recalled as the "torture" of woolen long underwear, the children often lost not only their possessions but also their names: Hehakaavita (Yellow Elk) became Thomas Goodwood; Polingaysi Qoyawayma became Elizabeth White.

The **Carlisle Indian School** in Pennsylvania, founded in 1879, became the model for later institutions. To encourage assimilation, Carlisle pioneered the "outing system" — sending students to live with white families during summer vacations. The policy reflected the school's slogan: "To civilize the Indian, get him into civilization. To keep him civilized, let him stay."

Carlisle Indian School
▶ Institution established in Pennsylvania in 1879 to educate and assimilate American Indians. It pioneered the "outing system" in which Indian students were sent to live with white families in order to accelerate acculturation.

Merrill Gates, a member of the Board of Indian Commissioners, summed up the goal of Indian education: "To get the Indian out of the blanket and into trousers, — *and trousers with a pocket in them, and with a pocket that aches to be filled with dollars!*" Gates's faith in the "civilizing" power of the dollar reflected the unabashed materialism of the age.

The Dawes Act and Indian Land Allotment

In the 1880s, the practice of rounding up Indians and herding them onto reservations lost momentum in favor of allotment — a new policy designed to encourage assimilation through farming and the ownership of private property. Americans vowing to avenge Custer urged the government to get tough with the Indians. Reservations, they argued, took up too much good land that white settlers could put to better use. At the same time, people sympathetic to the Indians were appalled at the desperate poverty on the reservations and feared for the Indians' survival. Helen Hunt Jackson, in her classic work *A Century of Dishonor* (1881), convinced many readers that the Indians had been treated unfairly. "Our Indian policy," the *New York Times* concluded, "is usually spoliation behind the mask of benevolence."

The Indian Rights Association, a group of mainly white easterners formed in 1882, campaigned for the dismantling of the reservations, now viewed as obstacles to progress. To "cease to treat the Indian as a red man and treat him as a man" meant putting an end to tribal communalism and fostering individualism. "Selfishness," declared Senator Henry Dawes of Massachusetts, "is at the bottom of civilization." Dawes called for "allotment in severalty" — the institution of private property.

In 1887, Congress passed the **Dawes Allotment Act**, dividing up reservations and allotting parcels of land to individual Indians as private property.

Dawes Allotment Act
▶ 1887 law that divided up reservations and allotted parcels of land to individual Indians as private property. In the end, the U.S. government sold almost two-thirds of "surplus" Indian land to white settlers. The Dawes Act dealt a crippling blow to traditional tribal culture.

> **> Provisions of the Dawes Allotment Act**

- Indian heads of household received an allotment of 160 acres from reservation lands.
- Single persons over eighteen and orphans under eighteen received 80 acres.
- Indians who took allotments earned U.S. citizenship.
- The government reserved the right to sell "surplus" reservation lands to white settlers.

The Dawes Act effectively reduced Indian land from 138 million acres to a scant 48 million. The legislation, in the words of one critic, worked "to despoil the Indians of their lands and to make them vagabonds on the face of the earth." By 1890, the United States controlled 97.5 percent of the territory formerly occupied by Native Americans.

Indian Resistance and Survival

Faced with the extinction of their entire way of life, different groups of Indians responded in different ways. In the 1870s, Comanche and Kiowa raiding parties

CHAPTER LOCATOR | What did U.S. expansion mean for Native Americans?

496 CHAPTER 17
CONTESTING THE WEST

frustrated the U.S. Army by brazenly using the reservations as a seasonal supply base during the winter months. When spring came, they resumed their nomadic hunting way of life.

Some tribes, including the Crow and Shoshoni, chose to fight alongside the army against their old enemies, the Sioux. The Crow chief Plenty Coups explained why he allied with the United States: "Not because we loved the white man . . . or because we hated the Sioux . . . but because we plainly saw that this course was the only one which might save our beautiful country for us." The Crow and Shoshoni got to stay in their homelands and avoided the fate of other tribes shipped to reservations far away.

Indians who refused to stay on reservations risked being hunted down. The Nez Percé war is perhaps the most harrowing example of the army's policy. In 1863, the government dictated a treaty drastically reducing Nez Percé land. Most of the chiefs refused to sign the treaty and did not move to the reservation. When the army cracked down in 1877, some eight hundred Nez Percé people, many of them women and children, fled across the mountains of Idaho, Wyoming, and Montana, heading for the safety of Canada. At the end of their 1,300-mile trek, 50 miles from freedom, they stopped to rest in the snow. The army caught up with them and attacked. Yellow Wolf recalled their plight: "Children crying with cold. No fire. There could be no light. Everywhere the crying, the death wail." After a five-day siege, the Nez Percé leader, Chief Joseph, surrendered. His speech, reported by a white soldier, would become famous. "I am tired of fighting," he said as he surrendered his rifle. "Our chiefs are killed. It is cold and we have no blankets. The little children are freezing to death. . . . I am tired. My heart is sick and sad. From where the sun now stands, I will fight no more forever."

In the Southwest, the Apaches resorted to armed resistance. They roamed the Sonoran Desert of southern Arizona and northern Mexico, perfecting a hit-and-run guerrilla warfare that terrorized white settlers and bedeviled the army in the 1870s and 1880s. General George Crook combined a policy of dogged pursuit with judicious diplomacy. Crook relied on Indian scouts to track the raiding parties, recruiting nearly two hundred Apaches, Navajos, and Paiutes. By 1882, Crook had succeeded in persuading most of the Apaches to settle on the San Carlos Reservation in Arizona Territory. A desolate piece of desert inhabited by scorpions and rattlesnakes, San Carlos, in the words of one Apache, was "the worst place in all the great territory stolen from the Apaches."

Geronimo, a respected shaman (medicine man) of the Chiricahua Apache, refused to stay at San Carlos and repeatedly led raiding parties in the early 1880s. His warriors attacked ranches to obtain ammunition and horses. Among

Chief Joseph

Chief Joseph came to symbolize the heroic resistance of the Nez Percé. General Nelson Miles promised the Nez Percé that they could return to their homeland if they surrendered. But he betrayed them, as he would betray the Apache people seven years later. The Nez Percé were shipped off to Indian Territory (Oklahoma). National Anthropological Archives, Smithsonian Institution, Washington, D.C. (#2906).

In what ways did different Indian groups defy and resist colonial rule?

How did mining shape American expansion?

How did the fight for land and resources in the West unfold?

Conclusion: How did the West set the tone for the Gilded Age?

☑ LearningCurve Check what you know. bedfordstmartins.com /roarkunderstanding

Geronimo's band was Lozen, a woman who rode with the warriors, armed with a rifle and a cartridge belt. The sister of a great chief described her as being as "strong as a man, braver than most, and cunning in strategy." In the spring of 1885, Geronimo and his followers, including Lozen, went on a ten-month offensive, moving from the Apache sanctuary in the Sierra Madre to raid and burn ranches and towns on both sides of the Mexican border. General Crook caught up with Geronimo in the fall and persuaded him to return to San Carlos, only to have him slip away on the way back to the reservation. Chagrined, Crook resigned his post. General Nelson Miles, Crook's replacement, adopted a policy of hunt and destroy.

Geronimo's band of thirty-three Apaches, including women and children, eluded Miles's troops for more than five months. The pursuit left Miles's cavalry ragged. Over time, Lieutenant Leonard Wood had discarded his horse and was reduced to wearing nothing "but a pair of canton flannel drawers, and an old blouse, a pair of moccasins and a hat without a crown." Eventually, Miles's scouts cornered Geronimo in 1886 at Skeleton Canyon, where he agreed to march north and negotiate a settlement. "We have not slept for six months," he admitted, "and we are worn out." After General Miles induced them to surrender, the government rounded up nearly five hundred Apaches and sent them as prisoners to the South, even though fewer than three dozen Apaches had been considered "hostile." By 1889, more than a quarter of them had died, some as a result of illnesses contracted in the damp lowland climate of Florida and Alabama and some by suicide. Their plight roused public opinion, and in 1892 they were moved to Fort Sill in Oklahoma and later to New Mexico.

Geronimo lived to become something of a celebrity. He appeared at the St. Louis Exposition in 1904, and he rode in President Theodore Roosevelt's inaugural parade in 1905. In a newspaper interview, he confessed, "I want to go to my old home before I die. . . . Want to go back to the mountains again. I asked the Great White Father to allow me to go back, but he said no." None of the Apaches were permitted to return to Arizona; when Geronimo died in 1909, he was buried in Oklahoma.

On the plains, many tribes turned to a nonviolent form of resistance — a compelling new religion called the **Ghost Dance**. The Paiute shaman Wovoka, drawing on a cult that had developed in the 1870s, combined elements of Christianity and traditional Indian religion to found the Ghost Dance religion in 1889. Wovoka claimed that he had received a vision in which the Great Spirit spoke through him to all Indians, prophesying that if they would unite in the Ghost Dance ritual, whites would be destroyed in an apocalypse and the buffalo would return. His religion, born of despair and with a message of hope, spread like wildfire over the plains. The Ghost Dance was performed in Idaho, Montana, Utah, Wyoming, Colorado, Nebraska, Kansas, the Dakotas, and Indian Territory by tribes as diverse as the Sioux, Arapaho, Cheyenne, Pawnee, and Shoshoni. Dancers often went into hypnotic trances, dancing until they dropped from exhaustion.

The Ghost Dance was nonviolent, but it frightened whites, especially when the Sioux taught that wearing a white ghost shirt made Indians immune to soldiers' bullets. Soon whites began to fear an uprising. "Indians are dancing in the snow and are wild and crazy," wrote the Bureau of Indian Affairs agent at the Pine Ridge Reservation in South Dakota. Frantic, he pleaded for reinforcements.

Ghost Dance

▶ Religion founded in 1889 by Paiute shaman Wovoka. It combined elements of Christianity and traditional Indian religion and served as a nonviolent form of resistance for Indians in the late nineteenth century. The Ghost Dance frightened whites and was violently suppressed.

CHAPTER LOCATOR | What did U.S. expansion mean for Native Americans?

"We are at the mercy of these dancers. We need protection, and we need it now." President Benjamin Harrison dispatched several thousand federal troops to Sioux country to handle any outbreak.

In December 1890, when Sitting Bull attempted to join the Ghost Dance, he was killed by Indian police as they tried to arrest him at his cabin on the Standing Rock Reservation. His people, fleeing the scene, joined with a larger group of Miniconjou Sioux, who were apprehended by the Seventh Cavalry, Custer's old regiment, near Wounded Knee Creek, South Dakota. As the Indians laid down their arms, a soldier attempted to take a rifle from a deaf Miniconjou man, and the gun went off. The soldiers opened fire. In the ensuing melee, more than two hundred Indian men, women, and children were mowed down in minutes by the army's brutally efficient Hotchkiss rapid-fire guns. Settler Jules Sandoz surveyed the scene the day after the massacre at **Wounded Knee**. "Here in ten minutes an entire community was as the buffalo that bleached on the plains," he wrote. "There was something loose in the world that hated joy and happiness as it hated brightness and color, reducing everything to drab agony and gray."

It had taken Euro-Americans 250 years to wrest control of the eastern half of the United States from the Indians. It took them less than 40 years to take the western half. The subjugation of the American Indians marked the first chapter in a national mission of empire that would anticipate overseas imperialistic adventures in Asia, Latin America, the Caribbean, and the Pacific islands.

Wounded Knee

▶ 1890 massacre of Sioux Indians by the Seventh Cavalry at Wounded Knee Creek, South Dakota. Sent to suppress the Ghost Dance, the soldiers opened fire on the Sioux as they attempted to surrender. More than two hundred Sioux men, women, and children were killed.

QUICK REVIEW <

How and why did U.S. Indian policy change between 1870 and 1890?

In what ways did different Indian groups defy and resist colonial rule?

How did mining shape American expansion?

How did the fight for land and resources in the West unfold?

Conclusion: How did the West set the tone for the Gilded Age?

☑ LearningCurve
Check what you know.
bedfordstmartins.com
/roarkunderstanding

How did mining shape American expansion?

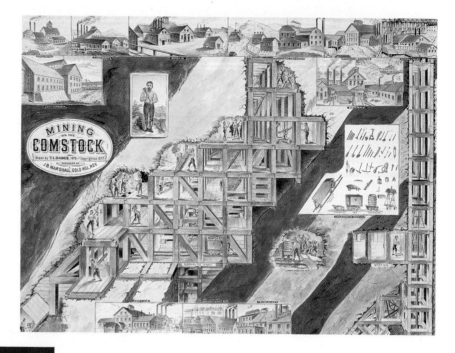

"Mining on the Comstock" This illustration, made at Gold Hill, Nevada, in 1876, shows a sectional view of a mine, highlighting the square-set timber method. Note also the tunnels, incline, cooling-off room, blower, and air shaft, along with a collection of miner's tools. Mines like this one honeycombed the hills of Gold City and neighboring Virginia City on the Comstock Lode in Nevada. University of California at Berkeley, Bancroft Library.

MINING STOOD AT THE CENTER of the United States' quest for empire in the West. The California gold rush of 1849 touched off the frenzy. The four decades following witnessed equally frenetic rushes for gold and other metals, most notably on the **Comstock Lode** in Nevada and later in New Mexico, Colorado, the Dakotas, Montana, Idaho, Arizona, and Utah (**Map 17.2**). At first glance, the mining West may seem much different from the East, but by the 1870s the term *urban industrialism* described Virginia City, Nevada, as accurately as it did Pittsburgh or Cleveland. A close look at life on the Comstock Lode indicates some of the patterns and paradoxes of western mining. The diversity of peoples drawn to the West by the promise of mining riches and land made the region the most cosmopolitan in the nation, as well as the most contested.

Comstock Lode
▶ Silver ore deposit discovered in 1859 in Nevada. Discovery of the Comstock Lode touched off a mining rush that brought a diverse population into the region and led to the establishment of a number of boomtowns, including Virginia City, Nevada.

Life on the Comstock Lode

By 1859, refugees from California's played-out goldfields flocked to the Washoe basin in Nevada. While searching for gold, Washoe miners stumbled on the richest vein of silver ore on the continent — the legendary Comstock Lode, named for prospector Henry Comstock.

CHAPTER LOCATOR | What did U.S. expansion mean for Native Americans?

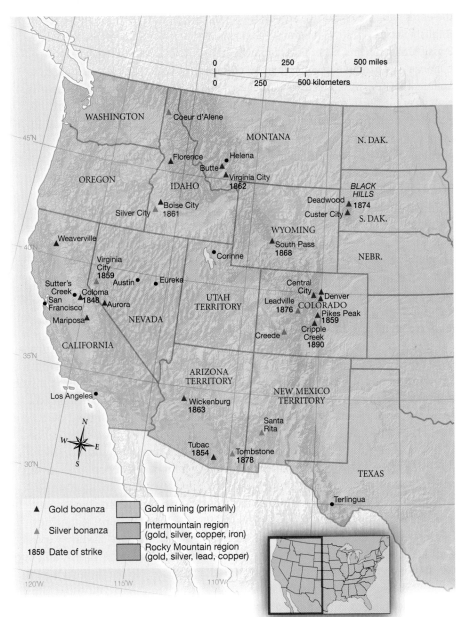

MAP 17.2 ■ Western Mining, 1848–1890

Rich deposits of gold, silver, copper, lead, and iron larded the mountains of the West. Miners from all over the world flocked to the mines. Few struck it rich, but many stayed on as paid workers in the increasingly mechanized corporate mines.

To exploit even potentially valuable silver claims required capital and expensive technology well beyond the means of the prospector. An active San Francisco stock market sprang up to finance operations on the Comstock. Shrewd businessmen soon recognized that the easiest way to get rich was to sell their claims or to form mining companies and sell shares of stock. The most unscrupulous mined the wallets of gullible investors by selling shares in bogus mines. Speculation, misrepresentation, and outright thievery ran rampant. In twenty years, more than $300 million poured from the earth in Nevada alone, most of it going to speculators in San Francisco.

The promise of gold and silver drew thousands to the mines of the West. As Mark Twain observed in Virginia City's *Territorial Enterprise*, "All the peoples of

| In what ways did different Indian groups defy and resist colonial rule? | **How did mining shape American expansion?** | How did the fight for land and resources in the West unfold? | Conclusion: How did the West set the tone for the Gilded Age? | ✔️ LearningCurve Check what you know. bedfordstmartins.com /roarkunderstanding |

501

> CHRONOLOGY

1873
– "Big Bonanza" is discovered on Comstock Lode.

1882
– Chinese Exclusion Act.

the earth had representative adventures in the Silverland." Irish, Chinese, Germans, English, Scots, Welsh, Canadians, Mexicans, Italians, Scandinavians, French, Swiss, Chileans, and other South and Central Americans came to share in the bonanza. With them came a sprinkling of Russians, Poles, Greeks, Japanese, Spaniards, Hungarians, Portuguese, Turks, Pacific Islanders, and Moroccans, as well as other North Americans, African Americans, and American Indians. This polyglot population, typical of mining boomtowns, made Virginia City in the 1870s more cosmopolitan than New York or Boston. In the part of Utah Territory that eventually became Nevada, as many as 30 percent of the people came from outside the United States, compared with 25 percent in New York and 21 percent in Massachusetts.

Irish immigrants formed the largest ethnic group in the mining district. In Virginia City, fully one-third of the population claimed at least one parent from Ireland. Irish women constituted the largest group of women on the Comstock. As servants, boardinghouse owners, and washerwomen, they made up a significant part of the workforce. By contrast, the Chinese community, numbering 642 in 1870, remained overwhelmingly male. Virulent anti-Chinese sentiment barred the men from work in the mines, but despite the violent anti-Asian rhetoric, the mining community came to depend on Chinese labor.

The discovery of precious metals on the Comstock spelled disaster for the Indians. No sooner had the miners struck pay dirt than they demanded that army troops "hunt Indians" and establish forts to protect transportation to and from the diggings. This sudden and dramatic intrusion left Nevada's native tribes — the Northern Paiute and Bannock Shoshoni — exiles in their own land. At first they resisted, but over time they adapted and preserved their culture and identity despite the havoc wreaked by western mining and settlement.

In 1873, Comstock miners uncovered a new vein of ore, a veritable cavern of gold and silver. This "Big Bonanza" speeded the transition from small-scale industry to corporate oligopoly, creating a radically new social and economic environment. The Comstock became a laboratory for new mining technology. Huge stamping mills pulverized rock with pistonlike hammers driven by steam engines. Enormous Cornish pumps sucked water from the mine shafts, and huge ventilators circulated air in the underground chambers. No backwoods mining camp, Virginia City was an industrial center with more than 1,200 stamping mills working on average a ton of ore every day. Almost 400 men worked in milling, nearly 300 labored in manufacturing industries, and roughly 3,000 toiled in the mines. The Gould and Curry mine covered sixty acres. Most of the miners who came to the Comstock ended up as laborers for the big companies.

New technology eliminated some of the dangers of mining but often created new ones. In the hard-rock mines of the West, accidents in the 1870s disabled one out of every thirty miners and killed one in eighty. Ross Moudy, who worked as a miner in Cripple Creek, Colorado, recalled how a stockholder visiting the mine nearly fell to his death. The terrified visitor told the miner next to him that "instead of being paid $3 a day, they ought to have all the gold they could take out." On the Comstock Lode, because of the difficulty of obtaining skilled labor, the richness of the ore, and the need for a stable workforce, labor unions formed early and held considerable bargaining power. Comstock miners commanded $4 a day, the highest wage in the mining West.

CHAPTER LOCATOR | What did U.S. expansion mean for Native Americans?

502 CHAPTER 17 CONTESTING THE WEST

The mining towns of the "Wild West" are often portrayed as lawless outposts, filled with saloons and rough gambling dens and populated almost exclusively by men. The truth is more complex, as Virginia City's development attests. An established urban community built to serve an industrial giant, Virginia City in its first decade boasted churches, schools, theaters, an opera house, and hundreds of families. By 1870, women composed 30 percent of the population, and 75 percent of the women listed their occupation in the census as housekeeper. Mary McNair Mathews, a widow from Buffalo, New York, who lived on the Comstock in the 1870s, worked as a teacher, nurse, seamstress, laundress, and lodging-house operator. She later published a book on her adventures.

By 1875, Virginia City boasted a population of 25,000 people, making it one of the largest cities between St. Louis and San Francisco. The city, dubbed the "Queen of the Comstock," hosted American presidents as well as legions of lesser dignitaries. Virginia City represented, in the words of a recent chronicler, "the distilled essence of America's newly established course — urban, industrial, acquisitive, and material-istic, on the move, 'a living polyglot' of cultures that collided and converged."

The Diverse Peoples of the West

The West of the late nineteenth century was a polyglot place, as much so as the big cities of the East. The sheer number of peoples who mingled in the West produced a complex blend of racism and prejudice. One historian has noted, not entirely facetiously, that there were at least eight oppressed "races" in the West — Indians, Latinos, Chinese, Japanese, blacks, Mormons, strikers, and radicals.

African Americans who ventured out to the territories faced hostile settlers determined to keep the West "for whites only." In response, they formed all-black communities such as Nicodemas, Kansas. That settlement, founded by thirty black Kentuckians in 1877, grew to a community of seven hundred by 1880. Isolated and often separated by great distances, small black settlements grew up throughout the West, in Nevada, Utah, and the Pacific Northwest, as well as in Kansas. Black soldiers who served in the West during the Indian wars often stayed on as settlers. Called buffalo soldiers because Native Americans thought their hair resembled that of the bison, these black troops numbered up to 25,000. In the face of discrimination, poor treatment, and harsh conditions, the buffalo soldiers served with distinction and boasted the lowest desertion rate in the army.

Hispanic peoples had lived in Texas and the Southwest since Juan de Oñate led pioneer settlers up the Rio Grande in 1598. Hispanics had occupied the Pacific coast since San Diego was founded in 1769. Overnight, they were reduced to a "minority" after the United States annexed Texas in 1845 and took land stretching to California after the Mexican-American War ended in 1848. At first, the Hispanic owners of large *ranchos* in California, New Mexico, and Texas greeted conquest as an economic opportunity. But racial prejudice soon ended their optimism. Califor-nios (Mexican residents of California), who had been granted American citizenship by the Treaty of Guadalupe Hidalgo (1848), faced discrimination by Anglos who sought to keep them out of California's mines and commerce. Whites illegally squat-ted on *rancho* land while protracted litigation over Spanish and Mexican land grants forced the Californios into court. Although the U.S. Supreme Court eventually

| In what ways did different Indian groups defy and resist colonial rule? | **How did mining shape American expansion?** | How did the fight for land and resources in the West unfold? | Conclusion: How did the West set the tone for the Gilded Age? | ☑ LearningCurve Check what you know. bedfordstmartins.com /roarkunderstanding |

503

validated most of their claims, it took so long — seventeen years on average — that many Californios sold their property to pay taxes and legal bills.

Swindles, trickery, and intimidation dispossessed scores of Californios. Many ended up segregated in urban barrios (neighborhoods) in their own homeland. Their percentage of California's population declined from 82 percent in 1850 to 19 percent in 1880 as Anglos migrated to the state. In New Mexico and Texas, Mexicans remained a majority of the population but became increasingly impoverished as Anglos dominated business and took the best jobs. Skirmishes between Hispanics and whites in northern New Mexico over the fencing of the open range lasted for decades. Groups of Hispanics with names such as *Las Manos Negras* (the Black Hands) cut fences and burned barns. In Texas, violence along the Rio Grande pitted Tejanos (Mexican residents of Texas) against the Texas Rangers, who saw their role as "keeping Mexicans in their place."

Like the Mexicans, the Mormons faced prejudice and hostility. The followers of Joseph Smith, the founder and prophet of the Church of Jesus Christ of Latter-Day Saints, fled west to Utah Territory in 1844 to avoid religious persecution. They believed they had a divine right to the land, and their messianic militancy made others distrust them. The Mormon practice of polygamy (church leader Brigham Young had twenty-seven wives) also came under attack. To counter the criticism of polygamy, the Utah territorial legislature gave women the right to vote in 1870, the first universal woman suffrage act in the nation. (Wyoming had granted suffrage to white women in 1869.) Although women's rights advocates argued that the newly enfranchised women would "do away with the horrible institution of polygamy," it remained in force. Not until 1890 did the church hierarchy yield to pressure and renounce polygamy. The fierce controversy over polygamy postponed statehood for Utah until 1896.

Of all the newcomers, the Chinese suffered the most brutal treatment at the hands of employers and other laborers. Drawn by the promise of gold, more than 20,000 Chinese had joined the rush to California by 1852. Miners determined to keep "California for Americans" succeeded in passing prohibitive foreign license laws to keep the Chinese out of the mines. But Chinese immigration continued. In the 1860s, when white workers moved on to find riches in the bonanza mines of Nevada, Chinese laborers took jobs abandoned by the whites. Railroad magnate Charles Crocker hired Chinese gangs to work on the Central Pacific, reasoning that "the race that built the Great Wall" could lay tracks across the treacherous Sierra Nevada. Some 12,000 Chinese, representing 90 percent of Crocker's workforce, completed America's first transcontinental railroad in 1869.

By 1870, more than 63,000 Chinese immigrants lived in America, 77 percent of them in California. A 1790 federal statute that limited naturalization to "white persons" was modified after the Civil War to extend naturalization to blacks ("persons of African descent"). But the Chinese and other Asians continued to be denied access to citizenship. As perpetual aliens, they constituted a reserve army of transnational laborers that many saw as a threat to American labor.

In 1876, the Workingmen's Party formed to fight for Chinese exclusion. Racial and cultural animosities stood at the heart of anti-Chinese agitation. Denis Kearney, the fiery San Francisco leader of the movement, made clear this racist bent when he urged legislation to "expel every one of the moon-eyed lepers." Nor

was California alone in its anti-immigrant nativism. As the country confronted growing ethnic and racial diversity with the rising tide of global immigration in the decades following the Civil War, many questioned the principle of racial equality at the same time they argued against the assimilation of "nonwhite" groups. In this climate, Congress passed the **Chinese Exclusion Act** in 1882, effectively barring Chinese immigration and setting a precedent for further immigration restrictions.

The Chinese Exclusion Act led to a sharp drop in the Chinese population — from 105,465 in 1880 to 89,863 in 1900 — because Chinese immigrants, overwhelmingly male, did not have families to sustain their population. Eventually, Japanese immigrants, including women as well as men, replaced the Chinese, particularly in agriculture. As "nonwhite" immigrants, they could not become naturalized citizens, but their children born in the United States claimed the rights of citizenship. Japanese parents, seeking to own land, purchased it in their children's names. Although anti-Asian prejudice remained strong in California and elsewhere in the West, Asian immigrants formed an important part of the economic fabric of the western United States.

Chinese Exclusion Act

▶ 1882 law that effectively barred Chinese immigration and set a precedent for further immigration restrictions. The Chinese population in America dropped sharply as a result of the passage of the act, which was fueled by racial and cultural animosities.

QUICK REVIEW <

What role did mining play in shaping the society and economy of the American West?

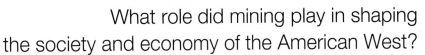

In what ways did different Indian groups defy and resist colonial rule?

How did mining shape American expansion?

How did the fight for land and resources in the West unfold?

Conclusion: How did the West set the tone for the Gilded Age?

☑ LearningCurve
Check what you know.
bedfordstmartins.com
/roarkunderstanding

How did the fight for land and resources in the West unfold?

Railroad Locomotive In the years following the Civil War, the locomotive replaced the covered wagon, enabling settlers to travel from Chicago or St. Louis to the West Coast in two days. The first transcontinental railroad, completed in 1869, soon led to the creation of competing systems, so that by the 1880s travelers going west could choose from four railroad lines. Library of Congress.

Homestead Act of 1862
▶ An act that promised 160 acres in the trans-Mississippi West free to any citizen or prospective citizen who settled on the land for five years. The act spurred American settlement of the West. Altogether, nearly one-tenth of the United States was granted to settlers.

first transcontinental railroad
▶ Railroad completed in 1869 that was the first to span the North American continent. Built in large part by Chinese laborers, this railroad and others opened access to new areas, fueled land speculation, and actively recruited settlers.

IN THE THREE DECADES following 1870, more land was settled than in all the previous history of the country. Americans by the hundreds of thousands packed up and moved west, goaded if not by the hope of striking gold, then by the promise of owning land to farm or ranch. The agrarian West shared with the mining West a persistent restlessness, an equally pervasive addiction to speculation, and a penchant for exploiting natural resources and labor.

Two factors stimulated the land rush in the trans-Mississippi West. The **Homestead Act of 1862** promised 160 acres free to any citizen or prospective citizen, male or female, who settled on the land for five years. Even more important, transcontinental railroads opened up new areas and actively recruited settlers. After the completion of the **first transcontinental railroad** in 1869, homesteaders abandoned the covered wagon, and by the 1880s they could choose from four competing rail lines and make the trip west in a matter of days.

CHAPTER LOCATOR | What did U.S. expansion mean for Native Americans?

Although the country was rich in land and resources, not all who wanted to own land achieved their goal. During the transition from the family farm to large commercial farming, small farms and ranches gave way to vast spreads worked by migrant labor or paid farmworkers and cowhands. Just as industry corporatized and consolidated in the East, the period from 1870 to 1900 witnessed corporate consolidation in mining, ranching, and agriculture.

Moving West: Homesteaders and Speculators

A Missouri homesteader remembered packing as her family pulled up stakes and headed west to Oklahoma in 1890. "We were going to God's Country," she wrote. "You had to work hard on that rocky country in Missouri. I was glad to be leaving it. . . . We were going to a new land and get rich."

Settlers who headed west in search of "God's Country" faced hardship, loneliness, and deprivation. To carve a farm from the raw prairie of Iowa, the plains of Nebraska, or the forests of the Pacific Northwest took more than fortitude and backbreaking toil. It took luck. Blizzards, tornadoes, grasshoppers, hailstorms, drought, prairie fires, accidental death, and disease were only a few of the catastrophes that could befall even the best farmer. Homesteaders on free land still needed as much as $1,000 for a house, a team of farm animals, a well, fencing, and seed. Poor farmers called "sodbusters" did without even these basics, living in houses made from sod (blocks of grass-covered earth) or dugouts carved into hillsides and using muscle instead of machinery.

"Father made a dugout and covered it with willows and grass," one Kansas girl recounted. When it rained, the dugout flooded, and "we carried the water out in buckets, then waded around in the mud until it dried." Rain wasn't the only problem. "Sometimes the bull snakes would get in the roof and now and then one would lose his hold and fall down on the bed. . . . Mother would grab the hoe . . . and after the fight was over Mr. Bull Snake was dragged outside."

For women on the frontier, obtaining simple daily necessities such as water and fuel meant backbreaking labor. Out on the plains, where water was scarce, women often had to trudge to the nearest creek or spring. "A yoke was made to place across [Mother's] shoulders, so as to carry at each end a bucket of water," one daughter recollected, "and then water was brought a half mile from spring to house." Gathering fuel was another heavy chore. Without ready sources of coal or firewood, the most prevalent fuel was "chips" — chunks of dried cattle and buffalo dung, found in abundance on the plains.

Despite the hardships, some homesteaders succeeded in building comfortable lives. The dugout made way for the sod hut — a more substantial dwelling; the log cabin yielded to a white clapboard home with a porch and a rocking chair. For others, the promise of the West failed to materialize. Already by the 1870s, much of the best land had been taken. Too often, homesteaders found that only the least desirable tracts were left — poor land, far from markets, transportation, and society. "There is plenty of land for sale in California," one migrant complained in 1870, but "the majority of the available lands are held by speculators, at prices far beyond the reach of a poor man." The railroads, flush from land grants provided by the state and federal governments, owned huge swaths of

> **CHRONOLOGY**

1862
– Homestead Act.

1869
– First transcontinental railroad is completed.

1879
– Exodusters move to Kansas.

1886–1887
– Severe blizzards decimate cattle.

1889
– Two million acres in Oklahoma are opened for settlement.

1893
– Last land rush in Oklahoma Territory.

Midwestern Settlement before 1862

In what ways did different Indian groups defy and resist colonial rule?

How did mining shape American expansion?

How did the fight for land and resources in the West unfold?

Conclusion: How did the West set the tone for the Gilded Age?

✓ LearningCurve
Check what you know.
bedfordstmartins.com /roarkunderstanding

507

land in the West and actively recruited buyers. Altogether, the land grants totaled approximately 180 million acres — an area almost one-tenth the size of the United States (**Map 17.3**). Of the 2.5 million farms established between 1860 and 1900, homesteading accounted for only one in five; the vast majority of farmland sold for a profit.

As land grew scarce on the prairie in the 1870s, farmers began to push farther west, moving into western Kansas, Nebraska, and eastern Colorado — the region called the Great American Desert by settlers who had passed over it on their way to California and Oregon. Many agricultural experts warned that the semiarid land (where less than twenty inches of rain fell annually) would not support a farm on the 160 acres allotted to homesteaders. But their words of caution were drowned out by the extravagant claims of western promoters, many employed by the railroads to sell off their land grants. "Rain follows the plow" became the slogan of western boosters, who insisted that cultivation would alter the climate of the region and bring more rainfall. Instead, drought followed the plow. Droughts were a cyclical fact of life on the Great Plains. Plowed up, the dry topsoil blew away in the wind. A period of relatively good rainfall in the early 1880s encouraged farming; then a protracted drought in the late 1880s and early 1890s sent starving farmers reeling back from the plains. Thousands left, some in wagons carrying the slogan "In God we trusted, in Kansas we busted."

Fever for fertile land set off a series of spectacular land runs in Oklahoma. When two million acres of land in former Indian Territory opened for settlement in 1889, thousands of homesteaders massed on the border. At the opening pistol shot, "with a shout and a yell the swift riders shot out, then followed the light buggies or wagons," a reporter wrote. "Above all, a great cloud of dust hover[ed] like smoke over a battlefield." By nightfall, Oklahoma boasted two tent cities with more than ten thousand residents. In the last frenzied land rush on Oklahoma's Cherokee strip in 1893, several settlers were killed in the stampede, and nervous men guarded their claims with rifles. As public land grew scarce, the hunger for land grew fiercer for both farmers and ranchers.

Ranchers and Cowboys

Cattle ranchers followed the railroads onto the plains, establishing a cattle kingdom from Texas to Wyoming between 1865 and 1885. Cowboys drove huge herds, as many as three thousand head of cattle that grazed on public lands as they followed cattle tracks like the Chisholm Trail from Texas to railheads in Kansas.

Barbed wire, invented in 1874, revolutionized the cattle business and sounded the death knell for the open range. As the largest ranches in Texas began to fence, nasty fights broke out between big ranchers and "fence cutters," who resented the end of the open range. One old-timer observed, "Those persons, Mexicans and Americans, without land but who had cattle were put out of business by fencing." Fencing forced small-time ranchers who owned land but could not afford to buy barbed wire or sink wells to sell out for the best price they could get. The displaced ranchers, many of them Mexicans,

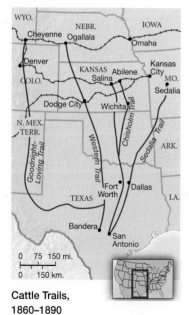

Cattle Trails, 1860–1890

CHAPTER LOCATOR | What did U.S. expansion mean for Native Americans?

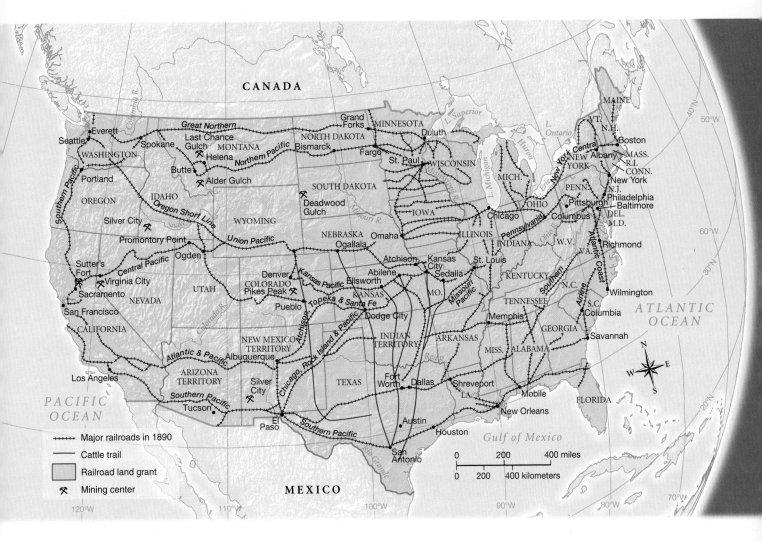

MAP 17.3 ■ Federal Land Grants to Railroads and the Development of the West, 1850–1900

Railroads received land grants totaling more than 180 million acres, an area as large as Texas. Built well ahead of demand, the western railroads courted settlers, often onto land not fit for farming.

> MAP ACTIVITY

READING THE MAP: Which mining cities and towns were located directly on a railroad line? Which towns were located at the junction of more than one line or railroad branch?
CONNECTIONS: In what ways did the growth of the railroads affect the population of the West? What western goods and products did the railroads help bring east and to ports for shipping around the world?

ended up as wageworkers on the huge spreads owned by Anglos or by European syndicates.

On the range, the cowboy gave way to the cattle king and, like the miner, became a wage laborer. Many cowboys were African Americans (as many as five thousand in Texas alone). Writers of western literature chose to ignore the presence of black cowboys like Deadwood Dick (Nat Love), who was portrayed as a white man in the dime novels of the era.

| In what ways did different Indian groups defy and resist colonial rule? | How did mining shape American expansion? | **How did the fight for land and resources in the West unfold?** | Conclusion: How did the West set the tone for the Gilded Age? | ✓ LearningCurve Check what you know. bedfordstmartins.com /roarkunderstanding |

By 1886, cattle overcrowded the range. Severe blizzards during the winter of 1886–87 decimated the herds. "A whole generation of cowmen," wrote one chronicler, "went dead broke." Fencing worsened the situation. During blizzards, cattle stayed alive by keeping on the move. But when they ran up against barbed wire fences, they froze to death. In the aftermath of the "Great Die Up," new labor-intensive forms of cattle ranching replaced the open-range model.

Tenants, Sharecroppers, and Migrants

In the post–Civil War period, as agriculture became a big business tied by the railroads to national and global markets, an increasing number of laborers worked land that they would never own. In the southern United States, farmers labored under particularly heavy burdens. The Civil War wiped out much of the region's capital, which had been invested in slaves, and crippled the plantation economy. Newly freed slaves rarely obtained land of their own and often ended up as farm laborers. "The colored folks stayed with the old boss man and farmed and worked on the plantations," a black Alabama sharecropper observed bitterly. "They were still slaves, but they were free slaves." Some freed people did manage to pull together enough resources to go west. In 1879, more than fifteen thousand black Exodusters, as the black settlers were known, moved from Mississippi and Louisiana to take up land in Kansas.

California's Mexican cowboys, or *vaqueros*, commanded decent wages throughout the Southwest. But by 1880, as the coming of the railroads ended the long cattle drives and as large feedlots began to replace the open range, the value of their skills declined. Many vaqueros ended up as migrant laborers, often on land their families had once owned. Similarly, in Texas, Tejanos (Mexican residents of Texas) found themselves displaced. After the heyday of cattle ranching ended in the late 1880s, cotton production rose in the southeastern regions of the state. Ranchers turned their pastures into sharecroppers' plots and hired displaced cowboys, most of them Mexicans, as seasonal laborers for as little as seventy-five cents a day, thereby creating a growing army of agricultural wageworkers.

Land monopoly and large-scale farming fostered tenancy and migratory labor on the West Coast. By the 1870s, less than 1 percent of California's population owned half the state's available agricultural land. The rigid economics of large-scale commercial agriculture and the seasonal nature of the crops spawned a ragged army of migratory agricultural laborers. Derisively labeled "blanket men" or "bindle stiffs," these transients worked the fields in the growing season and wintered in the flophouses of San Francisco. After passage of the Chinese Exclusion Act of 1882, Mexicans, Filipinos, and Japanese immigrants filled the demand for migratory workers.

Commercial Farming and Industrial Cowboys

In the late nineteenth century, the population of the United States remained overwhelmingly rural. The 1870 census showed that nearly 80 percent of the nation's people lived on farms and in villages of fewer than 8,000 inhabitants. By 1900, the figure had dropped to 66 percent (**Figure 17.1**). At the same time, the number of farms rose. Rapid growth in the West increased the number of the nation's farms from 2 million in 1860 to more than 5.7 million in 1900.

CHAPTER LOCATOR | What did U.S. expansion mean for Native Americans?

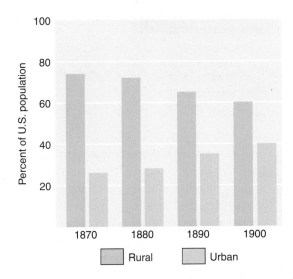

FIGURE 17.1 ■ Changes in Rural and Urban Populations, 1870–1900

Between 1870 and 1900, the number of urban dwellers increased; however, even as the number of rural inhabitants fell, the number of farms increased. Mechanization made it possible to farm with fewer hands, fueling the exodus from farm to city throughout the second half of the nineteenth century.

New technology and farming techniques revolutionized American farm life. Mechanized farm machinery halved the time and labor cost of production and made it possible to cultivate vast tracts of land. Meanwhile, urbanization provided farmers with expanding markets for their produce, and railroads carried crops to markets thousands of miles away. Even before the start of the twentieth century, American agriculture had entered the era of what would come to be called agribusiness — farming as a big business — with the advent of huge commercial farms.

As farming moved onto the prairies and plains, mechanization took command. Steel plows, reapers, mowers, harrows, seed drills, combines, and threshers replaced human muscle. Horse-drawn implements gave way to steam-powered machinery. By 1880, a single combine could do the work of twenty men, vastly increasing the acreage a farmer could cultivate. Mechanization spurred the growth of bonanza wheat farms, some more than 100,000 acres, in California and the Red River Valley of North Dakota and Minnesota. This agricultural revolution meant that Americans raised more than four times the corn, five times the hay, and seven times the wheat and oats they had before the Civil War.

Like cotton farmers in the South, western grain and livestock farmers increasingly depended on foreign markets for their livelihood. A fall in global market prices meant that a farmer's entire harvest went to pay off debts. In the depression that followed the panic of 1893, many heavily mortgaged farmers lost their land to creditors. As a Texas cotton farmer complained, "By the time the World Gets their Liveing out of the Farmer as we have to Feed the World, we the Farmer has nothing Left but a Bear Hard Liveing." Commercial farming, along with mining, represented another way in which the West developed its own brand of industrialism. The far West's industrial economy sprang initially from California gold and the vast territory that came under American control following the Mexican-American War. In the ensuing rush on land and resources, environmental factors interacted with economic and social forces to produce enterprises as vast in scale and scope as anything found in the East.

Two Alsatian immigrants, Henry Miller and Charles Lux, pioneered the West's mix of agriculture and industrialism. Beginning as meat wholesalers, Miller and Lux quickly expanded their business to encompass cattle, land, and

In what ways did different Indian groups defy and resist colonial rule? | How did mining shape American expansion? | **How did the fight for land and resources in the West unfold?** | Conclusion: How did the West set the tone for the Gilded Age? | ✓ LearningCurve Check what you know. bedfordstmartins.com /roarkunderstanding

511

land reclamation projects such as dams and irrigation systems. With a labor force of migrant workers, a highly coordinated corporate system, and large sums of investment capital, the firm of Miller & Lux became one of America's industrial behemoths. Eventually, these "industrial cowboys" grazed a herd of 100,000 cattle on 1.25 million acres of company land in California, Oregon, and Nevada and employed more than 1,200 migrant laborers on their corporate ranches. Miller & Lux dealt with the labor problem by offering free meals to migratory workers, thus keeping wages low while winning goodwill among an army of unemployed who competed for the work. When the company's Chinese cooks rebelled at washing the dishes resulting from the free meals, the migrant laborers were forced to eat after the ranch hands and use their dirty plates. By the 1890s, more than eight hundred migrants a year followed what came to be known as the "Dirty Plate Route" on Miller & Lux ranches throughout California.

Since the days of Thomas Jefferson, agrarian life had been linked with the highest ideals of a democratic society. Now agrarianism itself had been transformed. The farmer was no longer a self-sufficient yeoman but often a businessman or a wage laborer tied to a global market. And even as farm production soared, industrialization outstripped it. More and more farmers left the fields for urban factories or found work in the "factories in the fields" of the new industrialized agribusiness. Now that the future seemed to lie not with the small farmer but with industrial enterprises, was democracy itself at risk? This question would ignite a farmers' revolt in the 1880s and dominate political debate in the 1890s.

> QUICK REVIEW

Why did many homesteaders find it difficult to acquire good land in the West?

CHAPTER LOCATOR | What did U.S. expansion mean for Native Americans?

512 CHAPTER 17 CONTESTING THE WEST

Conclusion: How did
the West set the tone
for the Gilded Age?

IN 1871, **AUTHOR MARK TWAIN** published *Roughing It*, a chronicle of his days spent in mining towns in California and Nevada. There he found corrupt politics, vulgar display, and mania for speculation, the same cupidity he later skewered in *The Gilded Age* (1873), his biting satire of greed and corruption in the nation's capital. Far from being an antidote to the tawdry values of the East — an innocent idyll out of place and time — the American West, with its get-rich-quick ethos and its addiction to gambling and speculation, helped set the tone for the Gilded Age.

Twain's view countered that of Frederick Jackson Turner and perhaps better suited a West that witnessed the reckless overbuilding of railroads; the consolidation of business in mining and ranching; the rise of commercial farming; corruption and a penchant for government handouts; racial animosity, whether in the form of Indian wars or Chinese exclusion; the exploitation of labor and natural resources, which led to the decimation of the great bison herds, the pollution of rivers with mining wastes, and the overgrazing of the plains; and the beginnings of an imperial policy that would provide a template for U.S. adventures abroad. Turner, intent on promoting what was unique about the frontier, failed to note that the same issues that came to dominate debate east of the Mississippi — the growing power of big business, the exploitation of land and labor, corruption in politics, and ethnic and racial tensions exacerbated by colonial expansion and unparalleled immigration — took center stage in the West at the end of the nineteenth century.

| In what ways did different Indian groups defy and resist colonial rule? | How did mining shape American expansion? | How did the fight for land and resources in the West unfold? | **Conclusion: How did the West set the tone for the Gilded Age?** | ✔ **LearningCurve** Check what you know. bedfordstmartins.com /roarkunderstanding |

513

CHAPTER 17 STUDY GUIDE

STEP 1 **GET STARTED ONLINE**

✓ LearningCurve ▪ bedfordstmartins.com/roarkunderstanding

Now that you've read the chapter, make it stick by completing the LearningCurve activity.

STEP 2 **EXPLAIN WHY IT MATTERS**

Put your reading into practice. Identify each term below, and then explain why it matters in U.S. history.

TERM	WHO OR WHAT & WHEN	WHY IT MATTERS
reservations (p. 490)		
Comanchería (p. 492)		
Black Hills (p. 492)		
Battle of the Little Big Horn (p. 493)		
Carlisle Indian School (p. 495)		
Dawes Allotment Act (p. 496)		
Ghost Dance (p. 498)		
Wounded Knee (p. 499)		
Comstock Lode (p. 500)		
Chinese Exclusion Act (p. 505)		
Homestead Act of 1862 (p. 506)		
first transcontinental railroad (p. 506)		

STEP 3 **MOVE BEYOND THE BASICS**

To demonstrate a more advanced understanding, describe the policies and goals of the federal government with respect to the West in the late nineteenth century.

	Federal policies and legislation	Goals
Indian peoples		
Diverse peoples of the West		
Land and natural resources		
Transportation		

PUT IT ALL TOGETHER

Now, take a step back and try to explain the big picture. Remember to use specific examples from the chapter in your answers.

NATIVE AMERICANS

▶ How did American Indians respond to the flood of westward migration after the Civil War?

▶ How did American Indians respond to changes in federal Indian policy between 1865 and 1900?

NATURAL RESOURCES AND TRANSPORTATION IN THE WEST

▶ Why was mining so important in the economy and society of the West and of the nation?

▶ What role did the railroad play in the development of the West?

THE WEST AND ETHNIC DIVERSITY

▶ What was the impetus for and impact of the Chinese Exclusion Act?

▶ How did racial and ethnic prejudice affect relations among westerners?

LOOKING BACKWARD, LOOKING AHEAD

▶ How did western expansion before the Civil War differ from western expansion after the Civil War?

  ▶ What new political and economic issues and tensions did American expansion raise?

  ▶ How did American lives and livelihoods change as a result of migration to the West?

> **IN YOUR OWN WORDS**

Imagine that you must give an oral report to the class answering the following question: **What was most significant about American expansion after the Civil War?** What would be the most important points to include and why?

18

DEFINING THE GILDED AGE IN BUSINESS AND POLITICS

1865–1900

> **What were the most important business and political developments of the Gilded Age?**

Chapter 18 explores the years between 1865 and 1895, the era commonly known as the Gilded Age. It examines the acceleration of industrialization and the growing interplay of business and politics. This chapter also examines the role of race and gender in social and political life and explores the impact of economic changes on the politics and culture of the late nineteenth century.

✓ **LearningCurve**

bedfordstmartins.com/roarkunderstanding
After reading the chapter, use LearningCurve to retain what you've read.

The Lost Bet, **1893.** Artist Joseph Klir painted this scene of a Chicago parade after a local Republican agreed to pull his Democratic friend if Grover Cleveland won the 1892 presidential election. Library of Congress.

> How did the railroads stimulate big business?

> Why did the ideas of social Darwinism appeal to many Americans in the late nineteenth century?

> What factors influenced political life in the late nineteenth century?

> What issues shaped party politics in the late nineteenth century?

> What role did economic issues play in party realignment?

> Conclusion: Why did business dominate the Gilded Age?

How did the railroads stimulate big business?

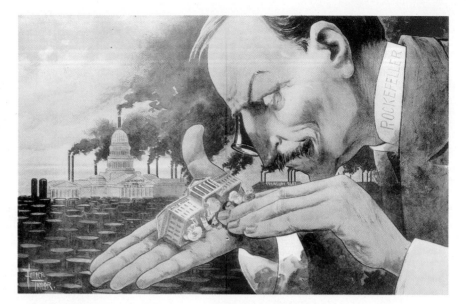

The power wielded by John D. Rockefeller and his Standard Oil Company is satirized here by cartoonist Horace Taylor. Rockefeller is pictured holding the White House and the Treasury Department in the palm of his hand, while in the background the U.S. Capitol has been converted into an oil refinery. Collection of the New-York Historical Society.

> VISUAL ACTIVITY

READING THE IMAGE: According to Horace Taylor, what kind of relationship did John D. Rockefeller have with the federal government? What did the public think of it?

CONNECTIONS: How much influence did industrialists such as Rockefeller exert over the national government in the late nineteenth century?

Gilded Age
► A period of enormous economic growth and ostentatious displays of wealth during the last quarter of the nineteenth century. Industrialization dramatically changed in U.S. society and created a newly dominant group of rich entrepreneurs and an impoverished working class.

I**N THE YEARS** following the Civil War, the American economy underwent a transformation. Where once wealth had been measured in tangible assets — property, livestock, buildings — the economy now ran on money and the new devices of business — paper currency, securities, and anonymous corporate entities. Wall Street, the heart of the country's financial system, increasingly affected Main Street. The scale and scope of American industry expanded dramatically. Old industries like iron transformed into modern industries typified by the behemoth U.S. Steel. Discovery and invention stimulated new industries, from oil refining to electric light and power. The reckless expansion of the railroad in the decades after the Civil War played the key role in the transformation of the American economy.

Jay Gould, Andrew Carnegie, John D. Rockefeller, and other business leaders pioneered new strategies to seize markets and consolidate power. Always with an eye to making the most of their opportunities, these tycoons set the tone in the get-rich-quick era of freewheeling capitalism that came to be called the **Gilded Age**.

CHAPTER LOCATOR | **How did the railroads stimulate big business?** | Why did the ideas of social Darwinism appeal to many Americans in the late nineteenth century?

518 CHAPTER 18 DEFINING THE GILDED AGE IN BUSINESS AND POLITICS

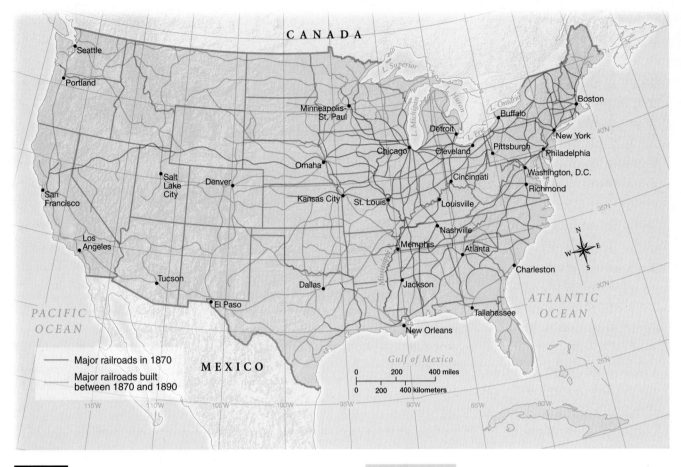

MAP 18.1 ■ Railroad Expansion, 1870–1890

Railroad mileage nearly quadrupled between 1870 and 1890, with the greatest growth occurring in the trans-Mississippi West. New transcontinental lines were completed in the 1880s. Fueled by speculation and built ahead of demand, the western railroads made fortunes for individual speculators. But they rarely paid for themselves and speeded the decline of Native Americans.

> MAP ACTIVITY

READING THE MAP: Where were most of the railroad lines located in 1870? By 1890, how many railroads reached the West Coast? What was the end point of the only western route? **CONNECTIONS:** Why were so many rails laid between 1870 and 1890? How did the railroads affect the nation's economy?

Railroads: America's First Big Business

The military conquest of America's inland empire and the dispossession of Native Americans (see chapter 17) were fed by an elaborate new railroad system built on speculation and government giveaways. Between 1870 and 1880, overbuilding doubled the amount of track in the country; in the following decade, the nation's railroad mileage nearly doubled again. By 1900, the nation boasted more than 193,000 miles of railroad track — more than in all of Europe and Russia combined (**Map 18.1** and **Figure 18.1**). Privately owned but publicly financed by enormous land grants from the federal government and the states, the railroads epitomized the insidious nexus of business and politics in the Gilded Age.

| What factors influenced political life in the late nineteenth century? | What issues shaped party politics in the late nineteenth century? | What role did economic issues play in party realignment? | Conclusion: Why did business dominate the Gilded Age? | ✓ LearningCurve Check what you know. bedfordstmartins.com /roarkunderstanding |

FIGURE 18.1 ■ Railroad Track Mileage, 1890

By 1850, the railway network in Great Britain was already well established, and most of the main lines in Germany had been built. France was slower to invest in railroads, but during the period 1850 to 1860, the government invested heavily in laying track, and the French soon caught up with, and then bypassed, their European neighbors. Russia's railway development experienced its greatest growth in the late nineteenth century. This growth was driven by the country's need to access its newly developing industrial regions and the vast natural resources of its far-flung territories in Asia. Like Russia, most of India's railroad growth occurred late in the century. This development was financed by the British, who were eager to tap the economic potential of their profitable overseas colony. By 1890, the United States had laid more railroad track than Britain, Germany, France, Russia, and India combined. Most of this growth occurred in the period 1870 to 1890, when railroad mileage in the United States nearly quadrupled. The vast area of the United States and its western territories accounted for some of the disparity between railroad mileage here and in Europe. England, France, and Germany combined contained less land than the states east of the Mississippi River.

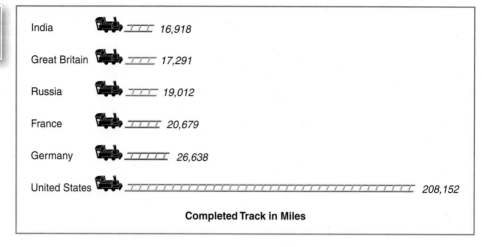

	Completed Track in Miles
India	16,918
Great Britain	17,291
Russia	19,012
France	20,679
Germany	26,638
United States	208,152

To understand how the railroads came to dominate American life, there is no better place to start than with the career of Jay Gould, the era's most notorious speculator. Jason "Jay" Gould bought his first railroad before he turned twenty-five. It was only sixty-two miles long, in bad repair, and on the brink of failure, but within two years he sold it at a profit of $130,000.

The secretive Gould operated in the stock market like a shark, looking for vulnerable railroads, buying enough stock to take control, and threatening to undercut his competitors until they bought him out at a high profit. The railroads that fell into his hands fared badly and often went bankrupt. Gould's genius lay not in providing transportation, but in cleverly buying and selling railroad stock on Wall Street. Millionaires like Gould adopted the strategy of expansion and consolidation, which in turn encouraged overbuilding of the railroads and stimulated a national market.

The New York Stock Exchange expanded as the volume of stock increased sixfold between 1869 and 1901. As the scale and complexity of the financial system increased, the line between investment and speculation blurred, causing many Americans to question if speculators manipulating paper profits fueled the boom and bust cycles that led to panic and depression, putting hardworking Americans out of jobs.

The dramatic growth of the railroads created the country's first big business. Before the Civil War, even the largest textile mill in New England employed no more than 800 workers. By contrast, the Pennsylvania Railroad by the 1870s boasted a payroll of more than 55,000 workers. Capitalized at more than $400 million, the Pennsylvania Railroad constituted the largest private enterprise in the world.

The big business of railroads bestowed enormous riches on a handful of tycoons. Both Gould and his competitor "Commodore" Cornelius Vanderbilt amassed fortunes estimated at $100 million. Such staggering wealth eclipsed that of upper-class Americans from previous generations and left a legacy of lavish spending for an elite crop of ultra-rich heirs.

The Republican Party, firmly entrenched in Washington, worked closely with business interests, subsidizing the transcontinental railroad system with

CHAPTER LOCATOR | **How did the railroads stimulate big business?** | Why did the ideas of social Darwinism appeal to many Americans in the late nineteenth century?

land grants of a staggering 100 million acres of public land and $64 million in tax incentives and direct aid. States and local communities joined the railroad boom, knowing that only those towns and villages along the tracks would grow and flourish.

A revolution in communication accompanied and supported the growth of the railroads. The telegraph, developed by Samuel F. B. Morse, marched across the continent alongside the railroad. By transmitting coded messages along electrical wire, the telegraph formed the "nervous system" of the new industrial order. Telegraph service quickly replaced Pony Express mail carriers in the West and transformed business by providing instantaneous communication. Again, Jay Gould took the lead. In 1879, through stock manipulation, he seized control of Western Union, the company that monopolized the telegraph industry.

The railroads soon fell on hard times. Already by the 1870s, lack of planning led to overbuilding. Across the nation, railroads competed fiercely for business. A manufacturer in an area served by competing railroads could get substantially reduced shipping rates in return for promises of steady business. Because railroad owners lost money through this kind of competition, they tried to set up agreements, or "pools," to divide up territory and set rates. But these informal gentlemen's agreements invariably failed because men like Jay Gould, intent on undercutting all competitors, refused to play by the rules.

The public's alarm at the control wielded by the new railroad magnates and the tactics they employed provided a barometer of attitudes toward big business itself. When Gould died in 1892, he was, as he himself admitted, "the most hated man in America."

Andrew Carnegie, Steel, and Vertical Integration

If Jay Gould was the man Americans loved to hate, Andrew Carnegie became one of America's heroes. Unlike Gould, Carnegie turned his back on speculation and worked to build something enduring — Carnegie Steel, the biggest steel business in the world during the Gilded Age.

The growth of the steel industry proceeded directly from railroad building. The first railroads ran on iron rails, which cracked and broke with alarming frequency. Steel, both stronger and more flexible than iron, remained too expensive for use in rails until Englishman Henry Bessemer developed a way to make steel more cheaply. Andrew Carnegie, among the first to champion the new "King Steel," came to dominate the emerging industry.

Carnegie, a Scottish immigrant, landed in New York in 1848 at the age of twelve. He rose from a job cleaning bobbins in a textile factory to become one of the richest men in America. Before he died, he gave away more than $300 million, most notably to public libraries. His generosity, combined with his own rise from poverty, burnished his public image.

While Carnegie was a teenager, his skill as a telegraph operator caught the attention of Tom Scott, superintendent of the Pennsylvania Railroad. Scott hired Carnegie, soon promoted him, and lent him the money for his first foray into

> **CHRONOLOGY**

1869
- First transcontinental railroad is completed.

1870
- John D. Rockefeller incorporates Standard Oil Company.

1872
- Andrew Carnegie builds world's largest steel plant.

1876
- Alexander Graham Bell demonstrates the telephone.

1882
- John D. Rockefeller develops the trust.

| What factors influenced political life in the late nineteenth century? | What issues shaped party politics in the late nineteenth century? | What role did economic issues play in party realignment? | Conclusion: Why did business dominate the Gilded Age? | ✓ LearningCurve Check what you know. bedfordstmartins.com /roarkunderstanding |

521

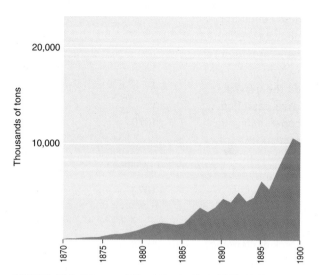

FIGURE 18.2 ■ Iron and Steel Production, 1870–1900

Iron and steel production in the United States grew from nearly none in 1870 to 10 million tons a year by 1900. The secrets to the great increase in steel production were the use of the Bessemer process and vertical integration, pioneered by Andrew Carnegie. By 1900, Carnegie's mills alone produced more steel than did all of Great Britain. With corporate consolidation after 1900, the rate of growth in steel proved even more spectacular.

Wall Street investment. As a result of this crony capitalism, Carnegie became a millionaire before his thirtieth birthday. At that point, Carnegie turned away from speculation. "My preference was always manufacturing," he wrote. "I wished to make something tangible." By applying the lessons of cost accounting and efficiency that he had learned with the Pennsylvania Railroad, Carnegie turned steel into the nation's first manufacturing big business (**Figure 18.2**).

In 1872, Andrew Carnegie built the world's largest, most up-to-date steel mill in Braddock, Pennsylvania. At that time, steelmakers produced about 70 tons a week. Within two decades, Carnegie's blast furnaces poured out an incredible 10,000 tons a week. His formula for success was simple: "Cut the prices, scoop the market, run the mills full; watch the costs and profits will take care of themselves." Carnegie pioneered a system of business organization called vertical integration, in which all aspects of the business were under Carnegie's control — from the mining of iron ore, to its transport on the Great Lakes, to the production of steel. As one observer noted, "There was never a price, profit, or royalty paid to any outsider."

The great productivity Carnegie encouraged came at a high price. He deliberately pitted his managers against one another, firing the losers and rewarding the winners with a share in the company. Workers achieved the output Carnegie demanded by enduring low wages, dangerous working conditions, and twelve-hour days six days a week. One worker, observing the contradiction between Carnegie's generous endowment of public libraries and his labor policy, observed, "After working twelve hours, how can a man go to a library?"

By 1900, Andrew Carnegie had become the best-known manufacturer in the nation, and the age of iron had yielded to an age of steel. Steel from Carnegie's mills supported the elevated trains in New York and Chicago, formed the skeleton of the Washington Monument, supported the first steel bridge to span the Mississippi, and girded America's first skyscrapers. As a captain of industry, Carnegie's only rival was the titan of the oil industry, John D. Rockefeller.

John D. Rockefeller, Standard Oil, and the Trust

In the days before the automobile and gasoline, crude oil was refined into lubricating oil for machinery and kerosene for lamps, the major source of lighting in the nineteenth century. The amount of capital needed to buy or build an oil refinery in the 1860s and 1870s remained relatively low — roughly what it cost to lay one mile of railroad track. As a result, the new petroleum industry experienced

CHAPTER LOCATOR | **How did the railroads stimulate big business?** | Why did the ideas of social Darwinism appeal to many Americans in the late nineteenth century?

522 CHAPTER 18
DEFINING THE GILDED AGE IN BUSINESS AND POLITICS

riotous competition. Ultimately, John D. Rockefeller and his Standard Oil Company succeeded in controlling nine-tenths of the oil-refining business.

Rockefeller grew up the son of a shrewd Yankee who peddled quack cures for cancer. Under his father's rough tutelage, Rockefeller learned how to drive a hard bargain. In 1865, at the age of twenty-five, he controlled the largest oil refinery in Cleveland. Like a growing number of business owners, Rockefeller abandoned partnership or single proprietorship to embrace the corporation as the business structure best suited to maximize profit and minimize personal liability. In 1870, he incorporated his oil business, founding the Standard Oil Company.

As the largest refiner in Cleveland, Rockefeller demanded illegal rebates from the railroads in exchange for his steady business. The secret rebates enabled Rockefeller to drive out his competitors through predatory pricing. The railroads needed Rockefeller's business so badly that they gave him a share of the rates that his competitors paid. A Pennsylvania Railroad official later confessed that Rockefeller extracted such huge rebates that the railroad, which could not risk losing his business, sometimes ended up paying him to transport Standard's oil. Rebates enabled Rockefeller to undercut his competitors and pressure competing refiners to sell out or face ruin.

To gain legal standing for Standard Oil's secret deals, Rockefeller in 1882 pioneered a new form of corporate structure — the **trust**. The trust differed markedly from Carnegie's vertical approach in steel. Rockefeller used horizontal integration to control not the entire process, but just one aspect of oil production — refining. Several trustees held stock in various refinery companies "in trust" for Standard's stockholders. This elaborate stock swap allowed the trustees to coordinate policy among the refineries by gobbling up all the small, competing refineries. Buyers often did not know they were actually selling out to Standard. By the end of the century, Rockefeller enjoyed a virtual monopoly of the oil-refining business. The Standard Oil trust, valued at more than $70 million, paved the way for trusts in sugar, whiskey, matches, and many other products.

When the federal government responded to public pressure to outlaw the trust in 1890, Standard Oil changed tactics and reorganized as a holding company. Instead of stockholders in competing companies acting through trustees to set prices and determine territories, the holding company simply brought competing companies under one central administration. Now one business, not an assortment of individual refineries, Standard Oil controlled competition without violating antitrust laws that forbade competing companies from forming "combinations in restraint of trade." By the 1890s, Standard Oil ruled more than 90 percent of the oil business, employed 100,000 people, and was the biggest, richest, most feared, and most admired business organization in the world.

John D. Rockefeller enjoyed enormous success in business, but he was not well liked by the public. Editor and journalist Ida M. Tarbell's "History of the Standard Oil Company," which ran for three years (1902–1905) in serial form in *McClure's Magazine*, largely shaped the public's harsh view of Rockefeller. Her history chronicled the illegal methods Rockefeller had used to take over the oil industry. By the time Tarbell finished her story, Rockefeller slept with a loaded revolver by his bed. Standard Oil and the man who created it had become the symbol of heartless monopoly.

trust
▶ A system in which corporations give shares of their stock to trustees who hold the stocks "in trust" for their stockholders, thereby coordinating the industry to ensure profits to the participating corporations and to curb competition.

| What factors influenced political life in the late nineteenth century? | What issues shaped party politics in the late nineteenth century? | What role did economic issues play in party realignment? | Conclusion: Why did business dominate the Gilded Age? |

✔ **LearningCurve**
Check what you know.
bedfordstmartins.com
/roarkunderstanding

TABLE 18.1 ■ Notable American
Inventions, 1865–1899

Year	Invention
1865	Railroad sleeping car
1867	Typewriter
1868	Railroad refrigerator car
1870	Stock ticker
1874	Barbed wire
1876	Telephone
1877	Phonograph
1879	Electric lightbulb
1882	Electric fan
1885	Adding machine
1886	Coca-Cola
1888	Kodak camera
1890	Electric chair
1891	Zipper
1895	Safety razor
1896	Electric stove
1899	Tape recorder

New Inventions: The Telephone and the Telegraph

The second half of the nineteenth century was an age of invention (**Table 18.1**). Men like Thomas Alva Edison and Alexander Graham Bell became folk heroes. But no matter how dramatic the inventors or the inventions, the new electric and telephone industries pioneered by Edison and Bell soon eclipsed their inventors and fell under the control of bankers and industrialists.

Alexander Graham Bell came to America from Scotland at the age of twenty-four with a passion to find a way to teach the deaf to speak (his wife and mother were deaf). Instead, he developed a way to transmit voice over wire — the telephone. Bell's invention astounded the world when he demonstrated it at the Philadelphia Centennial Exposition in 1876. In 1880, Bell's company, American Bell, pioneered "long lines" (long-distance telephone service), creating American Telephone and Telegraph (AT&T) as a subsidiary. In 1900, AT&T developed a complicated structure that enabled Americans to communicate not only locally but also across the country. And unlike a telegraph message, the telephone connected

AN UNRESTRAINED DEMON.

The Dangers of Electricity

This 1889 cartoon graphically portrays the dangers of electricity. Innocent pedestrians are electrocuted by the wires as a policeman runs for help. The skull in the wires attached to the electric lightbulb warns that this new technology can be deadly. And the carnage portrayed illustrates the point. Granger Collection.

CHAPTER LOCATOR | How did the railroads stimulate big business? | Why did the ideas of social Darwinism appeal to many Americans in the late nineteenth century?

CHAPTER 18
524 DEFINING THE GILDED AGE IN BUSINESS AND POLITICS

both parties immediately and privately. Bell's invention proved a boon to business, contributing to speed and efficiency. The number of telephones soared, reaching 310,000 in 1895 and more than 1.5 million in 1900.

Even more than Alexander Graham Bell, inventor Thomas Alva Edison embodied the old-fashioned virtues of Yankee ingenuity and rugged individualism that Americans most admired. A self-educated dynamo, he worked twenty hours a day in his laboratory in Menlo Park, New Jersey, vowing to turn out "a minor invention every ten days and a big thing every six months or so." He almost made good on his promise. At the height of his career, he averaged a patent every eleven days and invented such "big things" as the phonograph, the motion picture camera, and the filament for the incandescent lightbulb.

Edison, in competition with George W. Westinghouse, pioneered the use of electricity as an energy source. By the late nineteenth century, electricity had become a part of American urban life. It powered trolley cars and lighted factories, homes, and office buildings. Indeed, electricity became so prevalent in urban life that it symbolized the city, whose bright lights contrasted with rural America, left largely in the dark.

The day of the inventor quietly yielded to the heyday of the corporation. In 1892, the electric industry consolidated. Reflecting a nationwide trend in business, Edison General Electric dropped the name of its inventor, becoming simply General Electric (GE). For years, an embittered Edison refused to set foot inside a GE building. GE, a prime example of the trend toward business consolidation, soon dominated the market.

QUICK REVIEW

What tactics and strategies did American business owners employ during the Gilded Age?

| What factors influenced political life in the late nineteenth century? | What issues shaped party politics in the late nineteenth century? | What role did economic issues play in party realignment? | Conclusion: Why did business dominate the Gilded Age? | ☑ LearningCurve Check what you know. bedfordstmartins.com /roarkunderstanding |

Why did the ideas of social Darwinism appeal to many Americans in the late nineteenth century?

Homestead Steelworks

The Homestead steelworks, outside Pittsburgh, is pictured shortly after J. P. Morgan created U.S. Steel, the precursor of today's USX. Try to count the smokestacks in the picture. Air pollution on this scale posed a threat to the health of citizens and made for a dismal landscape. Workers complained that trees would not grow in Homestead. Hagley Museum & Library.

finance capitalism

▶ Investment sponsored by banks and bankers that typified the American business scene at the end of the nineteenth century. After the panic of 1893, bankers stepped in and reorganized major industries to stabilize them, leaving power concentrated in the hands of a few influential capitalists.

EVEN AS ROCKEFELLER and Carnegie built their empires, the era of the "robber barons," as they were dubbed by their detractors, was drawing to a close. Increasingly, businesses replaced partnerships and sole proprietorships with the anonymous corporate structure that would come to dominate the twentieth century. At the same time, mergers led to the creation of huge new corporations.

Banks and financiers played a key role in this consolidation, so much so that the decades at the turn of the twentieth century can be characterized as a period of **finance capitalism** — investment sponsored by banks and bankers. When the depression that followed the panic of 1893 bankrupted many businesses, bankers stepped in to bring order and to reorganize major industries. During these years, a new social philosophy later known as social Darwinism helped to justify consolidation and to inhibit state or federal regulation of business. A conservative Supreme Court further frustrated attempts to control business by consistently declaring unconstitutional legislation designed to regulate railroads or to outlaw trusts and monopolies.

CHAPTER LOCATOR | How did the railroads stimulate big business? | **Why did the ideas of social Darwinism appeal to many Americans in the late nineteenth century?**

526 CHAPTER 18
DEFINING THE GILDED AGE IN BUSINESS AND POLITICS

J. P. Morgan and Finance Capitalism

John Pierpont Morgan, the preeminent finance capitalist of the late nineteenth century, loathed competition and sought whenever possible to eliminate it by substituting consolidation and central control. Morgan's passion for order made him the architect of business mergers. At the turn of the twentieth century, he dominated American banking, exerting an influence so powerful that his critics charged he controlled a vast "money trust" even more insidious than Rockefeller's Standard Oil.

Morgan acted as a power broker in the reorganization of the railroads and the creation of industrial giants such as General Electric and U.S. Steel. When the railroads collapsed, Morgan quickly took over and eliminated competition by creating what he called "a community of interest." By the time he finished "Morganizing" the railroads, a handful of directors controlled two-thirds of the nation's track.

In 1898, Morgan moved into the steel industry, directly challenging Andrew Carnegie. The pugnacious Carnegie cabled his partners in the summer of 1900: "Action essential: crisis has arrived . . . have no fear as to the result; victory certain." The press trumpeted news of the impending fight between the feisty Scot and the haughty Wall Street banker. But for all his belligerence, the sixty-six-year-old Carnegie yearned to retire to Scotland. Morgan, who disdained haggling, agreed to pay Carnegie's asking price, $480 million (the equivalent of about $10 billion in today's currency). According to legend, when Carnegie later teased Morgan, saying that he should have asked $100 million more, Morgan replied, "You would have got it if you had."

Morgan's acquisition of Carnegie Steel signaled the passing of the old entrepreneurial order personified by Andrew Carnegie and the arrival of a new, anonymous corporate world. Morgan quickly moved to pull together Carnegie's chief competitors to form a huge new corporation, United States Steel, known today as USX. Created in 1901 and capitalized at $1.4 billion, U.S. Steel was the largest corporation in the world.

Even more than Carnegie or Rockefeller, Morgan left his stamp on the twentieth century and formed the model for corporate consolidation that economists and social scientists justified with a new social theory later known as social Darwinism.

Social Darwinism, Laissez-Faire, and the Supreme Court

John D. Rockefeller Jr., the son of the founder of Standard Oil, once remarked to his Baptist Bible class that the Standard Oil Company, like the American Beauty rose, resulted from "pruning the early buds that grew up around it." The elimination of competition, he declared, was "merely the working out of a law of nature

> **CHRONOLOGY**

1883
– William Graham Sumner articulates his philosophy of social Darwinism in *What Social Classes Owe to Each Other*.

1889
– Andrew Carnegie publishes "The Gospel of Wealth."

1901
– U.S. Steel is incorporated and capitalized at $1.4 billion.

What factors influenced political life in the late nineteenth century? | What issues shaped party politics in the late nineteenth century? | What role did economic issues play in party realignment? | Conclusion: Why did business dominate the Gilded Age? | ☑ LearningCurve Check what you know. bedfordstmartins.com /roarkunderstanding

527

and a law of God." The comparison of the business world to the natural world resembled the theory of evolution formulated by the British naturalist Charles Darwin. In his monumental work *On the Origin of Species* (1859), Darwin theorized that in the struggle for survival, adaptation to the environment triggered among species a natural selection process that led to evolution. Herbert Spencer in Britain and William Graham Sumner in the United States developed the theory of **social Darwinism**. The social Darwinists insisted that societal progress came about as a result of relentless competition in which the strong survived and the weak died out.

In social terms, the idea of the "survival of the fittest," coined by Herbert Spencer, had profound significance, as Sumner, a professor of political economy at Yale University, made clear in his book *What Social Classes Owe to Each Other* (1883). "The drunkard in the gutter is just where he ought to be, according to the fitness and tendency of things," Sumner insisted. Conversely, "millionaires are the product of natural selection," and although "they get high wages and live in luxury," Sumner claimed, "the bargain is a good one for society."

Social Darwinists equated wealth and power with "fitness" and believed that any efforts by the rich to aid the poor would only tamper with the laws of nature and slow down evolution. Social Darwinism acted to curb social reform while at the same time glorifying great wealth. In an age when Rockefeller and Carnegie amassed hundreds of millions of dollars (billions in today's currency) and the average worker earned $500 a year, social Darwinism justified economic inequality.

Andrew Carnegie softened some of the harshness of social Darwinism in his essay "The Gospel of Wealth," published in 1889. The millionaire, Carnegie wrote, acted as a "mere trustee and agent for his poorer brethren, bringing to their service his superior wisdom, experience, and ability to administer, doing for them better than they could or would do for themselves." Carnegie preached philanthropy and urged the rich to "live unostentatious lives" and "administer surplus wealth for the good of the people." His **gospel of wealth** earned much praise but won few converts. Most millionaires followed the lead of J. P. Morgan, who contributed to charity but hoarded private treasures in his marble library.

With its emphasis on the free play of competition and the survival of the fittest, social Darwinism encouraged the economic theory of laissez-faire (French for "let it alone"). Business argued that government should not meddle in economic affairs, except to protect private property (or support high tariffs and government subsidies). A conservative Supreme Court agreed. During the 1880s and 1890s, the Court increasingly reinterpreted the Constitution, judging corporations to be "persons" in order to protect business from taxation, regulation, labor organization, and antitrust legislation.

Only in the arena of politics did Americans tackle the social issues raised by corporate capitalism.

social Darwinism

▶ A social theory popularized in the late nineteenth century by Herbert Spencer and William Graham Sumner. Proponents believed that only relentless competition could produce social progress and that wealth was a sign of "fitness" and poverty a sign of "unfitness" for survival.

gospel of wealth

▶ The idea that the financially successful should use their wisdom, experience, and wealth to help the poor. Andrew Carnegie promoted this view in an 1889 essay in which he maintained that the wealthy should serve as stewards for society as a whole.

> **QUICK REVIEW**

How did social Darwinism shape American society and business in the late nineteenth century?

CHAPTER LOCATOR | How did the railroads stimulate big business? | Why did the ideas of social Darwinism appeal to many Americans in the late nineteenth century?

528 CHAPTER 18 DEFINING THE GILDED AGE IN BUSINESS AND POLITICS

What factors influenced political life in the late nineteenth century?

"Woman's Holy War"

This political cartoon styles the temperance campaign as "Woman's Holy War" and shows a woman knight in armor (demurely seated sidesaddle on her charger), wielding a battle-ax and trampling on barrels of liquor. The image of temperance women as ax-wielding Amazons proved a popular satiric image. The cartoon appeared in 1874, the year the Woman's Christian Temperance Union was founded. Picture Research Consultants & Archives.

FOR MANY AMERICANS, politics provided a source of identity, a means of livelihood, and a ready form of entertainment. No wonder voter turnout averaged a hefty 77 percent (compared with roughly 60 percent in the 2008 presidential election). A variety of factors contributed to the complicated interplay of politics and culture. Patronage provided an economic incentive for voter participation, but ethnicity, religion, sectional loyalty, race, and gender all influenced the political life of the period.

Political Participation and Party Loyalty

Political parties in power doled out federal, state, and local government jobs to their loyal supporters. With hundreds of thousands of jobs to be filled, the choice of party affiliation could mean the difference between a paycheck and an empty pocket. Money greased the wheels of this system of patronage, dubbed the **spoils system** from the adage "to the victor go the spoils." With their livelihoods tied to their party identity, government employees had a powerful incentive to vote in great numbers.

spoils system
▶ System in which politicians doled out government positions to their loyal supporters. This patronage system led to widespread corruption during the Gilded Age.

> **CHRONOLOGY**

1869
– National Woman Suffrage Association is founded.

1874
– Woman's Christian Temperance Union (WCTU) is founded.

1890
– General Federation of Women's Clubs (GFWC) is founded.

1892
– Ida B. Wells launches antilynching campaign.

Political affiliation provided a sense of group identity for many voters proud of their loyalty to the Democrats or the Republicans. Democrats, who traced the party's roots back to Thomas Jefferson, called theirs "the party of the fathers." The Republican Party, founded in the 1850s, still claimed strong loyalties in the North as a result of its alignment with the Union during the Civil War. Republicans proved particularly adept at evoking Civil War loyalty, using a tactic called "waving the bloody shirt."

Religion and ethnicity also played a significant role in politics. In the North, Protestants from the old-line denominations, particularly Presbyterians and Methodists, flocked to the Republican Party, which championed a series of moral reforms, including local laws requiring businesses to close on Sunday in observance of the Sabbath. In the cities, the Democratic Party courted immigrants and working-class Catholic and Jewish voters and charged, rightly, that Republican moral crusades often masked attacks on immigrant culture.

Sectionalism and the New South

After the end of Reconstruction, most white voters in the former Confederate states remained loyal Democrats, creating the so-called solid South that lasted for the next seventy years. Labeling the Republican Party the agent of "Negro rule," Democrats urged white southerners to "vote the way you shot." Yet the South proved far from solid for the Democrats on the state and local levels, leading to shifting political alliances and to third-party movements that challenged Democratic attempts to define politics along race lines and maintain the Democrats as the white man's party.

The South's economy, devastated by the war, foundered at the same time the North experienced an unprecedented industrial boom. Soon an influential group of southerners called for a New South modeled on the industrial North. Henry Grady, the ebullient young editor of the *Atlanta Constitution,* used his paper's influence to exhort the South to use its natural advantages — cheap labor and abundant natural resources — to go head-to-head in competition with northern industry. And even as southern Democrats took back control of state governments, they embraced northern promoters who promised prosperity and profits.

The railroads came first, opening up the region for industrial development. Southern railroad mileage grew fourfold from 1865 to 1890. The number of cotton spindles also soared as textile mill owners abandoned New England in search of the cheap labor and proximity to raw materials promised in the South. By 1900, the South had become the nation's leading producer of cloth, and more than 100,000 southerners, many of them women and children, worked in the region's textile mills.

The New South prided itself most on its iron and steel industry, which grew up in the area surrounding Birmingham, Alabama. During this period, the smokestack replaced the white-pillared plantation as the symbol of the New South. Andrew Carnegie toured the region in 1889 and observed, "The South is Pennsylvania's most formidable industrial enemy." But southern industry remained controlled by northern investors, who had no intention of letting the South beat the North at its own game. Elaborate mechanisms rigged the price of southern steel, inflating it, as one northern insider confessed, "for the purpose of

CHAPTER LOCATOR | How did the railroads stimulate big business? | Why did the ideas of social Darwinism appeal to many Americans in the late nineteenth century?

530   CHAPTER 18
DEFINING THE GILDED AGE IN BUSINESS AND POLITICS

protecting the Pittsburgh mills and in turn the Pittsburgh steel users." Similarly, in the lumber and mining industries, investors in the North and abroad, not southerners, reaped the lion's share of the profits.

In only one industry did the South truly dominate — tobacco. Capitalizing on the invention of a machine for rolling cigarettes, the American Tobacco Company, founded by the Duke family of North Carolina, eventually dominated the industry. As cigarettes replaced chewing tobacco in popularity at the turn of the twentieth century, a booming market developed for Duke's "ready mades." Soon the company sold 400,000 cigarettes a day.

In practical terms, the industrialized New South proved an illusion. Much of the South remained agricultural, caught in the grip of the insidious crop lien system (see chapter 16). White southern farmers, desperate to get out of debt, sometimes joined with African Americans to pursue their goals politically. Between 1865 and 1900, voters in every southern state experimented with political alliances that crossed the color line and threatened the status quo.

Gender, Race, and Politics

Gender — society's notion of what constitutes acceptable masculine or feminine behavior — influenced politics throughout the nineteenth century. From the early days of the Republic, citizenship had been defined in male terms. Citizenship and its prerogatives (voting and officeholding) served as a badge of manliness and rested on its corollary, patriarchy — the power and authority men exerted over their wives and families. With the advent of universal (white) male suffrage in the early nineteenth century, gender eclipsed class as the defining feature of citizenship; men's dominance over women provided the common thread that knit all white men together politically. The concept of separate spheres dictated political participation for men only. Once the public sphere of political participation became equated with manhood, women found themselves increasingly restricted to the private sphere of the home.

Women were not alone in their limited access to the public sphere. Blacks continued to face discrimination well after Reconstruction, especially in the New South. Segregation, commonly practiced through **Jim Crow** laws (as discussed in chapter 21), prevented ex-slaves from riding in the same train cars as whites, from eating in the same restaurants, or from using the same toilet facilities.

Amid the turmoil of the post-Reconstruction South, some groups struck cross-racial alliances. In Virginia, the "Readjusters," a coalition of blacks and whites determined to "readjust" (lower) the state debt and spend more money on public education, captured state offices from 1879 to 1883. Groups like the Readjusters believed that universal political rights could be extended to black males while maintaining racial segregation in the private sphere. Democrats fought back by arguing that black voting would lead to racial mixing, and many whites returned to the Democratic fold to protect "white womanhood."

The notion that black men threatened white southern womanhood reached its most vicious form in the practice of lynching — the killing and mutilation of black men by white mobs. By 1892, the practice had become so prevalent that a courageous black editor, Ida B. Wells, launched an antilynching movement. That year, a white mob lynched a friend of Wells's whose grocery store competed too successfully

Jim Crow

▶ System of racial segregation in the South lasting from after the Civil War into the twentieth century. Jim Crow laws segregated African Americans in public facilities such as trains and streetcars, curtailed their voting rights, and denied other basic civil rights.

| What factors influenced political life in the late nineteenth century? | What issues shaped party politics in the late nineteenth century? | What role did economic issues play in party realignment? | Conclusion: Why did business dominate the Gilded Age? | ☑ LearningCurve Check what you know. bedfordstmartins.com /roarkunderstanding |

531

Ida B. Wells

Ida B. Wells began her antilynching campaign in 1892 after a friend's murder led her to examine lynching in the South. She spread her message in lectures and pamphlets like this one, distributed for fifteen cents. Wells brought the horror of lynching to a national and international audience and became a founding member of the National Association for the Advancement of Colored People (NAACP). Manuscript, Archives, and Rare Books Division, Schomburg Center for Research in Black Culture, The New York Public Library, Astor, Lenox, and Tilden Foundations.

with a white-owned store. Wells shrewdly concluded that lynching served "as an excuse to get rid of Negroes who were acquiring wealth and property and thus keep the race terrorized." She began to collect data on lynching and discovered that in the decade between 1882 and 1892 lynching rose in the South by an overwhelming 200 percent, with at least 241 black people killed. The vast increase in lynching testified to the retreat of the federal government following Reconstruction and to white southerners' determination to maintain supremacy through terrorism and intimidation.

Wells articulated lynching as a problem of gender as well as race. She insisted that the myth of black attacks on white southern women masked the reality that mob violence had more to do with economics and the shifting social structure of the South than with rape. She demonstrated in a sophisticated way how the southern patriarchal system, having lost its control over blacks with the end of slavery, used its control over white women to circumscribe the liberty of black men.

Wells's outspoken stance immediately resulted in reprisal. While she was traveling in the North, vandals ransacked her office in Tennessee and destroyed her printing equipment. Yet the warning that she would be killed on sight if she ever returned to Memphis only stiffened her resolve. As she wrote in her autobiography, *Crusade for Justice* (1928), "Having lost my paper, had a price put on my life and been made an exile . . . , I felt that I owed it to myself and to my race to tell the whole truth now that I was where I could do so freely."

Lynching did not end during Wells's lifetime, but her forceful voice brought the issue to national and international prominence. At her funeral in 1931, black leader W. E. B. Du Bois eulogized Wells as the woman who "began the awakening of the conscience of the nation." Wells's determined campaign against lynching provided just one example of women's political activism during the Gilded Age. The suffrage and temperance movements, along with the growing popularity of women's clubs, dramatized how women refused to be relegated to a separate sphere that kept them out of politics.

Women's Activism

In 1869, Elizabeth Cady Stanton and Susan B. Anthony formed the National Woman Suffrage Association, the first independent woman's rights organization in the United States, to fight for the vote for women. But women found ways to act politically long before they voted and cleverly used their moral authority as wives and mothers to move from the domestic sphere into the realm of politics.

The extraordinary activity of women's clubs in the period following the Civil War provides just one example. Women's clubs proliferated beginning in the 1860s. Newspaper reporter Jane Cunningham Croly (pen name Jennie June)

CHAPTER LOCATOR | How did the railroads stimulate big business? | Why did the ideas of social Darwinism appeal to many Americans in the late nineteenth century?

CHAPTER 18

532 DEFINING THE GILDED AGE IN BUSINESS AND POLITICS

founded the Sorosis Club in New York City in 1868, after the New York Press Club denied entry to women journalists wishing to attend a banquet honoring the British author Charles Dickens. In 1890, Croly brought state and local clubs together under the umbrella of the General Federation of Women's Clubs (GFWC). Not wishing to alienate southern women, the GFWC barred black women's clubs from joining, despite vehement objections. Women's clubs soon abandoned literary pursuits to devote themselves to "civic usefulness," endorsing an end to child labor, supporting the eight-hour workday, and helping pass pure food and drug legislation.

The temperance movement (the movement to end drunkenness) attracted by far the largest number of organized women in the late nineteenth century. By the late 1860s and the 1870s, the liquor business was flourishing, with about one saloon for every fifty males over the age of fifteen. During the winter of 1873–74, temperance women adopted a radical new tactic. Armed with Bibles and singing hymns, they marched on taverns and saloons and refused to leave until the proprietors signed a pledge to quit selling liquor. Known as the Woman's Crusade, the movement spread like a prairie fire through small towns in Ohio, Indiana, Michigan, and Illinois and soon moved east into New York, New England, and Pennsylvania. Before it was over, more than 100,000 women had marched in more than 450 cities and towns.

The women's tactics may have been new, but the temperance movement dated back to the 1820s. Originally, the movement was led by Protestant men who organized clubs to pledge voluntary abstinence from liquor. By the 1850s, temperance advocates won significant victories when states, starting with Maine, passed laws to prohibit the sale of liquor. The Woman's Crusade dramatically brought the issue of temperance back into the national spotlight and led to the formation of a new organization, the **Woman's Christian Temperance Union (WCTU)** in 1874. Composed entirely of women, the WCTU advocated total abstinence from alcohol.

Temperance provided women with a respectable outlet for their increasing resentment of women's inferior status and their growing recognition of women's capabilities. In its first five years, the WCTU relied on education and moral suasion, but when Frances Willard became president in 1879, she politicized the organization (as discussed in chapter 20). When the women of the WCTU joined with the Prohibition Party (formed in 1869 by a group of evangelical clergymen), one wag observed, "Politics is a man's game, an' women, childhern, and prohyibition- ists do well to keep out iv it." By sharing power with women, the Prohibitionist men violated the old political rules and risked attacks on their honor and manhood.

Even though women found ways to affect the political process, especially in third parties, it remained true that politics, particularly presidential politics, remained an exclusively male prerogative.

Woman's Christian Temperance Union (WCTU)

▶ All-women organization founded in 1874 to advocate for total abstinence from alcohol. The WCTU provided important political training for women, which many used in the suffrage movement.

QUICK REVIEW <

How did race and gender influence politics?

| What factors influenced political life in the late nineteenth century? | What issues shaped party politics in the late nineteenth century? | What role did economic issues play in party realignment? | Conclusion: Why did business dominate the Gilded Age? | ✔️ LearningCurve Check what you know. bedfordstmartins.com /roarkunderstanding |

What issues shaped party politics in the late nineteenth century?

Civil Service Exam In this 1890s photograph, prospective police officers in Chicago take the written civil service exam. Civil service meant that politicians and party bosses could no longer use jobs in the government to reward the party faithful. Chicago Historical Society.

THE PRESIDENTS OF THE GILDED AGE, from Rutherford B. Hayes (1877–1881) to William McKinley (1897–1901), are largely forgotten men, primarily because so little was expected of them. The dominant creed of laissez-faire, coupled with the dictates of social Darwinism, warned the president and the government to leave business alone. Still, presidents in the Gilded Age grappled with corruption and party strife, and they struggled toward the creation of new political ethics designed to replace patronage with a civil service system that promised to award jobs on the basis of merit, not party loyalty.

Corruption and Party Strife

The political corruption and party factionalism that characterized the administration of Ulysses S. Grant (1869–1877) (see chapter 16) continued to trouble the nation in the 1880s. The spoils system remained the driving force in party politics at all levels of government. Pro-business Republicans generally held a firm grip on the White House, while Democrats had better luck in Congress. Both parties relied on patronage to cement party loyalty.

A small but determined group of reformers championed a new ethics that would preclude politicians from getting rich from public office. The selection of

CHAPTER LOCATOR | How did the railroads stimulate big business? | Why did the ideas of social Darwinism appeal to many Americans in the late nineteenth century?

CHAPTER 18
534 DEFINING THE GILDED AGE IN BUSINESS AND POLITICS

U.S. senators particularly concerned them. Under the Constitution, senators were selected by state legislatures, not directly elected by the voters. Powerful business interests often contrived to control state legislatures and through them U.S. senators. As journalist Henry Demarest Lloyd quipped, Standard Oil "had done everything to the Pennsylvania legislature except to refine it." In this climate, a constitutional amendment calling for the direct election of senators faced stiff opposition from entrenched interests.

Republican president Rutherford B. Hayes, whose disputed election in 1876 signaled the end of Reconstruction in the South (see chapter 16), tried to steer a middle course between spoilsmen and reformers. Hayes proved a hardworking, well-informed executive who wanted peace, prosperity, and an end to party strife. Yet the Republican Party remained divided into factions led by strong party bosses who boasted that they could make or break any president.

> CHRONOLOGY

1880
– James A. Garfield is elected president.

1881
– Garfield is assassinated; Vice President Chester A. Arthur becomes president.

1883
– Pendleton Civil Service Act.

1884
– Grover Cleveland is elected president.

> Republican Factions in 1880	
Stalwarts	Supporters of the patronage system, led by master spoilsman Senator Roscoe Conkling of New York.
Half Breeds	Less openly corrupt than the Stalwarts, led by Conkling's archrival, Senator James G. Blaine of Maine.
Mugwumps	Reform-minded Republicans from Massachusetts and New York who deplored the spoils system and advocated civil service reform.

President Hayes's middle course pleased no one, and he soon managed to alienate all factions of his party. Few were surprised when he announced that he would not seek reelection in 1880. To avoid choosing among its factions, the Republican Party in 1880 nominated a dark-horse candidate, Representative James A. Garfield of Ohio. To foster party unity, they picked Stalwart Chester A. Arthur as the vice presidential candidate. The Democrats made an attempt to overcome sectionalism by selecting former Union general Winfield Scott Hancock. Hancock garnered only lukewarm support, receiving just 155 electoral votes to Garfield's 214, although the popular vote was less lopsided.

Garfield's Assassination and Civil Service Reform

Garfield, like Hayes, faced the difficult task of remaining independent while pacifying the party bosses and placating the reformers. On July 2, 1881, less than four months after taking office, Garfield was shot and died two months later. His assailant, Charles Guiteau, though clearly insane, turned out to be a disappointed office seeker, motivated by political partisanship. He told the police officer who arrested him, "I did it; I will go to jail for it: Arthur is president, and I am a Stalwart."

The press almost universally condemned Republican factionalism for creating the political climate that produced Guiteau. Attacks on the spoils system increased, and both parties claimed credit for passage of the Pendleton Civil

| What factors influenced political life in the late nineteenth century? | **What issues shaped party politics in the late nineteenth century?** | What role did economic issues play in party realignment? | Conclusion: Why did business dominate the Gilded Age? | ✓ LearningCurve Check what you know. bedfordstmartins.com /roarkunderstanding |

535

Service Act of 1883, which established a permanent Civil Service Commission consisting of three members appointed by the president. Some fourteen thousand jobs came under a merit system that required examinations for office and made it impossible to remove jobholders for political reasons. The new law also prohibited federal jobholders from contributing to political campaigns, thus drying up the major source of the party bosses' revenue. Businesses soon stepped in as the nation's chief political contributors. Ironically, **civil service reform** gave business an even greater influence in political life.

civil service reform

▶ Effort in the 1880s to end the spoils system and reduce government corruption. The Pendleton Civil Service Act of 1883 created the Civil Service Commission to award government jobs under a merit system that required examinations for office and made it impossible to remove jobholders for political reasons.

Reform and Scandal: The Campaign of 1884

James G. Blaine assumed leadership of the Republican Party and at long last captured the presidential nomination in 1884. A magnetic Irish American, Blaine inspired such devotion that his supporters called themselves Blainiacs. But Mugwump reformers bolted the party and embraced the Democrats' presidential nominee, Governor Grover Cleveland of New York. The burly, beer-drinking Cleveland distinguished himself from a generation of politicians by the simple

Campaign Pins, 1884

These gilt campaign pins from the election of 1884 show Republican candidate James G. Blaine, on the right, thumbing his nose at Democratic candidate Grover Cleveland. The gilt pins are a symbol for Gilded Age politics, an era characterized by corruption and party strife. Collection of Janice L. and David J. Frent.

motto "A public office is a public trust." First as mayor of Buffalo and later as governor of New York, he built a reputation for honesty, economy, and administrative efficiency. The Democrats, who had not won the presidency since 1856, had high hopes for his candidacy, especially after the Mugwumps threw their support to Cleveland, announcing, "The paramount issue this year is moral rather than political."

The Mugwumps soon regretted their words. In July, Cleveland's hometown paper, the *Buffalo Telegraph*, dropped the bombshell that the candidate had fathered an illegitimate child in an affair with a local widow. Cleveland, a bachelor, stoically accepted responsibility for the child. Crushed by the scandal, the Mugwumps lost much of their enthusiasm. At public rallies, Blaine's partisans taunted Cleveland, chanting, "Ma, Ma, where's my Pa?"

Blaine set a new campaign style by launching a whirlwind national tour. On a last-minute stop in New York City, the exhausted candidate committed a misstep that may have cost him the election. He overlooked a remark by a supporter, a local clergyman who cast a slur on Catholic voters by styling the Democrats as the party of "Rum, Romanism, and Rebellion." Linking drinking (rum) and Catholicism (Romanism) offended Irish Catholic voters, whom Blaine had counted on to desert the Democratic Party and support him because of his Irish background.

With less than a week to go until the election, Blaine had no chance to recover from the negative publicity. He lost New York State by fewer than 1,200 votes and with it the election. In the final tally, Cleveland defeated Blaine by a scant 23,005 votes nationwide but won with 219 electoral votes to Blaine's 182 (**Map 18.2**), ending twenty-four years of Republican control of the presidency. Cleveland's followers had the last word. To the chorus of "Ma, Ma, where's my Pa?" they retorted, "Going to the White House, ha, ha, ha."

Candidate	Electoral Vote	Popular Vote	Percent of Popular Vote
Grover Cleveland (Democrat)	219	4,874,986	48.5*
James G. Blaine (Republican)	182	4,851,981	48.3

*Percentages do not total 100 because some popular votes went to other parties.

MAP 18.2 ■ The Election of 1884

QUICK REVIEW

How did the question of civil service reform contribute to divisions within the Republican Party?

What factors influenced political life in the late nineteenth century?

What issues shaped party politics in the late nineteenth century?

What role did economic issues play in party realignment?

Conclusion: Why did business dominate the Gilded Age?

☑ LearningCurve
Check what you know.
bedfordstmartins.com
/roarkunderstanding

537

> What role did economic issues play in party realignment?

FOUR YEARS LATER, in the election of 1888, fickle voters turned Cleveland out, electing Republican Benjamin Harrison, the grandson of President William Henry Harrison. Then, in the only instance in American history when a president once defeated at the polls returned to office, the voters brought Cleveland back in the election of 1892. What factors account for such a surprising turnaround? The 1880s witnessed a remarkable political realignment as a set of economic concerns replaced appeals to Civil War sectional loyalties. The tariff, federal regulation of the railroads and trusts, and the campaign for free silver restructured American politics. Then a Wall Street panic in 1893 set off a major depression that further fed political unrest.

The Tariff and the Politics of Protection

The tariff became a potent political issue in the 1880s. The concept of a protective tariff to raise the price of imported goods and stimulate American industry dated back to the founding days of the Republic. Republicans turned the tariff to political ends in 1861 by enacting a measure that both raised revenues for the Civil War and rewarded their industrial supporters, who wanted protection from foreign competition. After the war, the pro-business Republicans continued to raise the tariff. Manufactured goods such as steel and textiles, and some agricultural products, including sugar and wool, benefited from protection. Most farm products, notably wheat and cotton, did not. By the 1880s, the tariff produced more than $2.1 billion in revenue. Not only did the high tariff pay off the nation's Civil War debt and fund pensions for Union soldiers, but it also created a huge surplus that sat idly in the Treasury's vaults while the government argued about how (or even whether) to spend it.

To many Americans, particularly southern and midwestern farmers who sold their crops in a world market but had to buy goods priced artificially high because of the protective tariff, the answer was simple: Reduce the tariff. But the Republican Party seized on the tariff question to forge a new national coalition. "Fold up the bloody shirt and lay it away," James G. Blaine advised a colleague in 1880. "It's of no use to us. You want to shift the main issue to protection." By encouraging an alliance among industrialists, labor, and western producers of raw materials — groups seen to benefit from the tariff — Blaine hoped to solidify the North, Midwest, and West against the solidly Democratic South. Although the tactic failed for Blaine in the presidential election of 1884, it worked for the Republicans four years later.

Cleveland, who had straddled the tariff issue in the election of 1884, startled the nation in 1887 by calling for tariff reform. The president attacked the tariff as a tax levied on American consumers by powerful industries. And he pointed out that high tariffs impeded the expansion of American markets abroad at a time when American industries needed to expand. The Republicans countered by arguing that "tariff tinkering" would only unsettle prosperous industries, drive down wages, and shrink the farmers' home market. Republican Benjamin Harrison, who supported the high tariff, ousted Cleveland from the White House in 1888, carrying all the western and northern states except Connecticut and New Jersey.

Back in power, the Republicans brazenly passed the highest tariff in the nation's history in 1890. The new tariff, sponsored by Republican representative William McKinley of Ohio, stirred up a hornet's nest of protest across the United States. The American people had elected Harrison to preserve protection but not to enact a higher tariff. Democrats condemned the McKinley tariff and labeled the Republican Congress that passed it the "Billion Dollar Congress" for its carnival of spending, which depleted the nation's surplus by enacting a series of pork barrel programs shamelessly designed to bring federal money to congressmen's constituencies. In the congressional election of 1890, angry voters swept the hapless Republicans, including tariff sponsor McKinley, out of office. Two years later, Harrison himself was defeated, and Grover Cleveland returned to the White House. Such were the changes in the political winds whipped up by the tariff issue.

Controversy over the tariff masked deeper divisions in American society. Conflict between workers and farmers on the one side and bankers and corporate giants on the other erupted throughout the 1880s and came to a head in the 1890s. Both sides in the tariff debate spoke to concern over class conflict when they insisted that their respective plans, whether McKinley's high tariff or Cleveland's tariff reform, would bring prosperity and harmony. For their part, many working

> **CHRONOLOGY**

1873
– Wall Street panic leads to major economic depression.

1887
– Interstate Commerce Act.

1890
– McKinley tariff.
– Sherman Antitrust Act.

1893
– Wall Street panic touches off national depression.

1895
– J. P. Morgan bails out U.S. Treasury.

What factors influenced political life in the late nineteenth century?

What issues shaped party politics in the late nineteenth century?

What role did economic issues play in party realignment?

Conclusion: Why did business dominate the Gilded Age?

✓ LearningCurve
Check what you know.
bedfordstmartins.com
/roarkunderstanding

539

people shared the sentiment voiced by one labor leader that the tariff was "only a scheme devised by the old parties to throw dust in the eyes of laboring men."

Railroads, Trusts, and the Federal Government

American voters may have divided on the tariff, but increasingly they agreed on the need for federal regulation of the railroads and federal legislation to curb the power of the "trusts" (a term loosely applied to all large business combinations). As early as the 1870s, angry farmers in the Midwest who suffered from the unfair shipping practices of the railroads organized to fight for railroad regulation. The Patrons of Husbandry, or the Grange, founded in 1867 as a social and educational organization for farmers, soon became an independent political movement. By electing Grangers to state office, farmers made it possible for several midwestern states to pass laws in the 1870s and 1880s regulating the railroads. At first, the Supreme Court ruled in favor of state regulation (*Munn v. Illinois*, 1877). But in 1886, the Court reversed itself, ruling that because railroads crossed state boundaries, they fell outside state jurisdiction (*Wabash v. Illinois*). With more than three-fourths of railroads crossing state lines, the Supreme Court's decision effectively quashed the states' attempts at railroad regulation.

Anger at the *Wabash* decision finally led to the first federal law regulating the railroads, the Interstate Commerce Act, passed in 1887 during Cleveland's first administration. The act established the nation's first federal regulatory agency, the **Interstate Commerce Commission (ICC)**, to oversee the railroad industry. In its early years, the ICC was never strong enough to pose a serious threat to the railroads. For example, it could not end rebates to big shippers. In its early decades, the ICC proved more important as a precedent than effective as a watchdog.

Concern over the growing power of the trusts led Congress to pass the **Sherman Antitrust Act** in 1890. The act outlawed pools and trusts, ruling that businesses could no longer enter into agreements to restrict competition. It did nothing to restrict huge holding companies such as Standard Oil, however, and proved to be a weak sword against the trusts. In the following decade, the government successfully struck down only six trusts but used the law four times against labor by outlawing unions as a "conspiracy in restraint of trade." In 1895, the conservative Supreme Court dealt the antitrust law a crippling blow in *United States v. E. C. Knight Company*. In its decision, the Court ruled that "manufacture" did not constitute "trade." This semantic quibble drastically narrowed the law, in this case allowing the American Sugar Refining Company, which had bought out a number of other sugar companies (including E. C. Knight) and controlled 98 percent of the production of sugar, to continue its virtual monopoly.

Both the ICC and the Sherman Antitrust Act testified to the nation's concern about corporate abuses of power and to a growing willingness to use federal measures to intervene on behalf of the public interest. As corporate capitalism became more and more powerful, public pressure toward government intervention grew. Yet not until the twentieth century would more active presidents sharpen and use these weapons effectively against the large corporations.

Interstate Commerce Commission (ICC)

▶ Federal regulatory agency designed to oversee the railroad industry. Congress created it through the 1887 Interstate Commerce Act after the Supreme Court decision in *Wabash v. Illinois* (1886) effectively denied states the right to regulate railroads. The ICC proved weak and did not immediately pose a threat to the industry.

Sherman Antitrust Act

▶ 1890 act that outlawed pools and trusts, ruling that businesses could no longer enter into agreements to restrict competition. Government inaction, combined with the Supreme Court's narrow reading of the act in the *United States v. E. C. Knight Company* decision, undermined the law's effectiveness.

CHAPTER LOCATOR | How did the railroads stimulate big business? | Why did the ideas of social Darwinism appeal to many Americans in the late nineteenth century?

540 CHAPTER 18 DEFINING THE GILDED AGE IN BUSINESS AND POLITICS

The Fight for Free Silver

While the tariff and regulation of the trusts gained many backers, the silver issue stirred passions like no other issue of the day. On one side stood those who believed that gold constituted the only honest money. Many who supported the gold standard were eastern creditors who did not wish to be paid in devalued dollars. On the opposite side stood a coalition of western silver barons and poor farmers from the West and South who called for **free silver**. Farmers from the West and South hoped to increase the money supply with silver dollars and create inflation, which would give them some debt relief by enabling them to pay off their creditors with cheaper dollars. The mining interests, who had seen the silver bonanza in the West drive down the price of the precious metal, wanted the government to buy silver and mint silver dollars.

During the depression following the panic of 1873, critics of hard money organized the Greenback Labor Party, an alliance of farmers and urban wage laborers. The Greenbackers favored issuing paper currency not tied to the gold supply, citing the precedent of the greenbacks issued during the Civil War. The government had the right to define what constituted legal tender, the Greenbackers reasoned: "Paper is equally money, when . . . issued according to law." They proposed that the nation's currency be based on its wealth — land, labor, and capital — and not simply on its reserves of gold. The Greenback Labor Party captured more than a million votes and elected fourteen members to Congress in 1878. Although conservatives considered the Greenbackers dangerous cranks, their views eventually prevailed in the 1930s, when the country abandoned the gold standard.

After the Greenback Labor Party collapsed, proponents of free silver came to dominate the monetary debate in the 1890s. Advocates of free silver pointed out that until 1873 the country had enjoyed a system of bimetallism — the minting of both silver and gold into coins. In that year, at the behest of those who favored gold, the Republican Congress had voted to stop buying and minting silver, an act silver supporters denounced as the "crime of '73." By sharply contracting the money supply at a time when the nation's economy was burgeoning, the Republicans had enriched bankers and investors at the expense of cotton and wheat farmers and industrial wageworkers. In 1878 and again in 1890, with the Sherman Silver Purchase Act, Congress took steps to ease the tight money policy

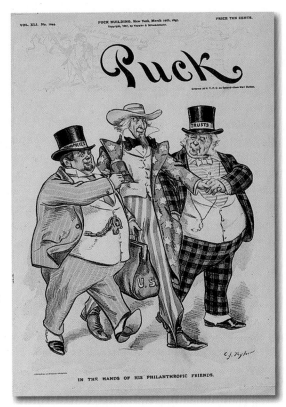

VOL. XLI. No. 1044.   PUCK BUILDING, New York, March 10th, 1897.   PRICE TEN CENTS.

Puck

IN THE HANDS OF HIS PHILANTHROPIC FRIENDS.

The Corruption of Government by Big Business

In this cartoon from the British magazine *Puck*, a gullible Uncle Sam is being led by trusts and monopolies satirically styled as "his philanthropic friends." Picture Research Consultants & Archives.

free silver

▶ Term used in the late nineteenth century by those who advocated minting silver dollars in addition to supporting the gold standard and the paper currency backed by gold. Poor farmers from the West and South hoped this would result in inflation, effectively providing them with debt relief. Western silver barons wanted the government to buy silver and mint silver dollars, thereby raising the price of silver.

What factors influenced political life in the late nineteenth century? | What issues shaped party politics in the late nineteenth century? | **What role did economic issues play in party realignment?** | Conclusion: Why did business dominate the Gilded Age? | ✓ LearningCurve Check what you know. bedfordstmartins.com /roarkunderstanding

541

and appease advocates of silver by passing legislation requiring the government to buy silver and issue silver certificates. Though good for the mining interests, the laws did little to promote the inflation desired by farmers. Soon monetary reformers began to call for "the free and unlimited coinage of silver," a plan whereby nearly all the silver mined in the West would be minted into coins, with sixteen ounces of silver equal in value to one ounce of gold.

By the 1890s, the silver issue crossed party lines. The Democrats hoped to use it to achieve a union between western and southern voters. Unfortunately for them, Democratic president Grover Cleveland supported the gold standard as vehemently as any Republican. After a panic on Wall Street in the spring of 1893, Cleveland called a special session of Congress and bullied the legislature into repealing the Silver Purchase Act because he believed it threatened economic confidence. Repeal proved disastrous for Cleveland. It did nothing to bring prosperity and dangerously divided the country. Angry farmers warned Cleveland not to travel west of the Mississippi River if he valued his life.

Panic and Depression

President Cleveland had scarcely begun his second term in 1893 when the country plunged into the worst depression it had yet seen. In the face of economic disaster, Cleveland clung to the economic orthodoxy of the gold standard. In the winter of 1894–95, the president walked the floor of the White House, sleepless over the prospect that the United States might go bankrupt. Individuals and investors, rushing to trade in their banknotes for gold, strained the country's monetary system. The Treasury's gold reserves dipped so low that unless they could be buttressed, the unthinkable might happen: The U.S. Treasury might not be able to meet its obligations.

At this juncture, J. P. Morgan stepped in. A group of bankers would purchase $65 million in U.S. government bonds, paying in gold. Cleveland knew that such a scheme would unleash a thunder of protest, yet to save the gold standard, the president had no choice. But if President Cleveland's action managed to salvage the gold standard, it did not save the country from hardship. In the winter of 1894–95, people faced unemployment, cold, and hunger. Cleveland, a firm believer in limited government, insisted that nothing could be done to help: "I do not believe that the power and duty of the General Government ought to be extended to the relief of individual suffering which is in no manner properly related to the public service or benefit." Nor did it occur to Cleveland that his great faith in the gold standard prolonged the depression, favored creditors over debtors, and caused immense hardship for millions of Americans.

> ## QUICK REVIEW

What role did the gold standard play in the economic crisis of the 1890s?

CHAPTER LOCATOR | How did the railroads stimulate big business? | Why did the ideas of social Darwinism appeal to many Americans in the late nineteenth century?

CHAPTER 18
542   DEFINING THE GILDED AGE IN BUSINESS AND POLITICS

Conclusion: Why did business dominate the Gilded Age?

THE GOLD DEAL BETWEEN J. P. Morgan and Grover Cleveland underscored a dangerous reality: The federal government was so weak that its solvency depended on a private banker. This lopsided power relationship signaled the dominance of business in the era Mark Twain satirically but accurately characterized as the Gilded Age. Birthed by the railroads, the new economy spawned greed, corruption, and vulgarity on a grand scale. Speculators like Jay Gould not only built but also wrecked railroads to turn paper profits; the get-rich-quick ethic of the gold miner infused the whole continent; and business boasted openly of buying politicians, who in turn lined their pockets at the public's expense.

Nevertheless, the Gilded Age was not without its share of solid achievements. Where dusty roads and cattle trails once sprawled across the continent, steel rails now bound the country together, creating a national market that enabled America to make the leap into the industrial age. Factories and refineries poured out American steel and oil at unprecedented rates. Businessmen like Carnegie, Rockefeller, and Morgan developed new strategies to consolidate American industry. New inventions, including the telephone and electric light and power, changed Americans' everyday lives. By the end of the nineteenth century, the country had achieved industrial maturity. It boasted the largest, most innovative, most productive economy in the world. No other era in the nation's history witnessed such a transformation.

Yet the changes that came with these developments worried many Americans and gave rise to the era's political turmoil. Race and gender profoundly influenced American politics, leading to new political alliances. The fearless activist Ida B. Wells fought racism in its most brutal form — lynching. Women's organizations championed causes, notably suffrage and temperance, and challenged prevailing views of woman's proper sphere. Reformers fought corruption by instituting civil service. And new issues — the tariff, the regulation of the trusts, and currency reform — restructured the nation's politics.

The Gilded Age witnessed a nation transformed. Fueled by expanding industry, cities grew exponentially, bulging at the seams with new inhabitants from around the globe and bristling with new bridges, subways, and skyscrapers. The frenzied growth of urban America brought wealth and opportunity, but also the exploitation of labor, racism toward newcomers, and social upheaval that lent a new urgency to calls for social reform.

| What factors influenced political life in the late nineteenth century? | What issues shaped party politics in the late nineteenth century? | What role did economic issues play in party realignment? | Conclusion: Why did business dominate the Gilded Age? | ✓ LearningCurve Check what you know. bedfordstmartins.com /roarkunderstanding |

543

CHAPTER 18 STUDY GUIDE

STEP 1 GET STARTED ONLINE

 LearningCurve ■ bedfordstmartins.com/roarkunderstanding
Now that you've read the chapter, make it stick by completing the LearningCurve activity.

STEP 2 EXPLAIN WHY IT MATTERS

Put your reading into practice. Identify each term below, and then explain why it matters in U.S. history.

TERM	WHO OR WHAT & WHEN	WHY IT MATTERS
Gilded Age (p. 518)		
trust (p. 523)		
finance capitalism (p. 526)		
social Darwinism (p. 528)		
gospel of wealth (p. 528)		
spoils system (p. 529)		
Jim Crow (p. 531)		
Woman's Christian Temperance Union (WCTU) (p. 533)		
civil service reform (p. 536)		
Interstate Commerce Commission (ICC) (p. 540)		
Sherman Antitrust Act (p. 540)		
free silver (p. 541)		

STEP 3 MOVE BEYOND THE BASICS

To demonstrate a more advanced understanding, describe the positions that various political parties held on the key economic issues of the Gilded Age and assess the impact of regional differences on these issues.

Key economic issues	Democrats	Republicans	Third parties	Regional differences
Tariffs				
Railroads				
Trusts				
Free silver				

PUT IT ALL TOGETHER

Now, take a step back and try to explain the big picture. Remember to use specific examples from the chapter in your answers.

THE RISE OF BIG BUSINESS

▶ What role did railroads and new technologies play in the rise of American big business?

▶ How did the business pioneers of the late nineteenth century organize and grow their businesses?

LATE-NINETEENTH-CENTURY POLITICS

▶ How did ideas about gender and race shape late-nineteenth-century politics?

▶ How did new social philosophical theories justify business and political practices in the late nineteenth century?

ECONOMIC ISSUES AND POLITICAL CONFLICT

▶ How did each Gilded Age president react to economic issues? How did Supreme Court decisions affect economic issues?

▶ What made free silver such a powerful and emotional issue in the late nineteenth century?

LOOKING BACKWARD, LOOKING AHEAD

▶ How did the role of business in politics in the late nineteenth century differ from its role in the first half of the century?

▶ How did the rise of big business affect the economic and political landscape of early-twentieth-century America? In what ways did Americans try to deal with the excesses of big business?

> **IN YOUR OWN WORDS**

Imagine that you must give an oral report to the class answering the following question: **What were the most important business and political developments of the Gilded Age?** What would be the most important points to include and why?

 Do it online at the Student Site ▪ bedfordstmartins.com/roarkunderstanding

19

THE GROWTH OF AMERICA'S CITIES

1870–1900

> What were the most important outcomes of the expansion of American cities in the late nineteenth century? Chapter 19 explores urban growth and its consequences. It focuses on the nature of industrial labor and tensions between workers and employers and assesses the impact of urbanization on daily life. Finally, the chapter examines efforts by city government and private citizens to respond to the demands of rapid population growth.

**LearningCurve**

bedfordstmartins.com/roarkunderstanding
After reading the chapter, use LearningCurve to
retain what you've read.

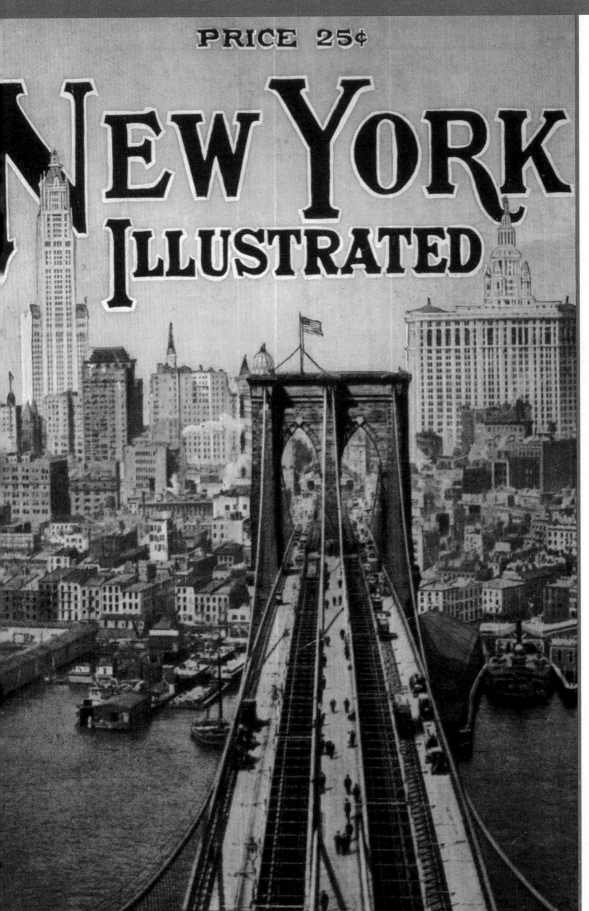

PRICE 25¢

NEW YORK ILLUSTRATED

> Why did American cities experience explosive growth in the late nineteenth century?

> What kinds of work did people do in industrial America?

> Why did the fortunes of the Knights of Labor rise in the late 1870s and decline in the 1890s?

> How did urban industrialism shape home life and the world of leisure?

> How did municipal governments respond to the challenges of urban expansion?

> Conclusion: Who built the cities?

Brooklyn Bridge. Completed in 1883, the Brooklyn Bridge realized builder John Roebling's dream of creating "a great work of art" as well as a superbly engineered bridge. Picture Research Consultants & Archives.

Why did American cities experience explosive growth in the late nineteenth century?

Russian Immigrant Family

A Russian immigrant family is shown leaving Ellis Island in 1900. The white slips of paper pinned to their coats indicate that they have been processed. The family is well dressed, but the scarcity of their possessions testifies to their struggles. The woman carries her belongings in a white cloth sack, and the man holds a suitcase and bedding. Keystone-Mast Collection, UCR/California Museum of Photography, University of California, Riverside.

global migration

▶ Movement of populations across large distances such as oceans and continents. In the late nineteenth century, large-scale immigration from southern and eastern Europe into the United States contributed to the growth of cities and changes in American demographics.

"WE CANNOT ALL LIVE IN CITIES, yet nearly all seem determined to do so," New York editor Horace Greeley complained. The last three decades of the nineteenth century witnessed an urban explosion. Cities and towns grew more than twice as rapidly as the total population. By 1900, the United States boasted three cities with more than a million inhabitants—New York, Chicago, and Philadelphia.

Patterns of **global migration** contributed to the rise of the city. In the port cities of the East Coast, more than fourteen million people arrived, many from southern and eastern Europe, and huddled together in dense urban ghettos. The word *slum* entered the American vocabulary along with a growing concern over the rising tide of newcomers. In the city, the widening gap between rich and poor became more visible. The gap was made more visible by changes in the city landscape brought about by advances in transportation and technology.

The Urban Explosion: A Global Migration

The United States grew up in the country and moved to the city, or so it seemed by the end of the nineteenth century. Between 1870 and 1900, eleven million people moved into cities. Burgeoning industrial centers such as Pittsburgh, Chicago, New York, and Cleveland acted as giant magnets, attracting workers from the countryside. But rural Americans were by no means the only ones migrating to cities.

CHAPTER LOCATOR | Why did American cities experience explosive growth in the late nineteenth century? | What kinds of work did people do in industrial America?

548 CHAPTER 19
THE GROWTH OF AMERICA'S CITIES

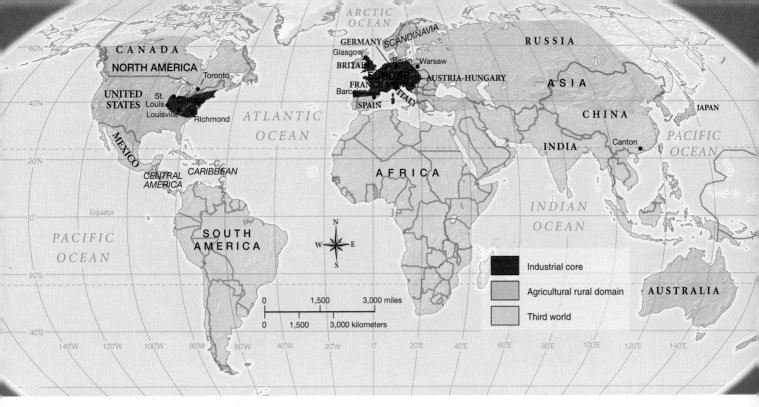

The global nature of the world economy at the turn of the twentieth century is indicated by three interconnected geographic regions. At the center stands the industrial core — western Europe and the northeastern United States. The second region — the agricultural periphery — supplied immigrant laborers to the industries in the core. Beyond these two regions lay a vast area tied economically to the industrial core by colonialism.

> MAP ACTIVITY

READING THE MAP: What types of economic regions were contained in the United States in this period? Which continents held most of the industrial core? Which held most of the agricultural rural domain? Which held the greatest portion of the third world?

CONNECTIONS: Which of these three regions provided the bulk of immigrant workers to the United States? What major changes prompted the global migration at the end of the nineteenth century?

Worldwide in scope, the movement from rural areas to urban industrial centers attracted millions of immigrants to American shores.

By the 1870s, the world could be conceptualized as three interconnected geographic regions (**Map 19.1**). At the center stood an industrial core that encompassed the eastern United States and western Europe. Surrounding this industrial core lay a vast agricultural domain from the Canadian wheat fields to the hinterlands of northern China. Capitalist development in the late nineteenth century shattered traditional patterns of economic activity in this rural periphery. As old patterns broke down, these rural areas exported, along with other raw materials, new recruits for the industrial labor force.

Beyond this second circle lay an even larger third world. Colonial ties between this part of the world and the industrial core strengthened in the late nineteenth century, but most of the people living there stayed put. They worked on plantations and railroads, and in mines and ports, as part of a huge export network managed by foreign powers that staked out spheres of influence and colonies in this vast region.

Why did the fortunes of the Knights of Labor rise in the late 1870s and decline in the 1890s?

How did urban industrialism shape home life and the world of leisure?

How did municipal governments respond to the challenges of urban expansion?

Conclusion: Who built the cities?

✓ LearningCurve
Check what you know.
bedfordstmartins.com
/roarkunderstanding

Immigrants: foreign-born and children of foreign or mixed parentage; by county

- Less than 10%
- 10% to 25%
- 25% to 50%
- 50% to 75%
- More than 75%
- N.Y. 2,748,011 — Total foreign-born population in 1910

MAP 19.2 ■ The Impact of Immigration, to 1910

Immigration flowed in all directions — south from Canada, north from Mexico and Latin America, east from Asia, and west from Europe.

> **MAP ACTIVITY**

READING THE MAP: Which states had high percentages of immigrants? Which cities attracted the most immigrants? Which cities attracted the fewest?

CONNECTIONS: Why did most immigrants gravitate toward the cities? Why do you think the South drew such a low percentage of immigrants?

In the 1870s, railroad expansion and low steamship fares gave the world's peoples a newfound mobility, enabling industrialists to draw on a global population for cheap labor. When Andrew Carnegie opened his first steel mill in 1872, his superintendent hired workers he called "buckwheats" — young American boys just off the farm. By the 1890s, however, Carnegie's workforce was liberally sprinkled with other rural boys, Hungarians and Slavs who had migrated to the United States, willing to work for low wages.

Altogether, more than 25 million immigrants came to the United States between 1850 and 1920. They came from all directions: east from Asia, south from Canada, north from Latin America, and west from Europe (**Map 19.2**). Part of a worldwide migration, immigrants traveled to South America and Australia as well as to the United States. Yet more than 70 percent of all European immigrants chose North America as their destination.

The largest number of immigrants to the United States came from the British Isles and from German-speaking lands (**Figure 19.1**). The vast majority of immigrants were white; Asians accounted for fewer than one million immigrants, and other people

CHAPTER LOCATOR | Why did American cities experience explosive growth in the late nineteenth century? | What kinds of work did people do in industrial America?

550 CHAPTER 19 THE GROWTH OF AMERICA'S CITIES

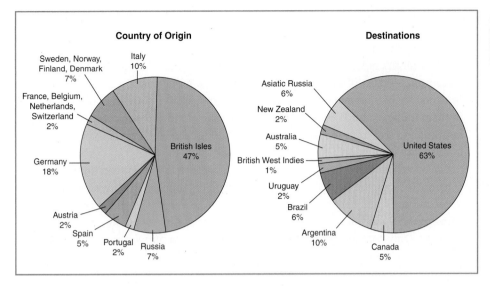

Country of Origin

- Sweden, Norway, Finland, Denmark 7%
- Italy 10%
- France, Belgium, Netherlands, Switzerland 2%
- British Isles 47%
- Germany 18%
- Austria 2%
- Spain 5%
- Portugal 2%
- Russia 7%

Destinations

- Asiatic Russia 6%
- New Zealand 2%
- Australia 5%
- British West Indies 1%
- Uruguay 2%
- Brazil 6%
- Argentina 10%
- United States 63%
- Canada 5%

FIGURE 19.1 ■ European Emigration, 1870–1890

European emigration between 1870 and 1890 shows that people from Germany, Austria, and the British Isles formed the largest group of out-migrants. After 1890, the origin of European emigrants tilted south and east, with Italians and eastern Europeans growing in number. The United States took in nearly two-thirds of the European emigrants. What factors account for the popularity of the United States?

of color numbered even fewer. Yet ingrained racial prejudices increasingly influenced the country's perception of immigration patterns. One of the classic formulations of the history of European immigration divided immigrants into two distinct waves that have been called the "old" and the "new" immigration. According to this theory, before 1880 the majority of immigrants came from northern and western Europe, with Germans, Irish, English, and Scandinavians making up approximately 85 percent of the newcomers. After 1880, the pattern shifted, with more and more ships carrying passengers from southern and eastern Europe. Italians, Hungarians, eastern European Jews, Turks, Armenians, Poles, Russians, and other Slavic peoples accounted for more than 80 percent of all immigrants by 1896. Implicit in the distinction was an invidious comparison between "old" pioneer settlers and "new" unskilled laborers. Yet this sweeping generalization spoke more to perception than to reality. In fact, many of the earlier immigrants from Ireland, Germany, and Scandinavia came not as settlers or farmers, but as wageworkers, and they were met with much the same disdain as the Italians and Slavs who followed them.

Steamship companies courted immigrants—a highly profitable, self-loading cargo. By the 1880s, the price of a ticket from Liverpool had dropped to less than $25. Would-be immigrants eager for information about the United States relied on letters from friends and relatives, advertisements, and word of mouth—sources that were not always dependable or truthful. Even photographs proved deceptive: Workers dressed in their Sunday best looked more prosperous than they actually were to relatives in the old country, where only the very wealthy wore white collars or silk dresses. No wonder people left for the United States believing, as one Italian immigrant observed, "that if they were ever fortunate enough to reach America, they would fall into a pile of manure and get up brushing the diamonds out of their hair."

Most of the newcomers stayed in the nation's cities. By 1900, almost two-thirds of the country's immigrant population resided in cities. Many of the immigrants were too poor to move on. (The average laborer immigrating to the United States carried only about $21.50.) Although the foreign-born rarely outnumbered the native-born population, taken together immigrants and their American-born

| Why did the fortunes of the Knights of Labor rise in the late 1870s and decline in the 1890s? | How did urban industrialism shape home life and the world of leisure? | How did municipal governments respond to the challenges of urban expansion? | Conclusion: Who built the cities? | ☑ **LearningCurve** Check what you know. bedfordstmartins.com /roarkunderstanding |

551

children did constitute a majority in some areas, particularly in the nation's largest cities: Philadelphia, 55 percent; Boston, 66 percent; Chicago, 75 percent; and New York City, an amazing 80 percent in 1900.

Not all the newcomers came to stay. Perhaps eight million European immigrants—most of them young men—worked for a year or a season and then returned to their homelands. Immigration officers called these immigrants, many of them Italians, "birds of passage" because they followed a regular pattern of migration to and from the United States. By 1900, almost 75 percent of the new immigrants were young, single men.

Women generally had less access to funds for travel and faced tighter family control. Because the traditional sexual division of labor relied on women's unpaid domestic labor and care of the very young and the very old, women most often came to the United States as wives, mothers, or daughters, not as single wage laborers. Only among the Irish did women immigrants outnumber men by a small margin from 1871 to 1891.

Jews from eastern Europe most often came with their families and came to stay. Beginning in the 1880s, a wave of violent pogroms, or persecutions, in Russia and Poland prompted the departure of more than a million Jews in the next two decades. Most of the Jewish immigrants settled in the port cities of the East, creating distinct ethnic enclaves, like Hester Street in the heart of New York City's Lower East Side, which rang with the calls of pushcart peddlers and vendors hawking their wares, from pickles to feather beds.

Racism and the Cry for Immigration Restriction

Ethnic diversity and racism played a role in dividing skilled workers (those with a craft or specialized ability) from the globe-hopping proletariat of unskilled workers (those who supplied muscle or tended machines). Skilled workers, frequently members of older immigrant groups, criticized the newcomers. One Irish worker complained, "There should be a law . . . to keep all the Italians from comin' in and takin' the bread out of the mouths of honest people."

The Irish worker's resentment brings into focus the impact of racism on America's immigrant laborers. Throughout the nineteenth century and into the twentieth, members of the educated elite as well as the uneducated viewed ethnic and even religious differences as racial characteristics, referring to the Polish or the Jewish "race." Americans judged "new" immigrants of southern and eastern European "races" as inferior. Each wave of newcomers was deemed somehow inferior to the established residents. The Irish who criticized the Italians so harshly had themselves been stigmatized as a lesser "race" a generation earlier.

Immigrants not only brought their own religious and racial prejudices to the United States but also absorbed the popular prejudices of American culture. Social Darwinism, with its strongly racist overtones, decreed that whites stood at the top of the evolutionary ladder. But who was "white"? Skin color supposedly served as a marker for the "new" immigrants—"swarthy" Italians; dark-haired, olive-skinned Jews. But even blond, blue-eyed Poles were not considered white. The social construction of "race" is nowhere more apparent than in the testimony of an Irish dockworker who boasted that he hired only "white

CHAPTER LOCATOR | **Why did American cities experience explosive growth in the late nineteenth century?** | What kinds of work did people do in industrial America?

CHAPTER 19
552   THE GROWTH OF AMERICA'S CITIES

men," a category that he insisted excluded "Poles and Italians." For the new immigrants, Americanization and assimilation would prove inextricably part of becoming "white."

For African Americans, the cities of the North promised not just economic opportunity but also an escape from institutionalized segregation and persecution. Throughout the South, Jim Crow laws—restrictions that segregated blacks—became common in the decades following Reconstruction. Intimidation and lynching terrorized blacks. "To die from the bite of frost is far more glorious than at the hands of a mob," proclaimed the *Defender*, Chicago's largest African American newspaper. In the 1890s, many blacks moved north, settling for the most part in the growing cities. Racism relegated them to poor jobs and substandard living conditions, but by 1900 New York, Philadelphia, and Chicago had the largest black communities in the nation. Although the most significant African American migration out of the South would occur during and after World War I, the great exodus was already under way.

On the West Coast, Asian immigrants became scapegoats of the changing economy. Hard times in the 1870s made them a target for disgruntled workers. Prohibited from owning land, the Chinese migrated to the cities. In 1870, San Francisco housed a Chinese population estimated at 12,022, and it continued to grow until passage of the Chinese Exclusion Act in 1882 (see chapter 17). For the first time in the nation's history, U.S. law excluded an immigrant group on the basis of race.

Huang Zunxian came to San Francisco in 1882 as Chinese consul general. Disillusioned with the anti-Chinese violence he saw all around him, he wrote a series of angry poems that took Americans to task for their hypocrisy. One of them read:

> They have sealed the gates tightly,
> Door after door with guards beating alarms.
>
> . . . .
>
> Anyone with a yellow-colored face
> Is beaten even if guiltless.
>
> . . . .
>
> The American eagle strides the heavens soaring,
> With half of the globe clutched in his claw.
> Although the Chinese arrived later,
> Couldn't you leave them a little space?

Despite the Chinese Exclusion Act, some Chinese managed to come to America using a loophole that allowed relatives to join their families. Meanwhile, the number of Japanese immigrants rapidly grew, leading to the creation in 1910 of an immigration station at Angel Island in San Francisco Bay through which many Asians entered the United States.

On the East Coast, the volume of immigration from Europe in the last two decades of the century proved unprecedented. In 1888 alone, more than half a million Europeans landed in America, 75 percent of them in New York City. The Statue of Liberty, a gift from the people of France erected in 1886, stood sentinel in the harbor.

| Why did the fortunes of the Knights of Labor rise in the late 1870s and decline in the 1890s? | How did urban industrialism shape home life and the world of leisure? | How did municipal governments respond to the challenges of urban expansion? | Conclusion: Who built the cities? | ✓ LearningCurve Check what you know. bedfordstmartins.com /roarkunderstanding |

553

Ellis Island

▶ Immigration facility opened in 1892 in New York harbor that processed new immigrants coming into New York City. In the late nineteenth century, some 75 percent of European immigrants to America came through New York.

When the federal government took over immigration in 1890, it built a facility on **Ellis Island** in New York harbor, which opened in 1892. After fire gutted the wooden building, a new brick edifice replaced it in 1900. Its overcrowded halls became the gateway to the United States for millions. To many Americans, the "new" immigrants seemed impossible to assimilate. "These people are not Americans," editorialized the popular journal *Public Opinion;* "they are the very scum and offal of Europe." Terence V. Powderly, head of the broadly inclusive Knights of Labor, complained that the newcomers "herded together like animals and lived like beasts." Blue-blooded Yankees led by Senator Henry Cabot Lodge of Massachusetts formed an unlikely alliance with leaders of organized labor—who feared that immigrants would drive down wages—to press for immigration restrictions. In 1896, Congress approved a literacy test for immigrants, but President Grover Cleveland promptly vetoed it. "It is said," the president reminded Congress, "that the quality of recent immigration is undesirable. The time is quite within recent memory when the same thing was said of immigrants, who, with their descendants, are now numbered among our best citizens."

The Social Geography of the City

During the Gilded Age, the social geography of the city changed enormously. Cleveland, Ohio, provides a good example. In the 1870s, Cleveland was a small city in both population and area. Oil magnate John D. Rockefeller could, and often did, walk from his large brick house on Euclid Avenue to his office downtown. On his way, he passed the small homes of his clerks and other middle-class families. Behind these homes ran miles of alleys crowded with the dwellings of Cleveland's working class. Farther out, on the shores of Lake Erie, close to the factories and foundries, clustered the shanties of the city's poorest laborers.

Within two decades, the Cleveland that Rockefeller knew no longer existed. The coming of mass transit transformed the walking city. In its place emerged a central business district surrounded by concentric rings of residences organized by ethnicity and income. First the horsecar in the 1870s and then the electric streetcar in the 1880s made it possible for those who could afford the five-cent fare to work downtown and flee after work to the "cool green rim" of the city. Social segregation—the separation of rich and poor, and of recent immigrants and old-stock Americans—became one of the major social changes engendered by the rise of the industrial metropolis.

Race and ethnicity affected the way cities evolved. Newcomers to the nation's cities faced hostility and not surprisingly sought out their kin and country folk as they struggled to survive. Distinct ethnic neighborhoods often formed around a synagogue or church. African Americans typically experienced the greatest residential segregation, but every large city had its ethnic enclaves—Little Italy, Chinatown, Bohemia Flats, Germantown—where English was rarely spoken.

Poverty, crowding, dirt, and disease constituted the daily reality of New York City's immigrant poor—a plight documented by photojournalist Jacob Riis in his best-selling book *How the Other Half Lives* (1890). By taking his camera into the hovels of the poor, Riis opened the nation's eyes to conditions in the city's slums.

While Riis's audience shivered at his revelations about the "other half," many middle-class Americans worried equally about the excesses of the wealthy. They

CHAPTER LOCATOR | Why did American cities experience explosive growth in the late nineteenth century? | What kinds of work did people do in industrial America?

554 CHAPTER 19 THE GROWTH OF AMERICA'S CITIES

The gap between the rich and poor documented in Jacob Riis's best seller, *How the Other Half Lives*, is underscored here by juxtaposing the photographs of two women. Riis took the photograph of a "scrub" or washerwoman (left) in one of the notorious Police Station lodging houses, the shelters of last resort for the city's poor. On the right is Alice Vanderbilt costumed as the "Spirit of Electricity" for her sister-in-law Alva Vanderbilt's costume ball in 1883. Washerwoman: Museum of the City of New York; Vanderbilt: Collection of the New-York Historical Society.

feared the class antagonism fueled by the growing chasm between rich and poor and shared Riis's view that "the real danger to society comes not only from the tenements, but from the ill-spent wealth which reared them."

The excesses of the Gilded Age's newly minted millionaires were nowhere more visible than in the lifestyle of the Vanderbilts. Alva Vanderbilt launched herself into New York society in 1883 with a costume party so opulent that her sister-in-law Alice Vanderbilt appeared as that miraculous new invention, the electric light, resplendent in a white satin evening dress studded with diamonds.

Such ostentatious displays of wealth became especially alarming when they were coupled with disdain for the well-being of ordinary people. When a reporter in 1882 asked William Vanderbilt whether he considered the public good when running his railroads, he shot back, "The public be damned." The fear that America had become a plutocracy—a society ruled by the rich—gained credence from the fact that the wealthiest 1 percent of the population owned more than half the real and personal property in the country. As the new century dawned, reformers would form a progressive movement to address the problems of urban industrialism and the substandard living and working conditions it produced.

QUICK REVIEW

What global trends were reflected in the growth of America's cities in the late nineteenth century?

 LearningCurve
Check what you know.
bedfordstmartins.com
/roarkunderstanding

What kinds of work did people do in industrial America?

Clerical Worker A stenographer takes dictation in an 1890s office. Notice that the apron, that symbol of feminine domesticity, accompanied women into the workplace. In the 1880s, with the invention of the typewriter, many women put their literacy skills to use in the nation's offices. Brown Brothers.

THE NUMBER OF INDUSTRIAL WAGEWORKERS in the United States exploded in the second half of the nineteenth century, more than tripling from 5.3 million in 1860 to 17.4 million in 1900. These workers toiled in a variety of settings. Many skilled workers and artisans still earned a living in small workshops. But with the rise of corporate capitalism, large factories, mills, and mines increasingly dotted the landscape. Sweatshops and the contracting out of pieces of assembly work, including finishing garments by hand, provided work experiences different from those of factory operatives and industrial workers. Pick-and-shovel labor constituted the lowest-paid labor, while managers, as well as women "typewriters" and salesclerks, formed a new white-collar segment of America's workforce. Children also worked in growing numbers in mills and mines across the country.

America's Diverse Workers

Common laborers formed the backbone of the American labor force. They built the railroads and subways, tunneled under New York's East River to anchor the Brooklyn Bridge, and helped lay the foundation of industrial America. These "human machines" generally came from the most recent immigrant groups. Initially, the Irish wielded the picks and shovels that built American cities, but by the turn of the century, as the Irish bettered their lot, Slavs and Italians took up their tools.

CHAPTER LOCATOR | Why did American cities experience explosive growth in the late nineteenth century? | **What kinds of work did people do in industrial America?**

At the opposite end of labor's hierarchy stood skilled craftsmen like iron puddler James J. Davis, a Welsh immigrant who worked in the Pennsylvania mills. Using brains along with brawn, puddlers earned good wages—Davis drew up to $7 a day, when there was work. But most industry and manufacturing work in the nineteenth century remained seasonal; few workers could count on year-round pay. In addition, two major depressions twenty years apart—one beginning in 1873, the other in 1893—brought unemployment and hardship. With no social safety net, even the best worker could not guarantee security for his family. "The fear of ending in the poor-house is one of the terrors that dog a man through life," Davis confessed.

Employers attempted to replace people with machines, breaking down skilled work into ever-smaller tasks that could be performed by unskilled factory operatives. New England's textile mills provide a classic example. Mary, a weaver at the mills in Fall River, Massachusetts, went to work in the 1880s at the age of twelve. Mechanization of the looms had reduced the job of the weaver to watching for breaks in the thread. "At first the noise is fierce, and you have to breathe the cotton all the time, but you get used to it," Mary told a reporter from *Independent* magazine. "When the bobbin flies out and a girl gets hurt, you can't hear her shout—not if she just screams, you can't. She's got to wait, 'till you see her. . . . Lots of us is deaf."

During the 1880s, the number of foreign-born mill workers almost doubled. At Fall River, Mary and her Scots-Irish family resented the new immigrants. "The Polaks learn weavin' quick," she remarked, using a common derogatory term to identify a rival group. "They just as soon live on nothin' and work like that. But it won't do 'em much good for all they'll make out of it." Employers encouraged racial and ethnic antagonism because it inhibited labor organization.

Mechanization transformed the garment industry as well. The introduction of the foot-pedaled sewing machine in the 1850s and the use of mechanical cloth-cutting knives drove out independent tailors, who were replaced by pieceworkers. Sadie Frowne, a sixteen-year-old Polish Jew, worked in a Brooklyn **sweatshop** in the 1890s. Frowne sewed for eleven hours a day in a 20-by-14-foot room containing fourteen machines. "The machines go like mad all day, because the faster you work the more money you get," she recalled. She earned about $4.50 a week and, by rigid economy, tried to save $2 from her weekly pay. Young and single, Frowne typified the woman wage earner in the late nineteenth century. In 1890, the average workingwoman was twenty-two and had been working since the age of fifteen, laboring twelve hours a day six days a week and earning less than $6 a week.

The Family Economy: Women and Children

In 1900, the typical male worker in manufacturing earned $500 a year, about $12,000 in today's dollars. Many working-class families, whether native-born or immigrant, lived in or near poverty, their economic survival dependent on the contributions of all family members, regardless of sex or age. "Father," asked one young immigrant girl, "does everybody in America live like this? Go to work early, come home late, eat and go to Sleep? And the next day again work, eat, and sleep?" Most workers did. The **family economy** meant that everyone contributed to maintain even the most meager household.

sweatshops
► Small rooms used for clothing piecework beginning in the later nineteenth century. As mechanization transformed the garment industry with the introduction of foot-pedaled sewing machines and mechanical cloth-cutting knives, independent tailors were replaced with sweatshop workers hired by contractors to sew pieces into clothing.

family economy
► Economic contributions of multiple members of a household that were necessary to the survival of the family. From the late nineteenth century into the twentieth, many working-class families depended on the wages of all family members, regardless of sex or age.

Why did the fortunes of the Knights of Labor rise in the late 1870s and decline in the 1890s? | How did urban industrialism shape home life and the world of leisure? | How did municipal governments respond to the challenges of urban expansion? | Conclusion: Who built the cities? | ☑ LearningCurve Check what you know. bedfordstmartins.com /roarkunderstanding

557

Bootblacks

The faces and hands of the two bootblacks shown here with a third boy on a New York City street in 1896 testify to their grimy trade. Boys as young as six worked on city streets as bootblacks and newsboys. For these child workers, education was a luxury they could not afford. Alice Austin photo, Staten Island Historical Society.

In the cities, boys as young as six years old plied their trades as bootblacks and newsboys. Often working under an adult contractor, these children earned as little as fifty cents a day. Many of them were homeless—orphaned or cast off by their families. "We wuz six, and we ain't got no father," a child of twelve told reporter Jacob Riis. "Some of us had to go."

Child labor increased each decade after 1870. The percentage of children under fifteen engaged in paid labor did not drop until after World War I. The 1900 census estimated that 1,750,178 children ages ten to fifteen were employed, an increase of more than a million over thirty years. Children in this age range constituted more than 18 percent of the industrial labor force.

The number of women working for wages in nonagricultural occupations more than doubled between 1870 and 1900 (**Figure 19.2**). Yet white married women, even among the working class, rarely worked for wages outside the home. In 1890, only 3 percent were employed. Black women, married and unmarried, worked out of the home for wages in much greater numbers. The 1890 census showed that 25 percent of married African American women were employed, often as domestics in the houses of white families.

White-Collar Workers: Managers, "Typewriters," and Salesclerks

In the late nineteenth century, a managerial revolution created a new class of white-collar workers who worked in offices and stores. As skilled workers saw their crafts replaced by mechanization, some moved into management positions.

CHAPTER LOCATOR | Why did American cities experience explosive growth in the late nineteenth century? | **What kinds of work did people do in industrial America?**

CHAPTER 19
558 THE GROWTH OF AMERICA'S CITIES

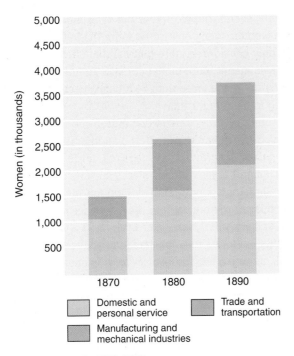

FIGURE 19.2 ■ Women and Work, 1870–1890

In 1870, close to 1.5 million women worked in nonagricultural occupations. By 1890, that number had more than doubled to 3.7 million. More and more women sought work in manufacturing and mechanical industries, although domestic service still constituted the largest employment arena for women.

"The middle class is becoming a salaried class," a writer for the *Independent* magazine observed, "and is rapidly losing the economic and moral independence of former days." As large business organizations consolidated, corporate development separated management from ownership, and the job of directing the firm became the province of salaried executives and managers, the majority of whom were white men drawn from the 8 percent of Americans who held high school diplomas.

The new white-collar workforce also included women **"typewriters"** and salesclerks. In the decades after the Civil War, as businesses became larger and more far-flung, the need for more elaborate and exact records, as well as the greater volume of correspondence, led to the hiring of more office workers. The adding machine, the cash register, and the typewriter came into general use in the 1880s. Employers seeking literate workers soon turned to nimble-fingered women. Educated men had many other career choices, but for middle-class white women, secretarial work constituted one of the very few areas where they could put their literacy to use for wages.

Sylvie Thygeson was typical of the young women who went to work as secretaries. Thygeson grew up in an Illinois prairie town and went to work as a country schoolteacher after graduating from high school in 1884. Realizing that teaching school did not pay a living wage, she mastered typing and stenography and found work as a secretary to help support her family. According to her account, she made "a fabulous sum of money" (possibly $25 a month). Nevertheless, she gave up her job after a few years when she met and married her husband.

"typewriters"

► Women who were hired by businesses in the decades after the Civil War to keep records and conduct correspondence, often using equipment such as typewriters. Secretarial work constituted one of the very few areas where middle-class women could use their literacy for wages.

Why did the fortunes of the Knights of Labor rise in the late 1870s and decline in the 1890s?

How did urban industrialism shape home life and the world of leisure?

How did municipal governments respond to the challenges of urban expansion?

Conclusion: Who built the cities?

LearningCurve
Check what you know.
bedfordstmartins.com
/roarkunderstanding

But by the 1890s, secretarial work was the overwhelming choice of native-born, single white women, who constituted more than 90 percent of the female clerical force. Not only considered more genteel than factory work or domestic labor, office work also meant more money for shorter hours. In 1883, Boston's clerical workers on average made more than $6 a week, compared with less than $5 for women working in manufacturing.

As a new consumer culture came to dominate American urban life in the late nineteenth century, department stores offered another employment opportunity for women in the cities. Boasting ornate facades, large plate-glass display windows, and marble and brass fixtures, stores such as Macy's in New York, Wanamaker's in Philadelphia, and Marshall Field in Chicago stood as monuments to the material promise of the era. Within these palaces of consumption, cash girls, stock clerks, and wrappers earned as little as $3 a week, while at the top of the scale, buyers like Belle Cushman of the fancy goods department at Macy's earned $25 a week, an unusually high salary for a woman in the 1870s. Salesclerks counted themselves a cut above factory workers. Their work was neither dirty nor dangerous, and even when they earned less than factory workers, they felt a sense of superiority.

> **QUICK REVIEW**

How did business expansion and consolidation change workers' occupations in the late nineteenth century?

CHAPTER LOCATOR | Why did American cities experience explosive growth in the late nineteenth century? | What kinds of work did people do in industrial America?

560 CHAPTER 19
THE GROWTH OF AMERICA'S CITIES

Pictures of the devastation caused in Pittsburgh during the Great Railroad Strike shocked many Americans. When militiamen fired on striking workers, killing more than twenty strikers, the mob retaliated by destroying a two-mile area along the track, reducing it to a smoldering rubble. Property damage totaled $2 million. In the aftermath, the curious came out to view the destruction. Carnegie Library of Pittsburgh.

Why did the fortunes of the Knights of Labor rise in the late 1870s and decline in the 1890s?

BY THE LATE NINETEENTH CENTURY, industrial workers were losing ground in the workplace. In the fierce competition to reduce prices and cut costs, industrialists invested heavily in new machinery that replaced skilled workers with unskilled labor. The erosion of skills and the redefinition of labor as mere "machine tending" left the worker with a growing sense of individual helplessness that spurred collective action. The 1870s and 1880s witnessed the emergence of two labor unions—the Knights of Labor and the American Federation of Labor. In 1877, in the midst of a depression, labor flexed its muscle in the Great Railroad Strike. But unionism would suffer a major setback after the mysterious Haymarket bombing in 1886.

The Great Railroad Strike of 1877

Economic depression following the panic of 1873 threw as many as three million people out of work. Those who were lucky enough to keep their jobs watched as pay cuts eroded wages until they could no longer feed their families. In the summer of 1877, the Baltimore and Ohio (B&O) Railroad announced a 10 percent wage cut at the same time it declared a 10 percent dividend to its stockholders. Angry

| **Why did the fortunes of the Knights of Labor rise in the late 1870s and decline in the 1890s?** | How did urban industrialism shape home life and the world of leisure? | How did municipal governments respond to the challenges of urban expansion? | Conclusion: Who built the cities? | ✓ **LearningCurve** Check what you know. bedfordstmartins.com /roarkunderstanding |

561

MAP 19.3 ■ The Great Railroad Strike of 1877

Starting in West Virginia and Pennsylvania, the strike spread as far north as Albany, New York, and as far west as San Francisco, bringing rail traffic to a standstill. Called the Great Uprising, the strike heralded the beginning of a new era of working-class protest and trade union organization.

Great Railroad Strike

▶ Nationwide strike that began in 1877 with West Virginia railroad brakemen who protested against sharp wage reductions. The strike quickly spread to include roughly 600,000 workers. When it grew violent, President Rutherford B. Hayes used federal troops to break the strike. Despite the strike's failure, union membership surged.

> CHRONOLOGY

1869
– Knights of Labor is founded.

1873
– Panic on Wall Street touches off a depression.

1877
– Great Railroad Strike.

1886
– American Federation of Labor (AFL) is founded.
– Haymarket bombing.

brakemen in West Virginia, whose wages had already fallen from $70 to $30 a month, walked out on strike. One B&O worker described the hardship that drove him to take such desperate action: "We eat our hard bread and tainted meat two days old on the sooty cars up the road, and when we come home, find our wives complaining that they cannot even buy hominy and molasses for food."

The West Virginia brakemen's strike touched off the **Great Railroad Strike** of 1877, a nationwide uprising that spread rapidly to Pittsburgh and Chicago, St. Louis and San Francisco (**Map 19.3**). Within a few days, nearly 100,000 railroad workers had walked off the job. An estimated 500,000 sympathetic laborers soon joined the train workers. In Reading, Pennsylvania, militiamen refused to fire on the strikers, saying, "We may be militiamen, but we are workmen first." Rail traffic ground to a halt; the nation lay paralyzed.

Violence erupted as the strike spread. In Pittsburgh, militia brought in from Philadelphia fired on the crowds, killing twenty people. Angry workers retaliated by reducing an area two miles long beside the tracks to rubble. Before the day ended, the militia had shot twenty more workers, and the railroad had sustained more than $2 million in property damage.

Within eight days, the governors of nine states, acting at the prompting of the railroad owners and managers, defined the strike as an "insurrection" and called for federal troops. President Rutherford B. Hayes, after hesitating briefly, called out the army. By the time the troops arrived, the violence had run its course. Federal troops did not shoot a single striker in 1877. But they struck a blow against labor by acting as strikebreakers—opening rail traffic, protecting nonstriking

CHAPTER LOCATOR | Why did American cities experience explosive growth in the late nineteenth century? | What kinds of work did people do in industrial America?

562 CHAPTER 19 THE GROWTH OF AMERICA'S CITIES

"scab" train crews, and maintaining peace along the line. In three weeks, the strike was over.

Middle-class Americans initially sympathized with the conditions that led to the strike. But they quickly condemned the strikers for the violence and property damage that occurred. The *New York Times* editorialized about the "dangerous classes," and the *Independent* magazine offered the following advice on how to deal with "rioters": "If the club of a policeman, knocking out the brains of the rioter, will answer then well and good; but if it does not promptly meet the exigency, then bullets and bayonets . . . constitutes [*sic*] the one remedy and one duty of the hour."

"The strikes have been put down by force," President Hayes noted in his diary on August 5. "But now for the real remedy. Can't something be done by education of the strikers, by judicious control of the capitalists, by wise general policy to end or diminish the evil? The railroad strikers, as a rule, are good men, sober, intelligent, and industrious." While Hayes acknowledged the workers' grievances, most businessmen condemned the idea of labor unions as agents of class warfare. For their part, workers quickly recognized that they held little power individually and flocked to join unions. As labor leader Samuel Gompers noted, the nation's first national strike dramatized the frustration and unity of the workers and served as an alarm bell to labor "that sounded a ringing message of hope to us all."

The Knights of Labor and the American Federation of Labor

The **Knights of Labor**, the first mass organization of America's working class, proved the chief beneficiary of labor's newfound consciousness. The Noble and Holy Order of the Knights of Labor had been founded in 1869 as a secret society of workers who envisioned a "universal brotherhood" of all workers, from common laborers to master craftsmen. Secrecy and ritual served to bind Knights together at the same time that it discouraged company spies and protected members from reprisals.

Although the Knights played no active role in the 1877 railroad strike, membership swelled as a result of the growing interest in labor organizing that followed the strike. In 1878, the Knights abandoned secrecy and launched an ambitious campaign to organize workers. The Knights attempted to bridge the boundaries of ethnicity, gender, ideology, race, and occupation. Leonora Barry served as general investigator for women's work from 1886 to 1890, helping the Knights recruit teachers, waitresses, housewives, and domestics along with factory and sweatshop workers. Women composed perhaps 20 percent of the membership. The Knights also recruited more than 95,000 black workers. That the Knights of Labor often fell short of its goals to unify the working class proved less surprising than the scope of its efforts. Under the direction of Grand Master Workman Terence V. Powderly, the Knights became the dominant force in labor during the 1880s.

The Knights of Labor was not without rivals. Many skilled workers belonged to craft unions organized by trade. Among the largest and richest of these unions stood the Amalgamated Association of Iron and Steel Workers, founded in 1876 and counting twenty thousand skilled workers as members. Trade unionists spurned the broad reform goals of the Knights and focused on workplace issues. Samuel Gompers founded the Organized Trades and Labor Unions in 1881 and reorganized it in 1886 into the **American Federation of Labor (AFL)**, which

Knights of Labor
▶ The first mass organization of America's working class. Founded in 1869, the Knights of Labor attempted to bridge the boundaries of ethnicity, gender, ideology, race, and occupation to build a "universal brotherhood" of all workers.

American Federation of Labor (AFL)
▶ Organization created by Samuel Gompers in 1886 that coordinated the activities of craft unions throughout the United States. The AFL worked to achieve immediate benefits for skilled workers. Its narrow goals for unionism became popular after the Haymarket bombing.

Why did the fortunes of the Knights of Labor rise in the late 1870s and decline in the 1890s? | How did urban industrialism shape home life and the world of leisure? | How did municipal governments respond to the challenges of urban expansion? | Conclusion: Who built the cities? | ✓ LearningCurve Check what you know. bedfordstmartins.com /roarkunderstanding

563

- Public ownership of railroads
- An income tax
- Equal pay for women workers
- Abolition of child labor
- One union of all workers (except gamblers, stockbrokers, lawyers, bankers, and liquor dealers) without class distinctions

coordinated the activities of craft unions throughout the United States. His plan was simple: Organize skilled workers such as machinists and locomotive engineers—those with the most bargaining power—and use strikes to gain immediate objectives such as higher pay and better working conditions. At first, Gompers drew few converts. The AFL had only 138,000 members in 1886, compared with 730,000 for the Knights of Labor. But events soon brought down the Knights, and Gompers's brand of unionism came to prevail.

Haymarket and the Specter of Labor Radicalism

While the AFL and the Knights of Labor competed for members, more radical labor groups, including socialists and anarchists, believed that reform was futile and called instead for social revolution. Both the socialists and the anarchists, sensitive to criticism that they preferred revolution in theory to improvements here and now, rallied around the popular issue of the eight-hour workday.

Since the 1840s, labor had sought to end the twelve-hour workday, which was standard in industry and manufacturing. By the mid-1880s, it seemed clear to many workers that labor shared too little in the new prosperity of the decade, and pressure mounted for the eight-hour workday. Labor championed the popular issue and launched major rallies in cities across the nation. Supporters of the movement set May 1, 1886, as the date for a nationwide general strike in support of the eight-hour workday.

All factions of the labor movement came together in Chicago on May Day. A group of labor radicals led by anarchist Albert Parsons, a *Mayflower* descendant, and August Spies, a German socialist, spearheaded the eight-hour movement in Chicago. Chicago's Knights of Labor rallied to the cause even though Terence Powderly and the union's national leadership, worried about the increasing activism of the rank and file, refused to endorse the movement for shorter hours. Samuel Gompers was on hand, too, to lead the city's trade unionists, although he privately urged the AFL assemblies not to participate in the general strike.

The cautious labor leaders stood in sharp contrast to the dispossessed workers out on strike across town at Chicago's huge McCormick reaper works. There strikers watched helplessly as the company brought in strikebreakers to take their jobs and marched the "scabs" to work under the protection of the Chicago police and security guards supplied by the Pinkerton Detective Agency. Cyrus McCormick Jr., son of the inventor of the mechanical reaper, viewed labor organization as a threat to his power as well as to his profits; he was determined to smash the union.

Haymarket bombing

▶ May 4, 1886, conflict in which both workers and policemen were killed or wounded during a labor demonstration in Chicago. The violence began when someone threw a bomb into the ranks of police at the gathering. The incident created a backlash against labor activism.

CHAPTER LOCATOR | Why did American cities experience explosive growth in the late nineteenth century? | What kinds of work did people do in industrial America?

564   CHAPTER 19
THE GROWTH OF AMERICA'S CITIES

During the May Day rally, 45,000 workers paraded peacefully down Michigan Avenue in support of the eight-hour day. Trouble came two days later, when strikers attacked strikebreakers outside the McCormick works and police opened fire, killing or wounding six men. Angry radicals urged workers to "arm yourselves and appear in full force" at a rally in Haymarket Square.

On the evening of May 4, the turnout at Haymarket was disappointing. No more than two or three thousand gathered in the drizzle to hear Spies, Parsons, and the other speakers. Mayor Carter Harrison, known as a friend of labor, mingled conspicuously in the crowd, pronounced the meeting peaceable, and went home to bed. Sometime later, police captain John "Blackjack" Bonfield marched his men into the crowd, by now fewer than three hundred people, and demanded that it disperse. Suddenly, someone threw a bomb into the police ranks. After a moment of stunned silence, the police drew their revolvers. "Fire and kill all you can," shouted a police lieutenant. When the melee ended, seven policemen and an unknown number of others lay dead. An additional sixty policemen and thirty or forty civilians suffered injuries.

News of the "Haymarket riot" provoked a nationwide convulsion of fear, followed by blind rage directed at anarchists, labor unions, strikers, immigrants, and the working class in general. Eight men, including Parsons and Spies, went on trial in Chicago. "Convict these men," thundered the state's attorney, Julius S. Grinnell, "make examples of them, hang them, and you save our institutions." Although the state could not link any of the defendants to the **Haymarket bombing**, the jury nevertheless found them all guilty. Four men were hanged, one committed suicide, and three received prison sentences.

The bomb blast at Haymarket had lasting repercussions. To commemorate the death of the Haymarket martyrs, labor made May 1 an annual international celebration of the worker. But the Haymarket bomb, in the eyes of one observer, proved "a godsend to all enemies of the labor movement." It effectively scotched the eight-hour movement and dealt a blow to the Knights of Labor. With the labor movement everywhere under attack, many skilled workers turned to the American Federation of Labor. Gompers's narrow economic strategy made sense at the time and enabled one segment of the workforce—the skilled—to organize effectively and achieve tangible gains.

"The Chicago Riot"

Inflammatory pamphlets published in the wake of the Haymarket bombing aimed to scare the public. In this charged atmosphere, the anarchist speakers at the rally were tried and convicted for the bombing even though witnesses testified that none of them had thrown the bomb. Even today, the identity of the bomb thrower remains uncertain. Chicago Historical Society.

> **VISUAL ACTIVITY**

READING THE IMAGE: What does the cover suggest about the views of the author of the pamphlet?
CONNECTIONS: In what ways does this pamphlet reflect the public climate following the Haymarket bombing?

QUICK REVIEW ‹

What were the long-term effects of the Great Railroad Strike of 1877 and the Haymarket bombing of 1886?

| Why did the fortunes of the Knights of Labor rise in the late 1870s and decline in the 1890s? | How did urban industrialism shape home life and the world of leisure? | How did municipal governments respond to the challenges of urban expansion? | Conclusion: Who built the cities? | ✓ LearningCurve Check what you know. bedfordstmartins.com /roarkunderstanding |

565

How did urban industrialism shape home life and the world of leisure?

Beach Scene at Coney Island

Coney Island became a symbol of commercialized leisure and mechanical excitement at the turn of the twentieth century. This fanciful rendering of Coney Island captures men and women frolicking in the waves. Notice the modest woolen bathing outfits. Men box and play ball, a woman flies on a parachute, a uniformed policeman wades into the fray, while the Ferris wheel dominates onshore. Sunday crowds reportedly reached 100,000. Library of Congress.

THE GROWTH OF URBAN INDUSTRIALISM not only dramatically altered the workplace but also transformed home and family life, and it gave rise to new forms of commercialized leisure. Industrialization redefined the very concepts of work and home. Increasingly, men went out to work for wages, while most white married women stayed home, either working in the home without pay—cleaning, cooking, and rearing children—or supervising paid domestic servants who did the housework.

Domesticity and "Domestics"

The separation of the workplace and the home that marked the shift to industrial society led to a new ideology, one that sentimentalized the home and women's role in it. The cultural ideal dictating that a woman's place was in the home, where she would create a haven for her family, began to develop in the early nineteenth century. It has been called the **cult of domesticity**, a phrase used to prescribe an ideal of middle-class, white womanhood that dominated the period from 1820 to the end of the nineteenth century.

cult of domesticity
▶ Nineteenth-century belief that women's place was in the home, where they should create havens for their families. This sentimentalized ideal led to an increase in the hiring of domestic servants, thus freeing white middle-class women to spend time in pursuits outside the home.

CHAPTER LOCATOR | Why did American cities experience explosive growth in the late nineteenth century? | What kinds of work did people do in industrial America?

The cult of domesticity and the elaboration of the middle-class home led to a major change in patterns of hiring household help. The live-in servant, or domestic, became a fixture in the North, replacing the hired girl of the previous century. In American cities by 1870, 15 to 30 percent of all households included live-in domestic servants, more than 90 percent of them women. Earlier in the mid-nineteenth century, native-born women increasingly took up other work and left domestic service to immigrants. In the East, the maid was so often Irish that "Bridget" became a generic term for female domestics. The South continued to rely on poorly paid black female "help."

Servants by all accounts resented the long hours and lack of privacy. "She is liable to be rung up at all hours," one study of domestics reported. "Her very meals are not secure from interruption, and even her sleep is not sacred." Domestic service became the occupation of last resort, a "hard and lonely life" in the words of one female servant.

For women of the white middle class, domestics were a boon, freeing them from household drudgery and giving them more time to spend with their children, to pursue club work, or to work for reforms. Thus, while domestic service supported the cult of domesticity, it created for those women who could afford it opportunities that expanded their horizons outside the home. They became involved in women's clubs as well as the temperance and suffrage movements.

Cheap Amusements

Growing class divisions manifested themselves in patterns of leisure as well as in work and home life. The poor and working class took their leisure, when they had any, not in the crowded tenements that housed their families, but increasingly in the cities' new dance halls, music houses, ballparks, and amusement arcades, which by the 1890s formed a familiar part of the urban landscape.

Young workingwomen no longer met prospective husbands only through their families. Fleeing crowded tenements, the young sought each other's company in dance halls and other commercial retreats. Young workingwomen counted on being "treated" by men, a transaction that often implied sexual payback. Their behavior sometimes blurred the line between respectability and promiscuity. The dance halls became a favorite target of reformers who feared they lured teenage girls into prostitution.

For men, baseball became a national pastime in the 1870s—then, as now, one force in urban life capable of uniting a city across class lines. Cincinnati mounted the first entirely paid team, the Red Stockings, in 1869. Soon professional teams proliferated in cities across the nation, and Mark Twain hailed baseball as "the very symbol, the outward and visible expression, of the drive and push and rush and struggle of the raging, tearing, booming nineteenth century."

Why did the fortunes of the Knights of Labor rise in the late 1870s and decline in the 1890s?

How did urban industrialism shape home life and the world of leisure?

How did municipal governments respond to the challenges of urban expansion?

Conclusion: Who built the cities?

LearningCurve
Check what you know.
bedfordstmartins.com
/roarkunderstanding

567

The increasing commercialization of entertainment in the late-nineteenth-century city was best seen at Coney Island. A two-mile stretch of sand nine miles from Manhattan by trolley or steamship, Coney Island in the 1890s was transformed into the site of some of the largest and most elaborate amusement parks in the country. Promoter George Tilyou built Steeplechase Park in 1897, advertising "10 hours of fun for 10 cents." With its mechanical thrills and fun-house laughs, the amusement park encouraged behavior that one schoolteacher aptly described as "everyone with the brakes off." By 1900, as many as a million New Yorkers flocked to Coney Island on any given weekend, making the amusement park the unofficial capital of a new mass culture.

> **QUICK REVIEW**

How and why did recreation and leisure change in the last decades of the nineteenth century?

CHAPTER LOCATOR | Why did American cities experience explosive growth in the late nineteenth century? | What kinds of work did people do in industrial America?

568   CHAPTER 19
THE GROWTH OF AMERICA'S CITIES

How did municipal governments respond to the challenges of urban expansion?

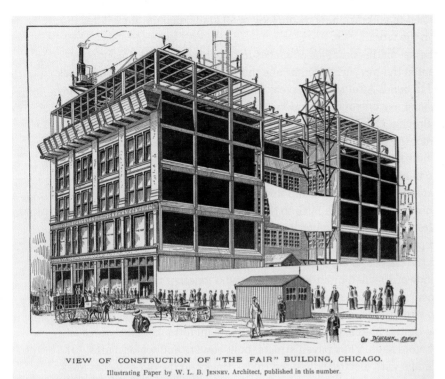

VIEW OF CONSTRUCTION OF "THE FAIR" BUILDING, CHICAGO.
Illustrating Paper by W. L. B. JENNEY, Architect, published in this number.

Chicago Skyscraper Going Up

With the advent of structural steel, skyscrapers like this one in progress in Chicago in 1891 became prominent features of the American urban landscape. This architect's rendering of the Fair Building, a department store designed by William Le Baron Jenney, shows a modern skyscraper whose foundations supported the structural steel skeleton so that the walls could simply "hang" on the outside of the building, because they no longer had to support the structure. Newberry Library (*Inland Architect*, Nov. 1891).

PRIVATE ENTERPRISE, not planners, built the cities of the United States. With a few notable exceptions, cities simply mushroomed, formed by the dictates of profit and the exigencies of local politics. With the rise of the city came the need for public facilities, transportation, and services that would tax the imaginations of America's architects and engineers and set the scene for the rough-and-tumble of big-city government, politics, and bossism.

Building Cities of Stone and Steel

Skyscrapers and mighty bridges dominated the imagination and the urban landscape. Less imposing but no less significant were the paved streets, the parks and public libraries, and the subways and sewers. In the late nineteenth century,

Why did the fortunes of the Knights of Labor rise in the late 1870s and decline in the 1890s?

How did urban industrialism shape home life and the world of leisure?

How did municipal governments respond to the challenges of urban expansion?

Conclusion: Who built the cities?

LearningCurve
Check what you know.
bedfordstmartins.com
/roarkunderstanding

569

Americans rushed to embrace new technology of all kinds, making their cities the most modern in the world.

Structural steel made enormous advances in building possible. No symbol better represented the new urban landscape than the Brooklyn Bridge, which took fourteen years to build. After the massive steel and stone structure opened in May 1883, it was hailed as "one of the wonders of the world." A decade after the completion of the Brooklyn Bridge, engineers used the new technology of structural steel to construct the Williamsburg Bridge. More prosaic and utilitarian than its neighbor, the new bridge was never as acclaimed, but it was longer by four feet and completed in half the time. It became the model for future building as the age of steel supplanted the age of stone and iron.

Chicago, not New York, gave birth to the modern skyscraper. Rising from the ashes of the Great Fire of 1871, which destroyed three square miles and left eighteen thousand people homeless, Chicago offered a generation of skilled architects and engineers the chance to experiment. Commercial architecture became an art form at the hands of a skilled group of architects who together constituted the "Chicago school." Employing the dictum "Form follows function," they built startlingly modern structures.

Across the United States, municipal governments undertook public works on a scale never before seen. They paved streets, built sewers and water mains, replaced gas lamps with electric lights, ran trolley tracks on the old horsecar lines, and dug underground to build subways, tearing down the unsightly elevated tracks that had clogged city streets. Boston completed the nation's first subway system in 1897, and New York and Philadelphia soon followed.

Cities became more beautiful with the creation of urban public parks to complement the new buildings that quickly filled city lots. Much of the credit for America's greatest parks goes to one man—landscape architect Frederick Law Olmsted. New York City's Central Park, completed in 1873, became the first landscaped public park in the United States. Olmsted and his partner, Calvert Vaux, directed the planting of more than five million trees, shrubs, and vines to transform the eight hundred acres between 59th Street and 110th Street into an oasis for urban dwellers. "We want a place," he wrote, where people "may stroll for an hour, seeing, hearing, and feeling nothing of the bustle and jar of the streets."

American cities did not overlook the mind in their efforts at improvement. They created a comprehensive free public school system that educated everyone from the children of the middle class to the sons and daughters of immigrant workers. Yet the exploding urban population strained the system and led to crowded and inadequate facilities. In 1899, more than 544,000 pupils attended school in New York City's five boroughs. Municipalities across the United States provided free secondary school education for all who wished to attend, even though only 8 percent of Americans completed high school.

To educate those who couldn't go to school, American cities created the most extensive free public library system in the world. In 1895, the Boston Public Library opened its bronze doors in its new Copley Square location under the inscription "Free to All." Designed in the style of a Renaissance palazzo, with more than 700,000 books on the shelves ready to be checked out, the library earned the description "a palace of the people."

CHAPTER LOCATOR | Why did American cities experience explosive growth in the late nineteenth century? | What kinds of work did people do in industrial America?

CHAPTER 19
570 THE GROWTH OF AMERICA'S CITIES

Despite the Boston Public Library's motto "Free to All," the poor did not share equally in the advantages of city life. The parks, the libraries, and even the subways and sewers benefited some city dwellers more than others. Few library cards were held by Boston's laborers, who worked six days a week and found the library closed on Sunday. And in the 1890s, there was nothing central about New York's Central Park. It was a four-mile walk from the tenements of Hester Street to the park's entrance at 59th Street and Fifth Avenue. Then, as now, the comfortable majority, not the indigent minority, reaped a disproportionate share of the benefits in the nation's big cities.

Any story of the American city, it seems, must be a tale of two cities — or, given the cities' great diversity, a tale of many cities within each metropolis. At the turn of the twentieth century, a central paradox emerged: The enduring monuments of America's cities — the bridges, skyscrapers, parks, and libraries — stood as the undeniable achievements of the same system of municipal government that reformers dismissed as boss-ridden, criminal, and corrupt.

City Government and the "Bosses"

The physical growth of the cities required the expansion of public services and the creation of entirely new facilities: streets, subways, elevated trains, bridges, docks, sewers, and public utilities. There was work to be done and money to be made. The rise of the professional politician — the colorful big-city boss — resulted from urban growth, and **bossism** became a national phenomenon. Though corrupt and often criminal, the boss saw to the building of the city and provided needed social services for the new residents in return for their political support. Yet not even the big-city boss could be said to rule the unruly city. The governing of America's cities resembled more a tug-of-war than boss rule.

The most notorious of all the city bosses was William Marcy "Boss" Tweed of New York City. At midcentury, Boss Tweed's Democratic Party "machine" held sway. A machine was really no more than a political party organized at the grassroots level. Its purpose was to win elections and reward its followers, often with jobs on the city's payroll. New York's citywide Democratic machine, Tammany Hall, commanded an army of party functionaries. They formed a shadow government more powerful than the city's elected officials.

As chairman of the Tammany general committee, Tweed kept the Democratic Party together and ran the city through the use of bribery and graft. "As long as I count the votes," he shamelessly boasted, "what are you going to do about it?" The excesses of the Tweed ring soon led to a clamor for reform and cries of "Throw the rascals out." Tweed's rule ended in 1871. Eventually, he was tried and convicted, and later died in jail. New York was not the only city to experience bossism and corruption. The British visitor James Bryce concluded in 1888, "There is no denying that the government of cities is the one conspicuous failure of the United States." More than 80 percent of the nation's thirty largest cities experienced some form of boss rule in the decades around the turn of the twentieth century. However, infighting among powerful ward bosses often meant that no single boss enjoyed exclusive power in the big cities.

bossism

▶ Pattern of urban political organization that arose in the late nineteenth century in which an often corrupt "boss" maintains an inordinate level of power through command of a political machine that distributes services to its constituents.

Why did the fortunes of the Knights of Labor rise in the late 1870s and decline in the 1890s?

How did urban industrialism shape home life and the world of leisure?

How did municipal governments respond to the challenges of urban expansion?

Conclusion: Who built the cities?

☑ LearningCurve
Check what you know.
bedfordstmartins.com
/roarkunderstanding

571

Urban reformers and proponents of good government (derisively called "goo goos" by their rivals) challenged machine rule and sometimes succeeded in electing reform mayors. But the reformers rarely managed to stay in office for long. Their detractors called them "mornin' glories," observing that they "looked lovely in the mornin' and withered up in a short time." The bosses enjoyed continued success largely because the urban political machine helped the cities' immigrants and poor, who remained the bosses' staunchest allies. "What tells in holding your district," a Tammany ward boss observed, "is to go right down among the poor and help them in the different ways they need help. It's philanthropy, but it's politics, too—mighty good politics."

The big-city boss, through the skillful orchestration of rewards, exerted powerful leverage and lined up support for his party from a broad range of constituents, from the urban poor to wealthy industrialists. In 1902, when journalist Lincoln Steffens began "The Shame of the Cities," a series of articles exposing city corruption, he found that business leaders who fastidiously refused to mingle socially with the bosses nevertheless struck deals with them. "He is a self-righteous fraud, this big businessman," Steffens concluded. "I found him buying boodlers [bribers] in St. Louis, defending grafters in Minneapolis, originating corruption in Pittsburgh, sharing with bosses in Philadelphia, deploring reform in Chicago, and beating good government with corruption funds in New York."

For all the color and flamboyance of the big-city boss, he was simply one of many actors in the drama of municipal government. Old-stock aristocrats, new professionals, saloon keepers, pushcart peddlers, and politicians all fought for their interests in the hurly-burly of city government. They didn't much like each other, and they sometimes fought savagely. But they learned to live with one another. Compromise and accommodation—not boss rule—best characterized big-city government by the turn of the twentieth century, although the cities' reputation for corruption left an indelible mark on the consciousness of the American public.

White City or City of Sin?

Americans have always been of two minds about the city. They like to boast of its skyscrapers and bridges, its culture and sophistication, and they pride themselves on its bigness and bustle. At the same time, they fear it as the city of sin, the home of immigrant slums, the center of vice and crime. Nowhere did the divided view of the American city take form more graphically than in Chicago in 1893. In that year, Chicago hosted the **World's Columbian Exposition**, the grandest world's fair in the nation's history. The fairground, only five miles down the shore of Lake Michigan from downtown Chicago, offered a lesson in what Americans on the eve of the twentieth century imagined a city might be. Christened the "White City," the fairground seemed light-years away from Chicago, with its stockyards, slums, and bustling terminals. Frederick Law Olmsted and architect Daniel Burnham supervised the transformation of a swampy wasteland into a pristine paradise of lagoons, fountains, wooded islands, gardens, and imposing white buildings.

World's Columbian Exposition

▶ World's fair held in Chicago in 1893 that attracted millions of visitors. The elaborately designed pavilions of the "White City" included exhibits of technological innovation and of cultural exoticism. The white buildings embodied an urban ideal that contrasted with the realities of Chicago life.

CHAPTER LOCATOR | Why did American cities experience explosive growth in the late nineteenth century? | What kinds of work did people do in industrial America?

CHAPTER 19
572 THE GROWTH OF AMERICA'S CITIES

Chicago's White City

This painting by H. D. Nichols captures the monumental architecture of the White City built for the World's Columbian Exposition in 1893. Monumental, harmonious, and pristine, the White City was designed by Daniel Burnham and Frederick Law Olmsted to awe and overwhelm fairgoers. And so it did, drawing millions of visitors from America and abroad. Chicago Historical Society.

"Sell the cookstove if necessary and come," novelist Hamlin Garland wrote to his parents on the farm. And come they did, in spite of the panic and depression that broke out only weeks after the fair opened in May 1893. In six months, fairgoers purchased more than 27 million tickets, turning a profit of nearly half a million dollars for promoters. Visitors from home and abroad strolled the elaborate grounds and visited the exhibits — everything from a model of the Brooklyn Bridge carved in soap to the latest goods and inventions. Half carnival, half culture, the great fair offered something for everyone. On the Midway Plaisance, crowds thrilled to the massive wheel built by G. W. G. Ferris and watched agog as Little Egypt danced the hootchy-kootchy.

In October, the fair closed its doors in the midst of the worst depression the country had yet seen. During the winter of 1894, Chicago's unemployed and homeless took over the grounds, vandalized the buildings, and frightened the city's comfortable citizens out of their wits. When reporters asked Daniel Burnham, its chief architect, what should be done with the moldering remains of the White City, he responded, "It should be torched." And it was. In July 1894, in a clash between federal troops and striking railway workers, incendiaries set fires that leveled the fairgrounds.

Why did the fortunes of the Knights of Labor rise in the late 1870s and decline in the 1890s?

How did urban industrialism shape home life and the world of leisure?

How did municipal governments respond to the challenges of urban expansion?

Conclusion: Who built the cities?

✓ LearningCurve
Check what you know.
bedfordstmartins.com
/roarkunderstanding

573

In the end, the White City remained what it had always been, a dream-scape. Buildings that looked like marble were actually constructed of staff, a plaster substance that began to crumble even before fire destroyed the fairgrounds. Perhaps it was not so strange, after all, that the legacy of the White City could be found on Coney Island, where two new amusement parks, Luna and Dreamland, sought to combine, albeit in a more tawdry form, the beauty of the White City and the thrill of the Midway Plaisance. More enduring than the White City itself was what it represented: the emergent industrial might of the United States, at home and abroad, with its inventions, manufactured goods, and growing consumer culture.

> ## QUICK REVIEW

How did city life change in the late nineteenth century?

CHAPTER LOCATOR | Why did American cities experience explosive growth in the late nineteenth century? | What kinds of work did people do in industrial America?

CHAPTER 19
574 THE GROWTH OF AMERICA'S CITIES

A S MUCH AS THE GREAT INDUSTRIALISTS and financiers, as much as engineers and landscape architects, it was common workers, most of them immigrants, who built the nation's cities. The unprecedented growth of urban, industrial America resulted from the labor of millions of men, women, and children who toiled in workshops and factories, in sweatshops and mines, on railroads and construction sites across America.

America's cities in the late nineteenth century teemed with life. Townhouses and tenements jostled for space with skyscrapers and great department stores, while parks, ball fields, amusement arcades, and public libraries provided the city masses with recreation and entertainment. Municipal governments, straining to build the new cities, experienced the rough-and-tumble of machine politics as bosses and their constituents looked to profit from city growth.

For America's workers, urban industrialism along with the rise of big business and corporate consolidation drastically changed the workplace. Industrialists replaced skilled workers with new machines that could be operated by cheaper unskilled labor. And during hard times, employers did not hesitate to cut workers' already meager wages. As the Great Railroad Strike of 1877 demonstrated, when labor united, it could bring the nation to attention. Organization held out the best hope for the workers; first the Knights of Labor and later the American Federation of Labor won converts among the nation's working class.

The rise of urban industrialism challenged the American promise, which for decades had been dominated by Jeffersonian agrarian ideals. Could such a promise exist in the changing world of cities, tenements, immigrants, and huge corporations? In the great depression that came in the 1890s, mounting anger and frustration would lead farmers and workers to join forces and create a grassroots movement to fight for change under the banner of a new People's Party.

Why did the fortunes of the Knights of Labor rise in the late 1870s and decline in the 1890s? | How did urban industrialism shape home life and the world of leisure? | How did municipal governments respond to the challenges of urban expansion? | **Conclusion: Who built the cities?** | ☑ LearningCurve Check what you know. bedfordstmartins.com /roarkunderstanding

575

CHAPTER 19 STUDY GUIDE

GET STARTED ONLINE

✓ **LearningCurve** ▪ bedfordstmartins.com/roarkunderstanding

Now that you've read the chapter, make it stick by completing the LearningCurve activity.

EXPLAIN WHY IT MATTERS

Put your reading into practice. Identify each term below, and then explain why it matters in U.S. history.

TERM	WHO OR WHAT & WHEN	WHY IT MATTERS
global migration (p. 548)		
Ellis Island, (p. 554)		
sweatshops (p. 557)		
family economy (p. 557)		
"typewriters" (p. 559)		
Great Railroad Strike (p. 562)		
Knights of Labor (p. 563)		
American Federation of Labor (AFL) (p. 563)		
Haymarket bombing (p. 565)		
cult of domesticity (p. 566)		
bossism (p. 571)		
World's Columbian Exposition (p. 572)		

MOVE BEYOND THE BASICS

To demonstrate a more advanced understanding, describe the key characteristics of American cities at the turn of the twentieth century and the impact that these characteristics had on city life.

Characteristic	The American city, ca. 1900	Impact on city life
Population		
Diversity		
Social structure		
Work and labor relations		
Politics		
Domestic life		
Leisure		

STEP 4 **PUT IT ALL TOGETHER**   Now, take a step back and try to explain the big picture. Remember to use specific examples from the chapter in your answers.

URBANIZATION

▶ What factors led immigrants to American cities in the late nineteenth century? How did their arrival change the cities in which they settled?

▶ How and why did the social geography of the American city change in the late nineteenth century?

INDUSTRY AND LABOR

▶ What new social divisions accompanied business expansion and industrialization?

▶ What kinds of organizations did workers form in the late nineteenth century, and why did they start them? How successful were they?

CITY LIFE

▶ How did urban industrialism transform home and family life?

▶ What led to the rise of the big-city boss? Whose interests did late-nineteenth-century city governments serve?

LOOKING BACKWARD, LOOKING AHEAD

▶ How did early-twentieth-century American cities differ from their early-nineteenth-century counterparts?

▶ How did the rise of urban industrialism change Americans' sense of themselves as a people?

> **IN YOUR OWN WORDS**   Imagine that you must give an oral report to the class answering the following question: **What were the most important outcomes of the expansion of American cities in the late nineteenth century?** What would be the most important points to include and why?

 Do it online at the Student Site ▪ **bedfordstmartins.com/roarkunderstanding**

20
DISSENT, DEPRESSION, AND WAR
1890–1900

> Why was the decade of the 1890s such a turbulent time in U.S. history? Chapter 20 explores the political and economic conflicts of the 1890s through the lenses of diverse groups of Americans. It also examines the major shift in U.S. foreign policy in the last decade of the nineteenth century.

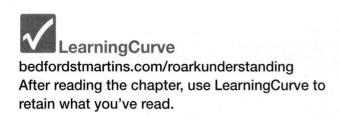

LearningCurve
bedfordstmartins.com/roarkunderstanding
After reading the chapter, use LearningCurve to
retain what you've read.

The Unemployed — Scene at a Country Railway Station. *The Graphic*, Chicago, September 9, 1893.
Chicago History Museum.

> Why did American farmers organize alliances in the late nineteenth century?

> What led to the labor wars of the 1890s?

> How were women involved in late-nineteenth-century politics?

> How did economic problems affect American politics in the 1890s?

> Why did the United States largely abandon its isolationist foreign policy in the 1890s?

> Conclusion: What was the connection between domestic strife and foreign policy?

Why did American farmers organize alliances in the late nineteenth century?

Nebraska Farm Family A Nebraska farm family poses in front of their sod hut in Custer County, Nebraska, in 1889. The house is formed of blocks of sod cut from the prairie. This photo testifies to the hard, lonely life of farmers on the Great Plains. Nebraska State Historical Society.

H HARD TIMES in the 1880s and 1890s created a groundswell of agrarian revolt. A bitter farmer wrote from Minnesota: "I settled on this Land in good Faith Built House and Barn. Broken up Part of the Land. Spent years of hard Labor in grubbing fencing and Improving." About to lose his farm to foreclosure, he lamented, "Are they going to drive us out like trespassers . . . and give us away to the Corporations?"

Farm prices fell decade after decade, even as American farmers' share of the world market grew (**Figure 20.1**). In parts of Kansas, corn sold for as little as ten cents a bushel, and angry farmers burned their crops for fuel rather than take them to market. At the same time, consumer prices soared (**Figure 20.2**). In Kansas alone, almost half the farms had fallen into the hands of the banks by 1894 through foreclosure. Farmers soon banded together into Farmers' Alliances, which gave birth to a broad political movement.

The Farmers' Alliance

At the heart of the farmers' problems stood a banking system dominated by eastern commercial banks committed to the gold standard, a railroad rate system both capricious and unfair, and rampant speculation that drove up the price of land. In the West, farmers rankled under a system that allowed railroads to charge them

> CHRONOLOGY

1876
– First Farmers' Alliance forms in Lampasas County, Texas.

1892
– Farmers' Alliance forms the People's Party and launches the Populist movement.

CHAPTER LOCATOR | Why did American farmers organize alliances in the late nineteenth century? | What led to the labor wars of the 1890s?

580 CHAPTER 20 DISSENT, DEPRESSION, AND WAR

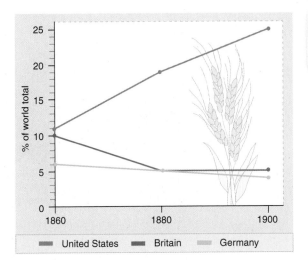

> GLOBAL COMPARISON

FIGURE 20.1 ■ Share of World Wheat Market, 1860–1900

Although many countries produced wheat for home markets, Britain, Germany, and the United States were among the largest wheat exporters. Exporting wheat worldwide became viable after the completion of the transcontinental railroad in 1869. The resulting growth of the railroads, coupled with the development of improved mechanical reapers throughout the second half of the century, led to the mechanization of U.S. agriculture, allowing wheat farmers to harvest ever-larger crops.

exorbitant freight rates while granting rebates to large shippers (see chapter 18). In the South, lack of currency and credit drove farmers to the stopgap credit system of the crop lien. Determined to do something, farmers banded together to fight for change.

Farm protest was not new. In the 1870s, farmers had supported the Grange and the Greenback Labor Party. As the farmers' situation grew more desperate, they organized, forming regional alliances. The first **Farmers' Alliance** came together in 1876 in Lampasas County, Texas, to fight "landsharks and horse thieves." In frontier farmhouses in Texas, in log cabins in the backwoods of Arkansas, and in the rural parishes of Louisiana, separate groups of farmers formed similar alliances for self-help.

As the movement grew in the 1880s, farmers' groups consolidated into two regional alliances: the Northwestern Farmers' Alliance, active in Kansas, Nebraska, and other midwestern Granger states; and the more radical Southern Farmers' Alliance. Traveling lecturers preached the Alliance message. Worn-out men and careworn women did not need to be convinced that something was wrong. By 1890, the Southern Farmers' Alliance alone counted more than three million members.

Radical in its inclusiveness, the Southern Alliance reached out to African Americans, women, and industrial workers. Through cooperation with the Colored Farmers' Alliance, an African American group founded in Texas in the 1880s, blacks and whites attempted to make common cause. As Georgia's Tom Watson, a Southern Alliance stalwart, pointed out, "The colored tenant is in the same boat as the white tenant, . . . and . . . the accident of color can make no difference in the interests of farmers, croppers, and laborers." Women rallied to the Alliance banner. "I am going to work for prohibition, the Alliance, and for Jesus as long as I live," swore one woman.

At the heart of the Alliance movement stood a series of farmers' cooperatives. By "bulking" their cotton — that is, selling it together — farmers could negotiate a better price. And by setting up trade stores and exchanges, they sought to escape the grasp of the merchant/creditor. Through the cooperatives, the Farmers'

Farmers' Alliance

▶ Movement to form local organizations to advance farmers' collective interests that gained popularity in the 1880s. Over time, farmers' groups consolidated into two regional alliances: the Northwestern Farmers' Alliance and the Southern Farmers' Alliance. In 1892, the Farmers' Alliance gave birth to the People's Party and launched the Populist movement.

How were women involved in late-nineteenth-century politics?

How did economic problems affect American politics in the 1890s?

Why did the United States largely abandon its isolationist foreign policy in the 1890s?

Conclusion: What was the connection between domestic strife and foreign policy?

✓ **LearningCurve**
Check what you know.
bedfordstmartins.com /roarkunderstanding

581

FIGURE 20.2 ■ Consumer Prices and Farm Income, 1865–1910

Around 1870, consumer prices and farm income were about equal. During the 1880s and 1890s, however, farmers suffered great hardships as prices for their crops steadily declined and the cost of consumer goods continued to rise.

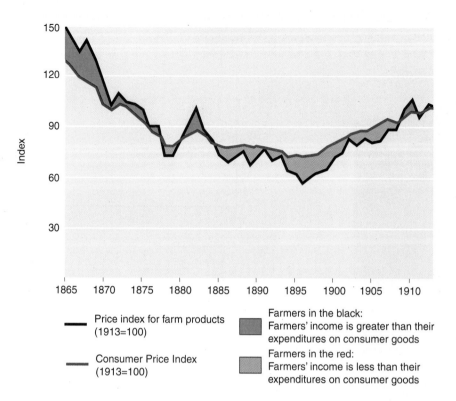

Index

Price index for farm products (1913=100)

Consumer Price Index (1913=100)

Farmers in the black: Farmers' income is greater than their expenditures on consumer goods

Farmers in the red: Farmers' income is less than their expenditures on consumer goods

Alliance promised to change the way farmers lived. "We are going to get out of debt and be free and independent people once more," exulted one Georgia farmer. But the Alliance faced insurmountable difficulties in running successful cooperatives. Opposition by merchants, bankers, wholesalers, and manufacturers made it impossible for the cooperatives to get credit. As the cooperative movement died, the Farmers' Alliance moved into politics.

The Populist Movement

In the earliest days of the Alliance movement, a leader of the Southern Farmers' Alliance insisted, "The Alliance is a strictly white man's nonpolitical, secret business association." But by 1892, it was none of those things. Advocates of a third party carried the day at a convention of laborers, farmers, and common folk in 1892 in St. Louis, where the Farmers' Alliance gave birth to the **People's Party** and launched the Populist movement. The same spirit of religious revival that animated the Farmers' Alliance infused the People's Party. Convinced that the money and banking systems worked to the advantage of the wealthy few, they demanded economic democracy. To help farmers get the credit they needed at reasonable rates, southern farmers hit on the ingenious idea of a subtreasury — a plan that would allow farmers to store their nonperishable crops until prices rose and to receive commodity credit from the federal government to obtain needed supplies.

People's Party (Populist Party)

▶ Political party formed in 1892 by the Farmers' Alliance to advance the goals of the Populist movement. Populists sought economic democracy, promoting land, electoral, banking, and monetary reform. Republican victory in the presidential election of 1896 effectively destroyed the People's Party.

CHAPTER LOCATOR | Why did American farmers organize alliances in the late nineteenth century? | What led to the labor wars of the 1890s?

582 CHAPTER 20
DISSENT, DEPRESSION, AND WAR

The sweeping array of Populist reforms enacted in the Populist platform changed the agenda of politics for decades to come. More than just a response to hard times, Populism presented an alternative vision of American economic democracy.

> **The Populist Platform**

- Championed land reform, including a plan to reclaim excessive land granted to railroads or sold to foreign investors.
- Proposed government ownership of the railroads and telegraph system to put an end to discriminatory rates.
- Supported free silver to ease the nation's tight money supply.
- Called for electoral reforms, such as the direct election of senators and the secret ballot, and the right to initiate legislation, to recall elected officials, and to submit issues to the people by means of a referendum.
- Supported the eight-hour workday.

QUICK REVIEW <

Why did the Farmers' Alliance decide to form a political party?

How were women involved in late-nineteenth-century politics?

How did economic problems affect American politics in the 1890s?

Why did the United States largely abandon its isolationist foreign policy in the 1890s?

Conclusion: What was the connection between domestic strife and foreign policy?

LearningCurve
Check what you know.
bedfordstmartins.com
/roarkunderstanding

What led to the labor wars of the 1890s?

National Guard Occupying Pullman, Illinois

After President Grover Cleveland called out troops to put down the Pullman strike in 1894, the National Guard occupied the town of Pullman. The intervention enabled owner George M. Pullman to bring in strikebreakers and defeat the unions. Chicago Historical Society.

WHILE FARMERS UNITED to fight for change, industrial laborers fought their own battles in a series of bloody strikes historians have called the "labor wars." Industrial workers took a stand in the 1890s. At issue was the right of workers to organize and to speak through unions, to bargain collectively, and to fight for better working conditions, higher wages, shorter hours, and greater worker control in the face of increased mechanization. Three major conflicts — the lockout of steelworkers in Homestead, Pennsylvania, in 1892; the miners' strike in Cripple Creek, Colorado, in 1894; and the Pullman boycott that same year — raised fundamental questions about the rights of labor and the sanctity of private property.

The Homestead Lockout

In 1892, steelworkers in Pennsylvania squared off against Andrew Carnegie in a decisive struggle over the right to organize in the Homestead steel mills. When the Amalgamated Iron and Steel Workers, one of the largest and richest craft unions in the American Federation of Labor (AFL), attempted to renew its contract at Carnegie's Homestead mill, Carnegie resolved to crush the union. The union's leaders were told that since "the vast majority of our employees are Non union, the Firm has decided that the minority must give place to the majority."

CHAPTER LOCATOR | Why did American farmers organize alliances in the late nineteenth century? | **What led to the labor wars of the 1890s?**

584 CHAPTER 20 DISSENT, DEPRESSION, AND WAR

While it was true that only 800 skilled workers belonged to the elite Amalgamated, the union had long enjoyed the support of the plant's 3,000 non-union workers. Slavs, who did much of the unskilled work, made common cause with the Welsh, Scottish, and Irish skilled workers who belonged to the union.

Carnegie preferred not to be directly involved in the union busting, so that spring he sailed to Scotland and left Henry Clay Frick, the toughest antilabor man in the industry, in charge. By summer, a strike looked inevitable. Frick prepared by erecting a fifteen-foot fence around the Homestead plant and topping it with barbed wire. Workers aptly dubbed it "Fort Frick." Frick then hired 316 mercenaries from the Pinkerton National Detective Agency at the rate of $5 per day, more than double the wage of the average Homestead worker.

On June 28, the Homestead lockout began when Frick locked the doors of the mills and prepared to bring in strikebreakers. Hugh O'Donnell, the young Irishman who led the union, vowed to prevent "scabs" from entering the plant. On July 6 at 4 a.m., a lookout spotted two barges moving up the Monongahela River in the fog. Frick was attempting to smuggle his Pinkertons into Homestead.

Workers sounded the alarm, and within minutes a crowd of more than a thousand, hastily armed with rifles, hoes, and fence posts, rushed to the riverbank. When the Pinkertons attempted to come ashore, gunfire broke out, and more than a dozen Pinkertons and some thirty strikers fell, killed or wounded. The Pinkertons retreated to the barges. For twelve hours, the workers, joined by their family members, threw everything they had at the barges, from fireworks to dynamite. Finally, the Pinkertons hoisted a white flag and arranged with O'Donnell to surrender. With three workers dead and scores wounded, the crowd, numbering perhaps ten thousand, was in no mood for conciliation. As the hated "Pinks" came up the hill, they were forced to run a gantlet of screaming, cursing men, women, and children. When a young guard dropped to his knees, weeping for mercy, a woman used her umbrella to poke out his eye. One Pinkerton had been killed in the siege on the barges. In the grim rout that followed their surrender, not one avoided injury. In the aftermath of the battle, the workers took control of the plant and elected a council to run the community. At first, public opinion favored their cause. A congressman castigated Carnegie for "skulking in his castle in Scotland." Populists, meeting in St. Louis, condemned the use of "hireling armies."

The action of the Homestead workers struck at the heart of the capitalist system, pitting the workers' right to their jobs against the rights of private property. The workers' insistence that "we are not destroying the property of the company — merely protecting our rights" did not prove as compelling to the courts and the state as the property rights of the owners. Four days after the confrontation, Pennsylvania's governor, who sympathized with the workers, nonetheless yielded to pressure from Frick and ordered eight thousand National Guard troops into Homestead to protect Carnegie's property. The workers, thinking they had nothing to fear from the militia, welcomed the troops with a brass band. But the troops' occupation not only protected Carnegie's property but also enabled Frick to reopen the mills and bring in strikebreakers. "We have been deceived," one worker complained bitterly. "We have stood idly by and let the town be occupied by soldiers who come here, not as our protectors, but as the protectors of non-union men. . . . If we undertake to resist the seizure of our jobs, we will be shot down like dogs."

> CHRONOLOGY

1892
– Homestead lockout.

1893
– Stock market crash touches off economic depression.

1894
– Miners' strike in Cripple Creek, Colorado.
– Pullman boycott is crushed.

Homestead lockout
▶ 1892 lockout of workers at the Homestead, Pennsylvania, steel mill after Andrew Carnegie refused to renew the union contract and workers prepared to strike. Union supporters attacked the Pinkerton National Detective Agency guards hired to protect the mill, but the National Guard soon broke the strike.

How were women involved in late-nineteenth-century politics?	How did economic problems affect American politics in the 1890s?	Why did the United States largely abandon its isolationist foreign policy in the 1890s?	Conclusion: What was the connection between domestic strife and foreign policy?	✓ LearningCurve Check what you know. bedfordstmartins.com /roarkunderstanding

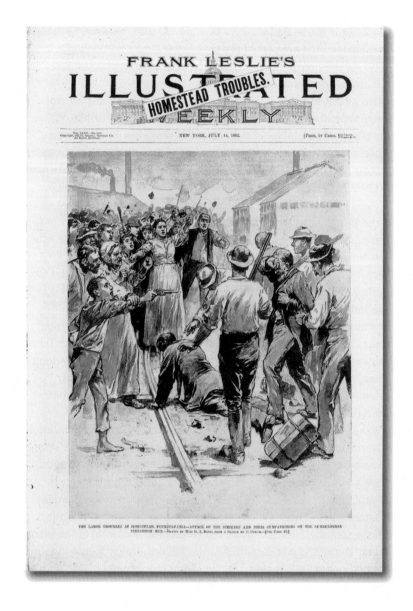

Then, in a misguided effort to ignite a general uprising, Alexander Berkman, a Russian immigrant and anarchist, attempted to assassinate Frick. Berkman bungled his attempt. Shot twice and stabbed with a dagger, Frick survived and showed considerable courage, allowing a doctor to remove the bullets but refusing to leave his desk until the day's work was completed. "I do not think that I shall die," Frick remarked coolly, "but whether I do or not, the Company will pursue the same policy and it will win."

After the assassination attempt, public opinion turned against the workers. Berkman was quickly tried and sentenced to prison. Although the Amalgamated and the AFL denounced his action, the incident linked anarchism and unionism. O'Donnell later wrote, "The bullet from Berkman's pistol, failing in its foul intent, went straight through the heart of the Homestead strike." The Homestead mill reopened in November, and the men returned to work, except for the union leaders,

CHAPTER LOCATOR | Why did American farmers organize alliances in the late nineteenth century? | **What led to the labor wars of the 1890s?**

now blacklisted in every steel mill in the country. With the owners firmly in charge, the company slashed wages, reinstated the twelve-hour workday, and eliminated five hundred jobs.

The workers at Homestead had been taught a lesson. They would never again, in the words of the National Guard commander, "believe the works are their's [sic] quite as much as Carnegie's." Another forty-five years would pass before steelworkers, unskilled as well as skilled, successfully unionized. In the meantime, Carnegie's production tripled, even in the midst of a depression. "Ashamed to tell you profits these days," Carnegie wrote a friend in 1899. And no wonder: Carnegie's profits had grown from $4 million in 1892 to $40 million in 1900.

The Cripple Creek Miners' Strike of 1894

Less than a year after the Homestead lockout, a panic on Wall Street in the spring of 1893 touched off a bitter economic depression. In the West, silver mines fell on hard times, leading to the **Cripple Creek miners' strike of 1894**. When mine owners moved to lengthen the workday from eight to ten hours, the newly formed Western Federation of Miners (WFM) vowed to hold the line in Cripple Creek, Colorado. In February 1894, the WFM threatened to strike all mines working more than eight-hour shifts. The mine owners divided: Some quickly settled with the WFM; others continued to demand ten-hour shifts, provoking a strike.

The striking miners received help from many quarters. Working miners paid $15 a month to a strike fund, and miners in neighboring districts sent substantial contributions. The miners enjoyed the support and assistance of local businesses and grocers, who provided credit to the strikers. With these advantages, the Cripple Creek strikers could afford to hold out for their demands.

Even more significant, Governor Davis H. Waite, a Populist elected in 1892, had strong ties to the miners and refused to use the power of the state against the strikers. Governor Waite asked the strikers to lay down their arms and demanded that the mine owners disperse their hired deputies. The miners agreed to arbitration and selected Waite as their sole arbitrator. By May, the recalcitrant mine owners capitulated, and the union won an eight-hour day.

Governor Waite's intervention demonstrated the pivotal power of the state in the nation's labor wars. Having a Populist in power made a difference. A decade later, in 1904, with Waite out of office, mine owners relied on state troops to take back control of the mines, defeating the WFM and blacklisting all of its members. In retrospect, the Cripple Creek miners' strike of 1894 proved the exception to the rule of state intervention on the side of private property.

Cripple Creek miners' strike of 1894

▶ Strike led by the Western Federation of Miners in response to an attempt to lengthen their workday to ten hours. With the support of local businessmen and the Populist governor of Colorado, the miners successfully maintained an eight-hour day.

Eugene V. Debs and the Pullman Strike

The economic depression that began in 1893 swelled the ranks of the unemployed to three million. "A fearful crisis is upon us," wrote a labor publication. Nowhere were workers more demoralized than in the model town of Pullman, on the outskirts of Chicago.

In the wake of the Great Railroad Strike of 1877, George M. Pullman, the builder of Pullman railroad cars, moved his plant and workers nine miles south

How were women involved in late-nineteenth-century politics?

How did economic problems affect American politics in the 1890s?

Why did the United States largely abandon its isolationist foreign policy in the 1890s?

Conclusion: What was the connection between domestic strife and foreign policy?

✓ LearningCurve
Check what you know.
bedfordstmartins.com /roarkunderstanding

587

A Pullman Craftsworker

Pullman Palace cars were known for their luxurious details. Here, a painter working in the 1890s applies elaborate decoration to the exterior of a Pullman car. The Pullman workers' strike in 1894 stemmed in part from the company's efforts to undermine the status of craftsworkers by reducing them to low-paid piecework. The fight to control the workplace contributed to the labor wars of the 1890s. Chicago Historical Society.

of Chicago and built a model town. The town of Pullman boasted parks, fountains, playgrounds, an auditorium, a library, a hotel, shops, and markets, along with 1,800 units of housing. Noticeably absent was a saloon.

The housing in Pullman was clearly superior to that in neighboring areas, but workers paid a high price to live there. Pullman's rents ran 10 to 20 percent higher than housing costs in nearby communities. In addition, George Pullman refused to "sell an acre under any circumstances." As long as he controlled the town absolutely, he held the powerful whip of eviction over his employees and could quickly get rid of "troublemakers." Although observers at first praised the beauty and orderliness of the town, critics by the 1890s compared Pullman's model town to a "gilded cage" for workers.

The depression brought hard times to Pullman. Workers saw their wages slashed five times between May and December 1893, with cuts totaling at least 28 percent. At the same time, Pullman refused to lower the rents in his model town, insisting that "the renting of the dwellings and the employment of workmen at Pullman are in no way tied together." When workers went to the bank to cash their paychecks, they found that the rent had been taken out. One worker discovered only forty-seven cents in his pay envelope for two weeks' work. When the bank teller asked him whether he wanted to apply it to his back rent, he retorted, "If Mr. Pullman needs that forty-seven cents worse than I do, let him have it." At the same time, Pullman continued to pay his stockholders an 8 percent dividend, and the company accumulated a $25 million surplus.

At the heart of the labor problems at Pullman lay not only economic inequity but also the company's attempt to control the work process, substituting piecework for day wages and undermining skilled craftsworkers. During the spring of 1894, Pullman's desperate workers, seeking help, flocked to the ranks of the American Railway Union (ARU), led by the charismatic Eugene V. Debs. The ARU,

CHAPTER LOCATOR | Why did American farmers organize alliances in the late nineteenth century? | **What led to the labor wars of the 1890s?**

588   CHAPTER 20
DISSENT, DEPRESSION, AND WAR

unlike the skilled craft unions of the AFL, pledged to organize all railway workers — from engineers to engine wipers.

George Pullman responded to union organization at his plant by firing three of the union's leaders the day after they protested wage cuts. Angry men and women walked off the job in disgust. What began as a spontaneous protest in May 1894 quickly blossomed into a strike that involved more than 90 percent of Pullman's 3,300 workers. Pullman countered by shutting down the plant. In June, the Pullman strikers appealed to the ARU to come to their aid. Debs pleaded with the workers to find another solution. But when George Pullman refused arbitration, the ARU membership voted to boycott all Pullman cars. Beginning on June 29, switchmen across the United States refused to handle any train that carried Pullman cars.

The conflict escalated quickly. The General Managers Association (GMA), an organization of managers from twenty-four different railroads, acted in concert to quash the **Pullman boycott**. They recruited strikebreakers and fired all the protesting switchmen. Their tactics set off a chain reaction. Entire train crews walked off the job in a show of solidarity with the Pullman workers. By July 2, rail lines from New York to California lay paralyzed. Even the GMA was forced to concede that the railroads had been "fought to a standstill."

The boycott remained surprisingly peaceful. In contrast to the Great Railroad Strike of 1877, no major riots broke out, and no serious property damage occurred. Debs fired off telegrams to all parts of the country advising his followers to avoid violence and respect law and order. But the nation's newspapers, fed press releases by the GMA, distorted the issues and misrepresented the strike. Across the country, papers ran headlines like "Wild Riot in Chicago" and "Mob Is in Control."

In Washington, Attorney General Richard B. Olney, a lawyer with strong ties to the railroads, determined to put down the strike. In his way stood the governor of Illinois, John Peter Altgeld, who, observing that the boycott remained peaceful, refused to call out troops. To get around Altgeld, Olney convinced President Grover Cleveland that federal troops had to intervene to protect the mails. To further cripple the boycott, two conservative Chicago judges issued an injunction so sweeping that it prohibited Debs from speaking in public. By issuing the injunction, the court made the boycott a crime punishable by a jail sentence for contempt of court, a civil process that did not require a jury trial. Even the conservative *Chicago Tribune* judged the injunction "a menace to liberty . . . a weapon ever ready for the capitalist." Furious, Debs risked jail by refusing to honor it.

Olney's strategy worked. President Grover Cleveland called out the army. On July 5, nearly 8,000 troops marched into Chicago. Violence immediately erupted. In one day, troops killed 25 workers and wounded more than 60. In the face of bullets and bayonets, the strikers held firm. "Troops cannot move trains," Debs reminded his followers, a fact that was borne out as the railroads remained paralyzed despite the military intervention. But if the army could not put down the boycott, the injunction did. Debs was arrested and imprisoned for contempt of court. With its leader in jail, its headquarters raided and ransacked, and its members demoralized, the ARU collapsed along with the boycott. Pullman reopened his factory, hiring new workers to replace many of the strikers and leaving 1,600 without jobs.

Pullman boycott
▶ Nationwide railroad workers' boycott of trains carrying Pullman cars in 1894 after Pullman workers, suffering radically reduced wages, joined the American Railway Union (ARU) and union leaders were fired in response. The boycott ended after the U.S. Army fired on strikers and ARU leader Eugene Debs was jailed.

How were women involved in late-nineteenth-century politics?

How did economic problems affect American politics in the 1890s?

Why did the United States largely abandon its isolationist foreign policy in the 1890s?

Conclusion: What was the connection between domestic strife and foreign policy?

✓ **LearningCurve**
Check what you know.
bedfordstmartins.com/roarkunderstanding

In the aftermath of the strike, a special commission investigated the events at Pullman, taking testimony from 107 witnesses, from the lowliest workers to George M. Pullman himself. Stubborn and self-righteous, Pullman spoke for the business orthodoxy of his era, steadfastly affirming the right of business to safeguard its interests through confederacies such as the GMA and at the same time denying labor's right to organize. "If we were to receive these men as representatives of the union," he stated, "they could probably force us to pay any wages which they saw fit."

From his jail cell, Eugene Debs reviewed the events of the Pullman strike. With the courts and the government ready to side with industrialists in defense of private property, strikes seemed futile, and unions remained helpless. Workers would have to take control of the state itself. Debs went into jail a trade unionist and came out six months later a socialist. At first, he turned to the Populist Party, but after its demise he formed the Socialist Party in 1900 and ran for president five times.

> **QUICK REVIEW**

Why were the labor conflicts of the 1890s so often marked by violence?

CHAPTER LOCATOR | Why did American farmers organize alliances in the late nineteenth century? | What led to the labor wars of the 1890s?

Woman's Christian Temperance Union Postcard

The Woman's Christian Temperance Union distributed postcards like this to attack the liquor trade. This card is typical in its portrayal of saloon backers as traitors to the nation. Notice the man trampling on the American flag as he casts his ballot — a sly allusion to the need for woman suffrage. Collection of Joyce M. Tice.

How were women involved in late-nineteenth-century politics?

"DO EVERYTHING," Frances Willard urged her followers in 1881. The new president of the Woman's Christian Temperance Union (WCTU) meant what she said. The WCTU followed a trajectory that was common for women in the late nineteenth century. As women organized to deal with issues that touched their homes and families, they moved into politics, lending new urgency to the cause of woman suffrage. Urban industrialism dislocated women's lives no less than men's. Like men, women sought political change and organized to promote issues central to their lives, campaigning for temperance and woman suffrage.

Frances Willard and the Woman's Christian Temperance Union

A visionary leader, Frances Willard spoke for a group left almost entirely out of the U.S. electoral process. In 1890, only one state, Wyoming, allowed women to vote in national elections. But lack of the franchise did not mean that women were apolitical. The Woman's Christian Temperance Union demonstrated the breadth of women's political activity in the late nineteenth century.

Women supported the temperance movement because they felt particularly vulnerable to the effects of drunkenness. Dependent on men's wages, women and children suffered when money went for drink. The drunken, abusive husband

✓ **LearningCurve**
Check what you know.
bedfordstmartins.com
/roarkunderstanding

1879
– Frances Willard becomes president of the Woman's Christian Temperance Union.

1884
– Frances Willard calls for woman suffrage.

1890
– National American Woman Suffrage Association is formed.
– Wyoming is the only state allowing women to vote in national elections.

epitomized the evils of a nation in which women remained second-class citizens. The WCTU, composed entirely of women, viewed all women's interests as essentially the same and therefore did not hesitate to use the singular *woman* to emphasize gender solidarity. Although mostly white and middle-class, WCTU members resolved to speak for their entire sex.

When Frances Willard became the WCTU's president in 1879, she radically changed the direction of the organization. Social action replaced prayer as women's answer to the threat of drunkenness. Viewing alcoholism as a disease rather than a sin and poverty as a cause rather than a result of drink, the WCTU became involved in labor issues, joining with the Knights of Labor to press for better working conditions for women workers. Describing workers in a textile mill, a WCTU member wrote in the organization's *Union Signal* magazine, "It is dreadful to see these girls, stripped almost to the skin . . . and running like racehorses from the beginning to the end of the day." She concluded, "The hard slavish work is drawing the girls into the saloon."

Willard capitalized on the cult of domesticity as a shrewd political tactic. Using "home protection" as her watchword, she argued as early as 1884 that women needed the vote to protect home and family. By the 1890s, the WCTU's grassroots network of local unions included 200,000 dues-paying members and had spread to all but the most isolated rural areas of the country.

Willard worked to create a broad reform coalition in the 1890s, embracing the Knights of Labor, the People's Party, and the Prohibition Party. Until her death in 1898, she led, if not a woman's rights movement, then the first organized mass movement of women united around a women's issue. By 1900, thanks largely to the WCTU, women could claim a generation of experience in political action — speaking, lobbying, organizing, drafting legislation, and running private charitable institutions. As Willard observed, "All this work has tended more toward the liberation of women than it has toward the extinction of the saloon."

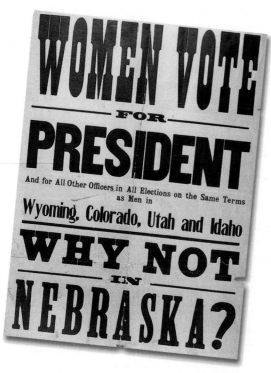

Campaigning for Woman Suffrage

In 1896, women voted in only four states — Wyoming, Colorado, Idaho, and Utah. The West led the way in the campaign for woman suffrage, with Wyoming Territory granting women the vote as early as 1869. The poster calls on Nebraska to join the suffrage column. Nebraska State Historical Society.

CHAPTER LOCATOR | Why did American farmers organize alliances in the late nineteenth century? | What led to the labor wars of the 1890s?

592 CHAPTER 20
DISSENT, DEPRESSION, AND WAR

Elizabeth Cady Stanton, Susan B. Anthony, and the Movement for Woman Suffrage

Unlike the WCTU, the organized movement for woman suffrage remained small and relatively weak in the late nineteenth century. In 1869, Elizabeth Cady Stanton and her ally, Susan B. Anthony, launched the National Woman Suffrage Association demanding the vote for women (see chapter 18). A more conservative group, the American Woman Suffrage Association (AWSA), formed the same year. Composed of men as well as women, the AWSA believed that women should vote in local but not national elections.

By 1890, the split had healed, and the newly united **National American Woman Suffrage Association (NAWSA)** launched campaigns on the state level to gain the vote for women. Twenty years had made a great change. Woman suffrage, though not yet generally supported, was no longer considered a crackpot idea, thanks in part to the WCTU's support of the "home protection" ballot. The NAWSA honored Elizabeth Cady Stanton by electing her its first president, but Susan B. Anthony, who took the helm in 1892, emerged as the leading figure in the new united organization.

Stanton and Anthony, both in their seventies, were coming to the end of their public careers. Since the days of the Seneca Falls woman's rights convention, they had worked for reforms for their sex, including property rights, custody rights, and the right to education and gainful employment. But the prize of woman suffrage still eluded them. Women suffered a bitter defeat in a California referendum on woman suffrage in 1896. Never losing faith, Susan B. Anthony remarked in her last public appearance, in 1906, "Failure is impossible."

National American Woman Suffrage Association (NAWSA)

▶ Organization formed in 1890 that united the National Woman Suffrage Association and the American Woman Suffrage Association. The NAWSA pursued state-level campaigns to gain the vote for women. With successes in Idaho, Colorado, and Utah, woman suffrage had become more accepted by the 1890s.

> **Nineteenth-Century Woman Suffrage Victories**

- 1869: Wyoming
- 1893: Colorado
- 1896: Idaho, Utah

QUICK REVIEW ◀

How did women's temperance activism contribute to the cause of woman suffrage?

| How were women involved in late-nineteenth-century politics? | How did economic problems affect American politics in the 1890s? | Why did the United States largely abandon its isolationist foreign policy in the 1890s? | Conclusion: What was the connection between domestic strife and foreign policy? | ✓ LearningCurve Check what you know. bedfordstmartins.com /roarkunderstanding |

How did economic problems affect American politics in the 1890s?

Coxey's Army A contingent of Coxey's army stops to rest on its way to Washington, D.C. A "petition in boots," Coxey's followers were well dressed. Music was an important component of the march, including the anthem "Marching with Coxey." Band members are pictured on the right with their instruments. Despite their peaceful pose, the marchers stirred the fears of many Americans, who predicted an uprising of the unemployed. Ohio Historical Society.

THE DEPRESSION that began in the spring of 1893 and lasted for more than four years put nearly half of the labor force out of work, a higher percentage than during the Great Depression of the 1930s. The human cost of the depression was staggering. "I Take my pen in hand to let you know that we are Starving to death," a Kansas farm woman wrote to the governor in 1894. "Last cent gone," wrote a young widow in her diary. "Children went to work without their breakfasts." Following the harsh dictates of social Darwinism and laissez-faire, the majority of America's elected officials believed that it was inappropriate for the government to intervene. But the scope of the depression made it impossible for churches and local agencies to supply sufficient relief, and increasingly Americans called on the federal government to take action. Armies of the unemployed marched on Washington to demand relief, and the Populist Party experienced a surge of support as the election of 1896 approached.

CHAPTER LOCATOR | Why did American farmers organize alliances in the late nineteenth century? | What led to the labor wars of the 1890s?

CHAPTER 20
594 DISSENT, DEPRESSION, AND WAR

Coxey's Army

Masses of unemployed Americans marched to Washington, D.C., in the spring of 1894 to call attention to their plight and to urge Congress to enact a public works program to end unemployment. Jacob S. Coxey of Massilon, Ohio, led the most publicized contingent. Convinced that men could be put to work building badly needed roads for the nation, Coxey proposed a scheme to finance public works through non-interest-bearing bonds. "What I am after," he maintained, "is to try to put this country in a condition so that no man who wants work shall be obliged to remain idle." His plan won support from the AFL and the Populists. Starting out from Ohio with one hundred men, **Coxey's army**, as it was dubbed, swelled as it marched east through the spring snows of the Alleghenies. In Pennsylvania, Coxey recruited several hundred from the ranks of those left unemployed by the Homestead lockout.

On May 1, Coxey's army arrived in Washington. When Coxey defiantly marched his men onto the Capitol grounds, police set upon the demonstrators with nightsticks, cracking skulls and arresting Coxey and his lieutenants. Coxey went to jail for twenty days and was fined $5 for "walking on the grass." But other armies of the unemployed, totaling possibly as many as five thousand people, were still on their way. The more daring contingents commandeered entire trains, stirring fears of revolution. Journalists who covered the march did little to quiet the nation's fears. They delighted in military terminology, describing themselves as "war correspondents." To boost newspaper sales, they gave to the episode a tone of urgency and heightened the sense of a nation imperiled.

By August, the leaderless, tattered armies dissolved. Although the "On to Washington" movement proved ineffective in forcing federal relief legislation, Coxey's army dramatized the plight of the unemployed and acted, in the words of one participant, as a "living, moving object lesson." Like the Populists, Coxey's army called into question the underlying values of the new industrial order and demonstrated how ordinary citizens turned to means outside the regular party system to influence politics in the 1890s.

The People's Party and the Election of 1896

Even before the depression of 1893, the Populists had railed against the status quo. "We meet in the midst of a nation brought to the verge of moral, political, and material ruin," Ignatius Donnelly had declared in his keynote address at the creation of the People's Party in St. Louis in 1892. "The fruits of the toil of millions are boldly stolen to build up colossal fortunes for a few. . . . From the same prolific womb of governmental injustice we breed the two great classes — tramps and millionaires."

The fiery rhetoric frightened many who saw in the People's Party a call not to reform but to revolution. Throughout the country, the press denounced the

> **CHRONOLOGY**

1894
– Coxey's army marches to Washington, D.C.

1896
– Democrats and Populists support William Jennings Bryan for president.
– William McKinley is elected president.

Coxey's army
▶ Unemployed men who marched to Washington, D.C., in 1894 to urge Congress to enact a public works program to end unemployment. Jacob S. Coxey of Ohio led the most publicized contingent. The movement failed to force federal relief legislation.

How were women involved in late-nineteenth-century politics?

How did economic problems affect American politics in the 1890s?

Why did the United States largely abandon its isolationist foreign policy in the 1890s?

Conclusion: What was the connection between domestic strife and foreign policy?

✓ LearningCurve
Check what you know.
bedfordstmartins.com /roarkunderstanding

595

Candidate	Electoral Vote	Popular Vote	Percent of Popular Vote
Grover Cleveland (Democrat)	277	5,555,426	46.1
Benjamin Harrison (Republican)	145	5,182,690	43.0
James B. Weaver (People's)	22	1,029,846	8.5

MAP 20.1 ■ The Election of 1892

Populists as "cranks, lunatics, and idiots." When one self-righteous editor dismissed them as "calamity howlers," Populist governor Lorenzo Lewelling of Kansas shot back, "If that is so I want to continue to howl until those conditions are improved."

The People's Party captured more than a million votes in the presidential election of 1892, a respectable showing for a new party (**Map 20.1**). But increasingly, sectional and racial animosities threatened its unity. Realizing that race prejudice obscured the common economic interests of black and white farmers, Populist Tom Watson of Georgia openly courted African Americans, appearing on platforms with black speakers and promising "to wipe out the color line." When angry Georgia whites threatened to lynch a black Populist preacher, Watson rallied two thousand gun-toting Populists to the man's defense. Although many Populists remained racist in their attitudes toward African Americans, the spectacle of white Georgians riding through the night to protect a black man from lynching was symbolic of the enormous changes the Populist Party promised in the South.

As the presidential election of 1896 approached, the depression intensified cries for reform not only from the Populists but also throughout the electorate. Depression worsened the tight money problem caused by the deflationary pressures of the gold standard. Once again, proponents of free silver stirred rebellion in the ranks of both the Democratic and the Republican parties. When the Republicans nominated Ohio governor William McKinley on a platform pledging the preservation of the gold standard, western advocates of free silver representing miners and farmers walked out of the convention. Open rebellion also split the Democratic Party as vast segments in the West and South repudiated President Grover Cleveland because of his support for gold. In South Carolina, Benjamin Tillman won his race for Congress by promising, "Send me to Washington and I'll stick my pitchfork into [Cleveland's] old ribs!"

The spirit of revolt animated the Democratic National Convention in Chicago in the summer of 1896. William Jennings Bryan of Nebraska, the thirty-six-year-old "boy orator from the Platte," whipped the convention into a frenzy with his passionate call for free silver with a ringing exhortation: "Do not crucify mankind upon a cross of gold." Pandemonium broke loose as delegates stampeded to nominate Bryan, the youngest candidate ever to run for the presidency.

The juggernaut of free silver rolled out of Chicago and on to St. Louis, where the People's Party met a week after the Democrats adjourned. Many western Populists urged the party to ally with the Democrats and endorse Bryan. A major obstacle in the path of fusion, however, was Bryan's running mate, Arthur M. Sewall. A Maine railway director and bank president, Sewall, who had been placed on the ticket to appease conservative Democrats, embodied everything the Populists detested. Moreover, die-hard southern Populists wanted no part of fusion. Southern Democrats had resorted to fraud and violence to steal elections from the Populists in southern states, and support for a Democratic ticket proved hard to swallow.

Populists struggled to work out a compromise. To show that they remained true to their principles, delegates first voted to support all the planks of the 1892

CHAPTER LOCATOR | Why did American farmers organize alliances in the late nineteenth century? | What led to the labor wars of the 1890s?

596 CHAPTER 20 DISSENT, DEPRESSION, AND WAR

platform, added to it a call for public works projects for the unemployed, and only narrowly defeated a plank for woman suffrage. To deal with the problem of fusion, the convention selected the vice presidential candidate first. The nomination of Tom Watson undercut opposition to Bryan's candidacy. And although Bryan quickly sent a telegram to protest that he would not drop Sewall as his running mate, mysteriously his message never reached the convention floor. Fusion triumphed. Bryan won nomination by a lopsided vote. The Populists did not know it, but their cheers for Bryan signaled the death knell for the People's Party.

Few contests in the nation's history have been as fiercely fought as the presidential election of 1896. On one side stood Republican William McKinley, backed by the wealthy industrialist and party boss Mark Hanna. Hanna played on the business community's fears of Populism to raise a Republican war chest more than double the amount of any previous campaign. On the other side, William Jennings Bryan, with few assets beyond his silver tongue, struggled to make up in energy and eloquence what his party lacked in campaign funds. He crisscrossed the country in a whirlwind tour, by his own reckoning visiting twenty-seven states and speaking to more than five million Americans.

On election day, four out of five voters went to the polls in an unprecedented turnout. The silver states of the Rocky Mountains lined up solidly for Bryan. The Northeast went for McKinley. The Midwest tipped the balance. In the end, the election hinged on between 100 and 1,000 votes in several key states, including Wisconsin, Iowa, and Minnesota. Although McKinley won twenty-three states to Bryan's twenty-two, the electoral vote showed a lopsided 271 to 176 in McKinley's favor (**Map 20.2**).

The biggest losers in 1896 turned out to be the Populists. On the national level, they polled fewer than 300,000 votes, a million less than in 1894. In the clamor to support Bryan, Populists in the South, determined to beat McKinley at any cost, swallowed their differences and drifted back to the Democratic Party.

But if Populism proved unsuccessful at the polls, it nevertheless set the domestic political agenda for the United States in the next decades, highlighting issues such as railroad regulation, banking and currency reform, electoral reforms, and an enlarged role for the federal government in the economy. Meanwhile, as the decade ended, the bugle call to arms turned America's attention to foreign affairs. The struggle for social justice gave way to a war for empire as the United States asserted its power on the world stage.

Candidate	Electoral Vote	Popular Vote	Percent of Popular Vote
William McKinley (Republican)	271	7,104,779	51.1
William J. Bryan (Democrat-People's)	176	6,502,925	47.7

MAP 20.2 ■ The Election of 1896

QUICK REVIEW <

Why was the People's Party unable to translate national support into victory in the 1896 election?

How were women involved in late-nineteenth-century politics?

How did economic problems affect American politics in the 1890s?

Why did the United States largely abandon its isolationist foreign policy in the 1890s?

Conclusion: What was the connection between domestic strife and foreign policy?

✔ LearningCurve
Check what you know.
bedfordstmartins.com
/roarkunderstanding

> Why did the United States largely abandon its isolationist foreign policy in the 1890s?

The Open Door

The trade advantage that the United States gained through the Open Door policy is portrayed in this political cartoon. Uncle Sam stands prominently in the "open door," while representatives of the other great powers seek admittance to the "Flowery Kingdom" of China. In fact, the Open Door policy promised equal access for all powers to the China trade, not U.S. preeminence as the cartoon implies. Culver Pictures.

> VISUAL ACTIVITY

READING THE IMAGE: How does the cartoon portray the role of the United States in international diplomacy?
CONNECTIONS: In what ways does this image misrepresent the reality of American and European involvement in China and of the Open Door policy?

THROUGHOUT MUCH OF THE SECOND HALF of the nineteenth century, U.S. interest in foreign policy took a backseat to territorial expansion in the American West. The United States fought the Indian wars while European nations carved out empires in Asia, Africa, Latin America, and the Pacific.

At the turn of the twentieth century, the United States pursued a foreign policy consisting of two currents — isolationism and expansionism. Although the determination to remain detached from European politics had been a hallmark of U.S. foreign policy since the nation's founding, Americans simultaneously believed in manifest destiny — the "obvious" right to expand the nation from ocean to ocean. With its own inland empire secured, the United States looked outward. Determined to protect its sphere of influence in the Western Hemisphere and to expand its trading in Asia, the nation moved away from isolationism and toward a more active role on the world stage that led to intervention in China's Boxer uprising and war with Spain.

Markets and Missionaries

The depression of the 1890s provided a powerful impetus to American commercial expansion. As markets weakened at home, American businesses looked abroad for profits. As the depression deepened, one diplomat warned that Americans "must turn [their] eyes abroad, or they will soon look inward upon discontent."

CHAPTER LOCATOR | Why did American farmers organize alliances in the late nineteenth century? | What led to the labor wars of the 1890s?

Exports constituted a small but significant percentage of the profits of American business in the 1890s (**Figure 20.3**). And where American interests led, businessmen expected the government's power and influence to follow to protect their investments. Companies like Standard Oil actively sought to use the U.S. government as their agent, often putting foreign service employees on the payroll. "Our ambassadors and ministers and consuls," wrote John D. Rockefeller appreciatively, "have aided to push our way into new markets and to the utmost corners of the world."

America's foreign policy often appeared little more than a sidelight to business development. In Hawai'i (first called the Sandwich Islands), American sugar interests fomented a rebellion in 1893, toppling the increasingly independent Queen Lili'uokalani. They pushed Congress to annex the islands to avoid the high McKinley tariff on sugar. When President Cleveland learned that Hawai'ians opposed annexation, he withdrew the proposal from Congress. But expansionists still coveted the islands and looked for an opportunity to push through annexation.

Business interests alone did not account for the new expansionism that seized the nation during the 1890s. As Alfred Thayer Mahan, leader of a growing group of American expansionists, confessed, "Even when material interests are the original exciting cause, it is the sentiment to which they give rise, the moral tone which emotion takes that constitutes the greater force." Much of that moral tone was set by American missionaries intent on spreading the gospel of Christianity to the "heathen." No area on the globe constituted a greater challenge than China.

> CHRONOLOGY

1894
- President Grover Cleveland nixes attempt to annex Hawai'i.

1895
- Cleveland enforces Monroe Doctrine in border dispute between British Guiana and Venezuela.

1898
- U.S. battleship *Maine* explodes in Havana harbor.
- Congress declares war on Spain.
- U.S. Navy destroys Spanish fleet in Manila Bay, the Philippines.
- U.S. troops defeat Spanish forces in Cuba.
- Treaty of Paris ends war with Spain.
- United States annexes Hawai'i.

1899–1900
- Secretary of State John Hay enunciates Open Door policy in China.
- Boxer uprising in China.

1901
- European powers impose Boxer Protocol on Chinese government.

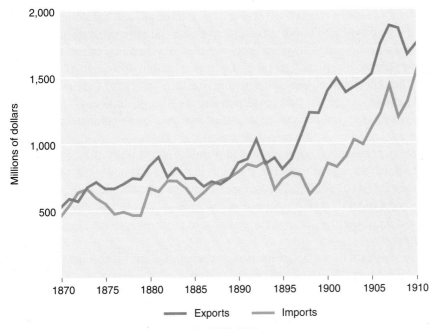

Exports — Imports

FIGURE 20.3 ■ **Expansion in U.S. Trade, 1870–1910**

Between 1870 and 1910, American exports more than tripled. Imports generally rose, but they were held in check by the high protective tariffs championed by Republican presidents from Ulysses S. Grant to William Howard Taft. A decline in imports is particularly noticeable after the passage of the prohibitive McKinley tariff in 1890.

How were women involved in late-nineteenth-century politics?

How did economic problems affect American politics in the 1890s?

Why did the United States largely abandon its isolationist foreign policy in the 1890s?

Conclusion: What was the connection between domestic strife and foreign policy?

✓ LearningCurve
Check what you know.
bedfordstmartins.com
/roarkunderstanding

Methodist women missionaries in China's Szechuan Province relied on traditional means of transportation, in this case "back chairs." Women constituted 60 percent of American foreign missionaries by 1890. Special Collections, Yale Divinity School Library.

An 1858 agreement, the Tianjin treaty admitted foreign missionaries to China. Although Christians converted only 100,000 in a population of 400 million, the Chinese nevertheless resented the interference of missionaries in village life. Opposition to foreign missionaries took the form of antiforeign secret societies, most notably the Boxers, whose Chinese name translated to "Righteous Harmonious Fist." In 1899, the Boxers hunted down and killed Chinese Christians and missionaries in northwestern Shandong Province. With the tacit support of China's Dowager Empress, the Boxers, shouting "Uphold the Ch'ing Dynasty, Exterminate the Foreigners," marched on the cities. Their rampage eventually led to the massacre of some 30,000 Chinese converts and 250 foreign nuns, priests, and missionaries. In August 1900, 2,500 U.S. troops joined an international force sent to rescue the foreigners and put down the uprising in the Chinese capital of Beijing. The European powers imposed the humiliating Boxer Protocol in 1901, giving themselves the right to maintain military forces in Beijing and requiring the Chinese government to pay an exorbitant indemnity of $333 million.

In the aftermath of the **Boxer uprising**, missionaries voiced no concern at the paradox of bringing Christianity to China at gunpoint. "It is worth any cost in money, worth any cost in bloodshed," argued one bishop, "if we can make millions of Chinese true and intelligent Christians." Merchants and missionaries alike shared such moralistic reasoning. Indeed, they worked hand in hand; trade and Christianity marched into Asia together. "Missionaries," admitted the American clergyman Charles Denby, "are the pioneers of trade and commerce. . . . The missionary, inspired by holy zeal, goes everywhere and by degrees foreign commerce and trade follow."

Boxer uprising

▶ 1899–1900 uprising in China led by the Boxers, an antiforeign society, in which 30,000 Chinese converts and 250 foreign Christians were killed. An international force rescued foreigners in Beijing, and European powers imposed the humiliating Boxer Protocol on China in 1901.

CHAPTER LOCATOR | Why did American farmers organize alliances in the late nineteenth century? | What led to the labor wars of the 1890s?

600 CHAPTER 20
DISSENT, DEPRESSION, AND WAR

The Monroe Doctrine and the Open Door Policy

The emergence of the United States as a world power pitted the nation against other colonial powers, particularly Germany and Japan, that posed a threat to the twin pillars of America's expansionist foreign policy. The first, the **Monroe Doctrine**, came to be interpreted as establishing the Western Hemisphere as an American "sphere of influence" and warned European powers to stay away or risk war. The second, the Open Door, dealt with maintaining market access to China.

American diplomacy actively worked to buttress the Monroe Doctrine, with its assertion of American hegemony (domination) in the Western Hemisphere. In the 1880s, Republican secretary of state James G. Blaine promoted hemispheric peace and trade through Pan-American cooperation but at the same time used American troops to intervene in Latin American border disputes. In 1895, President Cleveland risked war with Great Britain to enforce the Monroe Doctrine when a conflict developed between Venezuela and British Guiana. After American saber rattling, the British backed down and accepted U.S. mediation in the area despite their territorial claims in Guiana.

In Central America, American business triumphed in a bloodless takeover that saw French and British interests routed. The United Fruit Company of Boston virtually dominated the Central American nations of Costa Rica and Guatemala, while an importer from New Orleans turned Honduras into a "banana republic" (a country run by U.S. business interests). Thus, by 1895, the United States, through business as well as diplomacy, had successfully achieved hegemony in Latin America and the Caribbean, forcing even the British to concur that "the infinite resources [of the United States] combined with its isolated position render it master of the situation and practically invulnerable as against any or all other powers."

At the same time that American foreign policy warned European powers to stay out of the Western Hemisphere, the United States competed for trade in the Eastern Hemisphere. As American interests in China grew, the United States became more aggressive in defending its presence in Asia and the Pacific. In 1889, it risked war with Germany to guarantee U.S. naval access to Pago Pago in the Samoan Islands, a port for refueling on the way to Asia. Germany, seeking dominance over the islands, sent warships to the region. But before fighting broke out, a typhoon destroyed the German and American ships. The potential combatants later divided the islands amicably in the 1899 Treaty of Berlin.

In the 1890s, China, weakened by years of internal warfare, was partitioned into spheres of influence by Britain, Japan, Germany, France, and Russia. Concerned about the integrity of China and no less about American trade, Secretary of State John Hay in 1899–1900 wrote a series of notes calling for an "open door" policy that would ensure trade access to all and maintain Chinese sovereignty. The notes were greeted by the major powers with polite evasion. Nevertheless, Hay skillfully managed to maneuver them into doing his bidding, and in 1900 he boldly announced the Open Door as international policy. The United States, by insisting on the **Open Door policy**, managed to secure access to Chinese markets, expanding its economic power while avoiding the problems of maintaining a far-flung colonial empire on the Asian mainland. But as the Spanish-American War soon demonstrated, Americans found it hard to resist the temptations of overseas empire.

Monroe Doctrine

▶ President James Monroe's 1823 declaration that the Western Hemisphere was closed to further colonization or interference by European powers. In exchange, Monroe pledged that the United States would not become involved in European struggles. The United States strengthened the doctrine during the late nineteenth century.

Open Door policy

▶ Policy successfully insisted upon by Secretary of State John Hay in 1899–1900 recommending that the major powers of the United States, Britain, Japan, Germany, France, and Russia should all have access to trade with China and that Chinese sovereignty should be maintained.

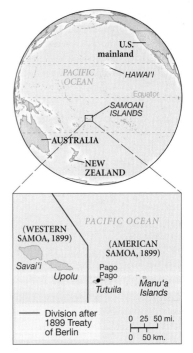

The Samoan Islands, 1889

How were women involved in late-nineteenth-century politics?

How did economic problems affect American politics in the 1890s?

Why did the United States largely abandon its isolationist foreign policy in the 1890s?

Conclusion: What was the connection between domestic strife and foreign policy?

☑ **LearningCurve**
Check what you know.
bedfordstmartins.com
/roarkunderstanding

"A Splendid Little War"

Spanish-American War

▶ 1898 war between Spain and the United States that began as an effort to free Cuba from Spain's colonial rule. This popular war left the United States an imperial power in control of Cuba and with colonies in Puerto Rico, Guam, and the Philippines.

The **Spanish-American War** began as a humanitarian effort to free Cuba from Spain's colonial grasp and ended with the United States itself acquiring territory overseas and fighting a dirty guerrilla war with Filipino nationalists who, like the Cubans, sought independence. Behind the contradiction stood the twin pillars of American foreign policy: The Monroe Doctrine made Spain's presence in Cuba unacceptable, and U.S. determination to keep open the door to Asia made the Philippines attractive. Precedent for the nation's imperial adventures also came from the recent Indian wars in the American West, which provided a template for the subjugation of native peoples in the name of civilization.

Looking back on the Spanish-American War of 1898, Secretary of State John Hay judged it "a splendid little war; begun with the highest motives, carried on with magnificent intelligence and spirit, favored by that fortune which loves the brave." At the close of a decade marred by bitter depression, social unrest, and political upheaval, the war offered Americans a chance to wave the flag and march in unison. War fever proved as infectious as the tune of a John Philip Sousa march. Few argued the merits of the conflict until it was over and the time came to divide the spoils.

Yellow Journalism

Most cartoonists followed the lead of William Randolph Hearst and Joseph Pulitzer in promoting war with Spain. Cartoonist Grant Hamilton drew this cartoon for *Judge* magazine in 1898. It shows a brutish Spain (the "Devil's Deputy") with bloody hands trampling on a sailor from the *Maine*. Cuba is prostrate, and a pile of skulls represents civilians "starved to death by Spain." Collection of the New-York Historical Society.

CHAPTER LOCATOR | Why did American farmers organize alliances in the late nineteenth century? | What led to the labor wars of the 1890s?

CHAPTER 20
602 DISSENT, DEPRESSION, AND WAR

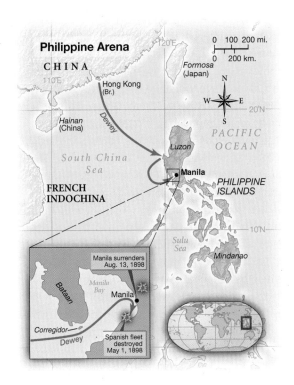

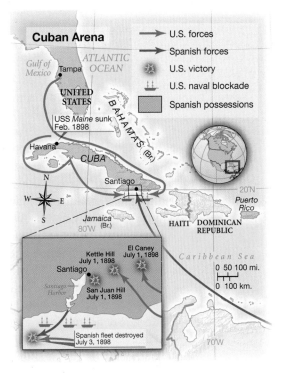

MAP 20.3 ■ The Spanish-American War, 1898

The Spanish-American War was fought in two theaters, the Philippine Islands and Cuba. Five days after President William McKinley called for a declaration of war, Admiral George Dewey captured Manila. The war lasted only eight months. Troops landed in Cuba in mid-June and by mid-July had destroyed the Spanish fleet.

> MAP ACTIVITY

READING THE MAP: Which countries held imperial control over countries and territories immediately surrounding the Philippine Islands and Cuba?

CONNECTIONS: What role did American newspapers play in the start of the war? How did the results of the war serve American aims in both Asia and the Western Hemisphere?

The war began with moral outrage over the treatment of Cuban revolutionaries, who had launched a fight for independence against the Spanish colonial regime in 1895. In an attempt to isolate the guerrillas, the Spanish general Valeriano Weyler herded Cubans into crowded and unsanitary concentration camps, where thousands died of hunger, disease, and exposure. Starvation soon spread to the cities. By 1898, fully a quarter of the island's population had perished in the Cuban revolution.

As the Cuban rebellion dragged on, pressure for American intervention mounted. American newspapers fueled public outrage at Spain. A fierce circulation war raged in New York City between William Randolph Hearst's *Journal* and Joseph Pulitzer's *World*. Their competition provoked what came to be called **yellow journalism**, named for the colored ink used in a popular comic strip. The Cuban war provided a wealth of dramatic copy. Newspapers fed the American people a daily diet of "Butcher" Weyler and Spanish atrocities. Hearst sent artist Frederic Remington to document the horror, and when Remington wired home, "There is no trouble here. There will be no war," Hearst shot back, "You furnish the pictures and I'll furnish the war."

American interests in Cuba were, in the words of the U.S. minister to Spain, more than "merely theoretical or sentimental." American business had more than

yellow journalism

▶ Term first given to sensationalistic newspaper reporting and cartoon images rendered in yellow. A circulation war between two New York City papers provoked the tactics of yellow journalism that fueled popular support for the Spanish-American War in 1898.

| How were women involved in late-nineteenth-century politics? | How did economic problems affect American politics in the 1890s? | **Why did the United States largely abandon its isolationist foreign policy in the 1890s?** | Conclusion: What was the connection between domestic strife and foreign policy? | ✔ LearningCurve Check what you know. bedfordstmartins.com /roarkunderstanding |

$50 million invested in Cuban sugar, and American trade with Cuba, a brisk $100 million a year before the rebellion, had dropped to near zero. Nevertheless, the business community balked, wary of a war with Spain. When industrialist Mark Hanna, the Republican kingmaker and senator from Ohio, urged restraint, a hotheaded Theodore Roosevelt exploded, "We will have this war for the freedom of Cuba, Senator Hanna, in spite of the timidity of commercial interests."

To expansionists like Roosevelt, more than Cuban independence was at stake. As assistant secretary of the navy, Roosevelt took the helm in the absence of his boss and in the summer of 1897 audaciously ordered the U.S. fleet to Manila in the Philippines. In the event of conflict with Spain, Roosevelt put the navy in a position to capture the islands and gain a stepping-stone to China.

President McKinley moved slowly toward intervention. In a show of American force, he dispatched the battleship *Maine* to Cuba. On the night of February 15, 1898, a mysterious explosion destroyed the *Maine*, killing 267 crew members. The source of the explosion remained unclear, but inflammatory stories in the press enraged Americans. Rallying to the cry "Remember the *Maine*," Congress declared war on Spain. In a surge of patriotism, more than a million men rushed to enlist. War brought with it a unity of purpose and national harmony that ended a decade of political dissent and strife. "In April, everywhere over this good fair land, flags were flying," wrote Kansas editor William Allen White. "At the stations, crowds gathered to hurrah for the soldiers, and to throw hats into the air, and to unfurl flags."

Five days after McKinley signed the war resolution, a U.S. Navy squadron destroyed the Spanish fleet in Manila Bay (**Map 20.3**). The stunning victory caught most Americans by surprise. Few had ever heard of the Philippines. Even McKinley confessed that he could not locate the archipelago on the map. Nevertheless, he dispatched U.S. troops to secure the islands.

The war in Cuba ended almost as quickly as it began. The first troops landed on June 22, and after a handful of battles the Spanish forces surrendered on July 17. The war lasted just long enough to elevate Theodore Roosevelt to the status of bona fide war hero. Roosevelt resigned his navy post and formed the Rough Riders, a regiment composed of a sprinkling of Ivy League polo players and a number of western cowboys Roosevelt befriended during his stint as a cattle rancher in the Dakotas. The Rough Riders' charge up Kettle Hill and Roosevelt's role in the decisive battle of San Juan Hill made front-page news. Overnight, Roosevelt became the most famous man in America. By the time he sailed home from Cuba, a coalition of independent Republicans was already plotting his political future.

The Debate over American Imperialism

After a few brief campaigns in Cuba and Puerto Rico brought the Spanish-American War to an end, the American people woke up in possession of an empire that stretched halfway around the globe. As part of the spoils of war, the United States acquired Cuba, Puerto Rico, Guam, and the Philippines. And Republicans quickly moved to annex Hawai'i in July 1898.

Contemptuous of the Cubans, whom General William Shafter declared "no more fit for self-government than gun-powder is for hell," the U.S. government directed a Cuban constitution and refused to give up military control of the

CHAPTER LOCATOR | Why did American farmers organize alliances in the late nineteenth century? | What led to the labor wars of the 1890s?

CHAPTER 20

604 DISSENT, DEPRESSION, AND WAR

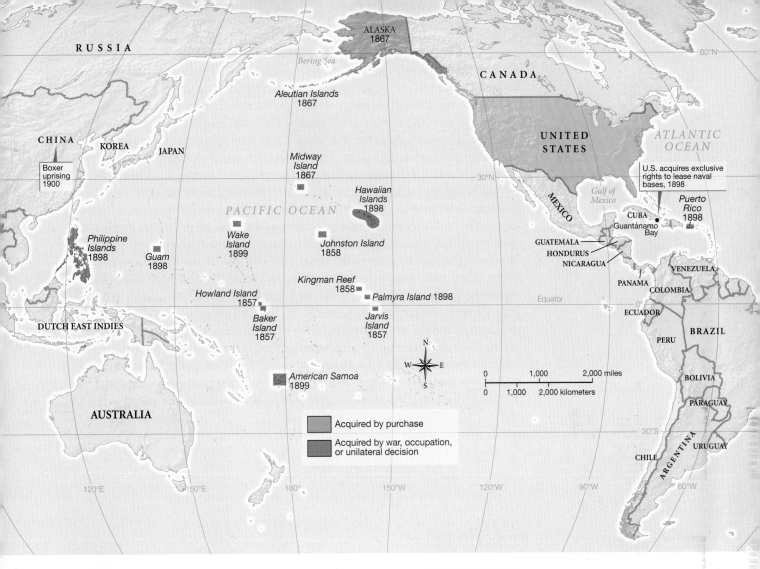

MAP 20.4 ■ U.S. Overseas Expansion through 1900

The United States extended its interests abroad with a series of territorial acquisitions. Although Cuba was granted independence, the Platt Amendment kept the new nation firmly under U.S. control. In the wake of the Spanish-American War, the United States woke up to find that it held an empire extending halfway around the globe.

> MAP ACTIVITY

READING THE MAP: Does the map indicate that more territory was acquired by purchase or by war, occupation, or unilateral decision? How many purchases of land outside the continental United States did the government make?

CONNECTIONS: What foreign policy developments occurred in the 1890s? How did American political leaders react to them? Where was U.S. expansion headed and why?

island until the Cubans accepted the so-called Platt Amendment — a series of provisions that granted the United States the right to intervene to protect Cuba's "independence," as well as the power to oversee Cuban debt so that European creditors would not find an excuse for intervention. For good measure, the United States gave itself a ninety-nine-year lease on a naval base at Guantánamo. In return, McKinley promised to implement an extensive sanitation program to clean up the island, making it more attractive to American investors.

In the formal Treaty of Paris (1898), Spain ceded the Philippines to the United States, along with the former Spanish colonies of Puerto Rico and Guam (**Map 20.4**).

How were women involved in late-nineteenth-century politics?

How did economic problems affect American politics in the 1890s?

Why did the United States largely abandon its isolationist foreign policy in the 1890s?

Conclusion: What was the connection between domestic strife and foreign policy?

✓ LearningCurve
Check what you know.
bedfordstmartins.com/roarkunderstanding

Empire did not come cheap. When Spain initially balked at these terms, the United States agreed to pay an indemnity of $20 million for the islands. Nor was the cost measured in money alone. Filipino revolutionaries under Emilio Aguinaldo, who had greeted U.S. troops as liberators, bitterly fought the new masters. It would take seven years and 4,000 American dead — almost ten times the number killed in Cuba — not to mention an estimated 20,000 Filipino casualties, to defeat Aguinaldo and secure American control of the Philippines.

At home, a vocal minority, mostly Democrats and former Populists, resisted the country's foray into overseas empire, judging it unwise, immoral, and unconstitutional. William Jennings Bryan, who enlisted in the army but never saw action, concluded that American expansionism only distracted the nation from problems at home. Pointing to the central paradox of the war, Representative Bourke Cockran of New York admonished, "We who have been the destroyers of oppression are asked now to become its agents." But the expansionists won the day. As Senator Knute Nelson of Minnesota assured his colleagues, "We come as ministering angels, not as despots." Fresh from the conquest of Native Americans in the West, the nation largely embraced the heady mixture of racism and missionary zeal that fueled American adventurism abroad. The *Washington Post* trumpeted, "The taste of empire is in the mouth of the people," thrilled at the prospect of "an imperial policy, the Republic renascent, taking her place with the armed nations."

> **QUICK REVIEW**

How did Americans respond to U.S. overseas expansion?

CHAPTER LOCATOR | Why did American farmers organize alliances in the late nineteenth century? | What led to the labor wars of the 1890s?

CHAPTER 20
606 DISSENT, DEPRESSION, AND WAR

A **DECADE OF DOMESTIC STRIFE** ended amid the blare of martial music and the waving of flags. The Spanish-American War drowned out the calls for social reform that had fueled the Populist politics of the 1890s. During that decade, angry farmers facing hard times looked to the Farmers' Alliance to fight for their vision of economic democracy, workers staged bloody battles across the country to assert their rights, and women like Frances Willard preached temperance and suffrage. Together, they formed a new People's Party to fight for change.

The bitter depression that began in 1893 led to increased labor strife. The Pullman boycott brutally dramatized the power of property and the conservatism of the laissez-faire state. But workers' willingness to confront capitalism on the streets of Chicago, Homestead, Cripple Creek, and a host of other sites across America eloquently testified to labor's growing determination, unity, and strength.

As the depression deepened, the sight of Coxey's army of unemployed marching on Washington to demand federal intervention in the economy signaled a growing shift in the public mind against the standpat politics of laissez-faire. The call for the government to take action to better the lives of workers, farmers, and the dispossessed manifested itself in the fiercely fought presidential campaign of William Jennings Bryan in 1896. With the outbreak of the Spanish-American War in 1898, the decade ended on a harmonious note with patriotic Americans rallying around the flag. But even though Americans basked in patriotism and contemplated empire, old grievances had not been laid to rest. The People's Party had been beaten, but the Populist spirit lived on in the demands for greater government involvement in the economy, expanded opportunities for direct democracy, and a more equitable balance of profits and power between the people and the big corporations. A new generation of progressive reformers took up the unfinished reform agenda in the first decades of the twentieth century.

How were women involved in late-nineteenth-century politics?	How did economic problems affect American politics in the 1890s?	Why did the United States largely abandon its isolationist foreign policy in the 1890s?	**Conclusion: What was the connection between domestic strife and foreign policy?**	✓ LearningCurve Check what you know. bedfordstmartins.com /roarkunderstanding

607

CHAPTER 20 STUDY GUIDE

STEP 1

GET STARTED ONLINE

 LearningCurve ■ bedfordstmartins.com/roarkunderstanding

Now that you've read the chapter, make it stick by completing the LearningCurve activity.

STEP 2

EXPLAIN WHY IT MATTERS

Put your reading into practice. Identify each term below, and then explain why it matters in U.S. history.

TERM	WHO OR WHAT & WHEN	WHY IT MATTERS
Farmers' Alliance (p. 581)		
People's Party (Populist Party) (p. 582)		
Homestead lockout (p. 585)		
Cripple Creek miners' strike of 1894 (p. 587)		
Pullman boycott (p. 589)		
National American Woman Suffrage Association (NAWSA) (p. 593)		
Coxey's army (p. 595)		
Boxer uprising (p. 600)		
Monroe Doctrine (p. 601)		
Open Door policy (p. 601)		
Spanish-American War (p. 602)		
yellow journalism (p. 603)		

STEP 3

MOVE BEYOND THE BASICS

To demonstrate a more advanced understanding, describe the issues, goals, actions, and successes and failures of activists, reformers, and foreign-policy makers in the 1890s.

Group	Issues and goals	Actions	Successes and failures
Farmers			
Laborers			
Women			
Foreign-policy makers			

STEP **4** **PUT IT ALL TOGETHER**   Now, take a step back and try to explain the big picture. Remember to use specific examples from the chapter in your answers.

ECONOMICS

▶ What key issues fueled farm protest in the late nineteenth century? How did the Farmers' Alliance attempt to address these issues?

▶ What strategies and tactics did unions employ in the late nineteenth century? How did companies fight back?

POLITICS

▶ How did reform movements provide a vehicle for women's involvement in public political life?

▶ How did the depression of the mid-1890s shape the politics of the decade?

EMPIRE

▶ How did U.S. foreign policy reflect the tension between American tendencies toward isolationism and expansionism?

▶ How did the Spanish-American War change the place of the United States in global politics?

LOOKING BACKWARD, LOOKING AHEAD

▶ What were the United States' most important strengths and weaknesses in 1900? How had the nation's place in the world changed since 1800?

▶ Defend or refute the following statement: "With its victory in the Spanish-American War in 1898, the United States became an imperial power."

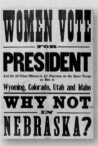

> **IN YOUR OWN WORDS**   Imagine that you must give an oral report to the class answering the following question: **Why was the decade of the 1890s such a turbulent time in U.S. history?** What would be the most important points to include and why?

21

PROGRESSIVISM FROM THE GRASS ROOTS UP

1890–1916

> What were the most significant changes in the United States as a result of the Progressive Era? Chapter 21 examines the efforts of progressive reformers to combat the ills of industrial America. It explores the initiatives of reformers at the grassroots level and examines their core values and beliefs. The chapter then considers the impact that the progressive agenda had on local, state, and national politics. Finally, it looks at the limits of progressive reform.

LearningCurve
bedfordstmartins.com/roarkunderstanding
After reading the chapter, use LearningCurve to
retain what you've read.

Progressive social work. An Infant Welfare Society nurse instructs an immigrant mother on clean home care in 1910. Chicago History Museum.

> How did grassroots progressives attack the problems of industrial America?

> What were the key tenets of progressive theory?

> How did Theodore Roosevelt advance the progressive agenda?

> How did progressivism evolve during Woodrow Wilson's first term?

> What were the limits of progressive reform?

> Conclusion: How did the liberal state transform during the Progressive Era?

> How did grassroots progressives attack the problems of industrial America?

Jane Addams Jane Addams was twenty-nine years old when she founded Hull House in 1889. Her insistence that settlement house work benefited educated women as well as her immigrant neighbors marked the distance from philanthropy to progressive reform. *Twenty Years at Hull-House*, her autobiography published in 1910, is shown in the inset. Photo: Jane Addams Memorial Collection (JAMC neg. 14), Special Collections, University of Illinois at Chicago, photographer: Max Platz; book: Newberry Library.

progressivism
▶ A reform movement that often advocated government activism to mitigate the problems created by urban industrialism. Progressivism reached its peak in 1912 with the creation of the Progressive Party. The term *progressivism* has come to mean any general effort advocating for social welfare programs.

AS THE GAP BETWEEN RICH and poor widened in the 1890s, a group of reformers demonstrated a willingness to use the government to counterbalance the power of private interests and in doing so redefined liberalism in the twentieth century. Faith in activism united an otherwise diverse group of progressive reformers. A sense of Christian mission inspired some. Others, fearing social upheaval, sought to remove some of the worst evils of urban industrialism — tenements, child labor, and harsh working conditions.

Much of progressive reform began at the grassroots level and percolated upward into local, state, and eventually national politics as reformers attacked the social problems fostered by urban industrialism. Although progressivism flourished in many different settings across the country, urban problems inspired the progressives' greatest efforts. In their zeal to "civilize the city," reformers founded settlement houses, professed a new Christian social gospel, and campaigned against vice and crime in the name of "social purity." Allying with the working class, women progressives sought to better the lot of sweatshop garment workers

CHAPTER LOCATOR | How did grassroots progressives attack the problems of industrial America? | What were the key tenets of progressive theory?

CHAPTER 21
612 PROGRESSIVISM FROM THE GRASS ROOTS UP

and to end child labor. These local reform efforts often ended up being debated in state legislatures and in the U.S. Congress.

Civilizing the City

Progressives attacked the problems of the city on many fronts. The settlement house movement, which began in England, came to the United States in 1886 with the opening of the University Settlement House in New York City. Other **settlement houses** soon followed. In the summer of 1889, reformer Jane Addams leased two floors of a dilapidated mansion on Chicago's West Side. For Addams, personal action marked the first step in her search for solutions to the social problems created by urban industrialism. She wanted to help her immigrant neighbors, and she wanted to offer meaningful work to educated women like herself. Addams's emphasis on the reciprocal relationship between the social classes made Hull House different from other philanthropic enterprises. She wished to do things with, not just for, Chicago's poor.

In the next decade, Hull House expanded from two rented floors in the old brick mansion to some thirteen buildings housing a remarkable variety of activities. Addams provided public baths, opened a restaurant for working women too tired to cook after their long shifts, and sponsored a nursery and kindergarten. Hull House offered classes, lectures, art exhibits, musical instruction, and college extension courses. It boasted a gymnasium, a theater, a manual training workshop, a labor museum, and the first public playground in Chicago.

In 1893, the needs of poor urban neighborhoods that had motivated Jane Addams led Lillian Wald, a nurse, to recruit several other nurses to move to New York City's Lower East Side "to live in the neighborhood as nurses, identify ourselves with it socially, and . . . contribute to it our citizenship." Wald's Henry Street settlement pioneered public health nursing.

Women, particularly college-educated women like Addams and Wald, formed the backbone of the settlement house movement and stood in the vanguard of the progressive movement. Settlement houses gave college-educated women eager to use their knowledge a place to put their talents to work in the service of society and to champion progressive reform. Settlements grew in number from six in 1891 to more than four hundred in 1911. In the process, settlement house women created a new profession — social work.

> ### > Progressives and Urban Reform

Settlement house movement	Effort by reformers to bridge the social divide by living and working among the poor.
Social gospel	Call for churches and their members to play an active role in social reform. Advocates questioned social Darwinism and the gospel of wealth.
Social purity movement	Campaign to attack vice, particularly prostitution. The movement brought together ministers who wished to stamp out sin, doctors concerned about the spread of sexually transmitted diseases, and women reformers. Advanced progressives linked prostitution to poverty and championed higher wages for women.

> CHRONOLOGY

1889
– Jane Addams opens Hull House in Chicago.

1893
– Lillian Wald opens Henry Street settlement house in New York.

1903
– Women's Trade Union League (WTUL) is founded.

1908
– *Muller v. Oregon.*

1909
– Garment workers' strike.

1911
– Triangle fire.

settlement houses
▶ Settlements established in poor neighborhoods beginning in the 1880s. Reformers like Jane Addams and Lillian Wald believed that only by living among the poor could they help bridge the growing class divide. College-educated women formed the backbone of the settlement house movement.

How did Theodore Roosevelt advance the progressive agenda?

How did progressivism evolve during Woodrow Wilson's first term?

What were the limits of progressive reform?

Conclusion: How did the liberal state transform during the Progressive Era?

☑ LearningCurve
Check what you know.
bedfordstmartins.com
/roarkunderstanding

social gospel

▶ A vision of Christianity that saw its mission not simply to reform individuals but to reform society. Emerging in the early twentieth century, it offered a powerful corrective to social Darwinism and the gospel of wealth, which fostered the belief that riches signaled divine favor.

For their part, churches confronted urban social problems by enunciating a new **social gospel**, one that saw its mission as not simply to reform individuals but to reform society. Charles M. Sheldon's popular book *In His Steps* (1898) called on men and women to Christianize capitalism by asking the question "What would Jesus do?" Ministers also played an active role in the social purity movement, the campaign to attack vice.

Attacks on alcohol went hand in hand with the push for social purity. The Anti-Saloon League, formed in 1895 under the leadership of Protestant clergy, added to the efforts of the Woman's Christian Temperance Union in campaigning to end the sale of liquor. Reformers pointed to links between drinking and a variety of other problems, including prostitution, wife and child abuse, unemployment, and industrial accidents. The powerful liquor lobby fought back, spending liberally in election campaigns, fueling the charge that liquor corrupted the political process.

An element of nativism (dislike of foreigners) ran through the movement for prohibition, as it did in a number of progressive reforms. The Irish, the Italians, and the Germans were among the groups stigmatized by temperance reformers for their drinking. Progressives campaigned to enforce the Sunday closing of taverns, stores, and other commercial establishments and pushed for state legislation to outlaw the sale of liquor. By 1912, seven states were "dry."

> ### > Core Progressive Attitudes

- A willingness to take action
- The belief that environment, not heredity alone, determined human behavior
- Optimism that reform could be achieved through government action without radically altering America's economy or institutions

Progressives and the Working Class

Day-to-day contact with their neighbors made settlement house workers particularly sympathetic to labor. When Mary Kenney O'Sullivan complained that her bookbinders' union met in a dirty, noisy saloon, Jane Addams invited them to meet at Hull House. And during the Pullman strike in 1894, Hull House residents organized strike relief. "Hull-House has been so unionized," grumbled one Chicago businessman, "that it has lost its usefulness and become a detriment and harm to the community." But to the working class, the support of middle-class reformers marked a significant gain.

Attempts to forge a cross-class alliance became institutionalized in 1903 with the creation of the Women's Trade Union League (WTUL). The WTUL brought together women workers and middle-class "allies." Its goal was to organize workingwomen into unions under the auspices of the American Federation of Labor (AFL). Although the alliance between workingwomen, primarily immigrants and daughters of immigrants, and their middle-class allies was not without tension, the WTUL helped workingwomen achieve significant gains.

The WTUL's most notable success came in 1909 in the "uprising of the twenty thousand," when hundreds of women employees of the Triangle Shirtwaist Company in New York City went on strike to protest low wages, dangerous working conditions,

CHAPTER LOCATOR | How did grassroots progressives attack the problems of industrial America? | What were the key tenets of progressive theory?

614 CHAPTER 21 PROGRESSIVISM FROM THE GRASS ROOTS UP

and management's refusal to recognize their union, the International Ladies' Garment Workers Union. In support, an estimated twenty thousand garment workers, most of them teenage girls and many of them Jewish and Italian immigrants, stayed out on strike through the winter, picketing in the bitter cold. By the time the strike ended in February 1910, the workers had won important demands in many shops. The solidarity shown by the women workers proved to be the strike's greatest achievement. As Clara Lemlich, one of the strike's leaders, exclaimed, "They used to say that you couldn't even organize women. They wouldn't come to union meetings. They were 'temporary' workers. Well we showed them!"

But for all its success, the uprising of the twenty thousand failed fundamentally to change conditions for women workers, as the tragic Triangle fire dramatized in 1911. A little over a year after the shirtwaist makers' strike ended, fire alarms sounded at the Triangle Shirtwaist factory. The ramshackle building, full of lint and combustible cloth, burned to rubble in half an hour. A WTUL member described the scene below on the street: "Two young girls whom I knew to be working in the vicinity came rushing toward me, tears were running from their eyes and they were white and shaking as they caught me by the arm. 'Oh,' shrieked one of them, 'they are jumping. Jumping from ten stories up! They are going through the air like bundles of clothes.'"

The terrified Triangle workers had little choice but to jump. Flames blocked one exit, and the other door had been locked to prevent workers from pilfering. The flimsy, rusted fire escape collapsed under the weight of fleeing workers, killing dozens. Trapped, 54 workers on the top floors jumped to their deaths. Of 500 workers, 146 died and scores of others were injured. The owners of the Triangle firm went to trial for negligence, but they avoided conviction when authorities determined that a careless smoker had started the fire. The Triangle Shirtwaist Company reopened in another firetrap within a matter of weeks.

14. Viewing the unfortunates at the Morgue

Triangle Fire Morgue

After the Triangle fire on March 26, 1911, New York City set up a makeshift morgue at the end of Manhattan's Charities Pier. There, the remains of more than a hundred young women and two dozen young men were laid out in coffins for their friends and relatives to identify. Small personal items often provided the only clues to the victims' identity. Hadwin Collection, Kheel Center, Cornell University, Ithaca, NY.

How did Theodore Roosevelt advance the progressive agenda?

How did progressivism evolve during Woodrow Wilson's first term?

What were the limits of progressive reform?

Conclusion: How did the liberal state transform during the Progressive Era?

✓ LearningCurve
Check what you know.
bedfordstmartins.com
/roarkunderstanding

615

Outrage and a sense of futility overwhelmed Rose Schneiderman, a leading WTUL organizer, who made a bitter speech at the memorial service for the dead Triangle workers. "I would be a traitor to those poor burned bodies if I came here to talk good fellowship," she told her audience. "We have tried you good people of the public and we have found you wanting. . . . I know from my experience it is up to the working people to save themselves . . . by a strong working class movement." The Triangle fire severely tested the bonds of the cross-class alliance. Schneiderman and other WTUL leaders determined that organizing and striking were no longer enough, particularly when the AFL paid so little attention to women workers. Increasingly, the WTUL turned its efforts to lobbying for protective legislation — laws that would limit hours and regulate women's working conditions.

The National Consumers League (NCL) also fostered cross-class alliance and advocated for protective legislation. When Florence Kelley took over the leadership of the NCL in 1899, she urged middle-class women to boycott stores and exert pressure for decent wages and working conditions for women employees. Frustrated by the reluctance of the private sector to reform, the NCL promoted protective legislation to better working conditions for women.

Advocates of protective legislation had won a major victory in 1908 when the U.S. Supreme Court, in *Muller v. Oregon*, reversed its previous rulings and upheld an Oregon law that limited to ten the number of hours women could work in a day. A mass of sociological evidence put together by Florence Kelley of the NCL and Josephine Goldmark of the WTUL convinced the Court that long hours endangered women and therefore the entire human race. The Court's ruling set a precedent, but one that separated the well-being of women workers from that of men by arguing that women's reproductive role justified special treatment. Later generations of women fighting for equality would question the effectiveness of this strategy and argue that it ultimately closed good jobs to women. The WTUL, however, greeted protective legislation as a first step in the attempt to ensure the safety of all workers.

Reform also fueled the fight for woman suffrage. For women like Jane Addams, involvement in social reform inevitably led to support for woman suffrage. These new suffragists emphasized the reforms that could be accomplished if women had the vote. Addams insisted that in an urban, industrial society, a good housekeeper could not be sure the food she fed her family, or the water and milk they drank, were pure unless she became involved in politics and wielded the ballot — and not just the broom — to protect her family.

> ## QUICK REVIEW

What types of people were drawn to the progressive movement, and why?

CHAPTER OVERVIEW | How did grassroots progressives attack the problems of industrial America? | What were the key tenets of progressive theory?

Tom Johnson

The reform mayor of Cleveland from 1901 to 1909, Tom Johnson is shown here campaigning in Cleveland's Wade Park in 1908. To get a three-cent streetcar fare and win the support of the working classes, Johnson instituted municipal ownership of the transit system. The Western Reserve Historical Society, Cleveland, Ohio.

What were the key tenets of progressive theory?

PROGRESSIVISM EMPHASIZED action and experimentation. Dismissing the view that humans should leave progress to the dictates of natural selection, a new group of reform Darwinists argued that evolution could be advanced more rapidly if men and women used their intellects to improve society. In their zeal for action, progressives often showed an unchecked admiration for speed and efficiency that promoted scientific management and a new cult to improve productivity. These varied strands of progressive theory found practical application in state and local politics, where reformers challenged traditional laissez-faire government.

Reform Darwinism and Social Engineering

The active, interventionist approach of the progressives directly challenged social Darwinism, with its insistence on survival of the fittest. A new group of sociologists argued that progress could be advanced more rapidly if people used their intellects to alter their environment. The best statement of this **reform Darwinism** came from sociologist Lester Frank Ward, who, in his book

reform Darwinism

▶ Sociological theory developed in the 1880s that argued humans could speed up evolution by altering their environment. A challenge to the laissez-faire approach of social Darwinism, reform Darwinism insisted that the liberal state should play an active role in solving social problems.

How did Theodore Roosevelt advance the progressive agenda?

How did progressivism evolve during Woodrow Wilson's first term?

What were the limits of progressive reform?

Conclusion: How did the liberal state transform during the Progressive Era?

✓ **LearningCurve**
Check what you know.
bedfordstmartins.com
/roarkunderstanding

> CHRONOLOGY

1883
– Lester Frank Ward champions reform Darwinism in *Dynamic Sociology*.

1910
– Progressive Hiram Johnson is elected governor of California.

1911
– Frederick Winslow Taylor pioneers "systematized shop management."

1914
– Journalist Walter Lippmann calls for scientific techniques to control social change.

Dynamic Sociology (1883), insisted that the "blind natural forces in society must give way to human foresight." This theory condemned the laissez-faire approach, insisting that the liberal state should play a more active role in solving social problems.

Efficiency and *expertise* became progressives' watchwords. In *Drift and Mastery* (1914), journalist and critic Walter Lippmann called for skilled "*technocrats*" to use scientific techniques to control social change. Unlike the Populists, who advocated a greater voice for the masses, progressives, for all their interest in social justice, insisted that experts be put in charge. At its extreme, the application of expertise and social engineering took the form of scientific management. In 1911, Frederick Winslow Taylor pioneered "systematized shop management." Obsessed with making humans and machines produce more and faster, he meticulously timed workers with a stopwatch and attempted to break down their work into its simplest components, one repetitious action after another. He won many converts among corporate managers, but workers hated the monotony of systematized shop management and argued that it led to speedup — pushing workers to produce more in less time and for less pay. Nevertheless, many progressives applauded the increased productivity and efficiency of Taylor's system.

Progressive Government: City and State

Progressivism burst forth at every level of government in 1900, but nowhere more forcefully than in Cleveland with the election of Democrat Thomas Loftin Johnson as mayor. A self-made millionaire by age forty, Johnson moved to Cleveland in 1899, where he began his career in politics. During his mayoral campaign, he pledged to reduce the streetcar fare from five cents to three cents. His election touched off a seven-year war between Johnson and the streetcar moguls. To get his three-cent fare, Johnson had Cleveland buy the streetcar system, a tactic of municipal ownership progressives called "gas and water socialism." Reelected four times, Johnson fought for fair taxation and championed greater democracy through the use of the initiative and referendum to let voters introduce legislation, and the recall to get rid of elected officials and judges. These devices allowed voters to have a direct say in legislative and judicial matters. Under Johnson's administration, Cleveland became, in the words of journalist Lincoln Steffens, the "best governed city in America."

In Wisconsin, Republican Robert M. La Follette converted to the progressive cause early in the twentieth century. La Follette capitalized on the grassroots movement for reform to launch his long political career as governor (1901–1905) and U.S. senator (1906–1925). La Follette brought scientists and professors into his administration and used the university, just down the street from the statehouse in Madison, as a resource. As governor, La Follette lowered railroad rates, raised railroad taxes, improved education, preached conservation, established factory regulation and workers' compensation, instituted the first direct primary in the country, and inaugurated the first state income tax. Under his leadership, Wisconsin earned the title "laboratory of democracy." A fiery orator, "Fighting Bob" La Follette united his supporters around issues that transcended party

CHAPTER OVERVIEW | How did grassroots progressives attack the problems of industrial America? | **What were the key tenets of progressive theory?**

loyalties. Democrats and Republicans like Tom Johnson and Robert La Follette crossed party lines to work for reform.

West of the Rockies, progressivism arrived somewhat later and found a champion in Republican Hiram Johnson of California, who served as governor from 1911 to 1917 and later as a U.S. senator. Since the 1870s, the Southern Pacific Railroad had dominated California politics. Johnson ran for governor in 1910 on the promise to "kick the Southern Pacific out of politics." With the support of the reform wing of the Republican Party and the promise "to return the government to the people," he won handily. As governor, he introduced the direct primary; supported the initiative, referendum, and recall; strengthened the state's railroad commission; supported conservation; and signed an employer's liability law.

QUICK REVIEW ◁

How did progressives justify their demand for a more activist government?

| How did Theodore Roosevelt advance the progressive agenda? | How did progressivism evolve during Woodrow Wilson's first term? | What were the limits of progressive reform? | Conclusion: How did the liberal state transform during the Progressive Era? | ☑ LearningCurve Check what you know. bedfordstmartins.com /roarkunderstanding |

How did Theodore Roosevelt advance the progressive agenda?

Theodore Roosevelt Aptly described by a contemporary observer as "a steam engine in trousers," Theodore Roosevelt, at forty-two, was the youngest president ever to occupy the White House. He brought to the office energy, intellect, and activism in equal measure. Roosevelt boasted that he used the presidency as a "bully pulpit"—a forum from which he advocated reforms ranging from trust-busting to conservation. Library of Congress.

ON SEPTEMBER 6, 1901, President William McKinley was shot by Leon Czolgosz, an anarchist, while attending the Pan-American Exposition in Buffalo, New York. Eight days later, McKinley died, and Theodore Roosevelt became president. Roosevelt immediately reassured the shocked nation that he intended "to continue absolutely unbroken" the policies of McKinley. But Roosevelt was quite different from McKinley. An activist and a moralist, imbued with the progressive spirit, Roosevelt would turn the White House into a "bully pulpit," advocating conservation and antitrust reforms and championing the nation's emergence as a world power. In the process, Roosevelt would work to shift the nation's center of power from Wall Street to Washington.

After serving nearly two full terms as president, Roosevelt left office at the height of his powers. Any man would have found it difficult to follow in his footsteps, but his handpicked successor, William Howard Taft, proved hopelessly ill suited to the task. Taft's presidency was marked by a progressive stalemate, a bitter break with Roosevelt, and a schism in the Republican Party.

CHAPTER OVERVIEW | How did grassroots progressives attack the problems of industrial America? | What were the key tenets of progressive theory?

The Square Deal

At age forty-two, Theodore Roosevelt became the youngest man ever to move into the White House. A patrician by birth and an activist by temperament, Roosevelt brought to the job enormous talent and energy.

Roosevelt recognized that the path to power did not lie in the good government leagues formed by his well-bred friends. "If it is the muckers that govern," he wrote, "then I want to see if I cannot hold my own with them." Roosevelt's rise in politics was swift and sure. He went from the New York assembly at the age of twenty-three to the presidency in less than twenty years, with time out as a cowboy in the Dakotas, police commissioner of New York City, assistant secretary of the navy, and a colonel of the Rough Riders. Elected governor of New York in 1898, he alienated the state's Republican boss, who finagled to get him "kicked upstairs" as a candidate for the vice presidency in 1900. The party bosses reasoned that Roosevelt could do little harm as vice president. But one bullet proved the error of their logic.

Once president, Roosevelt would harness his explosive energy to strengthen the power of the federal government, putting business on notice that it could no longer count on a laissez-faire government to give it free rein. In Roosevelt's eyes, self-interested capitalists like John D. Rockefeller, whose Standard Oil trust monopolized the refinery business, constituted "the most dangerous members of the criminal class — the criminals of great wealth." The "absolutely vital question" facing the country, Roosevelt wrote to a friend in 1901, was "whether or not the government has the power to control the trusts." The Sherman Antitrust Act of 1890 had been badly weakened by a conservative Supreme Court and by attorneys general more willing to use it against labor unions than against monopolies. To determine whether the law had any teeth left, Roosevelt, in one of his first acts as president, ordered his attorney general to begin a secret antitrust investigation of the Northern Securities Company, a behemoth that monopolized railroad traffic in the Northwest.

Just five months after Roosevelt took office, Wall Street rocked with the news that the government had filed an antitrust suit against Northern Securities. As one newspaper editor sarcastically observed, "Wall Street is paralyzed at the thought that a President of the United States would sink so low as to try to enforce the law." Roosevelt's thunderbolt put Wall Street on notice that the new president expected to be treated as an equal and was willing to use government as a weapon to curb business excesses. Perhaps sensing the new mood, the Supreme Court, in a significant turnaround, upheld the Sherman Act and called for the dissolution of Northern Securities in 1904.

"Hurrah for Teddy the Trustbuster," cheered the papers. Roosevelt went on to use the Sherman Act against forty-three trusts, including such giants as American Tobacco, Du Pont, and Standard Oil. Always the moralist, he insisted on a "rule of reason." He would punish "bad" trusts (those that broke the law) and leave "good" ones alone. In practice, he preferred regulation to antitrust suits. In 1903, he pressured Congress to pass the Elkins Act, outlawing railroad rebates. And he created the new cabinet-level Department of Commerce and Labor, with the subsidiary Bureau of Corporations to act as a corporate watchdog.

> CHRONOLOGY

1901
- William McKinley is assassinated; Theodore Roosevelt becomes president.

1902
- Antitrust lawsuit is filed against Northern Securities Company.
- Roosevelt mediates anthracite coal strike.

1903
- Panama Canal construction begins.

1904
- Roosevelt Corollary to Monroe Doctrine.

1906
- Pure Food and Drug Act and Meat Inspection Act.
- Hepburn Act.

1907
- Panic on Wall Street.
- "Gentlemen's Agreement" with Japan.

1908
- William Howard Taft is elected president.

How did Theodore Roosevelt advance the progressive agenda?

How did progressivism evolve during Woodrow Wilson's first term?

What were the limits of progressive reform?

Conclusion: How did the liberal state transform during the Progressive Era?

☑ **LearningCurve**
Check what you know.
bedfordstmartins.com /roarkunderstanding

621

In his handling of the anthracite coal strike in 1902, Roosevelt again demonstrated his willingness to assert the authority of the presidency, this time to mediate between labor and management. In May, 147,000 coal miners in Pennsylvania went on strike. The United Mine Workers (UMW) demanded a reduction in the workday from twelve to ten hours, an equitable system of weighing each miner's output, and a 10 percent wage increase, along with recognition of the union. When asked about the appalling conditions in the mines that led to the strike, George Baer, the mine operators' spokesman, scoffed, "The miners don't suffer, why they can't even speak English."

The strike dragged on through the summer and into the fall. Hoarding and profiteering drove the price of coal from $2.50 to $6.00 a ton. As winter approached, coal shortages touched off near riots in the nation's big cities. At this juncture, Roosevelt stepped in. Instead of sending in troops, he determined to mediate. His unprecedented intervention served notice that government counted itself an independent force in business and labor disputes. At the same time, it gave unionism a boost by granting the UMW a place at the table.

At the meeting, Baer and the mine owners refused to talk with the union representative — a move that angered the attorney general and insulted the president. Beside himself with rage over the "woodenheaded obstinacy and stupidity" of management, Roosevelt threatened to seize the mines and run them with federal troops. This quickly brought management to the table. In the end, the miners won a reduction in hours and a wage increase, but the owners succeeded in preventing formal recognition of the UMW.

Taken together, Roosevelt's actions in the Northern Securities case and the anthracite coal strike marked a dramatic departure from the presidential passivity of the Gilded Age. Roosevelt's actions demonstrated conclusively that government intended to act as a countervailing force to the power of the big corporations. Pleased with his role in the anthracite strike, Roosevelt announced that all he had tried to do was give labor and capital a "square deal."

The phrase "Square Deal" became Roosevelt's campaign slogan in the 1904 election. Roosevelt easily defeated the Democrats, who abandoned their former candidate, William Jennings Bryan, to support Judge Alton B. Parker, a "safe" choice they hoped would lure business votes away from Roosevelt. In the months before the election, the president prudently toned down his criticism of big business. Roosevelt swept into office with the largest popular majority — 57.9 percent — any candidate had polled up to that time.

Roosevelt the Reformer

"Tomorrow I shall come into my office in my own right," Roosevelt is said to have remarked on the eve of his election. "Then watch out for me!" Roosevelt's stunning victory gave him a mandate for reform. He would need all the popularity and political savvy he could muster, however, to guide his reform measures through Congress. The Senate remained controlled by a staunchly conservative Republican "old guard," with many senators on the payrolls of the corporations Roosevelt sought to curb. Roosevelt's pet project remained railroad regulation. The Elkins Act prohibiting rebates had not worked. Roosevelt determined that the only solution lay in giving the Interstate Commerce Commission (ICC) real power to set rates and prevent discriminatory practices. But the right to determine the price of goods or services was an age-old prerogative of private enterprise, and one that business had no intention of yielding to government.

The Hepburn Act of 1906 marked the crowning legislative achievement of Roosevelt's presidency. It gave the ICC the power to set rates subject to court review. Committed progressives like Robert La Follette judged the law a defeat for reform. Die-hard conservatives branded it a "piece of populism." Both sides exaggerated. The law left the courts too much power and failed to provide adequate means for the ICC to determine rates, but its passage proved a landmark in federal control of private industry. For the first time, a government commission had the power to investigate private business records and to set rates.

Always an apt reader of the public temper, Roosevelt witnessed a growing appetite for reform. Revelations of corporate and political wrongdoing as well as social injustice filled the papers and boosted the sales of popular magazines. Roosevelt counted many of the new investigative journalists among his friends. But he warned them against going too far, citing the allegorical character in *Pilgrim's Progress* who was too busy raking muck to notice higher things. Roosevelt's criticism gave the American vocabulary a new word, *muckraker*, which journalists soon appropriated as a title of honor.

Muckraking, as Roosevelt well knew, provided enormous help in securing progressive legislation. In the spring of 1906, publicity generated by the muckrakers about poisons in patent medicines goaded the Senate, with Roosevelt's backing, into passing a pure food and drug bill. Opponents in the House of Representatives hoped to keep the legislation locked up in committee. There it would have died, were it not for the publication of Upton Sinclair's novel *The Jungle* (1906), with its sensational account of filthy conditions in meatpacking plants. A massive public outcry led to the passage of the Pure Food and Drug Act and the Meat Inspection Act in 1906.

In the waning years of his administration, Roosevelt allied with the more progressive elements of the Republican Party. In speech after speech, he attacked "malefactors of great wealth." Styling himself a "radical," he claimed credit for leading the "ultra conservative" party of McKinley to a position of "progressive conservatism and conservative radicalism."

When an economic panic developed in the fall of 1907, business interests quickly blamed the president. Once again, J. P. Morgan stepped in to avert disaster, this time switching funds from one bank to another to prop up weak institutions. For his services, he claimed the Tennessee Coal and Iron Company, an independent steel business that U.S. Steel had long coveted. Morgan dispatched his lieutenants to Washington, where they told Roosevelt that the sale of the company would aid the economy "but little benefit" U.S. Steel. Willing to take the word of a gentleman, Roosevelt tacitly agreed not to institute antitrust proceedings against U.S. Steel over the acquisition. Roosevelt's promise would give rise to the charge that he acted as a tool of the Morgan interests.

The Jungle

Novelist Upton Sinclair, a lifelong socialist, wrote *The Jungle* to expose the evils of capitalism. But readers were more horrified by his descriptions of the unsanitary conditions in the meatpacking industry, where the novel's hapless hero sees rats, filth, and diseased animals processed into meat products. The public outcry surrounding *The Jungle* contributed to the enactment of pure food and drug legislation and a federal meat inspection law.
Picture Research Consultants, Inc.

muckraking

▶ Early-twentieth-century style of journalism that exposed the corruption of big business and government. Theodore Roosevelt coined the term after a character in *Pilgrim's Progress* who was too busy raking muck to notice higher things.

How did Theodore Roosevelt advance the progressive agenda?

How did progressivism evolve during Woodrow Wilson's first term?

What were the limits of progressive reform?

Conclusion: How did the liberal state transform during the Progressive Era?

✓ **LearningCurve**
Check what you know.
bedfordstmartins.com
/roarkunderstanding

The charge of collusion between business and government underscored the extent to which corporate leaders like Morgan found federal regulation preferable to unbridled competition or harsher state measures. During the Progressive Era, enlightened business leaders cooperated with government in the hope of avoiding antitrust prosecution. Convinced that regulation and not trust-busting offered the best way to deal with big business, Roosevelt never acknowledged that his regulatory policies fostered an alliance between business and government that today is called corporate liberalism.

Roosevelt and Conservation

In the area of conservation, Roosevelt proved indisputably ahead of his time. When he took office, some 43 million acres of forestland remained as government reserves. He more than quadrupled that number to 194 million acres. To conserve natural resources, he fought western cattle barons, lumber kings, mining interests, and powerful leaders in Congress, including Speaker of the House Joseph Cannon, who vowed to spend "not one cent for scenery."

As the first president to have lived and worked in the West, Roosevelt came to the White House convinced of the need for better management of the nation's rivers and forests as well as the preservation of wildlife and wilderness. During his presidency, he placed the nation's conservation policy in the hands of scientifically trained experts like his chief forester, Gifford Pinchot. Pinchot preached conservation — the efficient use of natural resources. Willing to permit grazing, lumbering, and the development of hydroelectric power, conservationists fought private interests only when they felt business acted irresponsibly or threatened to monopolize water and electric power. Preservationists like John Muir, founder of the Sierra Club, believed that the wilderness needed to be protected. Roosevelt — a fervent Darwinian naturalist and an (overly) enthusiastic game hunter, a conservationist who built big dams, and a preservationist who saved the redwoods — aimed to have it both ways.

In 1907, Congress attempted to put the brakes on Roosevelt's conservation program by passing a law limiting his power to create forest reserves in six western states. In the days leading up to the law's enactment, Roosevelt feverishly created twenty-one new reserves and enlarged eleven more, saving 16 million acres from development. Once again, Roosevelt had outwitted his adversaries. "Opponents of the forest service turned handsprings in their wrath," he wrote, "but the threats . . . were really only a tribute to the efficiency of our action." Worried that private utilities were gobbling up waterpower sites and creating a monopoly of hydroelectric power, he connived with Pinchot to withdraw 2,565 power sites from private use by designating them "ranger stations." Firm in his commitment to wild America, Roosevelt proved willing to stretch the law when it served his ends. His legacy is more than 234 million acres of American wilderness saved for posterity (**Map 21.1**).

The Big Stick

Roosevelt's activism extended to his foreign policy. A fierce proponent of America's interests abroad, he relied on executive power to pursue a vigorous for-

CHAPTER OVERVIEW | How did grassroots progressives attack the problems of industrial America? | What were the key tenets of progressive theory?

624   CHAPTER 21
PROGRESSIVISM FROM THE GRASS ROOTS UP

eign policy, sometimes stretching the powers of the presidency beyond legal limits. In his relations with the European powers, he relied on military strength and diplomacy, a combination he aptly described with the aphorism "Speak softly but carry a big stick."

A strong supporter of the Monroe Doctrine, Roosevelt jealously guarded the U.S. sphere of influence in the Western Hemisphere. His proprietary attitude toward the Caribbean became evident in the case of the Panama Canal. Roosevelt had long been a supporter of a canal linking the Caribbean and the Pacific. By enabling ships to move quickly from the Atlantic to the Pacific, a canal would trim 8,000 miles from a coast-to-coast voyage and effectively double the U.S. Navy's power. Having decided on a route across the Panamanian isthmus (a narrow strip

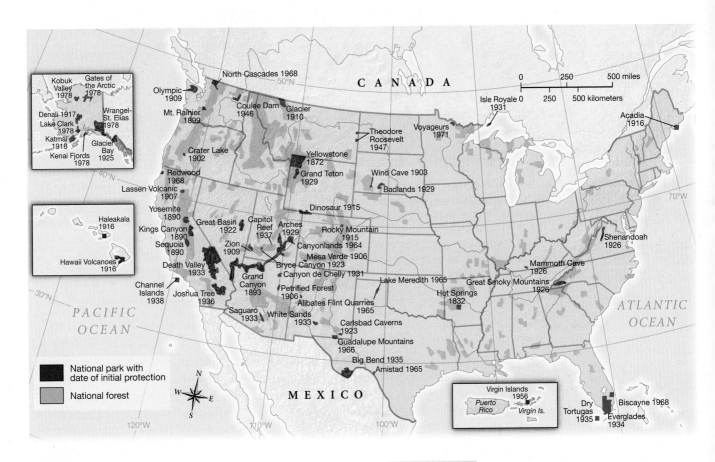

MAP 21.1 ■ National Parks and Forests

The national park system in the West began with Yellowstone in 1872. Grand Canyon, Yosemite, Kings Canyon, and Sequoia followed in the 1890s. During his presidency, Theodore Roosevelt added six parks— Crater Lake, Wind Cave, Petrified Forest, Lassen Volcanic, Mesa Verde, and Zion. Even more significant were the 234 million acres of wilderness he saved for posterity.

> MAP ACTIVITY

READING THE MAP: Collectively, do national parks or national forests encompass more land? According to the map, how many national parks were created before 1910? How many were created after 1910?

CONNECTIONS: How do conservation and preservation differ? Why did Roosevelt believe that saving land in the West was important? What principles guided the national land use policy of the Roosevelt administration?

| How did Theodore Roosevelt advance the progressive agenda? | How did progressivism evolve during Woodrow Wilson's first term? | What were the limits of progressive reform? | Conclusion: How did the liberal state transform during the Progressive Era? | ✓ LearningCurve Check what you know. bedfordstmartins.com /roarkunderstanding |

THE WORLD'S CONSTABLE.

"The World's Constable" In this political cartoon from 1905, President Theodore Roosevelt, dressed as a constable, wields the club of "The New Diplomacy" in one hand, with "Arbitration" tucked under his arm. The Roosevelt Corollary to the Monroe Doctrine made the United States the Western Hemisphere's policeman, a role Roosevelt relished. The Granger Collection, NYC.

> VISUAL ACTIVITY

READING THE IMAGE: How does this political cartoon visually represent Roosevelt's foreign policy? Does it appear to be supportive or critical of his policies? How does it treat the other peoples of the world?
CONNECTIONS: What aspects of Roosevelt's foreign policy ideas and actions are depicted in the cartoon?

of land connecting North and South America), then part of Colombia, Roosevelt in 1902 offered the Colombian government a one-time sum of $10 million and an annual rent of $250,000. When the government in Bogotá refused to accept the offer, Roosevelt became incensed at what he called the "homicidal corruptionists" in Colombia for trying to "blackmail" the United States. At the prompting of a group of New York investors, the Panamanians staged an uprising in 1903, and with unseemly haste the U.S. government recognized the new government within twenty-four hours. The Panamanians promptly accepted the $10 million, and the building got under way. The canal would take eleven years and $375 million to complete; it opened in 1914 (**Map 21.2**).

In the wake of the Panama affair, a confrontation with Germany over Venezuela, and yet another default on a European debt, this time in the Dominican Republic, Roosevelt grew concerned that financial instability in Latin America would lead European powers to interfere. In 1904, he announced the **Roosevelt Corollary** to the Monroe Doctrine.

Roosevelt Corollary
▶ Theodore Roosevelt's 1904 follow-up to the Monroe Doctrine in which he declared that the United States had the right to intervene in Latin America to stop "brutal wrongdoing" and protect American interests. The corollary warned European powers to keep out of the Western Hemisphere.

CHAPTER OVERVIEW | How did grassroots progressives attack the problems of industrial America? | What were the key tenets of progressive theory?

- The United States had a right to act as "an international police power" in the Western Hemisphere.

- The United States would not intervene in Latin America as long as nations there conducted their affairs with "decency," but it would step in to stop "brutal wrongdoing."

- The Roosevelt Corollary served notice to European powers to stay out of the Western Hemisphere.

In Asia, Roosevelt inherited the Open Door policy initiated by Secretary of State John Hay in 1899, designed to ensure U.S. commercial entry into China. As European powers raced to secure Chinese trade and territory, Roosevelt was tempted to use force to gain economic or possibly territorial concessions. Realizing that Americans would not support an aggressive Asian policy, the president sensibly held back.

MAP 21.2 ■ The Panama Canal, 1914

The Panama Canal, completed in 1914, bisects the isthmus in a series of massive locks and dams. As Theodore Roosevelt had planned, the canal greatly strengthened the U.S. Navy by allowing ships to move from the Atlantic to the Pacific in a matter of days.

> **MAP ACTIVITY**

READING THE MAP: How long was the trip from New York to San Francisco before the Panama Canal was built? After it was built?

CONNECTIONS: How did Roosevelt's desire for a canal lead to independence for Panama? How did the canal benefit the U.S. Navy?

| How did Theodore Roosevelt advance the progressive agenda? | How did progressivism evolve during Woodrow Wilson's first term? | What were the limits of progressive reform? | Conclusion: How did the liberal state transform during the Progressive Era? | ✓ LearningCurve Check what you know. bedfordstmartins.com /roarkunderstanding |

The Roosevelt Corollary in Action

In his relations with Europe, Roosevelt sought to establish the United States as a rising force in world affairs. When tensions flared between France and Germany in Morocco in 1905, Roosevelt mediated at a conference in Algeciras, Spain, where he worked to maintain a balance of power that helped neutralize German ambitions. His skillful mediation gained him a reputation as an astute player on the world stage and demonstrated the nation's new presence in world affairs.

Roosevelt earned the Nobel Peace Prize in 1906 for his role in negotiating an end to the Russo-Japanese War, which had broken out when the Japanese invaded Chinese Manchuria, threatening Russia's sphere of influence in the area. Once again, Roosevelt sought to maintain a balance of power, in this case working to curb Japanese expansionism. Roosevelt admired the Japanese, judging them "the most dashing fighters in the world," but he did not want Japan to become too strong in Asia.

When good relations with Japan were jeopardized by discriminatory legislation in California calling for segregated public schools for Asians, Roosevelt smoothed over the incident and negotiated the "Gentlemen's Agreement" in 1907, which allowed the Japanese to save face by voluntarily restricting immigration to the United States. To demonstrate America's naval power and to counter Japan's growing bellicosity, Roosevelt dispatched the Great White Fleet, sixteen of the navy's most up-to-date battleships, on a "goodwill mission" around the world. U.S. relations with Japan improved, and in the 1908 Root-Takahira agreement the two nations pledged to maintain the Open Door and support the status quo in the Pacific. Roosevelt's show of American force constituted a classic example of his dictum "Speak softly but carry a big stick."

The Troubled Presidency of William Howard Taft

On the eve of his election in 1904, Roosevelt promised that he would not seek another term. So he retired from the presidency in 1909 at age fifty and removed himself from the political scene by going on safari in Africa. He turned the White House over to his handpicked successor, William Howard Taft, a lawyer who had served as governor-general of the Philippines. In the presidential election of 1908, Taft soundly defeated the perennial Democratic candidate, William Jennings Bryan.

A genial man with a talent for law, Taft had no experience in elective office, no feel for politics, and no nerve for controversy. His ambitious wife coveted the office and urged him to seek it. He would have been better off listening to his mother, who warned, "Roosevelt is a good fighter and enjoys it, but the malice of politics would make you miserable."

Once in office, Taft proved a perfect tool in the hands of Republicans who yearned for a return to the days of a less active executive. A lawyer by training and instinct, Taft believed that it was up to the courts, not the president, to arbitrate social issues. Roosevelt had carried presidential power to a new level, often flouting the separation of powers and showing thinly veiled contempt for Congress and the courts. Taft found it difficult to condone Roosevelt's actions. Wary of the progressive insurgents in Congress, Taft relied increasingly on

CHAPTER OVERVIEW | How did grassroots progressives attack the problems of industrial America? | What were the key tenets of progressive theory?

CHAPTER 21
628 PROGRESSIVISM FROM THE GRASS ROOTS UP

William Howard Taft

When President Theodore Roosevelt tapped William Howard Taft as his successor in 1908, Taft had never held an elected office. Taft had little aptitude for politics, and his actions angered progressives, leading Roosevelt to challenge him for the presidency in 1912. Library of Congress.

conservatives in the Republican Party. As a progressive senator lamented, "Taft is a ponderous and amiable man completely surrounded by men who know exactly what they want."

Taft's troubles began on the eve of his inaugural, when he called a special session of Congress to deal with the tariff. Roosevelt had been too politically astute to tackle the troublesome tariff issue, even though he knew that rates needed to be lowered. Taft blundered into the fray. The Payne-Aldrich bill that emerged was amended in the Senate so that it actually raised the tariff, benefiting big business and the trusts at the expense of consumers. As if paralyzed, Taft neither fought for changes nor vetoed the measure. On a tour of the Midwest in 1909, he was greeted with jeers when he claimed, "I think the Payne bill is the best bill that the Republican Party ever passed." In the eyes of a growing number of Americans, Taft's praise of the tariff made him either a fool or a liar.

Taft's legalism soon got him into hot water in the area of conservation. He undid Roosevelt's work to preserve hydroelectric power sites when he learned that they had been improperly designated as ranger stations. And when Gifford Pinchot publicly denounced Taft's secretary of the interior as a tool of western land-grabbers, Taft fired Pinchot, touching off a storm of controversy that damaged Taft and alienated Roosevelt.

When Roosevelt returned to the United States in June 1910, he received a hero's welcome and attracted a stream of visitors and reporters seeking his advice and opinions. Hurt, Taft kept his distance. By late summer, Roosevelt had taken sides with the progressive insurgents in his party. "Taft is utterly hopeless as a leader," Roosevelt confided to his son as he set out on a speaking tour of the West. Reading the mood of the country, Roosevelt began to sound more and more like a candidate.

How did Theodore Roosevelt advance the progressive agenda?　How did progressivism evolve during Woodrow Wilson's first term?　What were the limits of progressive reform?　Conclusion: How did the liberal state transform during the Progressive Era?　☑ LearningCurve Check what you know. bedfordstmartins.com /roarkunderstanding

629

Taft's "Dollar Diplomacy"

With the Republican Party divided, the Democrats swept the congressional elections of 1910. Branding the Payne-Aldrich tariff "the mother of trusts," they captured a majority in the House of Representatives and won several key governorships. The revitalized Democratic Party could look to new leaders, among them the progressive governor of New Jersey, Woodrow Wilson.

The new Democratic majority in the House, working with progressive Republicans in the Senate, achieved a number of key reforms, including legislation to regulate mine and railroad safety, to create the Children's Bureau in the Department of Labor, and to establish an eight-hour day for federal workers. Two significant constitutional amendments — the Sixteenth Amendment, which provided for a modest graduated income tax, and the Seventeenth Amendment, which called for the direct election of senators (formerly chosen by state legislatures) — went to the states, where they would win ratification in 1913. While Congress rode the high tide of progressive reform, Taft sat on the sidelines.

In foreign policy, Taft continued Roosevelt's policy of extending U.S. influence abroad, but here, too, Taft had a difficult time following Roosevelt. Taft's "dollar diplomacy" championed commercial goals rather than the strategic aims Roosevelt had pursued. Taft naively assumed he could substitute "dollars for bullets." In the Caribbean, he provoked anti-American feeling by dispatching U.S. Marines to Nicaragua and the Dominican Republic in 1912 pursuant to the Roosevelt Corollary. In Asia, he openly avowed his intent to promote "active intervention to secure for . . . our capitalists opportunity for profitable investment." Lacking Roosevelt's understanding of power politics, Taft failed to recognize that an aggressive commercial policy could not exist without the willingness to use military might to back it up.

Taft faced the limits of dollar diplomacy when revolution broke out in Mexico in 1911. Under pressure to protect American investments, he mobilized troops along the border. In the end, however, with no popular support for a war with Mexico, he had to fall back on diplomatic pressure to salvage American interests.

Taft's greatest dream was to encourage world peace through the use of a world court and arbitration. He unsuccessfully sponsored a series of arbitration treaties that Roosevelt, who prized national honor more than international law, vehemently opposed as weak and cowardly. By 1910, Roosevelt had become a vocal critic of Taft's foreign policy.

The final breach between Taft and Roosevelt came in 1911, when Taft's attorney general filed an antitrust suit against U.S. Steel. In its brief against the corporation, the government cited Roosevelt's agreement with the Morgan interests in the 1907 acquisition of Tennessee Coal and Iron. The incident greatly embarrassed Roosevelt. Thoroughly enraged, he lambasted Taft's "archaic" antitrust policy and hinted that he might be persuaded to run for president again.

> **QUICK REVIEW**

What advances in the progressive agenda were made at the federal level between 1901 and 1913?

CHAPTER OVERVIEW | How did grassroots progressives attack the problems of industrial America? | What were the key tenets of progressive theory?

1912 Election Cartoon

In this 1912 political cartoon, an elephant—the mascot of the Republican Party (the Grand Old Party, or GOP)—and a donkey—representing the Democratic Party—react in alarm as a bull moose charges into the fray. The bull moose, with its spectacles and gleaming teeth, caricatures Theodore Roosevelt, the new Progressive Party's presidential candidate. Granger Collection.

How did progressivism evolve during Woodrow Wilson's first term?

DISILLUSIONMENT WITH TAFT resulted in a split in the Republican Party and the creation of a new Progressive Party that rallied around Theodore Roosevelt. In the election of 1912, four candidates styled themselves "progressives," but it was Democrat Woodrow Wilson who, with a minority of the popular vote, won the presidency.

Born in Virginia and raised in Georgia, Woodrow Wilson became the first southerner elected president since 1844 and only the second Democrat to occupy the White House since Reconstruction. A believer in states' rights, Wilson nevertheless promised legislation to break the hold of the trusts. This lean, ascetic scholar was, as one biographer conceded, a man whose "political convictions were never as fixed as his ambition." Building on the base built by Roosevelt in strengthening presidential power, Wilson exerted leadership to achieve banking reform and worked through his party in Congress to accomplish the Democratic agenda. Before he was finished, Wilson presided over progressivism at high tide and lent his support to many of the Progressive Party's social reforms.

> **CHRONOLOGY**

1912
– Roosevelt runs for president on Progressive Party ticket.
– Woodrow Wilson is elected president.

1913
– Federal Reserve Act.

1914
– Federal Trade Commission (FTC) is created.
– Clayton Antitrust Act.

How did Theodore Roosevelt advance the progressive agenda?

How did progressivism evolve during Woodrow Wilson's first term?

What were the limits of progressive reform?

Conclusion: How did the liberal state transform during the Progressive Era?

✓ LearningCurve
Check what you know.
bedfordstmartins.com
/roarkunderstanding

631

Progressive Insurgency and the Election of 1912

Convinced that Taft was inept, in February 1912 Roosevelt announced his candidacy for the Republican nomination. Taft, with uncharacteristic strength, refused to step aside. Roosevelt took advantage of newly passed primary election laws and ran in thirteen states, winning 278 delegates to Taft's 48. But at the Chicago convention, Taft's bosses refused to seat the Roosevelt delegates. Fistfights broke out on the convention floor as Taft won nomination on the first ballot. Crying robbery, Roosevelt's supporters bolted the party.

Seven weeks later, in the same Chicago auditorium, the hastily organized Progressive Party met to nominate Roosevelt. Full of reforming zeal, the delegates chose Roosevelt and Hiram Johnson to head the new party and approved the most ambitious platform since that of the Populists.

> ## > Progressive Party Platform

- Woman suffrage
- Presidential primaries
- Conservation of natural resources
- An end to child labor
- Workers' compensation
- A minimum wage that would include women workers
- Social security
- A federal income tax

Roosevelt arrived in Chicago to accept the nomination and announced that he felt "as fit as a bull moose," giving the new party a nickname and a mascot. But for all the excitement and the cheering, the new Progressive Party was doomed, and the candidate knew it. The people may have supported the party, but the politicians, even progressives such as La Follette, stayed within the Republican fold. "I am under no illusion about it," Roosevelt confessed to a friend. "It is a forlorn hope." But he had gone too far to turn back. The Democrats, delighted at the split in the Republican ranks, nominated Woodrow Wilson, the governor of New Jersey. After only eighteen months in office, the former professor of political science and president of Princeton University found himself running for president of the United States.

Voters in 1912 could choose among four candidates who claimed to be progressives. Taft, Roosevelt, and Wilson each embraced the label, and even the Socialist candidate, Eugene V. Debs, styled himself a progressive. That the term *progressive* could stretch to cover these diverse candidates underscored major disagreements in progressive thinking about the relationship between business and government. Taft, in spite of his trust-busting, was generally viewed as the candidate of the old guard. The real contest for the presidency was between Roosevelt and Wilson and the two political philosophies summed up in their respective campaign slogans: **"The New Nationalism"** and **"The New Freedom."**

The New Nationalism
▶ Theodore Roosevelt's 1912 campaign slogan, which reflected his commitment to federal planning and regulation. Roosevelt wanted to use the federal government to act as a "steward for the people" to regulate giant corporations.

The New Freedom
▶ Woodrow Wilson's 1912 campaign slogan, which reflected his belief in limited government and states' rights. Wilson promised to use antitrust legislation to eliminate big corporations and to improve opportunities for small businesses and farmers.

CHAPTER OVERVIEW | How did grassroots progressives attack the problems of industrial America? | What were the key tenets of progressive theory?

The New Nationalism expressed Roosevelt's belief in federal planning and regulation. He accepted the inevitability of big business but demanded that government act as "a steward of the people" to regulate the giant corporations. Wilson, schooled in the Democratic principles of limited government and states' rights, set a markedly different course with his New Freedom. Wilson promised to use antitrust legislation to get rid of big corporations and to give small businesses and farmers better opportunities in the marketplace.

The energy and enthusiasm of the Bull Moosers made the race seem closer than it was. In the end, the Republican vote split, while the Democrats remained united. No candidate claimed a majority in the race. Wilson captured a bare 42 percent of the popular vote. Roosevelt and his Bull Moose Party won 27 percent, an unprecedented tally for a new party. Taft came in third with 23 percent. The Socialist Party, led by Debs, captured 6 percent (**Map 21.3**). The Republican Party moved in a conservative direction, while the Progressive Party essentially collapsed after Roosevelt's defeat. It had always been, in the words of one astute observer, "a house divided against itself and already mortgaged."

Candidate	Electoral Vote	Popular Vote	Percent of Popular Vote
Woodrow Wilson (Democrat)	435	6,293,454	41.9
Theodore Roosevelt (Progressive)	88	4,119,538	27.4
William H. Taft (Republican)	8	3,484,980	23.2
Eugene V. Debs (Socialist)	0	900,672	6.1

MAP 21.3 ■ The Election of 1912

Wilson's Reforms: Tariff, Banking, and the Trusts

With the Democrats thoroughly in control of Congress, Wilson immediately called for tariff reform. "The object of the tariff," Wilson told Congress, "must be effective competition." The Democratic House of Representatives hastily passed the Underwood tariff, which lowered rates by 15 percent. To compensate for lost revenue, the House approved a moderate federal income tax made possible by the ratification of the Sixteenth Amendment a month earlier. In the Senate, lobbyists for industries quietly went to work to get the tariff raised, but Wilson rallied public opinion by attacking the "industrious and insidious lobby." In the harsh glare of publicity, the Senate passed the Underwood tariff.

Wilson next turned his attention to banking. During the panic of 1907, the government once again had to turn to J. P. Morgan to avoid economic catastrophe. But by the time Wilson came to office, Morgan's legendary power had come under close scrutiny. In 1913, a Senate committee investigated the "money trust," calling J. P. Morgan himself to testify. The committee uncovered an alarming concentration of banking power. J. P. Morgan and Company and its affiliates held 341 directorships in 112 corporations, controlling assets of more than $22 billion (more than $1 trillion in today's dollars). The sensational findings led to reform.

The Federal Reserve Act of 1913 marked the most significant piece of domestic legislation of Wilson's presidency.

How did Theodore Roosevelt advance the progressive agenda? | **How did progressivism evolve during Woodrow Wilson's first term?** | What were the limits of progressive reform? | Conclusion: How did the liberal state transform during the Progressive Era? | LearningCurve Check what you know. bedfordstmartins.com /roarkunderstanding

633

- Established a national banking system composed of twelve regional banks, privately controlled but regulated and supervised by the Federal Reserve Board, which was appointed by the president.
- Gave the United States its first efficient banking and currency system.
- Provided for a greater degree of government control over banking.
- Made currency more elastic and credit adequate for the needs of business and agriculture.

Wilson, flush with success, tackled the trust issue next. When Congress reconvened in January 1914, he supported the introduction and passage of the Clayton Antitrust Act to outlaw "unfair competition" — practices such as price discrimination and interlocking directorates (directors from one corporation sitting on the board of another). In the midst of the successful fight for the Clayton Act, Wilson changed course and threw his support behind the creation of the Federal Trade Commission (FTC), precisely the kind of federal regulatory agency that Roosevelt had advocated in his New Nationalism. The FTC, created in 1914, had not only wide investigatory powers but also the authority to prosecute corporations for "unfair trade practices" and to enforce its judgments by issuing "cease and desist" orders. Despite his campaign promises, Wilson's antitrust program worked to regulate rather than to break up big business.

Wilson, Reluctant Progressive

By the fall of 1914, Wilson declared that the progressive movement had fulfilled its mission and that the country needed "a time of healing." Progressives watched in dismay as Wilson repeatedly obstructed or obstinately refused to endorse further reforms. He failed to support labor's demand for an end to court injunctions against labor unions. He twice threatened to veto legislation providing farm credits for nonperishable crops. He refused to support child labor legislation or woman suffrage. Wilson used the rhetoric of the New Freedom to justify his actions, claiming that his administration would condone "special privileges to none." But, in fact, his stance often reflected the interests of his small-business constituency.

In the face of Wilson's obstinacy, reform might have ended in 1913 had not politics intruded. In the congressional elections of 1914, the Republican Party, no longer split by Roosevelt's Bull Moose faction, won substantial gains. Democratic strategists recognized that Wilson needed to pick up support in the Midwest and the West by capturing votes from former Bull Moose progressives. Wilson responded belatedly by lending his support to reform in the months leading up to the election of 1916. In a sharp about-face, he cultivated union labor, farmers, and social reformers. To please labor, he appointed progressive Louis Brandeis to the Supreme Court. To woo farmers, he threw his support behind legislation to obtain rural credits. And he won praise from labor by supporting workers' compensation

CHAPTER OVERVIEW | How did grassroots progressives attack the problems of industrial America? | What were the key tenets of progressive theory?

and the Keating-Owen child labor law (1916), which outlawed the regular employment of children younger than sixteen. When a railroad strike threatened in the months before the election, Wilson ordered Congress to establish an eight-hour day on the railroads. He had moved a long way from his New Freedom of 1912, and as Wilson noted, the Democrats had "come very near to carrying out the platform of the Progressive Party." Wilson's shift toward reform, along with his claim that he had kept the United States out of the war in Europe (as discussed in chapter 22), helped him win reelection in 1916.

QUICK REVIEW <

How did party politics change between 1912 and 1916, and what impact did this change have on progressivism?

How did Theodore Roosevelt advance the progressive agenda?

How did progressivism evolve during Woodrow Wilson's first term?

What were the limits of progressive reform?

Conclusion: How did the liberal state transform during the Progressive Era?

☑ LearningCurve
Check what you know.
bedfordstmartins.com
/roarkunderstanding

635

What were the limits of progressive reform?

Booker T. Washington and Theodore Roosevelt Dine at the White House

Theodore Roosevelt invited Booker T. Washington to the White House in 1901, stirring up a hornet's nest of controversy that continued into the election of 1904. This Republican campaign piece shows Roosevelt and a light-skinned Washington sitting under a portrait of Abraham Lincoln. Democrats' campaign buttons pictured Washington with darker skin and implied that Roosevelt had "painted the White House black" and favored "race mingling." Collection of Janice L. and David J. Frent.

WHILE PROGRESSIVISM CALLED for a more active role for the liberal state, at heart it was a movement that sought reforms designed to preserve American institutions and stem the tide of more radical change. Its basic conservatism can be seen by comparing it with the more radical movements of socialism, radical labor, and birth control — and by looking at the groups progressive reform left behind, including women, Asians, and African Americans.

Radical Alternatives

The year 1900 marked the birth of the Social Democratic Party in America, later called simply the **Socialist Party**. Like the progressives, the socialists were middle-class and native-born. They had broken with the older, more militant Socialist Labor Party precisely because of its dogmatic approach and immigrant constituency. The new group of socialists proved eager to appeal to a broad mass of disaffected Americans.

Socialist Party

▶ Political party formed in 1900 that advocated cooperation over competition and promoted the breakdown of capitalism. Its members, who were largely middle-class and native-born, saw both the Republican and the Democratic parties as hopelessly beholden to capitalism.

CHAPTER OVERVIEW | How did grassroots progressives attack the problems of industrial America? | What were the key tenets of progressive theory?

The Socialist Party chose as its presidential standard-bearer Eugene V. Debs, whose experience in the Pullman strike of 1894 (see chapter 20) convinced him that "there is no hope for the toiling masses of my countrymen, except by the pathways mapped out by Socialism." Debs would run for president five times, in every election (except 1916) from 1900 to 1920. The socialism Debs advocated preached cooperation over competition and urged men and women to liberate themselves from "the barbarism of private ownership and wage slavery." In the 1912 election, Debs indicted both old parties as "Tweedledee and Tweedledum," each dedicated to the preservation of capitalism and the continuation of the wage system. Styling the Socialist Party the "revolutionary party of the working class," he urged voters to rally to his standard. Debs's best showing came in 1912, when his 6 percent of the popular vote totaled more than 900,000 votes.

Farther to the left and more radical than the socialists stood the **Industrial Workers of the World (IWW)**, nicknamed the Wobblies. In 1905, Debs, along with Western Federation of Miners leader William Dudley "Big Bill" Haywood, created the IWW, "one big union" dedicated to organizing the most destitute segment of the workforce, the unskilled workers disdained by Samuel Gompers's AFL: western miners, migrant farmworkers, lumbermen, and immigrant textile workers. Haywood, a craggy-faced miner with one eye (he had lost the other in a childhood accident), was a charismatic leader and a proletarian intellectual. Seeing workers on the lowest rung of the social ladder as the victims of violent repression, the IWW advocated direct action, sabotage, and the general strike — tactics designed to trigger a workers' uprising and overthrow the capitalist state. The IWW never had more than 10,000 members at any one time, although possibly as many as 100,000 workers belonged to the union at one time or another in the early twentieth century. Nevertheless, the IWW's influence on the country extended far beyond its numbers (as discussed in chapter 22).

In contrast to political radicals like Debs and Haywood, Margaret Sanger promoted the **birth control movement** as a means of social change. Sanger, a nurse who had worked among the poor on New York's Lower East Side, coined the term *birth control* in 1915 and launched a movement with broad social implications. Sanger and her followers saw birth control not only as a sexual and medical reform but also as a means to alter social and political power relationships and to alleviate human misery. By having fewer babies, the working class could constrict the size of the workforce and make possible higher wages and at the same time refuse to provide "cannon fodder" for the world's armies.

The desire for family limitation was widespread, and in this sense birth control was nothing new. The birthrate in the United States had been falling consistently throughout the nineteenth century. The average number of children per family dropped from 7.0 in 1800 to 3.6 by 1900. But the open advocacy of contraception, the use of artificial means to prevent pregnancy, struck many people as both new and shocking. And it was illegal. Anthony Comstock, New York City's commissioner of vice, promoted laws in the 1870s making it a felony not only to sell contraceptive devices like condoms and cervical caps but also to publish information on how to prevent pregnancy.

When Margaret Sanger used her militant feminist paper, the *Woman Rebel,* to promote birth control, the Post Office confiscated Sanger's publication and

Industrial Workers of the World (IWW)
▶ Umbrella union and radical political group founded in 1905 that was dedicated to organizing unskilled workers to oppose capitalism. Nicknamed the Wobblies, the IWW advocated direct action by workers, including sabotage and general strikes, in hopes of triggering a widespread workers' uprising.

birth control movement
▶ Movement launched in 1915 by Margaret Sanger in New York City's Lower East Side. Birth control advocates hoped that contraception would alter social and political power relationships: By having fewer babies, the working class could constrict the size of the workforce, thus making possible higher wages, and at the same time refuse to provide soldiers for the world's armies.

How did Theodore Roosevelt advance the progressive agenda?

How did progressivism evolve during Woodrow Wilson's first term?

What were the limits of progressive reform?

Conclusion: How did the liberal state transform during the Progressive Era?

LearningCurve Check what you know. bedfordstmartins.com /roarkunderstanding

637

brought charges of obscenity against her. Facing arrest, she fled to Europe, only to return in 1916 as something of a national celebrity. In her absence, birth control had become linked with free speech and had been taken up as a liberal cause. Under public pressure, the government dropped the charges against Sanger, who undertook a nationwide tour to publicize the birth control cause.

Sanger then took direct action, opening the nation's first birth control clinic in the Brownsville section of Brooklyn in October 1916. Located in the heart of a Jewish and Italian immigrant neighborhood, the clinic attracted 464 clients. On the tenth day, police shut down the clinic and threw Sanger in jail. By then, she had become a national figure, and the cause she championed had gained legitimacy, if not legality. Sanger soon reopened her clinic. After World War I, the birth control movement would become much less radical as Sanger turned to medical doctors for support and mouthed popular racist genetic theories. But in its infancy, birth control was part of a radical vision for reforming the world that made common cause with the socialists and the IWW in challenging the limits of progressive reform.

Progressivism for White Men Only

The day before President Woodrow Wilson's inauguration in March 1913, the largest mass march to that date in the nation's history took place as more than five thousand demonstrators took to the streets in Washington to demand the vote for women. A rowdy crowd on hand to celebrate the Democrats' triumph attacked the marchers. Men spat at the suffragists and threw lighted cigarettes and matches at their clothing. "If my wife were where you are," a burly cop told one suffragist, "I'd break her head." But for all the marching, Wilson pointedly ignored woman suffrage in his inaugural address the next day.

The march served as a reminder that the political gains of progressivism were not spread equally throughout the population. As the twentieth century dawned, women still could not vote in most states, although they had won major victories in the West. Increasingly, however, woman suffrage had become an international movement.

Alice Paul, a Quaker social worker who had visited England and participated in suffrage activism there, returned to the United States in 1910 in time to plan the mass march on the eve of Wilson's inauguration and to lobby for a federal amendment to give women the vote. Paul's dramatic tactics alienated many in the National American Woman Suffrage Association. In 1916, Paul founded the militant National Woman's Party, which became the radical voice of the suffrage movement.

Women weren't the only group left out in progressive reform. Progressivism, as it was practiced in the West and South, was tainted with racism by seeking to limit the rights of Asians and African Americans. Anti-Asian bigotry in the West led to a

Woman Suffrage Parade

Women marched in a suffrage parade in Washington, D.C., in 1913. The women had to fend off angry crowds who attacked them and tried to break up the parade. Inez Milholland led the march on horseback, replicating the "white knight" on this program. Attacked by the mob, Milholland spurred her horse into the crowd shouting, "You men ought to be ashamed of yourselves." The Granger Collection, New York.

CHAPTER OVERVIEW | How did grassroots progressives attack the problems of industrial America? | What were the key tenets of progressive theory?

CHAPTER 21

638 PROGRESSIVISM FROM THE GRASS ROOTS UP

renewal of the Chinese Exclusion Act in 1902. At first, California governor Hiram Johnson stood against the strong anti-Asian prejudice of his state. But in 1913, he caved in to popular pressure and signed the Alien Land Law, which barred Japanese immigrants from purchasing land in California.

South of the Mason-Dixon line, the progressives' racism targeted African Americans. Progressives preached the disfranchisement of black voters as a "reform." During the bitter electoral fights that had pitted Populists against Democrats in the 1890s, the party of white supremacy held its power by votes purchased or coerced from African Americans. Southern progressives proposed to reform the electoral system by eliminating black voters. Beginning in 1890 with Mississippi, southern states curtailed the African American vote through devices such as poll taxes (fees required for voting) and literacy tests.

The Progressive Era also witnessed the rise of Jim Crow laws to segregate public facilities. The new railroads precipitated segregation in the South where it had rarely existed before, at least on paper. Soon, separate railcars, separate waiting rooms, separate bathrooms, and separate dining facilities for blacks sprang up across the South. In courtrooms in Mississippi, blacks were required to swear on a separate Bible.

In the face of this growing repression, Booker T. Washington, the preeminent black leader of the day, urged caution and restraint. A former slave, Washington opened the Tuskegee Institute in Alabama in 1881 to teach vocational skills to African Americans. He emphasized education and economic progress for his race and urged African Americans to put aside issues of political and social equality. In an 1895 speech in Atlanta that came to be known as the Atlanta Compromise, he stated, "In all things that are purely social we can be as separate as the fingers, yet one as the hand in all things essential to mutual progress." Washington's accommodationist policy appealed to whites and elevated "the wizard of Tuskegee" to the role of national spokesman for African Americans.

The year after Washington proclaimed the Atlanta Compromise, the Supreme Court upheld the legality of racial segregation, affirming in *Plessy v. Ferguson* (1896) the constitutionality of the doctrine of "separate but equal." Blacks could be segregated in separate schools, restrooms, and other facilities as long as the facilities were "equal" to those provided for whites. Of course, facilities for blacks rarely proved equal.

Woodrow Wilson brought to the White House southern attitudes toward race and racial segregation. He instituted segregation in the federal workforce, especially the Post Office, and approved segregated drinking fountains and restrooms in the nation's capital. When critics attacked the policy, Wilson insisted that segregation was "in the interest of the Negro."

In 1906, a major race riot in Atlanta called into question Booker T. Washington's strategy of uplift and accommodation. For three days in September, the streets of Atlanta ran red with blood as angry white mobs chased and cornered any blacks they happened upon. An estimated 250 African Americans died in the riots — members of Atlanta's black middle class along with the poor and derelict. Professor William Crogman of Clark College noted the central irony of the riot: "Here we have worked and prayed and tried to make good men and women of our colored population," he observed, "and at our very doorstep the whites kill these

Plessy v. Ferguson
▶ 1896 Supreme Court ruling that upheld the legality of racial segregation. According to the ruling, blacks could be segregated in separate schools, restrooms, and other facilities as long as the facilities were "equal" to those provided for whites.

How did Theodore Roosevelt advance the progressive agenda?

How did progressivism evolve during Woodrow Wilson's first term?

What were the limits of progressive reform?

Conclusion: How did the liberal state transform during the Progressive Era?

☑ LearningCurve
Check what you know.
bedfordstmartins.com
/roarkunderstanding

639

good men." The riot caused many African Americans to question Washington's strategy of gradualism and accommodation.

Foremost among Washington's critics stood W. E. B. Du Bois, a Harvard graduate who urged African Americans to fight for civil rights and racial justice. In *The Souls of Black Folk* (1903), Du Bois attacked the "Tuskegee Machine," comparing Washington to a political boss who used his influence to silence his critics and reward his followers. Du Bois founded the Niagara movement in 1905, calling for universal male suffrage, civil rights, and leadership composed of a black intellectual elite. The Atlanta riot only bolstered his resolve. In 1909, the Niagara movement helped found the National Association for the Advancement of Colored People (NAACP), a coalition of blacks and whites that sought legal and political rights for African Americans through the courts. In the decades that followed, the NAACP came to represent the future for African Americans, while Booker T. Washington, who died in 1915, represented the past.

> **QUICK REVIEW**

How did race, class, and gender shape the limits of progressive reform?

Conclusion: How did the liberal state transform during the Progressive Era?

PROGRESSIVISM'S GOAL WAS TO REFORM the existing system — by government intervention if necessary — but without uprooting any of the traditional American political, economic, or social institutions. As Theodore Roosevelt, the bellwether of the movement, insisted, "The only true conservative is the man who resolutely sets his face toward the future." Roosevelt was such a man, and progressivism was such a movement. But although progressivism was never radical, progressives' willingness to use the power of government to regulate business and achieve a measure of social justice redefined liberalism in the twentieth century, tying it to the expanded power of the state.

Progressivism contained many paradoxes. A diverse coalition of individuals and interests, the progressive movement began at the grass roots but left as its legacy a stronger presidency and unprecedented federal involvement in the economy and social welfare. A movement that believed in social justice, progressivism often promoted social control. And while progressives called for greater democracy, they fostered elitism with their worship of experts and efficiency, and they often failed to champion equality for women and minorities.

Whatever its inconsistencies and limitations, progressivism took action to deal with the problems posed by urban industrialism. Progressivism saw grassroots activists address social problems on the local and state levels and search for national solutions. By increasing the power of the presidency and expanding the power of the state, progressives worked to bring about greater social justice and to achieve a better balance between government and business. Jane Addams and Theodore Roosevelt could lay equal claim to the movement that redefined liberalism and launched the liberal state of the twentieth century. War on a global scale would provide progressivism with yet another challenge even before it had completed its ambitious agenda.

| How did Theodore Roosevelt advance the progressive agenda? | How did progressivism evolve during Woodrow Wilson's first term? | What were the limits of progressive reform? | **Conclusion: How did the liberal state transform during the Progressive Era?** | ✓ LearningCurve Check what you know. bedfordstmartins.com /roarkunderstanding |

641

STEP 1 — GET STARTED ONLINE

✓ **LearningCurve** ■ bedfordstmartins.com/roarkunderstanding
Now that you've read the chapter, make it stick by completing the LearningCurve activity.

STEP 2 — EXPLAIN WHY IT MATTERS

Put your reading into practice. Identify each term below, and then explain why it matters in U.S. history.

TERM	WHO OR WHAT & WHEN	WHY IT MATTERS
progressivism (p. 612)		
settlement houses (p. 613)		
social gospel (p. 614)		
reform Darwinism (p. 617)		
muckraking (p. 623)		
Roosevelt Corollary (p. 626)		
The New Nationalism (p. 632)		
The New Freedom (p. 632)		
Socialist Party (p. 636)		
Industrial Workers of the World (IWW) (p. 637)		
birth control movement (p. 637)		
Plessy v. Ferguson (p. 639)		

STEP 3 — MOVE BEYOND THE BASICS

To demonstrate a more advanced understanding, describe the actions and successes of the progressives at the local, state, and national levels between 1890 and 1916. Then, consider the limitations of the progressive movement

Decade	Key actions	Resulting reforms	Limitations/setbacks
1890s			
1900s			
1910s			

STEP 4 PUT IT ALL TOGETHER

Now, take a step back and try to explain the big picture. Remember to use specific examples from the chapter in your answers.

PROGRESSIVES AND PROGRESSIVISM

▶ How did progressivism differ from earlier reform movements?

▶ Why was grassroots activism so important to the progressive movement?

THEODORE ROOSEVELT AND PROGRESSIVISM

▶ What progressive ideals were embodied in Roosevelt's Square Deal?

▶ What were the limits of progressive reform during Roosevelt's presidency?

WOODROW WILSON AND PROGRESSIVISM

▶ How did Wilson's progressivism differ from Roosevelt's?

▶ How did Wilson's progressive agenda change during his presidency?

LOOKING BACKWARD, LOOKING AHEAD

▶ To what extent, in both the short term and the long term, did progressivism reflect the agendas of African Americans, working-class Americans, and women?

▶ What progressive ideas and policies continue to influence American social and political life today?

> ## IN YOUR OWN WORDS

Imagine that you must give an oral report to the class answering the following question: **What were the most significant changes in the United States as a result of the Progressive Era?** What would be the most important points to include and why?

 Do it online at the Student Site ▪ **bedfordstmartins.com/roarkunderstanding**

22

THE UNITED STATES AND WORLD WAR I

1914–1920

> What were the most important outcomes of World War I for the United States? Chapter 22 explores the nature and impact of U.S. involvement in World War I. It examines Woodrow Wilson's role in taking the country to war and in shaping the peace that followed. The chapter also considers the contribution of American armed forces to the Allied victory, the impact of the war on the home front, and the domestic tensions during and immediately following the war.

LearningCurve

bedfordstmartins.com/roarkunderstanding
After reading the chapter, use LearningCurve to
retain what you've read.

> What was Woodrow Wilson's foreign policy agenda?

> What role did the United States play in World War I?

> What impact did the war have on the home front?

> What part did Woodrow Wilson play at the Paris peace conference?

> Why was America's transition from war to peace so turbulent?

> Conclusion: What was the domestic cost of foreign victory?

Writing home. A Salvation Army worker writes a letter for a wounded American soldier, 1918.
National Archives.

What was Woodrow Wilson's foreign policy agenda?

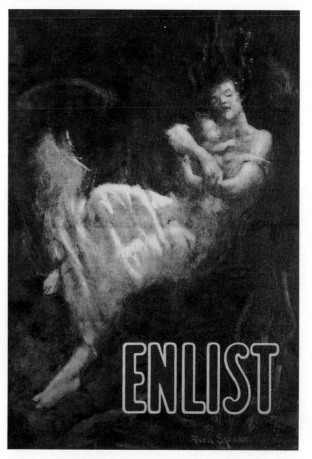

"Enlist"

This poster depicting a young mother and her baby beneath the cold waters of the Atlantic Ocean brought home the terrible cost of Germany's sinking of the British passenger liner *Lusitania* in 1915. Burned into American memory, the *Lusitania* remained a compelling reason to enlist in the armed forces after the United States entered the war in 1917.
Library of Congress.

SHORTLY AFTER WINNING election to the presidency in 1912, Woodrow Wilson confided to a friend: "It would be an irony of fate if my administration had to deal with foreign affairs." Indeed, Wilson had focused his life and career on domestic concerns, and in his campaign for the presidency hardly mentioned the world abroad.

Wilson, however, could not avoid the world and the rising tide of militarism, nationalism, and violence that beat against American shores. Economic interests compelled the nation outward. Moreover, Wilson was drawn abroad by his own progressive political principles. He believed that the United States had a moral duty to champion national self-determination, peaceful free trade, and political democracy. "We have no selfish ends to serve," he proclaimed. "We desire no conquest, no dominion. . . . We are but one of the champions of the rights of mankind." Yet as president, Wilson was as ready as any American president to apply military solutions to problems of foreign policy. This readiness led Wilson and the United States into military conflict in Mexico and then in Europe.

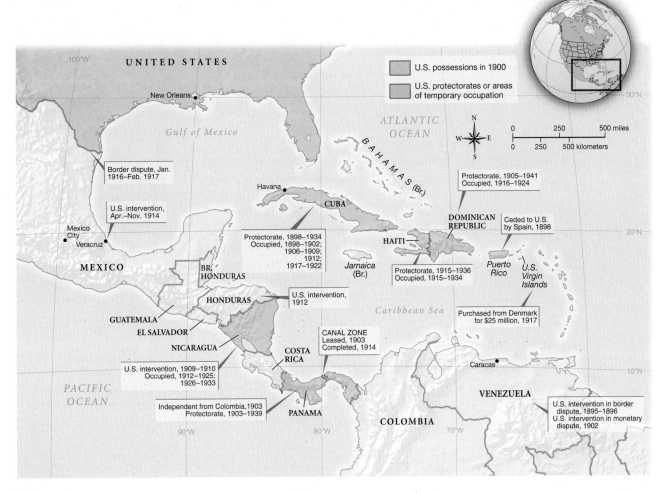

Gulf of Mexico

UNITED STATES

New Orleans

100°W

ATLANTIC
OCEAN

30°N

U.S. possessions in 1900

U.S. protectorates or areas
of temporary occupation

B A H A M A S (Br.)

Border dispute, Jan.
1916–Feb. 1917

U.S. intervention,
Apr.–Nov. 1914

Mexico
City
Veracruz

MEXICO

BR.
HONDURAS

GUATEMALA

EL SALVADOR

NICARAGUA

U.S. intervention, 1909–1910
Occupied, 1912–1925;
1926–1933

Independent from Colombia,1903
Protectorate, 1903–1939

PACIFIC
OCEAN

90°W

Havana

CUBA

Protectorate, 1898–1934
Occupied, 1898–1902;
1906–1909;
1912;
1917–1922

HONDURAS

U.S. intervention,
1912

COSTA
RICA

PANAMA

80°W

CANAL ZONE
Leased, 1903
Completed, 1914

COLOMBIA

Jamaica
(Br.)

HAITI

Protectorate, 1915–1936
Occupied, 1915–1934

Caribbean Sea

Protectorate, 1905–1941
Occupied, 1916–1924

DOMINICAN
REPUBLIC

Ceded to U.S.
by Spain, 1898

Puerto
Rico

U.S.
Virgin
Islands

Purchased from Denmark
for $25 million, 1917

Caracas

VENEZUELA

20°N

U.S. intervention in border
dispute, 1895–1896
U.S. intervention in monetary
dispute, 1902

10°N

70°W

0   250   500 miles
0   250   500 kilometers

MAP 22.1 ■ U.S. Involvement in Latin America and the Caribbean, 1895–1941

Victory against Spain in 1898 made Puerto Rico an American possession and Cuba a protectorate. The United States later gained control of the Panama Canal Zone. The nation protected its expanding economic interests with military force by propping up friendly, though not necessarily democratic, governments.

Taming the Americas

When he took office, Wilson sought to distinguish his foreign policy from that of his Republican predecessors. To Wilson, Theodore Roosevelt's "big stick" and William Howard Taft's "dollar diplomacy" appeared crude flexing of military and economic muscle. To signal a new direction, Wilson appointed William Jennings Bryan, a pacifist, as secretary of state.

But Wilson and Bryan, like Roosevelt and Taft, also believed that the Monroe Doctrine gave the United States special rights and responsibilities in the Western Hemisphere. Wilson thus authorized U.S. military intervention in Nicaragua, Haiti, and the Dominican Republic, paving the way for U.S. banks and corporations to take financial control. All the while, Wilson believed that U.S. actions were promoting order and democracy. "I am going to teach the South American Republics to elect good men!" he declared (**Map 22.1**).

Wilson's most serious involvement in Latin America came in Mexico. When General Victoriano Huerta seized power by violent means, most European nations

What impact did the war have on the home front?

What part did Woodrow Wilson play at the Paris peace conference?

Why was America's transition from war to peace so turbulent?

Conclusion: What was the domestic cost of foreign victory?

✓ LearningCurve
Check what you know.
bedfordstmartins.com
/roarkunderstanding

647

1914
- U.S. Marines occupy Veracruz, Mexico.
- Archduke Franz Ferdinand is assassinated.
- Austria-Hungary declares war on Serbia.
- Germany attacks Russia and France.
- Great Britain declares war on Germany.

1915
- German U-boat sinks the *Lusitania*.

1916
- Pancho Villa attacks Americans in Mexico and New Mexico.
- Wilson is reelected.

1917
- Zimmermann telegram is intercepted.
- United States declares war on Germany.

Triple Alliance

▶ Early-twentieth-century alliance among Germany, Austria-Hungary, and Italy, which was formed as part of a complex network of military and diplomatic agreements intended to prevent war in Europe by balancing power. In actuality, such alliances made large-scale conflict more likely.

Triple Entente

▶ Early-twentieth-century alliance among Great Britain, France, and Russia. The Triple Entente stood opposed to the Triple Alliance.

promptly recognized Mexico's new government, but Wilson refused, declaring that he would not support a "government of butchers." In April 1914, Wilson sent 800 Marines to seize the port of Veracruz to prevent the unloading of a large shipment of arms for Huerta. Huerta fled to Spain, and the United States welcomed a more compliant government.

But a rebellion erupted among desperately poor farmers who believed that the new government, aided by U.S. business interests, had betrayed the revolution's promise to help the common people. In January 1916, the rebel army, commanded by Francisco "Pancho" Villa, seized a train carrying gold to Texas from an American-owned mine in Mexico and killed the 17 American engineers aboard. In March, Villa's men crossed the border for a predawn raid on Columbus, New Mexico, where they killed 18 Americans. Wilson promptly dispatched 12,000 troops, led by Major General John J. Pershing. But Villa avoided capture, and in January 1917 Wilson recalled Pershing so that he might prepare the army for the possibility of fighting in the Great War.

U.S. Intervention In Mexico, 1916–1917

The European Crisis

Before 1914, Europe had enjoyed decades of peace, but just beneath the surface lay the potentially destructive forces of nationalism and imperialism. The consolidation of the German and Italian states into unified nations and the similar ambition of Russia to create a Pan-Slavic union initiated new rivalries throughout Europe. As the conviction spread that colonial possessions were a mark of national greatness, competition expanded onto the world stage. Most ominously, Germany's efforts under Kaiser Wilhelm II to challenge Great Britain's world supremacy by creating industrial muscle at home, an empire abroad, and a mighty navy threatened the balance of power and thus the peace.

European nations sought to avoid an explosion by developing a complex web of military and diplomatic alliances. By 1914, Germany, Austria-Hungary, and Italy (the **Triple Alliance**) stood opposed to Great Britain, France, and Russia (the **Triple Entente**, also known as "the Allies"). But in their effort to prevent war through a balance of power, Europeans had actually magnified the possibility of large-scale conflict (**Map 22.2**). Treaties, some of them secret, obligated members of the alliances to come to the aid of another member if attacked.

The fatal sequence began on June 28, 1914, in the city of Sarajevo, when a Bosnian Serb terrorist assassinated Archduke Franz Ferdinand, heir to the Austro-Hungarian throne. On July 18, Austria-Hungary declared war on Serbia. The elaborate alliance system meant that the war could not remain local. Russia announced that it would back the Serbs. Compelled by treaty to support Austria-Hungary, Germany on August 3 attacked Russia and France. In response, on

CHAPTER LOCATOR | **What was Woodrow Wilson's foreign policy agenda?** | What role did the United States play in World War I?

CHAPTER 22
648 THE UNITED STATES AND WORLD WAR I

MAP 22.2 ■ European Alliances after the Outbreak of World War I

With Germany and Austria-Hungary wedged between their Entente rivals and all parties fully armed, Europe was poised for war when Archduke Franz Ferdinand of Austria-Hungary was assassinated in Sarajevo in June 1914.

August 4, Great Britain, upholding its pact with France, declared war on Germany. Within weeks, Europe was engulfed in war. The conflict became a world war when Japan, seeing an opportunity to rid itself of European competition in China, joined the cause against Germany.

The Ordeal of American Neutrality

Woodrow Wilson promptly announced that because the war engaged no vital American interest and involved no significant principle, the United States would remain neutral. Neutrality entitled the United States to trade safely with all nations at war, he declared. Unfettered trade, Wilson believed, was not only a right under international law but also a necessity because in 1913 the U.S. economy had slipped into a recession that wartime disruption of European trade could drastically worsen.

What impact did the war have on the home front?

What part did Woodrow Wilson play at the Paris peace conference?

Why was America's transition from war to peace so turbulent?

Conclusion: What was the domestic cost of foreign victory?

✓ LearningCurve
Check what you know.
bedfordstmartins.com
/roarkunderstanding

Sinking of the *Lusitania*, 1915

German submarine blockade

Lusitania
▶ British passenger liner torpedoed by a German U-boat on May 7, 1915. The attack killed 1,198 passengers, including 128 Americans. The incident challenged American neutrality during World War I and moved the United States on a path toward entering the war.

Although Wilson proclaimed neutrality, his sympathies, like those of many Americans, lay with Great Britain and France. Americans gratefully remembered crucial French assistance in the American Revolution and shared with the British a language, a culture, and a commitment to liberty. Germany, by contrast, was a monarchy with strong militaristic traditions. Still, Wilson insisted on neutrality, in part because he feared the conflict's effects on the United States as a nation of immigrants. As he told the German ambassador, "We definitely have to be neutral, since otherwise our mixed populations would wage war on each other."

Britain's powerful fleet controlled the seas and quickly set up an economic blockade of Germany. The United States vigorously protested, but Britain refused to give up its naval advantage. The blockade actually had little economic impact on the United States. Between 1914 and the spring of 1917, while trade with Germany evaporated, war-related exports to Britain — food, clothing, steel, and munitions — escalated by some 400 percent. Although the British blockade violated American neutrality, the Wilson administration gradually acquiesced, thus beginning the fateful process of alienation from Germany.

Germany retaliated with a submarine blockade of British ports. German *Unterseebooten*, or U-boats, threatened notions of "civilized" warfare. Unlike surface warships that could harmlessly stop freighters and prevent them from entering a war zone, submarines relied on sinking their quarry. And once they sank a ship, the tiny U-boats could not pick up survivors. Nevertheless, in February 1915, Germany announced that it intended to sink on sight enemy ships en route to the British Isles. On May 7, 1915, a German U-boat torpedoed the British passenger liner *Lusitania*, killing 1,198 passengers, 128 of them U.S. citizens.

American newspapers featured drawings of drowning women and children, and some demanded war. Calmer voices pointed out that Germany had warned prospective passengers and that the *Lusitania* carried millions of rounds of ammunition and so was a legitimate target. Secretary of State Bryan resisted the hysteria and declared that a ship carrying war materiel "should not rely on passengers to protect her from attack — it would be like putting women and children in front of an army." He counseled Wilson to warn American citizens that they traveled on ships of belligerent countries at their own risk.

Wilson sought a middle course that would retain his commitment to peace and neutrality without condoning German attacks on passenger ships. On May 10, 1915, he announced that any further destruction of ships would be regarded as "deliberately unfriendly" and might lead the United States to break diplomatic relations with Germany. Wilson essentially demanded that Germany abandon unrestricted submarine warfare. Bryan resigned, predicting that the president had placed the United States on a collision course with Germany. Wilson replaced Bryan with Robert Lansing, who believed that Germany's antidemocratic character and goal of "world dominance" meant that it "must not be permitted to win this war."

After Germany apologized for the civilian deaths on the *Lusitania*, tensions subsided. And in 1916, Germany went further, promising no more submarine attacks without warning and without provisions for the safety of civilians. Wilson's supporters celebrated the success of his middle-of-the-road strategy.

Wilson's diplomacy proved helpful in his bid for reelection in 1916. In the contest against Republican Charles Evans Hughes, the Democratic Party ran Wilson under the slogan "He kept us out of war." The Democrats' case for Wilson's neutrality

CHAPTER LOCATOR | **What was Woodrow Wilson's foreign policy agenda?** | What role did the United States play in World War I?

CHAPTER 22
650 THE UNITED STATES AND WORLD WAR I

appealed to enough of those in favor of peace to eke out a majority. Wilson won, but only by the razor-thin margins of 600,000 popular and 23 electoral votes.

The United States Enters the War

Step-by-step, the United States backed away from "absolute neutrality." The consequence of protesting the German blockade of Great Britain but accepting the British blockade of Germany was that by 1916 the United States was supplying the Allies with 40 percent of their war materiel. When France and Britain ran short of money to pay for U.S. goods and asked for loans, Wilson argued that "loans by American bankers to any foreign government which is at war are inconsistent with the true spirit of neutrality." But rather than jeopardize America's wartime prosperity, Wilson allowed billions of dollars in loans that kept American goods flowing to Britain and France.

In January 1917, Germany decided that it could no longer afford to allow neutral shipping to reach Great Britain and announced that its navy would resume unrestricted submarine warfare and sink without warning any ship, enemy or neutral, found in the waters off Great Britain. Germany understood that the decision would probably bring the United States into the war but gambled that the submarines would strangle the British economy and allow German armies to win a military victory in France before American troops arrived in Europe.

Resisting demands for war, Wilson continued to hope for a negotiated peace and only broke off diplomatic relations with Germany. Then on February 25, 1917, British authorities informed Wilson of a secret telegram sent by the German foreign secretary, Arthur Zimmermann, to the German minister in Mexico. It promised that in the event of war between Germany and the United States, Germany would see that Mexico regained its "lost provinces" of Texas, New Mexico, and Arizona if Mexico would declare war against the United States. Wilson angrily responded to the Zimmermann telegram by asking Congress to approve a policy of "armed neutrality" that would allow merchant ships to fight back against any attackers.

In March, German submarines sank five American vessels off Britain, killing 66 Americans. On April 2, the president asked Congress to issue a declaration of war. He accused Germany of "warfare against all mankind" and declared that America fought to "vindicate the principles of peace and justice." He promised a world made "safe for democracy." On April 6, 1917, Congress voted to declare war.

Wilson feared what war would do at home. He said despairingly, "Once lead this people into war, and they'll forget there ever was such a thing as tolerance. To fight you must be brutal and ruthless, and the spirit of ruthless brutality will infect Congress, the courts, the policeman on the beat, the man in the street."

QUICK REVIEW <

Why did President Wilson fail to maintain U.S. neutrality during World War I?

| What impact did the war have on the home front? | What part did Woodrow Wilson play at the Paris peace conference? | Why was America's transition from war to peace so turbulent? | Conclusion: What was the domestic cost of foreign victory? | ☑ LearningCurve Check what you know. bedfordstmartins.com /roarkunderstanding |

What role did the United States play in World War I?

Life in the Trenches

One U.S. soldier in a rat-infested trench watches for danger, while others sit or lie in exhausted sleep. This trench is dry for the moment, but with the rains came mud so deep that wounded men drowned in it. Barbed wire, machine-gun nests, and mortars backed by heavy artillery protected the trenches. Trenches with millions of combatants stretched from French ports on the English Channel all the way to Switzerland. Such holes were miserable, but a decent shave with a Gillette safety razor and a friendly game of checkers offered temporary relief to doughboys (as the American soldiers were called). Inevitably, however, the whistles would blow, sending the young men rushing toward enemy lines. Photo: Imperial War Museum; shaving kit and checkers set: Collection of Colonel Stuart S. Corning Jr./ Picture Research Consultants, Inc.

> **VISUAL ACTIVITY**

READING THE IMAGE: What do these images suggest about the reality of life for American soldiers during World War I?

CONNECTIONS: How do you suppose the photograph of the trench compares with the doughboys' expectations of military service in France?

AMERICAN SOLDIERS SAILED FOR FRANCE filled with a sense of democratic mission. Some of them maintained their idealism to the end. American soldiers, many of whom had been drafted, joined the fighting just after the Russians had withdrawn from the war, leaving France as the main battleground. Although black soldiers faced discrimination, many eventually won respect under the French command. The majority of American soldiers, however, found little that was gallant in rats, lice, and poison gas and — despite the progressives' hopes — little to elevate the human soul in a landscape of utter destruction and death.

The Call to Arms

When America entered the war, Britain and France were nearly exhausted after almost three years of conflict. Millions of soldiers had perished; food and morale

CHAPTER LOCATOR | What was Woodrow Wilson's foreign policy agenda? | **What role did the United States play in World War I?**

CHAPTER 22
652 THE UNITED STATES AND WORLD WAR I

were dangerously low. Another Allied power, Russia, was in turmoil. In March 1917, a revolution had forced Czar Nicholas II to abdicate, and eight months later, in a separate peace with Germany, the **Bolshevik** revolutionary government withdrew Russia from the war. Peace with Russia allowed Germany to withdraw hundreds of thousands of its soldiers from the eastern front and to deploy them against the Allies on the western front in France.

On May 18, 1917, Wilson signed a sweeping Selective Service Act, authorizing a draft of all young men into the armed forces. Conscription transformed a tiny volunteer armed force of 80,000 men into a vast army and navy. Draft boards eventually inducted 2.8 million men into the armed services, in addition to the 2 million who volunteered.

Among the 4.8 million men under arms, 370,000 were black Americans. Although African Americans remained understandably skeptical about President Wilson's war for democracy, most followed W. E. B. Du Bois's advice to "close ranks" and to temporarily "forget our special grievances" until the nation had won the war. During training, black recruits suffered the same prejudices that they encountered in civilian life. Rigidly segregated, they faced abuse and miserable conditions, and they usually shouldered shovels rather than rifles.

Training camps sought to transform raw white recruits into fighting men. Progressives in the government were also determined that the camps turn out soldiers with the highest moral and civic values. YMCA workers and veterans of the settlement house and playground movements led recruits in games, singing, and college extension courses. The army asked soldiers to stop thinking about sex, explaining that a "man who is thinking below the belt is not efficient." Wilson's choice to command the army on the battlefields of France, Major General John "Black Jack" Pershing, was as morally upright as he was militarily uncompromising. Described by one observer as "lean, clean, keen," he gave progressives perfect confidence.

The War in France

At the front, the **American Expeditionary Force (AEF)** discovered a desperate situation. The war had degenerated into a stalemate of armies dug into hundreds of miles of trenches that stretched across France. Huddling in the mud among the corpses and rats, soldiers were separated from the enemy by only a few hundred yards of "no-man's-land." When ordered "over the top," troops raced desperately toward the enemy's trenches, only to be entangled in barbed wire, enveloped in poison gas, and mowed down by machine guns. The three-day battle of the Somme in 1916 cost the French and British forces 600,000 dead and wounded and the Germans 500,000. The deadliest battle of the war allowed the Allies to advance their trenches only a few meaningless miles.

Still, U.S. troops saw almost no combat in 1917. The major exception was the 92nd Division of black troops. When Pershing received an urgent call for troops from the French, he sent the 92nd to the front to be integrated with the French army because he did not want to lose command over the white troops he valued more. In the 191 days they spent in battle — longer than any other American outfit — the 369th Regiment of the 92nd Division won more medals than any other American combat unit. Black soldiers recognized the irony of having to serve with the French to gain respect.

> CHRONOLOGY

1917
– Selective Service Act.

1918
– Russia arranges separate peace with Germany.

1918
– U.S. Marines see first major combat.
– Armistice ending World War I is signed.

Bolshevik
▶ Russian revolutionary. Bolsheviks forced Czar Nicholas II to abdicate and seized power in Russia in 1917. In a separate peace with Germany, the Bolshevik government withdrew Russia from World War I.

American Expeditionary Force (AEF)
▶ U.S. armed forces under the command of General John Pershing who fought under a separate American command in Europe during World War I. They helped defeat Germany when they entered the conflict in full force in 1918.

What impact did the war have on the home front?

What part did Woodrow Wilson play at the Paris peace conference?

Why was America's transition from war to peace so turbulent?

Conclusion: What was the domestic cost of foreign victory?

✓ LearningCurve
Check what you know.
bedfordstmartins.com/roarkunderstanding

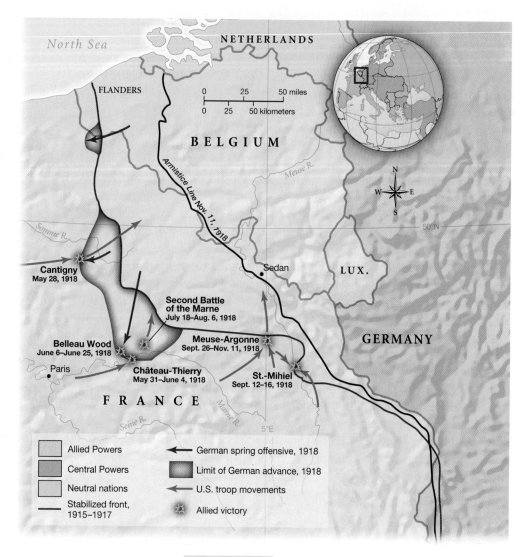

MAP 22.3 ■ The American Expeditionary Force, 1918

In the last year of the war, the AEF joined the French army on the western front to respond to the final German offensive and pursue the retreating enemy until surrender.

> MAP ACTIVITY

READING THE MAP: Across which rivers did the Germans advance in 1918? Where did the armistice line of November 11, 1918, lie in relation to the stabilized front of 1915–1917? Through which countries did the armistice line run?

CONNECTIONS: What events paved the way for the AEF to join the combat effort in 1918? What characteristic(s) differentiated American troops from other Allied forces and helped them achieve victory?

White troops continued to train and sightsee until March 1918, when a million German soldiers punched a hole in the Allied lines. Pershing finally committed the AEF to combat. In May and June, at Cantigny and then at Château-Thierry, the eager but green Americans checked the German advance with a series of assaults (**Map 22.3**). Then they headed toward the forest stronghold of Belleau Wood, moving against streams of retreating Allied soldiers who cried defeat: "La guerre est finie!" (The war is over!). A French officer commanded the Americans to retreat

CHAPTER LOCATOR | What was Woodrow Wilson's foreign policy agenda? | **What role did the United States play in World War I?**

with them, but the American commander replied sharply, "Retreat, hell. We just got here." After charging through a wheat field against withering machine-gun fire, the Marines plunged into hand-to-hand combat. Victory came hard, but a German report praised the enemy's spirit, noting that "the Americans' nerves are not yet worn out." Indeed, it was German morale that was on the verge of cracking.

In the summer of 1918, the Allies launched a massive counteroffensive that would end the war. A quarter of a million U.S. troops joined in the rout of German forces along the Marne River. In September, more than a million Americans took part in the assault that threw the Germans back from positions along the Meuse River. In November, a revolt against the German government sent Kaiser Wilhelm II fleeing to Holland. On November 11, 1918, a delegation from the newly established German republic met with the French high command to sign an armistice that brought the fighting to an end.

The adventure of the AEF was brief, bloody, and victorious. When Germany had resumed unrestricted U-boat warfare in 1917, it had been gambling that it could defeat Britain and France before the Americans could raise and train an army and ship it to France. The German military had miscalculated badly. By the end, 112,000 AEF soldiers perished from wounds and disease, while another 230,000 Americans suffered injuries but survived. European nations, however, suffered much greater losses: 2.2 million Germans, 1.9 million Russians, 1.4 million French, and 900,000 Britons had been killed. Where they had fought, the landscape was as blasted and barren as the moon.

QUICK REVIEW <

How did the American Expeditionary Force contribute to the defeat of Germany?

What impact did the war have on the home front?

What part did Woodrow Wilson play at the Paris peace conference?

Why was America's transition from war to peace so turbulent?

Conclusion: What was the domestic cost of foreign victory?

☑️ LearningCurve
Check what you know.
bedfordstmartins.com
/roarkunderstanding

What impact did the war have on the home front?

Picketing the White House for the Vote

Mrs. William L. Colt pickets the White House to demand women's right to vote. Because of such direct pressure and in recognition of women's service to the defense industry at home and as nurses and Red Cross workers in France, Woodrow Wilson finally pledged support for the suffrage amendment. © Bettmann/Corbis.

MANY PROGRESSIVES HOPED that the war would improve the quality of American life as well as free Europe from tyranny and militarism. Mobilization helped propel the crusades for woman suffrage and prohibition to success. Progressives enthusiastically channeled industrial and agricultural production into the vast war effort. Labor shortages caused by workers entering the military provided new opportunities for women in the booming wartime economy. With labor at a premium, unionized workers gained higher pay and shorter hours. To instill loyalty in Americans whose ancestry was rooted in the belligerent nations, President Wilson launched a campaign to foster patriotism. But fanning patriotism led to suppressing dissent. When the government launched a harsh assault on civil liberties, mobs gained license to attack those whom they considered disloyal. As Wilson feared, democracy took a beating at home when the nation undertook its crusade for democracy abroad.

The Progressive Stake in the War

Progressives embraced the idea that the war could be an agent of national improvement. The Wilson administration, realizing that the federal government would have to assert greater control to mobilize the nation's human and physical resources, created new agencies to manage the war effort. Bernard Baruch

CHAPTER LOCATOR | What was Woodrow Wilson's foreign policy agenda? | What role did the United States play in World War I?

656 CHAPTER 22
THE UNITED STATES AND WORLD WAR I

headed the War Industries Board, charged with stimulating and directing industrial production. Baruch brought industrial management and labor together into a team that produced everything from boots to bullets and made U.S. troops the best-equipped soldiers in the world.

Herbert Hoover headed the Food Administration. He led remarkably successful "Hooverizing" campaigns for "meatless" Mondays and "wheatless" Wednesdays and other ways of conserving resources. With farmers guaranteed high prices, the American heartland not only supplied the needs of U.S. citizens and armed forces but also became the breadbasket of America's allies. As the war went on, wartime agencies multiplied.

> Wartime Agencies

Railroad Administration	Directed railroad traffic
Fuel Administration	Coordinated the coal industry and other fuel suppliers
Shipping Board	Organized the merchant marine
National War Labor Policies Board	Resolved labor disputes

Industrial leaders found that wartime agencies enforced efficiency, which helped corporate profits triple. Some working people also had cause to celebrate. Mobilization meant high prices for farmers and plentiful jobs at high wages in the new war industries (**Figure 22.1**). Because increased industrial production required

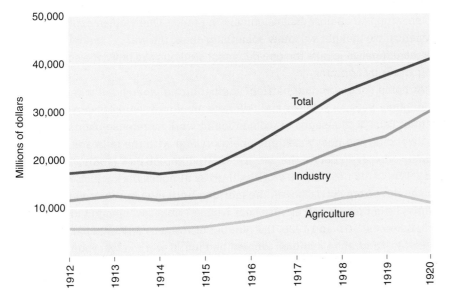

Agriculture: cash receipts.
Industry: includes mining, electric power, manufacturing, construction, and communications.

FIGURE 22.1 ■ Industrial Wages, 1912–1920

With help from unions and progressive reformers, wageworkers gradually improved their economic condition. The entry of millions of young men into the armed forces during World War I caused labor shortages and led to a rapid surge in industrial wages.

> CHRONOLOGY

1916
– Republican and Progressive parties endorse woman suffrage.

1917
– Committee on Public Information is created.
– Espionage Act and Trading with the Enemy Act.

1918
– President Wilson endorses woman suffrage.
– Sedition Act.
– Republicans win a majority in both houses of Congress.

1920
– Prohibition begins.
– American women get the vote.

| **What impact did the war have on the home front?** | What part did Woodrow Wilson play at the Paris peace conference? | Why was America's transition from war to peace so turbulent? | Conclusion: What was the domestic cost of foreign victory? | ✔ LearningCurve Check what you know. bedfordstmartins.com /roarkunderstanding |

657

peaceful labor relations, the National War Labor Policies Board enacted the eight-hour day, a living minimum wage, and collective bargaining rights in some industries. The American Federation of Labor (AFL) saw its membership soar from 2.7 million to more than 5 million.

The war also provided a huge boost to the crusade to ban alcohol. By 1917, prohibitionists had convinced nineteen states to go dry. Liquor's opponents now argued that banning alcohol would make the cause of democracy powerful and pure. At the same time, shutting down the distilleries would save millions of bushels of grain that could feed the United States and its allies. "Shall the many have food or the few drink?" the drys asked. In December 1917, Congress passed the **Eighteenth Amendment**, which banned the manufacture, transportation, and sale of alcohol. After swift ratification by the states, the prohibition amendment went into effect on January 1, 1920.

Eighteenth Amendment (prohibition)

▶ Constitutional amendment banning the manufacture, transportation, and sale of alcohol. Congress passed the amendment in December 1917, and it was ratified in January 1920. World War I provided a huge boost to the crusade to ban alcohol.

Women, War, and the Battle for Suffrage

Women had made real strides during the Progressive Era, and war presented new opportunities. More than 25,000 women served in France. About half were nurses. The others drove ambulances; ran canteens for the Salvation Army, Red Cross, and YMCA; worked with French civilians in devastated areas; and acted as telephone operators and war correspondents. Like men who joined the war effort, they believed that they were taking part in a great national venture. "I am more than willing to live as a soldier and know of the hardships I would have to undergo," one canteen worker declared when applying to go overseas, "but I want to help my country. . . . I want . . . to do the *real* work." And like men, women struggled against disillusionment in France. One woman explained: "Over in America, we thought we knew something about the war . . . but when you get here the difference is [like the one between] studying the laws of electricity and being struck by lightning."

At home, long-standing barriers against hiring women fell when millions of workingmen became soldiers and few new immigrant workers crossed the Atlantic. Tens of thousands of women found work in defense plants as welders, metalworkers, and heavy machine operators and with the railroads. A black woman, a domestic before the war, celebrated her job as a laborer in a railroad yard: "We . . . do not have to work as hard as at housework which requires us to be on duty from six o'clock in the morning until nine or ten at night, with might[y] little time off and at very poor wages." Other women found white-collar work. Between 1910 and 1920, the number of women clerks doubled. Before the war ended, more than a million women had found work in war industries.

The most dramatic advance for women came in the political arena. Adopting a state-by-state approach before the war, suffragists had achieved some success (**Map 22.4**). More commonly, voting rights for women met strong hostility and defeat. After 1910, suffrage leaders added a federal campaign to amend the Constitution to the traditional state-by-state strategy for suffrage.

The radical wing of the suffragists, led by Alice Paul, picketed the White House, where the marchers unfurled banners that proclaimed "America Is Not a Democracy. Twenty Million Women Are Denied the Right to Vote." They

CHAPTER LOCATOR | What was Woodrow Wilson's foreign policy agenda? | What role did the United States play in World War I?

CHAPTER 22
658 THE UNITED STATES AND WORLD WAR I

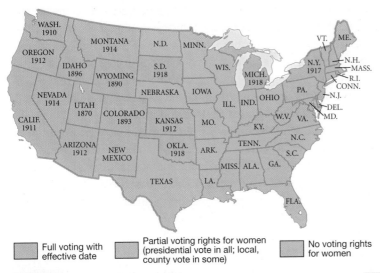

Full voting with effective date

Partial voting rights for women (presidential vote in all; local, county vote in some)

No voting rights for women

MAP 22.4 ■ Women's Voting Rights before the Nineteenth Amendment

The long campaign for women's voting rights reversed the pioneer epic that moved from east to west. From its first successes in the new democratic West, suffrage rolled eastward toward the entrenched, male-dominated public life of the Northeast and South.

> MAP ACTIVITY

READING THE MAP: What was the first state to grant woman suffrage? How many states extended full voting rights to women before 1914? How many extended these rights during World War I (1914–1918)?

CONNECTIONS: Suffragists redirected their focus during the war. What strategies did they use then?

chained themselves to fences and went to jail, where many engaged in hunger strikes. But membership in the mainstream organization, the National American Woman Suffrage Association, led by Carrie Chapman Catt, soared to some two million. Seeing the handwriting on the wall, the Republican and Progressive parties endorsed woman suffrage in 1916.

In 1918, Wilson gave his support to suffrage, calling the amendment "vital to the winning of the war." He conceded that it would be wrong not to reward the wartime "partnership of suffering and sacrifice" with a "partnership of privilege and right." By linking their cause to the wartime emphasis on national unity, the advocates of woman suffrage finally triumphed. In 1919, Congress passed the **Nineteenth Amendment (woman suffrage)**, granting women the vote, and by August 1920 the required two-thirds of the states had ratified it.

Rally around the Flag — or Else

When Congress committed the nation to war, only a handful of peace advocates resisted the tide of patriotism. A group of professional women, led by settlement house leader Jane Addams and economics professor Emily Greene Balch, denounced what Addams described as "the pathetic belief in the regenerative results of war." After America entered the conflict, advocates for peace were labeled cowards and traitors.

Nineteenth Amendment (woman suffrage)

► Constitutional amendment granting women the vote. Congress passed the amendment in 1919, and it was ratified in August 1920. Like proponents of prohibition, the advocates of woman suffrage triumphed by linking their cause to the war.

What impact did the war have on the home front?	What part did Woodrow Wilson play at the Paris peace conference?	Why was America's transition from war to peace so turbulent?	Conclusion: What was the domestic cost of foreign victory?	✓ LearningCurve Check what you know. bedfordstmartins.com /roarkunderstanding

659

To suppress criticism of the war, Wilson stirred up patriotic fervor. In 1917, the president created the Committee on Public Information under the direction of George Creel. Creel sent "Four-Minute Men," a squad of 75,000 volunteers, around the country to give brief pep talks that celebrated successes on the battle-fields and in the factories. Posters, pamphlets, and cartoons depicted brave American soldiers and sailors defending freedom and democracy against the evil "Huns," the derogatory nickname applied to German soldiers.

America rallied around Creel's campaign. The film industry cranked out pro-war melodramas and taught audiences to hiss at the German kaiser. Colleges and universities generated war propaganda in the guise of scholar-ship. When Professor James McKeen Cattell of Columbia University urged that America seek peace with Germany short of victory, university president Nicholas Murray Butler fired him on the grounds that "what had been folly is now treason."

A firestorm of anti-German passion erupted. Across the nation, "100% American" campaigns enlisted ordinary people to sniff out disloyalty. German, the most widely taught foreign language in 1914, practically disappeared from the nation's schools. Targeting German-born Americans, the *Saturday Evening Post* declared that it was time to rid the country of "the scum of the melting pot." Anti-German action reached its extreme with the lynching of Robert Prager, a German-born baker with socialist leanings. Persuaded by the defense lawyer who praised what he called a "patriotic murder," the jury at the trial of the killers took only twenty-five minutes to acquit.

D. W. Griffith's *Hearts of the World*

Hollywood joined the government's efforts to stir up rage against the Germans. In a 1918 film made by D. W. Griffith for the British and French governments, a hulking German is about to whip a defenseless farm woman. Library of Congress.

CHAPTER LOCATOR | What was Woodrow Wilson's foreign policy agenda? | What role did the United States play in World War I?

As hysteria increased, the campaign reached absurd levels. Menus across the nation changed German toast to French toast and sauerkraut to liberty cabbage. In Milwaukee, vigilantes mounted a machine gun outside the Pabst Theater to prevent the staging of Schiller's *Wilhelm Tell*, a powerful protest against tyranny. The fiancée of one of the war's leading critics, caught dancing on the dunes of Cape Cod, was held on suspicion of signaling to German submarines.

The Wilson administration's zeal in suppressing dissent contrasted sharply with its war aims of defending democracy. In the name of self-defense, the Espionage Act (June 1917), the Trading with the Enemy Act (October 1917), and the Sedition Act (May 1918) gave the government sweeping powers to punish any opinion or activity it considered "disloyal, profane, scurrilous, or abusive." When Postmaster General Albert Burleson blocked mailing privileges for dissenting publications, dozens of journals were forced to close down. Of the 1,500 individuals eventually charged with sedition, all but a dozen had merely spoken words the government found objectionable. One of them was Eugene V. Debs, the leader of the Socialist Party, who was convicted under the Espionage Act for speeches condemning the war as a capitalist plot and sent to the Atlanta penitentiary.

The president hoped that national commitment to the war would silence partisan politics, but his Republican rivals used the war as a weapon against the Democrats. The trick was to oppose Wilson's conduct of the war but not the war itself. Republicans outshouted Wilson on the nation's need to mobilize for war but then complained that Wilson's War Industries Board was a tyrannical agency that crushed free enterprise. As the war progressed, Republicans gathered power against the Democrats, who had narrowly reelected Wilson in 1916.

In 1918, Republicans gained a narrow majority in both the House and the Senate. The end of Democratic control of Congress not only halted further domestic reform but also meant that the United States would advance toward military victory in Europe with political power divided between a Democratic president and a Republican Congress likely to challenge Wilson's plans for international cooperation.

QUICK REVIEW <

How did progressive ideals fare during wartime?

What impact did the war have on the home front?	What part did Woodrow Wilson play at the Paris peace conference?	Why was America's transition from war to peace so turbulent?	Conclusion: What was the domestic cost of foreign victory?	☑ LearningCurve Check what you know. bedfordstmartins.com /roarkunderstanding

661

What part did Woodrow Wilson play at the Paris peace conference?

Leaders of the Paris Peace Conference

The three leaders in charge of putting the world back together after the Great War — from left to right, British prime minister David Lloyd George, French premier Georges Clemenceau, and U.S. president Woodrow Wilson — stride toward the peace conference at the Versailles palace. Clemenceau is caught offering animated instruction to Wilson, whom he considered naively idealistic. Gamma Liaison/Getty Images.

Fourteen Points

▶ Woodrow Wilson's plan, proposed in 1918, to create a new democratic world order with lasting peace. Wilson's plan affirmed basic liberal ideals, supported the right to self-determination, and called for the creation of a League of Nations. Wilson compromised on his plan at the 1919 Paris peace conference, and the U.S. Senate refused to ratify the resulting treaty.

League of Nations

▶ International organization proposed in Woodrow Wilson's Fourteen Points designed to secure political independence and territorial integrity for all states and thus ensure enduring peace. The U.S. Senate refused to ratify the Treaty of Versailles, and the United States never became a member.

WILSON DECIDED TO REAFFIRM his noble war ideals by announcing his peace aims before the end of hostilities. He hoped the victorious Allies would adopt his plan for international democracy, but he was sorely disappointed. America's allies understood that Wilson's principles jeopardized their own postwar plans for the acquisition of enemy territory, new colonial empires, and reparations. Wilson also faced strong opposition at home from those who feared that his enthusiasm for international cooperation would undermine American sovereignty.

Wilson's Fourteen Points

On January 8, 1918, President Wilson revealed to Congress his **Fourteen Points**, his blueprint for a new democratic world order. The first five points affirmed basic liberal ideals: an end to secret treaties; freedom of the seas; removal of economic barriers to free trade; reduction of weapons of war; and recognition of the rights of colonized peoples. The next eight points supported the right to self-determination of European peoples who had been dominated by Germany or its allies. Wilson's fourteenth point called for a "general association of nations" — a **League of Nations**—to provide "mutual guarantees of political independence and territorial integrity to great and small states alike." A League of Nations reflected Wilson's

CHAPTER LOCATOR | What was Woodrow Wilson's foreign policy agenda? | What role did the United States play in World War I?

lifelong dream of a "parliament of man." Only such an organization of "peace-loving nations," he believed, could justify the war and secure a lasting peace.

The Paris Peace Conference

From January 18 to June 28, 1919, the eyes of the world focused on Paris. Wilson, inspired by his mission, decided to head the U.S. delegation. He said he owed it to the American soldiers. "It is now my duty," he announced, "to play my full part in making good what they gave their life's blood to obtain." A dubious British diplomat retorted that Wilson was drawn to Paris "as a debutante is entranced by the prospect of her first ball." The decision to leave the country at a time when his political opponents challenged his leadership was risky enough, but his stubborn refusal to include prominent Republicans in the delegation proved foolhardy and eventually cost him his dream of a new world order.

> Allied Leaders at the Paris Peace Conference	
United States	Woodrow Wilson
Great Britain	David Lloyd George
France	Georges Clemenceau
Italy	Vittorio Orlando

After four terrible years of war, the common people of Europe almost worshipped Wilson, believing that he would create a safer, more decent world. When the peace conference convened at Louis XIV's magnificent palace at Versailles, however, Wilson encountered a different reception. To the Allied leaders, Wilson appeared a naive and impractical moralist. His desire to gather former enemies within a new international democratic order showed how little he understood hard European realities. Georges Clemenceau, premier of France, claimed that Wilson "believed you could do everything by formulas" and "empty theory." Disparaging the Fourteen Points, he added, "God himself was content with ten commandments."

The Allies wanted to fasten blame for the war on Germany, totally disarm it, and make it pay so dearly that it would never threaten its neighbors again. The French demanded retribution in the form of territory containing Germany's richest mineral resources. The British made it clear that they were not about to give up the powerful weapon of naval blockade for the vague principle of freedom of the seas.

The Allies forced Wilson to make drastic compromises. In return for France's moderating its territorial claims, he agreed to support Article 231 of the peace treaty, assigning war guilt to Germany. Though saved from permanently losing Rhineland territory to the French, Germany was outraged at being singled out as the instigator of the war and being saddled with more than $33 billion in damages. Many Germans felt that their nation had been betrayed. After agreeing to an armistice in the belief that peace terms would be based in Wilson's generous Fourteen Points, they faced hardship and humiliation instead.

Wilson had better success in establishing the principle of self-determination. But from the beginning, Secretary of State Robert Lansing knew that the president's concept of self-determination was "simply loaded with dynamite." Lansing

> CHRONOLOGY

1918
– Wilson gives Fourteen Points speech.

1919
– Paris peace conference begins.
– Treaty of Versailles is signed.

1920
– Senate votes against ratification of Treaty of Versailles.

What impact did the war have on the home front?

What part did Woodrow Wilson play at the Paris peace conference?

Why was America's transition from war to peace so turbulent?

Conclusion: What was the domestic cost of foreign victory?

✓ LearningCurve
Check what you know.
bedfordstmartins.com /roarkunderstanding

663

wondered, "What unit has he in mind? Does he mean a race, a territorial area, or a community?" Even Wilson was vague about what self-determination actually meant. "When I gave utterance to those words," he admitted, "I said them without the knowledge that nationalities existed, which are coming to us day after day." Lansing suspected that the notion "will raise hopes which can never be realized. It will, I fear, cost thousands of lives. In the end it is bound to be discredited, to be called the dream of an idealist who failed to realize the danger until it was too late."

Yet partly on the basis of self-determination, the conference redrew the map of Europe and parts of the rest of the world. Portions of Austria-Hungary were ceded to Italy, Poland, and Romania, and the remainder was reassembled into Austria, Hungary, Czechoslovakia, and Yugoslavia — independent republics whose boundaries were drawn with attention to concentrations of major ethnic groups. More arbitrarily, the Ottoman empire was carved up into small mandates (including Palestine) run by local leaders but under the control of France and Great Britain. The conference reserved the mandate system for those regions it deemed insufficiently "civilized" to have full independence. Thus, the reconstructed nations — each beset with ethnic and nationalist rivalries — faced the challenge of making a new democratic government work (**Map 22.5**). Many of today's bitterest disputes — in the Balkans and Iraq, between Greece and Turkey, between Arabs and Jews — have roots in the decisions made in Paris in 1919.

MAP 22.5 ■ Europe after World War I

The post–World War I settlement redrew boundaries to create new nations based on ethnic groupings. Within defeated Germany and Russia, this outcome left bitter peoples who resolved to recover the territory taken from them.

CHAPTER LOCATOR | What was Woodrow Wilson's foreign policy agenda? | What role did the United States play in World War I?

664   CHAPTER 22
THE UNITED STATES AND WORLD WAR I

Wilson hoped that self-determination would also dictate the fate of Germany's colonies in Asia and Africa. But the Allied nations, which had taken over the colonies during the war, allowed the League of Nations only a mandate to administer them. Technically, the mandate system rejected imperialism, but in reality it allowed the Allies to maintain control. Thus, while denying Germany its colonies, the Allies retained and added to their own empires.

The cause of democratic equality suffered another setback when the peace conference rejected Japan's call for a statement of racial equality in the treaty. Wilson's belief in the superiority of whites, as well as his apprehension about how white Americans would respond to such a declaration, led him to oppose the clause. To soothe hurt feelings, Wilson agreed to grant Japan a mandate over the Shantung Peninsula in northern China, which had formerly been controlled by Germany. The gesture mollified Japan's moderate leaders, but the military faction preparing to take over the country used bitterness toward racist Western colonialism to build support for expanding Japanese power throughout Asia.

Closest to Wilson's heart was finding a new way to manage international relations. In Wilson's view, war had discredited the old strategy of balance of power. Instead, he proposed a League of Nations that would provide collective security. The league would establish rules of international conduct and resolve conflicts between nations through rational and peaceful means. When the Allies agreed to the league, Wilson was overjoyed. He believed that the league would rectify the errors his colleagues had forced on him in Paris.

To some Europeans and Americans, the **Versailles treaty** came as a bitter disappointment. Wilson's admirers were shocked that the president dealt in compromise like any other politician. But without Wilson's presence, the treaty that was signed on June 28, 1919, surely would have been more vindictive. Wilson returned home in July 1919 consoled that, despite his frustrations, he had gained what he most wanted — a League of Nations. In Wilson's judgment, "We have completed in the least time possible the greatest work that four men have ever done."

The Fight for the Treaty

The tumultuous reception Wilson received when he arrived home persuaded him, probably correctly, that the American people supported the treaty. When the president submitted the treaty to the Senate in July 1919, he warned that failure to ratify it would "break the heart of the world." By then, however, criticism of the treaty was mounting, especially from Americans convinced that their countries of ethnic origin — Ireland, Italy, and Germany — had not been given fair treatment. Others worried that the president's concessions at Versailles had jeopardized the treaty's capacity to provide a workable plan for rebuilding Europe and to guarantee world peace.

In the Senate, Republican "irreconcilables" condemned the treaty for entangling the United States in world affairs. A larger group of Republicans did not object to American participation in world politics but feared that membership in the League of Nations would jeopardize the nation's ability to act independently. No Republican, in any case, was eager to hand Wilson and the Democrats a foreign policy victory with the 1920 presidential election little more than a year away.

At the center of Republican opposition was Wilson's archenemy, Senator Henry Cabot Lodge of Massachusetts. Lodge was no isolationist, but he thought

Versailles treaty

▶ Treaty signed on June 28, 1919, that ended World War I. The agreement redrew the map of the world and assigned Germany sole responsibility for the war and saddled it with a debt of $33 billion in war damages. Many Germans felt betrayed by the treaty.

What impact did the war have on the home front?

What part did Woodrow Wilson play at the Paris peace conference?

Why was America's transition from war to peace so turbulent?

Conclusion: What was the domestic cost of foreign victory?

☑ LearningCurve
Check what you know.
bedfordstmartins.com
/roarkunderstanding

665

"Refusing to Give the Lady a Seat"

When stiff opposition to American membership in the League of Nations developed in the United States, friends of the league mounted a counterattack. This cartoon skewers the three leading Republican opponents of the league — Senators William Borah of Idaho, Henry Cabot Lodge of Massachusetts, and Hiram Johnson of California — who stubbornly refuse to budge an inch for the angel of peace. Picture Research Consultants & Archives.

that much of the Fourteen Points was a "general bleat about virtue being better than vice." Lodge expected the United States' economic and military power to propel the nation into a major role in world affairs. But he insisted that membership in the League of Nations, which would require collective action to maintain peace, threatened the nation's independence in foreign relations.

With Lodge as its chairman, the Senate Foreign Relations Committee produced several amendments, or "reservations," that sought to limit the consequences of American membership in the league. For example, several reservations required approval of both the House and the Senate before the United States could participate in league-sponsored economic sanctions or military action.

It gradually became clear that ratification of the treaty depended on acceptance of the Lodge reservations. Democratic senators, who overwhelmingly supported the treaty, urged Wilson to accept Lodge's terms, arguing that they left the essentials of the treaty intact. Wilson, however, insisted that the reservations cut "the very heart out of the treaty."

Wilson decided to take his case directly to the people. On September 3, 1919, still exhausted from the peace conference, he set out by train on the most ambitious speaking tour ever undertaken by a president. On September 25 in Pueblo, Colorado, Wilson collapsed and had to return to Washington. There, he suffered a massive stroke that partially paralyzed him. From his bedroom, Wilson sent messages instructing Democrats in the Senate to hold firm against any and all reservations. Wilson commanded enough loyalty to ensure a vote against the Lodge reservations. But when the treaty without reservations came before the Senate in March 1920, the combined opposition of the Republican irreconcilables and reservationists left Wilson six votes short of the two-thirds majority needed for passage.

The nations of Europe organized the League of Nations at Geneva, Switzerland. Although Woodrow Wilson received the Nobel Peace Prize in 1920 for his central role in creating the league, the United States never became a member. Whether American membership could have prevented the world war that would begin in Europe in 1939 is highly unlikely, but the United States' failure to join certainly weakened the league from the start. In refusing to accept relatively minor compromises with Senate moderates, Wilson lost his treaty and American membership in the league.

> **QUICK REVIEW**

Why did the Senate fail to ratify the Versailles treaty?

CHAPTER LOCATOR | What was Woodrow Wilson's foreign policy agenda? | What role did the United States play in World War I?

CHAPTER 22
666 THE UNITED STATES AND WORLD WAR I

Why was America's transition from war to peace so turbulent?

African Americans Migrate North

Wearing their Sunday best and carrying the rest of what they owned in two suitcases, this southern family waits to board a northern-bound train in 1912. In Chicago, the League on Urban Conditions among Negroes, which became the Urban League, sought to ease the transition of southern blacks to life in the North. Photographs and Prints Division, Schomburg Center for Research in Black Culture, New York Public Library, Astor, Lenox, and Tilden Foundations.

THE DEFEAT OF WILSON'S plan for international democracy proved the crowning blow to progressives who had hoped that the war could boost reform at home. When the war ended, Americans wanted to demobilize swiftly. In the process, servicemen, defense workers, and farmers lost their war-related jobs. The volatile combination — of unemployed veterans returning home, a stalled economy, and leftover wartime patriotism looking for a new cause — threatened to explode. Wartime anti-German passion was quickly succeeded by the Red scare, an anti-radical campaign broad enough to ensnare unionists, socialists, dissenters, and African Americans and Mexicans who had committed no offense but to seek to escape rural poverty as they moved north.

Economic Hardship and Labor Upheaval

Americans demanded that the nation return to a peacetime economy. The government abruptly abandoned its wartime economic controls and canceled war contracts. In a matter of months, 3 million soldiers mustered out of the military and flooded the job market just as war production ceased.

| What impact did the war have on the home front? | What part did Woodrow Wilson play at the Paris peace conference? | **Why was America's transition from war to peace so turbulent?** | Conclusion: What was the domestic cost of foreign victory? | ☑ LearningCurve Check what you know. bedfordstmartins.com /roarkunderstanding |

667

> CHRONOLOGY

1915–1920
- Great migration of half a million blacks out of the South.

1918
- Global influenza epidemic starts.

1919
- Wave of labor strikes.
- Red scare.
- U.S. Supreme Court limits free speech in *Schenck v. United States*.

1920
- American Civil Liberties Union is founded.
- Palmer raids.
- Warren G. Harding is elected president.

Unemployment soared. At the same time, consumers went on a postwar spending spree that drove inflation skyward. In 1919 alone, prices rose 75 percent over prewar levels.

Most of the gains workers had made during the war evaporated. Business turned against the eight-hour day and attacked labor unions. With inflation eating up their paychecks, workers fought back. The year 1919 witnessed nearly 3,600 strikes involving 4 million workers. The most spectacular strike occurred in February 1919 in Seattle, where shipyard workers had been put out of work by demobilization. When a coalition of the radical Industrial Workers of the World (IWW, known as Wobblies) and the moderate American Federation of Labor called a general strike, the largest work stoppage in American history shut down the city. Newspapers claimed that the walkout was "a Bolshevik effort to start a revolution." The suppression of the Seattle general strike by city officials cost the AFL many of its wartime gains and contributed to the destruction of the IWW soon afterward.

A strike by Boston policemen in the fall of 1919 underscored postwar hostility toward labor militancy. Although the police were paid less than pick-and-shovel laborers, they won little sympathy. Once the officers stopped walking their beats, looters sacked the city. Massachusetts governor Calvin Coolidge called in the National Guard to restore order. The public welcomed Coolidge's anti-union assurance that "there is no right to strike against the public safety by anybody, anywhere, any time."

Labor strife climaxed in the grim steel strike of 1919. Faced with the industry's plan to revert to seven-day weeks, twelve-hour days, and weekly wages of about $20, Samuel Gompers, head of the AFL, called for a strike. In September, 350,000 workers in fifteen states walked out. The steel industry hired 30,000 strikebreakers and convinced the public that the strikers were radicals bent on subverting democracy and capitalism. In January 1920, after 18 striking workers were killed, the strike collapsed. That devastating defeat initiated a sharp decline in the fortunes of the labor movement, a trend that would continue for almost twenty years.

The Red Scare

Red scare

▶ The widespread fear of internal subversion and Communist revolution that swept the United States in 1919 and resulted in suppression of dissent. Labor unrest, postwar recession, the difficult peacetime readjustment, and the Soviet establishment of the Comintern all contributed to the scare.

Suppression of labor strikes was one response to the widespread fear of internal subversion that swept the nation in 1919. The **Red scare** ("Red" referred to the color of the Bolshevik flag) had homegrown causes: the postwar recession, labor unrest, terrorist acts, and the difficulties of reintegrating millions of returning veterans. But unsettling events abroad also added to Americans' anxieties.

Two epidemics swept the globe in 1918. One was Spanish influenza, which brought on a lethal accumulation of fluid in the lungs. A nurse near the front lines in France observed that victims "run a high temperature, so high that we can't believe it's true. . . . It is accompanied by vomiting and dysentery. When they die, as about half of them do, they turn a ghastly dark gray and are taken out at once and cremated." Before the flu virus had run its course, 40 million people had died worldwide, including some 700,000 Americans.

The other epidemic was Russian bolshevism, which seemed to most Americans equally contagious and deadly. Bolshevism became even more menacing in March 1919, when the new Soviet leaders created the Comintern, a worldwide association of Communists sworn to revolution in capitalist countries. A Communist revolution in the United States was extremely unlikely, but edgy Americans, faced with a flurry of

CHAPTER LOCATOR | What was Woodrow Wilson's foreign policy agenda? | What role did the United States play in World War I?

668 CHAPTER 22 THE UNITED STATES AND WORLD WAR I

terrorist acts, believed otherwise. Dozens of prominent individuals had received bombs through the mail. On September 16, 1920, a wagon filled with dynamite and iron exploded on Wall Street, killing 38 and maiming 143 others.

Even before the Wall Street bombing, the government had initiated a hunt for domestic revolutionaries. Led by Attorney General A. Mitchell Palmer, the campaign targeted men and women who harbored ideas that Palmer believed could lead to violence, even though the individuals may not have done anything illegal. In January 1920, Palmer ordered a series of raids that netted 6,000 alleged subversives. Finding no revolutionary conspiracies, Palmer nevertheless ordered 500 noncitizen suspects deported.

His action came in the wake of a campaign against the most notorious radical alien, Russian-born Emma Goldman. Before the war, Goldman's passionate support of labor strikes, women's rights, and birth control had made her a symbol of radicalism. In 1919, after a stay in prison for denouncing military conscription, she was ordered deported by J. Edgar Hoover, the director of the Justice Department's Radical Division.

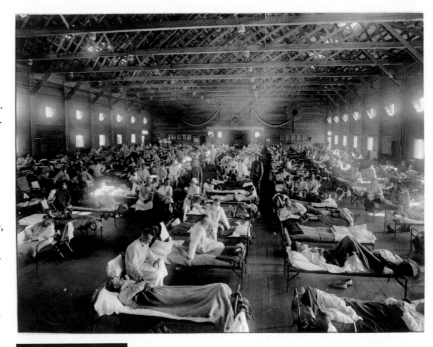

Emergency Hospital

Despite its name, the Spanish flu was first observed in 1918 in Kansas. Army camps, with their close troop quarters, proved perfect incubators. This emergency hospital at Camp Funston, Kansas, is filled with some of the flu's early victims. Crowded troopships quickly spread the virus to Europe. Civilians were not immune. In October 1918 in Philadelphia, more than 4,500 people died in a single week. National Museum of Health & Medicine, Armed Forces Institute of Pathology.

The effort to rid the country of alien radicals was matched by efforts to crush troublesome citizens. Law enforcement officials and vigilante groups joined hands against so-called Reds. In November 1919 in the rugged lumber town of Centralia, Washington, a menacing crowd gathered in front of the IWW hall. Nervous Wobblies inside opened fire, killing three people. Three IWW members were arrested and later convicted of murder, but another, ex-soldier Wesley Everett, was carried off by the mob, which castrated him, hung him from a bridge, and then riddled his body with bullets. His death was officially ruled a suicide.

Public institutions joined the attack on civil liberties. Local libraries removed dissenting books. Schools fired unorthodox teachers. Police shut down radical newspapers. State legislatures refused to seat elected representatives who professed socialist ideas. And in 1919, Congress removed its lone socialist representative, Victor Berger, on the pretext that he was a threat to national safety.

That same year, the Supreme Court provided a formula for restricting free speech. In upholding the conviction of socialist Charles Schenck for publishing a pamphlet urging resistance to the draft during wartime (*Schenck v. United States*), the Court established a "clear and present danger" test. Utterances such as Schenck's during a time of national peril, Justice Oliver Wendell Holmes wrote, were equivalent to shouting "Fire!" in a crowded theater.

Schenck v. United States
▶ 1919 Supreme Court decision that established a "clear and present danger" test for restricting free speech. The Court upheld the conviction of socialist Charles Schenck for urging resistance to the draft during wartime.

| What impact did the war have on the home front? | What part did Woodrow Wilson play at the Paris peace conference? | **Why was America's transition from war to peace so turbulent?** | Conclusion: What was the domestic cost of foreign victory? | ✓ LearningCurve Check what you know. bedfordstmartins.com /roarkunderstanding |

In 1920, the assault on civil liberties provoked the creation of the American Civil Liberties Union (ACLU), which was dedicated to defending an individual's constitutional rights. One of the ACLU's founders, Roger Baldwin, declared, "So long as we have enough people in this country willing to fight for their rights, we'll be called a democracy." The ACLU championed the targets of Attorney General Palmer's campaign — politically radical immigrants, trade unionists, socialists and Communists, and antiwar activists who still languished in jail.

The Red scare eventually collapsed because of its excesses. In particular, the antiradical campaign lost credibility after Palmer warned that radicals were planning to celebrate the Bolshevik Revolution with a nationwide wave of violence on May 1, 1920. Officials called out state militias, mobilized bomb squads, and even placed machine-gun nests at major city intersections. When May 1 came and went without a single disturbance, the public mood turned from fear to scorn.

The Great Migrations of African Americans and Mexicans

Before the Red scare lost steam, the government raised alarms about the loyalty of African Americans. A Justice Department investigation concluded that Reds were fomenting racial unrest among blacks. Although the report was wrong about Bolshevik influence, it was correct in noticing a new stirring among African Americans.

In 1900, nine of every ten blacks still lived in the South, where poverty, disfranchisement, segregation, and violence dominated their lives. Whites remained committed to keeping blacks down. "If we own a good farm or horse, or cow, or bird-dog, or yoke of oxen," a black sharecropper in Mississippi observed in 1913, "we are harassed until we are bound to sell, give away, or run away, before we can have any peace in our lives."

The First World War provided African Americans with the opportunity to escape the South's cotton fields and kitchens. When war channeled almost 5 million American workers into military service and almost ended European immigration, northern industrialists turned to black labor. Black men found work in northern steel mills, shipyards, munitions plants, railroad yards, automobile factories, and mines. From 1915 to 1920, half a million blacks (approximately 10 percent of the South's black population) boarded trains bound for Philadelphia, Detroit, Cleveland, Chicago, St. Louis, and other industrial cities.

Thousands of migrants wrote home to tell family and friends about their experiences in the North. One man announced proudly that he had recently been promoted to "first assistant to the head carpenter." He added, "I should have been here twenty years ago. I just begin to feel like a man. . . . My children are going to the same school with the whites and I don't have to [h]umble to no one. I have registered — will vote the next election and there ain't any 'yes sir' — it's all yes and no and Sam and Bill."

But the North was not the promised land. Black men stood on the lowest rungs of the labor ladder. Jobs of any kind proved scarce for black women, and most worked as domestic servants as they did in the South. The existing black middle class sometimes shunned the less educated, less sophisticated rural southerners crowding into northern cities. Many whites, fearful of losing jobs and status, lashed out against the new migrants. Savage race riots ripped through two

CHAPTER LOCATOR | What was Woodrow Wilson's foreign policy agenda? | What role did the United States play in World War I?

CHAPTER 22
670 THE UNITED STATES AND WORLD WAR I

Mexican Women Arriving in El Paso, 1911

These Mexican women, carrying bundles and wearing traditional shawls, try to get their bearings upon arriving in El Paso, Texas — the Ellis Island for Mexican immigrants. They were part of the first modern wave of Mexican immigration to the United States. Women like them found work in the fields, canneries, and restaurants of the Southwest, as well as at home taking in sewing, laundry, and boarders. Courtesy of the Rio Grande Historical Collections, New Mexico State University, Las Cruces, NM.

dozen northern cities. In 1918, the nation witnessed ninety-six lynchings of blacks, some of them decorated war veterans still in uniform.

Still, most black migrants stayed in the North and encouraged friends and family to follow. By 1940, more than one million blacks had left the South, profoundly changing their own lives and the course of the nation's history. Black enclaves such as Harlem in New York and the South Side of Chicago, "cities within cities," emerged in the North. These assertive communities provided a foundation for black protest and political organization in the years ahead.

At nearly the same time, another migration was under way in the American Southwest. Between 1910 and 1920, the Mexican-born population in the United States soared from 222,000 to 478,000. Mexican immigration resulted from developments on both sides of the border. When Mexicans revolted against dictator Porfirio Díaz in 1910, initiating a ten-year civil war, migrants flooded northward. In the United States, the Chinese Exclusion Act of 1882 and later the disruption of World War I cut off the supply of cheap foreign labor and caused western employers in the expanding rail, mining, construction, and agricultural industries to look south to Mexico for workers.

Like immigrants from Europe and black migrants from the South, Mexicans in the American Southwest dreamed of a better life. And like the others, they found both opportunity and disappointment. Wages were better than in Mexico, but life in the fields, mines, and factories was hard, and living conditions — in boxcars, labor camps, or urban barrios — were dismal. Signs warning "No Mexicans Allowed" increased rather than declined. Mexicans were considered excellent prospects for manual labor but not for citizenship. Among Mexican Americans, some of whom had lived in the Southwest for more than a century, *los recién llegados* (the recent arrivals) encountered mixed reactions. One Mexican American expressed this ambivalence: "We are all Mexicans anyway because the gueros [Anglos] treat us all alike." But he also called for immigration quotas because the recent arrivals drove down wages and incited white prejudice that affected all Mexican Americans.

Despite friction, large-scale immigration into the Southwest meant a resurgence of the Mexican cultural presence, which became the basis for

What impact did the war have on the home front? | What part did Woodrow Wilson play at the Paris peace conference? | **Why was America's transition from war to peace so turbulent?** | Conclusion: What was the domestic cost of foreign victory? | ☑ LearningCurve Check what you know. bedfordstmartins.com /roarkunderstanding

671

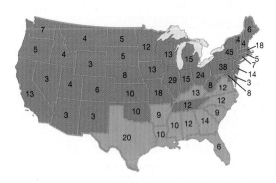

Candidate	Electoral Vote	Popular Vote	Percent of Popular Vote
Warren G. Harding (Republican)	404	16,143,407	60.5
James M. Cox (Democrat)	127	9,130,328	34.2
Eugene V. Debs (Socialist)	0	919,799	3.4

MAP 22.6 ■ The Election of 1920

greater solidarity and political action for the ethnic Mexican population. In 1929 in Texas, Mexican Americans formed the League of United Latin American Citizens.

Postwar Politics and the Election of 1920

A thousand miles away in Washington, D.C., President Woodrow Wilson, bedridden and paralyzed, ignored the mountain of domestic troubles — labor strikes, the Red scare, race riots, immigration backlash — and insisted that the 1920 election would be a "solemn referendum" on the League of Nations. Dutifully, the Democratic nominees for president, James M. Cox of Ohio, and for vice president, Franklin Delano Roosevelt of New York, campaigned on Wilson's international ideals. The Republican Party chose the handsome, gregarious Warren Gamaliel Harding, a senator from Ohio.

Harding found the winning formula when he declared that "America's present need is not heroics, but healing; not nostrums [questionable remedies] but normalcy." But what was "normalcy"? Harding explained: "By 'normalcy' I don't mean the old order but a regular steady order of things. I mean normal procedure, the natural way, without excess." Eager to put wartime crusades and postwar strife behind them, voters responded by giving Harding the largest presidential victory ever: 60.5 percent of the popular vote and 404 out of 531 electoral votes (**Map 22.6**). Harding's election lifted the national pall, signaling a new, more easygoing era.

> **QUICK REVIEW**

How did the Red scare contribute to the erosion of civil liberties after the war?

CHAPTER LOCATOR | What was Woodrow Wilson's foreign policy agenda? | What role did the United States play in World War I?

AMERICA'S EXPERIENCE IN WORLD WAR I was exceptional. For much of the world, the Great War produced great destruction — blackened fields, ruined factories, and millions of casualties. But in the United States, war and prosperity marched hand in hand. America emerged from the war with the strongest economy in the world and a position of international preeminence.

Still, the nation paid a heavy price both at home and abroad. American soldiers and sailors encountered unprecedented horrors — submarines, poison gas, machine guns — and more than 100,000 died. But rather than redeeming the sacrifice of these men as Woodrow Wilson promised, the peace that followed the armistice tarnished it.

At home, rather than permanently improving working conditions, advancing public health, and spreading educational opportunity, as progressives had hoped, the war threatened to undermine the achievements of the previous two decades. Moreover, rather than promoting democracy, the war bred fear, intolerance, and repression that led to a crackdown on dissent and a demand for conformity. Reformers could count only woman suffrage as a permanent victory.

Woodrow Wilson had promised more than anyone could deliver. Progressive hopes of extending democracy and liberal reform nationally and internationally were dashed. In 1920, a bruised and disillusioned society stumbled into a new decade. The era coming to an end had called on Americans to crusade and sacrifice. The new era promised peace, prosperity, and a good time.

| What impact did the war have on the home front? | What part did Woodrow Wilson play at the Paris peace conference? | Why was America's transition from war to peace so turbulent? | **Conclusion: What was the domestic cost of foreign victory?** | ☑ LearningCurve Check what you know. bedfordstmartins.com /roarkunderstanding |

673

CHAPTER 22 STUDY GUIDE

STEP 1

GET STARTED ONLINE

✓ **LearningCurve** ■ bedfordstmartins.com/roarkunderstanding

Now that you've read the chapter, make it stick by completing the LearningCurve activity.

STEP 2

EXPLAIN WHY IT MATTERS

Put your reading into practice. Identify each term below, and then explain why it matters in U.S. history.

TERM	WHO OR WHAT & WHEN	WHY IT MATTERS
Triple Alliance (p. 648)		
Triple Entente (p. 648)		
Lusitania (p. 650)		
Bolshevik (p. 653)		
American Expeditionary Force (AEF) (p. 653)		
Eighteenth Amendment (prohibition) (p. 658)		
Nineteenth Amendment (woman suffrage) (p. 659)		
Fourteen Points (p. 662)		
League of Nations (p. 662)		
Versailles treaty (p. 665)		
Red scare (p. 668)		
Schenck v. United States (p. 669)		

STEP 3

MOVE BEYOND THE BASICS

To demonstrate a more advanced understanding, describe U.S. entry into World War I and list the government initiatives in three areas: wartime agencies, legislation, and propaganda. How did these various initiatives help the war effort?

	Description or list	Reasons for	Effects of
U.S. entry into World War I			
Wartime agencies			
Legislation			
Propaganda			

PUT IT ALL TOGETHER

Now, take a step back and try to explain the big picture. Remember to use specific examples from the chapter in your answers.

THE PATH TO WAR

▶ Describe Woodrow Wilson's foreign policy during his first term in office. How did Wilson see the relationship between the United States and the rest of the world?

▶ Is it fair to describe the American people as "isolationist" prior to America's entry into World War I? Why or why not?

THE HOME FRONT

▶ How did the war affect the progressive agenda? How did progressives use the war to achieve their goals?

▶ To what extent did U.S. participation in World War I involve the domestic efforts of the American people?

A TROUBLED PEACE

▶ What vision did Wilson have of the postwar world? Why did the Senate refuse to endorse his vision, as embodied in the Treaty of Versailles?

▶ What led to the Red scare, and why did it eventually subside?

LOOKING BACKWARD, LOOKING AHEAD

▶ Why did a majority of Americans initially oppose the country's entry into World War I? What events and experiences in the country's past helped shape prewar public opinion?

▶ How did World War I change the place of the United States in the world? What role in world affairs was America poised to take as it entered the 1920s?

> ## IN YOUR OWN WORDS

Imagine that you must give an oral report to the class answering the following question: **What were the most important outcomes of World War I for the United States?** What would be the most important points to include and why?

23

FROM NEW ERA TO GREAT DEPRESSION

1920–1932

> **What were the high points and the low points of the 1920s?** Chapter 23 examines the central role of business in the 1920s, the cultural change and conflicts of the decade, and the events that led to the collapse of the American economy by the end of the decade. The chapter also explores the policies of the Republican administrations of the era and the failure of the federal government to respond effectively to the economic catastrophe.

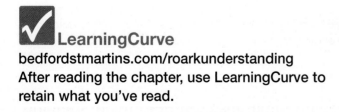

LearningCurve
bedfordstmartins.com/roarkunderstanding
After reading the chapter, use LearningCurve to
retain what you've read.

> How did big business shape the "New Era" of the 1920s?

> In what ways did the Roaring Twenties challenge traditional values?

> Why did the relationship between urban and rural America deteriorate in the 1920s?

> How did President Hoover respond to the economic crash of 1929?

> What was life like in the early years of the depression?

> Conclusion: Why did the hope of the 1920s turn to despair?

"Sheik with Sheba." Cover of *Judge* magazine, by A. John Held Jr. The Granger Collection, New York.

How did big business shape the "New Era" of the 1920s?

Henry and Edsel Ford

In this 1924 photograph, Henry Ford looks fondly at his first car while his son, Edsel, stands next to the ten millionth Model T. Henry Ford Museum and Greenfield Village.

O**NCE WOODROW WILSON LEFT** the White House, energy flowed away from government activism and civic reform and toward private economic endeavor. The rise of a freewheeling economy and a heightened sense of individualism caused Secretary of Commerce Herbert Hoover to declare that America had entered a "New Era," one of many labels used to describe the complex 1920s. Some terms focus on the decade's high-spirited energy and cultural change: Roaring Twenties, Jazz Age, Flaming Youth. Others echo the rising importance of money — Dollar Decade, Golden Twenties — or reflect the sinister side of gangster profiteering — Lawless Decade. Still others emphasize the lonely confusion of the Lost Generation and the stress and anxiety of the Aspirin Age.

America in the twenties was many things, but President Calvin Coolidge got at an essential truth when he declared: "The business of America is business." Politicians and diplomats proclaimed business the heart of American civilization as they promoted its products at home and abroad. Average men and women bought into the idea that business and its wonderful goods were what made America great, as they snatched up the flood of new consumer items American factories sent forth. Nothing caught Americans' fancy more powerfully than the automobile.

CHAPTER LOCATOR | **How did big business shape the "New Era" of the 1920s?** | In what ways did the Roaring Twenties challenge traditional values?

678 CHAPTER 23
FROM NEW ERA TO GREAT DEPRESSION

A Business Government

Republicans controlled the White House from 1921 to 1933. The first of the three Republican presidents was Warren Gamaliel Harding, the Ohio senator who in his 1920 campaign called for a "return to normalcy," by which he meant the end of public crusades and a return to private pursuits. Harding appointed a few men of real stature to his cabinet. Herbert Hoover, the former head of the wartime Food Administration, became secretary of commerce. But wealth and friendship also counted: Andrew Mellon, one of the richest men in America, became secretary of the treasury, and Harding handed out jobs to his friends, members of his old "Ohio gang." This curious combination of merit and cronyism made for a disjointed administration.

When Harding was elected in 1920 (see chapter 22, Map 22.6), the unemployment rate hit 20 percent, the highest ever up to that point. The bankruptcy rate of farmers increased tenfold. Harding pushed measures to regain national prosperity — high tariffs to protect American businesses, price supports for agriculture, and the dismantling of wartime government control over industry in favor of unregulated private business. "Never before, here or anywhere else," the U.S. Chamber of Commerce said proudly, "has a government been so completely fused with business."

Harding's policies to boost American enterprise made him very popular, but ultimately his small-town congeniality and trusting ways did him in. Some of his friends in the Ohio gang were up to their necks in lawbreaking. Three of Harding's appointees would go to jail. Interior Secretary Albert Fall was convicted of accepting bribes of more than $400,000 for leasing oil reserves on public land in Teapot Dome, Wyoming, and **Teapot Dome** became a synonym for political corruption.

On August 2, 1923, when Harding died from a heart attack, Vice President Calvin Coolidge became president. Coolidge, who once said that "the man who builds a factory builds a temple, the man who works there worships there," continued and extended Harding's policies of promoting business and limiting government. Secretary of the Treasury Andrew Mellon reduced the government's control over the economy and cut taxes for corporations and wealthy individuals. New rules for the Federal Trade Commission severely restricted its power to regulate business. Secretary of Commerce Herbert Hoover hedged government authority by encouraging trade associations that ideally would keep business honest and efficient through voluntary cooperation.

Coolidge found an ally in the Supreme Court. The Court ruled against closed shops — businesses where only union members could be employed — while confirming the right of owners to form exclusive trade associations. In 1923, the Court declared unconstitutional the District of Columbia's minimum-wage law for women, asserting that the law interfered with the freedom of employer and employee to make labor contracts. The Court and the president attacked government intrusion in the free market, even when the prohibition of government regulation threatened the welfare of workers.

The election of 1924 confirmed the defeat of the progressive principle that the state should take a leading role in ensuring the general welfare. To oppose Coolidge, the Democrats nominated John W. Davis, a corporate lawyer whose conservative views differed little from Republican principles. Only the Progressive Party and its presidential nominee, Senator Robert La Follette of Wisconsin, offered

> CHRONOLOGY

1920
– Warren G. Harding is elected president.

1922
– Teapot Dome scandal.
– Five-Power Naval Treaty.

1923
– Harding dies; Vice President Calvin Coolidge becomes president.

1924
– Dawes Plan.
– Coolidge is elected president.

1928
– Kellogg-Briand pact.

1929
– Publication of *Middletown*.

Teapot Dome

▶ Nickname for the scandal in which Interior Secretary Albert Fall accepted $400,000 in bribes for leasing oil reserves on public land in Teapot Dome, Wyoming. It was part of a larger pattern of corruption that marred Warren G. Harding's presidency.

Why did the relationship between urban and rural America deteriorate in the 1920s?

How did President Hoover respond to the economic crash of 1929?

What was life like in the early years of the depression?

Conclusion: Why did the hope of the 1920s turn to despair?

LearningCurve
Check what you know.
bedfordstmartins.com
/roarkunderstanding

a genuine alternative. When La Follette championed labor unions, regulation of business, and protection of civil liberties, Republicans coined the slogan "Coolidge or Chaos." Voters chose Coolidge in a landslide. Coolidge was right when he declared, "This is a business country, and it wants a business government." What was true of the government's relationship to business at home was also true abroad.

Promoting Prosperity and Peace Abroad

After orchestrating the Senate's successful effort to block U.S. membership in the League of Nations, Henry Cabot Lodge boasted, "We have torn Wilsonism up by the roots." But repudiation of Wilsonian internationalism and rejection of collective security through the League of Nations did not mean that the United States retreated into isolationism. The United States emerged from World War I with its economy intact and enjoyed a decade of stunning growth. New York replaced London as the center of world finance, and the United States became the world's chief creditor. Economic involvement in the world and the continuing chaos in Europe made withdrawal impossible.

One of the Republicans' most ambitious foreign policy initiatives was the Washington Disarmament Conference, which convened in 1921 to establish a global balance of naval power. Secretary of State Charles Evans Hughes shaped the **Five-Power Naval Treaty of 1922** committing Britain, France, Japan, Italy, and the United States to a proportional reduction of naval forces. The treaty led to the scrapping of more than two million tons of warships, by far the world's greatest success in disarmament. By fostering international peace, President Harding also helped make the world a safer place for American trade.

A second major effort on behalf of world peace came in 1928, when Secretary of State Frank Kellogg joined French foreign minister Aristide Briand to produce the Kellogg-Briand pact. Nearly fifty nations signed the solemn pledge to renounce war and settle international disputes peacefully.

But Republican administrations preferred private-sector diplomacy to state action. With the blessing of the White House, a team of American financiers led by Charles Dawes swung into action when Germany suspended its war reparation payments in 1923. Impoverished, Germany was staggering under the massive bill of $33 billion presented by the victorious Allies in the Versailles treaty. When Germany failed to meet its annual payment, France occupied Germany's industrial Ruhr Valley, creating the worst international crisis since the war. In 1924, the Dawes Plan halved Germany's annual reparation payments, initiated fresh American loans to Germany, and caused the French to retreat from the Ruhr. Although the United States failed to join the League of Nations, it continued to exercise significant economic and diplomatic influence abroad. These Republican successes overseas helped fuel prosperity at home.

Automobiles, Mass Production, and Assembly-Line Progress

The automobile industry emerged as the largest single manufacturing industry in the nation. The pioneer of the mass production of automobiles was Henry Ford.

Five-Power Naval Treaty of 1922

▶ Treaty that committed Britain, France, Japan, Italy, and the United States to a proportional reduction of naval forces, producing the world's greatest success in disarmament up to that time. Republicans orchestrated its development at the 1921 Washington Disarmament Conference.

CHAPTER LOCATOR | How did big business shape the "New Era" of the 1920s? | In what ways did the Roaring Twenties challenge traditional values?

680 CHAPTER 23 FROM NEW ERA TO GREAT DEPRESSION

When the 1920s began, he had already produced six million automobiles; by 1927, the figure reached fifteen million. In 1920, a Ford car cost $845; in 1928, the price was less than $300, within range of most of the country's skilled workingmen. Ford shrewdly located his company in Detroit, knowing that key materials for his automobiles were manufactured in nearby states (**Map 23.1**). Keystone of the American economy, the automobile industry not only employed hundreds of thousands of workers directly but also brought whole industries into being — filling stations, garages, fast-food restaurants, and "guest cottages" (motels). The need for tires, glass, steel, highways, oil, and refined gasoline for automobiles provided millions of related jobs. By 1929, one American in four found employment directly or indirectly in the automobile industry. "Give us our daily bread" was no longer addressed to the Almighty, one commentator quipped, but to Detroit.

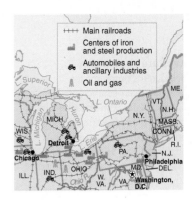

Detroit and the Automobile Industry in the 1920s

Automobiles changed where people lived, what work they did, how they spent their leisure, even how they thought. Hundreds of small towns decayed because the automobile enabled rural people to bypass them in favor of more distant cities and towns. In cities, streetcars began to disappear as workers moved to the suburbs and commuted to work along crowded highways. Nothing shaped modern America more than the automobile, and efficient mass production made the automobile revolution possible.

Mass production by the assembly-line technique became standard in almost every factory, from automobiles to meatpacking to cigarettes. To improve efficiency, corporations reduced assembly-line work to the simplest, most repetitive tasks. Changes on

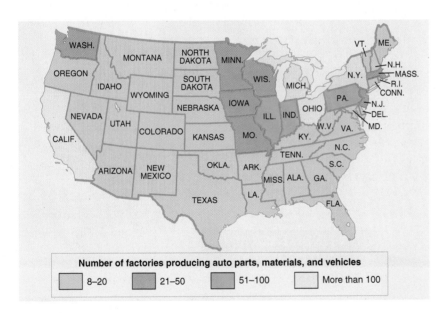

Number of factories producing auto parts, materials, and vehicles

| 8–20 | 21–50 | 51–100 | More than 100 |

MAP 23.1 ■ Auto Manufacturing

By the mid-1920s, the massive coal and steel industries of the Midwest had made that region the center of the new automobile industry. A major road-building program by the federal government carried the thousands of new cars produced each day to every corner of the country.

> **MAP ACTIVITY**

READING THE MAP: How many states had factories involved with the manufacture of automobiles? In what regions was auto manufacturing concentrated?

CONNECTIONS: On what related industries did auto manufacturing depend? How did the integration of the automobile into everyday life affect American society?

| Why did the relationship between urban and rural America deteriorate in the 1920s? | How did President Hoover respond to the economic crash of 1929? | What was life like in the early years of the depression? | Conclusion: Why did the hope of the 1920s turn to despair? | ✓ LearningCurve Check what you know. bedfordstmartins.com /roarkunderstanding |

the assembly line and in management, along with technological advances, significantly boosted overall efficiency. Between 1922 and 1929, productivity in manufacturing increased 32 percent. Average wages, however, increased only 8 percent.

Industries also developed programs for workers that came to be called **welfare capitalism**. Some businesses improved safety and sanitation inside factories. They also instituted paid vacations and pension plans. Welfare capitalism encouraged loyalty to the company and discouraged traditional labor unions. One labor organizer in the steel industry bemoaned the success of welfare capitalism. "So many workmen here had been lulled to sleep by the company union, the welfare plans, the social organizations fostered by the employer," he declared, "that they had come to look upon the employer as their protector, and had believed vigorous trade union organization unnecessary for their welfare."

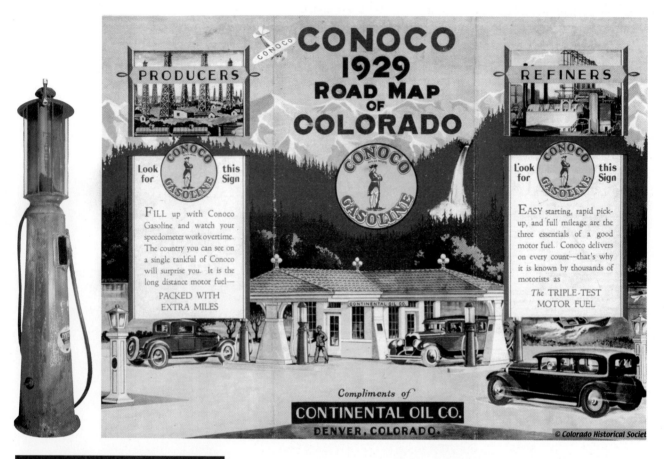

Colorado Filling Station and Gas Pump

By 1929, when Conoco (Continental Oil Company) produced this lavish map featuring Colorado's spectacular mountains, nearly every oil company was supplying road maps as part of its campaign to boost tourism. This appealing drive-through station is a far cry from the first retail outlets for gas — blacksmith shops and hardware stores, the same places individuals bought kerosene for their lamps. Because motorists did not trust what they could not see, companies in the 1910s introduced glass-cylinder, gravity-flow gas pumps. Courtesy, Colorado Historical Society.

> VISUAL ACTIVITY

READING THE IMAGE: What do this road map and accompanying image of a gravity-flow gasoline pump tell us about American consumer culture on the eve of the Great Depression?

CONNECTIONS: Does the road map accurately reflect the economic direction of the U.S. economy in 1929?

CHAPTER LOCATOR | How did big business shape the "New Era" of the 1920s? | In what ways did the Roaring Twenties challenge traditional values?

682   CHAPTER 23
FROM NEW ERA TO GREAT DEPRESSION

Consumer Culture

Mass production fueled corporate profits and national economic prosperity. During the 1920s, per capita income increased by a third, the cost of living stayed the same, and unemployment remained low. But the rewards of the economic boom were not evenly distributed. Americans who labored with their hands inched ahead, while white-collar workers enjoyed significantly more spending money and more leisure time to spend it. Mass production of a broad range of new products — automobiles, radios, refrigerators, electric irons, washing machines — produced a consumer goods revolution.

In this new era of abundance, more people than ever conceived of the American dream in terms of the things they could acquire. *Middletown* (1929), a study of the inhabitants of Muncie, Indiana, revealed that Muncie had become, above all, "a culture in which everything hinges on money." Moreover, faced with technological and organizational change beyond their comprehension, many citizens had lost confidence in their ability to play an effective role in civic affairs. More and more they became passive consumers, deferring to the supposed expertise of leaders in politics and economics.

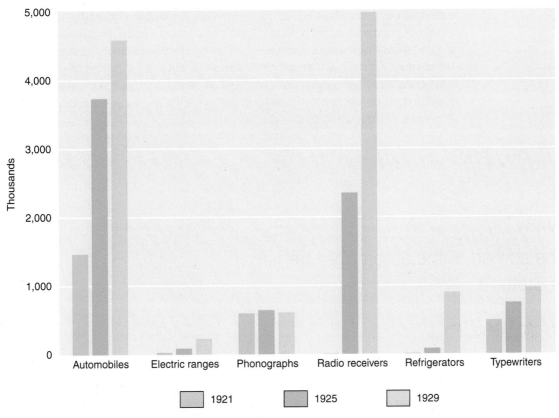

FIGURE 23.1 ■ **Production of Consumer Goods, 1920–1929**

Transportation, communications, and entertainment changed the lives of consumers in the 1920s. Laborsaving devices for the home were popular, but the vastly greater sales of automobiles and radios showed that consumerism was powerful in moving people's attention beyond their homes.

| Why did the relationship between urban and rural America deteriorate in the 1920s? | How did President Hoover respond to the economic crash of 1929? | What was life like in the early years of the depression? | Conclusion: Why did the hope of the 1920s turn to despair? | ✔ LearningCurve Check what you know. bedfordstmartins.com /roarkunderstanding |

The rapidly expanding business of advertising stimulated the desire for new products and attacked the traditional values of thrift and saving. Advertising linked material goods to the fulfillment of every spiritual and emotional need. Americans increasingly defined and measured their social status, and indeed their personal worth, on the yardstick of material possessions. Happiness itself rode on owning a car and choosing the right cigarettes and toothpaste.

By the 1920s, the United States had achieved the physical capacity to satisfy Americans' material wants (**Figure 23.1**, page 683). The economic problem shifted from production to consumption: Who would buy the goods flying off American assembly lines? One solution was to expand America's markets in foreign countries, and government and business joined in that effort. Another solution to the problem of consumption was to expand the market at home.

Henry Ford realized early on that "mass production requires mass consumption." He understood that automobile workers not only produced cars but would also buy them if they made enough money. "One's own employees ought to be one's own best customers," Ford said. In 1914, he raised wages in his factories to $5 a day, more than twice the going rate. High wages made for workers who were more loyal and more exploitable, and high wages returned as profits when workers bought Fords.

Many people's incomes, however, were too puny to satisfy the growing desire for consumer goods. The solution was installment buying — a little money down, a payment each month — which allowed people to purchase expensive items they could not otherwise afford or to purchase items before saving the necessary money. As one newspaper announced, "The first responsibility of an American to his country is no longer that of a citizen, but of a consumer." During the 1920s, America's motto became spend, not save. Old values — "Use it up, wear it out, make it do or do without" — seemed about as pertinent as a horse and buggy. American culture had shifted.

> ## QUICK REVIEW

How did the spread of the automobile transform the United States?

CHAPTER LOCATOR | How did big business shape the "New Era" of the 1920s? | In what ways did the Roaring Twenties challenge traditional values?

CHAPTER 23
684   FROM NEW ERA TO GREAT DEPRESSION

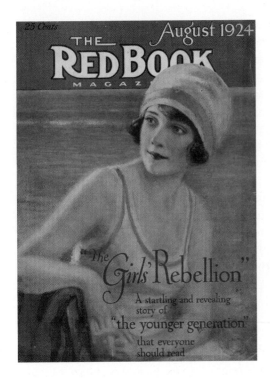

In what ways did the Roaring Twenties challenge traditional values?

A NEW ETHIC OF PERSONAL FREEDOM excited many Americans to seek pleasure without guilt in a whirl of activity that earned the decade the name "Roaring Twenties." Prohibition made lawbreakers of millions of otherwise decent folk. Flappers and "new women" challenged traditional gender boundaries. Other Americans enjoyed the Roaring Twenties through the words and images of vastly expanded mass communication, especially radio and movies. In America's big cities, particularly New York, a burst of creativity produced the "New Negro," who confounded and disturbed white Americans. The "Lost Generation" of writers, profoundly disillusioned with mainstream America's cultural direction, fled the country.

Prohibition

Republicans generally sought to curb the powers of government, but the twenties witnessed a great exception to this rule when the federal government implemented one of the last reforms of the Progressive Era: the Eighteenth Amendment, which banned the manufacture and sale of alcohol and took effect in January 1920 (see chapter 22). Drying up the rivers of liquor that Americans consumed, supporters of **prohibition** claimed, would eliminate crime, boost production, and lift the nation's morality. Instead, prohibition initiated a fourteen-year orgy of lawbreaking unparalleled in the nation's history.

prohibition
▶ The ban on the manufacture and sale of alcohol that went into effect in January 1920 with the Eighteenth Amendment. Prohibition proved almost impossible to enforce. By the end of the 1920s, most Americans wished it to end, and it was finally repealed in 1933.

Why did the relationship between urban and rural America deteriorate in the 1920s?

How did President Hoover respond to the economic crash of 1929?

What was life like in the early years of the depression?

Conclusion: Why did the hope of the 1920s turn to despair?

☑ **LearningCurve**
Check what you know.
bedfordstmartins.com
/roarkunderstanding

The Treasury Department agents charged with enforcing prohibition faced a staggering task. Although they smashed more than 172,000 illegal stills in 1925 alone, loopholes in the law almost guaranteed failure. Sacramental wine was permitted, allowing fake clergy to party with bogus congregations. Farmers were allowed to ferment their own "fruit juices." Doctors and dentists could prescribe liquor for medicinal purposes.

In 1929, a Treasury agent in Indiana reported intense local resistance to enforcement of prohibition. "Conditions in most important cities very bad," he declared. "Lax and corrupt public officials great handicap . . . prevalence of drinking among minor boys and the . . . middle or better classes of adults." The "speakeasy," an illegal nightclub, became a common feature of the urban landscape. Speakeasies' dance floors led to the sexual integration of the formerly all-male drinking culture, changing American social life forever. Detroit, probably America's wettest city, was home to more than 20,000 illegal drinking establishments, making the alcohol business the city's second-largest industry, behind automobile manufacturing.

Eventually, serious criminals took over the liquor trade. During the first four years of prohibition, Chicago witnessed more than two hundred gang-related killings as rival mobs struggled for control of the lucrative liquor trade. The most notorious event came on St. Valentine's Day 1929, when Alphonse "Big Al" Capone's Italian-dominated mob machine-gunned seven members of a rival Irish

Confiscated Liquor

Revenue agents, some holding rifles, proudly display the bootleg liquor they have confiscated during a raid in Washington, D.C., in 1922. The carefully staged scene and the photographer on the roof indicate that the agents were eager to publicize their success. Successes like this were common during prohibition, but the criminalization of liquor could not permanently defeat "Satan in a bottle." The Granger Collection, NYC.

CHAPTER LOCATOR | How did big business shape the "New Era" of the 1920s? | **In what ways did the Roaring Twenties challenge traditional values?**

CHAPTER 23
686 FROM NEW ERA TO GREAT DEPRESSION

gang. Federal authorities finally sent Capone to prison for income tax evasion. "I violate the Prohibition law — sure," he told a reporter. "Who doesn't? The only difference is, I take more chances than the man who drinks a cocktail before dinner."

Americans overwhelmingly favored the repeal of the Eighteenth Amendment. In 1931, a panel of distinguished experts reported that prohibition, which supporters had defended as "a great social and economic experiment," had failed. The social and political costs of prohibition outweighed the benefits. Prohibition fueled criminal activity, corrupted the police, demoralized the judiciary, and caused ordinary citizens to disrespect the law. In 1933, the nation ended prohibition, making the Eighteenth Amendment the only constitutional amendment to be repealed.

The New Woman

Of all the changes in American life in the 1920s, none sparked more heated debate than the alternatives offered to the traditional roles of women. Increasing numbers of women worked and went to college, defying older gender norms. Even mainstream magazines such as the *Saturday Evening Post* began publishing stories about young, college-educated women who drank gin cocktails, smoked cigarettes, and wore skimpy dresses and dangly necklaces. Before the Great War, the **new woman** dwelt in New York City's bohemian Greenwich Village, but afterward the mass media brought her into middle-class America's living rooms.

When the Nineteenth Amendment, ratified in 1920, granted women the vote, feminists felt liberated and expected women to reshape the political landscape. A Kansas woman declared, "I went to bed last night a slave[;] I awoke this morning a *free woman*." Women began pressuring Congress to pass laws that especially concerned women, including measures to protect women in factories and grant federal aid to schools. Black women lobbied particularly for federal courts to assume jurisdiction over the crime of lynching. But women's only significant national legislative success came in 1921 when Congress enacted the Sheppard-Towner Act, which extended federal assistance to states seeking to reduce high infant mortality rates.

A number of factors helped thwart women's political influence. Male domination of both political parties, the rarity of female candidates, and lack of experience in voting, especially among recent immigrants, kept many women away from the polls. In the South, poll taxes, literacy tests, and outright terrorism continued to decimate the vote of African Americans, men and women alike.

Most important, rather than forming a solid voting bloc, feminists divided. Some argued for women's right to special protection; others demanded equal protection. The radical National Woman's Party fought for an Equal Rights Amendment that stated flatly: "Men and women shall have equal rights throughout the United States." The more moderate League of Women Voters feared that the amendment's wording threatened state laws that provided women special protection, such as preventing them from working on certain machines. Put before Congress in 1923, the Equal Rights Amendment went down to defeat, and radical women were forced to work for the causes of birth control, legal equality for minorities, and the end of child labor through other means.

new woman
▶ Alternative image of womanhood that came into the American mainstream in the 1920s. The mass media frequently portrayed young, college-educated women who drank, smoked, and wore skimpy dresses. New women also challenged American convictions about separate spheres for women and men and the sexual double standard.

Why did the relationship between urban and rural America deteriorate in the 1920s?

How did President Hoover respond to the economic crash of 1929?

What was life like in the early years of the depression?

Conclusion: Why did the hope of the 1920s turn to despair?

✓ LearningCurve
Check what you know.
bedfordstmartins.com
/roarkunderstanding

687

Economically, more women worked for pay — approximately one in four by 1930 — but they clustered in "women's jobs." The proportion of women working as secretaries, stenographers, and typists skyrocketed. Women almost monopolized the occupations of librarian, nurse, elementary school teacher, and telephone operator. Women also represented 40 percent of salesclerks by 1930. More female white-collar workers meant that fewer women were interested in protective legislation for women; new women wanted salaries and opportunities equal to men's.

Increased earnings gave working women more buying power in the new consumer culture. A stereotype soon emerged of the flapper, so called because of the short-lived fad of wearing unbuckled galoshes. The flapper had short "bobbed" hair, and she wore lipstick and rouge. She spent freely on the latest styles — dresses with short skirts, drop waists, bare arms, and no petticoats — and she danced all night to wild jazz.

The new woman both reflected and propelled the modern birth control movement. Margaret Sanger, the crusading pioneer for contraception during the Progressive Era (see chapter 21), restated her principal conviction in 1920: "No woman can call herself free until she can choose consciously whether she will or will not be a mother." By shifting strategy in the twenties, Sanger courted the conservative American Medical Association; linked birth control with the eugenics movement, which advocated limiting reproduction among "undesirable" groups; and thus made contraception a respectable subject for discussion.

Flapper style and values spread from coast to coast through films, novels, magazines, and advertisements. New women challenged American convictions about separate spheres for women and men, the double standard of sexual conduct, and Victorian ideas of proper female appearance and behavior. Although only a minority of American women became flappers, all women, even those who remained at home, felt the great changes of the era.

The New Negro

The 1920s witnessed the emergence not only of the "new woman" but also of the "New Negro." African Americans who challenged the caste system that confined dark-skinned Americans to the lowest levels of society confronted whites who insisted that race relations would not change.

The prominent African American intellectual W. E. B. Du Bois and the National Association for the Advancement of Colored People (NAACP) aggressively pursued the passage of a federal antilynching law to counter mob violence against blacks in the South. At the same time, the Jamaican-born visionary Marcus Garvey urged African Americans to rediscover the heritage of Africa, take pride in their own achievements, and maintain racial purity by avoiding miscegenation. In 1917, Garvey launched the Universal Negro Improvement Association (UNIA) to help African Americans gain economic and political independence entirely outside white society. In 1919, the UNIA created its own shipping company, the Black Star Line, to support the "Back to Africa" movement among black Americans. In 1927, the federal government pinned charges of illegal practices on Garvey and deported him to Jamaica. Nevertheless, the issues Garvey raised about racial pride, black identity, and the search for equality persisted, and his legacy remains at the center of black nationalist thought.

CHAPTER LOCATOR | How did big business shape the "New Era" of the 1920s?

In what ways did the Roaring Twenties challenge traditional values?

688   CHAPTER 23
FROM NEW ERA TO GREAT DEPRESSION

Still, most African Americans maintained hope in the American promise. In New York City, hope and talent came together. New York City's black population jumped 115 percent (from 152,000 to 327,000) in the 1920s, and in Harlem in uptown Manhattan an extraordinary mix of black artists, sculptors, novelists, musicians, and poets set out to create a distinctive African American culture that drew on their identities as Americans and Africans. As scholar Alain Locke put it in 1925, they introduced to the world the **New Negro**, who rose from the ashes of slavery and segregation to proclaim African Americans' creative genius.

The emergence of the New Negro came to be known as the Harlem Renaissance. Building on the independence and pride displayed by black soldiers during the war, black artists sought to defeat the fresh onslaught of racial discrimination and violence with poems, paintings, and plays. "We younger Negro artists . . . intend to express our individual dark-skinned selves without fear or shame," poet Langston Hughes said of the Harlem Renaissance. "If white people are pleased, we are glad. If they are not, it doesn't matter. We know we are beautiful. And ugly, too."

The Harlem Renaissance produced dazzling talent. Despite such vibrancy, Harlem for most whites remained a separate black ghetto known only for its lively nightlife. Fashionable whites crowded into Harlem's segregated nightclubs, the most famous of which was the Cotton Club, where they believed they could hear

New Negro
▶ Term referring to African Americans who, through the arts, challenged American racial hierarchy. The New Negro emerged in New York City in the 1920s in what became known as the Harlem Renaissance, which produced dazzling literary, musical, and artistic talent.

Duke Ellington at the Cotton Club

Duke Ellington, at the piano, presides over the floor show at the Cotton Club in Harlem, where black performers played for white audiences. During the years from 1927 to 1931, when his orchestra was the house band at the Cotton Club, Ellington recorded more than one hundred of his compositions, establishing him as America's greatest composer and bandleader. The Frank Driggs Collection.

Why did the relationship between urban and rural America deteriorate in the 1920s?

How did President Hoover respond to the economic crash of 1929?

What was life like in the early years of the depression?

Conclusion: Why did the hope of the 1920s turn to despair?

✓ LearningCurve
Check what you know.
bedfordstmartins.com /roarkunderstanding

689

"real" jazz, a relatively new musical form, in its "natural" surroundings. The vigor of the Harlem Renaissance left a powerful legacy for black Americans, but the creative burst did little in the short run to dissolve the prejudice of white society.

> Leaders of the Harlem Renaissance	
James Weldon Johnson	writer, civil rights leader
Langston Hughes, Claude McKay, Countee Cullen	poets
Zora Neale Hurston	novelist
Aaron Douglas	artist

Entertainment for the Masses

In the 1920s, popular culture, like consumer goods, was mass-produced and mass-consumed. The proliferation of movies, radios, music, and sports meant that Americans found plenty to do, and in doing the same things, they helped create a national culture.

Nothing offered escapist delights like the movies. Hollywood, California, discovered the successful formula of combining opulence, sex, and adventure. Admission was cheap, and by 1929 the movies were drawing more than 80 million people in a single week, as many as lived in the entire country. Rudolph Valentino, described as "catnip to women," and Clara Bow, the "It Girl" (everyone knew what *it* was), became household names. Most loved of all was the comic Charlie Chaplin, whose famous character, the wistful Little Tramp, showed an endearing inability to cope with the rules and complexities of modern life.

Americans also found heroes in sports. Baseball solidified its place as the national pastime in the 1920s. It remained essentially a game played by and for the working class. In George Herman "Babe" Ruth, baseball had the most cherished free spirit of the time. The rowdy escapades of the "Sultan of Swat" demonstrated that sports offered a way to break out of the ordinariness of everyday life. By "his sheer exuberance," one sportswriter declared, Ruth "has lightened the cares of the world."

The public also fell in love with a young boxer from the grim mining districts of Colorado. As a teenager, Jack Dempsey had made his living hanging around saloons betting he could beat anyone in the house. When he took the heavy-weight crown just after World War I, he was revered as the people's champ, a stand-in for the average American who felt increasingly confined by bureaucracy and machine-made culture.

Football, essentially a college sport, held greater sway with the upper classes. But in keeping with the times, football moved toward a more commercial spectacle. Harold "Red" Grange, "the Galloping Ghost," led the way by going from stardom at the University of Illinois to the Chicago Bears in the new professional football league.

The decade's hero worship reached its zenith in the celebration of Charles Lindbergh, a young pilot who set out on May 20, 1927, to become the first person to fly nonstop across the Atlantic. Newspapers tagged Lindbergh "the Lone Eagle" — the perfect hero for an age that celebrated individual accomplishment. "Charles Lindbergh," one journalist proclaimed, "is the stuff out of which have

CHAPTER LOCATOR | How did big business shape the "New Era" of the 1920s?

In what ways did the Roaring Twenties challenge traditional values?

CHAPTER 23
690 FROM NEW ERA TO GREAT DEPRESSION

been made the pioneers that opened up the wilderness. His are the qualities which we, as a people, must nourish." Lindbergh realized, however, that technical and organizational complexity was fast reducing chances for solitary achievement. Consequently, he titled his book about the flight *We* (1927) to include the machine that had made it all possible.

Another machine — the radio — became crucial to mass culture in the 1920s. The nation's first licensed radio station, KDKA in Pittsburgh, began broadcasting in 1920, and soon American airwaves buzzed with news, sermons, soap operas, sports, comedy, and music. Because they could now reach prospective customers in their own homes, advertisers bankrolled radio's rapid growth. Between 1922 and 1929, the number of radio stations in the United States increased from 30 to 606. In just seven years, homes with radios jumped from 60,000 to a staggering 10.25 million.

The Lost Generation

Some writers and artists felt alienated from America's mass-culture society, which they found shallow, anti-intellectual, and materialistic. They believed that business culture blighted American life. Silly movie stars disgusted them. Young, white, and mostly college educated, these expatriates, as they came to be called, felt embittered by the war and renounced the progressives who had promoted it as a crusade. For them, Europe — not Hollywood or Harlem — seemed the place to seek their renaissance.

The American-born writer Gertrude Stein, long established in Paris, remarked famously as the young exiles gathered around her, "They are the lost generation." Most of the expatriates, however, believed to the contrary that they had finally found themselves. The Lost Generation helped launch the most creative period in American art and literature in the twentieth century. The novelist whose spare, clean style best exemplified the expatriate efforts to make art mirror basic reality was Ernest Hemingway. Admirers found the terse language and hard lessons of his novel *The Sun Also Rises* (1926) to be perfect expressions of a world stripped of illusions.

Many writers who remained in America were exiles in spirit. Before the war, intellectuals had eagerly joined progressive reform movements. Afterward, they were more likely critics of American cultural vulgarity. Novelist Sinclair Lewis in *Main Street* (1920) and *Babbitt* (1922) satirized his native Midwest as a cultural wasteland. Humorists such as James Thurber created outlandish characters to poke fun at American stupidity and inhibitions. And southern writers, led by William Faulkner, explored the South's grim class and race heritage. Worries about alienation surfaced as well. F. Scott Fitzgerald spoke sadly in *This Side of Paradise* (1920) of a disillusioned generation "grown up to find all Gods dead, all wars fought, all faiths in man shaken."

QUICK REVIEW <

How did the new freedoms of the 1920s challenge older conceptions of gender and race?

Why did the relationship between urban and rural America deteriorate in the 1920s?

How did President Hoover respond to the economic crash of 1929?

What was life like in the early years of the depression?

Conclusion: Why did the hope of the 1920s turn to despair?

☑ LearningCurve
Check what you know.
bedfordstmartins.com
/roarkunderstanding

Why did the relationship between urban and rural America deteriorate in the 1920s?

WKKK Badge

Half a million women were members of the Women of the Ku Klux Klan (WKKK). Klanswomen fit perfectly within the KKK because the organization proclaimed itself the defender of the traditional virtues of pure womanhood and decent homes. This badge from Harrisburg, Pennsylvania, advertises the local WKKK's support for a "home for orphan and dependent children." Collection of Janice L. and David J. Frent.

LARGE AREAS OF THE COUNTRY did not share in the wealth of the 1920s. By the end of the decade, 40 percent of the nation's farmers were landless, and 90 percent of rural homes lacked indoor plumbing, gas, or electricity. Rural America's traditional distrust of urban America turned to despair in the 1920s when the census reported that the majority of the population had shifted to the city (**Map 23.2**). Urban domination over the nation's political and cultural life and sharply rising economic disparity drove rural Americans in often ugly, reactionary directions.

Cities seemed to stand for everything rural areas stood against. Rural America imagined itself as solidly Anglo-Saxon (despite the presence of millions of African Americans in the South and Mexican Americans, Native Americans, and Asian Americans in the West), and the cities seemed to be filled with undesirable immigrants. Rural America was the home of old-time Protestant religion, and the cities teemed with Catholics, Jews, liberal Protestants, and atheists. Rural America championed old-fashioned moral standards — abstinence and self-denial — while the cities spawned every imaginable vice. In the 1920s, frustrated rural people sought to recapture their country by helping to push through prohibition, dam the flow of immigrants, revive the Ku Klux Klan, defend the Bible as literal truth, and defeat an urban Roman Catholic for president.

CHAPTER LOCATOR | How did big business shape the "New Era" of the 1920s? | In what ways did the Roaring Twenties challenge traditional values?

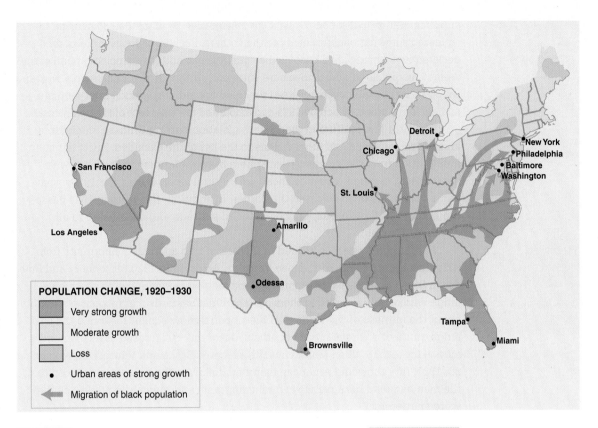

POPULATION CHANGE, 1920–1930

- Very strong growth
- Moderate growth
- Loss
- Urban areas of strong growth
- Migration of black population

MAP 23.2 ■ The Shift from Rural to Urban Population, 1920–1930

The movement of whites and Hispanics toward urban and agricultural opportunity made Florida, the West, and the Southwest the regions of fastest population growth. By contrast, large numbers of blacks left the rural South to find a better life in the North. Almost all migrating blacks went from the countryside to cities in distant parts of the nation, while white and Hispanic migrants tended to move shorter distances toward familiar places.

> **MAP ACTIVITY**

READING THE MAP: Which states had the strongest growth? To which cities did southern blacks predominantly migrate?
CONNECTIONS: What conditions in the countryside made the migration to urban areas appealing to many rural Americans? In what social and cultural ways did rural America view itself as different from urban America?

Rejecting the Undesirables

Before the war, when about a million immigrants arrived each year, some Americans warned that unassimilable foreigners were smothering the nation. War against Germany and its allies expanded nativist and antiradical sentiment. After the war, large-scale immigration resumed (another 800,000 immigrants arrived in 1921) at a moment when industrialists no longer needed new factory laborers. Returning veterans, as well as African American and Mexican migration, had relieved labor shortages. Moreover, union leaders feared that millions of poor immigrants would undercut their efforts to organize American workers. Rural America's God-fearing Protestants were particularly alarmed that most of the immigrants were Catholic or Jewish. In 1921, Congress responded by severely restricting immigration.

In 1924, Congress very nearly slammed the door shut. The **Johnson-Reed Act** limited the number of immigrants to no more than 161,000 a year and established quotas for each European nation. The act revealed the fear and bigotry that fueled

Johnson-Reed Act
▶ 1924 law that severely restricted immigration to the United States to no more than 161,000 a year, with quotas for each European nation. The racist restrictions were designed to staunch the flow of immigrants from southern and eastern Europe and from Asia.

| Why did the relationship between urban and rural America deteriorate in the 1920s? | How did President Hoover respond to the economic crash of 1929? | What was life like in the early years of the depression? | Conclusion: Why did the hope of the 1920s turn to despair? | ✓ LearningCurve Check what you know. bedfordstmartins.com /roarkunderstanding |

Ku Klux Klan

▶ Secret society that first thwarted black freedom after the Civil War but was reborn in 1915 to fight against perceived threats posed by blacks, immigrants, radicals, feminists, Catholics, and Jews. The new Klan spread well beyond the South in the 1920s.

anti-immigration legislation. While it cut immigration by more than 80 percent, it squeezed some nationalities far more than others. Backers of Johnson-Reed, who declared that America had become the "garbage can and the dumping ground of the world," manipulated quotas to ensure entry only to "good" immigrants from western Europe. The law effectively reversed the trend toward immigration from southern and eastern Europe, which by 1914 had amounted to 75 percent of the yearly total.

The 1924 law reaffirmed the 1880s legislation barring Chinese immigrants and added Japanese and other Asians to the list of the excluded. But it left open immigration from the Western Hemisphere because farmers in the Southwest demanded continued access to cheap agricultural labor. During the 1920s, some half a million Mexicans crossed the border. In addition, Congress in 1924 passed the Indian Citizenship Act, which extended suffrage and citizenship to all American Indians.

Antiforeign hysteria climaxed in the trial of two anarchist immigrants from Italy, Nicola Sacco and Bartolomeo Vanzetti. Arrested in 1920 for robbery and murder in South Braintree, Massachusetts, the men were sentenced to death by a judge who openly referred to them as "anarchist bastards." In response to doubts about the fairness of the verdict, a blue-ribbon review committee found the trial judge guilty of a "grave breach of official decorum" but refused to recommend a motion for retrial. When Massachusetts executed Sacco and Vanzetti on August 23, 1927, fifty thousand American mourners followed the caskets, convinced that the men had died because they were immigrants and radicals, not because they were murderers.

The Rebirth of the Ku Klux Klan

The nation's sour antiforeign mood struck a responsive chord in members of the secret society called the **Ku Klux Klan**. The Klan first appeared in the South during Reconstruction to thwart black freedom and expired with the reestablishment of white supremacy (see chapter 16). In 1915, the Klan was reborn at Stone Mountain, Georgia, but when the new Klan extended its targets beyond black Americans, it quickly spread beyond the South. Under a banner proclaiming "100 percent Americanism," the Klan promised to defend family, morality, and traditional American values against the threats posed by blacks, immigrants, radicals, feminists, Catholics, and Jews.

Building on the frustrations of rural America, the Klan in the 1920s spread throughout the nation, almost controlling Indiana and influencing politics in Illinois, California, Oregon, Texas, Louisiana, Oklahoma, and Kansas. In 1926, Klan imperial wizard Hiram Wesley Evans described the assault of modernity: "One by one all our traditional moral standards went by the boards or were so disregarded that they ceased to be binding," he explained. "The sacredness of our Sabbath, of our homes, of chastity, and finally even of our right to teach our own children in schools [represented] fundamental facts and truth torn away from us."

Eventually, social changes, along with lawless excess, crippled the Klan. Immigration restrictions eased the worry about invading foreigners, and sensational wrongdoing by Klan leaders cost it the support of traditional moralists. Grand Dragon David Stephenson of Indiana, for example, went to jail for the kidnapping and rape of a woman who subsequently committed suicide. Yet the

CHAPTER LOCATOR | How did big business shape the "New Era" of the 1920s? | In what ways did the Roaring Twenties challenge traditional values?

social grievances, economic problems, and religious anxieties of the countryside and small towns remained alive, ready to be ignited.

The Scopes Trial

In 1925 in a Tennessee courtroom, old-time religion and the new spirit of science went head-to-head. The confrontation occurred after several southern states passed legislation against the teaching of Charles Darwin's theory of evolution in the public schools. Scientists and civil liberties organizations clamored for a challenge to the law, and John Scopes, a young biology teacher in Dayton, Tennessee, offered to test his state's ban on teaching evolution. When Scopes came to trial, Clarence Darrow, a brilliant defense lawyer from Chicago, volunteered to defend him. Darrow, an avowed agnostic, took on the prosecution's William Jennings Bryan, three-time Democratic nominee for president, fervent fundamentalist, and symbol of rural America.

The **Scopes trial** quickly degenerated into a media circus. The first trial to be covered live on radio, it attracted a nationwide audience. When, under relentless questioning by Darrow, Bryan declared on the witness stand that he did indeed believe that the world had been created in six days and that Jonah had lived in the belly of a whale, his humiliation in the eyes of most urban observers was complete. Nevertheless, the Tennessee court upheld the law and punished Scopes with a $100 fine. Although fundamentalism won the battle, it lost the war. Baltimore journalist H. L. Mencken had the last word in a merciless obituary for Bryan, who died just a week after the trial ended. Portraying the "monkey trial" as a battle between the country and the city, Mencken flayed Bryan as a "charlatan, a mountebank, a zany without shame or dignity," motivated solely by "hatred of the city men who had laughed at him for so long."

As Mencken's acid prose indicated, Bryan's humiliation was not purely a victory of reason and science. It also revealed the disdain urban people felt for country people and the values they clung to. The Ku Klux Klan revival and the Scopes trial dramatized and inflamed divisions between city and country, intellectuals and the uneducated, the privileged and the poor, the scoffers and the faithful.

Scopes trial

▶ 1925 trial of John Scopes, a biology teacher in Dayton, Tennessee, for violating his state's ban on teaching evolution. The trial created a nationwide media frenzy and came to be seen as a showdown between urban and rural values.

Al Smith and the Election of 1928

The presidential election of 1928 brought many of the developments of the 1920s — prohibition, immigration, religion, and the clash of rural and urban values — into sharp focus. Republicans emphasized the economic success of their party's pro-business government and turned to Herbert Hoover, the energetic secretary of commerce and leading public symbol of 1920s prosperity. But because both parties generally agreed that the American economy was basically sound, the campaign turned on social issues that divided Americans.

The Democrats nominated four-time governor of New York Alfred E. Smith. Smith seemed to represent all that rural Americans feared and resented. A child of immigrants, Smith got his start in politics with the help of New York's Tammany Hall political machine, to many the epitome of big-city corruption. He denounced immigration quotas, signed New York State's anti-Klan bill, and opposed prohibition,

| Why did the relationship between urban and rural America deteriorate in the 1920s? | How did President Hoover respond to the economic crash of 1929? | What was life like in the early years of the depression? | Conclusion: Why did the hope of the 1920s turn to despair? | ✓ LearningCurve Check what you know. bedfordstmartins.com /roarkunderstanding |

695

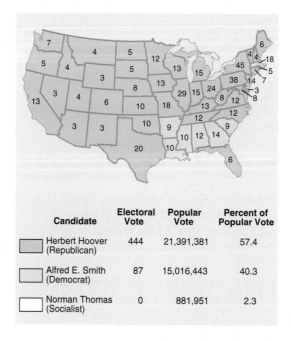

Candidate	Electoral Vote	Popular Vote	Percent of Popular Vote
Herbert Hoover (Republican)	444	21,391,381	57.4
Alfred E. Smith (Democrat)	87	15,016,443	40.3
Norman Thomas (Socialist)	0	881,951	2.3

MAP 23.3 ■ The Election of 1928

believing that it was a nativist attack on immigrant customs. Prohibition forces dubbed him "Alcohol Al," but Smith's greatest vulnerability in the heartland was his religion. He was the first Catholic to run for president. A Methodist bishop in Virginia denounced Roman Catholicism as "the Mother of ignorance, superstition, intolerance and sin" and begged Protestants not to vote for a candidate who represented "the kind of dirty people that you find today on the sidewalks of New York."

Hoover, who neatly combined the images of morality, efficiency, service, and prosperity, won the election by a landslide (**Map 23.3**). He received nearly 58 percent of the vote and gained 444 electoral votes to Smith's 87. The only bright spot for Democrats was the nation's cities, which voted Democratic, indicating the rising strength of ethnic minorities, including Smith's fellow Catholics.

> **QUICK REVIEW**

How did some Americans resist cultural change?

CHAPTER LOCATOR | How did big business shape the "New Era" of the 1920s? | In what ways did the Roaring Twenties challenge traditional values?

CHAPTER 23

696 FROM NEW ERA TO GREAT DEPRESSION

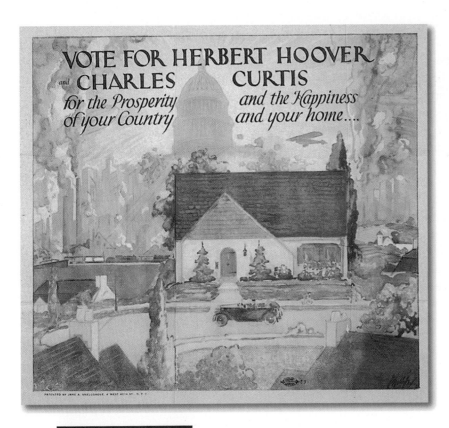

Hoover Campaign Poster

This poster effectively illustrates Herbert Hoover's 1928 campaign message: Republican administrations in the 1920s had produced middle-class prosperity, complete with a house in the suburbs and the latest automobile. To remind voters that Hoover as secretary of commerce had promoted industry that made the suburban dream possible, the poster portrays smoking chimneys at a discreet distance. Collection of Janice L. and David J. Frent.

How did President Hoover respond to the economic crash of 1929?

AT HIS INAUGURATION IN 1929, Herbert Hoover told the American people, "Given a chance to go forward with the policies of the last eight years, we shall soon with the help of God be in sight of the day when poverty will be banished from this nation." Those words came back to haunt Hoover when eight months later the prosperity he touted collapsed in the stock market crash of 1929. The nation ended nearly three decades of barely interrupted economic growth. Like much of the world, the United States fell into the most serious economic depression of all time. Hoover's limited response to economic catastrophe proved inadequate.

| Why did the relationship between urban and rural America deteriorate in the 1920s? | **How did President Hoover respond to the economic crash of 1929?** | What was life like in the early years of the depression? | Conclusion: Why did the hope of the 1920s turn to despair? | ✓ LearningCurve Check what you know. bedfordstmartins.com /roarkunderstanding |

697

1929
– Stock market collapses.

1930
– Congress authorizes $420 million for public works projects.
– Hawley-Smoot tariff.

1932
– Reconstruction Finance Corporation is established.

Herbert Hoover: The Great Engineer

When Herbert Hoover became president in 1929, he seemed the perfect choice to lead a prosperous business nation. His rise from poor Iowa orphan to one of the world's most celebrated mining engineers personified America's rags-to-riches ideal. His success in managing efforts to feed civilian victims of the fighting during World War I won him acclaim as "the Great Humanitarian" and led Woodrow Wilson to name him head of the Food Administration once the United States entered the war. Hoover's reputation soared even higher as secretary of commerce in the Harding and Coolidge administrations.

Hoover belonged to the progressive wing of his party. "The time when the employer could ride roughshod over his labor[ers] is disappearing with the doctrine of 'laissez-faire' on which it is founded," he declared in 1909. He urged a limited business-government partnership that would manage the sweeping changes Americans were experiencing. Hoover brought a reform agenda to the White House: "We want to see a nation built of home owners and farm owners. We want to see their savings protected. We want to see them in steady jobs. We want to see more and more of them insured against death and accident, unemployment and old age. We want them all secure."

But Hoover also had ideological and political liabilities. Principles that appeared strengths in the prosperous 1920s — individual self-reliance, industrial self-management, and a limited federal government — became straitjackets when economic catastrophe struck. Moreover, Hoover had never held an elected public office, had a poor political touch, and was too thin-skinned to be an effective politician. Prophetically, he confided to a friend his fear that "if some unprecedented calamity should come upon the nation . . . I would be sacrificed to the unreasoning disappointment of a people who expected too much." The distorted national economy set the stage for the calamity Hoover so feared.

The Distorted Economy

In the spring of 1929, the United States enjoyed a fragile prosperity. Although America had become the world's leading economy, it had done little to help rebuild Europe's shattered economy after World War I. Instead, the Republican administrations demanded that Allied nations repay their war loans, creating a tangled web of debts and reparations that sapped Europe's economic vitality. Moreover, to boost American business, the United States enacted tariffs that prevented other nations from selling their goods to Americans. Fewer sales meant that foreign nations had less money to buy American goods. American banks propped up the nation's export trade by extending credit to foreign customers, deepening their debt.

America's domestic economy was also in trouble. Wealth was unevenly distributed. Farmers continued to suffer from low prices and chronic indebtedness; the average income of farm families was only $240 per year. The wages of industrial workers, though rising during the decade, failed to keep up with productivity and corporate profits. Overall, nearly two-thirds of all American families lived on less than the $2,000 per year that economists estimated would "supply only basic necessities." In sharp contrast, the wealthiest 1 percent of the population

CHAPTER LOCATOR | How did big business shape the "New Era" of the 1920s? | In what ways did the Roaring Twenties challenge traditional values?

698 CHAPTER 23 FROM NEW ERA TO GREAT DEPRESSION

received 15 percent of the nation's income — the amount received by the poorest 42 percent. The Coolidge administration worsened the deepening inequality by cutting taxes on the wealthy.

By 1929, the inequality of wealth produced a serious problem in consumption. The rich spent lavishly, but they could absorb only a tiny fraction of the nation's output. For a time, the new device of installment buying — buying on credit — kept consumer demand up. By the end of the decade, four out of five cars and two out of three radios were bought on credit.

Signs of economic trouble began to appear at mid-decade. New construction slowed down. Automobile sales faltered. Companies began cutting back production and laying off workers. Between 1921 and 1928, as investment and loan opportunities faded, five thousand banks failed, wiping out the life savings of hundreds of thousands.

The Crash of 1929

Even as the economy faltered, Americans remained upbeat. Hoping for even bigger slices of the economic pie, Americans speculated wildly in the stock market on Wall Street. Between 1924 and 1929, the values of stocks listed on the New York

Stock Market Crash

Edward Laning, a mural painter who lost his personal fortune in the stock market crash, gained a measure of revenge in this melodramatic version of the panic on the Stock Exchange floor. Stock Exchange president Richard Whitney stands illuminated and unperturbed in the center as prices and brokers collapse around him. A few years later, however, Whitney went to prison for stealing from other people's accounts to cover his own losses. Collection of John. P. Axelrod/ Picture Research Consultants & Archives.

Why did the relationship between urban and rural America deteriorate in the 1920s?

How did President Hoover respond to the economic crash of 1929?

What was life like in the early years of the depression?

Conclusion: Why did the hope of the 1920s turn to despair?

☑ LearningCurve
Check what you know.
bedfordstmartins.com
/roarkunderstanding

Stock Exchange increased by more than 400 percent. Buying stocks on margin — that is, putting up only part of the money at the time of purchase — accelerated. Many people got rich this way, but those who bought on credit could finance their loans only if their stocks increased in value.

Finally, in the autumn of 1929, the market hesitated. Investors nervously began to sell their overvalued stocks. The dip quickly became a panic on October 24, the day that came to be known as Black Thursday. More panic selling came on Black Tuesday, October 29, the day the market suffered a greater fall than ever before. In the next six months, the stock market lost six-sevenths of its total value.

It was once thought that the crash alone caused the Great Depression. It did not. In 1929, the national and international economies were already riddled with severe problems. But the dramatic losses in the stock market crash and the fear of risking what was left acted as a great brake on economic activity. The collapse on Wall Street shattered the New Era's confidence that America would enjoy perpetually expanding prosperity.

Hoover and the Limits of Individualism

When the bubble broke, Americans expressed relief that Herbert Hoover resided in the White House. Not surprisingly for a man who had been such an active secretary of commerce, Hoover acted quickly to arrest the decline. In November 1929, to keep the stock market collapse from ravaging the entire economy, Hoover called a White House conference of business and labor leaders. He urged them to join in a voluntary plan for recovery: Businesses would maintain production and keep their workers on the job; labor would accept existing wages, hours, and conditions. Within a few months, however, the bargain fell apart. As demand for their products declined, industrialists cut production, sliced wages, and laid off workers. Poorly paid or unemployed workers could not buy much, and their decreased spending led to further cuts in production and further loss of jobs. Thus began the terrible spiral of economic decline.

> Hoover's Attempts to Deal with the Depression	
1929	• Agricultural Marketing Act allowed the federal government to buy surplus agricultural products to raise prices.
1930	• Hawley-Smoot tariff established the highest tariff rates in U.S. history. • Congress authorized $420 million for public works projects to give the unemployed jobs.
1932	• Reconstruction Finance Corporation was established to lend federal money to banks and corporations.

Reconstruction Finance Corporation (RFC)
▶ Federal agency established by Herbert Hoover in 1932 to help American industry by lending government funds to endangered banks and corporations, which Hoover hoped would benefit people at the bottom through trickle-down economics. In practice, this strategy provided little help to the poor.

But with each year of Hoover's term, the economy weakened. Tariffs did not end the suffering of farmers because foreign nations retaliated with increased tariffs of their own that crippled American farmers' ability to sell abroad. With the establishment of the **Reconstruction Finance Corporation (RFC)**, Hoover employed the theory of trickle-down economics: Pump money into the economy at

CHAPTER LOCATOR | How did big business shape the "New Era" of the 1920s? | In what ways did the Roaring Twenties challenge traditional values?

700 CHAPTER 23
FROM NEW ERA TO GREAT DEPRESSION

the top, and in the long run the people at the bottom would benefit. Or as one wag put it, "Feed the sparrows by feeding the horses." In the end, very little of what critics of the RFC called a "millionaires' dole" trickled down to the poor.

Meanwhile, hundreds of thousands of workers lost their jobs each month. By 1932, an astounding one-quarter of the American workforce — nearly thirteen million people — were unemployed. There was no direct federal assistance, and state services and private charities were swamped. The depression that began in 1929 devastated much of the world, but no other industrialized nation provided such feeble support to the jobless. Cries grew louder for the federal government to give hurting people relief.

Hoover's response revealed the limits of his conception of the government's proper role in fighting the economic disaster. He compared direct federal aid to the needy to the "dole" in Britain, which he thought destroyed the moral fiber of the chronically unemployed. The poor, he said, could rely on their neighbors to protect them "from hunger and cold." In 1931, he allowed the Red Cross to distribute government-owned agricultural surpluses to the hungry. In 1932, he relaxed his principles further to offer small federal loans, not gifts, to the states to help them in their relief efforts. But Hoover's circumscribed notions of legitimate government action proved vastly inadequate to address the problems of restarting the economy and ending human suffering.

QUICK REVIEW

Why did the American economy collapse in 1929?

| Why did the relationship between urban and rural America deteriorate in the 1920s? | **How did President Hoover respond to the economic crash of 1929?** | What was life like in the early years of the depression? | Conclusion: Why did the hope of the 1920s turn to despair? | ☑ LearningCurve Check what you know. bedfordstmartins.com /roarkunderstanding |

What was life like in the early years of the depression?

An Unemployed Youth Joblessness was frightening and humiliating. Brought up to believe that if you worked hard, you got ahead, the unemployed had difficulty seeing failure to find work as anything other than personal failure. We can only imagine this young man's story. Utterly alone, sitting on a bench that might be his bed, his head in his hands, he looks emotionally battered and perhaps defeated. Library of Congress.

IN 1930, SUFFERING on a massive scale set in. Men and women hollow-eyed with hunger grew increasingly bewildered and angry in the face of cruel contradictions. They saw agricultural surpluses pile up in the countryside and knew that their children were going to bed hungry. They saw factories standing idle, yet they knew that they and millions of others were willing to work. The gap between the American people and leaders who failed to resolve these contradictions widened as the depression deepened. By 1932, America's economic problems had created a dangerous social and political crisis.

The Human Toll

Statistics only hint at the human tragedy of the Great Depression. When Herbert Hoover took office in 1929, the American economy stood at its peak. When he left in 1933, it had reached its twentieth-century low (**Figure 23.2**). In 1929, national income was $88 billion. By 1933, it had declined to $40 billion. In 1929, unemployment was 3.1 percent, or 1.5 million workers. By 1933, unemployment stood at

CHAPTER LOCATOR

How did big business shape the "New Era" of the 1920s?

In what ways did the Roaring Twenties challenge traditional values?

702 CHAPTER 23
FROM NEW ERA TO GREAT DEPRESSION

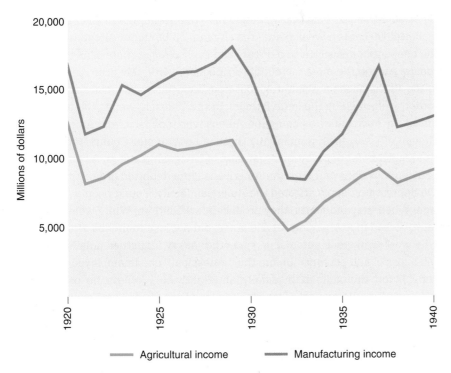

FIGURE 23.2 ■ Manufacturing and Agricultural Income, 1920–1940

After economic collapse, recovery in the 1930s began under New Deal auspices. The sharp declines in 1937–1938, when federal spending was reduced, indicated that New Deal stimuli were still needed to restore manufacturing and agricultural income.

> **CHRONOLOGY**

1931
– Scottsboro Boys are arrested.
– Harlan County, Kentucky, coal strike.

1932
– River Rouge factory demonstration.
– National Farmers' Holiday Association is formed.

25 percent, almost 13 million workers. By 1932, more than 9,000 banks had shut their doors, wiping out millions of savings accounts.

Jobless, homeless victims wandered in search of work, and the tramp, or hobo, became one of the most visible figures of the decade. Riding the rails or hitchhiking, a million vagabonds moved southward and westward looking for seasonal agricultural work. Other unemployed men and women, sick or less hopeful, huddled in doorways, overcome, one man remembered, by "helpless despair and submission." Scavengers haunted alleys behind restaurants in search of food. "I don't want to steal," a Pennsylvania man wrote to the governor in 1931, "but I won't let my wife and boy cry for something to eat. . . . How long is this going to keep up? I cannot stand it any longer."

Rural poverty was most acute. Tenant farmers and sharecroppers, mainly in the South, came to symbolize how poverty crushed the human spirit. Eight and a half million people, three million of them black, crowded into cabins without plumbing, electricity, or running water. They subsisted — just barely — on salt pork, cornmeal, molasses, beans, peas, and whatever they could hunt or fish. When economist John Maynard Keynes was asked whether anything like this degradation had existed before, he replied, "Yes, it was called the Dark Ages and it lasted four hundred years."

There was no federal assistance to meet this human catastrophe, only a patchwork of strapped charities and destitute state and local agencies. For a family of four without any income, the best the city of Philadelphia could do was

Why did the relationship between urban and rural America deteriorate in the 1920s?

How did President Hoover respond to the economic crash of 1929?

What was life like in the early years of the depression?

Conclusion: Why did the hope of the 1920s turn to despair?

✓ **LearningCurve**
Check what you know.
bedfordstmartins.com
/roarkunderstanding

703

provide $5.50 per week. That was not enough to live on but better than Detroit, which allotted 60 cents a week before the city ran out of money altogether.

The deepening crisis roused old fears and caused some Americans to look for scapegoats. Among the most thoroughly scapegoated were Mexican Americans. During the 1920s, cheap agricultural labor from Mexico flowed legally across the U.S. border, welcomed by the large farmers. In the 1930s, however, the public denounced the newcomers as dangerous aliens who took jobs from Americans. Government officials, most prominently those in Los Angeles County, targeted Mexican residents for deportation regardless of citizenship status. As many as half a million Mexicans and Mexican Americans were deported or fled to Mexico.

The depression deeply affected the American family. Young people postponed marriage. When they did marry, they produced few children. White women, who generally worked in low-paying service areas, did not lose their jobs as often as men who worked in steel, automobile, and other heavy industries. Idle husbands suffered a loss of self-esteem. "Before the depression," one unemployed man reported, "I wore the pants in this family, and rightly so." Jobless, he lost "self-respect" and also "the respect of my children, and I am afraid that I am losing my wife." Employers discriminated against married women workers, but necessity continued to drive women into the marketplace. As a result, by 1940 some 25 percent more women were employed for wages than in 1930.

Denial and Escape

President Hoover assured the American nation that economic recovery was on its way, but the president's optimism was contradicted by makeshift shantytowns, called "Hoovervilles," that sprang up on the edges of America's cities. Bitter jokes circulated about the increasingly unpopular president. One told of Hoover asking for a nickel to telephone a friend. Flipping him a dime, an aide said, "Here, call them both."

While Hoover practiced denial, other Americans sought refuge from reality at the movies. Throughout the depression, between 60 million and 75 million people (nearly two-thirds of the nation) scraped together enough change to fill the movie palaces every week. Box office hits such as *Forty-second Street* and *Gold Diggers of 1933* capitalized on the hope that prosperity lay just around the corner. But a few filmmakers grappled with realities rather than escape them. *The Public Enemy* (1931) taught hard lessons about gangsters' ill-gotten gains. Indeed, under the new production code of 1930, designed to protect public morals, all movies had to find some way to show that crime did not pay.

Despite Hollywood's efforts to keep Americans on the right side of the law, crime increased. In the countryside, the plight of people who had lost their farms to bank foreclosures led to the romantic idea that bank robbers were only getting back what banks had stolen from the poor. Woody Guthrie, the populist folksinger from Oklahoma, captured the public's tolerance for outlaws in his tribute to a murderous bank robber with a choirboy face, "The Ballad of Pretty Boy Floyd":

> Yes, as through this world I've wandered
> I've seen lots of funny men;
> Some will rob you with a six-gun,
> And some with a fountain pen.

CHAPTER LOCATOR | How did big business shape the "New Era" of the 1920s? | In what ways did the Roaring Twenties challenge traditional values?

CHAPTER 23
704 FROM NEW ERA TO GREAT DEPRESSION

And as through your life you travel,
Yes, as through your life you roam,
You won't never see an outlaw
Drive a family from their home.

Working-Class Militancy

The nation's working class bore the brunt of the economic collapse. By 1931, William Green, head of the American Federation of Labor, had turned militant. "I warn the people who are exploiting the workers," he shouted, "that they can drive them only so far before they will turn on them and destroy them. They are taking no account of the history of nations in which governments have been overturned. Revolutions grow out of the depths of hunger."

The American people were slow to anger, but on March 7, 1932, several thousand unemployed autoworkers massed at the gates of Henry Ford's River Rouge factory in Dearborn, Michigan, to demand work. Pelted with rocks, Ford's private security forces responded with gunfire, killing four demonstrators. Forty thousand outraged citizens turned out for the unemployed men's funerals.

Farmers mounted uprisings of their own. When Congress refused to guarantee farm prices, several thousand farmers created the National Farmers' Holiday Association in 1932, so named because its members planned to take a "holiday" from shipping crops to market. Farm militants also resorted to what they called "penny sales." When banks foreclosed and put farms up for auction, neighbors warned others not to bid, bought the foreclosed property for a few pennies, and returned it to the bankrupt owners. Militancy won farmers little in the way of long-term solutions, but one individual observed that "the biggest and finest crop of revolutions you ever saw is sprouting all over the country right now."

Even those who had proved their patriotism by serving in World War I rose up in protest against the government. In 1932, tens of thousands of unemployed veterans traveled to Washington, D.C., to petition Congress for the immediate payment of the pension (known as a "bonus") that Congress had promised them in 1924. Hoover feared that the veterans would spark a riot and ordered the U.S. Army to evict the **Bonus Marchers** from their camp on the outskirts of the city. Tanks destroyed the squatters' encampments while five hundred soldiers wielding bayonets and tear gas sent the protesters fleeing. The spectacle of the army driving peaceful, petitioning veterans from the nation's capital further undermined public support for the beleaguered Hoover.

The Great Depression — the massive failure of capitalism — catapulted the Communist Party to its greatest size and influence in American history. Some 100,000 Americans — workers, intellectuals, college students — joined the Communist Party in the belief that only an overthrow of the capitalist system could save the victims of the depression. In 1931, the party, through its National Miners Union, moved into Harlan County, Kentucky, to support a strike by brutalized coal miners. Mine owners unleashed thugs against the strikers and eventually beat the miners down. But the Communist Party gained a reputation as the most dedicated and fearless champion of the union cause.

The left also led the fight against racism. While both major parties refused to challenge segregation in the South, the Socialist Party, led by Norman Thomas,

Harlan County Coal Strike, 1931

Bonus Marchers

▶ World War I veterans who marched on Washington, D.C., in 1932 to lobby for immediate payment of the pension ("bonus") promised them in 1924. President Herbert Hoover believed the bonuses would bankrupt the government and sent the U.S. Army to evict the veterans from the city.

Why did the relationship between urban and rural America deteriorate in the 1920s?

How did President Hoover respond to the economic crash of 1929?

What was life like in the early years of the depression?

Conclusion: Why did the hope of the 1920s turn to despair?

LearningCurve
Check what you know.
bedfordstmartins.com
/roarkunderstanding

"Scottsboro Boys" Nine black youths, ranging in age from thirteen to twenty-one, were convicted of the rape of two white women and sentenced to death by an all-white jury in March 1931. None was executed, and eventually the state dropped the charges against the youngest four and granted paroles to the others. The last "Scottsboro Boy" left jail in 1950. © Bettmann/Corbis.

Scottsboro Boys

▶ Nine African American youths who were arrested for the alleged rape of two white women in Scottsboro, Alabama, in 1931. After an all-white jury sentenced the young men to death, the Communist Party took action that saved them from the electric chair.

attacked the system of sharecropping that left many African Americans in near servitude. The Communist Party also took action. When nine young black men in Scottsboro, Alabama (the **Scottsboro Boys**), were arrested on trumped-up rape charges in 1931, a team of lawyers sent by the party saved the defendants from the electric chair.

Radicals on the left often sparked action, but protests by moderate workers and farmers occurred on a far greater scale. Breadlines, soup kitchens, foreclosures, unemployment, government violence, and cold despair drove patriotic men and women to question American capitalism. "I am as conservative as any man could be," a Wisconsin farmer explained, "but any economic system that has in its power to set me and my wife in the streets, at my age — what can I see but red?"

> **QUICK REVIEW**

How did the depression reshape American politics?

CHAPTER LOCATOR | How did big business shape the "New Era" of the 1920s? | In what ways did the Roaring Twenties challenge traditional values?

Conclusion: Why did the hope of the 1920s turn to despair?

IN THE AFTERMATH of World War I, America turned its back on progressive crusades and embraced conservative Republican politics, the growing influence of corporate leaders, and business values. Changes in the nation's economy — Henry Ford's automobile revolution, mass production, advertising — propelled fundamental change throughout society. Living standards rose, economic opportunity increased, and Americans threw themselves into private pleasures — gobbling up the latest household goods and fashions, attending baseball and football games and boxing matches, gathering around the radio, and going to the movies. As big cities came to dominate American life, the culture of youth and flappers became the leading edge of what one observer called a "revolution in manners and morals." At home in Harlem and abroad in Paris, American literature, art, and music flourished.

For many Americans, however, none of the glamour and vitality had much meaning. The vast majority struggled to earn a decent living. Blue-collar America did not participate fully in white-collar prosperity. Country folk, deeply suspicious and profoundly discontented, championed prohibition, revived the Klan, attacked immigration, and defended old-time Protestant religion.

The crash of 1929 and the depression that followed starkly revealed the economy's crises of international trade and consumption. Hard times swept high living off the front pages of the nation's newspapers. Different images emerged: hoboes hopping freight trains, strikers confronting police, malnourished sharecroppers staring blankly into the distance, empty apartment buildings alongside cardboard shantytowns, and mountains of food rotting in the sun while guards with shotguns chased away the hungry.

The depression hurt everyone, but the poor were hurt most. As farmers and workers sank into aching hardship, businessmen rallied around Herbert Hoover to proclaim that private enterprise would get the country moving again. But things fell apart, and Hoover faced increasingly radical opposition. Membership in the Socialist and Communist parties surged, and more and more Americans contemplated desperate measures. By 1932, the depression had nearly brought the nation to its knees. America faced its greatest crisis since the Civil War, and citizens demanded new leaders who would save them from the "Hoover Depression."

Why did the relationship between urban and rural America deteriorate in the 1920s? | How did President Hoover respond to the economic crash of 1929? | What was life like in the early years of the depression? | **Conclusion: Why did the hope of the 1920s turn to despair?** | ☑ LearningCurve Check what you know. bedfordstmartins.com /roarkunderstanding

707

CHAPTER 23 STUDY GUIDE

STEP 1

GET STARTED ONLINE

✓ **LearningCurve** ▪ bedfordstmartins.com/roarkunderstanding

Now that you've read the chapter, make it stick by completing the LearningCurve activity.

STEP 2

EXPLAIN WHY IT MATTERS

Put your reading into practice. Identify each term below, and then explain why it matters in U.S. history.

TERM	WHO OR WHAT & WHEN	WHY IT MATTERS
Teapot Dome (p. 679)		
Five-Power Naval Treaty of 1922 (p. 680)		
welfare capitalism (p. 682)		
prohibition (p. 685)		
new woman (p. 687)		
New Negro (p. 689)		
Johnson-Reed Act (p. 693)		
Ku Klux Klan (p. 694)		
Scopes trial (p. 695)		
Reconstruction Finance Corporation (RFC) (p. 700)		
Bonus Marchers (p. 705)		
Scottsboro Boys (p. 706)		

STEP 3

MOVE BEYOND THE BASICS

To demonstrate a more advanced understanding, describe the social, cultural, and economic trends that marked the 1920s as a "New Era" and the changes that occurred as the nation entered the Great Depression.

	Characteristics/developments in the 1920s	Changes from 1929 to 1932
Business and manufacturing/ urban life		
Agriculture/rural life		
Society: consumerism, religion, mass culture		
Population: gender, race relations, immigrants		
Government and politics		
The economy		

PUT IT ALL TOGETHER

Now, take a step back and try to explain the big picture. Remember to use specific examples from the chapter in your answers.

POSTWAR DEVELOPMENTS

▶ What place did big business hold in the politics and culture of the 1920s?

▶ How did the economic changes of the 1920s contribute to challenges to social, cultural, and ethical norms?

RESISTANCE TO CHANGE

▶ What explains the rising anti-immigrant mood of America in the 1920s?

▶ What cultural divisions between rural and urban America were highlighted by the election of 1928?

THE CRASH AND THE GREAT DEPRESSION

▶ What underlying weaknesses in the American and world economies led to the Great Depression?

▶ How did Herbert Hoover respond to the economic crisis that engulfed his presidency? Why were his efforts unsuccessful?

▶ What was the "human toll" of the Great Depression?

LOOKING BACKWARD, LOOKING AHEAD

▶ Were the 1920s truly a New Era? Why or why not?

▶ How were American life and culture challenged by the economic collapse of 1929? How did economic disaster make political change possible?

> IN YOUR OWN WORDS

Imagine that you must give an oral report to the class answering the following question: **What were the high points and the low points of the 1920s?** What would be the most important points to include and why?

24
FORGING THE NEW DEAL
1932–1939

> Why was the New Deal so important in U.S. history? Chapter 24 traces the efforts of President Franklin D. Roosevelt to respond to the Great Depression through an effort known as the New Deal. The chapter explores the principles and political factors that shaped the New Deal and examines the successes and failures of the New Deal during the 1930s.

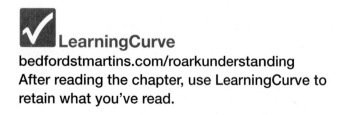

LearningCurve
bedfordstmartins.com/roarkunderstanding
After reading the chapter, use LearningCurve to retain what you've read.

> How did Franklin D. Roosevelt win the 1932 election?

> What were the goals and achievements of the first New Deal?

> Who opposed the New Deal and why?

> How did the second phase of the New Deal differ from the first?

> What major political trends changed during the late 1930s?

> Conclusion: What were the achievements and limitations of the New Deal?

"Work Pays America!" Poster from the New Deal's Works Progress Administration. Library of Congress.

How did Franklin D. Roosevelt win the 1932 election?

Sensing that his presentation of himself as a good neighbor was responsible for much of his popularity, Roosevelt arranged to have a friendly chat outside the polls in his hometown of Hyde Park with working-class voter Ruben Appel. In this photograph, Appel seems unaware that Roosevelt's standing was itself a feat of stagecraft. Franklin D. Roosevelt Library.

UNLIKE THE MILLIONS of impoverished Americans, Franklin Delano Roosevelt came from a wealthy and privileged background that contributed to his optimism, self-confidence, and vitality. He drew on these personal qualities in his political career to bridge the economic, social, and cultural chasm that separated him from the struggles of ordinary people. During the twelve years he served as president (1933–1945), many elites came to hate him as a traitor to his class, while millions more Americans in his New Deal coalition, especially the hardworking poor and dispossessed, revered him because he cared about them and their problems.

The Making of a Politician

Born in 1882, Franklin Delano Roosevelt grew up on his father's leafy estate at Hyde Park on the Hudson River, north of New York City. Roosevelt prepared for a career in politics, hoping to follow in the political footsteps of his fifth cousin, Theodore Roosevelt. Unlike cousin Teddy, Franklin Roosevelt sought his political

CHAPTER LOCATOR | How did Franklin D. Roosevelt win the 1932 election? | What were the goals and achievements of the first New Deal?

CHAPTER 24
712 FORGING THE NEW DEAL

fortune in the Democratic Party. In 1920, he catapulted to the second spot on the national Democratic ticket as the vice presidential running mate of presidential nominee James M. Cox. Although Cox lost the election (see chapter 22), Roosevelt's energetic campaigning convinced Democratic leaders that he had a bright future.

In the summer of 1921, at the age of thirty-nine, Roosevelt caught polio, which paralyzed both his legs. For the rest of his life, he wore heavy steel braces, and he could walk a few steps only by leaning on another person. Tireless physical therapy helped him regain his vitality and intense desire for high political office, although he carefully avoided being photographed in the wheelchair he used routinely.

After his polio attack, Roosevelt frequented a polio therapy facility at Warm Springs, Georgia. There, he got to know southern Democrats, which helped make him a rare political creature: a New Yorker from the Democratic Party's urban and immigrant wing who got along with whites from the party's entrenched southern wing.

By 1928, Roosevelt had recovered sufficiently to campaign for governor of New York, and he squeaked out a victory. As governor of the nation's most populous state, Roosevelt showcased his activist policies, which became a dress rehearsal for his presidency.

As the Great Depression spread hard times throughout the nation, Governor Roosevelt believed that government should intervene to protect citizens from economic hardships rather than wait for the law of supply and demand to improve the economy. According to the laissez-faire views of many conservatives — especially Republicans, but also numerous Democrats — the depression simply represented market forces separating strong survivors from weak losers. Unlike Roosevelt, conservatives believed that government help for the needy sapped individual initiative and impeded the self-correcting forces of the market by rewarding people for losing the economic struggle to survive. Roosevelt lacked a full-fledged counterargument to these conservative claims, but he sympathized with the plight of poor people. "To these unfortunate citizens," he proclaimed, "aid must be extended by governments, not as a matter of charity but as a matter of social duty. . . . [No one should go] unfed, unclothed, or unsheltered."

To his supporters, Roosevelt seemed to be a leader determined to attack the economic crisis without deviating from democracy — unlike the fascist parties gaining strength in Europe — or from capitalism — unlike the Communists in power in the Soviet Union. Roosevelt's ideas about how to revive the economy were vague, but his many supporters appreciated his energy and activism. His conviction that government should do something to help Americans climb out of the economic abyss propelled him into the front ranks of the national Democratic Party.

The Election of 1932

Democrats knew that Herbert Hoover's unpopularity gave them a historic opportunity to recapture the White House in 1932. Since Abraham Lincoln's election, Republicans had occupied the White House three-fourths of the time, a trend Democrats hoped to reverse. Democrats, however, had to overcome warring factions that divided the party by region, religion, culture, and commitment to the status quo.

> KEY FACTORS

The 1932 Election
- The election was held in the midst of the Great Depression.
- Franklin Roosevelt believed that government should intervene to protect citizens from economic hardship.
- President Herbert Hoover was highly unpopular.
- Democrats had to overcome divisiveness within the party.
- Roosevelt promised a "new deal" during the campaign but provided few details.

| Who opposed the New Deal and why? | How did the second phase of the New Deal differ from the first? | What major political trends changed during the late 1930s? | Conclusion: What were the achievements and limitations of the New Deal? | ✓ LearningCurve Check what you know. bedfordstmartins.com /roarkunderstanding |

Candidate	Electoral Vote	Popular Vote	Percent of Popular Vote
Franklin D. Roosevelt (Democrat)	472	22,821,857	57.4
Herbert C. Hoover (Republican)	59	15,761,841	39.7
Norman Thomas (Socialist)	0	881,951	2.2
William Z. Foster (Communist)	0	102,991	0.3

MAP 24.1 ■ The Election of 1932

The southern, native-born, white, rural, Protestant, conservative wing of the Democratic Party found little common ground with the northern, immigrant, urban, disproportionately Catholic, liberal wing. Eastern-establishment Democratic dignitaries shared few goals with angry farmers and factory workers. Still, this unruly coalition managed to agree on Franklin Roosevelt as its presidential candidate.

In his acceptance speech, Roosevelt vowed to help "the forgotten man at the bottom of the pyramid" with "bold, persistent experimentation." Highlighting his differences with Hoover and the Republicans, he pledged "a new deal for the American people." Few details about what Roosevelt meant by "a new deal" emerged in the presidential campaign. He declared that "the people of America want more than anything else . . . two things: work . . . and a reasonable measure of security." Voters decided that whatever Roosevelt's new deal might be, it was better than reelecting Hoover.

Roosevelt won the 1932 presidential election in a historic landslide. He received 57 percent of the nation's votes, the first time a Democrat had won a majority of the popular vote since 1852 (**Map 24.1**). He amassed 472 electoral votes to Hoover's 59, carrying state after state that had voted Republican for

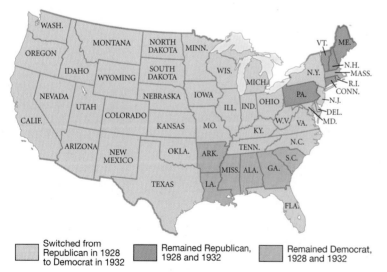

Switched from Republican in 1928 to Democrat in 1932

Remained Republican, 1928 and 1932

Remained Democrat, 1928 and 1932

MAP 24.2 ■ Electoral Shift, 1928–1932

The Democratic victory in 1932 signaled the rise of a New Deal coalition within which women and minorities, many of them new voters, made the Democrats the majority party for the first time in the twentieth century.

> MAP ACTIVITY

READING THE MAP: How many states voted Democratic in 1928? How many states voted Republican in 1932? How many states shifted from Republican to Democratic between 1928 and 1932?

CONNECTIONS: What factions within the Democratic Party opposed Franklin Roosevelt's candidacy in 1932, and why did they do so? To what do you attribute his landslide victory?

CHAPTER LOCATOR | How did Franklin D. Roosevelt win the 1932 election? | What were the goals and achievements of the first New Deal?

714 CHAPTER 24 FORGING THE NEW DEAL

years (**Map 24.2**). Roosevelt's coattails swept Democrats into control of Congress by large margins. The popular mandate for change was loud and clear.

Roosevelt's victory represented the emergence of what came to be known as the **New Deal coalition**. Attracting support from farmers, factory workers, immigrants, city folk, African Americans, women, and progressive intellectuals, Roosevelt launched a realignment of the nation's political loyalties. The New Deal coalition dominated American politics throughout Roosevelt's presidency and remained powerful long after his death in 1945. United less by ideology or support for specific policies, voters in the New Deal coalition instead expressed faith in Roosevelt's promise of a government that would somehow change things for the better. Nobody, including Roosevelt, knew exactly what the New Deal would change or whether the changes would revive the nation's ailing economy and improve Americans' lives. But Roosevelt and many others knew that the future of American capitalism and democracy was at stake.

New Deal coalition

▶ Political coalition that supported Franklin D. Roosevelt's New Deal and the Democratic Party, including farmers, factory workers, immigrants, city dwellers, women, African Americans, and progressive intellectuals. The coalition dominated American politics during and long after Roosevelt's presidency.

QUICK REVIEW

Why did Franklin D. Roosevelt win the 1932 presidential election by such a large margin?

Who opposed the New Deal and why?	How did the second phase of the New Deal differ from the first?	What major political trends changed during the late 1930s?	Conclusion: What were the achievements and limitations of the New Deal?	✅ **LearningCurve** Check what you know. bedfordstmartins.com /roarkunderstanding

> What were the goals and achievements of the first New Deal?

Eleanor Roosevelt Serving Unemployed Women

A tireless ambassador of the New Deal, Eleanor Roosevelt used her status as First Lady to highlight New Dealers' sympathy for the plight of the poor, unemployed, and neglected working people. Said one North Carolina woman, "One of my great pleasures was meeting Mrs. Roosevelt . . . she was so free of prejudice . . . she was always willing to take a stand." © Bettmann/Corbis.

AT NOON ON MARCH 4, 1933, Americans gathered around their radios to hear the inaugural address of the newly elected president. Roosevelt began by asserting his "firm belief that the only thing we have to fear is fear itself — nameless, unreasoning, unjustified terror which paralyzes needed efforts to convert retreat into advance." He promised "direct, vigorous action," and the first months of his administration, termed "the Hundred Days," fulfilled that promise in a whirlwind of government initiatives that launched the New Deal.

Roosevelt and his advisers had three interrelated objectives: relief, recovery, and reform. The New Deal never fully achieved these goals. But by aiming for them, Roosevelt's experimental programs enormously expanded government's role in the nation's economy and society.

CHAPTER LOCATOR | How did Franklin D. Roosevelt win the 1932 election? | **What were the goals and achievements of the first New Deal?**

Relief	Provide help to the millions of poor and unemployed Americans victimized by the depression.
Recovery	Foster economic recovery of farms and businesses, thereby creating jobs and reducing the need for relief.
Reform	Reshape government and the economy to protect citizens against future economic downturns.

The New Dealers

To design and implement the New Deal, Roosevelt needed ideas and people. He convened a "Brains Trust" of economists and other leaders to offer suggestions and advice about the problems facing the nation. No New Dealers were more important than the president and his wife, Eleanor. The gregarious president radiated charm and good cheer, giving the New Deal's bureaucratic regulations a benevolent human face. Eleanor Roosevelt became the New Deal's unofficial ambassador. She served, she said, as "the eyes and ears of the New Deal," traveling throughout the nation meeting Americans of all colors and creeds.

As Roosevelt's programs swung into action, the millions of beneficiaries of the New Deal became grassroots New Dealers who expressed their appreciation by voting Democratic on election day. In this way, the New Deal created a durable political coalition of Democrats that reelected Roosevelt in 1936, 1940, and 1944.

Four guiding ideas shaped New Deal policies. First, Roosevelt and his advisers sought capitalist solutions to the economic crisis. They had no desire to eliminate private property or impose socialist programs, such as public ownership of productive resources. Instead, they hoped to save the capitalist economy by remedying its flaws.

Second, Roosevelt's Brains Trust persuaded him that the greatest flaw of America's capitalist economy was **underconsumption**, the root cause of the current economic paralysis. Underconsumption, New Dealers argued, resulted from the gigantic productive success of capitalism. Factories and farms produced more than they could sell to consumers, causing factories to lay off workers and farmers to lose money on bumper crops. Workers without wages and farmers without profits shrank consumption and choked the economy. Somehow, the balance between consumption and production needed to be restored.

Third, New Dealers believed that the immense size and economic power of American corporations needed to be counterbalanced by government and by organization among workers and small producers. Unlike progressive trust-busters, New Dealers did not seek to splinter big businesses. Roosevelt and his advisers hoped to counterbalance big economic institutions with government programs focused on protecting individuals and the public interest.

Fourth, New Dealers felt that government must somehow moderate the imbalance of wealth created by American capitalism. Wealth concentrated in a few hands reduced consumption by most Americans and thereby contributed to the current economic gridlock. Government needed to find a way to permit ordinary working people to share more fully in the fruits of the economy.

underconsumption

▶ A situation in which factories and farms produce more than consumers buy, causing factories to lay off workers and farmers to lose money. New Dealers believed that underconsumption was the root cause of the country's economic paralysis. Workers without wages and farmers without profits shrank consumption and choked the economy. The only way to increase consumption, New Dealers believed, was to provide jobs that put wages in consumers' pockets.

| Who opposed the New Deal and why? | How did the second phase of the New Deal differ from the first? | What major political trends changed during the late 1930s? | Conclusion: What were the achievements and limitations of the New Deal? |

✔ **LearningCurve**
Check what you know.
bedfordstmartins.com
/roarkunderstanding

Banking and Finance Reform

Roosevelt wasted no time making good on his inaugural pledge for "action now." As he took the oath of office on March 4, the nation's banking system was on the brink of collapse. Roosevelt immediately declared a four-day "bank holiday" in order to devise a plan to shore up banks and restore depositors' confidence. Working round the clock, New Dealers drafted the Emergency Banking Act, which propped up the private banking system with federal funds and subjected banks to federal regulation and oversight. To secure the confidence of depositors, Congress passed the Glass-Steagall Banking Act, setting up the **Federal Deposit Insurance Corporation**, which guaranteed bank customers that the federal government would reimburse them for deposits if their banks failed. In addition, the act required the separation of commercial banks (which accept deposits and make loans to individuals and small businesses) and investment banks (which make speculative investments with their funds), in an effort to insulate the finances of Main Street America from the risky speculations of Wall Street wheeler-dealers.

On Sunday night, March 12, while the banks were still closed, Roosevelt broadcast the first of a series of **fireside chats**. Speaking in a friendly, informal manner, he explained the new banking legislation that, he said, made it "safer to keep your money in a reopened bank than under the mattress." With such plain talk, Roosevelt translated complex matters into common sense. This and subsequent fireside chats forged a direct connection — via radio — between Roosevelt and millions of Americans, a connection felt by a man from Paris, Texas, who wrote to Roosevelt, "You are the one & only President that ever helped a Working Class of People. . . . Please help us some way I Pray to God for relief."

The banking legislation and fireside chat worked. Within a few days, most of the nation's major banks reopened, and they remained solvent as reassured depositors switched funds from their mattresses to their bank accounts (**Figure 24.1**).

In his inaugural address, Roosevelt criticized financiers for their greed and incompetence. To prevent the fraud, corruption, and insider trading that had tainted Wall Street and contributed to the crash of 1929, New Dealers created the Securities and Exchange Commission (SEC) in 1934 to oversee financial markets by licensing investment dealers, monitoring all stock transactions, and requiring corporate officers to make full disclosures about their companies. The SEC helped clean up and regulate Wall Street, which slowly recovered.

Relief and Conservation Programs

Patching the nation's financial structure provided little relief for the hungry and unemployed. A poor man from Nebraska asked Eleanor Roosevelt "if the folk who was borned here in America . . . are this Forgotten Man, the President had in mind, [and] if we are this Forgotten Man then we are still Forgotten." Since its founding, the federal government had never assumed responsibility for needy people, except in moments of natural disaster or emergencies such as the Civil War. Instead, churches, private charities, county and municipal governments, and occasionally states assumed the burden of poor relief, usually with meager payments. The depression necessitated unprecedented federal relief efforts, according to New Dealers.

Federal Deposit Insurance Corporation
▶ Regulatory body established by the Glass-Steagall Banking Act that guaranteed the federal government would reimburse bank depositors if their banks failed. This key feature of the New Deal restored depositors' confidence in the banking system during the Great Depression.

fireside chats
▶ Series of informal radio addresses Franklin Roosevelt made to the nation in which he explained New Deal initiatives. The chats helped bolster Roosevelt's popularity and secured popular support for his reforms.

CHAPTER LOCATOR | How did Franklin D. Roosevelt win the 1932 election? | What were the goals and achievements of the first New Deal?

718 CHAPTER 24 FORGING THE NEW DEAL

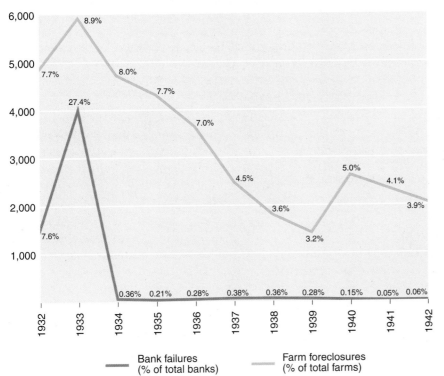

FIGURE 24.1 ■ Bank Failures and Farm Foreclosures, 1932–1942

New Deal legislation to stabilize the economy had its most immediate and striking effect in preventing banks, along with their depositors, from going under and farmers from losing their land.

Legend:
— Bank failures (% of total banks)
— Farm foreclosures (% of total farms)

The Federal Emergency Relief Administration (FERA), established in May 1933, supported four million to five million households with $20 or $30 a month. The FERA also created jobs for the unemployed on thousands of public works projects, organized into the Civil Works Administration (CWA), which put paychecks worth more than $800 million into the hands of previously jobless workers. Earning wages between 40 and 60 cents an hour, laborers renovated schools, dug sewers, and rebuilt roads and bridges.

The most popular work relief program was the **Civilian Conservation Corps (CCC)**, established in March 1933. It offered unemployed young men a chance to earn wages while working to conserve natural resources, a long-standing interest of Roosevelt. Women were excluded from working in the CCC until Eleanor Roosevelt demanded that a token number of young women be hired. By the end of the program in 1942, three million CCC workers had left a legacy of vast new recreation areas, along with roads that made those areas accessible to millions of Americans. Just as important, the CCC, CWA, and other work relief efforts replaced the stigma of welfare with the dignity of jobs. As one woman said about her husband's work relief job, "We aren't on relief anymore. My husband is working for the Government."

The New Deal's most ambitious and controversial natural resources development project was the Tennessee Valley Authority (TVA), created in May 1933 to build dams along the Tennessee River to supply impoverished rural communities with cheap electricity (**Map 24.3**). The TVA set out to demonstrate that a partnership between the federal government and local residents could overcome the barriers of state governments and private enterprises to make efficient use of

Civilian Conservation Corps (CCC)

▶ Federal relief program established in March 1933 that provided assistance in the form of jobs to millions of unemployed young men and a token number of women. CCC workers worked on conservation projects throughout the nation.

| Who opposed the New Deal and why? | How did the second phase of the New Deal differ from the first? | What major political trends changed during the late 1930s? | Conclusion: What were the achievements and limitations of the New Deal? | ✓ LearningCurve Check what you know. bedfordstmartins.com /roarkunderstanding |

719

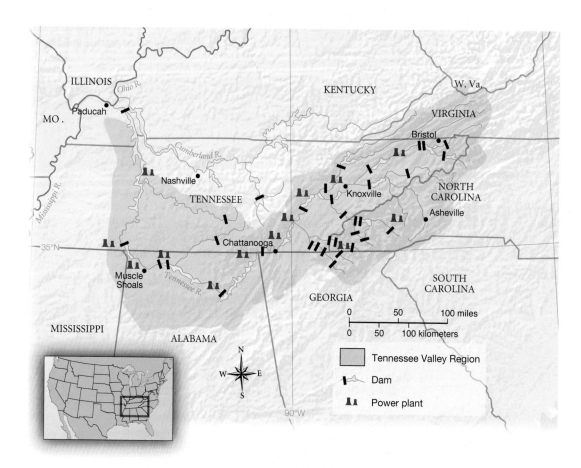

MAP 24.3 ■ The Tennessee Valley Authority

The New Deal created the Tennessee Valley Authority to modernize a vast impoverished region with hydroelectric power dams and, at the same time, to reclaim eroded land and preserve old folkways.

> **MAP ACTIVITY**

READING THE MAP: How many states were affected by the TVA? How many miles of rivers (approximately) were affected?

CONNECTIONS: What kinds of benefits—economic as well as social and cultural—did TVA programs bring to the region? How might the lives of a poor farming family in Alabama or Tennessee have changed after the mid-1930s owing to these programs?

abundant natural resources and break the ancient cycle of poverty. The TVA improved the lives of millions in the region with electric power, flood protection, soil reclamation, and jobs.

New sources of hydroelectric power helped the New Deal bring the wonders of electricity to country folk, fulfilling an old progressive dream. When Roosevelt became president, 90 percent of rural Americans lacked electricity. Private electric companies refused to build transmission lines into the sparsely settled country-side when they had a profitable market in more accessible and densely populated urban areas. Beginning in 1935, the Rural Electrification Administration (REA) made low-cost loans available to local cooperatives for power plants and transmission lines to serve rural communities. Within ten years, the REA delivered electricity to nine out of ten farms, giving rural Americans access for the first time to modern conveniences that urban people had enjoyed for decades.

CHAPTER LOCATOR | How did Franklin D. Roosevelt win the 1932 election? | What were the goals and achievements of the first New Deal?

CHAPTER 24
FORGING THE NEW DEAL

720

Agricultural Initiatives

Farmers had been mired in a depression since the end of World War I. New Dealers diagnosed the farmers' plight as a classic case of overproduction and underconsumption. Following age-old practices, farmers tried to compensate for low crop prices by growing more crops. Of course, producing more crops pushed prices lower still. Farm families' income sank to $167 a year, barely one-tenth of the national average in 1932.

New Dealers sought to cut agricultural production, thereby raising crop prices and farmers' income. With more money in their pockets, farm families — who made up one-third of all Americans — would then buy more goods and lift consumption in the entire economy. To reduce production, the **Agricultural Adjustment Act (AAA)**, passed in May 1933, authorized the "domestic allotment plan," which paid farmers *not* to grow crops. Individual farmers who agreed not to plant crops on a portion of their fields (their "allotment") would receive a government payment compensating them for the crops they did not plant. While millions of Americans went to bed hungry, farmers slaughtered livestock and destroyed crops to qualify for their allotment payments.

With the formation of the Commodity Credit Corporation, the federal government allowed farmers to hold their harvested crops off the market and wait for a higher price. New Dealers also sponsored the Farm Credit Act (FCA) to provide long-term credit on mortgaged farm property, allowing debt-ridden farmers to avoid foreclosures that were driving thousands off their land (see Figure 24.1).

Crop allotments, commodity loans, and mortgage credit made farmers major beneficiaries of the New Deal. Crop prices rose impressively, farm income jumped 50 percent by 1936, and FCA loans financed 40 percent of farm mortgage debt by the end of the decade. These gains were distributed fairly equally among farmers in the corn, hog, and wheat region of the Midwest. In the South's cotton belt, however, landlords controlled the distribution of New Deal agricultural benefits and shamelessly rewarded themselves while denying benefits to many sharecroppers and tenant farmers — blacks and whites — by taking the land they worked out of production and assigning it to the allotment program. As the president of the Oklahoma Tenant Farmers' Union explained, large farmers who got "Triple-A" payments often used the money to buy tractors and then "forced their tenants and [share]croppers off the land," causing these "Americans to be starved and dispossessed of their homes in our land of plenty."

Agricultural Adjustment Act (AAA)

▶ New Deal legislation passed in May 1933 aimed at cutting agricultural production and raising crop prices and, consequently, farmers' income. Through the "domestic allotment plan," the AAA paid farmers to not grow crops.

Industrial Recovery

Unlike farmers, industrialists cut production with the onset of the depression. Between 1929 and 1933, industrial production fell more than 40 percent in an effort to balance low demand with low supply and thereby maintain prices. But falling industrial production meant that millions of working people lost their jobs. Unlike farmers, most working people needed jobs to eat. Mass unemployment also reduced consumer demand for industrial products, contributing to a downward spiral in both production and jobs, with no end in sight. Industries responded by reducing wages for employees who still had jobs, further reducing demand—a

| Who opposed the New Deal and why? | How did the second phase of the New Deal differ from the first? | What major political trends changed during the late 1930s? | Conclusion: What were the achievements and limitations of the New Deal? | ☑ LearningCurve Check what you know. bedfordstmartins.com /roarkunderstanding |

721

trend made worse by competition among industrial producers. New Dealers struggled to find a way to break this cycle of unemployment and underconsumption — a way consistent with corporate profits and capitalism.

The New Deal's National Industrial Recovery Act opted for a government-sponsored form of industrial self-government through the **National Recovery Administration (NRA)**, established in June 1933. The NRA encouraged industrialists to agree on rules, known as codes, to define fair working conditions, to set prices, and to minimize competition. The idea behind NRA codes was to stabilize existing industries and maintain their workforces. Industry after industry wrote elaborate codes addressing detailed features of production, pricing, and competition. In exchange for the relaxation of federal antitrust regulations that prohibited such business agreements, the participating businesses promised to recognize the right of working people to organize and engage in collective bargaining. To encourage consumers to patronize businesses with NRA codes, posters with the NRA's Blue Eagle appeared in shop windows throughout the nation.

New Dealers hoped that NRA codes would yield businesses with a social conscience, ensuring fair treatment of workers and consumers as well as promotion of the general economic welfare. Instead, NRA codes tended to strengthen conventional business practices. Large corporations wrote codes that served primarily their own interests rather than the needs of workers or the welfare of the national economy.

Many business leaders criticized NRA codes as heavy-handed government regulation of private enterprise. In reality, compliance with NRA codes was voluntary, and government enforcement efforts were weak to nonexistent. The NRA did little to reduce unemployment, raise consumption, or relieve the depression. In effect, it represented a peace offering to business leaders by Roosevelt and his advisers, conveying the message that the New Deal did not intend to wage war against profits or private enterprise. The peace offering failed, however. Most corporate leaders became entrenched opponents of Roosevelt and the New Deal.

National Recovery Administration (NRA)

▶ Federal agency established in June 1933 to promote industrial recovery. The NRA encouraged industrialists to voluntarily adopt codes that defined fair working conditions, set prices, and minimized competition. In practice, large corporations developed codes that served primarily their own interests rather than those of workers or the economy.

> QUICK REVIEW

How did the New Dealers try to steer the nation toward recovery from the Great Depression?

CHAPTER LOCATOR | How did Franklin D. Roosevelt win the 1932 election? | What were the goals and achievements of the first New Deal?

Who opposed the New Deal and why?

Evicted Sharecroppers

The New Deal's Agricultural Adjustment Administration maintained farm prices by reducing acreage in production, often resulting in the eviction of tenant farmers when the land they worked was left idle. These African American sharecroppers protested AAA policies that caused cotton farmers to evict them from their homes. They were among the many rural laborers whose lives were made worse by New Deal agricultural policies. © Bettmann/Corbis.

THE FIRST NEW DEAL INITIATIVES engendered fierce criticism and political opposition. From the right, Republicans and business people charged that New Deal programs were too radical, undermining private property, economic stability, and democracy. Critics on the left faulted the New Deal for its failure to allay the human suffering caused by the depression and for its timidity in attacking corporate power and greed.

Resistance to Business Reform

New Deal programs rescued capitalism, but business leaders lambasted Roosevelt, even though their economic prospects improved more than those of most other Americans during the depression. Republicans and business leaders

| Who opposed the New Deal and why? | How did the second phase of the New Deal differ from the first? | What major political trends changed during the late 1930s? | Conclusion: What were the achievements and limitations of the New Deal? | ✓ LearningCurve Check what you know. bedfordstmartins.com /roarkunderstanding |

723

> CHRONOLOGY

1934
– Upton Sinclair loses California governorship bid.
– American Liberty League is founded.
– Dr. Francis Townsend devises Old Age Revolving Pension scheme.

1935
– Father Charles Coughlin founds National Union for Social Justice.

denounced New Deal efforts to regulate or reform what they considered their private enterprises.

By 1935, two major business organizations, the National Association of Manufacturers and the Chamber of Commerce, had become openly anti–New Deal. Their critiques were amplified by the American Liberty League, founded in 1934, which blamed the New Deal for betraying basic constitutional guarantees of freedom and individualism. To them, the Agricultural Adjustment Act was a "trend toward fascist control of agriculture," relief programs marked "the end of democracy," and the National Recovery Administration was a plunge into the "quicksand of visionary experimentation."

Economists who favored rational planning in the public interest and labor leaders who sought to influence wages and working conditions by organizing unions attacked the New Deal from the left. In their view, the National Recovery Administration stifled enterprise by permitting monopolistic practices. They pointed out that industrial trade associations twisted NRA codes to suit their aims, thwarted competition, and engaged in price gouging. Labor leaders especially resented the NRA's willingness to allow businesses to form company-controlled unions while blocking workers from organizing genuine grassroots unions to bargain for themselves.

The Supreme Court stepped into this cross fire of criticisms in May 1935 and declared that the NRA unconstitutionally conferred powers reserved to Congress on an administrative agency. The NRA codes soon lost the little authority they had. The failure of the NRA demonstrated the depth of many Americans' resistance to economic planning and the stubborn refusal of business leaders to yield to government regulations or reforms.

Casualties in the Countryside

The Agricultural Adjustment Act weathered critical battering by champions of the old order better than the National Recovery Administration. Allotment checks for keeping land fallow and crop prices high created loyalty among farmers with enough acreage to participate. As a white farmer in North Carolina declared, "I stand for the New Deal and Roosevelt . . . , the AAA . . . and crop control."

Protests stirred, however, among those who did not qualify for allotments. The Southern Farm Tenants Union argued passionately that the AAA enriched large farmers while it impoverished small farmers who rented rather than owned their land. Like the NRA, the AAA tended to help most those who least needed help. Roosevelt's political dependence on southern Democrats caused him to avoid confronting economic and racial inequities in the South.

Displaced tenants often joined the army of migrant workers who straggled across rural America during the 1930s, some to flee Great Plains dust storms. Many migrants came from Mexico to work Texas cotton, Michigan beans, Idaho sugar beets, and California crops of all kinds. But since the number of people willing to take agricultural jobs usually exceeded the number of jobs available, wages fell, and native-born white migrants fought to reserve even these low-wage jobs for themselves. Hundreds of thousands of "Okies" streamed out of the Dust Bowl of Oklahoma, Kansas, Texas, and Colorado, where chronic drought and harmful agricultural practices blasted crops and hopes. Parched, poor, and

CHAPTER LOCATOR | How did Franklin D. Roosevelt win the 1932 election? | What were the goals and achievements of the first New Deal?

724 CHAPTER 24 FORGING THE NEW DEAL

windblown, Okies — like the Joad family immortalized in John Steinbeck's novel *The Grapes of Wrath* (1939) — migrated to the lush fields and orchards of California, congregating in labor camps and hoping to find work and a future. But migrant laborers seldom found steady or secure work. As one Okie said, "When they need us they call us migrants, and when we've picked their crop, we're bums and we got to get out."

Politics on the Fringes

Politically, the New Deal's staunchest opponents were in the Republican Party — organized, well-heeled, mainstream, and determined to challenge Roosevelt at every turn. But the New Deal also faced challenges from the political fringes, fueled by the hardship of the depression and the hope for a cure-all.

Socialists and Communists accused the New Deal of being the handmaiden of business elites and of rescuing capitalism from its self-inflicted crisis. Socialist author Upton Sinclair ran for governor of California in 1934 on a plan that the state take ownership of idle factories and unused land and then give them to cooperatives of working people, a first step toward putting the needs of people above profits. Sinclair lost the election, ending the most serious socialist electoral challenge to the New Deal.

Some intellectuals and artists sought to advance the cause of more radical change by joining left-wing organizations, including the American Communist Party. At its high point in the 1930s, the party had only about thirty thousand members, the large majority of them immigrants, especially Scandinavians in the upper Midwest and eastern European Jews in major cities. Individual Communists worked to organize labor unions, protect the civil rights of black people, and help the destitute, but the party preached the overthrow of "bourgeois democracy" and the destruction of capitalism in favor of Soviet-style communism. Such talk attracted few followers among the nation's millions of poor and unemployed. They wanted jobs and economic security within American capitalism and democracy, not violent revolution to establish a dictatorship of the Communist Party.

More powerful radical challenges to the New Deal sprouted from homegrown roots. Many Americans felt overlooked by New Deal programs that concentrated on finance, agriculture, and industry but did little to produce jobs or aid the poor. The merciless reality of the depression also continued to erode the security of people who still had jobs but worried constantly that they, too, might be pushed into the legions of the unemployed and penniless.

A Catholic priest in Detroit named Charles Coughlin spoke to and for many worried Americans in his weekly radio broadcasts, which reached a nationwide audience of 40 million. Father Coughlin expressed outrage at the suffering and inequities that he blamed on Communists, bankers, and "predatory capitalists" who, he claimed, appealing to widespread anti-Semitic sentiments, were mostly Jews. Coughlin became frustrated by Roosevelt's refusal to grant him influence, turned against the New Deal, and in 1935 founded the National Union for Social Justice, or Union Party, to challenge Roosevelt in the 1936 presidential election.

Dr. Francis Townsend, of Long Beach, California, also criticized the timidity of the New Deal. Angry that many of his retired patients lived in misery, Townsend

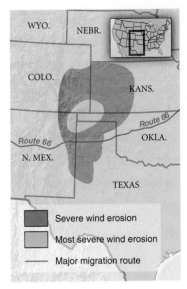

| Severe wind erosion |
| Most severe wind erosion |
| Major migration route |

The Dust Bowl

| **Who opposed the New Deal and why?** | How did the second phase of the New Deal differ from the first? | What major political trends changed during the late 1930s? | Conclusion: What were the achievements and limitations of the New Deal? | ✔ **LearningCurve** Check what you know. bedfordstmartins.com /roarkunderstanding |

725

Huey Long

Huey Long's ability to adapt his stump-speech style to the radio made him the one rival politician who gave Roosevelt considerable concern in the mid-1930s. Corbis.

proposed in 1934 the creation of the Old Age Revolving Pension, which would pay every American over age sixty a pension of $200 a month. To receive the pension, senior citizens had to agree to spend the entire amount within thirty days, thereby stimulating the economy.

Townsend organized pension clubs and petitioned the federal government to enact his scheme. When the major political parties ignored his impractical plan, Townsend merged his forces with Coughlin's Union Party in time for the 1936 election.

A more formidable challenge to the New Deal came from the powerful southern wing of the Democratic Party. Huey Long, son of a backcountry Louisiana farmer, was elected governor of the state in 1928 with his slogan "Every man a king, but no one wears a crown." Unlike nearly all other southern white politicians who harped on white supremacy, Long championed the poor over the rich, country people over city folk, and the humble over elites. As governor, "the Kingfish" — as he liked to call himself — delivered on his promises to provide jobs and build roads, schools, and hospitals, but he also behaved ruthlessly to achieve his goals. Long delighted his supporters, who elected him to the U.S. Senate in

CHAPTER LOCATOR | How did Franklin D. Roosevelt win the 1932 election? | What were the goals and achievements of the first New Deal?

CHAPTER 24
726 FORGING THE NEW DEAL

1932, where he introduced a sweeping "soak the rich" tax bill that would outlaw personal incomes of more than $1 million and inheritances of more than $5 million. When the Senate rejected his proposal, Long decided to run for president, mobilizing more than five million Americans behind his "Share Our Wealth" plan. Like Townsend's scheme, Long's program promised far more than it could deliver. The Share Our Wealth campaign died when Long was assassinated in 1935, but his constituency and the wide appeal of a more equitable distribution of wealth persisted.

The challenges to the New Deal from both right and left stirred Democrats to solidify their winning coalition. In the midterm congressional elections of 1934 — normally a time when a president loses support — voters gave New Dealers a landslide victory. Democrats increased their majority in the House of Representatives and gained a two-thirds majority in the Senate.

QUICK REVIEW <

Why did groups at both ends of the political spectrum criticize the New Deal?

| Who opposed the New Deal and why? | How did the second phase of the New Deal differ from the first? | What major political trends changed during the late 1930s? | Conclusion: What were the achievements and limitations of the New Deal? | ☑ LearningCurve Check what you know. bedfordstmartins.com /roarkunderstanding |

How did the second phase of the New Deal differ from the first?

During the 1930s, artists — many of them employed by New Deal agencies — painted thousands of murals depicting the variety of American life. These murals often appeared in public buildings. The mural shown here, by Missouri-born artist Thomas Hart Benton, illustrates the seductive pleasures and the spirit to be found in American cities. © AXA Financial, Inc. Thomas Hart Benton, *City Activities with Subway,* from *America Today,* 1930. Distemper and egg tempera on gessoed linen with oil glaze 92 x 134½". Collection of AXA Financial, Inc., through its subsidiary, The Equitable Life Assurance Society of the U.S.

> VISUAL ACTIVITY

READING THE IMAGE: What features of urban experience does Benton emphasize in this mural? What ideas and attitudes, if any, link the people shown here?
CONNECTIONS: To what extent does the mural highlight activities distinct to U.S. cities, compared with urban life in Europe, Africa, or Asia?

THE POPULAR MANDATE for the New Deal revealed by the congressional elections persuaded Roosevelt to press ahead with bold new efforts to achieve relief, recovery, and reform. Despite the initiatives of the Hundred Days, the depression still strangled the economy. In 1935, Roosevelt capitalized on his congressional majorities to enact major new programs that signaled the emergence of an American welfare state.

Taken together, these New Deal efforts stretched a safety net under the lives of ordinary Americans, including such landmark initiatives as Social Security, which provided modest pensions for the elderly, and the Wagner Act, which encouraged the organization of labor unions. Although many citizens remained unprotected, New Deal programs helped millions with jobs, relief, and government support. Knitting together the safety net was the idea that, when individual Americans

CHAPTER LOCATOR | How did Franklin D. Roosevelt win the 1932 election? | What were the goals and achievements of the first New Deal?

728 CHAPTER 24 FORGING THE NEW DEAL

suffered because of forces beyond their control, the federal government had the responsibility to support and protect them. The safety net of welfare programs tied the political loyalty of working people to the New Deal and the Democratic Party.

Relief for the Unemployed

First and foremost, Americans still needed jobs. Since the private economy left eight million people jobless by 1935, Roosevelt and his advisers launched a massive work relief program. With a congressional appropriation of nearly $5 billion — more than all government revenues in 1934 — the New Deal created the **Works Progress Administration (WPA)** in 1935 to give unemployed Americans government-funded jobs on public works projects. The WPA put millions of jobless citizens to work on roads, bridges, parks, public buildings, and more.

By 1936, WPA funds provided jobs for 7 percent of the nation's labor force. In effect, the WPA made the federal government the employer of last resort, creating useful jobs when the capitalist economy failed to do so. In hiring, WPA officials tended to discriminate in favor of white men and against women and racial minorities. Still, WPA jobs put thirteen million men and women to work and gave them paychecks worth $10 billion.

About three out of four WPA jobs involved construction and renovation of the nation's physical infrastructure. In addition, the WPA gave jobs to thousands of artists, musicians, actors, journalists, poets, and novelists. The WPA also organized sewing rooms for jobless women, giving them work and wages. These sewing rooms produced more than 100 million pieces of clothing that were donated to the needy. Throughout the nation, WPA projects displayed tangible evidence of the New Deal's commitment to public welfare.

Empowering Labor

During the Great Depression, factory workers who managed to keep their jobs worried constantly about being laid off while their wages and working hours were cut. When workers tried to organize labor unions to protect themselves, municipal and state governments usually sided with employers. Since the Gilded Age, state and federal governments had been far more effective at busting unions than at busting trusts. The New Deal dramatically reversed the federal government's stance toward unions. With legislation and political support, the New Deal encouraged an unprecedented wave of union organizing among the nation's working people. When the head of the United Mine Workers, John L. Lewis, told coal miners that "the President wants you to join a union," he exaggerated only a little. New Dealers believed that unions would counterbalance the organized might of big corporations by defending working people, maintaining wages, and replacing the bloody violence that often accompanied strikes with economic peace and commercial stability.

Violent battles on the nation's streets and docks showed the determination of militant labor leaders to organize unions that would protect jobs as well as wages. In 1934, striking workers in Toledo, Minneapolis, San Francisco, and elsewhere were beaten and shot by police and the National Guard. In Congress, labor leaders lobbied for the National Labor Relations Act, a bill sponsored by Senator Robert Wagner of New York that authorized the federal government to intervene in labor

Works Progress Administration (WPA)

▶ Federal New Deal program established in 1935 that provided government-funded public works jobs to millions of unemployed Americans during the Great Depression, in areas ranging from construction to the arts.

> **CHRONOLOGY**

1934
– Indian Reorganization Act.

1935
– Works Progress Administration (WPA) is created.
– Wagner Act.
– Committee for Industrial Organization (CIO) is founded.
– Social Security Act.

1937
– Sit-down strike at General Motors plant in Flint, Michigan.

Who opposed the New Deal and why?

How did the second phase of the New Deal differ from the first?

What major political trends changed during the late 1930s?

Conclusion: What were the achievements and limitations of the New Deal?

☑ LearningCurve
Check what you know.
bedfordstmartins.com
/roarkunderstanding

Wagner Act
▶ 1935 law that guaranteed industrial workers the right to organize into unions; also known as the National Labor Relations Act. Following passage of the act, union membership skyrocketed to 30 percent of the workforce, the highest in American history.

disputes and supervise the organization of labor unions. The **Wagner Act**, as it came to be called, guaranteed industrial workers the right to organize unions, putting the might of federal law behind the appeals of labor leaders. If the majority of workers at a company voted for a union, the union became the sole bargaining agent for the entire workplace, and the employer was required to negotiate with the elected union leaders. Roosevelt signed the Wagner Act in July 1935, for the first time providing federal support for labor organization — the most important New Deal reform of the industrial order.

The achievements that flowed from the Wagner Act and renewed labor militancy were impressive. When Roosevelt became president in 1933, union membership — composed almost entirely of skilled workers in trade unions affiliated with the American Federation of Labor (AFL) — stood at three million. With the support of the Wagner Act, union membership expanded to fourteen million by 1945. By then, 30 percent of the workforce was unionized, the highest in American history.

Most of the new union members were factory workers and unskilled laborers, many of them immigrants, women, and African Americans. For decades, established AFL unions had no desire to organize factory and unskilled workers. In 1935, under the aggressive leadership of the mine workers' John L. Lewis and the head of the Amalgamated Clothing Workers, Sidney Hillman, a coalition of unskilled workers formed the **Committee for Industrial Organization (CIO)**, later the Congress of Industrial Organizations). The CIO, helped by the Wagner Act, mobilized organizing drives in major industries, including the bitterly anti-union automobile and steel industries.

Committee for Industrial Organization (CIO)
▶ Coalition of mostly unskilled workers (later called Congress of Industrial Organizations) formed in 1935 that mobilized massive union organizing drives in major industries. By 1941, through the CIO-affiliated United Auto Workers, organizers had overcome violent resistance to unionize the entire automobile industry.

The bloody struggle by the CIO-affiliated United Auto Workers (UAW) to organize workers at General Motors climaxed in January 1937. Striking workers occupied the main assembly plant in Flint, Michigan, in a sit-down strike that slashed the plant's production of 15,000 cars a week to a mere 150. Stymied, General Motors eventually surrendered and agreed to make the UAW the sole bargaining agent for all the company's workers and to refrain from interfering with union activity. The UAW expanded its campaign until, after much violence, the entire industry was unionized by 1941.

The CIO hoped to ride organizing success in auto plants to victory in the steel mills. But after unionizing the giant U.S. Steel, the CIO ran up against determined opposition from smaller steel firms. Following a police attack that killed ten strikers at Republic Steel outside Chicago in May 1937, the battered steelworkers halted their organizing campaign. In steel and other major industries, such as the stridently anti-union southern textile mills, organizing efforts stalled until after 1941, when military mobilization created labor shortages that gave workers greater bargaining power.

Social Security and Tax Reform

The single most important feature of the New Deal's emerging welfare state was **Social Security**. An ambitious, far-reaching, and permanent reform, Social Security was designed to provide a modest income to relieve the poverty of elderly people. Only about 15 percent of older Americans had private pension plans, and during the depression corporations and banks often failed to pay the meager pensions they had promised. Corporations routinely fired or demoted employees to avoid or reduce pension payments. Prompted by the popular but impractical panaceas of

Social Security
▶ New Deal program created in August 1935 that was designed to provide a modest income for elderly people. The act also created unemployment insurance with modest benefits. Social Security provoked sharp opposition from conservatives and the wealthy.

CHAPTER LOCATOR | How did Franklin D. Roosevelt win the 1932 election? | What were the goals and achievements of the first New Deal?

730 CHAPTER 24 FORGING THE NEW DEAL

Dr. Townsend, Father Coughlin, and Huey Long, Roosevelt told Congress that "it is our plain duty to provide for that security upon which welfare depends . . . and undertake the great task of furthering the security of the citizen and his family through social insurance."

The political struggle for Social Security highlighted class differences among Americans. Support for the measure came from a coalition of advocacy groups for the elderly and the poor, traditional progressives, leftists, social workers, and labor unions. Arrayed against them were economic conservatives, including the American Liberty League, the National Association of Manufacturers, the Chamber of Commerce, and the American Medical Association. Enact the Social Security system, these conservatives and other Republicans warned, and the government will ruin private property, destroy initiative, and reduce proud individuals to spineless loafers. Despite this opposition, the large New Deal majority in Congress passed the Social Security Act in August 1935.

> ## > Key Provisions of Social Security

- Used tax contributions from workers and their employers to fund pensions for the elderly.
- Stipulated that, upon reaching retirement age, workers would earn benefits based on their contributions and years of work.
- Placed no means test on eligibility for benefits.
- Created unemployment insurance that provided modest benefits for workers who lost their jobs.

Not all workers benefited from the Social Security Act. It excluded domestic and agricultural workers, thereby making ineligible about half of all African Americans and more than half of all employed women — about five million people in all.

Although the first Social Security check (for $41.30) was not issued until 1940, the system gave millions of working people the assurance that when they became too old to work, they would receive a modest income from the federal government. This safety net protected many ordinary working people from fears of a penniless and insecure old age.

Fervent opposition to Social Security struck New Dealers as evidence that the rich had learned little from the depression. Roosevelt had long felt contempt for the moneyed elite who ignored the suffering of the poor. He looked for a way to redistribute wealth that would weaken conservative opposition, advance the cause of social equity, and defuse political challenges from Huey Long and Father Coughlin. Roosevelt charged in 1935 that large fortunes put "great and undesirable concentration of control in [the hands of] relatively few individuals." He urged a graduated tax on corporations, an inheritance tax, and an increase in maximum personal income taxes. Congress endorsed Roosevelt's basic principle by taxing those with higher incomes at a somewhat higher rate.

Neglected Americans and the New Deal

The patchwork of New Deal reforms erected a two-tier welfare state. In the top tier, organized workers in major industries were the greatest beneficiaries of New Deal

Who opposed the New Deal and why?

How did the second phase of the New Deal differ from the first?

What major political trends changed during the late 1930s?

Conclusion: What were the achievements and limitations of the New Deal?

LearningCurve
Check what you know.
bedfordstmartins.com
/roarkunderstanding

731

Mary McLeod Bethune

At the urging of Eleanor Roosevelt, Mary McLeod Bethune, a southern educational and civil rights leader, became director of the National Youth Administration's Division of Negro Affairs. The first black woman to head a federal agency, Bethune used her position to promote social change. Here, Bethune protests the discriminatory hiring practices of the Peoples Drug Store chain in the nation's capital. Moorland-Spingarn Research Center, Howard University.

initiatives. In the bottom tier, millions of neglected Americans — women, children, and old folks, along with the unorganized, unskilled, uneducated, and unemployed — often fell through the New Deal safety net. Many working people remained more or less untouched by New Deal benefits. The average unemployment rate for the 1930s stayed high — 17 percent. Workers in industries that resisted unions received little help from the Wagner Act or the WPA. Tens of thousands of women in southern textile mills, for example, commonly received wages of less than ten cents an hour and were fired if they protested. Domestic workers, almost all of them women, and agricultural workers — many of them African, Hispanic, or Asian Americans — were neither unionized nor eligible for Social Security.

The New Deal neglected few citizens more than African Americans. About half of black Americans in cities were jobless, more than double the unemployment rate among whites. In the rural South, where the vast majority of African Americans lived, conditions were worse, given the New Deal agricultural policies such as the AAA that favored landowners, who often pushed blacks off the land they farmed. Disfranchisement by intimidation and legal subterfuge prevented southern blacks from protesting their plight at the ballot box. Protesters risked vicious retaliation from local whites. Bitter critics charged that the New Deal's NRA stood for "Negro Run Around" or "Negroes Ruined Again."

Roosevelt responded to such criticisms with great caution, since New Deal reforms required the political support of powerful conservative, segregationist, southern white Democrats who would be alienated by programs that aided blacks. A white Georgia relief worker expressed the common view that "any Nigger who gets over $8 a week is a spoiled Nigger, that's all." Stymied by the political clout of entrenched white racism, New Dealers still attracted support from black voters. Roosevelt's overtures to African Americans prompted northern black voters in the 1934 congressional elections to shift from the Republican to the Democratic Party, helping elect New Deal Democrats.

Eleanor Roosevelt sponsored the appointment of Mary McLeod Bethune — the energetic cofounder of the National Council of Negro Women — as head of the Division of Negro Affairs in the National Youth Administration. The highest-ranking black official in Roosevelt's administration, Bethune used her position to guide a small number of black professionals and civil rights activists to posts within New Deal agencies. Ultimately, about one in four African Americans got access to New Deal relief programs.

Despite these gains, by 1940 African Americans still suffered severe handicaps. Most of the thirteen million black workers toiled at low-paying menial jobs, unprotected by the New Deal safety net. Segregated and unequal schools were the norm, and only 1 percent of black students earned college degrees. In southern

CHAPTER LOCATOR | How did Franklin D. Roosevelt win the 1932 election? | What were the goals and achievements of the first New Deal?

states, vigilante violence against blacks went unpunished. For these problems of black Americans, the New Deal offered few remedies.

Hispanic Americans fared no better. About a million Mexican Americans lived in the United States in the 1930s, most of them first- or second-generation immigrants who worked crops throughout the West. During the depression, field workers saw their low wages plunge lower still to about a dime an hour. To preserve scarce jobs for U.S. citizens, the federal government choked off immigration from Mexico, while state and local officials deported tens of thousands of Mexican Americans, many with their American-born children. New Deal programs throughout the West often discriminated against Hispanics and other people of color. A New Deal study concluded that "the Mexican is . . . segregated from the rest of the community as effectively as the Negro . . . [by] poverty and low wages."

Asian Americans had similar experiences. Asian immigrants were still excluded from U.S. citizenship and in many states were not permitted to own land. By 1930, more than half of Japanese Americans had been born in the United States, but they were still liable to discrimination. One young Asian American expressed the frustration felt by many others: "I am a fruit-stand worker. I would much rather it were doctor or lawyer . . . but my aspirations [were] frustrated long ago by circumstances. . . . I am only what I am, a professional carrot washer."

Native Americans also suffered neglect from New Deal agencies. As a group, they remained the poorest of the poor. Since the Dawes Act of 1887 (see chapter 17), the federal government had encouraged Native Americans to assimilate — to abandon their Indian identities and adopt the cultural norms of the majority society. Under the leadership of the New Deal's commissioner of Indian affairs, John Collier, the New Deal's Indian Reorganization Act (IRA) of 1934 largely reversed that policy. Collier claimed that "the most interesting and important fact about Indians" was that they "do not expect much, often they expect nothing at all; yet they are able to be happy." Given such views, the IRA provided little economic aid to Native Americans, but it did restore their right to own land communally and to have greater control over their own affairs. The IRA brought little immediate benefit to Native Americans, but it provided an important foundation for Indians' economic, cultural, and political resurgence a generation later.

Voicing common experiences among Americans neglected by the New Deal, singer and songwriter Woody Guthrie traveled the nation for eight years during the 1930s and heard other rambling men tell him "the story of their life": "how the home went to pieces, how . . . the crops got to where they wouldn't bring nothing, work in factories would kill a dog . . . and — always, always [you] have to fight and argue and cuss and swear . . . to try to get a nickel more out of the rich bosses."

QUICK REVIEW <

What features of a welfare state did the New Deal create and why?

Who opposed the New Deal and why?

How did the second phase of the New Deal differ from the first?

What major political trends changed during the late 1930s?

Conclusion: What were the achievements and limitations of the New Deal?

LearningCurve
Check what you know.
bedfordstmartins.com
/roarkunderstanding

What major political trends changed during the late 1930s?

Distributing Surplus Food to the Needy When bountiful harvests produced surplus crops that would depress prices if they were sent to market, the New Deal arranged to distribute some of them to needy Americans. Here, farmworkers in east-central Arizona near the New Mexico border line up to receive a ration of potatoes authorized by the New Deal agent checking the box of index cards. Library of Congress.

TO ACCELERATE the sputtering economic recovery, Roosevelt shifted the emphasis of the New Deal in the mid-1930s. Instead of seeking cooperation from conservative business leaders, he decided to rely on the growing New Deal coalition to enact reforms over the strident opposition of the Supreme Court, Republicans, and corporate interests.

Added to New Deal strength in farm states and big cities were some new allies on the left. Throughout Roosevelt's first term, socialists and Communists denounced the slow pace of change and accused the New Deal of failing to serve the interests of the workers who produced the nation's wealth. But by 1936, when Roosevelt won reelection in a landslide, many radicals switched from opposing the New Deal to supporting its relief programs and encouragement of labor unions. By 1937, Roosevelt believed the economy was improving and reduced government spending, triggering a sharp recession that undermined economic recovery and prolonged the depression.

CHAPTER LOCATOR | How did Franklin D. Roosevelt win the 1932 election? | What were the goals and achievements of the first New Deal?

The Election of 1936

Roosevelt believed that the presidential election of 1936 would test his leadership and progressive ideals. The depression still had a stranglehold on the economy. Conservative leaders believed that the New Deal's failure to lift the nation out of the depression indicated that Americans were ready for a change. Left-wing critics insisted that the New Deal had missed the opportunity to displace capitalism with a socialist economy and that voters would embrace candidates who recommended more radical remedies.

Republicans turned to Kansas governor Alfred (Alf) Landon as their presidential nominee, a moderate who stressed mainstream Republican proposals to achieve a balanced federal budget and less government bureaucracy. Roosevelt assailed his "old enemies . . . business and financial monopoly, speculation, reckless banking, [and] class antagonism" and proclaimed, "Never before in all our history have these forces been so united against one candidate. . . . They are unanimous in their hate for me — and I welcome their hatred."

Roosevelt triumphed spectacularly. He won 60.8 percent of the popular vote, making it the widest margin of victory in a presidential election to date. Third parties — including the Socialist and Communist parties — fell pitifully short of the support they expected and never again mounted a significant challenge to the New Deal. Congressional results were equally lopsided, with Democrats outnumbering Republicans more than three to one in both houses. In his inaugural address, Roosevelt announced, "I see one third of a nation ill-housed, ill-clad, [and] ill-nourished," and he promised to devote his second term to alleviating their hardship.

Court Packing

In the afterglow of his reelection triumph, Roosevelt pondered how to remove the remaining obstacles to New Deal reforms. He decided to target the Supreme Court. Conservative justices appointed by Republican presidents had invalidated eleven New Deal measures as unconstitutional interferences with free enterprise. Now, the justices were about to consider Social Security, the Wagner Act, the Securities and Exchange Commission, and other New Deal innovations.

To ensure that the Supreme Court did not dismantle the New Deal, Roosevelt proposed a **court-packing plan** that added one new justice for each existing judge who had served for ten years and was over the age of seventy. In effect, the proposed law would give Roosevelt the power to pack the Court with up to six New Dealers who could outvote the elderly, conservative, Republican justices.

But the president had not reckoned with Americans' deeply rooted deference to the independent authority of the Supreme Court. More than two-thirds of Americans believed that the Court should be free from political interference. Even New Deal supporters were disturbed by the court-packing scheme. The suggestion that individuals over age seventy had diminished mental capacity offended many elderly members of Congress, which defeated Roosevelt's plan in 1937.

Supreme Court justices still got the message. The four most conservative of the elderly justices retired. Roosevelt eventually named eight justices to the Court — more than any other president — ultimately giving New Deal laws safe passage through the Court.

> **CHRONOLOGY**

1936
- Franklin Roosevelt is reelected by a landslide.

1937
- Roosevelt's court-packing legislation is defeated.
- Economic recession.

1938
- Second Agricultural Adjustment Act.
- Fair Labor Standards Act.
- Congress rejects antilynching bill.

court-packing plan

▶ Law proposed by Franklin Roosevelt to add one new Supreme Court justice for each existing judge who had served for ten years and who was over the age of seventy. Roosevelt wanted to pack the Court with up to six New Dealers who could protect New Deal legislation, but the Senate defeated the bill in 1937.

Who opposed the New Deal and why?

How did the second phase of the New Deal differ from the first?

What major political trends changed during the late 1930s?

Conclusion: What were the achievements and limitations of the New Deal?

✓ LearningCurve
Check what you know.
bedfordstmartins.com
/roarkunderstanding

735

Reaction and Recession

Emboldened by their defeat of the court-packing plan, Republicans and southern Democrats rallied around their common conservatism to obstruct additional reforms. Former president Herbert Hoover proclaimed that the New Deal was the "repudiation of Democracy" and that "the Republican Party alone [was] the guardian of . . . the charter of freedom." Democrats' arguments over whether the New Deal needed to be expanded — and if so, how — undermined the consensus among reformers and sparked antagonism between Congress and the White House. The ominous rise of belligerent regimes in Germany, Italy, and Japan also slowed reform.

Roosevelt himself favored slowing the pace of the New Deal. He believed that existing New Deal measures had steadily boosted the economy and largely eliminated the depression crisis. In fact, the gross national product in 1937 briefly equaled the 1929 level before dropping lower for the rest of the decade. Unemployment declined to 14 percent in 1937 but quickly spiked upward and stayed higher until 1940. Roosevelt's unwarranted optimism about the economic recovery persuaded him that additional deficit spending by the federal government was no longer necessary.

Roosevelt's optimism failed to consider the stubborn realities of unemployment and poverty, and the reduction in deficit spending reversed the improving economy. Even at the high-water mark of recovery in the summer of 1937, seven million people lacked jobs. In the next few months, national income and production slipped so steeply that almost two-thirds of the economic gains since 1933 were lost by June 1938.

This economic reversal hurt the New Deal politically. Conservatives argued that this recession proved that New Deal measures produced only an illusion of progress. The way to weather the recession was to tax and spend less as well as to wait for the natural laws of supply and demand to restore prosperity. Many New Dealers insisted instead that the continuing depression demanded that Roosevelt revive federal spending and redouble efforts to stimulate the economy. In 1938, Congress heeded such pleas and enacted a massive new program of federal spending.

The recession scare of 1937–1938 taught the president the lesson that economic growth had to be carefully nurtured. The English economist John Maynard Keynes argued that only government intervention could pump enough money into the economy to restore prosperity, a concept that became known as Keynesian economics. Roosevelt never had the inclination or time to master Keynesian thought. But in a commonsense way, he understood that escape from the depression required a plan for large-scale spending to alleviate distress and stimulate economic growth (**Figure 24.2**).

The Last of the New Deal Reforms

From the moment he was sworn in, Roosevelt sought to expand the powers of the presidency. He believed that the president needed more authority to meet emergencies such as the depression and to administer the sprawling federal bureaucracy. Combined with a Democratic majority in Congress, a now-friendly Supreme Court, and the revival of deficit spending, the newly empowered White House seemed to be in a good position to move ahead with a revitalized New Deal.

Resistance to further reform was also on the rise, however. Conservatives argued that the New Deal had pressed government centralization too far. Even

CHAPTER LOCATOR | How did Franklin D. Roosevelt win the 1932 election? | What were the goals and achievements of the first New Deal?

CHAPTER 24

736 FORGING THE NEW DEAL

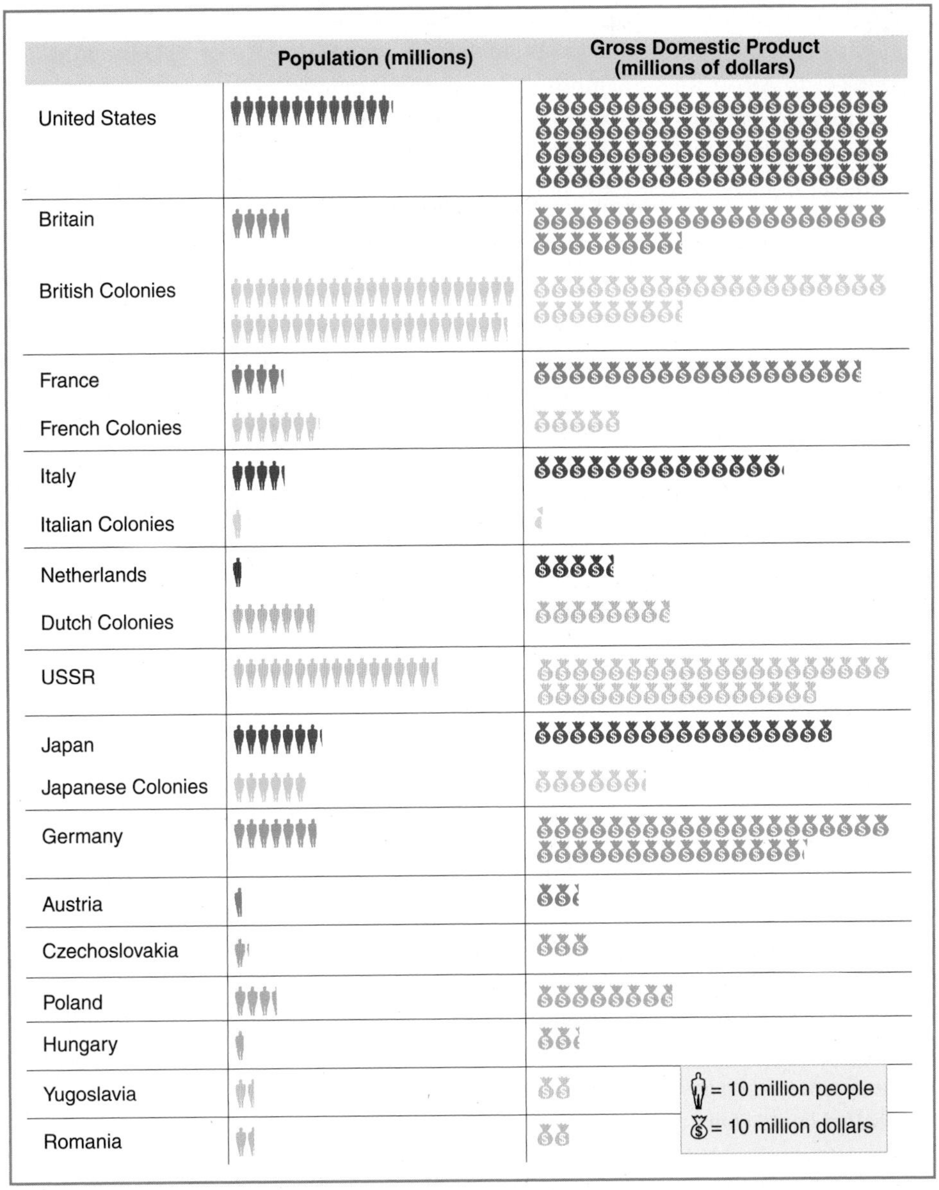

FIGURE 24.2 ■ National Populations and Economies, ca. 1938

Throughout the Great Depression, the United States remained more productive than any other nation in the world. Despite the lingering effects of the depression, by 1938 the United States produced more than twice as much as Germany and the Soviet Union, nearly three times as much as France and Japan, and more than five times as much as Italy. From the viewpoint of Germany, if the European nations listed here could be brought under German control, its economy would be greater than that of the United States and would become the mightiest in the world. Economically, how important were colonies to the major powers? In general, what do these data suggest about the relationship between population and gross domestic product?

the New Deal's friends became weary of one emergency program after another while economic woes continued to shadow New Deal achievements. By the midpoint of Roosevelt's second term, restive members of Congress balked at new initiatives. But enough support remained for one last burst of reform.

Agriculture still had strong claims on New Deal attention in the face of drought, declining crop prices, and impoverished sharecroppers and tenants. In 1937, the Agriculture Department created the Farm Security Administration (FSA) to provide housing and loans to help tenant farmers become independent. A black tenant farmer in North Carolina who received an FSA loan told a New Deal interviewer, "I wake up in the night sometimes and think I must be half-dead and gone to heaven." For those who owned farms, the New Deal offered renewed prosperity with a second Agricultural Adjustment Act (AAA) in 1938 that placed

---

Who opposed the New Deal and why? | How did the second phase of the New Deal differ from the first? | **What major political trends changed during the late 1930s?** | Conclusion: What were the achievements and limitations of the New Deal?

LearningCurve
Check what you know.
bedfordstmartins.com
/roarkunderstanding

737

production quotas on cotton, tobacco, wheat, corn, and rice while issuing food stamps to allow poor people to obtain surplus food. The AAA of 1938 brought stability to American agriculture and ample food to most — but not all — tables.

Advocates for the urban poor also made modest gains after decades of neglect. New York senator Robert Wagner convinced Congress to pass the National Housing Act in 1937. By 1941, some 160,000 residences had been made available to poor people at affordable rents. The program did not come close to meeting the need for affordable housing, but for the first time the federal government took an active role in providing decent urban housing.

The last major piece of New Deal labor legislation, the Fair Labor Standards Act of June 1938, reiterated the New Deal pledge to provide workers with a decent standard of living. The new law set standards for wages and hours and at long last curbed the use of child labor. The minimum-wage level was twenty-five cents an hour for a maximum of forty-four hours a week. To critics of the minimum wage law who said it was "government interference," one New Dealer responded: "It was. It interfered with the fellow running that pecan shelling plant . . . [and] told him he couldn't pay that little widow seven cents an hour." To attract enough conservative votes, the act exempted domestic help and farm laborers — relegating most women and African Americans to lower wages. Enforcement of the minimum-wage standards was weak and haphazard. Nevertheless, the Fair Labor Standards Act slowly advanced Roosevelt's inaugural promise to improve the living standards of the poorest Americans.

The final New Deal reform effort failed to make much headway against the hidebound system of racial injustice. Although Roosevelt denounced lynching as murder, he would not jeopardize his vital base of southern political support by demanding antilynching legislation, and Congress voted down attempts to make lynching a federal crime. Laws to eliminate the poll tax — used to deny blacks the opportunity to vote — encountered the same overwhelming resistance. The New Deal refused to confront racial injustice with the same vigor it brought to bear on economic hardship.

By the end of 1938, the New Deal had lost steam and encountered stiff opposition. In the congressional elections of 1938, Republicans made gains that gave them more congressional influence than they had enjoyed since 1932. New Dealers could claim unprecedented achievements since 1933, but nobody needed reminding that those achievements had not ended the depression. In his annual message to Congress in January 1939, Roosevelt signaled a halt to New Deal reforms by speaking about preserving the progress already achieved rather than extending it. Roosevelt pointed to the ominous threats posed by fascist aggressors in Germany and Japan, and he proposed defense expenditures that surpassed New Deal appropriations for relief and economic recovery.

> QUICK REVIEW

Why did political support for New Deal reforms decline?

CHAPTER LOCATOR | How did Franklin D. Roosevelt win the 1932 election? | What were the goals and achievements of the first New Deal?

738 CHAPTER 24 FORGING THE NEW DEAL

Conclusion: What were the achievements and limitations of the New Deal?

THE NEW DEAL demonstrated that a growing majority of Americans agreed with Roosevelt that the federal government should help those in need. Through programs that sought relief, recovery, and reform, the New Deal vastly expanded the size and influence of the federal government and changed the way many Americans viewed Washington. New Dealers achieved significant victories, such as Social Security, labor's right to organize, and guarantees that farm prices would be maintained through controls on production and marketing. New Deal measures marked the emergence of a welfare state, but its limits left millions of needy Americans with little aid.

Full-scale relief, recovery, and reform eluded the New Deal. Even though millions of Americans benefited from New Deal initiatives, both relief and recovery were limited and temporary. In 1940, the depression still plagued the economy. Perhaps the most impressive achievement of the New Deal was what did not happen. Although authoritarian governments and anticapitalist policies were common outside the United States during the 1930s, they were shunned by the New Deal. The greatest economic crisis the nation had ever faced did not cause Americans to abandon democracy, as happened in Germany, where Adolf Hitler seized dictatorial power. Nor did the nation turn to radical alternatives such as socialism or communism.

Republicans and other conservatives claimed that the New Deal amounted to a form of socialism that threatened democracy and capitalism. But rather than attack capitalism, Franklin Roosevelt sought to save it. And he succeeded. That success also marked the limits of the New Deal's achievements. Franklin Roosevelt believed that a shift of authority toward the federal government would allow capitalist enterprises to be balanced by the nation's democratic tradition. The New Deal stopped far short of challenging capitalism either by undermining private property or by imposing strict national planning.

New Dealers repeatedly described their programs as a kind of warfare against the depression of the 1930s. In the next decade, the Roosevelt administration had to turn from the economic crisis at home to participate in a worldwide conflagration to defeat the enemies of democracy abroad.

Nonetheless, many New Deal reforms continued for decades to structure the basic institutions of banking, the stock market, union organizations, agricultural markets, Social Security, minimum-wage standards, and more. Opponents of these measures and of the basic New Deal notion of an activist government remained powerful, especially in the Republican Party. They claimed that government was the problem, not the solution — a slogan that Republicans championed during and after the 1980s and that led, with the cooperation of some Democrats, to the dismantling of a number of New Deal programs, including the regulation of banking.

Who opposed the New Deal and why?

How did the second phase of the New Deal differ from the first?

What major political trends changed during the late 1930s?

Conclusion: What were the achievements and limitations of the New Deal?

LearningCurve
Check what you know.
bedfordstmartins.com
/roarkunderstanding

739

CHAPTER 24 STUDY GUIDE

STEP 1

GET STARTED ONLINE

✓ **LearningCurve** ▪ bedfordstmartins.com/roarkunderstanding

Now that you've read the chapter, make it stick by completing the LearningCurve activity.

STEP 2

EXPLAIN WHY IT MATTERS

Put your reading into practice. Identify each term below, and then explain why it matters in U.S. history.

TERM	WHO OR WHAT & WHEN	WHY IT MATTERS
New Deal coalition (p. 715)		
underconsumption (p. 717)		
Federal Deposit Insurance Corporation (p. 718)		
fireside chats (p. 718)		
Civilian Conservation Corps (CCC) (p. 719)		
Agricultural Adjustment Act (AAA) (p. 721)		
National Recovery Administration (NRA) (p. 722)		
Works Progress Administration (WPA) (p. 729)		
Wagner Act (p. 730)		
Committee for Industrial Organization (CIO) (p. 730)		
Social Security (p. 730)		
court-packing plan (p. 735)		

STEP 3

MOVE BEYOND THE BASICS

To demonstrate a more advanced understanding, describe the following New Deal programs and legislation and assess how successful or unsuccessful each was in achieving relief, recovery, or reform.

Program/legislation	Description	How successful/unsuccessful?
Agricultural Adjustment Act		
Civilian Conservation Corps		
Emergency Banking Act		
Indian Reorganization Act		
National Recovery Administration		
Public Works Administration		
Social Security		
Tennessee Valley Authority		
Wagner Act		
Works Progress Administration		

PUT IT ALL TOGETHER

Now, take a step back and try to explain the big picture. Remember to use specific examples from the chapter in your answers.

FRANKLIN D. ROOSEVELT

▶ Why was Franklin Roosevelt so popular? Why did he win the elections of 1932 and 1936?

▶ How was Eleanor Roosevelt a part of her husband's political career?

THE NEW DEAL

▶ What were the greatest achievements of the New Deal, both generally and specifically?

▶ What were the differences between the first phase of the New Deal and the second?

THE OPPOSITION

▶ Who initially opposed the New Deal and why?

▶ Why did general support for the New Deal decline?

LOOKING BACKWARD, LOOKING AHEAD

▶ What was distinctive about the New Deal compared with previous government reforms in the twentieth century?

▶ What was the long-term significance of the New Deal?

> ## IN YOUR OWN WORDS

Imagine that you must give an oral report to the class answering the following question: **Why was the New Deal so important in U.S. history?** What would be the most important points to include and why?

25

THE UNITED STATES AND THE SECOND WORLD WAR

1939–1945

> **How did the Second World War change the United States, both domestically and internationally?** Chapter 25 examines the involvement of the United States in World War II. It first examines isolationism and neutrality in the years before the nation's declaration of war in 1941 and then explains the most important wartime events, including the impact of the war on the American home front.

LearningCurve
bedfordstmartins.com/roarkunderstanding
After reading the chapter, use LearningCurve to
retain what you've read.

> How did the United States respond to international developments in the 1930s?

> How did the outbreak of war affect U.S. foreign policy?

> How did the United States mobilize for war?

> How did the Allies turn the tide in Europe and the Pacific?

> How did the war change life on the American home front?

> How did the Allies finally win the war?

> Conclusion: Why did the United States emerge as a superpower at the end of the war?

USS *Yorktown*. A Grumann F6F-3 "Hellcat" sits on the flight deck during Pacific operations, 1943. Photo by PhotoQuest/Getty Images.

How did the United States respond to international developments in the 1930s?

Promoting the Good Neighbor Policy

To encourage continuing friendly relations with Latin America during World War II, the Roosevelt administration urged Walt Disney to make the 1942 film *Saludos Amigos* — starring Donald Duck, Goofy, and "the Brazilian Jitterbird," Joe Carioca — largely for distribution south of the border. The good neighbor policy helped prevent Latin American nations from developing meaningful military alliances with the Axis powers during World War II. © Disney Enterprises, Inc.

THE FIRST WORLD WAR left a dangerous and ultimately deadly legacy. The victors — especially Britain, France, and the United States — sought to avoid future wars at almost any cost. The defeated nation, Germany, aspired to reassert its power and avenge its losses by means of renewed warfare. Italy and Japan felt humiliated by the Versailles peace settlement and saw war as a legitimate way to increase their global power. Japan invaded the northern Chinese province of Manchuria in 1931 with ambitions to expand throughout Asia. Italy, led by the fascist Benito Mussolini since 1922, hungered for an empire in Africa. In Germany, National Socialist Adolf Hitler rose to power in 1933 in a quest to dominate Europe and the world. These aggressive, militaristic, antidemocratic regimes seemed a smaller threat to most people in the United States during the 1930s than did the economic crisis at home. Shielded from external threats by the Atlantic and Pacific

CHAPTER LOCATOR | How did the United States respond to international developments in the 1930s? | How did the outbreak of war affect U.S. foreign policy?

oceans, Americans hoped to avoid entanglement in foreign woes and to concentrate on climbing out of the nation's economic abyss.

Roosevelt and Reluctant Isolation

Like most Americans during the 1930s, Franklin Roosevelt believed that the nation's highest priority was to attack the domestic causes and consequences of the Great Depression. But unlike most Americans, Roosevelt had long advocated an active role for the United States in international affairs.

The depression forced Roosevelt to retreat from his previous internationalism. He came to believe that energetic involvement in foreign affairs diverted resources and political support from domestic recovery. Once in office, Roosevelt sought to combine domestic economic recovery with a low-profile foreign policy that encouraged free trade and disarmament.

Roosevelt's pursuit of international amity was constrained by economic circumstances and American popular opinion. After an opinion poll demonstrated popular support for recognizing the Soviet Union, Roosevelt established formal diplomatic relations in 1933. But when the League of Nations condemned Japanese and German aggression, Roosevelt did not support the league's attempts to keep the peace because he feared jeopardizing isolationists' support for New Deal measures in Congress. America watched from the sidelines when Japan withdrew from the league and ignored the limitations on its navy imposed after World War I. The United States also looked the other way when Hitler rearmed Germany and recalled its representative to the league in 1933. Roosevelt worried that German and Japanese actions threatened world peace, but he reassured Americans that the nation would not "use its armed forces for the settlement of any [international] dispute anywhere."

The Good Neighbor Policy

In 1933, Roosevelt announced that the United States would pursue "the policy of the good neighbor" in international relations, which meant that no nation had the right to intervene in the internal or external affairs of another. The **good neighbor policy** did not indicate a U.S. retreat from empire in Latin America. Instead, it declared that, unlike in past decades, the United States would not depend on military force to exercise its influence in the region. Roosevelt refrained from sending troops to defend the interests of American corporations in Latin America. While Roosevelt's hands-off policy honored the principle of national self-determination, it also permitted the rise of dictators in Nicaragua, Cuba, and elsewhere, who exploited and terrorized their nations with private support from U.S. businesses.

Military nonintervention also did not prevent the United States from exerting its economic influence in Latin America. In 1934, Congress gave the president the power to reduce tariffs on goods imported into the United States from nations that agreed to lower their own tariffs on U.S. exports. By 1940, twenty-two nations had agreed to reciprocal tariff reductions, helping to double U.S. exports to Latin America and contributing to the New Deal's goal of boosting the domestic economy through free trade.

> CHRONOLOGY

1935–1937
– Neutrality acts.

1936
– Nazi Germany occupies the Rhineland.
– Italian armies conquer Ethiopia.
– Spanish civil war begins.

1937
– Japanese troops capture Nanjing.

good neighbor policy
▶ Foreign policy announced by Franklin Roosevelt in 1933 that promised the United States would not interfere in the internal or external affairs of another country, thereby ending U.S. military interventions in Latin America.

| How did the United States mobilize for war? | How did the Allies turn the tide in Europe and the Pacific? | How did the war change life on the American home front? | How did the Allies finally win the war? | Conclusion: Why did the United States emerge as a superpower at the end of the war? | ✔ LearningCurve Check what you know. bedfordstmartins.com /roarkunderstanding |

745

The Price of Noninvolvement

In Europe, fascist governments in Italy and Germany threatened military aggression. Britain and France made only verbal protests. Emboldened, Hitler plotted to avenge defeat in World War I by recapturing territories with German inhabitants, all the while accusing Jews of polluting the purity of the Aryan master race. The virulent anti-Semitism of Hitler and his Nazi Party unified non-Jewish Germans and attracted sympathizers among many other Europeans, even in France and Britain.

In Japan, a stridently militaristic government planned to follow the invasion of Manchuria in 1931 with conquests extending throughout Southeast Asia. The Manchurian invasion bogged down in a long and vicious war when Chinese Nationalists rallied around their leader, Jiang Jieshi (Chiang Kai-shek), to fight against the Japanese. Preparations for new Japanese conquests continued, however. In 1936, Japan openly violated naval limitation treaties and began to build a battle-ready fleet to seek naval superiority in the Pacific.

In the United States, the hostilities in Asia and Europe reinforced isolationist sentiments. Popular disillusionment with the failure of Woodrow Wilson's idealistic goals caused many Americans to question the nation's participation in World War I. In 1933, Gerald Nye, a Republican from North Dakota, chaired a Senate committee that concluded that greedy "merchants of death" — American weapons makers, bankers, and financiers — had dragged the nation into the war to line their own pockets. International tensions and the Nye committee report prompted Congress to pass a series of **neutrality acts** between 1935 and 1937 designed to avoid entanglement in foreign wars. The neutrality acts prohibited making loans and selling arms to nations at war.

By 1937, the growing conflicts overseas caused some Americans to call for a total embargo on all trade with warring countries. The Neutrality Act of 1937 attempted to reconcile the nation's desire for both peace and foreign trade with a "cash-and-carry" policy that required warring nations to pay cash for nonmilitary goods and to transport them in their own ships. This policy benefited the nation's economy, but it also helped foreign aggressors by supplying them with goods and thereby undermining peace.

The desire for peace in France, Britain, and the United States led Germany, Italy, and Japan to launch offensives on the assumption that the Western democracies lacked the will to oppose them. In March 1936, Nazi troops marched into the industry-rich Rhineland on Germany's western border, in blatant violation of the Treaty of Versailles. One month later, Italian armies completed their conquest of Ethiopia, projecting fascist power into Africa. In December 1937, Japanese invaders captured

neutrality acts

▶ Legislation passed in 1935 and 1937 that sought to avoid entanglement in foreign wars while protecting trade. The 1937 act prohibited selling arms to nations at war and required nations to pay cash for nonmilitary goods and to transport them in their own ships.

ATLANTIC OCEAN

Germans bomb civilians, 1937

FRANCE

Guernica

PORTUGAL

● Madrid

Barcelona

SPAIN

Surrendered March 28, 1939

Mediterranean Sea

SPANISH MOROCCO

ALGERIA

Nationalist, July 1936
Nationalist gains, Oct. 1937
Nationalist gains, July 1938
Nationalist gains, Feb. 1939
Republican, Feb. 1939

Spanish Civil War, 1936–1939

CHAPTER LOCATOR | How did the United States respond to international developments in the 1930s? | How did the outbreak of war affect U.S. foreign policy?

CHAPTER 25
746 THE UNITED STATES AND THE SECOND WORLD WAR

Nanjing (Nanking) and celebrated their triumph in the "Rape of Nanking," a deadly rampage that killed 200,000 Chinese civilians.

In Spain, a bitter civil war broke out in July 1936 when the Nationalists — fascist rebels led by General Francisco Franco — attacked the democratically elected Republican government. Both Germany and Italy reinforced Franco, while the Soviet Union provided much less aid to the Republican Loyalists. The Spanish civil war did not prompt European democracies or the U.S. government to help the Loyalists, despite sympathy for their cause. Abandoned by the Western nations, the Republican Loyalists were defeated in 1939, and Franco built a fascist bulwark in Spain.

Hostilities in Europe, Africa, and Asia alarmed Roosevelt and some Americans. The president sought to persuade most Americans to moderate their isolationism and find a way to support the victims of fascist aggression. Critics accused the president of seeking to replace "Americanism" with "internationalism." The popularity of isolationist sentiment convinced Roosevelt that he needed to maneuver carefully if the United States were to help prevent fascist aggressors from conquering Europe and Asia, leaving the United States an isolated island of democracy.

QUICK REVIEW

Why did isolationism during the 1930s concern Roosevelt?

| How did the United States mobilize for war? | How did the Allies turn the tide in Europe and the Pacific? | How did the war change life on the American home front? | How did the Allies finally win the war? | Conclusion: Why did the United States emerge as a superpower at the end of the war? | ✔ **LearningCurve** Check what you know. bedfordstmartins.com /roarkunderstanding |

747

How did the outbreak of war affect U.S. foreign policy?

Nazi Invasion of Poland

Adolf Hitler relished the early success of the German army's *blitzkrieg* against Poland in 1939. This photo shows Hitler reviewing a victory parade of his soldiers in Warsaw. After the conquest, Germans systematically murdered hundreds of thousands of Polish civilians and confined even more to slave labor camps. Photo by Hugo Jaeger/Timepix/Time Life Pictures/Getty Images.

BETWEEN 1939 AND 1941, fascist victories overseas eventually eroded American isolationism. At first, U.S. intervention was limited to providing material support to the enemies of Germany and Japan, principally Britain, China, and the Soviet Union. But Japan's surprise attack on Pearl Harbor eliminated that restraint, and the nation began to mobilize for an all-out assault on foreign foes.

Nazi Aggression and War in Europe

Under the spell of isolationism, Americans passively watched Hitler's relentless campaign to dominate Europe (**Map 25.1**). In 1938, Hitler incorporated Austria into Germany and turned his attention to the Sudetenland, which had been granted to Czechoslovakia by the World War I peace settlement. Hoping to avoid war, British prime minister Neville Chamberlain offered Hitler terms of **appeasement** that would give the Sudetenland to Germany if Hitler agreed to leave the rest of Czechoslovakia alone. Hitler accepted the terms but didn't keep his promise. By 1939, Hitler had annexed Czechoslovakia and demanded that Poland return the

appeasement

▶ British strategy aimed at avoiding a war with Germany in the late 1930s by not objecting to Hitler's policy of territorial expansion.

CHAPTER LOCATOR | How did the United States respond to international developments in the 1930s? | **How did the outbreak of war affect U.S. foreign policy?**

CHAPTER 25
748 THE UNITED STATES AND THE SECOND WORLD WAR

German territory it had gained after World War I. Recognizing that appeasement of Hitler had failed, Britain and France assured Poland that they would go to war with Germany if Hitler attacked. In turn, Hitler negotiated with Soviet premier Joseph Stalin, offering him concessions to prevent the Soviet Union from joining Britain and France in opposing a German attack on Poland. Despite the enduring hatred between fascist Germany and the Communist Soviet Union, the two powers signed the Nazi-Soviet treaty of nonaggression in August 1939, exposing Poland to an onslaught by both the German and Soviet armies.

At dawn on September 1, 1939, Hitler unleashed his *blitzkrieg* (literally, "lightning war") on Poland. "Act brutally!" Hitler exhorted his generals. "Send [every] man, woman, and child of Polish descent and language to their deaths, pitilessly and remorselessly." The attack triggered Soviet attacks on eastern Poland and declarations of war from France and Britain two days later, igniting a conflagration that raced around the globe. In September 1939, Germany seemed invincible, causing many people to fear that all of Europe would soon share Poland's fate.

After the Nazis overran Poland, Hitler soon launched a westward blitzkrieg. In the first six months of 1940, German forces smashed through Denmark, Norway, the Netherlands, Belgium, and France. The speed of the German attack trapped more than 300,000 British and French soldiers, who retreated to the port of Dunkirk, where an improvised armada of British vessels ferried them to safety across the English Channel. By mid-June 1940, France had surrendered the largest army in the world, signed an armistice that gave Germany control of nearly two-thirds of the countryside, and installed a collaborationist government at Vichy. With an empire that stretched across Europe from Poland to France, Hitler seemed poised to attack Britain.

The new British prime minister, Winston Churchill, vowed that Britain, unlike France, would never surrender to Hitler. "We shall fight on the seas and oceans [and] . . . in the air," he proclaimed, "whatever the cost may be, we shall fight on the beaches, . . . and in the fields and in the streets." Churchill's defiance stiffened British resolve against Hitler's attack, which began in mid-June 1940 when wave after wave of German bombers targeted British military installations and cities, killing tens of thousands of civilians. The outgunned Royal Air Force fought as doggedly as Churchill had predicted and finally won the Battle of Britain by November, clearing German bombers from British skies and handing Hitler his first defeat. Churchill praised the valiant British pilots, declaring that "never . . . was so much owed by so many to so few." Battered and exhausted by German attacks, Britain needed American help to continue to fight, as Churchill repeatedly wrote to Roosevelt in private.

From Neutrality to the Arsenal of Democracy

Most Americans condemned German aggression and favored Britain and France, but isolationism remained powerful. Roosevelt feared that if Congress did not repeal the arms embargo mandated by the Neutrality Act of 1937, France and Britain would soon succumb to the Nazi onslaught. Congress agreed in November 1939 to allow belligerent nations to buy arms, as well as nonmilitary supplies, on a cash-and-carry basis.

In practice, the revised neutrality law permitted Britain and France to purchase American war materiel and carry it across the Atlantic in their own ships,

1938
- Hitler annexes Austria.

1939
- German troops occupy Czechoslovakia.
- Nazi-Soviet nonaggression pact.
- Germany's attack on Poland begins World War II.

1940
- Germany invades Denmark, Norway, France, Belgium, Luxembourg, and the Netherlands.
- British and French troops evacuate from Dunkirk.
- Battle of Britain.
- Tripartite Pact.

1941
- Lend-Lease Act.
- Germany invades Soviet Union.
- Japanese attack Pearl Harbor.
- United States enters World War II.

| How did the United States mobilize for war? | How did the Allies turn the tide in Europe and the Pacific? | How did the war change life on the American home front? | How did the Allies finally win the war? | Conclusion: Why did the United States emerge as a superpower at the end of the war? | ✓ LearningCurve Check what you know. bedfordstmartins.com /roarkunderstanding |

749

thereby shielding American vessels from attack by German submarines lurking in the Atlantic. Roosevelt searched for a way to aid Britain short of entering a formal alliance or declaring war against Germany. Churchill pleaded for American destroyers, aircraft, and munitions, but he had no money to buy them under the

MAP 25.1 ■ Axis Aggression through 1941

Through a series of surprise military strikes before 1942, Mussolini sought to re-create the Roman empire in the Mediterranean while Hitler aimed to annex Austria and reclaim German territories occupied by France after World War I. When the German dictator began his campaign to rule "inferior" peoples by attacking Poland, World War II broke out.

CHAPTER LOCATOR | How did the United States respond to international developments in the 1930s? | **How did the outbreak of war affect U.S. foreign policy?**

CHAPTER 25
750 THE UNITED STATES AND THE SECOND WORLD WAR

prevailing cash-and-carry neutrality law. By late summer in 1940, Roosevelt concocted a scheme to deliver fifty old destroyers to Britain in exchange for American access to British bases in the Western Hemisphere, the first steps toward building a firm Anglo-American alliance against Hitler.

While German Luftwaffe (air force) pilots bombed Britain, Roosevelt decided to run for an unprecedented third term as president in 1940. But the presidential election, which Roosevelt won handily, provided no clear mandate for American involvement in the European war. The Republican candidate, Wendell Willkie, a former Democrat who generally favored New Deal measures and Roosevelt's foreign policy, attacked Roosevelt as a warmonger. Willkie's accusations caused the president to promise voters, "Your boys are not going to be sent into any foreign wars," a pledge counterbalanced by his repeated warnings about the threats to America posed by Nazi aggression.

Once reelected, Roosevelt maneuvered to support Britain in every way short of war. In a fireside chat shortly after Christmas 1940, he proclaimed that it was incumbent on the United States to become "the great arsenal of democracy" and send "every ounce and every ton of munitions and supplies that we can possibly spare to help the defenders who are in the front lines." In January 1941, Roosevelt proposed the **Lend-Lease Act.**

> ## > Lend-Lease Act

- Allowed the British to obtain arms from the United States without paying cash but with the promise to reimburse the United States when the war ended.
- Supported the defense of democracy and human rights throughout the world, according to Roosevelt.
- Provided Britain with more than $50 billion of support during the war.

Lend-Lease Act

▶ Legislation in 1941 that enabled Britain to obtain arms from the United States without cash but with the promise to reimburse the United States when the war ended. The act reflected Roosevelt's desire to assist the British in any way possible, short of war.

Stymied in his plans for an invasion of England, Hitler turned his massive army eastward and on June 22, 1941, sprang a surprise attack on the Soviet Union, his ally in the 1939 Nazi-Soviet nonaggression pact. Neither Roosevelt nor Churchill had any love for Joseph Stalin or communism, but they both welcomed the Soviet Union to the anti-Nazi cause. Both Western leaders understood that Hitler's attack on Russia would provide relief for the hard-pressed British. Roosevelt quickly persuaded Congress to extend Lend-Lease to the Soviet Union, beginning the shipment of millions of tons of trucks, jeeps, and other equipment that, in all, supplied about 10 percent of Russian war materiel.

As Hitler's Wehrmacht (armed forces) raced across the Russian plains and Nazi U-boats tried to choke off supplies to Britain and the Soviet Union, Roosevelt met with Churchill aboard a ship near Newfoundland to cement the Anglo-American alliance. In August 1941, the two leaders issued the Atlantic Charter, pledging the two nations to freedom of the seas and free trade as well as the right of national self-determination.

Japan Attacks America

Although the likelihood of war with Germany preoccupied Roosevelt, Hitler exercised a measure of restraint in directly provoking America. Japanese ambitions in

| How did the United States mobilize for war? | How did the Allies turn the tide in Europe and the Pacific? | How did the war change life on the American home front? | How did the Allies finally win the war? | Conclusion: Why did the United States emerge as a superpower at the end of the war? | ✓ LearningCurve Check what you know. bedfordstmartins.com /roarkunderstanding |

751

Asia clashed more openly with American interests and commitments, especially in China and the Philippines. And unlike Hitler, the Japanese high command planned to attack the United States in order to pursue Japan's aspirations to rule an Asian empire it termed the Greater East Asia Co-Prosperity Sphere. Appealing to widespread Asian bitterness toward white colonial powers such as the British

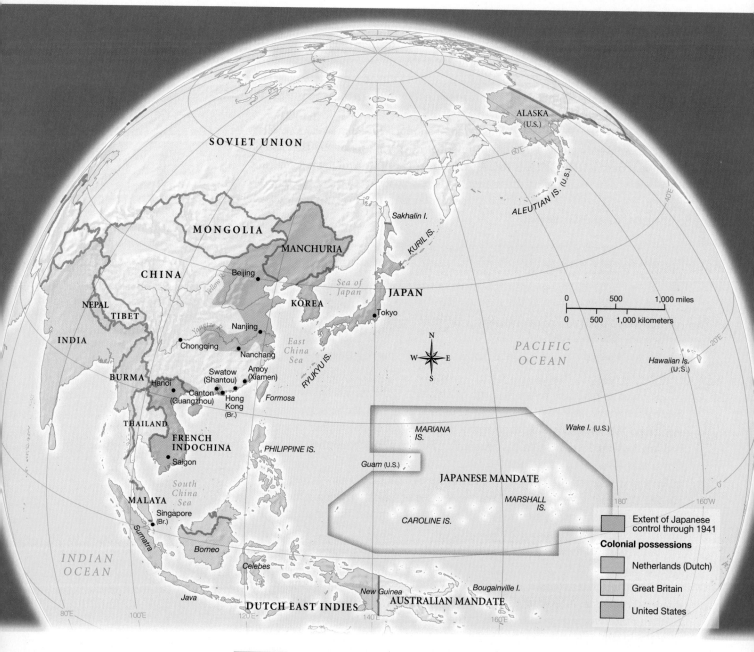

MAP 25.2 ■ Japanese Aggression through 1941

Beginning with the invasion of Manchuria in 1931, Japan sought to extend its imperialist control over most of East Asia. Japanese aggression was driven by the need for raw materials for the country's expanding industries and by the military government's devotion to martial honor.

CHAPTER LOCATOR | How did the United States respond to international developments in the 1930s? | **How did the outbreak of war affect U.S. foreign policy?**

CHAPTER 25
752 THE UNITED STATES AND THE SECOND WORLD WAR

in India and Burma, the French in Indochina (now Vietnam), and the Dutch in the East Indies (now Indonesia), the Japanese campaigned to preserve "Asia for the Asians." Japan's invasion of China — which had lasted for ten years by 1941 — proved that its true goal was Asia for the Japanese (**Map 25.2**). Japan coveted the raw materials available from China and Southeast Asia, and it ignored American demands to stop its campaign of aggression.

In 1940, Japan signaled a new phase of its imperial designs by entering a defensive alliance with Germany and Italy — the Tripartite Pact. To thwart Japanese plans to invade the Dutch East Indies, in July 1941 Roosevelt announced a trade embargo that denied Japan access to oil, scrap iron, and other goods essential for its war machines. Roosevelt hoped the embargo would strengthen factions within Japan that opposed the militarists.

Instead, the American embargo played into the hands of Japanese militarists headed by General Hideki Tojo, who seized control of the government in October 1941 and persuaded other leaders, including Emperor Hirohito, that swift destruction of American naval bases in the Pacific would leave Japan free to follow its destiny. On December 7, 1941, 183 aircraft lifted off six Japanese carriers and

吉岡堅二筆　　　ハイワ真珠湾強襲

Pearl Harbor Attack

This Japanese postcard celebrates the successful surprise attack on Pearl Harbor on December 7, 1941, highlighting the airborne supremacy of the Japanese, the weak defenses of the United States, and the smoking destruction caused by Japanese carrier-based aircraft. Brothers Wesley and Edward Heidt from Los Angeles were one of thirty-four pairs of brothers killed when Japanese warplanes sank the battleship *Arizona* at Pearl Harbor. www.museumofworldwarii.com.

| How did the United States mobilize for war? | How did the Allies turn the tide in Europe and the Pacific? | How did the war change life on the American home front? | How did the Allies finally win the war? | Conclusion: Why did the United States emerge as a superpower at the end of the war? | ☑ **LearningCurve** Check what you know. bedfordstmartins.com /roarkunderstanding |

Bombing of Pearl Harbor, December 7, 1941

Sunk
Damaged
Undamaged

attacked the U.S. Pacific Fleet at Pearl Harbor on the Hawai'ian island of Oahu. The devastating surprise attack sank all of the fleet's battleships, killed more than 2,400 Americans, and almost crippled U.S. war-making capacity in the Pacific. Luckily for the United States, Japanese pilots failed to destroy oil storage facilities at Pearl Harbor and any of the nation's aircraft carriers, which happened to be at sea during the attack.

The Japanese scored a stunning tactical victory at Pearl Harbor, but in the long run the attack proved a colossal blunder. The victory made many Japanese commanders overconfident about their military prowess. Worse for the Japanese, Americans instantly united in their desire to fight and avenge the attack. Roosevelt vowed that "this form of treachery shall never endanger us again." On December 8, Congress endorsed the president's call for a declaration of war. Both Hitler and Mussolini declared war against America on December 11, bringing the United States into all-out war with the Axis powers (Germany, Italy, and Japan) in both Europe and Asia.

> **QUICK REVIEW**

How did Roosevelt attempt to balance American isolationism with the military aggression of Germany and Japan in the late 1930s and early 1940s?

CHAPTER LOCATOR | How did the United States respond to international developments in the 1930s? | How did the outbreak of war affect U.S. foreign policy?

CHAPTER 25
754 THE UNITED STATES AND THE SECOND WORLD WAR

African American Machine Gunners

These African American soldiers prepare their machine gun for action on the side of a road near Pisa, Italy, in September 1944. They and other black soldiers who served in combat in segregated units repeatedly earned praise from their commanders for gallantry and courage under fire. © Bettmann/Corbis.

THE TIME HAD COME, Roosevelt announced, for the prescriptions of "Dr. New Deal" to be replaced by the stronger medicines of "Dr. Win-the-War." Military and civilian leaders rushed to secure the nation against possible attacks, causing Americans of Japanese descent to be stigmatized and sent to internment camps. Roosevelt and his advisers lost no time enlisting millions of Americans in the armed forces to bring the isolationist-era military to fighting strength for a two-front war. The war emergency also required economic mobilization unparalleled in the nation's history. As Dr. Win-the-War, Roosevelt set aside the New Deal goal of reform and plunged headlong into transforming the American economy into the world's greatest military machine, thereby achieving full employment and economic recovery, goals that had eluded the New Deal.

Home-Front Security

Shortly after declaring war against the United States, Hitler dispatched German submarines to hunt American ships along the Atlantic coast, where American pilots tried to destroy them. The U-boats had devastating success for about eight months, sinking hundreds of U.S. ships and threatening to disrupt the Lend-Lease

| How did the United States mobilize for war? | How did the Allies turn the tide in Europe and the Pacific? | How did the war change life on the American home front? | How did the Allies finally win the war? | Conclusion: Why did the United States emerge as a superpower at the end of the war? | ✔ LearningCurve Check what you know. bedfordstmartins.com /roarkunderstanding |

755

lifeline to Britain and the Soviet Union. But by mid-1942, the U.S. Navy had chased German submarines into the mid-Atlantic.

Within the continental United States, Americans remained sheltered from the chaos and destruction the war was bringing to hundreds of millions in Europe and Asia. Nevertheless, the government worried constantly about espionage and internal subversion. The campaign for patriotic vigilance focused on German and Japanese foes, but Americans of Japanese descent became targets of official and popular persecution because of Pearl Harbor and long-standing racial prejudice against people of Asian descent.

About 320,000 people of Japanese descent lived in U.S. territory in 1941, two-thirds of them in Hawai'i, where they largely escaped such wartime persecution because they were essential and valued members of society. On the mainland, however, Japanese Americans were a tiny minority — even along the West Coast, where most of them worked on farms and in small businesses. Although an official military survey concluded that Japanese Americans posed no danger, popular hostility fueled a campaign to round up all mainland Japanese Americans — two-thirds of them U.S. citizens. "A Jap's a Jap. . . . It makes no difference whether he is an American citizen or not," one official declared.

On February 19, 1942, Roosevelt issued Executive Order 9066, which authorized sending all Americans of Japanese descent to ten makeshift **internment camps** located in remote areas of the West (**Map 25.3**). Japanese Americans lost homes and businesses worth about $400 million and lived out the war penned in by barbed wire and armed guards. Although several thousand Japanese Americans served with distinction in the U.S. armed forces and no case of subversion by a Japanese American was ever uncovered, the Supreme Court, in its 1944 *Korematsu* decision, upheld Executive Order 9066's blatant violation of constitutional rights as justified by "military necessity."

Building a Citizen Army

In 1940, Roosevelt encouraged Congress to pass the **Selective Service Act** to register men of military age who would be subject to a draft if the need arose. When

internment camps
▶ Makeshift prison camps, to which Americans of Japanese descent were sent as a result of Roosevelt's Executive Order 9066, issued in February 1942. In 1944, the Supreme Court upheld this blatant violation of constitutional rights as a "military necessity."

Selective Service Act
▶ Law enacted in 1940 requiring all men who would be eligible for a military draft to register in preparation for the possibility of a future conflict. The act also prohibited discrimination based on "race or color."

MAP 25.3 ■ **Western Relocation Authority Centers**

Responding to prejudice and fear of sabotage, President Roosevelt authorized the roundup and relocation of all Americans of Japanese descent in 1942. Taken from their homes in the cities and fertile farmland of the far West, more than 120,000 Japanese Americans were confined in desolate camps scattered as far east as the Mississippi River.

▲ WRA relocation camp

☐ More than 1,000 Japanese Americans sent to relocation centers

CHAPTER LOCATOR | How did the United States respond to international developments in the 1930s? | How did the outbreak of war affect U.S. foreign policy?

CHAPTER 25
756 THE UNITED STATES AND THE SECOND WORLD WAR

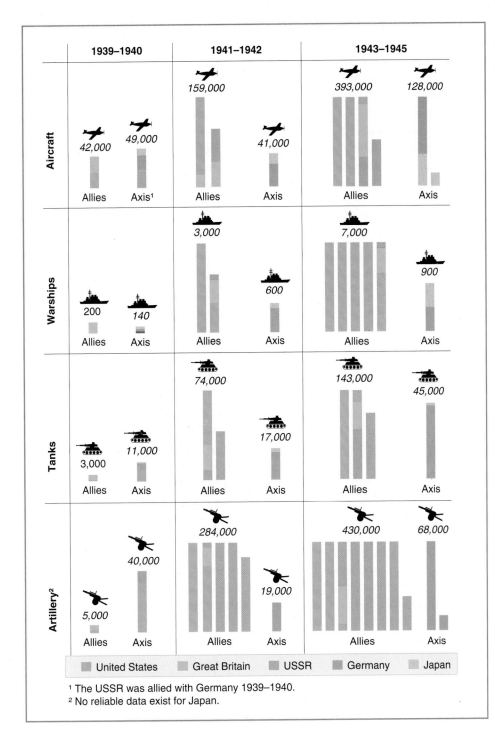

> GLOBAL COMPARISON

FIGURE 25.1 ■ Weapons Production by the Axis and Allied Powers during World War II

This chart demonstrates the massive contribution of the United States to Allied weapons production during World War II. In the air and on the sea, U.S. weapons predominated, after 1940 accounting for more aircraft and many more warships than those of Britain and the Soviet Union combined. Together, the three Allied powers produced about three times as many aircraft and five to eight times as many warships as the two Axis powers. On the ground, the Soviet Union led the other Allies in the production of tanks and artillery, an outgrowth of the colossal battles on the eastern front. What do these data suggest about the significance of America's entry into the war in December 1941? What do they suggest about the kind of warfare emphasized by each of the belligerents? What does the chronology of weapons production suggest about the course of the war?

war came, more than 16 million men and women served in uniform during the war, two-thirds of them draftees, mostly young men. Women were barred from combat duty, but they worked at nearly every noncombatant task, eroding traditional barriers to women's military service.

The Selective Service Act prohibited discrimination "on account of race or color," and almost a million African American men and women donned uniforms,

| How did the United States mobilize for war? | How did the Allies turn the tide in Europe and the Pacific? | How did the war change life on the American home front? | How did the Allies finally win the war? | Conclusion: Why did the United States emerge as a superpower at the end of the war? | ✓ LearningCurve Check what you know. bedfordstmartins.com /roarkunderstanding |

as did half a million Mexican Americans, 25,000 Native Americans, and 13,000 Chinese Americans. The racial insults and discrimination suffered by all people of color made some soldiers ask, as a Mexican American GI did on his way to the European front, "Why fight for America when you have not been treated as an American?" Only black Americans were trained in segregated camps, confined in segregated barracks, and assigned to segregated units. Homosexuals also served in the armed forces, although in much smaller numbers than black Americans. Allowed to serve as long as their sexual preferences remained covert, gay Americans, like other minorities, sought to demonstrate their worth under fire.

Conversion to a War Economy

In 1940, the American economy remained mired in the depression. Shortly after the attack on Pearl Harbor, Roosevelt announced the goal of converting the economy to produce "overwhelming . . . , crushing superiority of equipment in any theater of the world war." Factories were converted to assembling tanks and airplanes, and production soared to record levels. By the end of the war, jobs exceeded workers, and plants operated at full capacity.

To organize and oversee this tidal wave of military production, Roosevelt called upon business leaders to come to Washington and, for the token payment of a dollar a year, head new government agencies such as the War Production Board, which set production priorities and pushed for maximum output. Contracts flowed to large corporations, often on a basis that guaranteed their profits.

Booming wartime employment swelled union membership. To speed production, the government asked unions to pledge not to strike. Despite the relentless pace of work, union members kept their no-strike pledge, with the important exception of members of the United Mine Workers, who walked out of the coal mines in 1943, demanding a pay hike and earning the enmity of many Americans.

Overall, conversion to war production achieved Roosevelt's ambitious goal of "crushing superiority" in military goods. At a total cost of $304 billion during the war, the nation produced an avalanche of military equipment, more than double the combined production of Germany, Japan, and Italy (**Figure 25.1**). This outpouring of military goods supplied not only U.S. forces but also America's allies, giving tangible meaning to Roosevelt's pledge to make America the "arsenal of democracy."

> **QUICK REVIEW**

How did the Roosevelt administration mobilize the human and industrial resources necessary to fight a two-front war?

CHAPTER LOCATOR | How did the United States respond to international developments in the 1930s? | How did the outbreak of war affect U.S. foreign policy?

CHAPTER 25
758   THE UNITED STATES AND THE SECOND WORLD WAR

Marine Pinned Down on Saipan   More than 100,000 American GIs assaulted the Japanese garrison on Saipan in the Mariana Islands in June 1944. The battle lasted nearly a month and inflicted 14,000 casualties on American troops. The intensity of the fighting is visible on the face of the Marine shown here. Marine Corps Photo, National Archives.

THE UNITED STATES CONFRONTED a daunting military challenge in December 1941. The attack on Pearl Harbor destroyed much of its Pacific Fleet. In the Atlantic, Hitler's U-boats sank American ships, while German armies occupied most of western Europe and relentlessly advanced eastward into the Soviet Union. Roosevelt and his military advisers believed that defeating Germany took top priority. To achieve that victory required preventing Hitler from defeating America's allies, Britain and the Soviet Union. If they fell, Hitler would command all the resources of Europe in a probable assault on the United States. To fight back effectively against Germany and Japan, the United States had to coordinate military and political strategy with its allies and muster all its human and economic assets. Victory over the Japanese fleet at the Battle of Midway, the successful elimination of Germany's menace to Allied shipping in the prolonged battle of the Atlantic, and the Allied assault on North Africa and then Italy established Allied naval superiority in the Atlantic and Pacific and began to challenge German domination of southern Europe.

Turning the Tide in the Pacific

In the Pacific theater, the Japanese assaulted American airfields in the Philippines and captured U.S. outposts on Guam and Wake Island. After capturing Singapore and Burma, Japan sought to complete its domination of the southern Pacific with an attack in January 1942 on the American stronghold in the Philippines (see Map 25.5, page 772). American defenders surrendered to the Japanese in May. By the summer of 1942, the Japanese had conquered the Dutch East Indies and were poised to strike Australia and New Zealand.

How did the United States mobilize for war?

How did the Allies turn the tide in Europe and the Pacific?

How did the war change life on the American home front?

How did the Allies finally win the war?

Conclusion: Why did the United States emerge as a superpower at the end of the war?

✓ **LearningCurve** Check what you know. bedfordstmartins.com /roarkunderstanding

1942
- Japan captures the Philippines.
- Battles of Coral Sea and Midway.
- U.S. forces invade North Africa.

1943
- Allied leaders demand the unconditional surrender of the Axis powers.
- U.S. and British forces invade Sicily.

Battle of Midway
▶ June 3–6, 1942, naval battle in the Central Pacific in which American forces surprised and defeated the Japanese who had been massing an invasion force aimed at Midway Island. The battle put the Japanese at a disadvantage for the rest of the war.

In the spring of 1942, U.S. forces launched a major two-pronged counteroffensive that military officials hoped would reverse Japanese advances. Forces led by General Douglas MacArthur, commander of the U.S. armed forces in the Pacific theater, moved north from Australia and eventually attacked the Japanese in the Philippines. Far more decisively, Admiral Chester W. Nimitz sailed his battle fleet west from Hawai'i to retake Japanese-held islands in the southern and mid-Pacific. On May 7–8, 1942, in the Coral Sea just north of Australia, the American fleet and carrier-based warplanes defeated a Japanese armada that was sailing around the coast of New Guinea.

Nimitz then learned from an intelligence intercept that the Japanese were massing an invasion force aimed at Midway Island, an outpost guarding the Hawai'ian Islands. Nimitz maneuvered his carriers and cruisers to surprise the Japanese at the **Battle of Midway**. In a furious battle that raged on June 3–6, American ships and planes delivered a devastating blow to the Japanese navy. The Battle of Midway reversed the balance of naval power in the Pacific and put the Japanese at a disadvantage for the rest of the war. But the Japanese still occupied and defended the many places they had conquered.

The Campaign in Europe

After Pearl Harbor, Hitler's eastern-front armies marched ever deeper into the Soviet Union while his western-front forces prepared to invade Britain. As in World War I, the Germans attempted to starve the British into submission by destroying their seaborne lifeline. In 1941 and 1942, they sank Allied ships faster than new ones could be built.

Until mid-1943, the outcome of the war in the Atlantic remained in doubt. Then, newly invented radar detectors and production of sufficient destroyer escorts for merchant vessels allowed the Allies to prey upon the lurking U-boats. After U-boat crews suffered a 75 percent casualty rate, Hitler withdrew German submarines from the North Atlantic in late May 1943, allowing thousands of American supply ships to cross the Atlantic unimpeded. Winning the battle of the Atlantic allowed the United States to continue to supply its British and Soviet allies for the duration of the war and to reduce the imminent threat of a German invasion of Britain.

The most important strategic questions confronting the United States and its allies were when and where to open a second front against the Nazis. Stalin demanded that America and Britain mount an immediate and massive assault across the English Channel into western France to force Hitler to divert his armies from the eastern front and relieve the pressure on the Soviet Union. Churchill and Roosevelt instead delayed opening a second front, allowing the Germans and the Soviets to slug it out. Churchill and Roosevelt decided to strike first in North Africa to help secure Allied control of the Mediterranean.

In October and November 1942, British forces at El-Alamein in Egypt halted German general Erwin Rommel's drive to capture the Suez Canal, Britain's lifeline to the oil of the Middle East and to British colonies in India and South Asia (see Map 25.4, page 769). In November, an American army under General Dwight D. Eisenhower landed far to the west, in French Morocco. Propelled by American tank units commanded by General George Patton, the Allied armies defeated the Germans in North Africa in May 1943. The North African campaign pushed the Germans out of Africa, made the Mediterranean safe for Allied shipping, and opened the door for an Allied invasion of Italy.

CHAPTER LOCATOR | How did the United States respond to international developments in the 1930s? | How did the outbreak of war affect U.S. foreign policy?

760 CHAPTER 25
THE UNITED STATES AND THE SECOND WORLD WAR

Relief Column, Tunisia, North Africa

This eyewitness painting depicts a column of American soldiers moving toward the front lines to relieve exhausted and wounded comrades in Tunisia in 1943. The artist, Peter Sanfilippo, a twenty-three-year-old private from Brooklyn, New York, wrote that the "arrival of a relief column of fresh soldiers . . . reassures a battered man's faith in his fellow comrades. The unnerved and wounded are resurrected in spirit to thrive, and thus persevere into a new day." Peter Sanfilippo/Veterans History Project, Library of Congress.

In January 1943, while the North African campaign was still under way, Roosevelt and Churchill met in Casablanca and announced that they would accept nothing less than the "unconditional surrender" of the Axis powers, ruling out peace negotiations. They concluded that they should capitalize on their success in North Africa and strike against Italy, consigning the Soviet Union to continue to bear the brunt of the Nazi war machine.

In July 1943, American and British forces landed in Sicily. Soon afterward, Mussolini was deposed in Italy, ending the reign of Italian fascism. Quickly, the Allies invaded the mainland, and the Italian government surrendered unconditionally. The Germans responded by rushing reinforcements to Italy, turning the Allies' Italian campaign into a series of battles to liberate Italy from German occupation.

German troops dug into strong fortifications and fought to defend every inch of Italy's rugged terrain. Allied forces continued to battle against stubborn German defenses for the remainder of the war, making the Italian campaign the war's deadliest for American infantrymen. One soldier wrote that his buddies "died like butchered swine."

QUICK REVIEW <

How did the United States seek to counter the Japanese in the Pacific and the Germans in Europe?

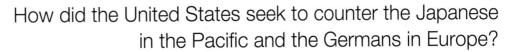

How did the United States mobilize for war?

How did the Allies turn the tide in Europe and the Pacific?

How did the war change life on the American home front?

How did the Allies finally win the war?

Conclusion: Why did the United States emerge as a superpower at the end of the war?

✓ LearningCurve
Check what you know.
bedfordstmartins.com
/roarkunderstanding

How did the war change life on the American home front?

This poster encourages women and children to contribute to the war effort by collecting scrap metal for recycling into weaponry. The poster highlights the middle-class prosperity of the war years, a sharp contrast to the hard times of the 1930s. Chicago Historical Society.

THE WAR EFFORT MOBILIZED Americans as never before. Factories churned out ever more bombs, bullets, tanks, ships, and airplanes, which workers rushed to assemble, leaving their farms and small towns and congregating in cities. Women took jobs with wrenches and welding torches, boosting the nation's workforce and fraying traditional notions that a woman's place was in the home rather than on the assembly line. Despite rationing and shortages, unprecedented government expenditures for war production brought prosperity to many Americans after years of depression-era poverty. Although Americans in uniform risked their lives on battlefields in Europe and Asia, Americans on the U.S. mainland enjoyed complete immunity from foreign attack — in sharp contrast to their Soviet and

CHAPTER LOCATOR | How did the United States respond to international developments in the 1930s? | How did the outbreak of war affect U.S. foreign policy?

762 CHAPTER 25 THE UNITED STATES AND THE SECOND WORLD WAR

British allies. The wartime ideology that contrasted Allied support for human rights with Axis tyranny provided justification for the many sacrifices Americans were required to make in support of the military effort. It also established a standard of basic human equality that became a potent weapon in the campaign for equal rights at home and in condemning the atrocities of the Holocaust perpetrated by the Nazis.

Women and Families, Guns and Butter

Millions of American women gladly took their places on assembly lines in defense industries. At the start of the war, about a quarter of adult women worked outside the home, but few women worked in factories, except for textile mills and sewing industries. But wartime mobilization of the economy and the siphoning of millions of men into the armed forces left factories begging for women workers.

Government advertisements urged women to take industrial jobs by assuring them that their household chores had prepared them for work on the "Victory Line." Millions of women responded. Advertisers often referred to a woman who worked in a war industry as "Rosie the Riveter," a popular wartime term. By the end of the war, women working outside the home numbered 50 percent more than in 1939. Contributing to the war effort also paid off in wages. A Kentucky woman remembered her job at a munitions plant, where she earned "the fabulous sum of $32 a week. To us it was an absolute miracle."

The majority of married women remained at home, occupied with domestic chores and child care. But they, too, supported the war effort, planting Victory Gardens, saving tin cans and newspapers for recycling into war materiel, and buying war bonds. Many families scrimped to cope with the 30 percent inflation during the war, but men and women in manufacturing industries enjoyed wages that grew twice as fast as inflation.

The war influenced how all families spent their earnings. Buying a new washing machine or car was out of the question, since factories that formerly built them now made military goods. Many other consumer goods — such as tires, gasoline, shoes, and meat — were rationed at home to meet military needs overseas. But most Americans readily found things to buy, including movie tickets, cosmetics, and music recordings.

The wartime prosperity and abundance enjoyed by most Americans contrasted with the experiences of their hard-pressed allies. Personal consumption fell by 22 percent in Britain, and food output plummeted to just one-third of prewar levels in the Soviet Union, creating widespread hunger and even starvation.

The Double V Campaign

Fighting against Nazi Germany and its ideology of Aryan racial supremacy, Americans were confronted with the extensive racial prejudice in their own country. The *Pittsburgh Courier*, a leading black newspaper, asserted that the wartime emergency called for a **Double V campaign** seeking "victory over our enemies at home and victory over our enemies on the battlefields abroad."

In 1941, black organizations demanded that the federal government require companies receiving defense contracts to integrate their workforces. A. Philip

> **CHRONOLOGY**

1942
– Congress of Racial Equality is founded.

1943
– 242 race riots erupt in 47 American cities.

1944
– GI Bill of Rights.
– Roosevelt is reelected to fourth term.

Double V campaign
▶ World War II campaign in America to attack racism at home and abroad. The campaign pushed the federal government to require defense contractors to integrate their workforces. In response, Franklin Roosevelt authorized a committee to investigate and prevent racial discrimination in employment.

How did the United States mobilize for war?

How did the Allies turn the tide in Europe and the Pacific?

How did the war change life on the American home front?

How did the Allies finally win the war?

Conclusion: Why did the United States emerge as a superpower at the end of the war?

✓ LearningCurve
Check what you know.
bedfordstmartins.com /roarkunderstanding

763

Randolph, head of the Brotherhood of Sleeping Car Porters, promised that 100,000 African American marchers would descend on Washington if the president did not eliminate discrimination in defense industries. Roosevelt decided to risk offending his white allies in the South and in unions, and he issued Executive Order 8802 in mid-1941. It authorized the Committee on Fair Employment Practices to investigate and prevent racial discrimination in employment.

Progress came slowly, however. In 1940, nine out of ten black Americans lived below the federal poverty line, and those who worked earned an average of just 39 percent of whites' wages. In search of better jobs and living conditions, 5.5 million black Americans migrated from the South to centers of industrial production in the North and West, making a majority of African Americans city dwellers for the first time in U.S. history. Severe labor shortages and government fair employment standards opened assembly-line jobs in defense plants to African Americans, causing black unemployment to drop by 80 percent during the war. But more jobs did not mean equal pay for blacks. The average income of black families rose during the war, but by the end of the conflict it still stood at only half of what white families earned.

Blacks' migration to defense jobs intensified racial antagonisms, which boiled over in the hot summer of 1943, when 242 race riots erupted in 47 cities. The worst mayhem occurred in Detroit, where a long-simmering conflict between whites and blacks over racially segregated housing ignited into a race war. In two days of violence, twenty-five blacks and nine whites were killed, and scores more were injured.

Racial violence created the impetus for the Double V campaign, officially supported by the National Association for the Advancement of Colored People (NAACP), which asserted black Americans' demands for the rights and privileges enjoyed by all other Americans — demands reinforced by the Allies' wartime ideology of freedom and democracy. While the NAACP focused on court challenges to segregation, a new organization founded in 1942, the Congress of Racial Equality, organized picketing and sit-ins against racially segregated restaurants and theaters. Still, the Double V campaign achieved only limited success against racial discrimination during the war.

Wartime Politics and the 1944 Election

Americans rallied around the war effort in unprecedented unity. In June 1944, Congress recognized the sacrifices made by millions of veterans, unanimously passing the landmark **GI Bill of Rights**, which put the financial resources of the federal government behind the abstract goals of freedom and democracy for which veterans were fighting.

GI Bill of Rights

▶ Legislation passed in 1944 authorizing the government to provide World War II veterans with funds for education, housing, and health care, as well as loans to start businesses and buy homes.

> **> GI Bill of Rights**

- Gave military veterans government funds for education, housing, and health care.
- Provided loans to help veterans start businesses and buy homes.
- Empowered millions of GIs to better themselves and their families after the war.

CHAPTER LOCATOR | How did the United States respond to international developments in the 1930s? | How did the outbreak of war affect U.S. foreign policy?

764   CHAPTER 25
THE UNITED STATES AND THE SECOND WORLD WAR

After twelve turbulent years in the White House, Roosevelt was exhausted and gravely ill with heart disease, but he was determined to remain president until the war ended. His poor health made the selection of a vice presidential candidate unusually important. Convinced that many Americans had soured on liberal reform, Roosevelt chose Senator Harry S. Truman of Missouri as his running mate. A reliable party man from a southern border state, Truman satisfied urban Democratic leaders while not worrying white southerners who were nervous about challenges to racial segregation.

The Republicans, confident of a strong conservative upsurge in the nation, nominated as their presidential candidate the governor of New York, Thomas E. Dewey, who had made his reputation as a tough crime fighter. In the 1944 presidential campaign, Roosevelt's failing health alarmed many observers, but his frailty was outweighed by Americans' unwillingness to change presidents in the midst of the war and by Dewey's failure to persuade most voters that the New Deal was a creeping socialist menace. Voters gave Roosevelt a 53.5 percent majority, his narrowest presidential victory, ensuring his continued leadership as Dr. Win-the-War.

Reaction to the Holocaust

Since the 1930s, the Nazis had persecuted Jews in Germany and every German-occupied territory, causing many Jews to seek asylum beyond Hitler's reach. Thousands of Jews sought to immigrate to the United States, but 82 percent of

Mass Execution of Jewish Women and Children

On October 14, 1942, Jewish women and children from the village of Mizocz in present-day Ukraine were herded into a ravine, forced to undress and lie facedown, and then shot at point-blank range by German police. This rare photograph, taken by one of the authorities at the scene, shows Germans killing the women who survived the initial gunfire. United States Holocaust Memorial Museum.

How did the United States mobilize for war? | How did the Allies turn the tide in Europe and the Pacific? | **How did the war change life on the American home front?** | How did the Allies finally win the war? | Conclusion: Why did the United States emerge as a superpower at the end of the war? | LearningCurve Check what you know. bedfordstmartins.com /roarkunderstanding

765

The Holocaust, 1933–1945

◆ Principal German concentration and extermination camp

Holocaust

▶ German effort during World War II to murder Europe's Jews, along with other groups the Nazis deemed "undesirable." Despite reports of the ongoing genocide, the Allies did almost nothing to interfere. In all, some 11 million people were killed in the Holocaust, most of them Jews.

Americans opposed admitting them, and they were turned away. In 1942, numerous reports reached the United States that Hitler was sending Jews, Gypsies, religious and political dissenters, homosexuals, and others to concentration camps, where old people, children, and others deemed too weak to work were systematically slaughtered and cremated, while the able-bodied were put to work at slave labor until they died of starvation and abuse. Other camps were devoted almost exclusively to murdering and cremating Jews. Despite reports of the brutal slave labor and killing camps, U.S. officials refused to grant asylum to Jewish refugees. Most Americans, including top officials, believed that reports were exaggerated.

Desperate to stem the killing, the World Jewish Congress appealed to the Allies to bomb the death camps and the railroad tracks leading to them in order to hamper the killing and block further shipments of victims. Intent on achieving military victory as soon as possible, the Allies repeatedly turned down such bombing requests, arguing that the air forces could not spare resources from their military missions.

The nightmare of the **Holocaust** was all too real. When Russian troops arrived at Auschwitz in Poland in January 1945, they found emaciated prisoners, skeletal corpses, gas chambers, pits filled with human ashes, and loot the Nazis had stripped from the dead, including hair, gold fillings, and false teeth. At last, the truth about the Holocaust began to be known beyond the Germans who had perpetrated and tolerated these atrocities and the men, women, and children who had succumbed to the genocide. By then, it was too late for the 11 million civilian victims — mostly Jews — of the Nazis' crimes against humanity.

> **QUICK REVIEW**

How did the war influence American society?

CHAPTER LOCATOR | How did the United States respond to international developments in the 1930s? | How did the outbreak of war affect U.S. foreign policy?

CHAPTER 25
766   THE UNITED STATES AND THE SECOND WORLD WAR

МЫ ЗЛОМУ ВРАГУ ВСЕ ОТРЕЖЕМ ПУТИ,
ИЗ ПЕТЛИ, ИЗ ЭТОЙ ЕМУ НЕ УЙТИ!

The Allied War Effort

The Russian poster shown here illustrates the combined efforts of the Allies, declaring, "We won't let the evil enemy escape the noose. He will not evade it." Museum of World War II, Natick, MA, www.museumofworldwarii.com.

> VISUAL ACTIVITY

READING THE IMAGE: What does the depiction of Hitler on this Russian poster suggest about his leadership and character?
CONNECTIONS: What does the poster suggest about the importance of the alliance among the major Allied powers?

B BY FEBRUARY 1943, Soviet defenders had finally defeated the massive German offensive against Stalingrad, turning the tide of the war in Europe. After gargantuan sacrifices in fighting that had lasted for eighteen months, the Red Army forced Hitler's Wehrmacht to turn back toward the west. In the Pacific, the Allies had halted the expansion of the Japanese empire but now had the deadly task of dislodging Japanese defenders from the outposts they still occupied. Allied military planners devised a strategy to annihilate Axis resistance by taking advantage of America's industrial superiority. A secret plan to develop a superbomb harnessing atomic power came to fruition too late to use against Germany. But when the atomic bomb devastated the cities of Hiroshima and Nagasaki, Japan finally surrendered, averting the planned assault on the

| How did the United States mobilize for war? | How did the Allies turn the tide in Europe and the Pacific? | How did the war change life on the American home front? | **How did the Allies finally win the war?** | Conclusion: Why did the United States emerge as a superpower at the end of the war? | ✓ LearningCurve Check what you know. bedfordstmartins.com /roarkunderstanding |

767

1944
– D Day.

1945
– Yalta Conference.
– Roosevelt dies; Vice President Harry Truman becomes president.
– Germany surrenders.
– United States joins United Nations.
– United States drops atomic bombs on Hiroshima and Nagasaki.
– Japan surrenders, ending World War II.

Japanese homeland by hundreds of thousands of American soldiers and sailors and their allies.

From Bombing Raids to Berlin

While the Allied campaigns in North Africa and Italy were under way, British and American pilots flew bombing missions from England to German-occupied territories and to Germany itself as an airborne substitute for the delayed second front on the ground. During night raids, British bombers targeted general areas, hoping to hit civilians, create terror, and undermine morale. Beginning in August 1942, American pilots flew heavily armored B-17s from English airfields in daytime raids on industrial targets vital for the German war machine.

German air defenses took a fearsome toll on Allied pilots and aircraft. In 1943, two-thirds of American airmen did not survive to complete their twenty-five-mission tours of duty. In all, 85,000 American airmen were killed in the skies over Europe. Many others were shot down and held as prisoners of war. In February 1944, the arrival of America's durable and deadly P-51 Mustang fighter gave Allied bombers superior protection. The Mustangs slowly began to sweep the Luftwaffe from the skies, allowing bombers to penetrate deep into Germany and pound civilian and military targets around the clock.

In November 1943, Churchill, Roosevelt, and Stalin met in Teheran to discuss wartime strategy and the second front.

> ### > Allied Agreement at Teheran

- Roosevelt conceded to Stalin that the Soviet Union would exercise de facto control of the eastern European countries that the Red Army occupied as it rolled back the German Wehrmacht.
- Stalin agreed to enter the war against Japan once Germany finally surrendered.
- Roosevelt and Churchill promised that they would launch a massive second-front assault in northern France, code-named Overlord, scheduled for May 1944.

General Dwight Eisenhower was assigned overall command of the Allied forces preparing to invade northern France, and mountains of military supplies were stockpiled in England. The huge deployment of Hitler's armies in the east, which were trying to halt the Red Army's westward offensive, left too few German troops to stop the millions of Allied soldiers waiting to attack France. More decisive, years of Allied air raids had decimated the German Luftwaffe, which could send aloft only 300 fighter planes against 12,000 Allied aircraft.

After frustrating delays caused by stormy weather, Eisenhower launched the largest amphibious assault in world history on **D Day**, June 6, 1944 (**Map 25.4**). Allied soldiers finally succeeded in securing the beachhead. An officer told his men, "The only people on this beach are the dead and those that are going to die — now let's get the hell out of here." And they did, finally surmounting the

D Day

▶ June 6, 1944, the date of the Allied invasion of northern France. D Day was the largest amphibious assault in world history. The invasion opened a second front against the Germans and moved the Allies closer to victory in Europe.

CHAPTER LOCATOR | How did the United States respond to international developments in the 1930s? | How did the outbreak of war affect U.S. foreign policy?

768 CHAPTER 25 THE UNITED STATES AND THE SECOND WORLD WAR

Legend:
- Axis powers, including annexed territory
- Extent of Axis control, early Nov. 1942
- Allied powers
- Neutral nations
- → Allied forces
- ✳ Major battle (Allied victory)

ICELAND

ATLANTIC OCEAN

NORWAY

SWEDEN

FINLAND

• Murmansk

• Archangel

North Sea

DENMARK

Baltic Sea

Leningrad
Besieged
Sept. 1942–Jan. 1943

Sept. 1944

• Moscow

GREAT BRITAIN

IRELAND

London •

NETH.

Berlin
Captured
May 2, 1945

• Danzig

Warsaw

July 1944

SOVIET UNION

Normandy
D Day
June 6, 1944

BELG.

Apr. 1945

GERMANY

POLAND

Mar. 1944

Aug. 1943

Stalingrad
Aug. 21, 1942–
Jan. 31, 1943

LUX.

Battle of
the Bulge
Dec. 16, 1944–
Jan. 31, 1945

SLOVAKIA

Aug. 1944

UKRAINE

Paris
Liberated
Aug. 25, 1944

FRANCE

AUSTRIA

HUNGARY

VICHY
FRANCE

SWITZ.

Aug. 1944

ROMANIA

Black Sea

PORTUGAL

SPAIN

CROATIA

SERBIA

N
W   E
S

Corsica

ITALY

Adriatic Sea

BULGARIA

T U R K E Y

Casablanca

Rome
Liberated
June 4, 1944

Sardinia

MONTENEGRO

Nov. 1942

SP. MOROCCO

ALBANIA
(It.)

GREECE

SYRIA   IRAQ

MOROCCO

FRENCH
NORTH AFRICA
(Vichy France)
Joined Allies Nov. 1942

Tunis
Occupied
May 12, 1943

Jul 1943

Sicily

Rhodes
(It.)

Cyprus
(Br.)

LEBANON
(Fr.)

Kasserine Pass
Feb. 14–26, 1943

TUNISIA

Crete (Gr.)

PALESTINE
(Br.)

TRANSJORDAN

Suez
Canal

ALGERIA

Mediterranean Sea

El-Alamein
Oct. 23–Nov. 5, 1942

• Alexandria

SAUDI
ARABIA

0   200   400 miles
0   200   400 kilometers

LIBYA
(It.)

Nov. 1942

EGYPT

MAP 25.4 ■ The European Theater of World War II, 1942–1945

The Russian reversal of the German offensive at Stalingrad and Leningrad, combined with Allied landings in North Africa and Normandy, trapped Germany in a closing vise of Allied armies on all sides.

> MAP ACTIVITY

READING THE MAP: By November 1942, which nations or parts of nations in the European theater were under Axis control? Which had been absorbed by the Axis powers before the war? Which nations remained neutral? Which ones were affiliated with the Allies?

CONNECTIONS: What were the three fronts in the European theater? When did the Allies initiate actions on each front, and why did Churchill, Stalin, and Roosevelt disagree on the timing of the opening of these fronts?

How did the United States mobilize for war? | How did the Allies turn the tide in Europe and the Pacific? | How did the war change life on the American home front? | **How did the Allies finally win the war?** | Conclusion: Why did the United States emerge as a superpower at the end of the war? | ✓ LearningCurve Check what you know. bedfordstmartins.com /roarkunderstanding

769

cliffs that loomed over the beach and destroying the German defenses. One GI who made the landing recalled the soldiers "were exhausted and we were exultant. We had survived D Day!"

Within a week, a flood of soldiers, tanks, and other military equipment propelled Allied forces toward Germany. On August 25, the Allies liberated Paris from four years of Nazi occupation. As the giant pincers of the Allied and Soviet armies closed on Germany in December 1944, Hitler ordered a counterattack to capture the Allies' essential supply port at Antwerp, Belgium. In the Battle of the Bulge (December 16, 1944, to January 31, 1945), as the Allies termed it, German forces drove fifty-five miles into Allied lines before being stopped at Bastogne. More than 70,000 Allied soldiers were killed, including more Americans than in any other battle of the war. The battle fatally depleted Hitler's reserves.

In February 1945, while Allied armies relentlessly pushed German forces backward, Churchill, Stalin, and Roosevelt met secretly at the Yalta Conference (named for the Russian resort town where it was held) to discuss their plans for the postwar world.

> ### > Results of the Yalta Conference

- Stalin promised to permit votes of self-determination in the eastern European countries occupied by the Red Army.
- The Allies pledged to support Jiang Jieshi (Chiang Kai-shek) as the leader of China.
- The Soviet Union obtained a role in the postwar governments of Korea and Manchuria in exchange for entering the war against Japan after the defeat of Germany.

The "Big Three" also agreed on the creation of a new international peacekeeping organization, the United Nations (UN). All nations would have a place in the UN General Assembly, but the Security Council would wield decisive power, and its permanent representatives from the Allied powers — China, France, Great Britain, the Soviet Union, and the United States — would possess a veto over UN actions. The Senate ratified the United Nations Charter in July 1945 by a vote of 89 to 2, reflecting the triumph of internationalism during the nation's mobilization for war.

While Allied armies sped toward Berlin, Allied warplanes dropped more bombs after D Day than in all the previous European bombing raids combined. By April 11, Allied armies reached the banks of the Elbe River and paused while the Soviets smashed into Berlin. The Red Army captured Berlin on May 2. Hitler had committed suicide on April 30, and the provisional German government surrendered unconditionally on May 7. The war in Europe was finally over, with the sacrifice of 135,576 American soldiers, nearly 250,000 British troops, and 9 million Russian combatants.

CHAPTER LOCATOR | How did the United States respond to international developments in the 1930s? | How did the outbreak of war affect U.S. foreign policy?

CHAPTER 25
770 THE UNITED STATES AND THE SECOND WORLD WAR

Roosevelt did not live to witness the end of the war. On April 12, he suffered a fatal stroke. Americans grieved for the man who had led them through years of depression and world war, and they worried about his untested successor, Vice President Harry Truman.

The Defeat of Japan

After the punishing defeats in the Coral Sea and at Midway, Japan had to fend off Allied naval and air attacks. In 1943, British and American forces, along with Indian and Chinese allies, launched an offensive against Japanese outposts in southern Asia, pushing through Burma and into China, where Jiang's armies continued to resist conquest. In the Pacific, Americans and their allies attacked Japanese strongholds by sea, air, and land, moving island by island toward the Japanese homeland (**Map 25.5**).

The island-hopping campaign began in August 1942, when American Marines landed on Guadalcanal in the southern Pacific. For the next six months, a savage battle raged for control of the strategic area. Finally, during the night of February 8, 1943, Japanese forces withdrew. The terrible losses on both sides indicated to the Marines how costly it would be to defeat Japan. After the battle, Joseph Steinbacher, a twenty-one-year-old from Alabama, sailed from San Francisco to New Guinea, where, he recalled, "all the cannon fodder waited to be assigned" to replace the killed and wounded.

In mid-1943, Allied forces launched offensives in New Guinea and the Solomon Islands that gradually secured the South Pacific. In the Central Pacific, amphibious forces conquered the Gilbert and Marshall islands, which served as forward bases for air assaults on the Japanese home islands. As the Allies attacked island after island, Japanese soldiers were ordered to refuse to surrender no matter how hopeless their plight.

While the island-hopping campaign kept pressure on Japanese forces, the Allies invaded the Philippines in the fall of 1944. In the four-day Battle of Leyte Gulf, one of the greatest naval battles in world history, the American fleet crushed the Japanese armada, clearing the way for Allied victory in the Philippines. While the Philippine campaign was under way, American forces captured two crucial islands — Iwo Jima and Okinawa — from which they planned to launch an attack on the Japanese homeland. To defend Okinawa, Japanese leaders ordered thousands of suicide pilots, known as *kamikaze*, to crash their bomb-laden planes into Allied ships. But instead of destroying the American fleet, they demolished the last vestige of the Japanese air force. By June 1945, the Japanese were nearly defenseless on the sea and in the air. Still, their leaders prepared to fight to the death for their homeland.

Joseph Steinbacher and other GIs who had suffered "horrendous" casualties in the Philippines were now told by their commanding officer: "Men, in a few short months we are going to invade [Japan]. . . . We will be going in on the first wave and are expecting ninety percent casualties the first day. . . . For the few of

How did the United States mobilize for war?

How did the Allies turn the tide in Europe and the Pacific?

How did the war change life on the American home front?

How did the Allies finally win the war?

Conclusion: Why did the United States emerge as a superpower at the end of the war?

LearningCurve Check what you know. bedfordstmartins.com /roarkunderstanding

771

Legend:
- Extent of Japanese control, Aug. 1942
- Allies
- Neutral nations
- Allied forces
- Major battle
- Atomic bomb explosion

MAP 25.5 ■ The Pacific Theater of World War II, 1941–1945

To drive the Japanese from their far-flung empire, the Allies launched two combined naval and military offensives — one to recapture the Philippines and then attack Japanese forces in China, the other to hop from island to island in the Central Pacific toward the Japanese mainland.

> **MAP ACTIVITY**

READING THE MAP: What was the extent of Japanese control up until August 1942? Which nations in the Pacific theater sided with the Allies? Which nations remained neutral?

CONNECTIONS: Describe the economic and military motivations behind Japanese domination of the region. How and when did Japan achieve this dominance? Judging from this map, what strategic and geographic concerns might have prompted Truman and his advisers to consider using the atomic bomb against Japan?

CHAPTER LOCATOR | How did the United States respond to international developments in the 1930s? | How did the outbreak of war affect U.S. foreign policy?

CHAPTER 25
772 THE UNITED STATES AND THE SECOND WORLD WAR

us left alive the war will be over." Steinbacher later recalled his mental attitude at that moment: "I know that I am now a walking dead man and will not have a snowball's chance in hell of making it through the last great battle to conquer the home islands of Japan."

Atomic Warfare

In mid-July 1945, as Allied forces prepared for the final assault on Japan, American scientists tested a secret weapon at an isolated desert site near Los Alamos, New Mexico. In 1942, Roosevelt had authorized the top-secret **Manhattan Project** to find a way to convert nuclear energy into a superbomb before the Germans added such a weapon to their arsenal. More than 100,000 Americans, led by scientists, engineers, and military officers at Los Alamos, worked frantically to win the race for an atomic bomb. Germany surrendered two and a half months before the test on July 16, 1945, when scientists first witnessed an atomic explosion that sent a mushroom cloud of debris eight miles into the atmosphere. After watching the successful test of the bomb, J. Robert Oppenheimer, the head scientist at Los Alamos, remarked soberly, "Lots of boys not grown up yet will owe their life to it."

Manhattan Project

▶ Top-secret project authorized by Franklin Roosevelt in 1942 to develop an atomic bomb ahead of the Germans. The thousands of Americans who worked on the project at Los Alamos, New Mexico, succeeded in producing a successful atomic bomb by July 1945.

Hiroshima

This photo shows part of Hiroshima shortly after the atomic bomb dropped from the B-29 bomber named the *Enola Gay*, leveling the densely populated city. Deadly radiation from the bomb maimed and killed Japanese civilians for years afterward. National Archives.

How did the United States mobilize for war? | How did the Allies turn the tide in Europe and the Pacific? | How did the war change life on the American home front? | **How did the Allies finally win the war?** | Conclusion: Why did the United States emerge as a superpower at the end of the war? | ☑ LearningCurve Check what you know. bedfordstmartins.com /roarkunderstanding

773

President Truman saw no reason not to use the atomic bomb against Japan if doing so would save American lives. Despite numerous defeats, Japan still had more than 6 million reserves at home for a last-ditch defense against the anticipated Allied assault, which U.S. military advisers estimated would kill at least 250,000 Americans. But first Truman issued an ultimatum: Japan must surrender unconditionally or face utter ruin. When the Japanese failed to respond by the deadline, Truman ordered that an atomic bomb be dropped on a Japanese city. The bomb that Colonel Paul Tibbets and his crew released over Hiroshima on August 6 leveled the city and incinerated about 100,000 people. Three days later, after the Japanese government still refused to surrender, the second atomic bomb killed nearly as many civilians at Nagasaki.

With American assurance that the emperor could retain his throne after the Allies took over, Japan surrendered on August 14. On a troop ship departing from Europe for what would have been the final assault on Japan, an American soldier spoke for millions of others when he heard the wonderful news that the killing was over: "We are going to grow to adulthood after all."

While all Americans welcomed peace, Robert Oppenheimer and others worried about the consequences of unleashing atomic power. Almost every American, including Oppenheimer, believed that the atomic bomb had brought peace in 1945, but nobody knew what it would bring in the future.

> **QUICK REVIEW**

Why did Truman elect to use the atomic bomb against Japan?

CHAPTER LOCATOR | How did the United States respond to international developments in the 1930s? | How did the outbreak of war affect U.S. foreign policy?

774   CHAPTER 25
THE UNITED STATES AND THE SECOND WORLD WAR

Conclusion: Why did the United States emerge as a superpower at the end of the war?

AT A COST OF 405,399 American lives, the nation united with its allies to crush the Axis aggressors into unconditional surrender. Almost all Americans believed they had won a "good war" against totalitarian evil. The Allies saved Asia and Europe from enslavement and finally halted the Nazis' genocidal campaign against Jews and many others whom the Nazis considered inferior. To secure human rights and protect the world against future wars, the Roosevelt administration took the lead in creating the United Nations.

Wartime production lifted the nation out of the Great Depression. The gross national product soared to four times what it had been when Roosevelt became president in 1933. Jobs in defense industries eliminated chronic unemployment, provided wages for millions of women workers and African American migrants from southern farms, and boosted Americans' prosperity. Ahead stretched the challenge of maintaining that prosperity while reintegrating millions of uniformed men and women, with help from the benefits of the GI Bill.

By the end of the war, the United States had emerged as a global superpower. Wartime mobilization made the American economy the strongest in the world, buttressed by the military clout of the nation's nuclear monopoly. Although the war left much of the world a rubble-strewn wasteland, the American mainland had enjoyed immunity from attack. The Japanese occupation of China had left 50 million people without homes and millions more dead, maimed, and orphaned. The German offensive against the Soviet Union had killed more than 20 million Russian soldiers and civilians. Germany and Japan lay in ruins, their economies and societies as shattered as their military forces. But in the gruesome balance sheet of war, the Axis powers had inflicted far more grief, misery, and destruction on the global victims of their aggression than they had suffered in return.

As the dominant Western nation in the postwar world, the United States asserted its leadership in the reconstruction of Europe while occupying Japan and overseeing its economic and political recovery. America soon confronted new challenges in the tense aftermath of the war, as the Soviets seized political control of eastern Europe, a Communist revolution swept China, and national liberation movements emerged in the colonial empires of Britain and France. The forces unleashed by World War II would shape the United States and the rest of the world for decades to come. Before the ashes of World War II had cooled, America's wartime alliance with the Soviet Union fractured, igniting a Cold War between the superpowers. To resist global communism, the United States became, in effect, the policeman of the free world, repudiating the pre–World War II legacy of isolationism.

| How did the United States mobilize for war? | How did the Allies turn the tide in Europe and the Pacific? | How did the war change life on the American home front? | How did the Allies finally win the war? | Conclusion: Why did the United States emerge as a superpower at the end of the war? | ☑ LearningCurve Check what you know. bedfordstmartins.com /roarkunderstanding |

775

STEP 1

GET STARTED ONLINE

✓ **LearningCurve** ▪ bedfordstmartins.com/roarkunderstanding
Now that you've read the chapter, make it stick by completing the LearningCurve activity.

 STEP 2

EXPLAIN WHY IT MATTERS

Put your reading into practice. Identify each term below, and then explain why it matters in U.S. history.

TERM	WHO OR WHAT & WHEN	WHY IT MATTERS
good neighbor policy (p. 745)		
neutrality acts (p. 746)		
appeasement (p. 748)		
Lend-Lease Act (p. 751)		
internment camps (p. 756)		
Selective Service Act (p. 756)		
Battle of Midway (p. 760)		
Double V campaign (p. 763)		
GI Bill of Rights (p. 764)		
Holocaust (p. 766)		
D Day (p. 768)		
Manhattan Project (p. 773)		

 STEP 3

MOVE BEYOND THE BASICS

To demonstrate a more advanced understanding, describe important developments in the United States and their impact during World War II. What impact did these developments have on women and racial minorities, on the New Deal and the political balance of power, and on the size and nature of the federal government?

	Developments	Impact
Economic activity		
Employment		
Government		
Politics and the New Deal		
Race relations		
Women's roles		

PUT IT ALL TOGETHER

Now, take a step back and try to explain the big picture. Remember to use specific examples from the chapter in your answers.

THE ONSET OF WORLD WAR II

▶ Why were the American people, as a whole, reluctant to become involved in World War II?

▶ How did Roosevelt use the economic power of the United States to aid Britain and the Soviet Union?

THE HOME FRONT

▶ How did the conversion to a war economy end the Great Depression? Who benefited most? What groups still struggled?

▶ What were the most important social consequences of America's involvement in World War II?

VICTORY

▶ How did the Allies achieve victory? What tensions among the Allies emerged in the final years of the war?

▶ What led to the decision to drop atomic bombs on Japan? In your opinion, was it a purely military decision, or were nonmilitary considerations important as well?

LOOKING BACKWARD, LOOKING AHEAD

▶ How did America's experience of World War I shape public opinion in 1939 and 1940 about U.S. involvement in World War II?

▶ How did World War II help set the stage for the social, economic, and political developments of the 1950s?

> ## IN YOUR OWN WORDS

Imagine that you must give an oral report to the class answering the following question: **How did the Second World War change the United States, both domestically and internationally? What would be the most important points to include and why?**

 Do it online at the Student Site ▪ bedfordstmartins.com/roarkunderstanding

26

COLD WAR POLITICS IN THE TRUMAN YEARS

1945–1953

> What was the impact of the Cold War on the United States? Chapter 26 examines American politics and foreign policy in the years immediately following World War II. It explores the origins and impact of the Cold War, President Harry Truman's domestic and foreign policy agendas, and the effect of the Korean War on U.S. domestic politics.

 **LearningCurve**

bedfordstmartins.com/roarkunderstanding
After reading the chapter, use LearningCurve to
retain what you've read.

IS THIS TOMORROW

AMERICA UNDER COMMUNISM!

Cold War comic book. Four million copies of this 1947 comic book painted a terrifying picture of what would happen to Americans if the Soviets took over the country. Collection of Charles H. Christensen.

> What factors contributed to the Cold War?

> Why did Truman have limited success in implementing his domestic agenda?

> How did U.S. Cold War policy lead to the Korean War?

> Conclusion: What were the costs and consequences of the Cold War?

> What factors contributed to the Cold War?

Joseph Stalin: From Ally to Enemy

These two portrayals indicate how quickly the World War II alliance disintegrated into the Cold War. The photograph on the left, from a 1944 issue of the popular magazine *Look*, shows Stalin with two adoring schoolchildren. Only four years later, in 1948, *Look* published Stalin's life story, framing his photo with communism's emblem, the hammer and sickle. The Michael Barson Collection/Past Perfect.

WITH JAPAN'S SURRENDER in August 1945, Americans besieged the government for the return of their loved ones. Americans wanted to dismantle the large military establishment and expected the Allies to cooperate in the management of international peace. Postwar realities quickly dashed these hopes. The wartime alliance forged by the United States, Great Britain, and the Soviet Union crumbled, giving birth to a Cold War. The United States began to develop the means for containing the spread of Soviet power around the globe, including an enormous aid program for Europe, known as the Marshall Plan.

The Cold War Begins

"The guys who came out of World War II were idealistic," reported Harold Russell, a young paratrooper who had lost both hands in a training accident. "We felt the day had come when the wars were all over." But these hopes were quickly dashed. Once the Allies had overcome a common enemy, the prewar mistrust and antagonism between the Soviet Union and the West resurfaced over their very different visions of the postwar world.

The Western Allies' delay in opening a second front in Western Europe aroused Soviet suspicions during the war. The Soviet Union made supreme wartime sacrifices, losing more than twenty million citizens and vast portions of its agricultural and industrial capacity. Soviet leader Joseph Stalin wanted to make Germany pay for Soviet economic reconstruction and to expand Soviet influence in the world. Above all, he wanted friendly governments on the Soviet Union's borders in Eastern Europe. A ruthless dictator, Stalin also wanted to maintain his own power.

In contrast to the Soviet devastation, the United States emerged from the war as the most powerful nation on the planet, with a vastly expanded economy and a monopoly on atomic weapons. That sheer power, along with U.S. economic interests and a belief in the superiority of American institutions and intentions, all affected how American leaders approached the Soviet Union.

American officials believed that a healthy economy depended on opportunities abroad. American companies needed access to raw materials, markets for their goods, and security for their investments overseas. These needs could be met best in countries with similar economic and political systems. As President Harry S. Truman put it in 1947, "The American system can survive in America only if it becomes a world system." Yet leaders and citizens alike regarded their foreign policy not as a self-interested campaign for economic advantage, but as the means to preserve national security and bring freedom, democracy, and capitalism to the rest of the world. Laura Briggs, a woman from Idaho, spoke for many Americans who believed "it was our destiny to prove that we were the children of God and that our way was right for the world."

Recent history also shaped postwar foreign policy. Americans believed that World War II might have been avoided had Britain and France resisted rather than appeased Hitler's initial aggression. Navy Secretary James V. Forrestal argued against trying to "buy [the Soviets'] understanding and sympathy. We tried that once with Hitler." The man with ultimate responsibility for U.S. policy was a keen student of history but came to the White House with little international experience. Harry S. Truman anticipated Soviet-American cooperation, as long as the Soviet Union conformed to U.S. plans for the postwar world. Proud of his ability to make quick decisions, Truman determined to take a firm hand if the Soviets tried to expand, confident that America's nuclear monopoly gave him the upper hand.

The **Cold War** first emerged over clashing Soviet and American interests in Eastern Europe. Stalin insisted that wartime agreements gave him a free hand in the countries defeated or liberated by the Red Army, just as the United States was unilaterally reconstructing governments in Italy and Japan. The Soviet dictator used harsh methods to install Communist governments in neighboring Poland and Bulgaria. Elsewhere, Stalin initially tolerated non-Communist governments in Hungary and Czechoslovakia. In early 1946, he responded to pressure from the West and removed troops from Iran on the Soviet Union's southwest border, allowing U.S. access to the rich oil fields there.

Stalin saw hypocrisy when U.S. officials demanded democratic elections in Eastern Europe while supporting dictatorships friendly to U.S. interests in Latin America. The United States clung to its sphere of influence while opposing Soviet efforts to create its own. But the Western Allies were unwilling to match tough words with military force against the largest army in the world. They protested strongly but failed to prevent the Soviet Union from establishing satellite countries throughout Eastern Europe.

> CHRONOLOGY

1945
- Franklin Roosevelt dies; Vice President Harry Truman becomes president.

1946
- George F. Kennan drafts containment policy.
- United States grants independence to the Philippines.

1947
- National Security Act.
- Truman announces Truman Doctrine.
- U.S. aid to Greece and Turkey.

1948
- Marshall Plan is approved.
- United States recognizes Israel.

1948–1949
- Berlin crisis and airlift.

1949
- Communists take over China.
- North Atlantic Treaty Organization (NATO) is formed.
- Soviet Union explodes atomic bomb.
- Truman approves development of hydrogen bomb.

1951
- U.S. occupation of Japan ends.

Cold War
▶ Term given to the tense and hostile relationship between the United States and the Soviet Union from 1947 to 1989. The term *cold* was apt because the hostility stopped short of direct armed conflict.

Why did Truman have limited success in implementing his domestic agenda?

How did U.S. Cold War policy lead to the Korean War?

Conclusion: What were the costs and consequences of the Cold War?

✓ LearningCurve
Check what you know.
bedfordstmartins.com
/roarkunderstanding

781

In 1946, the wartime Allies contended over Germany's future. Both sides wanted to demilitarize Germany, but U.S. policymakers sought rapid industrial revival there to foster European economic recovery and thus America's own long-term prosperity. By contrast, the Soviet Union wanted Germany weak both militarily and economically, and Stalin demanded heavy reparations from Germany to help rebuild the devastated Soviet economy. Unable to settle their differences, the Allies divided Germany. The Soviet Union installed a puppet Communist government in the eastern section, and Britain, France, and the United States began to unify their occupation zones, eventually establishing the Federal Republic of Germany — West Germany — in 1949 (**Map 26.1**).

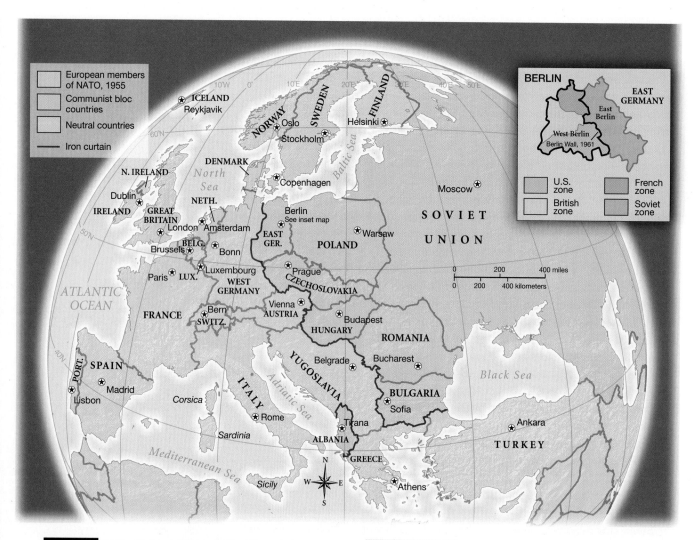

MAP 26.1 ■ The Division of Europe after World War II

The "iron curtain," a term coined by Winston Churchill to refer to the Soviet grip on Eastern and central Europe, divided the continent for nearly fifty years. Communist governments controlled the countries along the Soviet Union's western border, except for Finland, which remained neutral.

> MAP ACTIVITY

READING THE MAP: Is the division of Europe between NATO, Communist, and neutral countries about equal? Why would the location of Berlin pose a problem for the Western allies?

CONNECTIONS: When was NATO founded, and what was its purpose? How did the postwar division of Europe compare with the wartime alliances?

CHAPTER LOCATOR | What factors contributed to the Cold War?

The war of words escalated early in 1946. Boasting of the superiority of the Soviet system, Stalin told a Moscow audience in February that capitalism inevitably produced war. One month later, Truman accompanied Winston Churchill to Westminster College in Fulton, Missouri, where the former prime minister denounced Soviet interference in Eastern and central Europe. "From Stettin in the Baltic to Trieste in the Adriatic, an **iron curtain** has descended across the Continent," Churchill said. Stalin saw Churchill's proposal for joint British-American action to combat Soviet aggression as "a call to war against the USSR (the Soviet Union)."

In February 1946, George F. Kennan, a career diplomat and expert on Russia, wrote a comprehensive rationale for what came to be called the policy of **containment**. Downplaying the influence of Communist ideology in Soviet policy, he instead stressed Soviet insecurity and Stalin's need to maintain authority at home, which, he believed, prompted Stalin to exaggerate threats from abroad and expand Soviet power. Kennan believed that the Soviet Union would retreat from its expansionist efforts if the United States would respond with "unalterable counterforce." This approach, he predicted, would eventually end in "either the breakup or the gradual mellowing of Soviet power." Not all public figures agreed. In September 1946, Secretary of Commerce Henry A. Wallace urged greater understanding of the Soviets' national security concerns, insisting that "we have no more business in the political affairs of Eastern Europe than Russia has in the political affairs of Latin America." State Department officials were furious at Wallace for challenging the administration's hard line against the Soviet Union, and Truman fired Wallace.

The Truman Doctrine and the Marshall Plan

In 1947, the United States began to implement the doctrine of containment that would guide foreign policy for the next four decades. It was not an easy transition; Americans approved of taking a hard line against the Soviet Union but wanted to keep their soldiers and tax dollars at home. In addition to selling containment to the public, Truman had to gain the support of a Republican-controlled Congress.

Crises in two Mediterranean countries triggered the implementation of containment. In February 1947, Britain informed the United States that its crippled economy could no longer sustain military assistance to Greece, where the autocratic government faced a leftist uprising, and to Turkey, which was trying to resist Soviet pressures. Truman promptly sought congressional authority to send the two countries military and economic aid. Meeting with congressional leaders, Undersecretary of State Dean Acheson predicted that if Greece and Turkey fell, communism would soon consume three-fourths of the world. After a stunned silence, Michigan senator Arthur Vandenberg, the Republican foreign policy leader, warned that to get approval, Truman would have to "scare hell out of the country."

Truman did just that. He warned that if Greece fell to the rebels, "confusion and disorder might well spread throughout the entire Middle East" and then create instability in Europe. According to what came to be called the **Truman Doctrine**, the United States must not only resist Soviet military power but also "support free peoples who are resisting attempted subjugation by armed

iron curtain
▶ Metaphor coined by Winston Churchill in 1946 to demarcate the line dividing Soviet-controlled countries in Eastern Europe from democratic nations in Western Europe following World War II.

containment
▶ The post–World War II foreign policy strategy that committed the United States to resisting the influence and expansion of the Soviet Union and communism. The strategy of containment shaped American foreign policy throughout the Cold War.

Truman Doctrine
▶ President Harry S. Truman's commitment to "support free peoples who are resisting attempted subjugation by armed minorities or outside pressures." First applied to Greece and Turkey in 1947, the Truman Doctrine became the justification for U.S. intervention in many countries during the Cold War.

Why did Truman have limited success in implementing his domestic agenda?

How did U.S. Cold War policy lead to the Korean War?

Conclusion: What were the costs and consequences of the Cold War?

✓ LearningCurve
Check what you know.
bedfordstmartins.com
/roarkunderstanding

783

minorities or by outside pressures." The president failed to convince some liberal members of Congress who wanted the United States to work through the United Nations and opposed propping up the authoritarian Greek government. But the administration won the day, setting a precedent for forty years of Cold War interventions that would aid any kind of government if the only alternative appeared to be communism. A much larger assistance program for Europe followed aid to Greece and Turkey. In May 1947, Acheson described a war-ravaged Western Europe, with "factories destroyed, fields impoverished, transportation systems wrecked, populations scattered and on the borderline of starvation." American citizens were sending generous amounts of private aid, but Europe needed large-scale assistance to keep desperate citizens from turning to socialism or communism.

In March 1948, Congress approved such assistance, which came to be called the **Marshall Plan**, after Secretary of State George C. Marshall, who proposed it. Over the next five years, the United States spent $13 billion ($117 billion in 2010 dollars) to restore the economies of sixteen Western European nations. Marshall invited all European nations and the Soviet Union to cooperate in a request for aid, but the Soviets objected to the American terms of free trade and financial disclosure. They ordered their Eastern European satellites to reject the offer.

Marshall Plan

▶ Aid program begun in 1948 to help European economies recover from World War II. Between 1948 and 1953, the United States provided $13 billion to seventeen Western European nations in a project that helped its own economy as well.

Marshall Plan Bread for Greek Children

Greece was one of sixteen European nations that participated in the European Recovery Program, more commonly known as the Marshall Plan. In this photograph taken in 1949, Greek children receive loaves of bread made from the first shipment of Marshall Plan flour from the United States. © Bettmann/Corbis.

CHAPTER LOCATOR | What factors contributed to the Cold War?

Humanitarian impulses as well as the goal of keeping Western Europe free of communism drove the adoption of this enormous aid program. But the Marshall Plan also helped boost the U.S. economy because the participating European nations spent most of the dollars to buy American products and Europe's economic recovery created new markets and opportunities for American investment. And by insisting that the recipient nations work together, the Marshall Plan marked the first step toward the European Union.

In February 1948, the Soviets staged a brutal coup and installed a Communist regime in Czechoslovakia, the last democracy left in Eastern Europe. Next, Stalin threatened Western access to Berlin. That former capital of Germany lay within Soviet-controlled East Germany, but all four Allies jointly occupied it. As the Western Allies moved to organize West Germany as a separate nation, the Soviets retaliated by blocking roads and rail lines between West Germany and the Western-held sections of Berlin, cutting off food, fuel, and other essentials to two million inhabitants. "We stay in Berlin, period," Truman vowed. To avoid a confrontation with Soviet troops, for nearly a year U.S. and British pilots airlifted 2.3 million tons of goods to sustain the West Berliners. Stalin hesitated to shoot down these cargo planes, and in 1949 he lifted the blockade. The city was then divided into East Berlin, under Soviet control, and West Berlin, which became part of West Germany.

Berlin Divided, 1948

Building a National Security State

In September 1949, the Soviet Union detonated its own atomic bomb. Truman then approved the development of a hydrogen bomb — equivalent to five hundred atomic bombs — rejecting the counterarguments of several scientists who had worked on the atomic bomb and of George Kennan, who warned of an endless arms race. The "superbomb" was ready by 1954, but the U.S. advantage was brief. In November 1955, the Soviets exploded their own hydrogen bomb.

> **The Six-Pronged Containment Program**

- Development of atomic weapons
- Stronger traditional military forces
- Military alliances with other nations
- Military and economic aid to friendly nations
- An espionage network and secret means to subvert Communist expansion
- A propaganda offensive to win support for the United States around the world

From the 1950s through the 1980s, deterrence formed the basis of American nuclear strategy. To deter a Soviet attack, the United States strove to maintain a nuclear force more powerful than that of the Soviets. Because the Russians pursued a similar policy, the superpowers became locked in an ever-escalating nuclear weapons race. Albert Einstein, whose mathematical discoveries had laid the foundations for nuclear weapons, commented grimly that the war that came after World War III would "be fought with sticks and stones."

Why did Truman have limited success in implementing his domestic agenda?

How did U.S. Cold War policy lead to the Korean War?

Conclusion: What were the costs and consequences of the Cold War?

✓ LearningCurve
Check what you know.
bedfordstmartins.com
/roarkunderstanding

Implementing the second component of containment, the United States beefed up its conventional military power to deter Soviet threats that might not warrant nuclear retaliation. The National Security Act of 1947 united the military branches under a single secretary of defense and created the National Security Council (NSC) to advise the president. During the Berlin crisis in 1948, Congress hiked military appropriations and enacted a peacetime draft. In addition, Congress granted permanent status to the women's military branches, though it limited their numbers and rank. With 1.5 million men and women in uniform in 1950, the military strength of the United States had quadrupled since the 1930s, and defense expenditures claimed one-third of the federal budget.

Collective security, the third prong of containment strategy, marked a sharp reversal of the nation's traditional foreign policy. In 1949, the United States joined Canada and Western European nations in its first peacetime military alliance, the **North Atlantic Treaty Organization (NATO)**, designed to counter a Soviet threat to Western Europe (see Map 26.1). For the first time in its history, the United States pledged to go to war if one of its allies was attacked.

The fourth element of defense strategy involved foreign assistance programs to strengthen friendly countries, such as aid to Greece and Turkey and the Marshall Plan. In addition, in 1949 Congress approved $1 billion of

North Atlantic Treaty Organization (NATO)

▶ Military alliance formed in 1949 among the United States, Canada, and Western European nations to counter any possible Soviet threat. It represented an unprecedented commitment by the United States to go to war if one of its allies was attacked.

Cold War Spying

"Intelligence," the gathering of information about the enemy, took on new importance with the Cold War and the creation of the Central Intelligence Agency (CIA) in 1947. While much intelligence work took place in Washington, where analysts combed through Communist newspapers, official reports, and speeches, secret agents gathered information behind the iron curtain with bugs and devices such as these cameras hidden in cigarette packs. Jack Naylor Collection/Picture Research Consultants & Archives.

CHAPTER LOCATOR | What factors contributed to the Cold War?

military aid to its NATO allies, and the government began economic assistance to nations in other parts of the world.

The fifth ingredient of containment improved the government's espionage. The National Security Act of 1947 created the **Central Intelligence Agency (CIA)** to gather information and to perform any activities "related to intelligence affecting the national security" that the NSC might authorize. Such functions included propaganda, sabotage, economic warfare, and support for "anti-communist elements in threatened countries of the free world." In 1948, secret CIA operations helped defeat Italy's Communist Party. Subsequently, CIA agents would intervene even more actively, helping to topple legitimate foreign governments and violating the rights of U.S. citizens.

Finally, the U.S. government sought, through cultural exchanges and propaganda, to win "hearts and minds" throughout the world. Truman expanded the Voice of America, created during World War II to broadcast U.S. propaganda abroad. In addition, the State Department sent books, exhibits, jazz musicians, and other performers to foreign countries as "cultural ambassadors."

By 1950, the United States had abandoned age-old tenets of foreign policy. Isolationism and neutrality had given way to a peacetime military alliance and efforts to control events far beyond U.S. borders. Short of war, the United States could not stop the descent of the iron curtain, but it aggressively and successfully promoted economic recovery and a military shield for the rest of Europe.

Central Intelligence Agency (CIA)

▶ Agency created by the National Security Act of 1947 to expand the government's espionage capacities and ability to thwart communism through covert activities, including propaganda, sabotage, economic warfare, and support for anti-Communist forces around the world.

Superpower Rivalry around the Globe

Efforts to implement containment moved beyond Europe. In Africa, Asia, and the Middle East, World War II accelerated a tide of national liberation movements against war-weakened imperial powers. By 1960, forty countries had won their independence. These nations, along with Latin America, came to be referred to collectively as the third world.

Like Woodrow Wilson during World War I, Roosevelt and Truman promoted the ideal of self-determination. The United States granted independence to the Philippines in 1946 and applauded the British withdrawal from India. U.S. policymakers encouraged democracy and capitalism in emerging nations and sought to preserve opportunities for American trade, while U.S. corporations coveted the vast oil reserves in the Middle East. Yet leaders of many liberation movements, impressed with Russia's rapid economic growth, adopted socialist or Communist ideas. Although few of these movements had formal ties with the Soviet Union, American leaders saw them as a threatening extension of Soviet power. Seeking to hold communism at bay by fostering economic development and political stability, in 1949 the Truman administration began a small program of aid to developing nations. Meanwhile, civil war raged in China, where the Communists, led by Mao Zedong (Mao Tse-tung), fought the official Nationalist government under Jiang Jieshi (Chiang Kai-shek). While the Communists gained popular support for their land reforms and valiant stand against the Japanese, Jiang's corrupt, incompetent government alienated much of the population. Failing to promote a settlement between Jiang and Mao, the United States provided $3 billion in aid to the Nationalists. Yet, recognizing the ineptness of Jiang's government, Truman refused to divert further resources from Europe to China.

| Why did Truman have limited success in implementing his domestic agenda? | How did U.S. Cold War policy lead to the Korean War? | Conclusion: What were the costs and consequences of the Cold War? | ☑ LearningCurve Check what you know. bedfordstmartins.com /roarkunderstanding |

In October 1949, Mao established the People's Republic of China (PRC), and the Nationalists fled to the island of Taiwan. Fearing a U.S.-supported invasion to recapture China for the Nationalists, Mao signed a mutual defense treaty with the Soviet Union. The United States refused to recognize the PRC, blocked its admission to the United Nations, and supported the Nationalist government in Taiwan. Only a massive U.S. military commitment could have stopped the Chinese Communists, yet some Republicans charged that Truman and "pro-Communists in the State Department" had "lost" China. With China in turmoil, U.S. policy shifted to helping Japan rapidly reindustrialize. In a short time, the Japanese economy was flourishing, and the official military occupation ended when the two nations signed a peace treaty and a mutual security pact in September 1951. Like West Germany, Japan now sat squarely within the American orbit, ready to serve as an economic hub in a vital area.

The one place where Cold War considerations did not control American policy was Palestine. In 1943, then-senator Harry Truman spoke passionately about Nazi Germany's annihilation of the Jews, asserting, "This is not a Jewish problem, it is an American problem — and we must . . . face it squarely and honorably." As president, he made good on his words. Jews had been migrating to Palestine, their biblical homeland, since the nineteenth century, resulting in tension and hostilities with the Palestinian Arabs. After World War II, as hundreds of thousands of European Jews sought refuge and a national homeland in Palestine, fighting and terrorism escalated on both sides.

Truman's foreign policy experts sought American-Arab friendship to contain Soviet influence in the Middle East and to secure access to Arabian oil. Uncharacteristically defying his advisers, the president responded instead to pleas from Jewish organizations, his moral commitment to Holocaust survivors, and his interest in the American Jewish vote for the 1948 election. When Jews in Palestine declared the state of Israel in May 1948, Truman quickly recognized the new country and made its defense the cornerstone of U.S. policy in the Middle East.

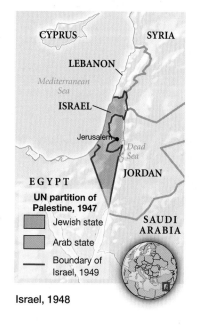

Israel, 1948

> **QUICK REVIEW**

Why did relations between the United States and the Soviet Union deteriorate after World War II?

Truman's Whistle-Stop Campaign

Harry Truman rallies a crowd from his campaign train in Bridgeport, Pennsylvania, in October 1948. As he campaigned across the country, supporters often shouted, "Give 'em hell, Harry." Truman's support for civil rights cost him four southern states but helped him win votes from liberals and blacks. Truman Library.

Why did Truman have limited success in implementing his domestic agenda?

REFERRING TO THE CIVIL WAR GENERAL who coined the phrase "War is hell," Truman said in December 1945, "Sherman was wrong. I'm telling you I find peace is hell." Challenged by crises abroad, Truman also faced shortages, strikes, inflation, and other problems as the economy shifted to peacetime production. At the same time, he tried to expand New Deal reform with his own Fair Deal agenda of initiatives in civil rights, housing, education, and health care — efforts hindered by the wave of anti-Communist hysteria sweeping the country.

Reconverting to a Peacetime Economy

Despite scarcities and deprivations, World War II had brought most Americans a higher standard of living than ever before. Economic experts as well as ordinary citizens worried about sustaining that standard and providing jobs for millions of returning soldiers. To that end, Truman asked Congress to enact a twenty-one-point program of social and economic reforms. He wanted the government to continue regulating the economy while it adjusted to peacetime production, and he sought government programs to provide basic essentials such as housing and

| Why did Truman have limited success in implementing his domestic agenda? | How did U.S. Cold War policy lead to the Korean War? | Conclusion: What were the costs and consequences of the Cold War? | ☑ LearningCurve Check what you know. bedfordstmartins.com /roarkunderstanding |

789

health care to those in need. "Not even President Roosevelt ever asked for as much at one sitting," exploded Republican leader Joseph W. Martin Jr.

Congress approved one of Truman's key proposals — full-employment legislation — only after watering it down. The Employment Act of 1946 called on the federal government "to promote maximum employment, production, and purchasing power," thereby formalizing government's responsibility for maintaining a healthy economy. But it authorized no new powers to translate that obligation into effective action.

Inflation, not unemployment, turned out to be the biggest problem. Consumers had $30 billion in wartime savings to spend, but shortages of meat, automobiles, housing, and other items persisted. Until industry could make more goods available, consumer demand would continue to drive up prices. With a basket of groceries on her arm to dramatize rising costs, Democratic congresswoman Helen Gahagan Douglas of California urged Congress to maintain price and rent controls. Those efforts, however, fell to pressures from business groups and others determined to trim government powers.

Labor relations were another thorn in Truman's side. Organized labor emerged from the war with its 14.5 million members making up 35 percent of the civilian workforce. Yet union members feared the erosion of wartime gains and turned to the weapon they had surrendered during the war. Five million workers went out on strike in 1946, affecting nearly every major industry. Shortly before voting to strike, a former Marine and his coworkers calculated that an executive had spent more on a party than they would earn in a whole year at the steel mill. "That sort of stuff made us realize, hell we had to bite the bullet. . . . The bosses sure didn't give a damn for us." Although most Americans approved of unions in principle, they became fed up with strikes, blamed unions for shortages and rising prices, and called for government restrictions on organized labor. When the

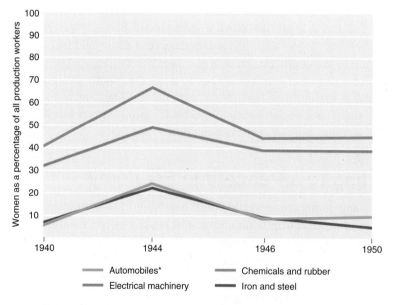

FIGURE 26.1 ■ Women Workers in Selected Industries, 1940–1950
Women demolished the idea that some jobs were "men's work" during World War II, but they failed to maintain their gains in the manufacturing sector after the war.

*During World War II, this industry did not produce cars, but rather military transportation such as jeeps, tanks, aircraft, etc.

CHAPTER LOCATOR | What factors contributed to the Cold War?

strikes subsided, workers had won wage increases of about 20 percent, but the loss of overtime pay along with rising prices left their purchasing power only slightly higher than in 1942.

Women workers fared even worse. Polls indicated that many women wanted to keep their wartime jobs, but most who remained in the workforce had to settle for relatively low-paying jobs in light industry or the service sector (**Figure 26.1**). Displaced from her shipyard work, Marie Schreiber took a cashier's job, lamenting, "You were back to women's wages, you know . . . practically in half." With the backing of women's organizations and union women, Congresswoman Douglas sponsored bills to require equal pay for equal work, to provide child care for employed mothers, and to create a government commission to study women's status. But at a time when women were viewed primarily as wives and mothers and opposition to further expansion of federal powers was strong, these initiatives went nowhere.

By 1947, the economy had stabilized, avoiding the postwar depression that so many had feared. Wartime profits enabled businesses to expand. Consumers could now spend their wartime savings on houses, cars, and appliances that had lain beyond their reach during the depression and war. Defense spending and foreign aid that enabled war-stricken countries to purchase American products also stimulated the economy. A soaring birthrate further sustained consumer demand. Although prosperity was far from universal, the United States entered into a remarkable economic boom that lasted through the 1960s (as discussed in chapter 27).

Another economic boost came from the only large welfare measure passed after the New Deal. The Servicemen's Readjustment Act (GI Bill), enacted in 1944, offered 16 million veterans job training and education; unemployment compensation until they found jobs; and low-interest loans to purchase homes, farms, and small businesses. By 1948, some 1.3 million veterans had bought houses with government loans. Helping 2.2 million ex-soldiers attend college, the subsidies sparked a boom in higher education. A drugstore clerk before his military service, Don Condren was able to get an engineering degree and buy his first house. "I think the GI Bill gave the whole country an upward boost economically," he said.

Yet the impact of the GI Bill was uneven. As wives and daughters of veterans, women benefited indirectly from the GI subsidies, but few women qualified for the employment and educational preferences available to some 15 million men. Moreover, GI programs were administered at the state and local levels, which resulted in routine discrimination especially in the South. Southern universities remained segregated, and historically black colleges could not accommodate all

Women's Role in Peacetime

Like many manufacturers during World War II, Proctor Electric Company was forced to convert to war production, so it switched from making appliances to producing bomb fuses, cartridges, and airplane wing flaps. After the war, the company hoped to profit from pent-up consumer demand. During the reconversion period, ads tempted consumers with products soon to come, as in this 1946 ad. What message about women's employment during and after the war is conveyed here? Picture Research Consultants & Archives.

Why did Truman have limited success in implementing his domestic agenda?

How did U.S. Cold War policy lead to the Korean War?

Conclusion: What were the costs and consequences of the Cold War?

✓ LearningCurve
Check what you know.
bedfordstmartins.com
/roarkunderstanding

791

who wanted to attend. Black veterans were shuttled into menial labor. One decorated veteran reported that "my color bars me from most decent jobs, and if, instead of accepting menial work, I collect my $20 a week readjustment allowance, I am classified as a 'lazy nigger.'" Thousands of black veterans did benefit, but the GI Bill did not help all ex-soldiers equally.

Blacks and Mexican Americans Push for Their Civil Rights

"I spent four years in the army to free a bunch of Frenchmen and Dutchmen," an African American corporal declared, "and I'm hanged if I'm going to let the Alabama version of the Germans kick me around when I get home." Black veterans along with civilians resolved not to return to the racial injustices of prewar America. The migration of two million African Americans to northern and western cities meant that they could now vote and participate in ongoing struggles to end discrimination in housing and education. Pursuing civil rights through the courts and Congress, the National Association for the Advancement of Colored People (NAACP) counted half a million members.

In the postwar years, individual African Americans broke through the color barrier, achieving several "firsts." Jackie Robinson integrated major league baseball, playing for the Brooklyn Dodgers, and won the Rookie of the Year Award in 1947. In 1950, Ralph J. Bunche received the Nobel Peace Prize for his United Nations work, and Gwendolyn Brooks won the Pulitzer Prize for poetry. Still, little had changed for most African Americans, especially in the South, where violence greeted their attempts to assert their rights. Armed white men prevented Medgar Evers (who would become a key civil rights leader in the 1960s) and four other veterans from voting in Mississippi. A mob lynched Isaac Nixon for voting in Georgia, and an all-white jury acquitted the men accused of his murder. Segregation and economic discrimination were widespread in the North as well.

In waging the Cold War, the superpowers vied for the allegiance of newly independent nations with nonwhite populations, and Soviet propaganda repeatedly highlighted racial injustice in the United States. Secretary of State Dean Acheson noted that systematic segregation and discrimination endangered "our moral leadership of the free and democratic nations of the world."

"My very stomach turned over when I learned that Negro soldiers just back from overseas were being dumped out of army trucks in Mississippi and beaten," wrote Truman. Risking support from southern white voters, Truman spoke more boldly on civil rights than any previous president had. In 1946, he created the President's Committee on Civil Rights, and in February 1948 he asked Congress to enact the committee's recommendations. The first president to address the NAACP, Truman asserted that all Americans should have equal rights to housing, education, employment, and the ballot.

As with much of his domestic program, Truman failed to act aggressively on his bold words. Congress rejected his proposals for national civil rights legislation, although some northern and western states did pass laws against discrimination in employment and public accommodations. Running for reelection in 1948 and hoping to appeal to northern black and liberal voters, Truman issued an executive

Segregation The segregation visible on this bus was a feature of life in the South from the late nineteenth century until the 1960s. African Americans could not use white hospitals, cemeteries, schools, libraries, swimming pools, restrooms, or drinking fountains. They were relegated to balconies in movie theaters and kept apart from whites in all public meetings. Stan Wayman/Time Life Pictures/ Getty Images.

order to desegregate the armed services, but it lay unimplemented until the Korean War, when the cost of segregation to military efficiency became apparent. Although actual accomplishments fell far short of Truman's proposals, desegregation of the military and the administration's support of civil rights cases in the Supreme Court contributed to far-reaching changes.

Discussion of race and civil rights usually focused on African Americans, but Mexican Americans fought similar injustices. In 1929, they had formed the League of United Latin American Citizens (LULAC) to combat discrimination and segregation in the Southwest. Like black soldiers, Mexican American veterans believed, as one insisted, that "we had earned our credentials as American citizens." Problems with getting their veterans' benefits spurred the formation of a new organization in 1948 in Corpus Christi, Texas — the American GI Forum. Dr. Héctor Peréz García, president of the local LULAC and a Bronze Star combat surgeon, led the GI Forum, which became a national force for battling discrimination and electing sympathetic officials.

"Education is our freedom," read the GI Forum's motto, yet Mexican American children were routinely segregated in public schools. In 1945, with the help of LULAC, parents filed a class action suit in southern California, challenging school districts that barred their children from white schools. In the resulting decision, *Mendez v. Westminster* (1947), a federal court for the first time struck down school segregation. NAACP lawyer Thurgood Marshall filed a supporting brief in

Why did Truman have limited success in implementing his domestic agenda?

How did U.S. Cold War policy lead to the Korean War?

Conclusion: What were the costs and consequences of the Cold War?

✓ LearningCurve
Check what you know.
bedfordstmartins.com
/roarkunderstanding

793

the case, which foreshadowed the landmark *Brown* decision of 1954 (as discussed in chapter 27). Efforts to gain equal education, challenges to job discrimination in employment, and campaigns for political representation all demonstrated a growing mobilization of Mexican Americans in the Southwest.

The Fair Deal Flounders

In the 1946 congressional elections, Republicans won control of Congress for the first time in fourteen years, capitalizing on public frustrations with strikes and shortages and accusing the administration of "confusion, corruption, and communism." Many Republicans had campaigned against the New Deal in 1946, and in the Eightieth Congress they weakened some reform programs and enacted tax cuts favoring higher-income groups.

Organized labor took the most severe blow when Congress passed the **Taft-Hartley Act** over Truman's veto in 1947. Called a "slave labor" law by unions, the measure amended the Wagner Act (see chapter 24). It reduced the power of organized labor and made it more difficult to organize workers. States could now pass "right-to-work" laws, which banned the practice of requiring all workers to join a union once a majority had voted for it. Many states, especially in the South and West, rushed to enact such laws, encouraging industries to relocate there. Taft-Hartley maintained the New Deal principle of government protection for collective bargaining, but it put the government more squarely between labor and management.

In the 1948 election, Truman faced not only a resurgent Republican Party headed by New York governor Thomas E. Dewey but also two revolts within his own party. On the left, Henry A. Wallace, whose foreign policy views had cost him his cabinet seat, led the new Progressive Party. On the right, South Carolina governor J. Strom Thurmond headed the States' Rights Party — the Dixiecrats — formed by southern Democrats who walked out of the 1948 Democratic Party convention when it passed a liberal civil rights plank.

Truman launched a vigorous campaign, yet his prospects were so bleak that on election night the *Chicago Daily Tribune* printed its next day's issue with the headline "Dewey Defeats Truman." But even though the Dixiecrats won four southern states, Truman took 303 electoral votes to Dewey's 189, and his party regained control of Congress (**Map 26.2**). His unexpected victory attested to the broad support for his foreign policy and the enduring popularity of New Deal reform.

While most New Deal programs survived Republican attacks, Truman failed to enact his Fair Deal agenda. Congress made modest improvements in Social Security and raised the minimum wage, but it passed only one significant reform measure. The **Housing Act of 1949** authorized 810,000 units of government-constructed housing over the next six years and represented a landmark commitment by the government to address the housing needs of the poor. Yet it fell far short of

Taft-Hartley Act

▶ Law passed by the Republican-controlled Congress in 1947 that amended the Wagner Act and placed restrictions on organized labor that made it more difficult for unions to organize workers.

Housing Act of 1949

▶ Law authorizing the construction of 810,000 units of government housing. This landmark effort marked the first significant commitment of the federal government to meet the housing needs of the poor.

Candidate	Electoral Vote	Popular Vote	Percent of Popular Vote
Harry S. Truman (Democrat)	303	24,105,695	49.5
Thomas E. Dewey (Republican)	189	21,969,170	45.1
J. Strom Thurmond (States' Rights)	39	1,169,021	2.4
Henry A. Wallace (Progressive)	0	1,156,103	2.4

MAP 26.2 ■ The Election of 1948

actual need, and slum clearance frequently displaced the poor without providing alternatives.

With southern Democrats posing a primary obstacle, Congress rejected Truman's proposals for civil rights, a powerful medical lobby blocked plans for a universal health care program, and conflicts over race and religion thwarted federal aid to education. Truman's efforts to revise immigration policy were mixed. The McCarran-Walter Act of 1952 ended the outright ban on immigration and citizenship for Japanese and other Asians, but it authorized the government to bar suspected Communists and homosexuals and maintained the discriminatory quota system established in the 1920s. By late 1950, the Korean War embroiled the president in controversy and depleted his power as a legislative leader (see pages 798–99). Truman's failure to make good on his domestic proposals set the United States apart from most European nations, which by the 1950s had in place comprehensive health, housing, and employment security programs to underwrite the material well-being of their populations.

The Domestic Chill: McCarthyism

Truman's domestic program also suffered from a wave of anticommunism that weakened liberals. "Red-baiting" (attempting to link individuals or ideas with communism) and official retaliation against leftist critics of the government had flourished during the Red scare at the end of World War I (see chapter 22). A second Red scare followed World War II, born of partisan politics, the collapse of the Soviet-American alliance, foreign policy setbacks, and disclosures of Soviet espionage.

Republicans who had attacked the New Deal as a plot of radicals now jumped on events such as the Soviet takeover of Eastern Europe and the Communist triumph in China to accuse Democrats of fostering internal subversion. Wisconsin senator Joseph R. McCarthy avowed that "the Communists within our borders have been more responsible for the success of Communism abroad than Soviet Russia." McCarthy's charges — such as the allegation that retired general George C. Marshall belonged to a Communist conspiracy — were reckless and often ludicrous, but the press covered him avidly, and *McCarthyism* became a term synonymous with the anti-Communist crusade.

Revelations of Soviet espionage lent credibility to fears of internal communism. A number of ex-Communists, including Whittaker Chambers and Elizabeth Bentley, testified that they and others had provided secret documents to the Soviets. Most alarming of all, in 1950 a British physicist working on the atomic bomb project confessed that he was a spy and implicated several Americans, including Ethel and Julius Rosenberg. The Rosenbergs pleaded not guilty but were convicted of conspiracy to commit espionage and electrocuted in 1953.

Records opened in the 1990s showed that the Soviet Union did receive secret documents from Americans that probably hastened its development of nuclear weapons by a year or two. Yet the vast majority of individuals hunted down in the Red scare had done nothing more than at one time joining the Communist Party, associating with Communists, or supporting radical causes. And most of those activities had taken place long before the Cold War had made the Soviet Union an enemy. The hunt for subversives was conducted by both Congress and the

Why did Truman have limited success in implementing his domestic agenda?

How did U.S. Cold War policy lead to the Korean War?

Conclusion: What were the costs and consequences of the Cold War?

☑ LearningCurve
Check what you know.
bedfordstmartins.com/roarkunderstanding

795

executive branch. Stung by charges of communism in the 1946 midterm elections, Truman issued Executive Order 9835 in March 1947, establishing loyalty review boards to investigate every federal employee. "A nightmare from which there [was] no awakening" was how State Department employee Esther Brunauer described it when both she and her husband, a chemist in the navy, lost their jobs because he had joined a Communist youth organization in the 1920s and associated with suspected radicals. Government investigators allowed anonymous informers to make charges and placed the burden of proof on the accused. More than two thousand civil service employees lost their jobs, and another ten thousand resigned as Truman's loyalty program continued into the mid-1950s. Years later, Truman admitted that it had been a mistake.

Congressional committees, such as the **House Un-American Activities Committee (HUAC)**, also investigated individuals' political associations. When those under scrutiny refused to name names, investigators charged that silence was tantamount to confession, and these "unfriendly witnesses" lost their jobs and suffered public ostracism. In 1947, HUAC investigated radical activity in Hollywood. Some actors and directors cooperated, but ten refused, citing their First Amendment rights. The "Hollywood Ten" served jail sentences for contempt of Congress and then found themselves blacklisted in the movie industry.

The domestic Cold War spread beyond the nation's capital. State and local governments investigated citizens, demanded loyalty oaths, fired employees suspected of disloyalty, banned books from public libraries, and more. Because the Communist Party had helped organize unions and championed racial justice, labor and civil rights activists fell prey to McCarthyism as well. African American activist Jack O'Dell remembered that segregationists pinned the tag of Communist on "anybody who supported the right of blacks to have civil rights."

McCarthyism caused untold harm to thousands of innocent individuals. Anti-Communist crusaders humiliated and discredited law-abiding citizens, hounded them from their jobs, and in some cases even sent them to prison. The anti-Communist crusade violated fundamental constitutional rights of freedom of speech and stifled the expression of dissenting ideas or unpopular causes.

House Un-American Activities Committee (HUAC)

▶ Congressional committee especially prominent during the early years of the Cold War that investigated Americans who might be disloyal to the government or might have associated with Communists or other radicals. It was one of the key institutions that promoted the second Red scare.

> **QUICK REVIEW**

What impact did the Cold War have on Truman's domestic agenda?

CHAPTER LOCATOR | What factors contributed to the Cold War?

How did U.S. Cold War policy lead to the Korean War?

POWs in Korea

These demoralized American soldiers reflect the grim situation for U.S. forces during the early months of the Korean War. Their North Korean captors forced them to march through Seoul in July 1950 carrying a banner proclaiming the righteousness of the Communist cause and attacking U.S. intervention. Wide World Photos, Inc.

THE COLD WAR ERUPTED into a shooting war in June 1950 when troops from Communist North Korea invaded South Korea. For the first time, Americans went into battle to implement containment. Confirming the global reach of the Truman Doctrine, U.S. involvement in Korea also marked the militarization of American foreign policy. The United States, in concert with the United Nations, ultimately held the line in Korea, but at a great cost in lives, dollars, and domestic unity.

Korea and the Military Implementation of Containment

The **Korean War** grew out of the artificial division of Korea after World War II. Having expelled the Japanese, the United States and the Soviet Union created two occupation zones separated by the thirty-eighth parallel (**Map 26.3**). With Moscow and Washington unable to agree on unification, the United Nations sponsored elections in South Korea in July 1948. The American-favored candidate, Syngman Rhee, was elected president, and the United States withdrew most of its troops. In the fall of 1948, the Soviets established the People's Republic of North Korea under Kim Il-sung and also withdrew. Although unsure whether Rhee's repressive government could sustain popular support, U.S. officials appreciated his anticommunism and provided economic and military aid to South Korea.

Korean War

▶ Conflict between North Korean forces, supported by China and the Soviet Union, and South Korean and U.S.-led UN forces over control of South Korea. Lasting from 1950 to 1953, the war represented the first time that the United States went to war to implement containment.

Why did Truman have limited success in implementing his domestic agenda?

How did U.S. Cold War policy lead to the Korean War?

Conclusion: What were the costs and consequences of the Cold War?

✓ LearningCurve
Check what you know.
bedfordstmartins.com
/roarkunderstanding

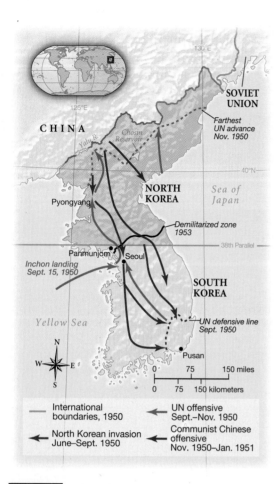

International boundaries, 1950

North Korean invasion June–Sept. 1950

UN offensive Sept.–Nov. 1950

Communist Chinese offensive Nov. 1950–Jan. 1951

MAP 26.3 ■ The Korean War, 1950–1953

Although each side had plunged deep into enemy territory, the war ended in 1953 with the dividing line between North and South Korea nearly where it had been before the fighting began.

> **MAP ACTIVITY**

READING THE MAP: How far south did the North Korean forces progress at the height of their invasion? How far north did the UN forces get? What countries border Korea?

CONNECTIONS: What dangers did the forays of MacArthur's forces to within forty miles of the Korean-Chinese border pose? Why did Truman forbid MacArthur to approach that border? What political considerations on the home front influenced Truman's policy and military strategy regarding Korea?

Skirmishes between North and South Korean troops at the thirty-eighth parallel began in 1948. Then, in June 1950, 90,000 North Koreans swept into South Korea. Truman's advisers assumed that the Soviet Union or China had instigated the attack (an assumption later proved incorrect), and he quickly decided to intervene, viewing Korea as "the Greece of the Far East." With the Soviet Union absent from the Security Council, the United States obtained UN sponsorship of a collective effort to repel the attack. Authorized to appoint a commander for the UN force, Truman named World War II hero General Douglas MacArthur.

Sixteen nations sent troops to Korea, but the United States furnished most of the personnel and weapons, deploying almost 1.8 million troops and dictating strategy. By dispatching troops without asking Congress for a declaration of war, Truman violated the spirit if not the letter of the Constitution and contributed to the expansion of executive power that would characterize the Cold War. The first American soldiers rushed to Korea unprepared and ill equipped, and U.S. forces suffered severe defeats early in the war. The North Koreans took the capital of Seoul and drove deep into South Korea, forcing UN troops to retreat to Pusan. Then, in September 1950, General MacArthur launched a bold counteroffensive at Inchon, 180 miles behind North Korean lines. By October, UN and South Korean forces had retaken Seoul and pushed the North Koreans back to the thirty-eighth parallel. Now Truman had to decide whether to invade North Korea and seek to unify the country.

From Containment to Rollback to Containment

"Troops could not be expected . . . to march up to a surveyor's line and stop," remarked Secretary of State Dean Acheson, reflecting support for transforming the military objective from containment to elimination of the enemy and unification of Korea. Thus, for the only time during the Cold War, the United States tried to roll back communism by force. With UN approval, on September 27, 1950, Truman authorized MacArthur to cross the thirty-eighth parallel. Concerned about possible intervention by China, the president directed him to keep UN troops away from the Korean-Chinese border. Disregarding the order, MacArthur sent them to within forty miles of China, whereupon 300,000 Chinese soldiers crossed into Korea. With Chinese help, the North Koreans recaptured Seoul.

After three months of grueling battle, UN forces fought their way back to the thirty-eighth parallel. At that point, Truman decided to seek a negotiated settlement. MacArthur was furious when the goal of the war reverted to containment, which to him represented defeat. Taking his case to the public, he challenged both the president's authority to conduct foreign policy and the principle of civilian control of the military. Fed up with MacArthur's insubordination, Truman fired him in April 1951. Many Americans sided with MacArthur, reflecting their frustration with containment. Why should Americans die simply to preserve the status quo? Why not destroy the enemy once and for all? Those siding with MacArthur assumed that the United States was all-powerful and blamed the stalemate in Korea on the government's ineptitude or willingness to shelter subversives.

When Congress investigated MacArthur's dismissal, all of the top military leaders supported the president. According to the chairman of the Joint Chiefs of Staff, MacArthur wanted to wage "the wrong war, at the wrong place, at the wrong time, with the wrong enemy." Yet Truman never recovered from the political fallout. Nor was he able to end the war. Negotiations began in July 1951, but peace talks dragged on for two more years while twelve thousand more U.S. soldiers died.

> CHRONOLOGY

1950
– Korean War begins.

1951
– Truman fires General Douglas MacArthur.

1952
– Dwight D. Eisenhower is elected president.

1953
– Korean War ends.

Korea, Communism, and the 1952 Election

Popular discontent with President Truman's war boosted Republicans in the 1952 election. Their presidential nominee, General Dwight D. Eisenhower, was a popular hero. As supreme commander in Europe, he won widespread acclaim for leading the Allied armies to victory over Germany in World War II. In 1950, Truman appointed Eisenhower the first supreme commander of NATO forces.

Although Eisenhower believed that professional soldiers should stay out of politics, he found compelling reasons to run in 1952. He largely agreed with Truman's foreign policy, but he deplored the Democrats' propensity to solve domestic problems with costly new federal programs. He also disliked the foreign policy views of the leading Republican presidential contender, Senator Robert A. Taft, who attacked containment and sought to cut defense spending. Eisenhower defeated Taft for the nomination, but the old guard prevailed on the party platform. It excoriated containment as "negative, futile, and immoral" and charged the Truman administration with shielding "traitors to the Nation in high places." By choosing thirty-nine-year-old Senator Richard M. Nixon for his running mate, Eisenhower helped to appease the right wing of the party.

Richard Milhous Nixon grew up in southern California, worked his way through college and law school, served in the navy, and briefly practiced law before winning election to Congress in 1946. Nixon quickly made a name for himself as a member of HUAC (see page 796) and a key anti-Communist, moving to the Senate in 1950.

With his public approval ratings plummeting, Truman decided not to run for reelection. The Democrats nominated Adlai E. Stevenson, the popular governor of Illinois, who was acceptable to both liberals and southerners. Stevenson could not escape the domestic fallout from the Korean War, however; nor could he match Eisenhower's widespread appeal. Shortly before the election, Eisenhower announced dramatically, "I shall go to Korea," and voters registered their confidence in his ability to end the war. Cutting sharply into traditional Democratic territory, Eisenhower won several southern states and garnered 55 percent of the popular vote overall. His coattails carried a narrow Republican majority to Congress.

Why did Truman have limited success in implementing his domestic agenda?

How did U.S. Cold War policy lead to the Korean War?

Conclusion: What were the costs and consequences of the Cold War?

✓ LearningCurve
Check what you know.
bedfordstmartins.com
/roarkunderstanding

An Armistice and the War's Costs

Eisenhower made good on his pledge to end the Korean War. In July 1953, the two sides reached an armistice that left Korea divided, again roughly at the thirty-eighth parallel, with North and South separated by a two-and-a-half-mile-wide demilitarized zone (see Map 26.3). The war fulfilled the objective of containment, since the United States had backed up its promise to help nations that were resisting communism. Both Truman and Eisenhower managed to contain what amounted to a world war — involving twenty nations altogether — within a single country and to avoid the use of nuclear weapons.

> ### > The Human Toll of the Korean War

- 36,000 Americans were killed, and 100,000 were wounded.
- South Korea lost more than 1 million people to war-related causes.
- More than 1.8 million North Koreans and Chinese were killed or wounded.

NSC 68

▶ Top-secret government report of April 1950 warning that national survival required a massive military buildup. The Korean War brought nearly all of the expansion that the report called for, and by 1952 defense spending claimed nearly 70 percent of the federal budget.

The Korean War had an enormous effect on defense policy and spending. In April 1950, just before the war began, the National Security Council completed a top-secret report, known as **NSC 68**, on the United States' military strength, warning that national survival required a massive military buildup. The Korean War brought about nearly all of the military expansion called for in NSC 68, vastly increasing U.S. capacity to act as a global power. Military spending shot up from $14 billion in 1950 to $50 billion in 1953 and remained above $40 billion thereafter. By 1952, defense spending claimed nearly 70 percent of the federal budget, and the size of the armed forces had tripled.

To General Matthew Ridgway, MacArthur's successor as commander of the UN forces, Korea taught the lesson that U.S. forces should never again fight a land war in Asia. Eisenhower concurred. Nevertheless, the Korean War induced the Truman administration to expand its role in Asia by increasing aid to the French, who were fighting to hang on to their colonial empire in Indochina. As U.S. Marines retreated from a battle against Chinese soldiers in 1950, they sang, prophetically, "We're Harry's police force on call, / So put back your pack on, / The next step is Saigon."

> QUICK REVIEW

How did the Korean War shape American foreign policy in the 1950s?

Conclusion: What were the costs and consequences of the Cold War?

HOPING FOR CONTINUED U.S.-Soviet cooperation rather than unilateral American intervention to resolve foreign crises, some liberal members of Congress had initially opposed the implementation of containment. By 1948, however, most had gotten behind Truman's decision to fight communism throughout the world, a decision that marked the most momentous foreign policy initiative in the nation's history.

More than any development in the postwar world, the Cold War defined American politics and society for decades to come. It transformed the federal government, shifting its priorities from domestic to external affairs, greatly expanding its budget, and substantially increasing the power of the president. Military spending helped transform the nation itself, as defense contracts promoted economic and population booms in the West and Southwest. The nuclear arms race put the people of the world at risk, consumed resources that might have been used to improve living standards, and skewed the economy toward dependence on military projects.

In sharp contrast to foreign policy, the domestic policies of the postwar years reflected continuity with the past. Some liberals in Congress avidly supported Truman's proposals for new programs in education, health, and civil rights, but a majority of members of Congress did not. Consequently, the poor and minorities suffered even while many other Americans enjoyed a higher standard of living in an economy boosted by Cold War spending and the reconstruction of Western Europe and Japan.

Another cost of the early Cold War years was the anti-Communist hysteria that swept the nation, narrowing the range of ideas acceptable for political discussion. Partisan politics and Truman's warnings about the Communist menace fueled McCarthyism, along with popular frustrations over the failure of containment to produce clear-cut victories. The Korean War, which ended in stalemate rather than the defeat of communism, exacerbated feelings of frustration. It would be a major challenge of the Eisenhower administration to restore national unity and confidence.

Why did Truman have limited success in implementing his domestic agenda?

How did U.S. Cold War policy lead to the Korean War?

Conclusion: What were the costs and consequences of the Cold War?

☑ **LearningCurve**
Check what you know.
bedfordstmartins.com
/roarkunderstanding

801

CHAPTER 26 STUDY GUIDE

GET STARTED ONLINE

 LearningCurve ■ bedfordstmartins.com/roarkunderstanding

Now that you've read the chapter, make it stick by completing the LearningCurve activity.

STEP 2

EXPLAIN WHY IT MATTERS

Put your reading into practice. Identify each term below, and then explain why it matters in U.S. history.

TERM	WHO OR WHAT & WHEN	WHY IT MATTERS
Cold War (p. 781)		
iron curtain (p. 783)		
containment (p. 783)		
Truman Doctrine (p. 783)		
Marshall Plan (p. 784)		
North Atlantic Treaty Organization (NATO) (p. 786)		
Central Intelligence Agency (CIA) (p. 787)		
Taft-Hartley Act (p. 794)		
Housing Act of 1949 (p. 794)		
House Un-American Activities Committee (HUAC) (p. 796)		
Korean War (p. 797)		
NSC 68 (p. 800)		

MOVE BEYOND THE BASICS

To demonstrate a more advanced understanding, describe the U.S. and Soviet actions and policies between 1945 and 1953 in Germany; Eastern Europe; Turkey, Greece, and the Middle East; China; and Korea.

The Cold War, 1945–1953	U.S. actions and policies	Soviet actions and policies
Germany		
Eastern Europe		
Turkey, Greece, and the Middle East		
Middle East		
China		
Korea		

STEP 4

**PUT IT ALL
TOGETHER**

Now, take a step back and try to explain the big picture. Remember to use specific examples from the chapter in your answers

THE UNITED STATES AND THE POSTWAR WORLD

▶ What interests did American and Soviet policymakers think were at stake in Eastern Europe? How did events in the region contribute to the growing Cold War?

▶ What was the policy of containment? What assumptions about Soviet power and intentions were at the heart of the policy?

TRUMAN AND THE FAIR DEAL

▶ How did Truman propose to expand the New Deal? In what areas did he succeed, and in what areas did he fail?

▶ What explains the rise of McCarthyism? Why did so many Americans believe that the country faced a grave internal threat to its security?

THE KOREAN WAR

▶ How did the policy of containment lead to American involvement in Korea?

▶ What impact did the Korean War have on American domestic politics?

LOOKING BACKWARD, LOOKING AHEAD

▶ How did American and Soviet experiences between 1918 and 1945 lay the groundwork for the Cold War?

▶ How did the Cold War set the stage for American life in the 1950s?

> **IN YOUR OWN WORDS**

Imagine that you must give an oral report to the class answering the following question: **What was the impact of the Cold War on the United States?** What would be the most important points to include and why?

27

THE POLITICS
AND CULTURE
OF ABUNDANCE

1952–1960

**> What were the successes and limitations
of America's "culture of abundance" in the
1950s?** Chapter 27 examines the politics and culture of
the 1950s. It explores President Dwight D. Eisenhower's
domestic and foreign policies, the causes and consequences
of the prosperity of the era, and the challenges to the status
quo, in particular the challenge to racial segregation and
discrimination.

LearningCurve
bedfordstmartins.com/roarkunderstanding
After reading the chapter, use LearningCurve to
retain what you've read.

A 1950s family poses proudly with their new sedan. Bettmann/Corbis BE042857.

> What was Eisenhower's "middle way" on domestic issues?

> How did Eisenhower's foreign policy differ from Truman's?

> What fueled the prosperity of the 1950s?

> How did prosperity affect American society and culture?

> How did African Americans fight for civil rights in the 1950s?

> Conclusion: What unmet challenges did peace and prosperity mask?

What was Eisenhower's "middle way" on domestic issues?

"I Like Ike" President Dwight D. Eisenhower's "middle way" earned him broad support, particularly among the white middle classes. The slogan "I Like Ike," coined for his bid for reelection, emphasized his personal appeal, which helped him easily defeat Adlai Stevenson in 1956. © Bettmann/Corbis.

MODERATION WAS THE GUIDING PRINCIPLE of Dwight D. Eisenhower's domestic agenda and leadership style. In 1953, he pledged a "middle way between untrammeled freedom of the individual and the demands for the welfare of the whole Nation," promising that his administration would "avoid government by bureaucracy as carefully as it avoids neglect of the helpless." Eisenhower generally resisted expanding the federal government's power, he acted reluctantly when the Supreme Court ordered schools to desegregate, and his administration terminated the federal trusteeship of dozens of Indian tribes. As a moderate Republican, however, Eisenhower supported the continuation of New Deal programs, and in some cases, such as the creation of a national highway system, he expanded federal action. Nicknamed "Ike," the confident war hero remained popular, but he was not able to lift the Republican Party to national dominance.

Modern Republicanism

In contrast to the old guard conservatives in his party who criticized containment and wanted to repeal much of the New Deal, Dwight D. Eisenhower preached "modern Republicanism." This meant resisting additional federal intervention in economic and social life but not turning the clock back to the 1920s. Democratic control of Congress after the elections of 1954 further contributed to Eisenhower's moderate approach.

CHAPTER LOCATOR | **What was Eisenhower's "middle way" on domestic issues?** | How did Eisenhower's foreign policy differ from Truman's?

806 CHAPTER 27 THE POLITICS AND CULTURE OF ABUNDANCE

The new president attempted to distance himself from the anti-Communist fervor that had plagued the Truman administration, even as he intensified Truman's loyalty program, allowing federal executives to dismiss thousands of employees on grounds of loyalty, security, or "suitability." Reflecting his inclination to avoid controversial issues, Eisenhower refused to denounce Senator Joseph McCarthy publicly. In 1954, McCarthy began to destroy himself when he hurled reckless charges of communism against military personnel during televised hearings. When the army's lawyer demanded of McCarthy, "Have you left no sense of decency?" those in the hearing room applauded. In 1954, the Senate voted to condemn him, marking the end of his influence but not the end of pursuing radicals.

Eisenhower sometimes echoed the conservative Republicans' conviction that government was best left to the states and economic decisions to private business. Yet he signed laws bringing ten million more workers under Social Security, increasing the minimum wage, and creating a new Department of Health, Education, and Welfare. And when the spread of polio neared epidemic proportions, Eisenhower obtained funds from Congress to distribute a vaccine, even though conservatives wanted to leave that responsibility to the states.

Eisenhower's greatest domestic initiative was the **Interstate Highway and Defense System Act of 1956** (**Map 27.1**). Promoted as essential to national defense and an impetus to economic growth, the act authorized construction of a national highway system, with the federal government paying most of the costs through increased fuel and vehicle taxes. The new highways accelerated the mobility of people and goods, and they benefited the trucking, construction, and automobile industries, which had lobbied hard for the law. Eventually, the monumental highway project exacted such unforeseen costs as air pollution, increased energy

> **CHRONOLOGY**

1952
– Dwight D. Eisenhower is elected president.

1954
– Senate condemns Senator Joseph McCarthy.

1956
– Interstate Highway and Defense System Act becomes law.
– Eisenhower is reelected.

Interstate Highway and Defense System Act of 1956
▶ Law authorizing the construction of a national highway system. Promoted as essential to national defense and an impetus to economic growth, the national highway system accelerated the movement of people and goods and changed the nature of American communities.

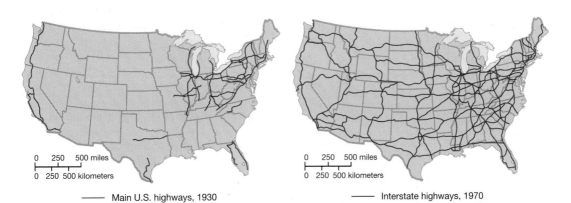

——— Main U.S. highways, 1930

0 250 500 miles
0 250 500 kilometers

——— Interstate highways, 1970

0 250 500 miles
0 250 500 kilometers

MAP 27.1 ■ The Interstate Highway System, 1930 and 1970

Built with federal funds authorized in the Interstate Highway and Defense System Act of 1956, superhighways soon crisscrossed the nation. Trucking, construction, gasoline, and travel were among the industries that prospered, but railroads suffered from the subsidized competition.

> **MAP ACTIVITY**

READING THE MAP: What regions of the United States had main highways in 1930? What regions did not? How had the situation changed by 1970?

CONNECTIONS: What impact did the growth of the interstate highway system have on migration patterns in the United States? What benefits did the new interstate highways bring to Americans and at what costs?

What fueled the prosperity of the 1950s? | How did prosperity affect American society and culture? | How did African Americans fight for civil rights in the 1950s? | Conclusion: What unmet challenges did peace and prosperity mask? | ✓ LearningCurve
Check what you know.
bedfordstmartins.com
/roarkunderstanding

consumption, declining railroads and mass transportation, and the decay of central cities.

In other areas, Eisenhower restrained federal activity in favor of state governments and private enterprise. His large tax cuts directed most benefits to business and the wealthy, and he resisted federal aid to primary and secondary education as well as strong White House leadership on behalf of civil rights. Eisenhower opposed national health insurance, preferring the growing practice of private insurance provided by employers. Although Democrats sought to keep nuclear power in government hands, Eisenhower signed legislation authorizing the private manufacture and sale of nuclear energy.

Termination and Relocation of Native Americans

Eisenhower's efforts to limit the federal government were consistent with a new direction in Indian policy, which reversed the New Deal emphasis on strengthening tribal governments and preserving Indian culture (see chapter 24). After World War II, when some 25,000 Indians had left their homes for military service and another 40,000 for work in defense industries, policymakers began to favor assimilating Native Americans and ending their special relationship with the government.

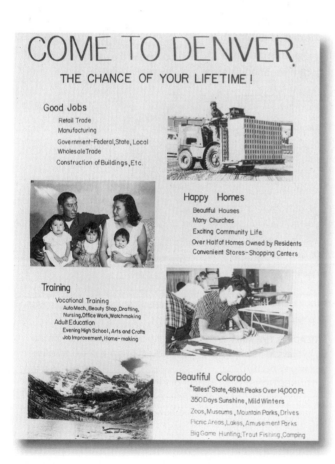

Indian Relocation

As part of its new emphasis on assimilation in the late 1940s and the 1950s, the Bureau of Indian Affairs distributed this leaflet to entice Native Americans to move from their reservations to cities. Thousands of Indians relocated in the years after World War II. The percentage of Indians living in urban areas grew from 13.4 in 1950 to 44 in 1970. National Archives.

> VISUAL ACTIVITY

READING THE IMAGE: Which of the features shown in this leaflet do you think would have been the most appealing to Native Americans living on reservations? Which might have evoked little interest?

CONNECTIONS: In what ways did the government's plan to assimilate Native Americans succeed? In what ways did it fail?

CHAPTER LOCATOR | What was Eisenhower's "middle way" on domestic issues? | How did Eisenhower's foreign policy differ from Truman's?

CHAPTER 27
808 THE POLITICS AND CULTURE OF ABUNDANCE

To some officials, the communal practices of Indians resembled socialism and stifled individual initiative. Eisenhower's commissioner of Indian affairs, Glenn Emmons, did not believe that tribal lands could produce income sufficient to eliminate poverty, but he also revealed the ethnocentrism of policymakers when he insisted that Indians wanted to "work and live like Americans." Moreover, Indians still held rights to water, land, minerals, and other resources that were increasingly attractive to state governments and private entrepreneurs.

By 1960, the government had implemented a three-part program of compensation, termination, and relocation. In 1946, Congress established the Indian Claims Commission to hear outstanding claims by Native Americans for land taken by the government. By the time it closed in 1978, the commission had settled 285 cases, with compensation exceeding $800 million. Yet the awards were based on land values at the time the land was taken and did not include interest.

The second policy, termination, also originated in the Truman administration, when Commissioner Dillon S. Myer asserted that his Bureau of Indian Affairs should do "nothing for Indians which Indians can do for themselves." Beginning in 1953, Eisenhower signed bills transferring jurisdiction over tribal land to state and local governments and ending the trusteeship relationship between Indians and the federal government. The loss of federal hospitals, schools, and other special arrangements devastated Indian tribes. As had happened after passage of the Dawes Act in 1887 (see chapter 17), some corporate interests and individuals took advantage of the opportunity to purchase Indian land cheaply. The government abandoned termination in the 1960s after some 13,000 Indians and more than one million acres of their land had been affected.

The Indian Relocation Program, the third piece of Native American policy, began in 1948 and involved more than 100,000 Native Americans by 1973. The government encouraged Indians to move to cities, where relocation centers were supposed to help with housing, job training, and medical care. Even though Indians were moved far from their reservations, about one-third returned.

Most who stayed in cities faced racism, unemployment, poor housing, and the loss of their traditional culture. "I wish we had never left home," said one woman whose husband was out of work and drinking heavily. "It's dirty and noisy, and people all around, crowded. . . . It seems like I never see the sky or trees." Reflecting long-standing disagreements among Indians themselves, some who overcame these obstacles applauded the program. But most urban Indians remained poor, and even many who had welcomed relocation worried that "we would lose our identity as Indian people, lose our culture and our [way] of living." Within two decades, a national pan-Indian movement — a by-product of this urbanization — emerged to resist assimilation and to demand much more for Indians (as discussed in chapter 28).

Major Indian Relocations, 1950–1970

The 1956 Election and the Second Term

Eisenhower easily defeated Adlai Stevenson in 1956, doubling his victory margin of 1952. Yet Democrats kept control of Congress, and in the midterm elections two years later, they all but wiped out the Republican Party, gaining a 64–34 majority

| What fueled the prosperity of the 1950s? | How did prosperity affect American society and culture? | How did African Americans fight for civil rights in the 1950s? | Conclusion: What unmet challenges did peace and prosperity mask? | ✓ LearningCurve Check what you know. bedfordstmartins.com /roarkunderstanding |

809

in the Senate and a 282–135 advantage in the House. Although Ike captured voters' hearts, a majority of Americans remained wedded to the programs and policies of the Democrats.

Eisenhower faced more serious leadership challenges in his second term. When the economy plunged into a recession in late 1957, he fought with Congress over the budget and vetoed bills to expand housing, urban development, and public works projects. The president and Congress did agree on the first, though largely symbolic, civil rights law in a century and on a larger federal role in education, largely in the interest of national security (as discussed on pages 815–16 and 828).

In the end, the first Republican administration after the New Deal left the functions of the federal government intact, though it tipped policy benefits somewhat toward corporate interests. Even with two recessions, unparalleled prosperity graced the Eisenhower years, and inflation was kept low. Eisenhower celebrated what he called the "wide diffusion of wealth and incomes" across the United States, yet amid the remarkable abundance were some forty million impoverished Americans. Rural deprivation was particularly pronounced, as was poverty among the elderly, African Americans, and other minorities.

> **QUICK REVIEW**

How did Eisenhower's domestic policies reflect his moderate political vision?

CHAPTER LOCATOR | What was Eisenhower's "middle way" on domestic issues? | How did Eisenhower's foreign policy differ from Truman's?

810   CHAPTER 27
THE POLITICS AND CULTURE OF ABUNDANCE

The Nuclear Arms Race

Soviet Premier Nikita Khrushchev speaks at his arrival at Andrews Air Force Base in September 1959 for talks with President Eisenhower that both hoped would defuse the nuclear threat. Behind the two leaders are the Soviet ambassador, Mikhail Menshikov, and the U.S. Secretary of State, Christian Herter. At the close of their summit Eisenhower and Khrushchev issued a statement declaring that "the question of general disarmament is the most important one facing the world today." © Bettmann/Corbis.

How did Eisenhower's foreign policy differ from Truman's?

AT HIS INAUGURATION IN 1953, Eisenhower warned that "forces of good and evil are massed and armed and opposed as rarely before in history." Like Truman, he saw communism as a threat to the nation's security and economic interests, and he wanted to keep the United States the most powerful country in the world. Eisenhower's foreign policy differed from Truman's, however, in three areas: its rhetoric, its means, and — after Stalin's death in 1953 — its movement toward accommodation with the Soviet Union.

Although some Republicans, such as Secretary of State John Foster Dulles, deplored containment as "negative, futile, and immoral," the Eisenhower administration practiced containment in Vietnam and intervened in Latin America and the Middle East. Eisenhower also pursued an ever-escalating arms race with the Soviet Union but sought to ease tensions between the superpowers toward the end of his presidency.

What fueled the prosperity of the 1950s?	How did prosperity affect American society and culture?	How did African Americans fight for civil rights in the 1950s?	Conclusion: What unmet challenges did peace and prosperity mask?	✓ LearningCurve Check what you know. bedfordstmartins.com /roarkunderstanding

mutually assured destruction (MAD)
▶ Term for the standoff between the United States and Soviet Union based on the assumption that a nuclear first strike by either nation would result in massive retaliation and mutual destruction for each. Despite this possibility, both countries pursued an ever-escalating arms race.

domino theory
▶ Theory of containment articulated by President Dwight Eisenhower in the context of Vietnam. He warned that the fall of a non-Communist government to communism would trigger the spread of communism to neighboring countries.

The "New Look" in Foreign Policy

To meet his goals of balancing the budget and cutting taxes, Eisenhower was determined to control military expenditures. Moreover, he feared that massive defense spending would threaten the nation's economic strength. Reflecting American confidence in technology and opposition to a large peacetime army, Eisenhower's "New Look" in defense strategy concentrated U.S. military strength in nuclear weapons and missiles to deliver them. Instead of maintaining large ground forces of its own, the United States would arm friendly nations and back them up with an ominous nuclear arsenal, providing, according to one defense official, "more bang for the buck." Dulles believed that America's willingness to "go to the brink" of war with its intimidating nuclear weapons — a strategy called brinksmanship — would block any Soviet efforts to expand.

Nuclear weapons could not stop a Soviet nuclear attack, but in response to one, they could inflict enormous destruction. This certainty of "massive retaliation" was meant to deter the Soviets from launching an attack. Because the Soviet Union could respond similarly to an American first strike, this nuclear standoff became known as **mutually assured destruction,** or **MAD**. Leaders of both nations pursued an ever-escalating arms race.

Nuclear weapons could not roll back the iron curtain. When a revolt against the Soviet-controlled government began in Hungary in 1956, Dulles's liberation rhetoric proved to be empty. A radio plea from Hungarian freedom fighters cried, "SOS! They just brought us a rumor that the American troops will be here within one or two hours." But help did not come. Eisenhower was unwilling to risk U.S. soldiers and possible nuclear war, and Soviet troops soon suppressed the insurrection, killing or wounding thousands of Hungarians.

Applying Containment to Vietnam

A major challenge to the containment policy came in Southeast Asia. During World War II, Ho Chi Minh, a Vietnamese nationalist, had founded a coalition called the Vietminh to fight both the occupying Japanese forces and the French colonial rulers. In 1945, the Vietminh declared Vietnam's independence from France, and when France fought back, the area plunged into war. Because Ho declared himself a Communist, the Truman administration quietly began to provide aid to the French (see chapter 29, Map 29.2). American principles of national self-determination took a backseat to the battle against communism.

Eisenhower viewed communism in Vietnam much as Truman had regarded it in Greece and Turkey. In what became known as the **domino theory,** Eisenhower explained, "You have a row of dominoes, you knock over the first one, and what will happen to the last one is the certainty that it will go over very quickly." A Communist victory in Southeast Asia, he warned, could trigger the fall of Japan, Taiwan, and the Philippines. By 1954, the United States was paying 75 percent of the cost of France's war, but Eisenhower resisted a larger role. When the French asked for American troops and planes to avert almost certain defeat at Dien Bien Phu, Eisenhower, remembering the Korean War (see chapter 26), said no.

CHAPTER LOCATOR | What was Eisenhower's "middle way" on domestic issues? | How did Eisenhower's foreign policy differ from Truman's?

Dien Bien Phu fell in May 1954, and two months later in Geneva a truce was signed. The Geneva accords recognized Vietnam's independence and temporarily partitioned it at the seventeenth parallel, separating the Vietminh in the north from the puppet government established by the French in the south. Within two years, the Vietnamese people were to vote in elections for a unified government. Some officials warned against U.S. involvement in Vietnam, envisioning "nothing but grief in store for us if we remained in that area." Eisenhower and Dulles nonetheless moved to prop up the dominoes with a new alliance and put the CIA to work infiltrating and destabilizing North Vietnam. Fearing a Communist victory in the elections mandated by the Geneva accords, they supported South Vietnamese prime minister Ngo Dinh Diem's refusal to hold the vote.

Between 1955 and 1961, the United States provided $800 million to the South Vietnamese army (ARVN). Yet the ARVN proved grossly unprepared for the guerrilla warfare that began in the late 1950s. With help from Ho Chi Minh's government in Hanoi, Vietminh rebels in the south stepped up their guerrilla attacks on the Diem government. The insurgents gained support from the largely Buddhist peasants, who were outraged by the repressive regime of the Catholic, Westernized Diem. Unwilling to abandon containment, Eisenhower left his successor with a deteriorating situation and a firm commitment to defend South Vietnam against communism.

Geneva Accords, 1954

Interventions in Latin America and the Middle East

While supporting friendly governments in Asia, the Eisenhower administration sought to topple unfriendly ones in Latin America and the Middle East. U.S. officials saw internal civil wars in terms of the Cold War conflict between the superpowers and often viewed nationalist uprisings as Communist threats to democracy. They also acted against governments that threatened U.S. economic interests. The Eisenhower administration took this course of action out of sight of Congress and the public, making the CIA an important arm of foreign policy.

Guatemala's government, under the popularly elected reformist president Jacobo Arbenz, was not Soviet controlled, but it accepted support from the local Communist Party (see chapter 29, Map 29.1). In 1953, Arbenz moved to help landless, poverty-stricken peasants by nationalizing uncultivated land owned by the United Fruit Company, a U.S. corporation whose annual profits were twice the size of Guatemala's budget. United Fruit refused Arbenz's offer to compensate the company at the value of the land it had declared for tax purposes. Then, in response to the nationalization program, the CIA supported an opposition army that overthrew the elected government and installed a military dictatorship in 1954. United Fruit kept its land, and Guatemala succumbed to destructive civil wars that lasted through the 1990s.

In 1959, when Cubans' desire for political and economic autonomy erupted into a revolution led by Fidel Castro, a CIA agent promised "to take care of Castro just like we took care of Arbenz." American companies controlled major Cuban resources, and decisions made in Washington directly influenced the lives of the Cuban people. The 1959 **Cuban revolution** drove out the U.S.-supported dictator Fulgencio Batista and led the CIA to warn Eisenhower

Cuban revolution
▶ Uprising led by Fidel Castro that drove out U.S.-supported dictator Fulgencio Batista and eventually allied Cuba with the Soviet Union.

| What fueled the prosperity of the 1950s? | How did prosperity affect American society and culture? | How did African Americans fight for civil rights in the 1950s? | Conclusion: What unmet challenges did peace and prosperity mask? | ✓ LearningCurve Check what you know. bedfordstmartins.com /roarkunderstanding |

813

that "Communists and other extreme radicals appear to have penetrated the Castro movement." When the United States denied Castro's requests for loans, he turned to the Soviet Union. And when U.S. companies refused Castro's offer to purchase their Cuban holdings at their assessed value, he began to nationalize their property. Many anti-Castro Cubans fled to the United States and reported his atrocities. Before leaving office, Eisenhower broke off diplomatic relations with Cuba and authorized the CIA to train Cuban exiles for an invasion.

In the Middle East, the CIA intervened in Iran to oust an elected government, support an unpopular dictatorship, and maintain Western access to Iranian oil (see chapter 30, Map 30.2). In 1951, the Iranian parliament, led by Prime Minister Mohammed Mossadegh, nationalized the country's oil fields and refineries, which had been held primarily by a British company. Britain strongly objected to the takeover and eventually sought help from the United States.

Advisers convinced Eisenhower that Mossadegh, whom *Time* magazine had called "the Iranian George Washington," left Iran vulnerable to communism, and the president wanted to keep oil-rich areas "under the control of people who are friendly." With his authorization, CIA agents instigated a coup. In August 1953, Iranian army officers captured Mossadegh and reestablished the authority of the shah, Mohammad Reza Pahlavi, known for favoring Western interests and the Iranian wealthy classes. U.S. companies received a 40 percent share of Iran's oil concessions. But resentment over the intervention would poison U.S.-Iranian relations into the twenty-first century.

Elsewhere in the Middle East, Eisenhower continued Truman's support of Israel but also pursued friendships with Arab nations to secure access to oil and build a bulwark against communism. U.S. officials demanded that smaller nations take the American side in the Cold War, even when those nations preferred neutrality. In 1955, as part of this effort to win Arab allies, Secretary of State Dulles began talks with Egypt about American support to build the Aswan Dam on the Nile River. The following year, Egypt's leader, Gamal Abdel Nasser, sought arms from Communist Czechoslovakia, formed a military alliance with other Arab nations, and recognized the People's Republic of China. In retaliation, Dulles called off the deal for the dam.

In July 1956, Nasser responded by seizing the Suez Canal, then owned by Britain and France but scheduled to revert to Egypt within seven years. In response to the seizure, Israel, whose forces had been skirmishing with Egyptian troops along their common border since 1948, attacked Egypt, with help from Britain and France. Eisenhower opposed the intervention, recognizing that the Egyptians had claimed their own territory and that Nasser "embodie[d] the emotional demands of the people . . . for independence." Calling on the United Nations to arrange a truce, he pressured Britain and France to pull back, forcing Israel to retreat.

Despite staying out of the Suez crisis, Eisenhower made it clear in a January 1957 speech that the United States would actively combat communism in the Middle East. In March, Congress approved aid to any Middle Eastern nation "requesting assistance against armed aggression from any country controlled by international communism." The president invoked this **Eisenhower Doctrine** to send aid to Jordan in 1957 and troops to Lebanon in 1958 to counter anti-Western pressures on those governments.

Eisenhower Doctrine

▶ President Dwight Eisenhower's 1957 declaration that the United States would actively combat communism in the Middle East. Congress approved the policy, and Eisenhower sent aid to Jordan in 1957 and troops to Lebanon in 1958.

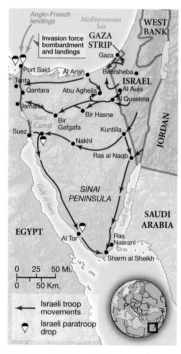

The Suez Crisis, 1956

CHAPTER LOCATOR | What was Eisenhower's "middle way" on domestic issues? | How did Eisenhower's foreign policy differ from Truman's?

CHAPTER 27
814 THE POLITICS AND CULTURE OF ABUNDANCE

The Nuclear Arms Race

While Eisenhower moved against perceived Communist inroads abroad, he also sought to reduce superpower tensions. After Stalin's death in 1953, Nikita Khrushchev emerged as a more moderate leader. Like Eisenhower, who remarked privately that the arms race would lead "at worst to atomic warfare, at best to robbing every people and nation on earth of the fruits of their own toil," Khrushchev wanted to reduce defense spending and the threat of nuclear devastation. Eisenhower and Khrushchev met in Geneva in 1955 at the first summit conference since the end of World War II. Although the meeting produced no new agreements, it symbolized what Eisenhower called "a new spirit of conciliation and cooperation."

In August 1957, the Soviets test-fired their first intercontinental ballistic missile (ICBM) and two months later beat the United States into space by launching *Sputnik*, the first man-made satellite to circle the earth. The United States launched a successful satellite of its own in January 1958, but *Sputnik* raised fears that the Soviets led not only in missile development and space exploration but also in science and education. In response, Eisenhower established the National

The Age of Nuclear Anxiety As schools routinely held "duck-and-cover" drills to prepare for possible Soviet attacks, children directly experienced the anxiety and insecurity of the 1950s nuclear arms race. The federal government distributed this pamphlet about how to protect oneself from an atomic attack. How effective do you think the strategy pictured here would be in a nuclear attack? Photo: Archive Photos/Getty Images; Pamphlet: Lynn Historical Society.

What fueled the prosperity of the 1950s?	How did prosperity affect American society and culture?	How did African Americans fight for civil rights in the 1950s?	Conclusion: What unmet challenges did peace and prosperity mask?	✓ LearningCurve Check what you know. bedfordstmartins.com /roarkunderstanding

Aeronautics and Space Administration (NASA) and signed the National Defense Education Act, providing support for students in math, foreign languages, and science and technology.

Eisenhower assured the public that the United States possessed nuclear superiority. In fact, during his presidency the stockpile of nuclear weapons more than quadrupled. Yet these weapons could not guarantee security because both superpowers possessed sufficient nuclear capacity to devastate each other. Most Americans did not follow Civil Defense Administration recommendations to construct home bomb shelters, but they did realize how precarious nuclear weapons had made their lives.

In the midst of the arms race, the superpowers continued to talk, and by 1960 the two sides were close to a ban on nuclear testing. But just before a planned summit in Paris, a Soviet missile shot down an American U-2 spy plane over Soviet territory. The State Department first denied that U.S. planes had been violating Soviet airspace, but the Soviets produced the pilot and the photos taken on his flight. Eisenhower and Khrushchev met briefly in Paris, but the U-2 incident dashed all prospects for a nuclear arms agreement.

As Eisenhower left office, he warned about the growing influence of the **military-industrial complex**. Eisenhower had struggled against persistent pressures from defense contractors who, in tandem with the military, sought more dollars for newer, more powerful weapons systems. In his farewell address, he warned that the "conjunction of an immense military establishment and a large arms industry . . . exercised a total influence . . . in every city, every state house, every office of the federal government." The Cold War had created a warfare state.

military-industrial complex
▶ A term President Eisenhower used to refer to the military establishment and defense contractors who, he warned, exercised undue influence in city, state, and federal government.

> **QUICK REVIEW**

Where and how did Eisenhower practice containment?

CHAPTER LOCATOR | What was Eisenhower's "middle way" on domestic issues? | How did Eisenhower's foreign policy differ from Truman's?

CHAPTER 27
816 THE POLITICS AND CULTURE OF ABUNDANCE

What fueled the prosperity of the 1950s?

Hotpoint Air Conditioner Ad, 1955

In 1902, Willis Haviland Carrier, a twenty-six-year-old American engineer, designed the first system to control temperature and humidity and installed it in a Brooklyn printing plant. Room air conditioners began to appear in the 1930s and spread rapidly in the 1950s, making possible the industrial and population explosion in the Sun Belt. While this ad promised consumers clean as well as cool air inside the house, it failed to note that air conditioning consumed large amounts of energy and contributed to outdoor air pollution. Hotpoint/General Electric Company.

STIMULATED BY COLD WAR spending and by technological advances, economic productivity increased enormously in the 1950s. A multitude of new items came on the market, and consumption became the order of the day. Millions of Americans enjoyed new homes in the suburbs, and higher education enrollments skyrocketed. Although every section of the nation enjoyed the new abundance, the Southwest and the South — the Sun Belt — especially boomed in production, commerce, and population.

Work itself was changing. Fewer people labored on farms, service-sector employment overtook manufacturing jobs, women's employment grew, and union membership soared. Not all Americans benefited from these changes; forty million lived in poverty. Most Americans, however, enjoyed a higher standard of living, prompting economist John Kenneth Galbraith to call the United States "the affluent society."

Technology Transforms Agriculture and Industry

Between 1940 and 1960, agricultural output mushroomed even while the number of farmworkers declined by almost one-third. Farmers achieved unprecedented

What fueled the prosperity of the 1950s?	How did prosperity affect American society and culture?	How did African Americans fight for civil rights in the 1950s?	Conclusion: What unmet challenges did peace and prosperity mask?	✔ **LearningCurve** Check what you know. bedfordstmartins.com /roarkunderstanding

1954
– Operation Wetback is launched.
– *Hernandez v. Texas.*

1960
– One-quarter of Americans live in suburbs.
– Women hold nearly one-third of all jobs.

Technology Transforms Agriculture

The years from 1945 to 1970 saw a second agricultural revolution in the United States. In 1954, tractors outnumbered mules and horses on farms for the first time. In 1940, one farmer could feed 10.7 people. By 1970, that ratio was 1 to 75.8. This advertisement shows how one person could plant several rows of corn by barely lifting a finger. International Harvester Company.

productivity through greater crop specialization, intensive use of fertilizers, and, above all, mechanization. A single mechanical cotton picker replaced fifty people and cut the cost of harvesting a bale of cotton from $40 to $5.

The decline of family farms and the growth of large commercial farming, or agribusiness, were both causes and consequences of mechanization. Benefiting handsomely from federal price supports begun in the New Deal, larger farmers could afford technological improvements, while smaller producers lacked capital to purchase the machinery necessary to compete. Consequently, average farm size more than doubled between 1940 and 1964, and the number of farms fell by more than 40 percent.

Many small farmers who hung on constituted a core of rural poverty. Southern landowners replaced sharecroppers and tenants with machines. Hundreds of thousands of African Americans moved to cities, where racial discrimination and a lack of jobs mired many in urban poverty. A Mississippi mother reported that most of her relatives headed for Chicago when they realized that "it was going to be machines now that harvest the crops." Worrying that "it might be worse up there" for her children, she agonized, "I'm afraid to leave and I'm afraid to stay."

New technologies also transformed industrial production. Between 1945 and 1960, the number of labor-hours needed to manufacture a car fell by 50 percent. Technology revolutionized industries such as electronics, chemicals, and air transportation. It also promoted the growth of television, plastics, computers, and other newer industries. American businesses enjoyed access to cheap oil, ample markets abroad, and little foreign competition. Even with Eisenhower's conservative fiscal policies, government spending reached $80 billion annually and created new jobs.

Labor unions enjoyed their greatest success during the 1950s, and real earnings for production workers shot up 40 percent. As one worker put it, "We saw continual improvement in wages, fringe benefits like holidays, vacation, medical plans . . . all sorts of things that provided more security for people." In most industrial nations, government programs underwrote their citizens' security, but the United States developed a mixed system in which company-funded programs won by unions provided for retirement, health care, and the like. This system, often called a private welfare state, resulted in wide disparities among workers, disadvantaging those not unionized and those with irregular employment.

While the number of organized workers continued to grow, union membership peaked at 27.1 percent of the labor force in 1957. Technological advances eliminated jobs in heavy industry. "You are going to have trouble collecting union dues from all of these machines," commented a Ford manager to union leader Walter Reuther. Moreover, the economy as a whole was shifting from production to service as more workers distributed goods, performed services, provided education, and carried out government work. Unions made some headway in these fields, especially among government employees, but most service industries resisted unionization.

The growing clerical and service occupations swelled the demand for female workers. By the end of the 1950s, women held nearly one-third of all jobs. The vast majority of them worked in offices, light manufacturing, domestic service, teaching, and nursing; because these occupations were occupied

CHAPTER LOCATOR | What was Eisenhower's "middle way" on domestic issues? | How did Eisenhower's foreign policy differ from Truman's?

CHAPTER 27
818 THE POLITICS AND CULTURE OF ABUNDANCE

primarily by women, wages were relatively low. In 1960, the average female full-time worker earned just 60 percent of the average male worker's wages. At the bottom of the employment ladder, black women took home only 42 percent of what white men earned.

Burgeoning Suburbs and Declining Cities

Although suburbs had existed since the nineteenth century, nothing symbolized the affluent society more than their tremendous expansion in the 1950s. Eleven million new homes went up in the suburbs, and by 1960 one in four Americans lived there. In 1949, families could purchase mass-produced houses in Levittown, a new 17,000-home development on Long Island, New York, for just under $8,000 each ($75,000 in 2012 dollars). Developments similar to Levittown, as well as more luxurious ones, quickly went up throughout the country. The government subsidized home ownership by guaranteeing low-interest mortgages and by making interest on mortgages tax deductible. Government-funded interstate highways running through urban areas also encouraged suburban development.

The growing suburbs helped polarize society, especially along racial lines. Each Levittown homeowner signed a contract pledging not to rent or sell to a non-Caucasian. The Supreme Court declared such covenants unenforceable in 1948, but suburban America remained dramatically segregated. Although some African Americans joined the suburban migration, most moved to cities in search of economic opportunity, doubling their numbers in most cities during the 1950s. These migrants, however, came to cities that were already in decline, losing not only population but also commerce and industry to the suburbs or to southern and western states.

The Rise of the Sun Belt

No regions experienced the postwar economic and population booms more intensely than the South and Southwest (**Map 27.2**). California overtook New York as the most populous state. Sports franchises followed fans: In 1958, the Brooklyn Dodgers moved to Los Angeles, joined by the Minneapolis Lakers three years later.

A pleasant natural environment attracted new residents, but no magnet proved stronger than economic opportunity. As railroads had fueled western growth in the nineteenth century, so the automobile and airplane spurred the post–World War II surge. Air-conditioning facilitated industrial development and by 1960 cooled nearly eight million homes in the **Sun Belt**, which stretched from Florida to California.

So important was the defense industry to the South and Southwest that the area was later referred to as the "Gun Belt." The aerospace industry boomed in such cities as Los Angeles and Dallas–Fort Worth, and military bases helped underwrite prosperity in cities such as San Diego and San Antonio. Although defense dollars benefited other regions, the Sun Belt captured the lion's share of Cold War spending. By the 1960s, nearly one of every three California workers held a defense-related job.

The surging populations and industries soon threatened the environment. Providing sufficient water and power to cities and to agribusiness meant building

Sun Belt
▶ Name applied to the Southwest and the South, an area that grew rapidly after World War II as a center of defense industries and non-unionized labor.

| What fueled the prosperity of the 1950s? | How did prosperity affect American society and culture? | How did African Americans fight for civil rights in the 1950s? | Conclusion: What unmet challenges did peace and prosperity mask? | ✓ LearningCurve Check what you know. bedfordstmartins.com /roarkunderstanding |

819

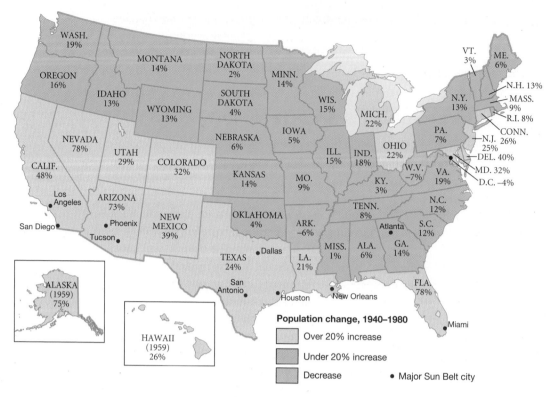

MAP 27.2 ■ The Rise of the Sun Belt, 1940–1980

The growth of defense industries, a non-unionized labor force, and the spread of air-conditioning all helped spur economic development and population growth in the Southwest and the South. This made the Sun Belt the fastest-growing region of the country between 1940 and 1980.

> MAP ACTIVITY

READING THE MAP: Which states experienced population growth of more than 20 percent? Which states experienced the largest population growth?

CONNECTIONS: What stimulated the population boom in the Southwest? What role did the Cold War play in this expansion? What developments made the Southwest diverse in the composition of its population?

dams and reservoirs on free-flowing rivers. Native Americans lost fishing sites on the Columbia River, and dams on the Upper Missouri displaced nine hundred Indian families. Sprawling suburban settlement without efficient public transportation contributed to blankets of smog over Los Angeles and other cities.

The high-technology basis of economic development drew well-educated, highly skilled workers to the West, but economic promise also attracted the poor. "We see opportunity all around us here. . . . We smell freedom here, and maybe soon we can taste it," commented a black mother in California. Between 1945 and 1960, more than one-third of the African Americans who left the South moved west.

The Mexican American population also grew, especially in California and Texas. To supply California's vast agribusiness industry, the government continued the *bracero* program begun in 1942, under which Mexicans were permitted to enter the United States to work for a limited period. Until the program ended in 1964, more than 100,000 Mexicans entered the United States each year to labor in the fields — and many of them stayed, legally or illegally. But permanent Mexican immigration was not as welcome as Mexicans' low-wage labor. In 1954, the

CHAPTER LOCATOR | What was Eisenhower's "middle way" on domestic issues? | How did Eisenhower's foreign policy differ from Truman's?

820 CHAPTER 27 THE POLITICS AND CULTURE OF ABUNDANCE

government launched a series of raids called "Operation Wetback," sending more than a million Mexicans back across the border.

At the same time, Mexican American citizens gained a victory in their ongoing struggle for civil rights in *Hernandez v. Texas*. In this 1954 case, the Supreme Court ruled unanimously that Mexican Americans constituted a distinct group and that their systematic exclusion from juries violated the Fourteenth Amendment guarantee of equal protection.

Free of the discrimination faced by minorities, white Americans enjoyed the fullest prosperity in the West. In April 1950, when California developers opened Lakewood, a large housing development in Los Angeles County, thirty thousand people lined up to buy houses at prices averaging $85,000 in 2012 dollars. Many of the new homeowners were veterans, blue-collar and lower-level white-collar workers whose defense-based jobs at aerospace corporations enabled them to fulfill the American dream of the 1950s. A huge shopping mall, Lakewood Center, offered myriad products of the consumer culture, and the workers' children lived at commuting distance from community colleges and six state universities.

Hernandez v. Texas
▶ 1954 Supreme Court decision that found that the systematic exclusion of Mexican Americans from juries violated the constitutional guarantee of equal protection.

The Democratization of Higher Education

California's university system exemplified a spectacular transformation of higher education. Between 1940 and 1960, college enrollments in the United States more than doubled, and more than 40 percent of young Americans attended college by the mid-1960s. The federal government subsidized the education of more than two million veterans, and the Cold War sent millions of federal dollars to universities for defense-related research. State governments vastly expanded the number of public colleges and universities, while municipalities began to build two-year community colleges.

All Americans did not benefit equally from the democratization of higher education. Although their college enrollments surged from 37,000 in 1941 to 90,000 in 1961, African Americans constituted only about 5 percent of all college students. For a time, the educational gap between white men and women grew, even though women's enrollments increased. In 1940, women had earned 40 percent of undergraduate degrees, but as veterans flocked to college campuses, women's proportion fell to 25 percent, rising to just 33 percent by 1960. Women were more likely than men to drop out of college after marriage, taking jobs to keep their husbands in school. Reflecting gender norms of the 1950s, most college women agreed that "it is natural for a woman to be satisfied with her husband's success and not crave personal achievement."

QUICK REVIEW <

How did technology contribute to changes in the economy, suburbanization, and the growth of the Sun Belt?

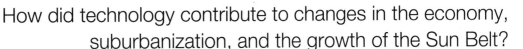

What fueled the prosperity of the 1950s?

How did prosperity affect American society and culture?

How did African Americans fight for civil rights in the 1950s?

Conclusion: What unmet challenges did peace and prosperity mask?

✔ LearningCurve
Check what you know.
bedfordstmartins.com
/roarkunderstanding

How did prosperity affect American society and culture?

The Made-for-TV Family

The Adventures of Ozzie and Harriet ran on television from 1952 to 1966. Like other family sitcoms, it idealized white family life, in which no one got divorced, no one took drugs or seriously misbehaved, fathers held white-collar jobs, and mothers did not work outside the home. Picture Research Consultants & Archives.

PROSPERITY IN THE 1950s intensified the transformation of the nation into a consumer society, changing the way Americans lived and converting the traditional work ethic into an ethic of consumption. The new medium of television both reflected and stimulated a consumer culture. People married at earlier ages, the birthrate soared, and dominant values celebrated family life and traditional gender roles. Undercurrents of rebellion, especially among young people, and women's increasing employment defied some of the dominant norms but did not greatly disrupt the complacency of the 1950s.

Consumption Rules the Day

Consumer items flooded American society in the 1950s. Although the purchase and display of consumer goods was not new (see chapter 23), by midcentury consumption had become a reigning value, vital for economic prosperity and essential to individuals' identity and status. In place of the traditional emphasis on work and savings, the consumer culture encouraged satisfaction and happiness through the acquisition of new products.

The consumer culture rested on a firm material base. Between 1950 and 1960, both the gross national product (the value of all goods and services produced) and median family income grew by 25 percent in constant dollars (**Figure 27.1**). Economists claimed that 60 percent of Americans enjoyed middle-class incomes in 1960. By then, nearly 90 percent of all families owned a television set, nearly all had a refrigerator, and most owned at least one car. The number of shopping centers quadrupled between 1957 and 1963.

CHAPTER LOCATOR | What was Eisenhower's "middle way" on domestic issues? | How did Eisenhower's foreign policy differ from Truman's?

822   CHAPTER 27
THE POLITICS AND CULTURE OF ABUNDANCE

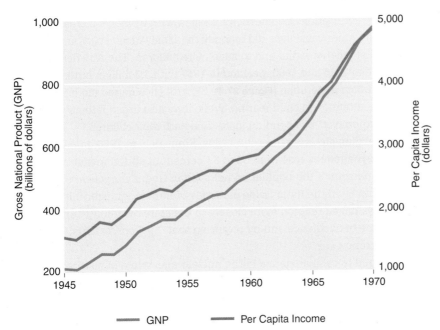

FIGURE 27.1 ■ The Postwar Economic Boom: GNP and Per Capita Income, 1945–1970

American dominance of the worldwide market, innovative technologies that led to new industries such as computers and plastics, population growth, and increases in worker productivity all contributed to the enormous economic growth of the United States after World War II.

Several forces spurred this unparalleled abundance. A population surge — from 152 million to 180 million during the 1950s — expanded demand for products and boosted industries ranging from housing to baby goods. Consumer borrowing also fueled the economic boom, as people made purchases on installment plans and began to use credit cards. Americans now enjoyed their possessions while they paid for them instead of saving their money for future purchases.

Although the sheer need to support themselves and their families explained most women's employment, a desire to secure some of the new abundance sent growing numbers of women to work. As one woman remarked, "My Joe can't put five kids through college . . . and the washer had to be replaced, and Ann was ashamed to bring friends home because the living room furniture was such a mess, so I went to work." The standards for family happiness imposed by the consumer culture increasingly required a second income.

The Revival of Domesticity and Religion

Despite married women's growing employment, a dominant ideology celebrated traditional family life and conventional gender roles. Both popular culture and public figures defined the ideal family as a male breadwinner, a full-time homemaker, and three or four children. Writer and feminist Betty Friedan gave a name to the idealization of women's domestic roles in her 1963 book *The Feminine Mystique*. Friedan criticized scholars, advertisers, and public officials for assuming that biological differences dictated different roles for men and women. According to this feminine mystique that they promulgated, women should find fulfillment in devotion to their homes, families, and serving others. Not many women directly challenged these ideas, but writer Edith Stern maintained that "many arguments about the joys of housewifery have been advanced, largely by those who have never had to work at it."

> CHRONOLOGY

1945–1960
– Baby boom.

1953
– *Playboy* begins publication.

1960
– Nearly 90 percent of American homes have a television set.

1963
– Betty Friedan publishes *The Feminine Mystique*.

What fueled the prosperity of the 1950s? | **How did prosperity affect American society and culture?** | How did African Americans fight for civil rights in the 1950s? | Conclusion: What unmet challenges did peace and prosperity mask? | ✓ LearningCurve Check what you know. bedfordstmartins.com /roarkunderstanding

823

Although the glorification of domesticity clashed with women's increasing employment, many Americans' lives did embody the family ideal. Postwar prosperity enabled people to marry earlier and to have more children. The American birthrate soared between 1945 and 1960, peaking in 1957 with 4.3 million births and producing the **baby boom** generation (**Figure 27.2**). Experts encouraged mothers to devote even more attention to child rearing, while they also urged fathers to cultivate family "togetherness" by spending more time with their children.

Interest in religion also surged in the 1950s. From 1940 to 1960, membership in churches and synagogues rose from 50 to 63 percent of all Americans. Polls reported that 95 percent of the population believed in God. Evangelism took on new life, most notably in the nationwide crusades of Baptist minister Billy Graham. Congress linked religion more closely to the state by adding "under God" to the pledge of allegiance and by requiring that "In God We Trust" be printed on all currency.

Religion helped to calm anxieties in the nuclear age, while ministers such as Graham made the Cold War a holy war, labeling communism "a great sinister anti-Christian movement masterminded by Satan." Some critics questioned the depth of the religious revival, attributing the growth in church membership to a desire for conformity and a need for social outlets. One commentator noted that 53 percent of Americans could not name any book of the New Testament.

Television Transforms Culture and Politics

Just as family life and religion offered a respite from Cold War anxieties, so too did the new medium of television. By 1960, nearly 90 percent of American

baby boom

▶ The surge in the American birthrate between 1945 and 1960, which peaked in 1957 with 4.3 million births. The baby boom both reflected and promoted Americans' postwar prosperity.

> **GLOBAL COMPARISON**

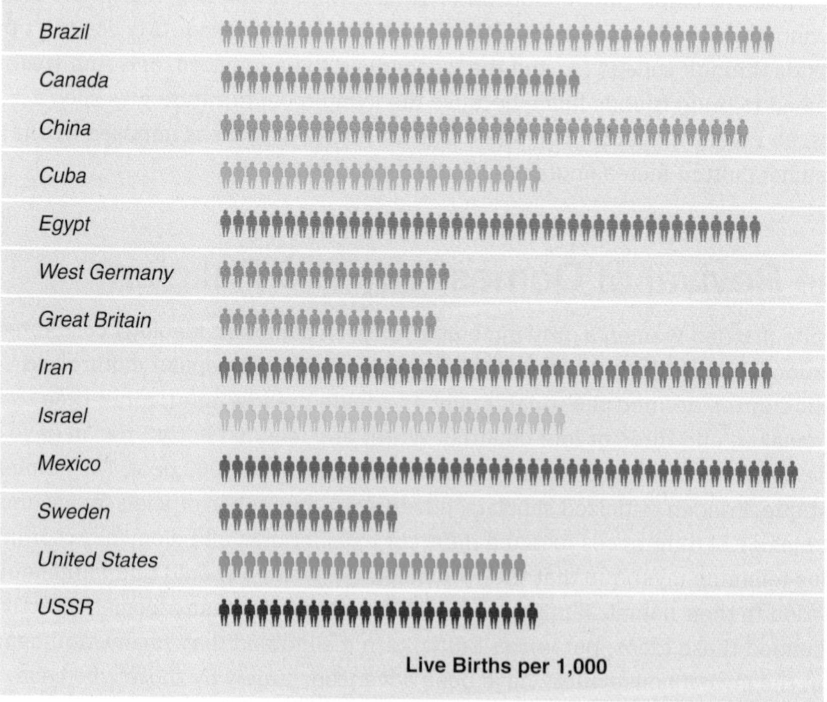

FIGURE 27.2 ■ **The Baby Boom in International Perspective**

The United States was not alone in welcoming bumper crops of babies in the 1950s. High fertility continued in nonindustrialized countries, while in Europe, as in the United States, birthrates rebounded from low levels during the Great Depression and World War II. Which countries had birthrates comparable to those of the United States? What might explain why countries such as Brazil, China, Iran, and Mexico had birthrates so much higher than those in the United States? What might explain why birthrates in Europe were lower than those in the United States?

Brazil
Canada
China
Cuba
Egypt
West Germany
Great Britain
Iran
Israel
Mexico
Sweden
United States
USSR

Live Births per 1,000

CHAPTER LOCATOR | What was Eisenhower's "middle way" on domestic issues? | How did Eisenhower's foreign policy differ from Truman's?

824 CHAPTER 27
THE POLITICS AND CULTURE OF ABUNDANCE

homes boasted a television set, and the average viewer spent more than five hours each day in front of the screen. Audiences were especially attracted to situation comedies, which projected the family ideal and the feminine mystique into millions of homes.

Television also began to affect politics. Eisenhower's 1952 presidential campaign used TV ads for the first time, although he was not happy that "an old soldier should come to this." By 1960, television played a key role in election campaigns. Reflecting on his narrow victory, president-elect John F. Kennedy remarked, "We wouldn't have had a prayer without that gadget."

Television transformed politics in other ways. Money played a much larger role in elections because candidates needed to pay for expensive TV spots. The ability to appeal directly to voters in their living rooms put a premium on personal attractiveness and encouraged candidates to build their own campaign organizations, relying less on political parties. The declining strength of parties and the growing power of money in elections were not new trends, but TV helped accelerate them.

Unlike government-financed television in Europe, private enterprise paid for American TV. What NBC called a "selling machine in every living room" became the major vehicle for fostering consumption, and advertisers did not hesitate to interfere with shows that might jeopardize the sale of their products. In 1961, Newton Minow, chairman of the Federal Communications Commission, called television a "vast wasteland." While acknowledging some of TV's achievements, particularly documentaries and drama, Minow depicted it as "a procession of game shows, . . . formula comedies about totally unbelievable families, blood and thunder, mayhem, violence, sadism, murder . . . and cartoons." But viewers kept tuning in. In little more than a decade, television came to dominate Americans' leisure time, influence their consumption patterns, and shape their perceptions of the nation's leadership.

Countercurrents

Pockets of dissent underlay the complacency of the 1950s. Some intellectuals took exception to the materialism and conformity of the era. In *The Lonely Crowd* (1950), sociologist David Riesman lamented a shift from the "inner-directed" to the "other-directed" individual, as Americans replaced independent thinking with an eagerness to adapt to external standards of behavior and belief. Sharing that distaste for the importance of "belonging," William H. Whyte Jr., in his popular book *The Organization Man* (1956), blamed the modern corporation for making employees tailor themselves to the group. Vance Packard's 1959 best seller, *The Status Seekers,* decried "the vigorous merchandising of goods as status-symbols."

Implicit in much of the critique of consumer culture was concern about the loss of traditional masculinity. Consumption was associated with women and their presumed greater susceptibility to manipulation. Men, required to conform to get ahead, moved farther away from the masculine ideals of individualism and aggressiveness. Moreover, the increase in married women's employment compromised the male ideal of breadwinner. Into this gender confusion came *Playboy*, which began publication in 1953 and quickly gained a circulation of one million.

| What fueled the prosperity of the 1950s? | **How did prosperity affect American society and culture?** | How did African Americans fight for civil rights in the 1950s? | Conclusion: What unmet challenges did peace and prosperity mask? | ☑ LearningCurve Check what you know. bedfordstmartins.com /roarkunderstanding |

825

The new magazine idealized masculine independence in the form of bachelorhood and assaulted the middle-class norms of domesticity and respectability. By associating the sophisticated bachelor with good wine, music, furnishings, and the like, the magazine made consumption more masculine while promoting sexual freedom, at least for men.

In fact, two books published by Alfred Kinsey and other researchers at Indiana University — *Sexual Behavior in the Human Male* (1948) and *Sexual Behavior in the Human Female* (1953) — disclosed that Americans' sexual behavior often departed from the postwar family ideal. Large numbers of men and women reported that they had engaged in premarital sex and adultery; one-third of the men and one-seventh of the women reported homosexual experiences. Although Kinsey's sampling procedures later cast doubt on his ability to generalize across the population, the books became best sellers.

Less direct challenges to mainstream standards appeared in the everyday behavior of young Americans. "Roll over Beethoven and tell Tchaikovsky the news!" belted out Chuck Berry in his 1956 hit record celebrating **rock and roll**, a new form of music that combined country music with black rhythm and blues. White teenagers lionized Elvis Presley, who shocked their parents with his tight pants, hip-rolling gestures, and sensuous rock-and-roll music. "Before there was Elvis . . . I started going crazy for 'race music,'" recalled a white man of his teenage years. His recollection underscored African Americans' contributions to rock and roll, as well as the rebellion expressed by white youths' attraction to black music.

The most blatant revolt against conventionality came from the self-proclaimed Beat generation, a small group of primarily male literary figures based in New York City and San Francisco. Rejecting nearly everything in mainstream culture — patriotism, consumerism, technology, conventional family life, discipline — writers such as Allen Ginsberg and Jack Kerouac celebrated spontaneity and absolute personal freedom, including drug consumption and freewheeling sex. The Beats' lifestyles shocked "square" Americans, but they would provide a model for a new movement of youthful dissidents in the 1960s.

Bold new styles in the visual arts also showed the 1950s to be more than a decade of bland conventionality. In New York City, "action painting" or "abstract expressionism" flowered, rejecting the idea that painting should represent recognizable forms. Jackson Pollock and other abstract expressionists poured, dripped, and threw paint on canvases or substituted sticks and other implements for brushes. The new form of painting so captivated and redirected the Western art world that New York replaced Paris as its center.

rock and roll

▶ A music genre created from country music and black rhythm and blues that emerged in the 1950s and captivated American youth.

> **QUICK REVIEW**

Why did American consumption expand so dramatically in the 1950s, and what aspects of society and culture did it influence?

CHAPTER LOCATOR | What was Eisenhower's "middle way" on domestic issues? | How did Eisenhower's foreign policy differ from Truman's?

826 CHAPTER 27 THE POLITICS AND CULTURE OF ABUNDANCE

How did African Americans fight for civil rights in the 1950s?

Montgomery Civil Rights Leaders

During the Montgomery bus boycott, local white officials sought to intimidate African Americans with arrests and lawsuits. Here Rosa Parks, one of ninety-two defendants, enters the Montgomery County courthouse. Parks later said of her actions: "People always say that I didn't give up my seat because I was tired, but that isn't true. I was not tired physically. . . . I was not old. . . . I was forty-two. No, the only tired I was, was tired of giving in." Wide World Photos.

BUILDING ON THE CIVIL RIGHTS initiatives begun during World War II, African Americans posed the most dramatic challenge to the status quo of the 1950s as they sought to overcome discrimination and segregation. Although black protest was as old as American racism, in the 1950s grassroots movements arose that attracted national attention and the support of white liberals. Pressed by civil rights groups, the Supreme Court delivered significant institutional reforms, but the most important changes occurred among blacks themselves. Ordinary African Americans in substantial numbers sought their own liberation, building a movement that would transform race relations in the United States.

African Americans Challenge the Supreme Court and the President

Several factors spurred black protest in the 1950s. Between 1940 and 1960, more than three million African Americans moved from the South into areas where they had a political voice. Black leaders made sure that foreign policy officials realized

> CHRONOLOGY

1954
– *Brown v. Board of Education.*

1955–1956
– Montgomery, Alabama, bus boycott.

1957
– Southern Christian Leadership Conference (SCLC) is founded.
– Civil Rights Act of 1957.

What fueled the prosperity of the 1950s?

How did prosperity affect American society and culture?

How did African Americans fight for civil rights in the 1950s?

Conclusion: What unmet challenges did peace and prosperity mask?

☑ LearningCurve
Check what you know.
bedfordstmartins.com
/roarkunderstanding

827

how racist practices at home tarnished the U.S. image abroad and handicapped the United States in its competition with the Soviet Union. The very system of segregation meant that African Americans controlled certain organizational resources, such as churches, colleges, and newspapers, where leadership skills could be honed and networks developed.

The legal strategy of the major civil rights organization, the National Association for the Advancement of Colored People (NAACP), reached its crowning achievement with the Supreme Court decision in *Brown v. Board of Education* in 1954, which consolidated five separate suits. Oliver Brown, a World War II veteran in Topeka, Kansas, filed suit because his daughter had to pass by a white school near their home to attend a black school more than a mile away. In Virginia, sixteen-year-old Barbara Johns initiated a student strike over wretched conditions in her black high school, leading to another of the suits joined in *Brown*. The NAACP's lead lawyer, future Supreme Court justice Thurgood Marshall, urged the Court to overturn the "separate but equal" precedent established in *Plessy v. Ferguson* in 1896 (see chapter 21). A unanimous Court, headed by Chief Justice Earl Warren, declared, "Separate educational facilities are inherently unequal" and thus violated the Fourteenth Amendment.

Ultimate responsibility for enforcement of the decision lay with President Eisenhower, but he refused to endorse *Brown*. He also kept silent in 1955 when whites murdered Emmett Till, a fourteen-year-old black boy who had allegedly whistled at a white woman in Mississippi. Reflecting his own prejudice, his preference for limited federal intervention in the states, and a leadership style that favored consensus and gradual progress, Eisenhower kept his distance from civil rights issues. Such inaction fortified southern resistance.

In September 1957, Arkansas governor Orval Faubus sent National Guard troops to block the enrollment of nine black students in Little Rock's Central High School. Later, he allowed them to enter but withdrew the National Guard, leaving the students to face an angry white mob. "During those years when we desperately needed approval from our peers," Melba Patillo Beals remembered, "we were victims of the most harsh rejection imaginable." As television cameras transmitted the ugly scene, Eisenhower was forced to send regular army troops to Little Rock, the first federal military intervention in the South since Reconstruction. Paratroopers escorted the "Little Rock Nine" into the school, but resistance to integration continued across the South.

School segregation outside the South was not usually sanctioned by law, but northern school districts separated black and white students by manipulating neighborhood boundaries and with other devices. Even before *Brown*, black parents in dozens of northern cities challenged the assignment of their children to inferior "colored" schools. While their protests reaped some successes, the structure of residential segregation, often supported by official action, made school segregation a reality for African Americans in both the North and the South.

Eisenhower ordered the integration of public facilities in Washington, D.C., and on military bases, and he supported the first federal civil rights legislation since Reconstruction. Yet the Civil Rights Acts of 1957 and 1960 were little more than symbolic. Baseball star Jackie Robinson spoke for many African Americans when he wired Eisenhower in 1957: "We disagree that half a loaf is better than

Brown v. Board of Education

▶ 1954 Supreme Court ruling that overturned the "separate but equal" precedent established in *Plessy v. Ferguson* in 1896. The Court declared that separate educational facilities were inherently unequal and thus violated the Fourteenth Amendment.

CHAPTER LOCATOR | What was Eisenhower's "middle way" on domestic issues? | How did Eisenhower's foreign policy differ from Truman's?

828 CHAPTER 27 THE POLITICS AND CULTURE OF ABUNDANCE

none. Have waited this long for a bill with meaning — can wait a little longer."
Eisenhower appointed the first black professional to his White House staff, but
E. Frederick Morrow confided in his diary, "I feel ridiculous . . . trying to defend
the administration's record on civil rights."

Montgomery and Mass Protest

What set the civil rights movement of the 1950s and 1960s apart from earlier acts of
black protest was its widespread presence in the South, the large number of people
involved, their willingness to confront white institutions directly, and the use of
nonviolent protest and civil disobedience to bring about change. The Congress of
Racial Equality and other groups had experimented with these tactics in the 1940s,
organizing to integrate movie theaters, restaurants, and swimming pools in northern cities. In the South, the first sustained protest to claim national attention began
in Montgomery, Alabama, on December 1, 1955.

School Integration in Little Rock, Arkansas

Nine African American teenagers — including Elizabeth Eckford, shown here — endured nearly three weeks
of threats and hateful taunts as they sought to integrate Central High School. Even after President Eisenhower intervened to enable the "Little Rock Nine" to attend school, they were called names, tripped, spat
on, and otherwise harassed by some white students. Francis Miller/TimePix/Getty.

| What fueled the prosperity of the 1950s? | How did prosperity affect American society and culture? | **How did African Americans fight for civil rights in the 1950s?** | Conclusion: What unmet challenges did peace and prosperity mask? | ✓ LearningCurve Check what you know. bedfordstmartins.com /roarkunderstanding |

829

That day, police arrested Rosa Parks for violating a local segregation ordinance. Riding a crowded bus home from work, she refused to give up her seat so that a white man could sit down. The bus driver called the police, who promptly arrested her. Parks had long been active in the local NAACP, headed by E. D. Nixon. They had already talked about challenging bus segregation. So had the Women's Political Council (WPC), led by Jo Ann Robinson, an English professor at Alabama State, who had once been humiliated by a bus driver when she accidentally sat in the white section.

When word came that Parks would fight her arrest, WPC leaders mobilized teachers and students to distribute fliers urging blacks to boycott the buses. E. D. Nixon called a mass meeting at a black church, where those assembled founded the Montgomery Improvement Association (MIA). The MIA arranged volunteer car pools and marshaled more than 90 percent of the black community to sustain the yearlong **Montgomery bus boycott.**

Elected to head the MIA was twenty-six-year-old Martin Luther King Jr., a young Baptist pastor with a doctorate in theology from Boston University. King addressed mass meetings at churches throughout the bus boycott, inspiring blacks' courage and commitment by linking racial justice to Christianity. He promised, "If you will protest courageously and yet with dignity and Christian love . . . historians will have to pause and say, 'There lived a great people — a black people — who injected a new meaning and dignity into the veins of civilization.'"

Montgomery blacks summoned their courage and determination in abundance. An older woman insisted, "I'm not walking for myself, I'm walking for my children and my grandchildren." Boycotters walked miles or carpooled to get to work, contributed their meager financial resources, and stood up to intimidation and police harassment. Authorities arrested several leaders, and whites firebombed King's house. Yet the movement persisted until November 1956, when the Supreme Court declared unconstitutional Alabama's laws requiring bus segregation. King's face on the cover of *Time* magazine in February 1957 marked his rapid rise to national and international fame. In January, black clergy from across the South had chosen King to head the Southern Christian Leadership Conference (SCLC), newly established to coordinate local protests against segregation and disfranchisement. The prominence of King and other ministers obscured the substantial numbers and critical importance of black women in the movement. King's fame and the media's focus on the South also hid the national scope of racial injustice and the struggles for racial equality in the North that both encouraged and benefited from the black freedom struggle in the South.

Montgomery bus boycott

▶ Yearlong boycott of Montgomery's segregated bus system in 1955–1956 by the city's African American population. The boycott brought Martin Luther King Jr. to national prominence and ended in victory when the Supreme Court declared segregated transportation unconstitutional.

> **QUICK REVIEW**

What were the goals and strategies of civil rights activists in the 1950s?

CHAPTER LOCATOR | What was Eisenhower's "middle way" on domestic issues? | How did Eisenhower's foreign policy differ from Truman's?

830 CHAPTER 27 THE POLITICS AND CULTURE OF ABUNDANCE

AT AN AMERICAN EXHIBIT in Moscow in 1959, the consumer goods that Nixon proudly displayed to Khrushchev and the Cold War competition that crackled through their dialogue reflected two dominant themes of the 1950s: American prosperity and the success of both the United States and the Soviet Union in keeping their antagonism within the bounds of peace. The tremendous economic growth of the 1950s, which raised the standard of living for most Americans, resulted in part from Cold War defense spending.

Prosperity changed the very landscape of the United States. Suburban housing developments sprang up, interstate highways cut up cities and connected the country, farms declined in number but grew in size, and population and industry moved south and west. Daily habits and even values shifted as the economy became more service oriented and as the appearance of a host of new products intensified the growth of a consumer culture.

The prosperity, however, masked a number of developments and problems that Americans would soon face head-on: rising resistance to racial injustice, a 20 percent poverty rate, married women's movement into the labor force, and the emergence of a youth rebellion. Although defense spending and housing, highway, and education subsidies helped to sustain the economic boom, in general President Eisenhower tried to curb domestic programs and let private enterprise have its way. His administration maintained the welfare state inherited from the New Deal but resisted the expansion of federal programs.

In global affairs, Eisenhower exercised restraint on large issues, recognizing the limits of U.S. power. In the name of deterrence, he promoted the development of more destructive atomic weapons, but he withstood pressures for even larger defense budgets. Still, Eisenhower shared Harry Truman's assumption that the United States must fight communism everywhere, and when movements in Iran, Guatemala, Cuba, and Vietnam seemed too radical, too friendly to communism, or too inimical to American economic interests, he tried to undermine them, often with secret operations. Eisenhower presided over eight years of peace and prosperity, but his foreign policy inspired anti-Americanism and forged commitments and interventions that future generations would deem unwise. As Eisenhower's successors took on the struggle against communism and grappled with the domestic challenges of race, poverty, and urban decay that he had avoided, the tranquility and consensus of the 1950s would give way to the turbulence and conflict of the 1960s.

CHAPTER 27 STUDY GUIDE

GET STARTED ONLINE

 ✓ LearningCurve ▪ bedfordstmartins.com/roarkunderstanding
Now that you've read the chapter, make it stick by completing the LearningCurve activity.

EXPLAIN WHY IT MATTERS

Put your reading into practice. Identify each term below, and then explain why it matters in U.S. history.

TERM	WHO OR WHAT & WHEN	WHY IT MATTERS
Interstate Highway and Defense System Act of 1956 (p. 807)		
mutually assured destruction (MAD) (p. 812)		
domino theory (p. 812)		
Cuban revolution (p. 813)		
Eisenhower Doctrine (p. 814)		
military-industrial complex (p. 816)		
Sun Belt (p. 819)		
Hernandez v. Texas (p. 821)		
baby boom (p. 824)		
rock and roll (p. 826)		
Brown v. Board of Education (p. 828)		
Montgomery bus boycott (p. 830)		

MOVE BEYOND THE BASICS

To demonstrate a more advanced understanding, describe the social, political, and cultural aspects of life in the 1950s as it affected a range of Americans: the suburban middle class, the counterculture, and African Americans and other minorities.

	Developments	Impact on suburban middle class	Impact on African Americans and other minorities	Impact on the counterculture
Economic growth and consumerism				
Suburban growth/ domesticity				
Culture/values				
The Cold War				

PUT IT ALL TOGETHER

Now, take a step back and try to explain the big picture. Remember to use specific examples from the chapter in your answers.

THE COLD WAR

▶ What was the "New Look" in U.S. foreign policy under President Eisenhower?

▶ How did the United States use military intervention or CIA covert activities as a tool of foreign policy in the 1950s?

CULTURAL CURRENTS

▶ How did prosperity shape living patterns in the 1950s?

▶ What developments challenged the dominant norms regarding consumer culture in the 1950s?

CIVIL RIGHTS

▶ Why was *Brown v. Board of Education* such a pivotal case in the history of the civil rights movement?

▶ Why did the Montgomery bus boycott succeed?

LOOKING BACKWARD, LOOKING AHEAD

▶ Compare and contrast the culture and society of the 1920s with that of the 1950s.

▶ What tensions in 1950s America suggest defining aspects of the 1960s?

> IN YOUR OWN WORDS

Imagine that you must give an oral report to the class answering the following question: **What were the successes and limitations of America's "culture of abundance" in the 1950s?** What would be the most important points to include and why?

28

REFORM, REBELLION, AND REACTION

1960–1974

> **How did protest movements change policies and society in the 1960s and 1970s?** Chapter 28 examines the efforts to reform and transform American society in the 1960s and early 1970s. It explores the domestic agenda of Lyndon B. Johnson's administration, the role of the Supreme Court, and the evolution of the black freedom movement. The chapter also examines other movements inspired by the struggle for black civil rights, the backlash against reform, and the transformation of the liberal agenda under President Richard M. Nixon.

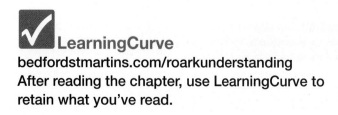

LearningCurve
bedfordstmartins.com/roarkunderstanding
After reading the chapter, use LearningCurve to retain what you've read.

Birmingham, Alabama. Police officers attack civil rights demonstrators with fire hoses at Kelley Ingram Park in 1963. © Bob Adelman.

> What liberal reforms were advanced during the Kennedy and Johnson administrations?

> How did the civil rights movement evolve in the 1960s?

> What other rights movements emerged in the 1960s?

> What were the goals of the new wave of feminism?

> How did liberalism fare under President Nixon?

> Conclusion: What were the achievements and limitations of liberalism?

What liberal reforms were advanced during the Kennedy and Johnson administrations?

A Tribute to Johnson for Medicare

George Niedermeyer, who lived in Hollywood, Florida, and received a Social Security pension, painted pieces of wood and glued them together to create this thank-you to President Lyndon Johnson for establishing Medicare. LBJ Library, photo by Henry Groskinsky.

AT THE DEMOCRATIC National Convention in 1960, John F. Kennedy announced "a New Frontier" that would confront "unsolved problems of peace and war, unconquered pockets of ignorance and prejudice, unanswered questions of poverty and surplus." Four years later, Lyndon B. Johnson invoked the ideal of a "Great Society, [which] rests on abundance and liberty for all [and] demands an end to poverty and racial injustice." Acting under the liberal faith that government should use its power to solve social and economic problems, end injustice, and promote the welfare of all citizens, the Democratic administrations of the 1960s won legislation on civil rights, poverty, education, medical care, housing, consumer safeguards, and environmental protection. These measures, along with pathbreaking Supreme Court decisions, responded to demands for rights from African Americans and other groups and addressed problems arising from rapid economic growth.

The Unrealized Promise of Kennedy's New Frontier

John F. Kennedy grew up in privilege, the child of an Irish Catholic businessman who became a New Deal official. Helped by a distinguished World War II navy

CHAPTER LOCATOR | **What liberal reforms were advanced during the Kennedy and Johnson administrations?** | How did the civil rights movement evolve in the 1960s?

836 CHAPTER 28 REFORM, REBELLION, AND REACTION

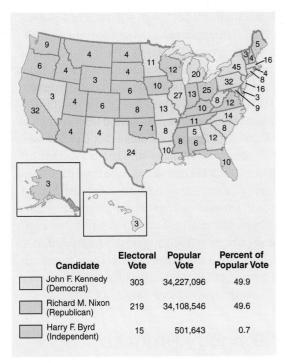

Candidate	Electoral Vote	Popular Vote	Percent of Popular Vote
John F. Kennedy (Democrat)	303	34,227,096	49.9
Richard M. Nixon (Republican)	219	34,108,546	49.6
Harry F. Byrd (Independent)	15	501,643	0.7

MAP 28.1 ■ The Election of 1960

record, Kennedy won election to the House of Representatives in 1946 and the Senate in 1952. With a powerful political machine, his family's fortune, and a dynamic personal appeal, Kennedy won the Democratic presidential nomination in 1960. He stunned many Democrats by choosing as his running mate Lyndon B. Johnson of Texas, whom liberals disparaged as a typical southern conservative.

In the general election, Kennedy narrowly defeated his Republican opponent, Vice President Richard M. Nixon, by a 118,550-vote margin (**Map 28.1**). African American voters contributed to his victory, and Kennedy also benefited from the nation's first televised presidential debates, at which he appeared cool and confident beside a nervous and pale Nixon.

The Kennedy administration projected energy, idealism, and glamour, although Kennedy was in most ways a cautious, pragmatic politician. At his inauguration, he called on Americans to serve the common good. "Ask not what your country can do for you," he implored, "ask what you can do for your country." Although Kennedy's idealism inspired many, he failed to persuade Congress to expand the welfare state with federal education and health care programs. Moreover, he resisted leadership on behalf of racial justice until civil rights activists gave him no choice.

Moved by the desperate conditions he observed while campaigning in Appalachia, Kennedy pushed poverty onto the national agenda. In 1962, he read Michael Harrington's *The Other America*, which described the poverty that left more than one in five Americans "maimed in body and spirit, existing at levels beneath those necessary for human decency." By 1962, Kennedy had won support for a $2 billion urban renewal program, providing incentives to businesses to locate in economically depressed areas and job training for the unemployed. In the summer of 1963, he asked aides to plan a full-scale attack on poverty.

Kennedy had promised to make economic growth a key objective, and he called for an enormous tax cut in 1963, which he promised would increase demand and create jobs. Passed in February 1964, the law contributed to an economic boom, as unemployment fell and the gross national product shot up. Some liberal critics of the tax cut, however, noted that it favored the well-off and argued instead for increased spending on social programs.

> CHRONOLOGY

1960
– John F. Kennedy is elected president.

1963
– In *Abington School District v. Schempp*, Supreme Court rules against requiring Bible reading and prayer in schools.
– Supreme Court rules that congressional districts must reflect "one person, one vote" in *Baker v. Carr*.
– President Kennedy is assassinated; Lyndon B. Johnson becomes president.

1964
– Civil Rights Act is passed.

1964–1966
– Congress passes most of Johnson's Great Society domestic programs.

1966
– *Miranda v. Arizona* ruling requires police officers to inform suspects of their rights.

1967
– Supreme Court strikes down state laws against interracial marriage in *Loving v. Virginia*.

| What other rights movements emerged in the 1960s? | What were the goals of the new wave of feminism? | How did liberalism fare under President Nixon? | Conclusion: What were the achievements and limitations of liberalism? | ✓ LearningCurve Check what you know. bedfordstmartins.com /roarkunderstanding |

Kennedy's domestic efforts were in their infancy when an assassin's bullets struck him down on November 22, 1963. Within minutes of the shooting—which occurred as Kennedy's motorcade passed through Dallas, Texas—radio and television broadcast the unfolding horror to the nation. Stunned Americans struggled to understand what had happened. Soon after the assassination, police arrested Lee Harvey Oswald and concluded that he had fired the shots from a nearby building. Two days later, while officers were transferring Oswald from one jail to another, a local nightclub operator killed him. Suspicions arose that Oswald was murdered to cover up a conspiracy by ultraconservatives who hated Kennedy or by Communists who supported Castro's Cuba (as discussed in chapter 29). To get at the truth, President Johnson appointed a commission headed by Chief Justice Earl Warren, which concluded that both Oswald and his assassin had acted alone.

Kennedy's domestic record had been unremarkable in his first two years, but his attention to taxes, civil rights, and poverty in 1963 suggested an important shift. Whether Kennedy could have persuaded Congress to enact them remained in question. Journalist James Reston commented, "What was killed was not only the president but the promise. . . . We saw him only as a rising sun."

Civil Rights Act of 1964
▶ Law that responded to demands of the civil rights movement by making discrimination in employment, education, and public accommodations illegal. It was the strongest such measure since Reconstruction and included a ban on sex discrimination in employment.

Johnson Fulfills the Kennedy Promise

Lyndon B. Johnson assumed the presidency with a wealth of political experience. A self-made man from the Texas Hill Country, he had won election in 1937 to the House of Representatives and in 1948 to the Senate, where he served skillfully as Senate majority leader. His modest upbringing, his admiration for Franklin Roosevelt, and his ambition to outdo the New Deal president all spurred his commitment to reform. Equally compelling were external pressures generated by the black freedom struggle and the host of movements it helped inspire.

Lacking Kennedy's sophistication, Johnson excelled behind the scenes, where he could entice, maneuver, or threaten legislators to support his objectives. The famous "Johnson treatment" became legendary. In his ability to achieve his legislative goals, Johnson had few peers in American history.

Johnson entreated Congress to act so that "John Fitzgerald Kennedy did not live or die in vain." He signed Kennedy's tax cut bill in February 1964. More remarkable was passage of the **Civil Rights Act of 1964**, which made discrimination in employment, education, and public accommodations illegal. The strongest such measure since reconstruction, the law required every ounce of

The "Johnson Treatment"

Abe Fortas, a distinguished lawyer who had argued a major criminal rights case, *Gideon v. Wainwright* (1963), before the Supreme Court, was a close friend of and adviser to President Johnson. This photograph of the president and Fortas taken in July 1965 illustrates how Johnson used his body as well as his voice to bend people to his will. Yoichi R. Okamoto/LBJ Library Collection.

CHAPTER LOCATOR | What liberal reforms were advanced during the Kennedy and Johnson administrations? | How did the civil rights movement evolve in the 1960s?

838 CHAPTER 28 REFORM, REBELLION, AND REACTION

Johnson's political skill to pry sufficient votes from Republicans to balance the "nays" of southern Democrats. Senate Republican leader Everett Dirksen's aide reported that Johnson "never left him alone for thirty minutes."

Antipoverty legislation followed fast on the heels of the Civil Rights Act. Johnson announced "an unconditional war on poverty" in his January 1964 State of the Union message, and in August Congress passed the Economic Opportunity Act. The law authorized ten new programs, allocating $800 million—about 1 percent of the federal budget—for the first year.

> ## > Programs of the Economic Opportunity Act

- Head Start for preschoolers
- Work-study grants for college students
- Job Corps for unemployed young people
- Volunteers in Service to America (VISTA) to work with the disadvantaged
- Legal services for the poor
- Community Action Program requiring participation by the poor in antipoverty projects

The most novel and controversial part of the law, the Community Action Program (CAP), required "maximum feasible participation" of the poor themselves in antipoverty projects. Poor people began to organize to take control of their neighborhoods and to make welfare agencies, school boards, police departments, and housing authorities more accountable to the people they served. Even though Johnson backed off from pushing genuine representation for the poor, CAP gave people usually excluded from government an opportunity to act on their own behalf and develop leadership skills.

Policymaking for a Great Society

As the 1964 election approached, Johnson projected stability and security in the midst of a booming economy. Few voters wanted to risk the dramatic change promised by his Republican opponent, Arizona senator Barry M. Goldwater, who attacked the welfare state and entertained the use of nuclear weapons in Vietnam. Johnson achieved a record-breaking 61 percent of the popular vote, and Democrats won resounding majorities in the House (295–140) and Senate (68–32). Still, Goldwater's considerable grassroots support marked a growing movement on the right (as discussed in chapter 30).

"I want to see a whole bunch of coonskins on the wall," Johnson told his aides, using a hunting analogy to stress his ambitious legislative goals for what he called the "Great Society." The large Democratic majorities in Congress, his own political skills, and pressure from the black freedom struggle enabled Johnson to obtain legislation on discrimination, poverty, education, medical care, housing, consumer and environmental protection, and more. Reporters called the legislation of the Eighty-ninth Congress (1965–1966) "a political miracle."

| What other rights movements emerged in the 1960s? | What were the goals of the new wave of feminism? | How did liberalism fare under President Nixon? | Conclusion: What were the achievements and limitations of liberalism? | ✓ LearningCurve Check what you know. bedfordstmartins.com /roarkunderstanding |

839

War on Poverty

▶ President Lyndon Johnson's efforts, organized through the Office of Economic Opportunity, to ameliorate poverty, primarily through education and training as well as by including the poor in decision making.

Medicare and Medicaid

▶ Social programs enacted as part of Lyndon Johnson's Great Society. Medicare provided the elderly with universal compulsory medical insurance financed primarily by Social Security taxes. Medicaid authorized federal grants to supplement state-paid medical care for poor people of all ages.

Voting Rights Act of 1965

▶ Law passed during Lyndon Johnson's administration that empowered the federal government to intervene to ensure minorities access to the voting booth. As a result of the act, black voting and officeholding in the South shot up, initiating a major transformation in southern politics.

Immigration and Nationality Act of 1965

▶ Legislation passed during Lyndon Johnson's administration abolishing discriminatory immigration quotas based on national origins. Although it did limit the number of immigrants, including those from Latin America for the first time, it facilitated a surge in immigration later in the century.

The Economic Opportunity Act of 1964 was the opening shot in the **War on Poverty**. Congress doubled the program's funding in 1965, enacted new economic development measures for depressed regions, and authorized more than $1 billion to improve the nation's slums. Direct aid included a new food stamp program, giving poor people greater choice in obtaining food, and rent supplements that provided alternatives to public housing. Moreover, a movement of welfare mothers, the National Welfare Rights Organization, assisted by antipoverty lawyers, pushed administrators of Aid to Families with Dependent Children (AFDC) to ease restrictions on welfare recipients. The number of families receiving assistance jumped from less than one million in 1960 to three million by 1972, benefiting 90 percent of those eligible.

Central to Johnson's War on Poverty were efforts to equip the poor with the skills necessary to find jobs. His Elementary and Secondary Education Act of 1965 marked a turning point by involving the federal government in K–12 education. The measure sent federal dollars to local school districts with high poverty populations and provided equipment and supplies to private and parochial schools serving the poor. That same year, Congress passed the Higher Education Act, vastly expanding federal assistance to colleges and universities for buildings, programs, scholarships, and loans.

The federal government's responsibility for health care marked an even greater watershed. Faced with a powerful medical lobby that opposed national health insurance as "socialized medicine," Johnson focused on the elderly, who constituted a large portion of the nation's poor. Congress responded with the **Medicare** program, providing the elderly with universal medical insurance financed largely through Social Security taxes. A separate program, **Medicaid**, authorized federal grants to supplement state-paid medical care for poor people. By the twenty-first century, these two programs covered 87 million Americans, nearly 30 percent of the population.

Whereas programs such as Medicare fulfilled New Deal and Fair Deal promises, the Great Society's civil rights legislation represented a break with tradition. Racial minorities were neglected or discriminated against in many New Deal programs, and Truman's civil rights proposals bore few results. By contrast, the Civil Rights Act of 1964 made discrimination in employment, education, and public accommodations illegal. The **Voting Rights Act of 1965** banned literacy tests and authorized federal intervention to ensure access to the voting booth.

Another form of bias fell with the **Immigration and Nationality Act of 1965**, which abolished quotas based on national origins that discriminated against non–western European immigrants. The law maintained caps on the total number of immigrants and for the first time limited those from the Western Hemisphere; preference was now given to immediate relatives of U.S. citizens and to those with desirable skills. The measure's unanticipated consequences triggered a surge of immigration near the end of the century (as discussed in chapter 31).

Great Society benefits reached well beyond victims of discrimination and the poor. Medicare covered the elderly, regardless of income. A groundswell of consumer activism won legislation making cars safer and raising standards for the food, drug, and cosmetics industries. Johnson insisted that the Great Society meet "not just the needs of the body but the desire for beauty and hunger for

CHAPTER LOCATOR | What liberal reforms were advanced during the Kennedy and Johnson administrations? | How did the civil rights movement evolve in the 1960s?

840 CHAPTER 28 REFORM, REBELLION, AND REACTION

community." In 1965, he sent Congress the first presidential message on the environment, obtaining measures to control water and air pollution and to preserve the natural beauty of the American landscape. In addition, the National Arts and Humanities Act of 1965 funded artists, musicians, writers, and scholars and brought their work to public audiences.

The flood of reform legislation dwindled after 1966, when Democratic majorities in Congress diminished and a backlash against government programs arose. The Vietnam War dealt the largest blow to Johnson's ambitions, diverting his attention, spawning an antiwar movement that crippled his leadership, and devouring tax dollars that might have been used for reform (as discussed in chapter 29).

In 1968, Johnson pried out of Congress one more civil rights law, which banned discrimination in housing and jury service. He also signed the National Housing Act of 1968, which authorized an enormous increase in low-income housing—1.7 million units over three years—and put construction and ownership in private hands.

Assessing the Great Society

The reduction in poverty in the 1960s was considerable. The number of poor Americans fell from more than 20 percent of the population in 1959 to around 13 percent in 1968. Those who in Johnson's words "live on the outskirts of hope" saw new opportunities. To Rosemary Bray, what turned her family of longtime welfare recipients into taxpaying workers "was the promise of the civil rights movement and the war on poverty." A Mexican American who learned to be a sheet metal worker through a jobs program reported, "[My children] will finish high school and maybe go to college. . . . I see my family and I know the chains are broken."

Certain groups, especially the aged, fared better than others. Many male-headed families rose out of poverty, but impoverishment among female-headed families actually increased. Whites escaped poverty faster than racial and ethnic minorities. Great Society programs contributed to a burgeoning black middle class, yet one out of three African Americans remained poverty-stricken (**Figure 28.1**).

Conservative critics charged that Great Society programs discouraged initiative by giving the poor "handouts." Liberal critics claimed that focusing on training and education wrongly blamed the poor themselves rather than an economic system that could not provide enough adequately paying jobs. In contrast to the New Deal, the Great Society avoided structural reform of the economy and spurned public works projects as a means of providing jobs for the disadvantaged.

Some critics insisted that ending poverty required raising taxes in order to create jobs, overhaul welfare systems, and rebuild slums. Great Society programs did invest more heavily in the public sector, but they were funded from economic growth rather than from new taxes on the rich or middle class. There was no significant redistribution of income, despite large increases in subsidies for food stamps, housing, medical care, and AFDC. Economic prosperity allowed spending for the poor to rise and improved the lives of millions, but that spending never approached the amounts necessary to claim victory in the War on Poverty.

What other rights movements emerged in the 1960s?

What were the goals of the new wave of feminism?

How did liberalism fare under President Nixon?

Conclusion: What were the achievements and limitations of liberalism?

LearningCurve
Check what you know.
bedfordstmartins.com
/roarkunderstanding

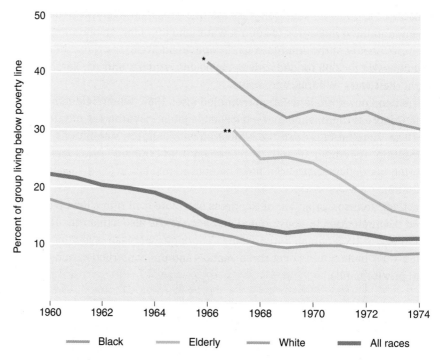

[*]Statistics on blacks for years 1960–1965 not available.
^{**}Statistics on the elderly for years 1960–1966 not available.

FIGURE 28.1 ■ **Poverty in the United States, 1960–1974**

The short-term effects of economic growth and the Great Society's attack on poverty are seen here. Which groups experienced the sharpest decline in poverty, and what might account for the differences?

The Judicial Revolution

A key element of liberalism's ascendancy emerged in the Supreme Court under Chief Justice Earl Warren (1953–1969). In contrast to the federal courts of the Progressive Era and New Deal, which blocked reform, the **Warren Court** often moved ahead of Congress and public opinion. Expanding the Constitution's promise of equality and individual rights, the Court's decisions supported an activist government to prevent injustice and provided new protections to disadvantaged groups and accused criminals.

Following the pathbreaking *Brown v. Board of Education* school desegregation decision of 1954 (see chapter 27), the Court struck down southern states' stratagems to avoid integration and defended civil rights activists' rights to freedom of assembly and speech. In addition, a unanimous Court in *Loving v. Virginia* (1967) invalidated state laws banning interracial marriage, calling that institution one of the "basic civil rights of man." Chief Justice Warren considered *Baker v. Carr* (1963) his most important decision. The case grew out of a complaint that inequitably drawn Tennessee electoral districts gave sparsely populated rural districts far more representatives than densely populated urban areas. Using the Fourteenth Amendment guarantee of "equal protection of the laws," *Baker* established the principle of "one person, one vote" for state legislatures and the House of

Warren Court

▶ The Supreme Court under Chief Justice Earl Warren (1953–1969), which expanded the Constitution's promise of equality and civil rights. The Court issued landmark decisions in the areas of civil rights, criminal rights, reproductive freedom, and separation of church and state.

CHAPTER LOCATOR | What liberal reforms were advanced during the Kennedy and Johnson administrations? | How did the civil rights movement evolve in the 1960s?

842 CHAPTER 28
REFORM, REBELLION, AND REACTION

Representatives. As states redrew electoral districts, legislatures became more responsive to metropolitan interests.

The Warren Court also reformed the criminal justice system, overturning a series of convictions on the grounds that the accused had been deprived of "life, liberty, or property, without due process of law," guaranteed in the Fourteenth Amendment. In decisions that dramatically altered law enforcement practices, the Court declared that states, as well as the federal government, were subject to the Bill of Rights. *Gideon v. Wainwright* (1963) ruled that when an accused criminal could not afford to hire a lawyer, the state had to provide one. *Miranda v. Arizona* (1966) required police officers to inform suspects of their rights upon arrest. The Court also overturned convictions based on evidence obtained by unlawful arrest, by electronic surveillance, or without a search warrant. Critics accused the justices of "handcuffing the police" and letting criminals go free; liberals argued that these rulings promoted equal treatment in the criminal justice system.

The Court's decisions on religion provoked even greater outrage. *Abington School District v. Schempp* (1963) ruled that requiring Bible reading and prayer in the schools violated the First Amendment principle of separation of church and state. Later judgments banned official prayer in public schools even if students were not required to participate. The Court's supporters declared that the religion cases protected the rights of non-Christians and atheists. They noted that the Court left students free to pray on their own, but the decisions infuriated many Christians. Billboards demanding "Impeach Earl Warren" spoke for critics of the Court, who joined a larger backlash mounting against Great Society liberalism.

QUICK REVIEW <

How did the Kennedy and Johnson administrations exemplify a liberal vision of the federal government?

What other rights movements emerged in the 1960s?

What were the goals of the new wave of feminism?

How did liberalism fare under President Nixon?

Conclusion: What were the achievements and limitations of liberalism?

LearningCurve Check what you know. bedfordstmartins.com /roarkunderstanding

> How did the civil rights movement evolve in the 1960s?

Lunch Counter Sit-in

John Salter Jr., a professor at Tougaloo College, and students Joan Trumpauer and Anne Moody take part in a 1963 sit-in at the Woolworth's lunch counter in Jackson, Mississippi. Shortly before this photograph was taken, whites had thrown two students to the floor, and police had arrested one student. Salter was spattered with mustard and ketchup. In 1968, Moody published *Coming of Age in Mississippi*, a popular book about her experiences in the black freedom struggle. State Historical Society of Wisconsin.

> VISUAL ACTIVITY

READING THE IMAGE: What does the photograph tell you about black civil rights activity of the early 1960s?

CONNECTIONS: How would you describe the changes in race relations between African Americans and whites in the United States in the first half of the 1960s?

AS MUCH AS SUPREME COURT DECISIONS, the black freedom struggle distinguished the liberalism of the 1960s from that of the New Deal. Before the Great Society reforms—and, in fact, contributing to them—African Americans had mobilized a movement that struck down legal separation and discrimination in the South and secured their voting rights. Whereas the first Reconstruction reflected the power of northern Republicans in the aftermath of the Civil War, the second Reconstruction depended heavily on the courage and determination of black people themselves to stand up to racist violence.

Civil rights activism that focused on the South and on legal rights won widespread acceptance. But when African Americans stepped up protest against racial injustice in the rest of the country and challenged the economic deprivation that equal rights left untouched, a strong backlash developed as the movement itself lost cohesion.

The Flowering of the Black Freedom Struggle

The Montgomery bus boycott of 1955–1956 gave racial issues national visibility and produced a leader in Martin Luther King Jr. In the 1960s, protest expanded dramatically, as blacks directly confronted the people and institutions that

CHAPTER LOCATOR | What liberal reforms were advanced during the Kennedy and Johnson administrations? | **How did the civil rights movement evolve in the 1960s?**

CHAPTER 28
844 REFORM, REBELLION, AND REACTION

segregated and discriminated against them: retail establishments, public parks and libraries, buses and depots, voting registrars, and police forces.

Massive direct action in the South began in February 1960, when four African American college students in Greensboro, North Carolina, requested service at the whites-only Woolworth's lunch counter. Within days, hundreds of young people joined them, and others launched sit-ins in thirty-one southern cities. From Southern Christian Leadership Conference headquarters, civil rights activist Ella Baker telephoned her young contacts at black colleges: "What are you going to do? It's time to move."

In April 1960, Baker helped student activists form a new organization, the Student Nonviolent Coordinating Committee (SNCC). Embracing civil disobedience and Martin Luther King Jr.'s principles of nonviolence, activists would confront their oppressors and stand up for their rights, but they would not respond if attacked. In the words of SNCC leader James Lawson, "Nonviolence nurtures the atmosphere in which reconciliation and justice become actual possibilities." SNCC, however, rejected the top-down leadership of King and the established civil rights organizations, adopting a structure that fostered decision making and leadership development at the grassroots level.

The activists' optimism and commitment to nonviolence soon underwent severe tests. Although some cities quietly met student demands, more typically activists encountered violence. Hostile whites poured food over demonstrators, burned them with cigarettes, called them "niggers," and pelted them with rocks. Local police attacked protesters with dogs, clubs, fire hoses, and tear gas, and they arrested thousands of demonstrators.

Another wave of protest occurred in May 1961, when the Congress of Racial Equality (CORE) organized Freedom Rides to integrate interstate transportation in the South. When a group of six whites and seven blacks reached Alabama, whites bombed their bus and beat them with baseball bats so fiercely that an observer "couldn't see their faces through the blood." CORE rebuffed President Kennedy's pleas to call off the rides. But after a huge mob attacked the riders in Montgomery, Alabama, Attorney General Robert Kennedy dispatched federal marshals to restore order. Freedom Riders arriving in Jackson, Mississippi, were promptly arrested, and several hundred spent weeks in jail. All told, more than four hundred blacks and whites participated in the Freedom Rides.

In the summer of 1962, SNCC and other groups began the Voter Education Project. They, too, met violence. Whites bombed black churches, threw tenant farmers out of their homes, and beat and jailed activists. In June 1963, a white man gunned down Mississippi NAACP leader Medgar Evers in front of his house. Similar violence met King's 1963 campaign in Birmingham, Alabama, to integrate public facilities and open jobs to blacks. The police attacked demonstrators with dogs, cattle prods, and fire hoses—brutalities that television broadcast around the world.

The largest demonstration drew 250,000 blacks and whites to the nation's capital in August 1963 in the March on Washington for Jobs and Freedom, inspired by the strategy of A. Philip Randolph in 1941 (see chapter 25). Speaking from the Lincoln Memorial, King put his indelible stamp on the day. "I have a dream," he repeated again and again, imagining the day "when all of God's children . . . will be able to join hands and sing . . . 'Free at last, free at last; thank God Almighty, we are free at last.'"

> CHRONOLOGY

1960
– Student Nonviolent Coordinating Committee (SNCC) is founded.

1961
– Freedom Rides.

1963
– March on Washington.

1964
– Civil Rights Act.
– Mississippi Freedom Summer Project.

1965
– Voting Rights Act.

1965–1968
– Riots in major cities.

1966
– Black Panther Party for Self-Defense is founded.

1968
– Martin Luther King Jr. is assassinated.

Civil Rights Freedom Rides, May 1961

| What other rights movements emerged in the 1960s? | What were the goals of the new wave of feminism? | How did liberalism fare under President Nixon? | Conclusion: What were the achievements and limitations of liberalism? | ☑ LearningCurve Check what you know. bedfordstmartins.com /roarkunderstanding |

The Children's Crusade

Children and teenagers played a key role in the civil rights campaign in Birmingham, Alabama, in May 1963. As shown here, police stopped the children and led them into jail. After more than a thousand young people filled the jails, police used water hoses and dogs against the next stream of demonstrators, bringing national attention to the protesters and some concessions from Birmingham's leaders. AP Photo/Bill Hudson.

The euphoria of the March on Washington faded as activists returned to face continued violence in the South. In 1964, the Mississippi Freedom Summer Project mobilized more than a thousand northern black and white college students to conduct voter registration drives. Resistance was fierce, and by the end of the summer only twelve hundred new voters had been allowed to register. Southern whites had killed several activists, beaten eighty, arrested more than a thousand, and burned thirty-five black churches. Hidden resistance came from the federal government itself, as the FBI spied on King and other leaders and expanded its activities to "expose, disrupt, misdirect, discredit, or otherwise neutralize" black protest.

Still, the movement persisted. In March 1965, Alabama state troopers used such violent force to turn back a voting rights march from Selma to the state capitol in Montgomery that the incident earned the name "Bloody Sunday" and com-

CHAPTER LOCATOR | What liberal reforms were advanced during the Kennedy and Johnson administrations? | How did the civil rights movement evolve in the 1960s?

CHAPTER 28
846 REFORM, REBELLION, AND REACTION

pelled President Johnson to call up the Alabama National Guard to protect the marchers. Battered and hospitalized on Bloody Sunday, John Lewis, chairman of SNCC (and later a congressman from Georgia), called the Voting Rights Act, which passed that October, "every bit as momentous as the Emancipation Proclamation." Referring to the Selma march, he said, "We all felt we'd had a part in it."

The Response in Washington

Civil rights leaders would have to wear sneakers, Lyndon Johnson said, if they were going to keep up with him. But both Kennedy and Johnson, reluctant to alienate southern voters and their congressional representatives, tended to move only when events gave them little choice. In June 1963, Kennedy finally made good on his promise to seek strong antidiscrimination legislation. Pointing to the injustice suffered by blacks, Kennedy asked white Americans, "Who among us would then be content with the counsels of patience and delay?" Johnson took up Kennedy's commitment with passion, as scenes of violence against peaceful demonstrators appalled television viewers across the nation. The resulting public support, the "Johnson treatment," and the president's appeal to memories of the martyred Kennedy all produced the most important civil rights law since reconstruction.

The Civil Rights Act of 1964 guaranteed access for all Americans to public accommodations, public education, employment, and voting, and it extended constitutional protections to Indians on reservations. Title VII of the measure, banning discrimination in employment, not only attacked racial discrimination but also outlawed discrimination against women. Because Title VII applied to every aspect of employment, including wages, hiring, and promotion, it represented a giant step toward equal employment opportunity for white women as well as for racial minorities.

Responding to black voter registration drives in the South, Johnson demanded legislation to remove "every remaining obstacle to the right and the opportunity to vote." In August 1965, he signed the Voting Rights Act, empowering the federal government to intervene directly to enable African Americans to register and vote, thereby launching a major transformation in southern politics. Black voting rates shot up dramatically (**Map 28.2**). In turn, the number of African Americans holding political office in the South increased from a handful in 1964 to more than a thousand by 1972. Such gains translated into tangible benefits as black officials upgraded public facilities, police protection, and other basic services for their constituents.

Johnson also declared the need to realize "not just equality as a right and theory, but equality as fact and result." To this end, he issued an executive order in 1965 to require employers holding government contracts (affecting about one-third of the labor force) to take affirmative action to ensure equal opportunity. Extended to cover women in 1967, the affirmative action program required employers to counter the effects of centuries of oppression by acting forcefully to align their labor force with the available pool of qualified candidates. Most corporations came to see affirmative action as a good employment practice.

In 1968, Johnson maneuvered one final bill through Congress. While those in other regions often applauded the gains made by the black freedom struggle in the South, they were just as likely to resist claims for racial justice in their own locations.

| What other rights movements emerged in the 1960s? | What were the goals of the new wave of feminism? | How did liberalism fare under President Nixon? | Conclusion: What were the achievements and limitations of liberalism? | ☑ LearningCurve Check what you know. bedfordstmartins.com /roarkunderstanding |

847

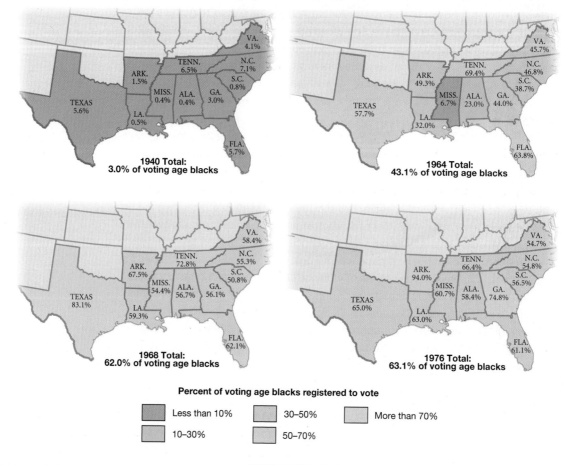

Percent of voting age blacks registered to vote

▨ Less than 10%	▨ 30–50%	▨ More than 70%
▨ 10–30%	▨ 50–70%	

MAP 28.2 ■ The Rise of the African American Vote, 1940–1976

Voting rates of southern blacks increased gradually in the 1940s and 1950s but shot up dramatically in the deep South after the Voting Rights Act of 1965 provided for federal agents to enforce African Americans' right to vote.

> MAP ACTIVITY

READING THE MAP: When did the biggest change in African American voter registration occur in the South? In 1968, which states had the highest and which had the lowest voter registration rates?

CONNECTIONS: What role did African American voters play in the 1960 election? What were the targets of two major voting drives in the 1960s?

In 1963, California voters rejected a law passed by the legislature banning discrimination in housing. And when Martin Luther King Jr. launched a campaign against de facto segregation in Chicago in 1966, thousands of whites jeered and threw stones at demonstrators. Johnson's efforts to get a federal open-housing law succeeded only in the wake of King's assassination in 1968. The Civil Rights Act of 1968 banned racial discrimination in housing and jury selection, and it authorized federal intervention when states failed to protect civil rights workers from violence.

Black Power and Urban Rebellions

By 1966, black protest engulfed the entire nation, demanding not just legal equality but also economic justice and abandoning passive resistance as a basic principle.

CHAPTER LOCATOR | What liberal reforms were advanced during the Kennedy and Johnson administrations? | How did the civil rights movement evolve in the 1960s?

848 CHAPTER 28
REFORM, REBELLION, AND REACTION

These developments were not completely new. African Americans had waged campaigns for decent jobs, housing, and education outside the South since the 1930s. Some African Americans had always armed themselves in self-defense, and many activists doubted that their passive suffering would change the hearts of racists. Still, the black freedom struggle began to appear more threatening to the white majority.

The new emphases resulted from a combination of heightened activism and unrealized promise. Legal equality could not quickly improve the material conditions of blacks, and black rage at oppressive conditions erupted in waves of urban uprisings from 1965 to 1968 (**Map 28.3**). In a situation where virtually all-white police forces patrolled black neighborhoods, incidents between police and local blacks typically sparked rioting and resulted in looting, destruction of property, injuries, and deaths. The worst riots occurred in Watts (Los Angeles) in August 1965, Newark and Detroit in July 1967, and the nation's capital in April 1968, but violence visited hundreds of cities.

In the North, Malcolm X posed a powerful challenge to the ethos of nonviolence. Calling for black pride and autonomy, separation from the "corrupt [white]

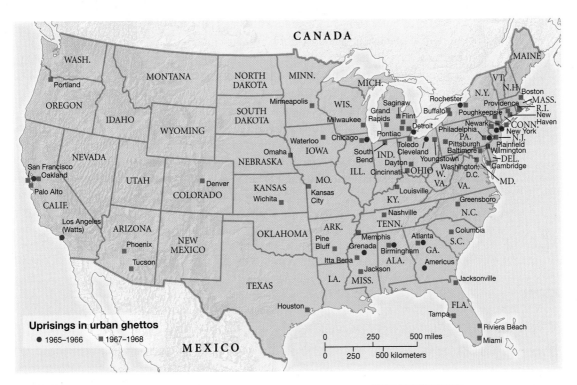

MAP 28.3 ■ Urban Uprisings, 1965–1968

When a white police officer in the Watts district of Los Angeles struck a twenty-one-year-old African American, whom he had just pulled over for driving drunk, one onlooker shouted, "We've got no rights at all — it's just like Selma." The altercation sparked a five-day uprising, during which young blacks set fires, looted, and attacked police and firefighters. When the riot ended, 34 people were dead, more than 3,000 were arrested, and scores of businesses had been wiped out. Similar but smaller-scale violence erupted in dozens of cities across the nation during the next three summers.

> MAP ACTIVITY

READING THE MAP: In what regions and cities of the United States were the 1960s uprisings concentrated? What years saw the greatest unrest?

CONNECTIONS: What were some of the causes of racial unrest in America's cities during this period? Whom did whites generally hold responsible for the violence and why?

| What other rights movements emerged in the 1960s? | What were the goals of the new wave of feminism? | How did liberalism fare under President Nixon? | Conclusion: What were the achievements and limitations of liberalism? | ✓ LearningCurve Check what you know. bedfordstmartins.com /roarkunderstanding |

society," and self-defense against white violence, Malcolm X attracted a large following, especially in urban ghettos. At a June 1966 rally in Greenwood, Mississippi, SNCC chairman Stokely Carmichael gave the ideas espoused by Malcolm X a new name when he shouted, "We want black power." Carmichael rejected integration and assimilation because that implied white superiority. African Americans were encouraged to develop independent businesses and control their own schools, communities, and political organizations. The phrase "Black is beautiful" emphasized pride in African American culture and connections to dark-skinned people around the world, who were claiming their independence from colonial domination. Black power quickly became the rallying cry in SNCC and CORE as well as other organizations such as the Black Panther Party for Self-Defense, organized in 1966 to combat police brutality.

black power movement

▶ Movement of the 1960s and 1970s that emphasized black racial pride and autonomy. Black power advocates encouraged African Americans to assert community control, and some within the movement also rejected the ethos of nonviolence.

The press paid inordinate attention to the **black power movement**, and civil rights activism encountered a severe white backlash. Although the urban riots of the mid-1960s erupted spontaneously, triggered by specific incidents of alleged police mistreatment, horrified whites blamed black power militants. By 1966, 85 percent of the white population—up from 34 percent two years earlier—thought that African Americans were pressing for too much too quickly.

Martin Luther King Jr. agreed with black power advocates about the need for "a radical reconstruction of society," yet he clung to nonviolence and integration as the means to this end. In 1968, the thirty-nine-year-old leader went to Memphis to support striking municipal sanitation workers. There, on April 4, he was murdered by an escaped white convict.

Although black power organizations captured the headlines, they failed to gain the massive support from African Americans that King and other leaders had attracted. Nor could they alleviate the poverty and racism entrenched in the entire country. Yet black power's emphasis on racial pride and its critique of American institutions resonated loudly and helped shape the protest activities of other groups.

> **QUICK REVIEW**

How and why did the civil rights movement change in the mid-1960s?

CHAPTER LOCATOR | What liberal reforms were advanced during the Kennedy and Johnson administrations? | How did the civil rights movement evolve in the 1960s?

850   CHAPTER 28
REFORM, REBELLION, AND REACTION

What other rights movements emerged in the 1960s?

Beginning in November 1969, some one hundred Native Americans occupied Alcatraz Island in San Francisco Bay. Calling themselves "Indians of All Tribes" to reflect their diversity, they demanded the deed to the island and the creation of an Indian university, museum, and cultural center. Although failing to achieve their goals, they brought attention to the Native American cause and spurred further activism. Photo by Ralph Crane/Time Life Pictures/Getty Images.

THE CIVIL RIGHTS MOVEMENT'S undeniable moral claims helped make protest more respectable, while its successes encouraged other groups with grievances. Native Americans, Latinos, college students, women, gay men and lesbians, and others drew on the black freedom struggle for inspiration and models of activism. Many of these groups engaged in direct-action protests, expressed their own cultural nationalism, and challenged dominant institutions and values. Their grievances gained attention in the political arena, and they expanded justice and opportunity for many of their constituents.

| What other rights movements emerged in the 1960s? | What were the goals of the new wave of feminism? | How did liberalism fare under President Nixon? | Conclusion: What were the achievements and limitations of liberalism? | LearningCurve Check what you know. bedfordstmartins.com /roarkunderstanding |

American Indian Movement (AIM)

▶ Organization established in 1968 to address the problems Indians faced in American cities, including poverty and police harassment. AIM organized Indians to end relocation and termination policies and to win greater control over their cultures and communities.

Native American Protest

The cry "red power" reflected the influence of black radicalism on young Native Americans, whose activism took on fresh militancy and goals in the 1960s. The termination and relocation programs of the 1950s, contrary to their intent, stirred a sense of Indian identity across tribal lines and a determination to preserve traditional culture. Native Americans demonstrated and occupied land and public buildings, claiming rights to natural resources and territory they had owned collectively before European settlement.

In 1969, Native American militants captured world attention when several dozen seized Alcatraz Island, an abandoned federal prison in San Francisco Bay, claiming their right of "first discovery" of this land. For nineteen months, they used the occupation to publicize injustices against Indians, promote pan-Indian cooperation, and celebrate traditional cultures. One of the organizers, Dr. LaNada Boyer, the first Native American to attend the University of California, Berkeley, said of Alcatraz, "We were able to reestablish our identity as Indian people, as a culture, as political entities."

In Minneapolis in 1968, two Chippewa Indians, Dennis Banks and George Mitchell, founded the **American Indian Movement (AIM)** to attack problems in cities, where about 300,000 Indians lived. AIM sought to protect Indians from police harassment, secure antipoverty funds, and establish "survival schools" to teach Indian history and values. The movement's appeal quickly spread and filled many Indians with a new sense of purpose. Lakota activist and author Mary Crow Dog wrote that AIM's visit to her South Dakota reservation "loosened a sort of earthquake inside me." AIM leaders helped organize the "Trail of Broken Treaties" caravan to the nation's capital in 1972, when activists occupied the Bureau of Indian Affairs to express their outrage at the bureau's policies and interference in Indians' lives. In 1973, a much longer siege occurred on the Lakota Sioux reservation in South Dakota. Conflicts there between AIM militants and older tribal leaders led AIM to take over for seventy-two days the village of Wounded Knee, where U.S. troops had massacred more than two hundred Sioux Indians in 1890 (see chapter 17).

Although these dramatic occupations failed to achieve their specific goals, Indians won the end of relocation and termination policies, greater tribal sovereignty and control over community services, protection of Indian religious practices, and a measure of respect and pride. A number of laws and court decisions restored rights to ancestral lands and compensated tribes for land seized in violation of treaties.

Latino Struggles for Justice

The fastest-growing minority group in the 1960s was Latino, or Hispanic American, an extraordinarily varied population encompassing people of Mexican, Puerto Rican, Caribbean, and other Latin American origins. (The term *Latino* stresses their common bonds as a minority group in the United States. The older, less political term *Hispanic* also includes people with origins in Spain.) People of

CHAPTER LOCATOR | What liberal reforms were advanced during the Kennedy and Johnson administrations? | How did the civil rights movement evolve in the 1960s?

852 CHAPTER 28 REFORM, REBELLION, AND REACTION

Puerto Rican and Caribbean descent populated East Coast cities, but more than half of the nation's Latino population—including some six million Mexican Americans—lived in the Southwest. In addition, thousands illegally crossed the border between Mexico and the United States yearly in search of economic opportunity.

Political organization of Mexican Americans dated back to the League of United Latin American Citizens (LULAC), founded in 1929, which fought segregation and discrimination through litigation (see chapter 26). In the 1960s, however, young Mexican Americans increasingly rejected traditional politics in favor of direct action. One symbol of this generational challenge was young activists' adoption of the term *Chicano* (from *mejicano*, the Spanish word for "Mexican").

The **Chicano movement** drew national attention to California, where Cesar Chavez and Dolores Huerta organized a movement to improve the wretched conditions of migrant agricultural workers. As the child of migrant farmworkers, Chavez lived in soggy tents, changed schools frequently, and encountered indifference and discrimination. One teacher, he recalled, "hung a sign on me that said, 'I am a clown, I speak Spanish.'" After serving in World War II, Chavez began to organize voter registration drives among Mexican Americans.

In contrast to Chavez, Dolores Huerta grew up in an integrated urban neighborhood and avoided the farmworkers' grinding poverty but witnessed subtle forms of discrimination. Once, a high school teacher challenged her authorship

Chicano movement

▶ Mobilization of Mexican Americans in the 1960s and 1970s to fight for civil rights, economic justice, and political power and to combat police brutality. Most notably, the movement worked to improve the lives of migrant farmworkers and to end discrimination in employment and education.

Cesar Chavez and Dolores Huerta

Under posters showing Senator Robert Kennedy and Mahatma Gandhi, Chavez and Huerta confer in 1968 during the United Farm Workers' struggle with grape growers for better wages and working conditions. Chavez, like Martin Luther King Jr., had studied the ideas of Gandhi, who used civil disobedience and nonviolence to gain independence for India. People across the country, including Robert Kennedy, supported the UFW's grape boycott. Arthur Schatz/TimePix/Getty Images.

What other rights movements emerged in the 1960s?

What were the goals of the new wave of feminism?

How did liberalism fare under President Nixon?

Conclusion: What were the achievements and limitations of liberalism?

✓ LearningCurve
Check what you know.
bedfordstmartins.com
/roarkunderstanding

of an essay because it was so well written. Believing that collective action was the key to progress, she and Chavez founded the United Farm Workers (UFW) in 1962. To gain leverage for striking workers, the UFW mounted a nationwide boycott of California grapes, winning support from millions of Americans and gaining a wage increase for the workers in 1970. Although the UFW struggled and lost membership during the 1970s, it helped politicize Mexican Americans and improve farmworkers' lives.

Other Chicanos pressed the Equal Employment Opportunity Commission (EEOC) to act against job discrimination against Mexican Americans. After LULAC, the American GI Forum (see chapter 26), and other groups picketed government offices, President Johnson responded in 1967 by appointing Vicente T. Ximenes as the first Mexican American EEOC commissioner and created a special committee on Mexican American issues.

Claiming "brown power," Chicanos organized to end discrimination in education, gain political power, and combat police brutality. In Denver, Rodolfo "Corky" Gonzales set up "freedom schools" where Chicano children learned Spanish and Mexican American history. The nationalist strains of Chicano protest were evident in La Raza Unida (the United Race), a political party founded in 1970 based on cultural pride and brotherhood. Along with blacks and Native Americans, Chicanos continued to be disproportionately impoverished, but they gradually won more political offices, more effective enforcement of antidiscrimination legislation, and greater respect for their culture.

Student Rebellion, the New Left, and the Counterculture

Although materially and legally more secure than their African American, Indian, and Latino counterparts, white youths also expressed dissent, participating in the black freedom struggle, student protests, the antiwar movement, and the new feminist movement. Challenging establishment institutions, young activists were part of a larger international phenomenon of student movements around the globe.

The central organization of white student protest was Students for a Democratic Society (SDS), formed in 1960. In 1962, the organizers wrote in their statement of purpose, "We are people of this generation, bred in at least modest comfort, housed now in universities, looking uncomfortably at the world we inherit." The idealistic students criticized the complacency of their elders, the remoteness of decision makers, and the powerlessness and alienation generated by a bureaucratic society. SDS aimed to mobilize a "New Left" around the goals of civil rights, peace, and universal economic security. Other forms of student activism soon followed.

The first large-scale white student protest arose at the University of California, Berkeley, in 1964, when university officials banned students from setting up tables to recruit support for various causes. Led by whites returning from civil rights work in the South, the "free speech" movement occupied the administration building, and more than seven hundred students were arrested before the California Board of Regents overturned the new restrictions.

CHAPTER LOCATOR | What liberal reforms were advanced during the Kennedy and Johnson administrations? | How did the civil rights movement evolve in the 1960s?

854   CHAPTER 28
REFORM, REBELLION, AND REACTION

Hundreds of student rallies and building occupations followed on campuses across the country, especially after 1965, when opposition to the Vietnam War mounted and students protested against universities' ties with the military (as discussed in chapter 29). Students also changed the collegiate environment. Women at the University of Chicago, for example, charged in 1969 that all universities "discriminate against women, impede their full intellectual development, deny them places on the faculty, exploit talented women and mistreat women students." At Howard University, African American students called for a "Black Awareness Research Institute," demanding that academic departments "place more emphasis on how these disciplines may be used to effect the liberation of black people."

> **Accomplishments of the Student Movement**

- Curricular reforms, such as the introduction of black studies, Latino studies, and women's studies programs
- Increased financial aid for minority and poor students
- Independence from paternalistic rules
- A larger voice in campus decision making

Student protest sometimes blended into a cultural revolution against nearly every conventional standard of behavior. Drawing on the ideas of the Beats of the 1950s (see chapter 27), the "hippies," as they were called, rejected mainstream values such as materialism, order, and sexual control. Seeking personal rather than political change, they advocated "Do your own thing" and drew attention with their long hair, wildly colorful clothing, and use of drugs. Across the country, thousands of radicals established communes in cities or on farms.

Rock and folk music defined both the counterculture and the political left. Music during the 1960s often carried insurgent political and social messages that reflected radical youth culture. "Eve of Destruction," a top hit of 1965, reminded young men at a time when the voting age was twenty-one, "You're old enough to kill but not for votin'." The 1969 Woodstock Music Festival, attended by 400,000 young people, epitomized the centrality of music to the youth rebellion. Hippies faded away in the 1970s, but many elements of the counterculture—rock music, jeans, and long hair, as well as new social attitudes—filtered into the mainstream. More tolerant approaches to sexual behaviors spawned what came to be called the "sexual revolution," with help from the birth control pill, which became available in the 1960s. Self-fulfillment became a dominant concern of many Americans, and questioning of authority became more widespread.

Gay Men and Lesbians Organize

More permissive sexual norms did not stretch easily to include tolerance of homosexuality. Gay men and lesbians escaped discrimination and ridicule only by concealing their very identities. Those who couldn't or wouldn't found themselves

| What other rights movements emerged in the 1960s? | What were the goals of the new wave of feminism? | How did liberalism fare under President Nixon? | Conclusion: What were the achievements and limitations of liberalism? | ✓ LearningCurve Check what you know. bedfordstmartins.com /roarkunderstanding |

855

fired from jobs, arrested for their sexual activities, deprived of their children, or accused of being "perverted." Nevertheless, some gays and lesbians began to organize.

Some of the first gay activism challenged the government's aggressive efforts to keep homosexuals out of the civil service. In October 1965, picketers outside the White House held signs calling discrimination against homosexuals "as immoral as discrimination against Negroes and Jews." Not until ten years later, however, did the Civil Service Commission formally end its anti-gay policy.

A turning point in gay activism came in 1969 when police raided a gay bar, the Stonewall Inn, in New York City's Greenwich Village, and gay men and lesbians fought back. "Suddenly, they were not submissive anymore," a police officer remarked. Energized by the defiance shown at the Stonewall riots, gay men and lesbians organized a host of new groups, such as the Gay Liberation Front and the National Gay and Lesbian Task Force.

In 1972, Ann Arbor, Michigan, passed the first antidiscrimination ordinance, and two years later Elaine Noble's election to the Massachusetts legislature marked the first time an openly gay candidate won state office. In 1973, gay activists persuaded the American Psychiatric Association to withdraw its designation of homosexuality as a mental disease. It would take decades for these initial gains to improve conditions for most homosexuals, but by the mid-1970s gay men and lesbians had a movement through which they could claim equal rights and express pride in their identities.

> ## QUICK REVIEW

How did the black freedom struggle influence other reform movements of the 1960s and 1970s?

CHAPTER LOCATOR | What liberal reforms were advanced during the Kennedy and Johnson administrations? | How did the civil rights movement evolve in the 1960s?

856 CHAPTER 28
REFORM, REBELLION, AND REACTION

In 1972, Gloria Steinem and other journalists and writers published the premier issue of the first mass-circulation magazine for and controlled by women. *Ms.: The New Magazine for Women* ignored the recipes and fashion tips of typical women's magazines. It featured literature by women writers and articles on a broad range of feminist issues. Courtesy, Lang Communications.

What were the goals of the new wave of feminism?

BECOMING VISIBLE by the late 1960s, a multifaceted women's movement reached its high tide in the 1970s and persisted into the twenty-first century. By that time, despite a powerful countermovement, women had experienced tremendous transformations in their legal status, public opportunities, and personal and sexual relationships, while popular expectations about appropriate gender roles had shifted dramatically.

A Multifaceted Movement Emerges

Beginning in the 1940s, large demographic changes laid the preconditions for a resurgence of feminism. As more and more women took jobs, the importance of their paid work to the economy and their families challenged traditional views of women and awakened many women workers, especially labor union women, to the inferior conditions of their employment. The democratization of higher education brought more women to college campuses, where their aspirations exceeded the confines of domesticity and of routine, subordinate jobs.

Policy initiatives in the early 1960s reflected both these larger transformations and the efforts of women's rights activists. In 1961, Assistant Secretary of Labor Esther Peterson persuaded President Kennedy to create the President's Commission on the Status of Women. Its 1963 report documented widespread discrimination against women and recommended remedies. One of the commission's concerns was addressed even before it issued its report, when Congress passed the Equal Pay Act of 1963, making it illegal to pay women less than men for the same work.

Like other movements, the rise of feminism owed much to the black freedom struggle. Women gained protection from employment discrimination through Title VII of the Civil Rights Act of 1964 and the extension of affirmative action to women by piggybacking onto civil rights measures. They soon grew impatient when the government failed to take these new policies seriously. Determined to speed the process of change, writer and feminist Betty Friedan, civil rights activist Pauli Murray, several union women, and others founded the **National Organization for Women (NOW)** in 1966.

Simultaneously, a more radical feminism grew among civil rights and New Left activists. Frustrated with the unwillingness of male activists to take sexism seriously, many women walked out of New Left organizations and created an independent women's liberation movement throughout the nation.

Women's liberation began to gain public attention, especially when dozens of women picketed the Miss America beauty pageant in 1968, protesting against being forced "to compete for male approval [and] enslaved by ludicrous 'beauty' standards." Women began to speak publicly about personal experiences that had always been shrouded in secrecy, such as rape and abortion. Throughout the country, women joined consciousness-raising groups, where they discovered that what they had considered "personal" problems reflected an entrenched system of discrimination against and devaluation of women.

Radical feminists, who called their movement "women's liberation," differed from feminists in NOW and other more mainstream groups in several ways. NOW focused on equal treatment for women in the public sphere; women's liberation emphasized ending women's subordination in family and other personal relationships. Groups such as NOW wanted to integrate women into existing institutions; radical groups insisted that women's liberation required a total transformation of economic, political, and social institutions. Differences between these two strands of feminism blurred in the 1970s, as NOW and other mainstream groups embraced many of the issues raised by radicals.

Although NOW elected a black president, Aileen Hernandez, in 1970, the new feminism's leadership and constituency were predominantly white and middle-class. Women of color criticized white feminists for their inadequate attention to the disproportionate poverty experienced by minority women and to the additional layers of discrimination based on race or ethnicity. To black women, who were much more frequently compelled to work in the lowest-paying jobs for their families' survival, employment did not necessarily look like liberation.

In addition to struggling with vast differences among women, feminism also contended with the refusal of the mass media to take women's grievances seriously. When the House of Representatives passed an Equal Rights Amendment to the U.S. Constitution in 1970, the *New York Times* criticized it in an editorial titled "The Henpecked House." After Gloria Steinem founded *Ms: The New Magazine for Women* in 1972, feminists had their own mass-circulation periodical controlled by women and featuring articles on a broad range of feminist issues. *Ms.* reported on a multifaceted movement that included numerous organizations, reflecting the diverse experiences, backgrounds, and goals of American women. New women's organizations represented ethnic and racial minorities, labor union

National Organization for Women (NOW)

▶ Women's civil rights organization formed in 1966. Initially, NOW focused on eliminating gender discrimination in public institutions and the workplace, but by the 1970s it also embraced many of the issues raised by more radical feminists.

women, religious women, welfare mothers, lesbians, and more. Other new groups focused on single issues such as health, education, abortion rights, and violence against women. Common threads underlay the great diversity of organizations, issues, and activities. Feminism represented the belief that women were barred from, unequally treated in, or poorly served by the male-dominated public arena, encompassing politics, medicine, law, education, culture, and religion. Many feminists also sought equality in the private sphere, challenging traditional norms that identified women primarily as wives and mothers or sex objects, subservient to men.

Feminist Gains Spark a Countermovement

Although more an effect than a cause of women's rising employment, feminism lifted female aspirations and helped lower barriers to posts monopolized by men. Between 1970 and 2000, women's share of law degrees shot up from 5 percent to nearly 50 percent, and their proportion of medical degrees from less than 10 percent to more than 35 percent. Women gained political offices very slowly; yet by 2010, they constituted about 17 percent of Congress and more than 20 percent of all state executives and legislators. Despite some inroads into male-dominated occupations, women still concentrated in low-paying, traditionally female jobs. Employed women continued to bear primary responsibility for their homes and families, thereby working a "double day."

By the mid-1970s, feminism faced a powerful countermovement, organized around opposition to an Equal Rights Amendment (ERA) to the Constitution that would outlaw differential treatment of men and women under all state and federal laws. After Congress passed the ERA in 1972, Phyllis Schlafly, a conservative activist in the Republican Party, mobilized thousands of antifeminist women. These women, marching on state capitols, persuaded enough male legislators to block ratification so that when the time limit ran out in 1982, only thirty-five states had done so, three short of the necessary three-fourths majority. Powerful opposition likewise arose to feminists' quest for abortion rights. "Without the full capacity to limit her own reproduction," abortion rights activist Lucinda Cisler insisted, "a woman's other 'freedoms' are tantalizing mockeries that cannot be exercised." In 1973, the Supreme Court ruled in the landmark **Roe v. Wade** decision that the Constitution protects the right to abortion, which states cannot prohibit in the early stages of pregnancy. This decision galvanized many Americans who equated abortion with murder. Like ERA opponents, with whom they often overlapped, right-to-life activists believed that abortion disparaged motherhood and that feminism threatened their traditional roles. Beginning in 1977, abortion foes pressured Congress to restrict the right to abortion by prohibiting coverage under Medicaid and other government-financed health programs, and the Supreme Court allowed states to impose additional obstacles.

Despite resistance, feminists won other lasting gains. Title IX of the Education Amendments Act of 1972 banned sex discrimination in all aspects of education, such as admissions, athletics, and hiring. Congress also outlawed sex discrimination in credit in 1974, opened U.S. military academies to women in 1976, and prohibited discrimination against pregnant workers in 1978. Moreover, the Supreme Court struck down laws that treated men and women differently in Social Security, welfare and military benefits, and workers' compensation.

> CHRONOLOGY

1963
- President's Commission on the Status of Women issues report.
- Equal Pay Act makes it illegal to pay women less than men for the same work.

1966
- National Organization for Women (NOW) is founded.

1972
- Title IX bans sex discrimination in education.

1973
- Supreme Court rules in favor of abortion rights for women in *Roe v. Wade*.

Roe v. Wade
▶ 1973 Supreme Court ruling that the Constitution protects the right to abortion, which states cannot prohibit in the early stages of pregnancy. The decision galvanized social conservatives and made abortion a controversial policy issue for decades to come.

What other rights movements emerged in the 1960s?

What were the goals of the new wave of feminism?

How did liberalism fare under President Nixon?

Conclusion: What were the achievements and limitations of liberalism?

✓ LearningCurve
Check what you know.
bedfordstmartins.com
/roarkunderstanding

859

At the state and local levels, women saw reforms in areas that radical feminists had first introduced. They won laws forcing police departments and the legal system to treat rape victims more justly and humanely. Activists also pushed domestic violence onto the public agenda, obtaining government financing for shelters for battered women as well as laws ensuring both greater protection for victims of domestic violence and more effective prosecution of abusers.

> **QUICK REVIEW**

What were the key goals of feminist reformers, and why did a countermovement arise to resist them?

CHAPTER LOCATOR | What liberal reforms were advanced during the Kennedy and Johnson administrations? | How did the civil rights movement evolve in the 1960s?

CHAPTER 28
860   REFORM, REBELLION, AND REACTION

How did liberalism fare under President Nixon?

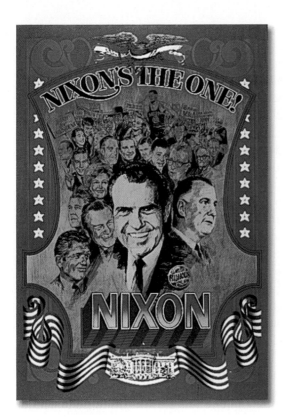

Poster for Nixon's 1968 Campaign

Seeking the presidency in 1968 — a turbulent year for protests, riots, and assassinations — Richard Nixon tried to appeal to a broad spectrum of voters, reflected in this campaign poster. While his slogan "Champion of the Forgotten America" spoke to white Americans alienated by the Great Society's programs for minorities and the poor, the appearance on the poster of the black Republican senator Edward Brooke and basketball player Wilt Chamberlain of the Los Angeles Lakers gave a nod to African Americans. Collection of Janice L. and David J. Frent.

OPPOSITION TO CIVIL RIGHTS MEASURES, Great Society reforms, and protest groups—along with frustrations over the war in Vietnam (as discussed in chapter 29)—delivered the White House to Republican Richard M. Nixon in 1968. Nixon attacked the Great Society for "pouring billions of dollars into programs that have failed" and promised to represent the "forgotten Americans, the non-shouters, the non-demonstrators." Yet his administration either promoted or accepted important elements of the liberal reform agenda, such as greater federal assistance to the poor and environmental reforms.

Extending the Welfare State and Regulating the Economy

A number of factors shaped the liberal policies of the Nixon administration. Democrats continued to control Congress, the Republican Party contained significant numbers of liberals and moderates, and Nixon saw political advantages in accepting some liberal programs. Serious economic problems also compelled new approaches, and although Nixon's real passion lay in foreign policy, he was eager to establish a domestic legacy.

| What other rights movements emerged in the 1960s? | What were the goals of the new wave of feminism? | **How did liberalism fare under President Nixon?** | Conclusion: What were the achievements and limitations of liberalism? | ✓ LearningCurve Check what you know. bedfordstmartins.com /roarkunderstanding |

861

Under Nixon, government assistance programs such as Social Security, housing, and food stamps grew, and Congress enacted a new billion-dollar program that provided Pell grants for low-income students to attend college. Noting the disparity between what Nixon said and what he did, his speechwriter, the arch-conservative Pat Buchanan, grumbled, "Vigorously did we inveigh against the Great Society, enthusiastically did we fund it."

Nixon also acted contrary to his antigovernment rhetoric when economic crises and energy shortages induced him to increase the federal government's power in the marketplace. By 1970, both inflation and unemployment had surpassed 6 percent, an unprecedented combination dubbed "stagflation." Domestic troubles were compounded by the decline of American dominance in the international economy. In 1971, for the first time in decades, the United States imported more than it exported. Because the amount of dollars in foreign hands exceeded U.S. gold reserves, the nation could no longer back up its currency with gold.

In 1971, Nixon abandoned the convertibility of dollars into gold and devalued the dollar to increase exports. To protect domestic manufacturers, he imposed a 10 percent surcharge on most imports, and he froze wages and prices, thus enabling the government to stimulate the economy without fueling inflation. In the short run, these policies worked, and Nixon was resoundingly reelected in 1972. Yet by 1974, unemployment had crept back up and inflation soared.

Skyrocketing energy prices intensified stagflation. Throughout the post–World War II economic boom, abundant domestic oil deposits and access to cheap Middle Eastern oil had encouraged the building of large cars and skyscrapers with no concern for fuel efficiency. By the 1970s, the United States was consuming one-third of the world's fuel resources.

In the fall of 1973, the United States faced its first energy crisis. Arab nations, furious at the administration's support of Israel during the Yom Kippur War (as discussed in chapter 29), cut off oil shipments to the United States. Long lines formed at gas stations, where prices had nearly doubled, and many homes were cold. In response, Nixon authorized temporary emergency measures allocating petroleum and establishing a national 55-mile-per-hour speed limit to save gasoline. The energy crisis eased, but the nation had yet to come to grips with its seemingly unquenchable demand for fuel and dependence on foreign oil.

Responding to Environmental Concerns

The oil crisis dovetailed with a rising environmental movement, which was pushing the government to conserve energy and protect nature and human beings from the hazards of rapid economic growth. Like the conservation movement born in the Progressive Era (see chapter 21), the new environmentalists sought to preserve natural areas for recreational and aesthetic purposes and to conserve natural resources for future use. Especially in the West, the post–World War II explosion of economic growth and mushrooming population, with the resulting demands for electricity and water, made such efforts seem even more critical.

The new environmentalists, however, went beyond conservationism to attack the ravaging effects of industrial development and technological advances on human life and health. Biologist Rachel Carson drew national attention in 1962 with her best seller *Silent Spring*, which described the harmful effects of toxic

CHAPTER LOCATOR | What liberal reforms were advanced during the Kennedy and Johnson administrations? | How did the civil rights movement evolve in the 1960s?

CHAPTER 28
862 REFORM, REBELLION, AND REACTION

Earth Day in the Nation's Capital

Democratic senator Gaylord Nelson of Wisconsin suggested the idea of Earth Day "to shake up the political establishment and force this issue [environmentalism] onto the national agenda." As a result, on April 22, 1970, some twenty million people participated in grassroots demonstrations all over the country. This banner displayed on the Mall in Washington, D.C., focused on clean air. Other activists dramatized oil spills, toxic dumps, pesticides, polluted rivers and lakes, the loss of wilderness, and the extinction of wildlife. Dennis Brack/Black Star/Stockphoto.com.

chemicals such as the pesticide DDT. The Sierra Club and other older conservation organizations expanded their agendas, and a host of new groups arose. Millions of Americans expressed environmental concerns on the first observation of Earth Day in April 1970.

Responding to these concerns, Nixon called "clean air, clean water, open spaces . . . the birthright of every American" and urged Congress to "end the plunder of America's natural heritage." In 1970, he created the **Environmental Protection Agency (EPA)** to enforce environmental laws, conduct research, and reduce environmental and human health risks from pollutants. He also signed the Occupational Safety and Health Act, protecting workers against job-related accidents and disease, and the Clean Air Act of 1970, restricting factory and automobile emissions of carbon dioxide and other pollutants. Environmentalists claimed that Nixon failed to do enough, pointing particularly to his veto of the Clean Water Act of 1972, which Congress overrode. Yet his environmental initiatives surpassed those of previous administrations.

Environmental Protection Agency (EPA)

▶ Federal agency created by President Nixon in 1970 to enforce environmental laws, conduct environmental research, and reduce environmental and human health risks from pollutants.

Expanding Social Justice

Nixon's 1968 campaign had appealed to southern Democrats and white workers by exploiting hostility to black protest and new civil rights policies, but his administration had to answer to the courts and to Congress. In 1968, fourteen years

What other rights movements emerged in the 1960s?

What were the goals of the new wave of feminism?

How did liberalism fare under President Nixon?

Conclusion: What were the achievements and limitations of liberalism?

✓ LearningCurve
Check what you know.
bedfordstmartins.com
/roarkunderstanding

863

after the *Brown* decision, school desegregation had barely touched the South. Like Eisenhower, Nixon was reluctant to use federal power to compel integration, but the Supreme Court overruled the administration's efforts to delay court-ordered desegregation. By the time Nixon left office, fewer than one in ten southern black children attended totally segregated schools.

Nixon also began to implement affirmative action among federal contractors and unions, and his administration awarded more government contracts and loans to minority businesses. Congress took the initiative in other areas. In 1970, it extended the Voting Rights Act of 1965, and in 1972 it strengthened the Civil Rights Act of 1964 by enlarging the powers of the Equal Employment Opportunity Commission. In 1971, Congress also responded to the massive youth movement with the Twenty-sixth Amendment to the Constitution, which reduced the voting age to eighteen.

Several measures of the Nixon administration also specifically attacked sex discrimination, as the president confronted a growing feminist movement that included Republican feminists. Nixon vetoed a comprehensive child care bill and publicly opposed abortion, but he signed the pathbreaking Title IX, guaranteeing equality in all aspects of education, and allowed his Labor Department to push affirmative action.

President Nixon gave more public support for justice to Native Americans than to any other protest group. While not bowing to radical demands, the administration dealt cautiously with extreme protests. Nixon signed measures recognizing claims of Alaskan and New Mexican Indians and set in motion legislation restoring tribal lands and granting Indians more control over their schools and other service institutions.

> **QUICK REVIEW**

Why and how did Republican president Richard Nixon expand the liberal reforms of previous administrations?

CHAPTER LOCATOR | What liberal reforms were advanced during the Kennedy and Johnson administrations? | How did the civil rights movement evolve in the 1960s?

864 CHAPTER 28 REFORM, REBELLION, AND REACTION

SENATE MAJORITY LEADER Mike Mansfield was not alone in concluding that Lyndon Johnson "has done more than FDR ever did, or ever thought of doing." Building on initiatives from John F. Kennedy's New Frontier, the Great Society expanded the New Deal's focus on economic security, refashioning liberalism to embrace individual rights and to extend material well-being to groups left out of or discriminated against in New Deal programs. Yet opposition to Johnson's leadership grew so strong that by 1968 his liberal vision lay in ruins. "How," he asked, "was it possible that all these people could be so ungrateful to me after I have given them so much?"

African Americans could have responded by pointing out how slowly the government acted when efforts to win black rights met with violence. In addition, failed attempts to use Johnson's antipoverty programs to help poor blacks in the South reflected, in part, some of the more general shortcomings of the War on Poverty. Hastily planned and inadequately funded, antipoverty programs focused more on remediating individual shortcomings than on reforms that would ensure adequately paying jobs for all. Because Johnson launched an all-out war in Vietnam and refused to ask for sacrifices from prosperous Americans, the Great Society never commanded the resources necessary for victory over poverty.

Furthermore, black aspirations exceeded white Americans' commitment to genuine equality. When the civil rights movement attacked racial barriers long entrenched throughout the nation and sought equality in fact as well as in law, it faced a powerful backlash. By the end of the 1960s, the revolution in the legal status of African Americans was complete, but the black freedom struggle had lost momentum, and African Americans remained, with Native Americans and Chicanos, at the bottom of the economic ladder.

Johnson's critics overlooked the Great Society's more successful and lasting elements. Medicare and Medicaid continue to provide access to health care for the elderly and the poor. Federal aid for education and housing became permanent elements of national policy. Moreover, Richard Nixon's otherwise conservative administration implemented school desegregation in the South and affirmative action, initiated environmental reforms, and secured new rights for Native Americans and women. Women benefited from the decline of discrimination, and significant numbers of African Americans and other minority groups began to enter the middle class.

Yet the perceived shortcomings of government programs contributed to social turmoil and fueled the resurgence of conservative politics. Young radicals launched direct confrontations with the government and universities that, together with racial conflict, escalated into political discord and social disorder. The Vietnam War polarized American society as much as did domestic change; it devoured resources that might have been used for social reform and undermined faith in presidential leadership.

| What other rights movements emerged in the 1960s? | What were the goals of the new wave of feminism? | How did liberalism fare under President Nixon? | **Conclusion: What were the achievements and limitations of liberalism?** | ✔ **LearningCurve** Check what you know. bedfordstmartins.com /roarkunderstanding |

865

CHAPTER 28 STUDY GUIDE

STEP 1

GET STARTED ONLINE

LearningCurve ■ bedfordstmartins.com/roarkunderstanding

Now that you've read the chapter, make it stick by completing the LearningCurve activity.

STEP 2

EXPLAIN WHY IT MATTERS

Put your reading into practice. Identify each term below, and then explain why it matters in U.S. history.

TERM	WHO OR WHAT & WHEN	WHY IT MATTERS
Civil Rights Act of 1964 (p. 838)		
War on Poverty (p. 840)		
Medicare and Medicaid (p. 840)		
Voting Rights Act of 1965 (p. 840)		
Immigration and Nationality Act of 1965 (p. 840)		
Warren Court (p. 842)		
black power movement (p. 850)		
American Indian Movement (AIM) (p. 852)		
Chicano movement (p. 853)		
National Organization for Women (NOW) (p. 858)		
Roe v. Wade (p. 859)		
Environmental Protection Agency (EPA) (p. 863)		

STEP 3

MOVE BEYOND THE BASICS

To demonstrate a more advanced understanding, describe the goals, strategies and tactics, and achievements of the major rights movements of the 1960s. Make sure to include a description of any divisions within the movements.

Rights movement	Goals	Strategies and tactics	Achievements
African Americans			
Latinos			
Native Americans			
Students			
Feminists			
Gays and lesbians			
Environmentalists			

PUT IT ALL TOGETHER

Now, take a step back and try to explain the big picture. Remember to use specific examples from the chapter in your answers.

LYNDON JOHNSON AND THE GREAT SOCIETY

▶ What were the most important domestic achievements of the Johnson administration? What were its most important failures?

▶ What assumptions about the relationship between government and society underlay Johnson's Great Society programs?

PROTEST AND REBELLION

▶ What role did students play in the civil rights struggles of the 1960s? How did the civil rights movement change toward the end of the decade?

▶ What were the key achievements of 1960s feminism? What goals did it fail to fulfill?

LIBERAL REFORM IN THE NIXON ADMINISTRATION

▶ What liberal initiatives did the Nixon administration embrace, and what explains these actions?

▶ Should Richard Nixon be considered an environmentalist? Why or why not?

LOOKING BACKWARD, LOOKING AHEAD

▶ How did the African American civil rights movement of the 1960s differ from the movement of the 1950s?

▶ What kinds of opposition emerged in the late 1960s to liberal reforms and radical protest? How might that trend influence politics in the decades after the 1960s?

> ## IN YOUR OWN WORDS

Imagine that you must give an oral report to the class answering the following question: **How did protest movements change policies and society in the 1960s and 1970s?** What would be the most important points to include and why?

 Do it online at the Student Site ■ bedfordstmartins.com/roarkunderstanding

29

VIETNAM AND THE END OF THE COLD WAR CONSENSUS

1961–1975

> Why was the United States unable to achieve its objectives in Vietnam? Chapter 29 explores U.S. foreign policy from 1961 to 1975, placing the Vietnam War in the larger context of American politics and relations with the Soviet Union, China, and developing nations. It examines the escalation of U.S. involvement in Vietnam under Presidents John F. Kennedy and Lyndon B. Johnson, the polarizing effect of the war on American society and politics, and the gradual American withdrawal from Vietnam under President Richard M. Nixon.

LearningCurve

bedfordstmartins.com/roarkunderstanding

After reading the chapter, use LearningCurve to retain what you've read.

> How did U.S. foreign policy change under Kennedy?

> Why did Johnson escalate American involvement in Vietnam?

> How did the war in Vietnam polarize the nation?

> How did U.S. foreign policy change under Nixon?

> Conclusion: Was Vietnam an unwinnable war?

Marines patrol near the DMZ. U.S. Marines patrol near the demilitarized zone in Vietnam during Operation Prairie, 1966. Larry Burrows.

How did U.S. foreign policy change under Kennedy?

Preparing for the Worst during the Cuban Missile Crisis Waiting out the tense days after President Kennedy issued the ultimatum to the Soviet Union to halt shipments of missile materials to Cuba, many Americans tried to prepare for the worst possible outcome. Owners of Chalet Suzanne, a hotel in Lake Wales, Florida, canned several thousand cases of well water, labeled "NASK" for Nuclear Attack Survival Kit. Photo by David Woods.

JOHN F. KENNEDY MOVED quickly to pursue containment more aggressively and with more flexible means than the Eisenhower administration had. Kennedy declared that the United States would "pay any price, bear any burden, meet any hardship, support any friend, oppose any foe to assure the survival and the success of liberty."

> ## Key Elements of Kennedy's Foreign Policy

- Expansion of the United States' ability to fight conventional battles and engage in guerrilla warfare
- Acceleration of the nation's space exploration program
- Increased attention to the third world
- Escalation of the nuclear arms race
- Commitment of U.S. arms and personnel to South Vietnam

Meeting the "Hour of Maximum Danger"

Underlying Kennedy's foreign policy was an assumption that the United States had "gone soft—physically, mentally, spiritually soft," as he put it in 1960. Calling the Eisenhower era "years of drift and impotency," Kennedy warned in his inaugural

CHAPTER LOCATOR | How did U.S. foreign policy change under Kennedy?

870 CHAPTER 29
VIETNAM AND THE END OF THE COLD WAR CONSENSUS

address that the nation faced a grave peril: "Each day the crises multiply. . . . Each day we draw nearer the hour of maximum danger."

Although the president exaggerated the threat to national security, several developments in 1961 heightened the sense of crisis and provided a rationalization for his military buildup. Shortly before Kennedy's inauguration, Soviet leader Nikita Khrushchev publicly encouraged "wars of national liberation," thereby aligning the Soviet Union with independence movements in the third world that were often anti-Western. His statement reflected in part the Soviet competition with China for the allegiance of emerging nations, but U.S. officials saw it as a threat to the status quo of containment.

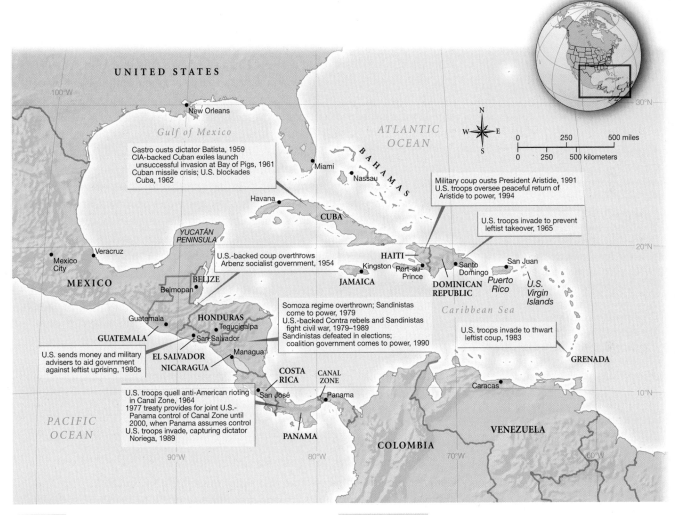

MAP 29.1 ■ U.S. Involvement in Latin America and the Caribbean, 1954–1994

During the Cold War, the United States frequently intervened in Central American and Caribbean countries to suppress Communist or leftist movements.

> **MAP ACTIVITY**

READING THE MAP: How many and which Latin American countries did the United States invade directly? What was the extent of indirect U.S. involvement in other upheavals in the region?

CONNECTIONS: What role, if any, did geographic proximity play in U.S. policy toward the region? What was the significance of the Cuban missile crisis for U.S. foreign policy?

| Why did Johnson escalate American involvement in Vietnam? | How did the war in Vietnam polarize the nation? | How did U.S. foreign policy change under Nixon? | Conclusion: Was Vietnam an unwinnable war? | ✓ LearningCurve Check what you know. bedfordstmartins.com /roarkunderstanding |

> CHRONOLOGY

1961
- Bay of Pigs invasion.
- Berlin Wall is erected.
- Kennedy increases military aid to South Vietnam.
- Peace Corps is created.

1962
- Cuban missile crisis.

1963
- President Kennedy is assassinated; Lyndon B. Johnson becomes president.

1969
- American astronauts land on the moon.

Bay of Pigs

▶ Failed U.S.-sponsored invasion of Cuba in 1961 by anti-Castro forces who planned to overthrow Fidel Castro's government. The disaster humiliated Kennedy and the United States. It alienated Latin Americans who saw the invasion as another example of Yankee imperialism.

Apollo program

▶ Project initiated by John F. Kennedy in 1961 to surpass the Soviet Union in space exploration and send a man to the moon.

Berlin Wall

▶ Structure erected by East Germany in 1961 to stop the massive exodus of East Germans into West Berlin, which was an embarrassment to the Communists.

Peace Corps

▶ Program launched by President Kennedy in 1961 through which young American volunteers helped with education, health, and other projects in developing countries around the world. More than 60,000 volunteers had served by the mid-1970s.

Cuba, just ninety miles off the Florida coast, posed the first crisis for Kennedy. The revolution led by Fidel Castro had moved Cuba into the Soviet orbit, and Eisenhower's Central Intelligence Agency (CIA) had been planning an invasion of the island by Cuban exiles living in Florida. Kennedy ordered the invasion to proceed even though his military advisers gave it only a fair chance of success.

On April 17, 1961, about 1,400 anti-Castro exiles trained and armed by the CIA landed at the **Bay of Pigs** on the south shore of Cuba (**Map 29.1**). Contrary to U.S. expectations, no popular uprising materialized to support the anti-Castro brigade. Kennedy refused to provide direct military support, and the invaders quickly fell to Castro's forces. The disaster humiliated Kennedy and the United States, posing a stark contrast to the president's inaugural promise of a new, more effective foreign policy. And it alienated Latin Americans who saw it as another example of Yankee imperialism.

Days before the Bay of Pigs invasion, the Soviet Union delivered a psychological blow when a Soviet astronaut became the first human to orbit the earth. Kennedy then called for a huge new commitment to the space program, with the goal of sending a man to the moon by 1970. Congress authorized the **Apollo program** and boosted appropriations for space exploration. John H. Glenn orbited the earth in 1962, and the United States beat the Soviets to the moon, landing two astronauts there in 1969.

Kennedy determined to show American toughness to Khrushchev, but when the two met in June 1961 in Vienna, Austria, Khrushchev took the offensive. The stunned Kennedy reported privately, "He just beat [the] hell out of me. . . . If he thinks I'm inexperienced and have no guts . . . we won't get anywhere with him." Khrushchev demanded an agreement recognizing the existence of two Germanys, and he threatened America's occupation rights in and access to West Berlin.

Khrushchev was concerned about the massive exodus of East Germans into West Berlin, a major embarrassment for the Communists. To stop this flow, in August 1961 East Germany erected a wall between East and West Berlin. With the **Berlin Wall** stemming the tide of escapees and Kennedy declaring West Berlin "the great testing place of Western courage and will," Khrushchev backed off from his threats.

Kennedy used the Berlin crisis to add $3.2 billion to the defense budget. He increased draft calls, and he also mobilized the reserves and National Guard, adding 300,000 troops to the military. This buildup of conventional forces provided for a "flexible response," offering "a wider choice than humiliation or all-out nuclear action."

New Approaches to the Third World

Complementing Kennedy's hard-line policy toward the Soviet Union were fresh approaches to the nationalist movements that had multiplied since the end of World War II. In 1960 alone, seventeen African nations gained their independence. Kennedy publicly supported third world aspirations, believing that the United States could win the hearts and minds of people in developing nations by helping to fulfill hopes for autonomy and democracy.

Kennedy launched his most dramatic third world initiative in 1961 with an idea borrowed from Senator Hubert H. Humphrey: the **Peace Corps**. The program recruited young people to work in developing countries, attracting many who had been moved by Kennedy's appeal for idealism and sacrifice in his inaugural

CHAPTER LOCATOR | How did U.S. foreign policy change under Kennedy?

address. Peace Corps volunteers worked directly with local people, opening schools, providing basic health care, and assisting with agriculture and small economic enterprises. By the mid-1970s, more than 60,000 volunteers had served in Latin America, Africa, and Asia. Peace Corps projects were generally welcomed, but they did not address the receiving countries' larger economic and political structures.

Kennedy also used direct military means to bring political stability to the third world. He rapidly expanded the elite special forces corps established under Eisenhower to aid groups fighting against Communist-leaning movements. These counterinsurgency forces, including the army's Green Berets and the navy's SEALs, were trained to wage guerrilla warfare and equipped with the latest technology. They would get their first test in Vietnam.

The Arms Race and the Nuclear Brink

The final piece of Kennedy's foreign policy was to strengthen American nuclear dominance. He increased the number of nuclear weapons based in Europe from 2,500 to 7,200 and multiplied fivefold the supply of intercontinental ballistic missiles (ICBMs). Concerned that this buildup would enable the United States to launch a first strike and wipe out Soviet missile sites before they could respond, the Soviet Union stepped up its own ICBM program. Thus began the most intense arms race in history.

The superpowers came perilously close to using their weapons during the **Cuban missile crisis** in 1962. Khrushchev decided to install nuclear missiles in Cuba to protect Castro's regime from further U.S. attempts at intervention and to balance the U.S. missiles aimed at the Soviet Union from Europe. On October 22, after the CIA showed Kennedy aerial photographs of missile launching sites under construction in Cuba, Kennedy announced that the military was on full alert and that the navy would turn back any Soviet vessel suspected of carrying offensive missiles to Cuba. He warned that any attack launched from Cuba would trigger a full nuclear assault against the Soviet Union.

With the superpowers on the brink of nuclear war, both Kennedy and Khrushchev also exercised caution. Kennedy refused advice from the military to bomb the missile sites. On October 24, Russian ships carrying nuclear warheads toward Cuba suddenly turned back. When one ship crossed the blockade line, Kennedy ordered the navy to follow the ship rather than attempt to stop it.

While Americans experienced the Cold War's most dangerous days, Kennedy and Khrushchev negotiated an agreement. The Soviets removed the missiles and pledged not to introduce new offensive weapons into Cuba. The United States promised not to invade the island. Secretly, Kennedy also agreed to remove U.S. missiles from Turkey. The Cuban crisis contributed to Khrushchev's fall from power two years later, while Kennedy emerged triumphant. The image of an inexperienced president fumbling the Bay of Pigs invasion gave way to that of a strong leader.

Having proved his toughness, Kennedy worked to ease superpower hostilities. In a major speech in June 1963, Kennedy called for a reexamination of Cold War assumptions, asking Americans "not to see conflict as inevitable." Acknowledging the superpowers' differences, Kennedy stressed what they had in common: "We all breathe the same air. We all cherish our children's future and we are all mortal."

Cuban missile crisis

▶ 1962 nuclear standoff between the Soviet Union and the United States when the Soviets attempted to deploy nuclear missiles in Cuba. In a negotiated settlement, the Soviet Union agreed to remove its missiles from Cuba, and the United States agreed to remove its missiles from Turkey.

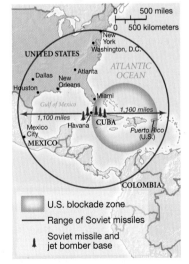

Cuban Missile Crisis, 1962

| Why did Johnson escalate American involvement in Vietnam? | How did the war in Vietnam polarize the nation? | How did U.S. foreign policy change under Nixon? | Conclusion: Was Vietnam an unwinnable war? | ✓ **LearningCurve** Check what you know. bedfordstmartins.com /roarkunderstanding |

In August 1963, the United States, the Soviet Union, and Great Britain signed a limited nuclear test ban treaty, reducing the threat of radioactive fallout from nuclear testing and raising hopes for further superpower accord.

A Growing War in Vietnam

In 1963, Kennedy criticized the idea of "a Pax Americana enforced on the world by American weapons of war," but he had already increased the flow of those weapons into South Vietnam. Kennedy's strong anticommunism and attachment to a vigorous foreign policy prepared him to expand the commitment that he had inherited from Eisenhower.

By the time Kennedy took office, more than $1 billion in aid and seven hundred U.S. military advisers had failed to stabilize South Vietnam. Two major obstacles stood in the way. First, the South Vietnamese insurgents—whom Americans called Vietcong—were an indigenous force whose initiative came from within. Because the Saigon government refused to hold elections, the rebels saw no choice but to take up arms. Increasingly, Ho Chi Minh's Communist government in North Vietnam supplied them with weapons and soldiers.

Second, the South Vietnamese government refused to satisfy insurgents' demands, but the Army of the Republic of Vietnam (ARVN) could not defeat them militarily. Ngo Dinh Diem, South Vietnam's premier from 1954 to 1963, chose self-serving military leaders for their personal loyalty rather than for their effectiveness. Many South Vietnamese, the majority of whom were Buddhists, saw the Catholic Diem as a corrupt and brutal tool of the West. The growing intervention by North Vietnam made matters worse. In 1960, the Hanoi government established the National Liberation Front, composed of South Vietnamese rebels but directed by the northern army. In addition, Hanoi constructed a network of infiltration routes, called the Ho Chi Minh Trail, in neighboring Laos and Cambodia, through which it sent people and supplies to help liberate the

MAP 29.2 ■ The Vietnam War, 1964–1975

The United States sent 2.6 million soldiers to Vietnam and spent more than $150 billion on the longest war in American history, but it was unable to prevent the unification of Vietnam under a Communist government.

> **MAP ACTIVITY**

READING THE MAP: What accords divided Vietnam into two nations? When were these accords signed, and where was the line of division drawn? Through what countries did the Ho Chi Minh Trail go?

CONNECTIONS: What was the Gulf of Tonkin incident, and how did the United States respond? What was the Tet Offensive, and how did it affect the war?

South (**Map 29.2**). Violence escalated between 1960 and 1963, bringing the Saigon government close to collapse.

In response, Kennedy gradually escalated the U.S. commitment. By the spring of 1963, military aid had doubled, and 9,000 Americans served in Vietnam as military advisers, occasionally participating in actual combat. The South Vietnamese government promised reform but never made good on its promises.

American officials assumed that technology and sheer power could win in Vietnam. Yet advanced weapons were ill suited to the guerrilla warfare practiced by the enemy, whose surprise attacks were designed to weaken support for the South Vietnamese government. Moreover, U.S. weapons and strategy harmed the very people they were intended to save. Thousands of peasants were uprooted or fell victim to bombs—containing the highly flammable substance napalm—dropped by the South Vietnamese air force to quell the Vietcong. In 1962, U.S. planes began to spray herbicides such as **Agent Orange** to destroy the Vietcong's jungle hideouts and food supply.

With tacit permission from Washington, South Vietnamese military leaders executed a coup against Diem and his brother, who headed the secret police, in November 1963. Kennedy expressed shock at the murders but indicated no change in policy. In a speech to be given on the day he was assassinated, Kennedy referred specifically to Southeast Asia and warned, "We dare not weary of the task." At his death, 16,700 Americans were stationed in Vietnam, and 100 had died there.

Agent Orange

▶ Herbicide used extensively during the Vietnam War to destroy the Vietcong's jungle hideouts and food supply. Its use was later linked to a wide range of illnesses that veterans and the Vietnamese suffered after the war, including birth defects, cancer, and skin disorders.

QUICK REVIEW

Why did Kennedy believe that engagement in Vietnam was crucial to his foreign policy?

| Why did Johnson escalate American involvement in Vietnam? | How did the war in Vietnam polarize the nation? | How did U.S. foreign policy change under Nixon? | Conclusion: Was Vietnam an unwinnable war? | ✓ **LearningCurve** Check what you know. bedfordstmartins.com /roarkunderstanding |

Why did Johnson escalate American involvement in Vietnam?

U.S. Military Helicopter

The particular conditions in Vietnam — the guerrilla tactics of the enemy, the conduct of fighting all over South Vietnam, and the mountains and dense jungles with limited landing areas — put a premium on helicopters' mobility and maneuverability. In addition to transporting troops and artillery, performing reconnaissance, picking up downed pilots, and evacuating the dead and wounded, helicopters mounted with machine guns and grenade launchers also served as attack vehicles. © Bettmann/Corbis.

LYNDON B. JOHNSON SHARED the Cold War assumptions that had shaped Kennedy's foreign policy. Retaining Kennedy's key advisers—Secretary of State Dean Rusk, Secretary of Defense Robert McNamara, and National Security Adviser McGeorge Bundy—Johnson continued the massive buildup of nuclear weapons as well as conventional and counterinsurgency forces. In 1965, he made the fateful decisions to order U.S. troops into combat in Vietnam and to initiate sustained bombing of the North. That same year, Johnson sent U.S. Marines to the Dominican Republic to crush a leftist rebellion.

An All-Out Commitment in Vietnam

The president who wanted to make his mark on domestic policy was compelled to deal with the commitments his predecessors had made in Vietnam. Some advisers, politicians, and international leaders questioned the wisdom of greater intervention there, viewing the situation as a civil war rather than Communist aggression. Most U.S. allies did not consider Vietnam crucial to containing communism and were not prepared to share the military burden. Senate majority leader Mike Mansfield wondered whether Vietnam could be won with a "limited expenditure

CHAPTER LOCATOR | How did U.S. foreign policy change under Kennedy?

of American lives and resources somewhere commensurate with our national interests." Disregarding the opportunity for disengagement that these critics saw in 1964, Johnson expressed his own doubt privately: "I don't think it's worth fighting for and I don't think we can get out."

Like Kennedy, Johnson remembered how Harry Truman had suffered politically when the Communists took over China. Along with most of his advisers, Johnson believed that American credibility was on the line, and he believed that conceding defeat in Vietnam would undermine his ability to achieve his Great Society.

Johnson understood the ineffectiveness of his South Vietnamese allies and agonized over sending young men into combat. Yet he continued to dispatch more military advisers, weapons, and economic aid and, in August 1964, seized an opportunity to increase the pressure on North Vietnam. While spying in the Gulf of Tonkin, off the coast of North Vietnam, two U.S. destroyers reported that North Vietnamese gunboats had fired on them (see Map 29.2). Johnson quickly ordered air strikes on North Vietnamese torpedo bases and oil storage facilities. Concealing the uncertainty about whether the second attack had even occurred, he won from Congress the **Gulf of Tonkin Resolution**, authorizing him to take "all necessary measures to repel any armed attacks against the forces of the United States and to prevent further aggression."

Soon after winning the election of 1964, Johnson widened the war. He rejected peace overtures from North Vietnam, which insisted on American withdrawal and a coalition government in South Vietnam as steps toward unification of the country. In February 1965, Johnson authorized Operation Rolling Thunder, a strategy of gradually intensified bombing of North Vietnam. Less than a month later, Johnson ordered the first U.S. combat troops to South Vietnam, and in July he shifted U.S. troops from defensive to offensive operations, dispatching 50,000 more soldiers (**Figure 29.1**). Although the administration downplayed the import of these decisions, they marked a critical turning point. Now it was genuinely America's war.

> CHRONOLOGY

1964
– Gulf of Tonkin Resolution.

1965
– Operation Rolling Thunder begins.
– First combat troops are sent to Vietnam.
– U.S. troops invade the Dominican Republic.

Gulf of Tonkin Resolution

▶ Resolution passed by Congress in 1964 in the wake of a naval confrontation in the Gulf of Tonkin. It gave the president virtually unlimited authority in conducting the Vietnam War. The Senate terminated the resolution following outrage over the U.S. invasion of Cambodia in 1970.

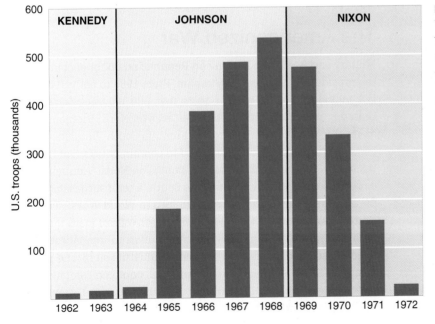

FIGURE 29.1 ■ U.S. Troops in Vietnam, 1962–1972

The steepest increases in the American military presence in Vietnam came with Johnson's escalation of the war in 1965 and 1966. Although Nixon reduced troop levels significantly in 1971 and 1972, the United States continued massive bombing attacks.

| Why did Johnson escalate American involvement in Vietnam? | How did the war in Vietnam polarize the nation? | How did U.S. foreign policy change under Nixon? | Conclusion: Was Vietnam an unwinnable war? | ✓ LearningCurve Check what you know. bedfordstmartins.com /roarkunderstanding |

Preventing Another Castro in Latin America

Closer to home, Johnson faced persistent problems in Latin America. Thirteen times during the 1960s, military coups toppled Latin American governments, and local insurgencies grew apace. The administration's response varied from case to case but centered on the determination to prevent any more Castro-type revolutions.

In 1964, riots erupted in the Panama Canal Zone, instigated by Panamanians who viewed the United States as a colonial power, since it had seized the land and made it a U.S. territory early in the century (see chapter 21). Johnson sent troops to quell the disturbance, but he also initiated negotiations that eventually returned the canal to Panamanian authority in 2000.

Elsewhere, Johnson's Latin American policy generated new cries of "Yankee imperialism." In 1961, voters in the Dominican Republic ousted a longtime dictator and elected a constitutional government headed by reformist Juan Bosch, who was overthrown by a military coup two years later. In 1965, when Bosch supporters launched an uprising against the military government, Johnson sent more than 20,000 soldiers to suppress what he perceived to be a leftist revolt and to take control of the island.

This first outright show of Yankee force in Latin America in four decades damaged the administration. Although Johnson had justified intervention as necessary to prevent "another Cuba," no Communists were found among the rebels, and U.S. intervention kept the reform-oriented Boschists from returning to power. Moreover, the president had not consulted the Dominicans or the Organization of American States, to which the United States had promised it would respect national sovereignty in Latin America.

U.S. Troops in the Dominican Republic

These U.S. paratroopers were among the 20,000 troops sent to the Dominican Republic in April and May 1965. The invasion restored peace but kept the popularly elected government of Juan Bosch from regaining office. Dominicans greeted the U.S. troops with anti-American slogans throughout the capital, Santo Domingo. Bosch himself said, "This was a democratic revolution smashed by the leading democracy in the world." © Bettmann/Corbis.

The Americanized War

Military success in the Dominican Republic no doubt encouraged the president to press on in Vietnam. From 1965 to early 1968, the U.S. military presence grew to more than 500,000 troops as the United States gradually escalated attacks on North Vietnam and on its ally, the National Liberation Front, in South Vietnam.

Even with restrictions imposed to contain criticism of the war, U.S. pilots dropped 643,000 tons of bombs on North Vietnam and more than twice that amount in the South, a total surpassing all the explosives the United States dropped in World War II. The North Vietnamese withstood monthly death tolls of more than 2,000. They applied ingenuity and sheer effort to compensate for the destruction of transportation lines, industrial sites, and power plants. In South Vietnam, the massive U.S. bombing campaign destroyed villages and fields, alienating the very population that the Americans had come to save.

CHAPTER LOCATOR | How did U.S. foreign policy change under Kennedy?

On the ground, General William Westmoreland's strategy of attrition was designed to seek out and kill the Vietcong and North Vietnamese regular army. With no fixed battlefront, helicopters carried troops to conduct offensives all over South Vietnam, and officials calculated progress not in territory seized but in "body counts" and "kill ratios"—the number of enemies killed relative to the cost in American and ARVN lives. According to Lieutenant Frederick Downs, "To win a battle, we had to kill them. For them to win, all they had to do was survive." The Americans "never owned anything except the ground they stood on."

Those Who Served

Teenagers fought the Vietnam War. In contrast to World War II, in which the average soldier was twenty-six years old, the average age for all soldiers in Vietnam was nineteen. Until the Twenty-sixth Amendment to the Constitution dropped the voting age from twenty-one to eighteen in 1971, most soldiers could not even vote for the officials who sent them to war. Men of all classes had fought in World War II,

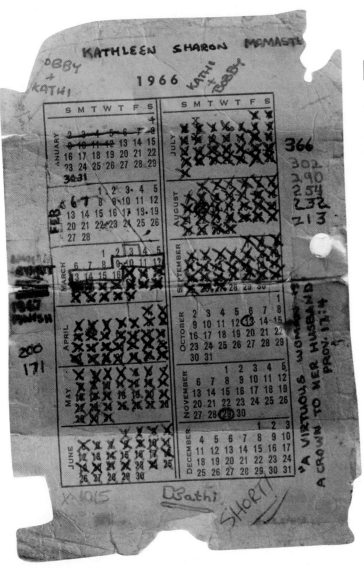

Counting the Days in Vietnam

Unlike previous wars, most soldiers served tours of duty in Vietnam lasting just one year. The soldier who carried this calendar expressed an obsession with time "in country" that many of his comrades shared. Soldiers considered themselves "short" when they had fewer than 100 days left. Bobby McMaster was thinking either of his wife or of the woman he would marry when, and if, he returned home. What might his inscription of the Bible verse on the right side of the calendar suggest about his feelings about the woman he left behind? © Bettmann/Corbis.

| Why did Johnson escalate American involvement in Vietnam? | How did the war in Vietnam polarize the nation? | How did U.S. foreign policy change under Nixon? | Conclusion: Was Vietnam an unwinnable war? | ☑ LearningCurve Check what you know. bedfordstmartins.com /roarkunderstanding |

879

but in Vietnam the poor and working class constituted about 80 percent of the troops. More privileged youths avoided the draft by using college deferments or family connections to get into the National Guard. Sent from Plainville, Kansas, to Vietnam in 1965, Mike Clodfelter could not recall "a single middle-class son of the town's businessmen, lawyers, doctors, or ranchers from my high school graduating class who experienced the Armageddon of our generation."

Much more than World War II, Vietnam was a men's war. Because the United States did not undergo full mobilization for Vietnam, officials did not seek women's sacrifices for the war effort. Still, between 7,500 and 10,000 women served in Vietnam, the vast majority of them nurses. Early in the war, African Americans constituted 31 percent of combat troops, often choosing the military over the meager opportunities in the civilian economy. Special forces ranger Arthur E. Woodley Jr. recalled, "The only way I could possibly make it out of the ghetto was to be the best soldier I possibly could." Death rates among black soldiers were disproportionately high until 1966, when the military adjusted personnel assignments to achieve a better racial balance.

The young troops faced extremely difficult conditions. Platoons fought in thick jungles filled with leeches, in rain and oppressive heat, always vulnerable to sniper bullets and land mines. Soldiers in previous wars had served "for the duration," but in Vietnam a soldier served a one-year tour of duty. A commander called it "the worst personnel policy in history," because men had less incentive to fight near the end of their tours, wanting merely to stay alive and whole.

American soldiers inflicted great losses on the enemy, yet the war remained a stalemate. The South Vietnamese government was an enormous obstacle to victory, as graft and corruption continued to flourish. In the intensified fighting and with the inability to distinguish friend from foe, ARVN and American troops killed and wounded thousands of South Vietnamese civilians and destroyed their villages. By 1968, nearly 30 percent of the population had become refugees. The failure to stabilize South Vietnam even as the U.S. military presence expanded enormously created grave challenges for the administration at home.

> **QUICK REVIEW**

Why did massive amounts of airpower and ground troops fail to bring U.S. victory in Vietnam?

How did the war in Vietnam polarize the nation?

Mothers against the War

Founded in 1961 to work for nuclear disarmament, Women Strike for Peace (WSP) began to protest the Vietnam War in 1963. Identifying themselves as "concerned housewives" and mothers, members mobilized around the slogan "Not Our Sons, Not Your Sons, Not Their Sons." In February 1967, WSP held the first antiwar protest at the Pentagon. More than 2,000 women, some shown here, banged their shoes on Pentagon doors, which were locked as they approached. © Bettmann/Corbis.

SOON PRESIDENT JOHNSON was fighting a war on two fronts, as domestic opposition to the war swelled after 1965. In March 1968, torn between his domestic critics and the military's clamor for more troops, Johnson announced a halt to the bombing, a new effort at negotiations, and his decision not to pursue reelection. Throughout 1968, demonstrations, violence, and assassinations convulsed the increasingly polarized nation. Vietnam took center stage in the election, and voters narrowly favored the Republican candidate, former vice president Richard Nixon, who promised to achieve "peace with honor."

The Widening War at Home

Johnson's authorization of Operation Rolling Thunder expanded the previously quiet doubts and criticism into a mass movement against the war. In April 1965, Students for a Democratic Society (SDS) recruited 20,000 people for the first major antiwar protest in Washington, D.C. Thousands of students protested against Reserve Officers Training Corps (ROTC) programs, CIA and defense industry recruiters, and military research projects on their campuses. Environmentalists attacked the use of chemical weapons, such as the deadly Agent Orange.

| Why did Johnson escalate American involvement in Vietnam? | **How did the war in Vietnam polarize the nation?** | How did U.S. foreign policy change under Nixon? | Conclusion: Was Vietnam an unwinnable war? | ✓ **LearningCurve** Check what you know. bedfordstmartins.com /roarkunderstanding |

881

> CHRONOLOGY

1968
– Demonstrations against Vietnam War increase.
– Tet Offensive.
– Johnson decides not to seek a second term.
– Violence erupts near the Democratic convention in Chicago.
– Richard Nixon is elected president.

Antiwar sentiment entered society's mainstream. By 1968, media critics included the *New York Times*, the *Wall Street Journal*, *Life* magazine, and popular TV anchorman Walter Cronkite. Clergy, business people, scientists, and physicians formed their own groups to pressure Johnson to stop the bombing and start negotiations. Prominent Democratic senators urged Johnson to substitute negotiation for force.

Although the peace movement never claimed a majority of the population, it focused media attention on the war and severely limited the administration's options. The twenty-year-old consensus around Cold War foreign policy had shattered.

Many refused to serve. The World Boxing Association stripped Muhammad Ali of his heavyweight title when he refused to fight in what he called a "white man's war." More than 170,000 men gained conscientious objector status and performed nonmilitary duties at home or in Vietnam. About 60,000 fled the country to escape the draft, and more than 200,000 were accused of failing to register or of committing other draft offenses.

Opponents of the war held diverse views. Those who saw the conflict in moral terms wanted total withdrawal, claiming that their country had no right to interfere in a civil war and stressing the suffering of the Vietnamese people. A larger segment of antiwar sentiment reflected practical considerations — the belief that the war could not be won at a bearable cost. Those activists wanted Johnson to stop bombing North Vietnam and seek negotiations. Working-class people were no more antiwar than other groups, but they recognized the class dimensions of the war and the antiwar movement. A firefighter whose son had died in Vietnam said bitterly, "It's people like us who give up our sons for the country."

The antiwar movement outraged millions of Americans who supported the war. Some members of the generation who had fought against Hitler could not understand younger men's refusal to support their government. They expressed their anger at war protesters with bumper stickers that read "America: Love It or Leave It."

By 1967, the administration realized that "discontent with the war is now wide and deep." President Johnson used various means to silence critics. He equated opposition to the war with communism and assistance to the enemy. His administration deceived the public by making optimistic statements and concealing officials' doubts about the possibility of success in Vietnam. Johnson ordered the CIA to spy on peace advocates, and without the president's specific authorization, the FBI infiltrated the peace movement, disrupted its work, and spread false information about activists.

The Tet Offensive and Johnson's Move toward Peace

The year 1968 was marked by violent confrontations around the world. Protests against governments erupted from Mexico City to Paris to Tokyo, usually led by students in collaboration with workers. American society became increasingly polarized. On one side, the so-called hawks charged that the United States was fighting with one hand tied behind its back and called for intensification of the war. The doves wanted de-escalation or withdrawal. As U.S. troop strength neared half a million and military deaths approached 20,000 by the end of 1967,

CHAPTER LOCATOR | How did U.S. foreign policy change under Kennedy?

CHAPTER 29
882 VIETNAM AND THE END OF THE COLD WAR CONSENSUS

most people were torn between weariness with the war and a desire to fulfill the United States' commitment. As one woman said, "I want to get out but I don't want to give up."

Grave doubts penetrated the administration itself. Secretary of Defense Robert McNamara, a principal architect of U.S. involvement, now believed that the North Vietnamese "won't quit no matter how much bombing we do." He feared for the image of the United States, "the world's greatest superpower, killing or seriously injuring 1,000 noncombatants a week, while trying to pound a tiny, backward nation into submission on an issue whose merits are hotly disputed." McNamara left the administration in early 1968 but did not publicly oppose the war.

A critical turning point came with the **Tet Offensive**. On January 30, 1968, the North Vietnamese and Vietcong launched a campaign of attacks on key cities, every major American base, and the U.S. Embassy in Saigon during Tet, the Vietnamese New Year holiday. Although the enemy lost ten times as many soldiers as ARVN and U.S. forces, Tet was psychologically devastating to the United States because it exposed the credibility gap between official statements and the war's reality. Newsman Walter Cronkite wondered, "What the hell is going on? I thought we were winning the war." The attacks created a million more South Vietnamese refugees as well as widespread destruction. Public approval of Johnson's handling of the war dropped to 26 percent.

In the aftermath of Tet, Johnson conferred with advisers in the Defense Department and an unofficial group of foreign policy experts who had been key architects of Cold War policies since the 1940s. Dean Acheson, Truman's secretary of state, summarized their conclusion: "We can no longer do the job we set out to do in the time we have left and we must begin to take steps to disengage."

On March 31, 1968, Johnson announced that the United States would sharply curtail its bombing of North Vietnam and that he was prepared to begin peace talks. He added the stunning declaration that he would not run for reelection. Thus, military strategy shifted from "Americanization" to "Vietnamization" of the war. But this was not a shift in policy. The goal remained a non-Communist South Vietnam; the United States would simply rely more heavily on the South Vietnamese to achieve it.

Negotiations began in Paris in May 1968. The United States would not agree to recognize the National Liberation Front, to a coalition government, or to American withdrawal. The North Vietnamese would agree to nothing less. Although the talks continued, so did the fighting.

Meanwhile, violence escalated at home. Protests struck two hundred college campuses in the spring of 1968. In the bloodiest action, students occupied buildings at Columbia University in New York City, condemning the university's war-related research and its treatment of African Americans. When negotiations failed, university officials called in the city police, who cleared the buildings, injuring scores of demonstrators and arresting hundreds. An ensuing student strike prematurely ended the academic year.

The Tumultuous Election of 1968

Disorder and violence also entered the election process. In June, two months after the murder of Martin Luther King Jr. and the riots that followed, Senator Robert F. Kennedy,

Tet Offensive
▶ Major campaign of attacks launched throughout South Vietnam in early 1968 by the North Vietnamese and Vietcong. A major turning point in the war, it exposed the credibility gap between official statements and the war's reality, and it shook Americans' confidence in the government.

Why did Johnson escalate American involvement in Vietnam?

How did the war in Vietnam polarize the nation?

How did U.S. foreign policy change under Nixon?

Conclusion: Was Vietnam an unwinnable war?

☑ **LearningCurve**
Check what you know.
bedfordstmartins.com
/roarkunderstanding

883

Protest in Chicago The worst violence surrounding the 1968 Democratic National Convention in Chicago came near the Hilton Hotel, where most of the delegates stayed. When some 3,000 protesters marching toward the convention site came up against a line of police, the police attacked not only the demonstrators but also reporters, hotel guests, and bystanders, driving a crowd through the plate-glass window of the hotel and injuring hundreds. AP Photo/Michael Boyer.

an antiwar candidate campaigning for the Democratic Party's presidential nomination, was killed by a Palestinian Arab refugee because of his support for Israel.

In August, protesters battled the police in Chicago, site of the Democratic National Convention. Several thousand demonstrators came to the city, some to support peace candidate Senator Eugene McCarthy, others to cause disruption. On August 25, when demonstrators jeered at orders to disperse, police attacked them with tear gas and clubs. Street battles continued for three days, culminating in a police riot on the night of August 28. Taunted by the crowd, the police sprayed Mace and clubbed not only those who had come to provoke violence but also reporters, peaceful demonstrators, and convention delegates.

The bloodshed in Chicago had little effect on the convention's outcome. Vice President Hubert H. Humphrey trounced McCarthy by nearly three to one for the Democratic nomination.

In contrast to the turmoil in Chicago, the Republican convention met peacefully and nominated former vice president Richard Nixon. In a bid for southern support, Nixon chose Maryland governor Spiro T. Agnew for his running mate. A strong third candidate entered the race when the American Independent Party nominated staunch segregationist George C. Wallace. The former Alabama

CHAPTER LOCATOR | How did U.S. foreign policy change under Kennedy?

CHAPTER 29
884 VIETNAM AND THE END OF THE COLD WAR CONSENSUS

governor appealed to Americans' dissatisfaction with the reforms and rebellions of the 1960s and their outrage at the assaults on traditional values. Nixon guardedly played on resentments that fueled the Wallace campaign, calling for "law and order" and attacking liberal Supreme Court decisions, busing for school desegregation, and protesters.

Nixon and Humphrey differed little on the central issue of Vietnam. Nixon promised "an honorable end" to the war but did not indicate how to achieve it. Humphrey had reservations about U.S. policy in Vietnam, yet as vice president he was tied to Johnson's policies. With nearly 13 percent of the total popular vote, Wallace produced the strongest third-party finish since 1924. Nixon edged out Humphrey by just half a million popular votes but won 301 electoral college votes to Humphrey's 191 and Wallace's 46. The Democrats maintained control of Congress.

The 1968 election revealed deep cracks in the coalition that had maintained Democratic dominance in Washington for the previous thirty years. Johnson's liberal policies on race shattered a century of Democratic Party rule in the South, which delivered all its electoral votes to Wallace and Nixon. Elsewhere, large numbers of blue-collar workers broke with labor's traditional alliance with the Democrats to vote for Wallace or Nixon, as did other groups that associated the Democrats with racial turmoil, poverty programs, changing sexual mores, and failure to turn the tide in Vietnam. These resentments would soon be mobilized into a resurging right in American politics (as discussed in chapter 30).

QUICK REVIEW <

How did the Vietnam War shape the election of 1968?

Why did Johnson escalate American involvement in Vietnam?

How did the war in Vietnam polarize the nation?

How did U.S. foreign policy change under Nixon?

Conclusion: Was Vietnam an unwinnable war?

☑ LearningCurve
Check what you know.
bedfordstmartins.com
/roarkunderstanding

885

How did U.S. foreign policy change under Nixon?

Nixon in China

"This was the week that changed the world," proclaimed President Nixon in February 1972, emphasizing the stunning turnaround in relations with America's former enemy, the People's Republic of China. Nixon's trip was planned to dramatize the event on television and, aside from criticism from some conservatives, won overwhelming support from Americans. Here, Nixon and his wife, Pat, visit the Great Wall of China. Nixon Presidential Materials Project, National Archives and Record Administration.

détente

▶ Term (from the French for "loosening") given to the easing of conflict between the United States and the Soviet Union during the Nixon administration by focusing on issues of common concern, such as arms control and trade.

Helsinki accords

▶ 1975 agreement signed by U.S., Canadian, Soviet, and European leaders, recognizing the post–World War II borders in Europe and pledging the signatories to respect human rights and fundamental freedoms.

RICHARD M. NIXON TOOK office hoping to make his mark on history by applying his broad understanding of international relations to a changing world. Diverging from Republican orthodoxy, he made dramatic overtures to the Soviet Union and China. Yet anticommunism remained central to U.S. policy. Nixon backed repressive regimes around the world and aggressively pursued the war in Vietnam, despite mounting opposition to his policies. He expanded the conflict into Cambodia and Laos and ferociously bombed North Vietnam. Yet in the end, he was forced to settle for peace without victory.

Moving toward Détente with the Soviet Union and China

Nixon perceived that the "rigid and bipolar world of the 1940s and 1950s" was changing, and America's European allies were seeking to ease East-West tensions. Moreover, Nixon and his national security adviser Henry A. Kissinger believed they could exploit the increasing conflict between the Soviet Union and

CHAPTER LOCATOR | How did U.S. foreign policy change under Kennedy?

China. In addition, these two nations might be used to help the United States extricate itself from Vietnam.

In February 1972, following two years of secret negotiations, Nixon became the nation's first president to set foot on Chinese soil. Although his visit was largely symbolic, cultural and scientific exchanges followed, and American manufacturers began to find markets in China—small steps in the process of globalization that would take giant strides in the 1990s.

As Nixon and Kissinger had hoped, the warming of U.S.-Chinese relations furthered their strategy of **détente**, their term for easing conflict with the Soviet Union. Détente (from the French for "loosening") did not mean abandoning containment; instead, it focused on issues of common concern, such as arms control and trade. Containment would be achieved not just by military threat but also by ensuring that the Soviets and Chinese had stakes in a stable international order. Nixon's goal was "a stronger healthy United States, Europe, Soviet Union, China, Japan, each balancing the other."

Arms control, trade, and stability in Europe were three areas where the United States and the Soviet Union had common interests. In May 1972, Nixon visited Moscow, signing agreements on trade and cooperation in science and space. Most significantly, Soviet and U.S. leaders concluded arms limitation treaties that had grown out of the Strategic Arms Limitation Talks begun in 1969, agreeing to limit antiballistic missiles (ABMs) to two each. Giving up pursuit of a defense against nuclear weapons was a crucial move, because it denied both nations an ABM defense so secure against a nuclear attack that they would risk a first strike.

Although détente made little progress after 1974, U.S., Canadian, Soviet, and European leaders signed a historic agreement in 1975 in Helsinki, Finland, that formally recognized the post–World War II boundaries in Europe. The **Helsinki accords** were controversial because they acknowledged Soviet domination over Eastern Europe. Yet they also committed the signing countries to recognize "the universal significance of human rights and fundamental freedoms." Dissidents in the Soviet Union and its Eastern European satellites used this official promise of rights to challenge the Soviet dictatorship and help force its overthrow fifteen years later.

Shoring Up U.S. Interests around the World

Despite the thawing in U.S. relations with the Soviet Union and China, in Vietnam and elsewhere Nixon and Kissinger continued to view left-wing movements as threats to U.S. interests and actively resisted social revolutions that might lead to communism. The Nixon administration helped overthrow Salvador Allende, a self-proclaimed Marxist who was elected president of Chile in 1970. Since 1964, the CIA and U.S. corporations concerned about nationalization of their Chilean properties had assisted Allende's opponents. After Allende became president, Nixon ordered the CIA director to destabilize his government, and in 1973 the CIA helped the Chilean military engineer a coup, killing Allende and establishing a brutal dictatorship under General Augusto Pinochet.

In other parts of the world, too, the Nixon administration backed repressive regimes. In southern Africa, it eased pressures on white minority governments that tyrannized blacks. In the Middle East, the United States sent massive arms

> **CHRONOLOGY**

1970
- Nixon orders invasion of Cambodia.
- Students are killed at Kent State and Jackson State.

1971
- Portions of *Pentagon Papers* are published.

1972
- Nixon visits China.
- Nixon signs arms limitation treaties with Soviets.

1973
- Paris Peace Accords.
- CIA-backed military coup in Chile.
- Arab oil embargo following Yom Kippur War.

1975
- North Vietnam takes over South Vietnam, ending the war.
- Helsinki accords.

Chile

| Why did Johnson escalate American involvement in Vietnam? | How did the war in Vietnam polarize the nation? | **How did U.S. foreign policy change under Nixon?** | Conclusion: Was Vietnam an unwinnable war? | ✓ LearningCurve Check what you know. bedfordstmartins.com /roarkunderstanding |

Israeli Territorial Gains in the Six-Day War, 1967

Six-Day War

▶ 1967 conflict between Israel and the Arab nations of Egypt, Syria, and Jordan. Israel attacked Egypt after Egypt had massed troops on its border and cut off the sea passage to Israel's southern port. Israel won a stunning victory, seizing territory that amounted to twice its original size.

shipments to support the shah of Iran's harsh regime because Iran had enormous petroleum reserves and seemed a stable anti-Communist ally. Like his predecessors, Nixon pursued a delicate balance between defending Israel's security and seeking the goodwill of Arab nations strategically and economically important to the United States. Conflict between Israel and the Arab nations had escalated into the **Six-Day War** in 1967, when Israel attacked Egypt after Egypt had massed troops on the Israeli border and cut off sea passage to Israel's southern port. Although Syria and Jordan joined the war on Egypt's side, Israel won a stunning victory, seizing the Sinai Peninsula and Gaza Strip from Egypt, the Golan Heights from Syria, and the West Bank, where hundreds of thousands of Palestinians lived, from Jordan.

That decisive victory did not quell Middle Eastern turmoil. In October 1973, on the Jewish holiday of Yom Kippur, Egypt and Syria surprised Israel with a full-scale attack. When the Nixon administration sided with Israel, Arab nations retaliated with an oil embargo that created severe shortages in the United States. After Israel repulsed the attack, tensions remained high. The Arab countries refused to recognize Israel's right to exist, Israel began to settle its citizens in the West Bank and other territories occupied during the Six-Day War, and no solution could be found for the Palestinian refugees who had been displaced by the creation of Israel in 1948. The simmering conflict contributed to anti-American sentiment among Arabs who viewed the United States as Israel's supporter.

Vietnam Becomes Nixon's War

"I'm going to stop that war. Fast," Nixon asserted. He gradually withdrew ground troops, but he was no more willing than his predecessors to be the president who let South Vietnam fall to the Communists. That goal was tied to the larger objective of maintaining American credibility. Regardless of the wisdom of the initial intervention, Kissinger asserted, "The commitment of 500,000 Americans has settled the importance of Vietnam. For what is involved now is confidence in American promises."

From 1969 to 1972, Nixon and Kissinger pursued a three-pronged approach. First, they tried to strengthen the South Vietnamese military and government. ARVN forces grew to more than a million, and the South Vietnamese air force became the fourth largest in the world. The United States also promoted land reform, village elections, and the building of schools, hospitals, and transportation facilities. Second, Nixon gradually reduced the U.S. presence in Vietnam, a move that somewhat disarmed the antiwar movement at home. American forces decreased from 543,000 in 1968 to 140,000 by the end of 1971, although casualties remained high. Third, the United States replaced U.S. ground forces with intensive bombing. In the spring of 1969, Nixon began a ferocious air war in Cambodia, hiding it from Congress and the public for more than a year. Seeking to knock out North Vietnamese sanctuaries in Cambodia, the United States dropped more than 100,000 tons of bombs but succeeded only in sending the enemy to other hiding places. Echoing Johnson, Kissinger believed that a "fourth-rate power like North Vietnam" had to have a "breaking point," but the massive bombing failed to find it.

To support a new, pro-Western Cambodian government installed through a military coup and "to show the enemy that we were still serious about our commitment in Vietnam," Nixon ordered a joint U.S.-ARVN invasion of Cambodia in April 1970. That order made Vietnam "Nixon's war" and provoked outrage at home. Nixon made a belligerent speech emphasizing the importance of U.S. credibility: "If when the chips are down, the world's most powerful nation acts like a pitiful helpless giant, the forces of totalitarianism and anarchy will threaten free nations" everywhere.

In response, more than 100,000 people protested in Washington, D.C., and students boycotted classes on hundreds of campuses. At a rally on May 4 at Kent State University in Ohio, National Guard troops opened fire after students threw rocks at them, killing four and wounding ten others. "They're starting to treat their own children like they treat us," commented a black woman in Harlem. In a confrontation at Jackson State College in Mississippi on May 14, police shot into a dormitory, killing two black students.

Congressional reaction to the invasion of Cambodia revealed increasing concern about abuses of presidential power. In the name of national security, presidents since Franklin Roosevelt had conducted foreign policy without the consent or sometimes even the knowledge of Congress—for example, Eisenhower in Iran and Johnson in the Dominican Republic. But in their determination to win the war in Vietnam, Johnson and Nixon had taken extreme measures to deceive the public and silence their critics. The bombing and invasion of Cambodia infuriated enough legislators that the Senate voted to terminate the Gulf of Tonkin Resolution, which had given the president virtually a blank check in Vietnam, and to cut off funds for the Cambodian operation. The House refused to go along, but by the end of June 1970 Nixon had pulled all U.S. troops out of Cambodia.

In 1971, Vietnam veterans became a visible part of the peace movement, the first men in U.S. history to protest a war in which they had fought. They held a public investigation of "war crimes" in Vietnam, rallied in front of the Capitol, and cast away their war medals. In May 1971, veterans numbered among the 40,000 protesters who engaged in civil disobedience in an effort to shut down Washington.

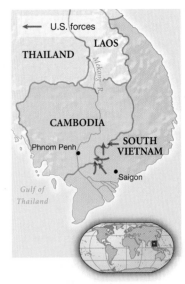

U.S. Invasion of Cambodia, 1970

Pro-War Demonstrators

Supporters as well as opponents of the war in Vietnam took to the streets, as these New Yorkers did in support of the U.S. invasion of Cambodia in May 1970. Construction workers — called "hard hats" — and other union members marched with American flags and posters championing President Nixon's policies and blasting New York mayor John Lindsay for his antiwar position. Paul Fusco/Magnum Photos, Inc.

> VISUAL ACTIVITY

READING THE IMAGE: What do the hard hats in the photograph symbolize in terms of identity and politics?

CONNECTIONS: How were these union members related to the unraveling of the Democratic Party coalition?

| Why did Johnson escalate American involvement in Vietnam? | How did the war in Vietnam polarize the nation? | **How did U.S. foreign policy change under Nixon?** | Conclusion: Was Vietnam an unwinnable war? | ✓ LearningCurve Check what you know. bedfordstmartins.com /roarkunderstanding |

Officials made more than 12,000 arrests, which courts later ruled violations of protesters' rights.

After the spring of 1971, there were fewer massive antiwar demonstrations, but protest continued. Public attention focused on the court-martial of Lieutenant William Calley, which began in November 1970. During the trial, Americans learned that in March 1968 Calley's company had killed every inhabitant of the hamlet of My Lai, even though it had encountered no enemy forces and the four hundred villagers were nearly all old men, women, and children. The military covered up the atrocity for more than a year before a journalist exposed it. Eventually, twelve officers and enlisted men were charged with murder or assault, but only Calley was convicted.

Administration policy suffered another blow in June 1971 when the *New York Times* published portions of the **Pentagon Papers**, a secret internal study of the war begun in 1967. Nixon sent government lawyers to court to stop further publication, in part out of fear that other information would be leaked. The Supreme Court, however, ruled that suppression of the publication violated the First Amendment. Subsequent circulation of the *Pentagon Papers*, which revealed pessimism among officials even as they made rosy promises, heightened disillusionment with the war by casting doubts on the government's credibility. More than 60 percent of Americans polled in 1971 considered it a mistake to have sent American troops to Vietnam; 58 percent believed the war to be immoral.

Military morale sank in the last years of the war. Having been exposed to the antiwar movement at home, many of the remaining soldiers had less faith in the war than their predecessors had had. Racial tensions among soldiers mounted, many soldiers sought escape in illegal drugs, and enlisted men committed hundreds of "fraggings," attacks on officers. In a 1971 report, "The Collapse of the Armed Forces," a retired Marine Corps colonel described the lack of discipline: "Our army that now remains in Vietnam [is] near mutinous."

The Peace Accords

Nixon and Kissinger continued to believe that intensive firepower could bring the North Vietnamese to their knees. In March 1972, responding to a North Vietnamese offensive, the United States resumed sustained bombing of the North, mined Haiphong and other harbors for the first time, and announced a naval blockade. With peace talks stalled, in December Nixon ordered the most devastating bombing yet. Though costly to both sides, it brought renewed negotiations. On January 27, 1973, representatives of the United States, North Vietnam, South Vietnam, and the Vietcong (now called the Provisional Revolutionary Government) signed a formal peace accord in Paris. The agreement required removal of all U.S. troops and military advisers from South Vietnam but allowed North Vietnamese forces to remain. Both sides agreed to return prisoners of war. Nixon called the agreement "peace with honor," but in fact it allowed only a face-saving withdrawal.

Fighting resumed immediately among the Vietnamese. Nixon's efforts to support the South Vietnamese government, and indeed his ability to govern at all, were increasingly eroded by what came to be known as the Watergate scandal, which forced him to resign in 1974 (as discussed in chapter 30). In 1975, North Vietnam launched a new offensive, seizing Saigon on April 30. The Americans

Pentagon Papers
▶ Secret government documents published in 1971 containing an internal study of the Vietnam War. The documents further disillusioned the public by revealing that officials harbored pessimism about the war even as they made rosy public pronouncements about its progress.

CHAPTER LOCATOR | How did U.S. foreign policy change under Kennedy?

890 CHAPTER 29 VIETNAM AND THE END OF THE COLD WAR CONSENSUS hastily evacuated, along with 150,000 of their South Vietnamese allies. Confusion, humiliation, and tragedy marked the rushed departure. The United States lacked sufficient transportation capabilities and time to evacuate all those who had supported the South Vietnamese government and were desperate to leave. A journalist reported that his departing helicopter "took some ground fire from South Vietnamese soldiers who probably felt that the Americans had betrayed them."

During the four years it took Nixon to end the war, he had expanded the conflict into Cambodia and Laos and launched massive bombing campaigns. Although increasing numbers of legislators criticized the war, Congress never denied the funds to fight it. Only after the peace accords did the legislative branch try to reassert its constitutional authority in the making of war. The War Powers Act of 1973 required the president to secure congressional approval for any substantial, long-term deployment of troops abroad. The new law, however, did little to dispel the distrust of and disillusionment with the government that resulted from Americans' realization that their leaders had not told the truth about Vietnam.

The Legacy of Defeat

Antigovernment sentiment was just one of the war's legacies. It left bitter divisions among Americans, diverted money from domestic programs, and sounded the death knell for Johnson's Great Society. The war created federal budget deficits and triggered inflation that contributed to ongoing economic crises throughout the 1970s (as discussed in chapter 30).

Four presidents had declared that the survival of South Vietnam was essential for U.S. containment policy, but their predictions that a Communist victory in South Vietnam would set the dominoes cascading did not materialize. Although Vietnam, Laos, and Cambodia all fell within the Communist camp in the spring of 1975, the rest of Southeast Asia did not. When China and Vietnam reverted to their historically hostile relationship, the myth of a monolithic Communist power overrunning Asia evaporated.

The long pursuit of victory in Vietnam complicated the United States' relations with other nations, as even its staunchest ally, Britain, doubted the wisdom of the war. The use of terrifying American power against a small Asian country compromised efforts to win the hearts and minds of people in developing nations.

The cruelest legacy of Vietnam fell on those who had served. "The general public just wanted to ignore us," remembered Frederick Downs, while opponents of the war "wanted to argue with us until we felt guilty about what we had done over there." Many veterans believed in the war's purposes and felt betrayed by the government for not letting them win it. Other veterans blamed the government for sacrificing the nation's youth in an immoral, unnecessary war, expressing their sense of the war's futility by referring to their dead comrades as having been "wasted." Some veterans belonging to minority groups had more reason to doubt the nobility of their purpose. A Native American soldier assigned to resettle Vietnamese civilians found it to be "just like when they moved us to the rez [reservation]. We shouldn't have done that."

Evacuating South Vietnam

As Communist troops rolled south toward Saigon in the spring of 1975, desperate South Vietnamese attempted to flee along with the departing Americans. These South Vietnamese, carrying little or nothing, attempt to scale the wall of the U.S. Embassy to reach evacuation helicopters. Thousands of Vietnamese who wanted to be evacuated were left behind. Even though space for evacuees was desperately limited, South Vietnamese president Nguyen Van Thieu fled to Taiwan on a U.S. plane, taking with him fifteen tons of baggage. AP Images.

Why did Johnson escalate American involvement in Vietnam?

How did the war in Vietnam polarize the nation?

How did U.S. foreign policy change under Nixon?

Conclusion: Was Vietnam an unwinnable war?

✓ LearningCurve
Check what you know.
bedfordstmartins.com
/roarkunderstanding

891

TABLE 29.1 ■ Vietnam War Casualties

United States	
Battle deaths	47,434
Other deaths	10,786
Wounded	153,303
South Vietnam	
Killed in action	110,357
Military wounded	499,026
Civilians killed	415,000
Civilians wounded	913,000
Communist Regulars and Guerrillas	
Killed in action	66,000

Source: U.S. Department of Defense.

Because the Vietnam War was a civil war involving guerrilla tactics, combat was especially brutal (**Table 29.1**). The terrors of conventional warfare were multiplied, and so were the motivations to commit atrocities. The 1968 massacre at My Lai was only the most widely publicized war crime. To demonstrate the immorality of the war, peace advocates stressed the atrocities, contributing to a distorted image of the Vietnam veteran as dehumanized and violent.

Most veterans came home to public neglect. Government benefits were less generous to Vietnam veterans than they had been to those of the previous two wars. While two-thirds of Vietnam veterans said that they would serve again, and while most veterans readjusted well to civilian life, some suffered long after the war ended. The Veterans Administration estimated that nearly one-sixth of the veterans suffered from post-traumatic stress disorder, experiencing recurring nightmares, feelings of guilt and shame, violence, substance abuse, and suicidal tendencies. Thirty years after performing army intelligence work in Saigon, Doris Allen "still hit the floor sometimes when [she heard] loud bangs." Some who had served in Vietnam began to report birth defects, cancer, severe skin disorders, and other ailments. Veterans claimed a link between those illnesses and Agent Orange, which had exposed many to the deadly poison dioxin in Vietnam. In 1991, Congress began to provide assistance to veterans with diseases linked to the poison.

By then, the climate had changed. The war began to enter the realm of popular culture, with novels, TV shows, and hit movies depicting a broad range of military experience—from soldiers reduced to brutality, to men and women serving with courage and integrity. The incorporation of the Vietnam War into the collective experience was symbolized most dramatically in the Vietnam Veterans Memorial unveiled in Washington, D.C., in November 1982. Designed by Yale architecture student Maya Lin, the black, V-shaped wall inscribed with the names of 58,200 men and women lost in the war became one of the most popular sites in the nation's capital. In an article describing the memorial's dedication, a Vietnam combat veteran spoke to and for his former comrades: "Welcome home. The war is over."

> ## QUICK REVIEW

What strategies did Nixon implement to bring American involvement in Vietnam to a close?

CHAPTER LOCATOR | How did U.S. foreign policy change under Kennedy?

CHAPTER 29
892 VIETNAM AND THE END OF THE COLD WAR CONSENSUS

Conclusion: Was Vietnam an unwinnable war?

THE UNITED STATES SPENT $111 billion (more than $600 billion in 2013 dollars) and sent 2.6 million men and women to Vietnam. Of those, 58,200 never returned, and 150,000 suffered serious injury. The war shattered consensus at home, increased presidential power at the expense of congressional authority and public accountability, weakened the economy, and contributed to the downfall of two presidents.

Even as Nixon and Kissinger took steps to ease Cold War tensions with the major Communist powers—the Soviet Union and China—they also acted vigorously throughout the third world to install or prop up anti-Communist governments. They embraced their predecessors' commitment to South Vietnam as a necessary Cold War engagement: To do otherwise would threaten American credibility and make the United States appear weak. Defeat in Vietnam did not make the United States the "pitiful helpless giant" predicted by Nixon, but it did mark a relative decline of U.S. power and the impossibility of containment on a global scale.

One of the constraints on U.S. power was the tenacity of revolutionary movements determined to achieve national independence. Overestimating the effectiveness of American technological superiority, U.S. officials badly underestimated the sacrifices that the enemy was willing to make and failed to realize how easily the United States could be perceived as a colonial intruder. A second constraint on Eisenhower, Kennedy, Johnson, and Nixon was their resolve to avoid a major confrontation with the Soviet Union or China. For Johnson, who conducted the largest escalation of the war, caution was critical so as not to provoke direct intervention by the Communist superpowers. After China exploded its first atomic bomb in 1964, the potential heightened for the Vietnam conflict to escalate into worldwide disaster.

Third, in Vietnam the United States sought to prop up an extremely weak ally engaged in a civil war. The South Vietnamese government failed to win the support of its people, and the intense devastation the war brought to civilians only made things worse. Short of taking over the South Vietnamese government and military, the United States could do little to strengthen South Vietnam's ability to resist communism.

Finally, domestic opposition to the war, which by 1968 had spread to mainstream America, constrained the options of Johnson and Nixon. As the war dragged on, with increasing American casualties and growing evidence of the damage being inflicted on innocent Vietnamese, more and more civilians wearied of the conflict. Even some who had fought in the war joined the peace movement, sending their military ribbons and bitter letters of protest to the White House. In 1973, Nixon and Kissinger bowed to the resoluteness of the enemy and the limitations of U.S. power. As the war wound down, passions surrounding it contributed to a rising conservative movement that would substantially alter the post–World War II political order.

| Why did Johnson escalate American involvement in Vietnam? | How did the war in Vietnam polarize the nation? | How did U.S. foreign policy change under Nixon? | Conclusion: Was Vietnam an unwinnable war? | ✔ LearningCurve Check what you know. bedfordstmartins.com /roarkunderstanding |

893

CHAPTER 29 STUDY GUIDE

STEP 1

GET STARTED ONLINE

☑ **LearningCurve** ▪ bedfordstmartins.com/roarkunderstanding
Now that you've read the chapter, make it stick by completing the LearningCurve activity.

STEP 2

EXPLAIN WHY IT MATTERS

Put your reading into practice. Identify each term below, and then explain why it matters in U.S. history.

TERM	WHO OR WHAT & WHEN	WHY IT MATTERS
Bay of Pigs (p. 872)		
Apollo program (p. 872)		
Berlin Wall (p. 872)		
Peace Corps (p. 872)		
Cuban missile crisis (p. 873)		
Agent Orange (p. 875)		
Gulf of Tonkin Resolution (p. 877)		
Tet Offensive (p. 883)		
détente (p. 886)		
Helsinki accords (p. 886)		
Six-Day War (p. 888)		
Pentagon Papers (p. 890)		

STEP 3

MOVE BEYOND THE BASICS

To demonstrate a more advanced understanding, describe the key American policy decisions regarding Vietnam between 1961 and 1974 and explain the rationale and impact of each decision. How was U.S. involvement in Vietnam shaped by policymakers' larger vision of global politics?

	Policy decision	Rationale	Impact
Kennedy administration			
Johnson administration			
Nixon administration			

KENNEDY'S FOREIGN POLICY

► How did Kennedy's view of America's place in the world affect his foreign policy decisions in 1961 and 1962?

► How were Kennedy's decisions with respect to Vietnam shaped by the Cold War?

JOHNSON AND VIETNAM

► Why did Lyndon Johnson disregard some of his advisers who urged him to disengage from Vietnam?

► How did the divisions over Vietnam contribute to Nixon's election in 1968?

NIXON'S FOREIGN POLICY

► What impact did Nixon's strategies in Vietnam have on the United States?

► How did Nixon's approach to foreign policy differ from that of his predecessors?

LOOKING BACKWARD, LOOKING AHEAD

► How did American foreign policy in the 1950s set the stage for the escalation of U.S. involvement in Vietnam in the 1960s?

► How did American foreign policy change between 1961 and 1975? What impact did the Vietnam conflict have on these changes?

> **IN YOUR OWN WORDS** Imagine that you must give an oral report to the class answering the following question: **Why was the United States unable to achieve its objectives in Vietnam?** What would be the most important points to include and why?

30
THE CONSERVATIVE TURN

1969–1989

> What were the effects of America's move to the political right on American society and on U.S. foreign policy? Chapter 30 explores the rise of conservatism as a major force in late-twentieth-century American politics. It examines the emergence of new strands of conservatism in the 1960s, the evolution of conservatism in the post-Watergate years, and its full expression in the politics and policies of Ronald Reagan.

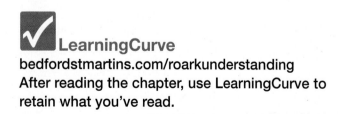

LearningCurve
bedfordstmartins.com/roarkunderstanding
After reading the chapter, use LearningCurve to retain what you've read.

> How did the Nixon presidency reflect the rise of postwar conservatism?

> Why did the "outsider" presidency of Jimmy Carter fail to gain broad support?

> What conservative goals were realized in the Reagan administration?

> What strategies did liberals use to fight the conservative turn?

> How did Ronald Reagan's foreign policy affect the Cold War?

> Conclusion: What was the long-term impact of the conservative turn?

Inauguration of Ronald Reagan, 1981. Chief Justice Warren Burger administers the oath of office to President Ronald Reagan. Dirck Halstead/Getty Images.

How did the Nixon presidency reflect the rise of postwar conservatism?

School Busing Controversy over busing as a means to integrate public schools erupted in Boston when the 1974–1975 school year started. Opposition was especially high in white ethnic neighborhoods such as South Boston. Residents there resented liberal judges from the suburbs assigning them the burden of integration. Clashes between blacks and whites in Boston, such as this one in February 1975 outside Boston's Hyde Park High School, prompted authorities to dispatch police to protect black students. AP/Wide World.

RICHARD NIXON ACQUIESCED IN CONTINUING most Great Society programs and even approved pathbreaking environmental, minority, and women's rights measures. Yet his public rhetoric and some of his actions signaled the country's rightward move. Whereas Kennedy had appealed to Americans to contribute to the common good, Nixon invited Americans to "ask—not just what will government do for me, but what can I do for myself?" His words invoked individualism and reliance on private enterprise rather than on government, preferences that would grow stronger in the nation during the 1970s and beyond, as a new strand of conservatism joined the older movement that focused on anticommunism, a strong national defense, and a limited federal role in domestic affairs. New conservatives wanted to restore what they considered traditional moral values.

Just two years after Nixon won reelection by a huge margin, his abuse of power and efforts to cover up crimes committed by subordinates, revealed in the so-called Watergate scandal, forced the first presidential resignation in history. His successor, Gerald Ford, faced the aftermath of Watergate and severe economic problems, which returned the White House to the Democrats in 1976.

Emergence of a Grassroots Movement

Hidden beneath Lyndon Johnson's landslide victory over Arizona senator Barry Goldwater in 1964 lay a rising conservative movement. Defining his purpose as

CHAPTER LOCATOR | How did the Nixon presidency reflect the rise of postwar conservatism? | Why did the "outsider" presidency of Jimmy Carter fail to gain broad support?

898 CHAPTER 30 THE CONSERVATIVE TURN

"enlarging freedom at home and safeguarding it from the forces of tyranny abroad," Goldwater argued that government intrusions into economic life hindered prosperity, stifled personal responsibility, and interfered with individuals' rights to determine their own values. Conservatives assailed big government in domestic affairs but demanded a strong military to eradicate "Godless communism."

The grassroots movement supporting Goldwater's nomination was especially vigorous in the South and West, and it included middle-class suburban women and men, members of the rabidly anti-Communist John Birch Society, and college students in the new Young Americans for Freedom. A number of Sun Belt characteristics made this movement strong in places such as Orange County, California; Dallas, Texas; and Scottsdale, Arizona. Such predominantly white areas contained relatively homogeneous, skilled, and economically comfortable populations, as well as military bases and defense production facilities. The West harbored a long-standing tradition of Protestant morality, individualism, and opposition to interference by a remote federal government. That tradition continued with the emergence of the New Right, even though it was hardly consistent with the Sun Belt's economic dependence on defense spending and on huge federal projects providing water and power for the burgeoning region.

The South, which also benefited from military bases and the space program, shared the West's antipathy toward the federal government. Hostility to racial change, however, was much more central to the South's conservatism. After signing the Civil Rights Act of 1964, President Lyndon Johnson remarked privately, "I think we just delivered the South to the Republican Party." Indeed, Barry Goldwater carried five southern states in 1964.

Grassroots movements proliferated around what conservatives believed marked the "moral decline" of their nation. For example, in 1962 Mel and Norma Gabler got the Texas board of education to drop books that they believed undermined "the Christian-Judeo morals, values, and standards as given to us by God through . . . the Bible." Sex education roused the ire of Eleanor Howe in Anaheim, California, who felt that "nothing [in the sex education curriculum] depicted my values. . . . It wasn't so much the information. It was the shift in values." The Supreme Court's liberal decisions on school prayer, obscenity, and abortion also galvanized conservatives to restore "traditional values."

In the 1970s, grassroots protests against taxes grew alongside concerns about morality. As Americans struggled with inflation and unemployment, many found themselves

The Tax Revolt

Neighbors gather in Los Angeles to rally for Proposition 13, an initiative launched by conservative Howard Jarvis in 1978. Many homeowners rallied to Jarvis's antitax movement because rising land values had increased their property taxes sharply. After Californians passed Proposition 13, some thirty-seven states cut property taxes, and twenty-eight reduced income taxes. The tax issue helped the Republican Party end decades of Democratic dominance. Tony Korody/Getty Images.

What conservative goals were realized in the Reagan administration?

What strategies did liberals use to fight the conservative turn?

How did Ronald Reagan's foreign policy affect the Cold War?

Conclusion: What was the long-term impact of the conservative turn?

☑ LearningCurve
Check what you know.
bedfordstmartins.com
/roarkunderstanding

Percent of black students statewide
attending schools more than 50% white

	60% or more		30–40%
	50–60%		20–30%
	40–50%		20% or less

Integration of Public Schools, 1968

paying higher taxes, especially higher property taxes as the value of their homes increased. In 1978, Californians revolted in a popular referendum, reducing property taxes by more than one-half and limiting the state legislature's ability to raise taxes. What a newspaper called a "primal scream by the People against Big Government" spread to other states.

Nixon Courts the Right

In his 1968 campaign, Richard Nixon exploited hostility to black protest and new civil rights policies, wooing white southerners and a considerable number of northern voters away from the Democratic Party. As president, he used this "southern strategy" to make further inroads into traditional Democratic strongholds in the 1972 election.

Nixon reluctantly enforced court orders to achieve high degrees of integration in southern schools, but he resisted efforts to deal with segregation outside the South. In northern and western cities, where segregation resulted from discrimination in housing and in the drawing of school district boundaries, half of all African American children attended nearly all-black schools. After courts began to order the transfer of students between schools in white and black neighborhoods to achieve desegregation, busing became a hot-button issue. "We've had all we can take of judicial interference with local schools," conservative spokeswoman Phyllis Schlafly railed in 1972.

Children had been riding buses to school for decades, but busing for racial integration provoked fury. Violence erupted in Boston in 1974 when a district judge found that school officials had maintained what amounted to a dual system based on race and ordered busing "if necessary to achieve a unitary school system." The whites most affected by busing came from working-class families left in cities abandoned by the more affluent and whose children often rode buses to predominantly black, overcrowded schools with deficient facilities. Clarence McDonough denounced the liberal officials who bused his "kid half way around Boston so that a bunch of politicians can end up their careers with a clear conscience." African Americans themselves were conflicted about sending their children on long rides to schools where white teachers might not welcome or respect them.

Whites eventually became more accepting of integration, especially after the creation of schools with specialized programs and other new mechanisms for desegregation offered greater choice. Nonetheless, integration propelled white flight to the suburbs. Nixon failed to persuade Congress to end court-ordered busing, but after he had appointed four new justices, the Supreme Court imposed strict limits on the use of that tool to achieve racial balance.

Nixon's judicial appointments also reflected the southern strategy. He criticized the Supreme Court under Chief Justice Earl Warren for being "unprecedentedly politically active . . . using their interpretation of the law to remake American society according to their own social, political, and ideological precepts." When Warren resigned in 1969, Nixon replaced him with Warren E. Burger, a federal appeals court judge who was a strict constructionist, inclined to interpret the Constitution narrowly and to limit government intervention on behalf of individual rights. The Burger Court restricted somewhat the protections of individual rights established by its predecessor, but it upheld many of the liberal programs of the 1960s. For

CHAPTER LOCATOR | **How did the Nixon presidency reflect the rise of postwar conservatism?** | Why did the "outsider" presidency of Jimmy Carter fail to gain broad support?

example, *Regents of the University of California v. Bakke* (1978) limited the range of affirmative action but allowed universities to attack the results of past discrimination if they avoided strict quotas and racial classifications.

Nixon's southern strategy and other repercussions of the civil rights revolution of the 1960s ended the Democratic hold on the "solid South." Beginning in 1964, a number of conservative southern Democrats changed their party affiliation, and by 2005 Republicans held the majority of southern seats in Congress and governorships in seven southern states.

In addition to exploiting racial fears, Nixon appealed to anxieties about women's changing roles and new demands. In 1971, he vetoed a bill providing federal funds for day care centers with a message that combined the old and new conservatism. Parents should purchase child care services "in the private, open market," he insisted, not rely on government. He appealed to social conservatives by warning about the measure's "family-weakening implications." In response to the movement to liberalize abortion laws, Nixon sided with "defenders of the right to life of the unborn," anticipating the Republican Party's eventual embrace of the issue.

The Election of 1972

Nixon's ability to attract Democrats and appeal to concerns about Vietnam, race, law and order, and traditional morality heightened his prospects for reelection in 1972. Although the war in Vietnam continued, antiwar protests diminished with the decrease in American ground forces and casualties. Nixon's economic initiatives had temporarily checked inflation and unemployment (see chapter 28), and his attacks on busing and antiwar protesters had won increasing support from the right.

A large field of contenders vied for the Democratic nomination, including New York congresswoman Shirley Chisholm, the first African American to make a serious bid for the presidency. South Dakota senator George S. McGovern came to the Democratic convention as the clear leader and was easily nominated, but he struggled against Nixon from the outset. Republicans portrayed McGovern as a left-wing extremist, and his support for busing, a generous welfare program, and immediate withdrawal from Vietnam alienated conservative Democrats.

Nixon achieved a landslide victory, winning 60.7 percent of the popular vote and every state except Massachusetts. Although the Democrats maintained control of Congress, Nixon won majorities among traditional Democrats—southerners, Catholics, urbanites, and blue-collar workers. The president, however, had little time to savor his triumph, as revelations began to emerge about crimes committed to ensure the victory.

Watergate

During the early-morning hours of June 17, 1972, five men working for Nixon's reelection crept into Democratic Party headquarters in the Watergate complex in Washington, D.C. Intending to repair a bugging device installed in an earlier break-in, they were discovered and arrested. Nixon and his aides then tried to cover up the intruders' connection to administration officials, setting in motion the scandal reporters dubbed **Watergate**.

Nixon was not the first president to lie to the public or to misuse power. Every president since Franklin D. Roosevelt had enlarged the powers of his office

Watergate
▶ Term referring to the 1972 break-in at Democratic Party headquarters in the Watergate complex in Washington, D.C., by men working for President Nixon's reelection, along with Nixon's efforts to cover it up. The Watergate scandal led to President Nixon's resignation.

| What conservative goals were realized in the Reagan administration? | What strategies did liberals use to fight the conservative turn? | How did Ronald Reagan's foreign policy affect the Cold War? | Conclusion: What was the long-term impact of the conservative turn? | ✓ LearningCurve Check what you know. bedfordstmartins.com /roarkunderstanding |

901

in the name of national security. This expansion of executive powers, often called the "imperial presidency," weakened the traditional checks and balances on the executive branch and opened the door to abuses. No president, however, had dared go as far as Nixon, who saw opposition to his policies as a personal attack and was willing to violate the Constitution to stop it.

Upon learning of the Watergate arrests, Nixon plotted to conceal links between the burglars and the White House, while publicly denying any connection. In April 1973, after investigations by a grand jury and the Senate suggested that White House aides had been involved in the cover-up effort, Nixon accepted official responsibility for Watergate but denied any knowledge of the break-in or cover-up. He also announced the resignations of three White House aides and the attorney general. In May, he authorized the appointment of an independent special prosecutor, Archibald Cox, to conduct an investigation.

Meanwhile, speaking before a Senate investigating committee, headed by Democrat Samuel J. Ervin of North Carolina, White House counsel John Dean described projects to harass "enemies" through tax audits and other illegal means and implicated the president in efforts to cover up the Watergate break-in. Another White House aide struck the decisive blow when he disclosed that all conversations in the Oval Office were taped. Both Cox and Ervin immediately asked for the tapes related to Watergate. When Nixon refused, citing executive privilege and separation of powers, Cox and Ervin won a unanimous decision from the Supreme Court ordering him to release the tapes.

Additional disclosures exposed Nixon's misuse of federal funds and tax evasion. In August 1973, Vice President Spiro Agnew resigned after an investigation revealed that he had taken bribes while governor of Maryland. Nixon's choice of House minority leader Gerald Ford of Michigan to succeed Agnew won widespread approval, but Agnew's resignation further tarnished the administration, and Nixon's popular support plummeted.

In February 1974, the House of Representatives voted to begin an impeachment investigation. In April, Nixon began to release edited transcripts of the tapes. The transcripts revealed Nixon's orders to aides in March 1973: "I don't give a shit what happens. I want you all to stonewall it, let them plead the Fifth Amendment, cover up or anything else, if it'll save it—save the plan." House Republican leader Hugh Scott of Pennsylvania called the documents a "deplorable, shabby, disgusting, and immoral performance by all."

In July 1974, the House Judiciary Committee voted to impeach the president on three counts: obstruction of justice, abuse of power, and contempt of Congress. Seven or eight Republicans on the committee sided with the majority, and it seemed certain that the House would follow suit. Georgia state legislator and civil rights activist Julian Bond commented, "The prisons of Georgia are full of people who stole $5 or $10, and this man tried to steal the Constitution."

To avoid impeachment, Nixon announced his resignation to a national television audience on August 8, 1974. Acknowledging some incorrect judgments, he insisted that he had always tried to do what was best for the nation. The next morning, Nixon ended a rambling, emotional farewell to his staff with some advice: "Always give your best, never get discouraged, never get petty; always remember, others may hate you, but those who hate you don't win unless you hate them, and then you destroy yourself."

CHAPTER LOCATOR | How did the Nixon presidency reflect the rise of postwar conservatism?

Why did the "outsider" presidency of Jimmy Carter fail to gain broad support?

CHAPTER 30
902   THE CONSERVATIVE TURN

The Ford Presidency and the 1976 Election

Upon taking office, Gerald R. Ford announced, "Our long national nightmare is over." But he shocked many Americans one month later by granting Nixon a pardon "for all offenses against the United States which he . . . has committed or may have committed or taken part in" during his presidency. Prompted by Ford's concern for Nixon's health and by his hope to get the country beyond Watergate, this sweeping pardon saved Nixon from nearly certain indictment and trial, and it provoked a tremendous outcry from Congress and the public. Democrats made impressive gains in the November congressional elections, while Ford's action gave Nixon a new political life. Without having to admit that he had violated the law, Nixon rebuilt his image over the next two decades into that of an elder statesman. Thirty of his associates ultimately pleaded guilty to or were convicted of crimes related to Watergate.

Congress's efforts to guard against the types of abuses revealed in the Watergate investigations had only limited effects. The Federal Election Campaign Act of 1974 established public financing of presidential campaigns and imposed some restrictions on contributions to curtail the selling of political favors. Yet politicians found other ways of raising money—for example, through political action committees (PACs), to which individuals could contribute more than they could to candidates. Moreover, the Supreme Court struck down limitations on campaign spending as violations of freedom of speech. Ever-larger campaign donations flowed to candidates from interest groups, corporations, labor unions, and wealthy individuals.

Congressional investigating committees discovered a host of illegal FBI and CIA activities stretching back to the 1950s, including harassment of political dissenters and plots to assassinate Fidel Castro and other foreign leaders. In response to these revelations, President Ford established new controls on covert operations, and Congress created permanent committees to oversee the

| What conservative goals were realized in the Reagan administration? | What strategies did liberals use to fight the conservative turn? | How did Ronald Reagan's foreign policy affect the Cold War? | Conclusion: What was the long-term impact of the conservative turn? | **LearningCurve** Check what you know. bedfordstmartins.com /roarkunderstanding |

intelligence agencies. Yet these measures did little to diminish the public's cynicism about their government.

Disillusionment grew as the Ford administration struggled with serious economic problems: a low growth rate, high unemployment, a foreign trade deficit, and soaring energy prices. Ford carried these burdens into the election campaign of 1976, while contending with a major challenge from the Republican right. Blasting Nixon's and Ford's foreign policy of détente for causing the "loss of U.S. military supremacy," California governor Ronald Reagan came close to capturing the nomination.

The Democrats nominated James Earl "Jimmy" Carter Jr., former governor of Georgia. A graduate of the U.S. Naval Academy, Carter spent seven years as a nuclear engineer in the navy before returning to Plains, Georgia, to run the family peanut farming business. Carter stressed his faith as a "born-again Christian" and his distance from the government in Washington. Although he selected liberal senator Walter F. Mondale of Minnesota as his running mate, Carter's nomination nonetheless marked a rightward turn in the party.

Carter had considerable appeal as a candidate who carried his own bags, lived modestly, and taught a Bible class at his Baptist church. He also benefited from Ford's failure to solve the country's economic problems, which helped him win the traditional Democratic coalition of blacks, organized labor, and ethnic groups and even recapture some of the white southerners who had voted for Nixon in 1972. Still, on election day, Carter received just 50 percent of the popular vote to Ford's 48 percent, while Democrats retained substantial margins in Congress.

> **QUICK REVIEW**

How did Nixon's policies reflect the increasing influence of conservatives on the Republican Party?

CHAPTER LOCATOR | How did the Nixon presidency reflect the rise of postwar conservatism? | Why did the "outsider" presidency of Jimmy Carter fail to gain broad support?

904 CHAPTER 30
THE CONSERVATIVE TURN

Why did the "outsider" presidency of Jimmy Carter fail to gain broad support?

Jimmy Carter Honors Martin Luther King Jr.

On January 14, 1979, the day before the anniversary of King's birthday, President Carter and his wife, Rosalyn, worshipped at Ebenezer Baptist Church in Atlanta, Georgia, where both King and his father had been pastors. Carter had been pushing to establish King's birthday as a national holiday, but Congress did not enact such a law until 1983. Jimmy Carter Presidential Library.

JIMMY CARTER PROMISED a government that was "competent" as well as "decent, open, fair, and compassionate." He also warned Americans "that even our great Nation has its recognized limits, and that we can neither answer all questions nor solve all problems." Carter's humility and personal integrity helped revive trust in the presidency, but he faltered in the face of domestic and foreign crises.

Energy shortages and stagflation worsened, exposing Carter's deficiencies in working with Congress and in rallying public opinion. He achieved notable advances in environmental and energy policies, and he oversaw foreign policy successes concerning the Panama Canal, China, and the Middle East. Yet near the end of his term, Soviet-American relations deteriorated, new crises emerged in the Middle East, and the economy plummeted.

Retreat from Liberalism

Jimmy Carter vowed "to help the poor and aged, to improve education, and to provide jobs," but at the same time "not to waste money." When these goals conflicted, reform took second place to budget balancing. Carter's approach pleased Americans unhappy about their tax dollars being used to benefit the

What conservative goals were realized in the Reagan administration?

What strategies did liberals use to fight the conservative turn?

How did Ronald Reagan's foreign policy affect the Cold War?

Conclusion: What was the long-term impact of the conservative turn?

☑ **LearningCurve**
Check what you know.
bedfordstmartins.com
/roarkunderstanding

disadvantaged while stagflation eroded their own standard of living. But his fiscal stringency frustrated liberal Democrats pushing for major welfare reform and a national health insurance program. Carter himself said, "In many cases I feel more at home with the conservative Democratic and Republican members of Congress than I do with the others."

Although Carter did fulfill liberals' desire to make government more inclusive by appointing unprecedented numbers of women and minorities to cabinet, judicial, and diplomatic posts, a number of factors thwarted Carter's policy goals. His outsider status helped him win the election but left him without strong ties to party leaders in Congress. Democrats complained that Carter flooded them with comprehensive proposals without consultation or a strategy to get them enacted. Even if he had possessed Lyndon Johnson's political skills, Carter might not have done much better. The economic problems he inherited—unemployment, inflation, and sluggish economic growth—confounded economic doctrine. Usually, rising prices accompanied a humming economy with a strong demand for labor. Now, however, stagflation burdened the economy with both steep inflation and high unemployment.

Carter first targeted unemployment, signing bills that pumped $14 billion into the economy through public works and public service jobs programs and cutting taxes by $34 billion. Unemployment receded, but then inflation surged. Working people, wrote one journalist, "winced and ached" as their paychecks bought less and less, "hollowing their hopes and dreams, their plans for a house or their children's college education." To curb inflation, Carter curtailed federal spending, and the Federal Reserve Board tightened the money supply. Not only did these measures fail to halt inflation, which surpassed 13 percent in 1980, but they also contributed to rising unemployment, reversing the gains made in Carter's first two years.

Carter's commitment to holding down the federal budget frustrated Democrats pushing for comprehensive welfare reform, national health insurance, and a substantial jobs program that would make government the employer of last resort. His refusal to propose a comprehensive national health insurance plan, long a key Democratic Party objective, led to a bitter split with Massachusetts senator Ted Kennedy, who fought Carter for the 1980 presidential nomination. Carter's agreement to legislation to ensure solvency in the Social Security system resulted in higher payroll taxes on lower- and middle-income Americans.

By contrast, corporations and wealthy individuals gained from new legislation, such as a sharp cut in the capital gains tax. When the Chrysler Corporation approached bankruptcy, Congress provided $1.5 billion in loan guarantees to bail out the auto giant. Congress also acted on Carter's proposals to deregulate airlines in 1978 and the banking, trucking, and railroad industries in 1980, beginning a policy turn toward implementing conservatives' attachment to a free market and unfettered private enterprise.

Energy and Environmental Reform

Complicating the government's battle with stagflation was the nation's enormous energy consumption and dependence on foreign nations to fill one-third of its energy demands. Consequently, Carter proposed a comprehensive program to

CHAPTER LOCATOR | How did the Nixon presidency reflect the rise of postwar conservatism? | **Why did the "outsider" presidency of Jimmy Carter fail to gain broad support?**

CHAPTER 30
906 THE CONSERVATIVE TURN

The Fuel Shortage

This billboard appeared in 1980, while Iran held Americans hostage in Teheran (see pages 911–12). Gasoline shortages and rising gas prices vexed motorists all over the country. The shortages and high prices were sparked by the Iranian revolution, which brought to power Ayatollah Ruholla Khomeini, pictured on the billboard. The ad appeals to drivers to observe the fuel-saving 55-mile-per-hour national speed limit imposed in 1974 during the first oil crisis. John W. Hartman Center/Duke University Special Collections Library.

> **VISUAL ACTIVITY**

READING THE IMAGE: What assumptions does the billboard make about Americans' reactions to the Iran hostage crisis? What reasons does the ad give for drivers to respect the speed limit? What reasons are not mentioned?

CONNECTIONS: What impact did the hostage and oil crises have on American politics?

conserve energy, and he elevated its importance by establishing the Department of Energy. Beset with competing demands among energy producers and consumers, Congress picked Carter's program apart. The **National Energy Act of 1978** penalized manufacturers of gas-guzzling automobiles and provided other incentives for conservation and development of alternative fuels, such as wind and solar power, but the act fell far short of a long-term, comprehensive program.

In 1979, a new upheaval in the Middle East, the Iranian revolution, created the most severe energy crisis yet. In midsummer, shortages caused 60 percent of gasoline stations to close down, resulting in long lines and high prices. In response, Congress reduced controls on the oil and gas industry to stimulate American production and imposed a windfall profits tax on producers to redistribute some of the profits they would reap from deregulation.

European nations were just as dependent on foreign oil as was the United States, but they more successfully controlled consumption. They levied high taxes on gasoline, causing people to rely more on public transportation and manufacturers to produce more energy-efficient cars. In the automobile-dependent United States, however, with inadequate public transit, a sprawling population, and an aversion to taxes, politicians dismissed that approach. By the end of the century, the United States, with 6 percent of the world's population, would consume more than 25 percent of global oil production (**Map 30.1** and **Figure 30.1**).

A vigorous environmental movement opposed nuclear energy as an alternative fuel, warning of radiation leakage, potential accidents, and the hazards of radioactive wastes. In 1976, hundreds of members of the Clamshell Alliance

National Energy Act of 1978

▶ Legislation that penalized manufacturers of gas-guzzling automobiles and provided additional incentives for energy conservation and development of alternative fuels, such as wind and solar power. However, the act fell short of the long-term, comprehensive program that President Carter advocated.

What conservative goals were realized in the Reagan administration?

What strategies did liberals use to fight the conservative turn?

How did Ronald Reagan's foreign policy affect the Cold War?

Conclusion: What was the long-term impact of the conservative turn?

☑ **LearningCurve**
Check what you know.
bedfordstmartins.com
/roarkunderstanding

went to jail for attempting to block construction of a nuclear power plant in Seabrook, New Hampshire; other groups sprang up across the country to demand an environment safe from nuclear radiation and waste. The perils of nuclear energy claimed international attention in March 1979, when a meltdown of the reactor core was narrowly averted at the nuclear facility near Harrisburg, Pennsylvania. Popular opposition and the great expense of building nuclear power plants stalled further development of the industry, which provided 10 percent of the nation's electricity in the 1970s. A disaster at Love Canal in Niagara Falls, New York, advanced other environmental goals by underscoring the human costs of unregulated development. Residents suffering high rates of serious illness discovered that their homes sat amid highly

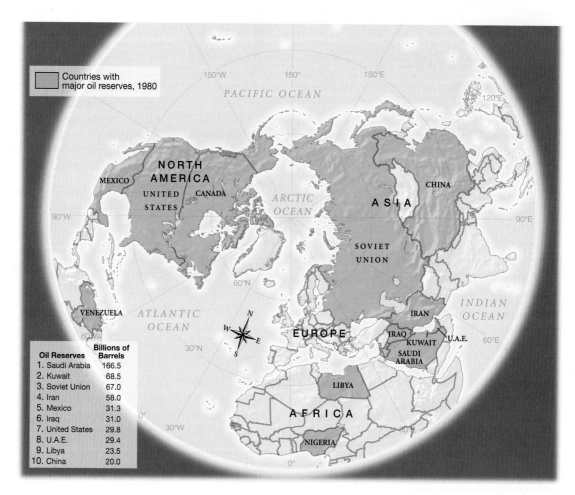

Oil Reserves	Billions of Barrels
1. Saudi Arabia	166.5
2. Kuwait	68.5
3. Soviet Union	67.0
4. Iran	58.0
5. Mexico	31.3
6. Iraq	31.0
7. United States	29.8
8. U.A.E.	29.4
9. Libya	23.5
10. China	20.0

MAP 30.1 ■ Worldwide Oil Reserves, 1980

Data produced by geologists and engineers enable experts to estimate the size of "proved oil reserves," quantities that are recoverable with existing technology and prices. In 1980, total worldwide reserves were estimated at 645 billion barrels. Recovery of reserves depends on many factors, including the location of the oil. Large portions of U.S. reserves, for example, lie under the Gulf of Mexico, where it is expensive to drill and where hurricanes can disrupt operations.

> MAP ACTIVITY

READING THE MAP: Where did the United States rank in 1980 in the possession of oil reserves? About what portion of the total oil reserves were located in the Middle East?

CONNECTIONS: When during the 1970s did the United States experience oil shortages? What caused these shortages?

CHAPTER LOCATOR | How did the Nixon presidency reflect the rise of postwar conservatism? | Why did the "outsider" presidency of Jimmy Carter fail to gain broad support?

908 CHAPTER 30 THE CONSERVATIVE TURN

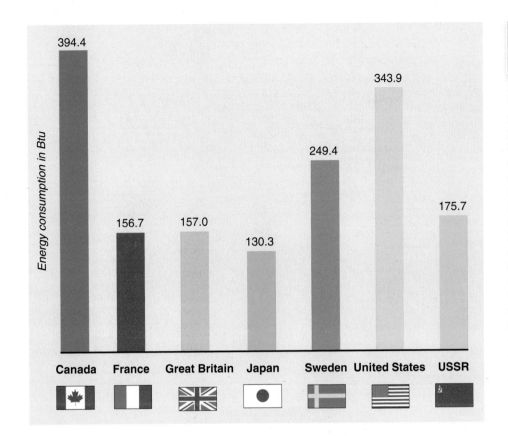

Relative to most other industrialized nations, the United States consumed energy voraciously, with a per capita rate of consumption in 1980 that was more than twice as high as that of Britain, France, and Japan and nearly twice as high as that of the Soviet Union. A number of factors influence a nation's energy consumption (shown here in British thermal units, or Btu), including standard of living, climate, size of landmass and dispersal of population, availability and price of energy, and government policies such as support for public transportation. What country had a per capita rate of consumption even higher than that of the United States?

toxic waste products from a nearby chemical company. Finally responding to the residents' claims in 1978, the state of New York agreed to help families relocate, and the Carter administration sponsored legislation in 1980 that created the so-called Superfund, $1.6 billion for cleanup of hazardous wastes left by the chemical industry around the country.

Carter also signed bills to improve clean air and water programs; to expand the Arctic National Wildlife Refuge preserve in Alaska; and to control strip-mining, which left destructive scars on the land. During the 1979 gasoline crisis, Carter attempted to balance the development of domestic fuel sources with environmental concerns, winning legislation to conserve energy and to provide incentives for the development of solar energy and environmentally friendly alternative fuels.

Promoting Human Rights Abroad

"We're ashamed of what our government is as we deal with other nations around the world," Jimmy Carter charged, promising to reverse U.S. support of dictators, secret diplomacy, interference in the internal affairs of other countries, and excessive reliance on military solutions. Human rights formed the cornerstone of his approach. The Carter administration applied economic pressure on governments that denied their citizens basic rights, refusing aid or trading privileges to nations such as Chile and El Salvador, as well as to the white minority governments of Rhodesia and South Africa. Yet in other instances, Carter sacrificed human rights

What conservative goals were realized in the Reagan administration?

What strategies did liberals use to fight the conservative turn?

How did Ronald Reagan's foreign policy affect the Cold War?

Conclusion: What was the long-term impact of the conservative turn?

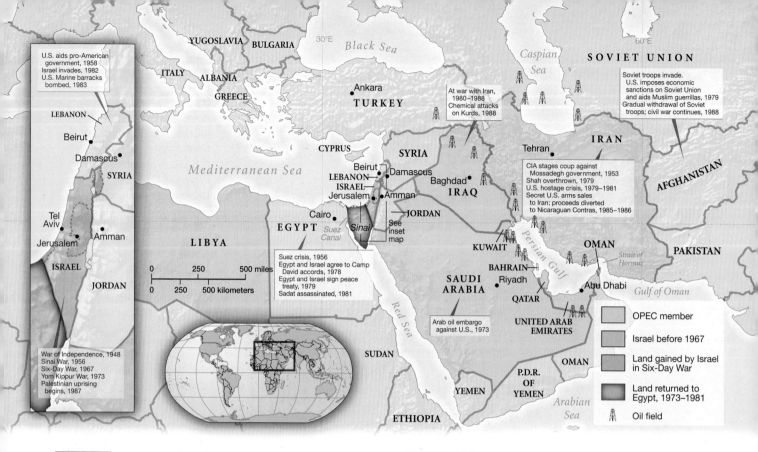

MAP 30.2 ■ The Middle East, 1948–1989

Determination to preserve access to the rich oil reserves of the Middle East and commitment to the security of Israel were the fundamental — and often conflicting — principles of U.S. foreign policy in that region.

> **MAP ACTIVITY**

READING THE MAP: Where did the United States become involved diplomatically or militarily in the Middle East between 1948 and 1989?

CONNECTIONS: What role did U.S. foreign policy regarding the Middle East and events in Israel play in provoking the 1973 Arab oil embargo against the United States? What precipitated the taking of U.S. hostages in Iran in 1979?

---

ideals to strategic and security considerations, invoking no sanctions against repressive governments in Iran, South Korea, and the Philippines.

Carter's human rights principles faced another test when a popular movement overthrew an oppressive dictatorship in Nicaragua. U.S. officials were uneasy about the leftist Sandinistas who led the rebellion and had ties to Cuba. Once they assumed power in 1979, however, Carter recognized the new government and sent economic aid, signaling that the way a government treated its citizens was as important as how anti-Communist and friendly to American interests it was.

Panama Canal treaty

▶ 1977 agreement that returned control of the Panama Canal from the United States to Panama in 2000. To pass the treaty, President Carter overcame stiff opposition in the Senate from conservatives who regarded control of the canal as vital to America's interests.

Applying moral principles to relations with Panama, Carter sped up negotiations over control of the Panama Canal and in 1977 signed a treaty providing for Panama's takeover of the canal in 2000. Supporters viewed the treaty as restitution for the U.S. seizure of Panamanian territory in 1903. Opponents insisted on retaining the vital waterway. "We bought it, we paid for it, it's ours," claimed Ronald Reagan during the presidential primaries of 1976. It took a massive effort by the administration to get Senate ratification of the **Panama Canal treaty**.

Seeking to promote peace in the Middle East, Carter seized on the courage of Egyptian president Anwar Sadat, the first Arab leader to risk his political

CHAPTER LOCATOR | How did the Nixon presidency reflect the rise of postwar conservatism? | Why did the "outsider" presidency of Jimmy Carter fail to gain broad support?

910 CHAPTER 30 THE CONSERVATIVE TURN

career by talking directly with Israeli officials. In 1979, Carter invited Sadat and Israeli prime minister Menachem Begin to Camp David, Maryland, where he applied his tenacious diplomacy for thirteen days. These talks led to the **Camp David accords**, whereby Egypt became the first Arab state to recognize Israel, and Israel agreed to gradual withdrawal from the Sinai Peninsula, which it had seized in the 1967 Six-Day War (**Map 30.2**). Although the issues of Palestinian self-determination in other Israeli-occupied territories (the West Bank and Gaza) and the plight of Palestinian refugees remained unresolved, Carter had nurtured the first meaningful steps toward peace in the Middle East.

The Cold War Intensifies

Consistent with his human rights approach, Carter preferred to pursue national security through nonmilitary means and initially sought accommodation with the nation's Cold War enemies. Following up on Nixon's initiatives, in 1979 he formally recognized the People's Republic of China. That same year, he and Soviet premier Leonid Brezhnev signed a second strategic arms reduction treaty.

Yet that same year, Carter decided to pursue a military buildup when the Soviet Union invaded neighboring Afghanistan, whose recently installed Communist government was threatened by Muslim opposition (see Map 30.2). Carter imposed economic sanctions on the Soviet Union, barred U.S. participation in the 1980 Summer Olympic Games in Moscow, and obtained legislation requiring all nineteen-year-old men to register for the draft.

Claiming that Soviet actions jeopardized oil supplies from the Middle East, the president announced the "Carter Doctrine," threatening the use of any means necessary to prevent an outside force from gaining control of the Persian Gulf. His human rights policy fell by the wayside as the United States stepped up aid to the military dictatorship in Afghanistan's neighbor, Pakistan, and the CIA funneled secret aid through Pakistan to the Afghan rebels. Finally, Carter called for hefty increases in defense spending.

Events in Iran also encouraged this hard-line approach. Generous U.S. arms and aid had not enabled the shah to crush Iranian dissidents who still resented the CIA's role in the overthrow of the Mossadegh government in 1953 (see chapter 27), condemned the shah's brutal attempts to silence opposition, and detested his adoption of Western culture and values. These grievances erupted into a revolution in 1979 that forced the shah out of Iran and brought to power Shiite Islamic fundamentalists led by Ayatollah Ruholla Khomeini, whom the shah had exiled in 1964.

Carter's decision to allow the shah into the United States for medical treatment enraged Iranians, who believed that the United States would restore the shah to power as it had done in 1953. On November 4, 1979, a crowd broke into the U.S. Embassy in Iran's capital, Teheran, and seized sixty-six U.S. diplomats, CIA officers, citizens, and military attachés. Refusing the captors' demands that the shah be returned to Iran for trial, Carter froze Iranian assets in U.S. banks and placed an embargo on Iranian oil. In April 1980, he sent a small military operation into Iran, but the rescue mission failed.

The disastrous rescue attempt and scenes of blindfolded U.S. citizens paraded before TV cameras fed Americans' feelings of impotence, simmering since the defeat in Vietnam. These frustrations in turn increased support for a

Camp David accords

▶ Agreements between Egypt and Israel reached at the 1979 talks hosted by President Carter at Camp David. In the accords, Egypt became the first Arab state to recognize Israel, and Israel agreed to gradual withdrawal from the Sinai Peninsula.

| What conservative goals were realized in the Reagan administration? | What strategies did liberals use to fight the conservative turn? | How did Ronald Reagan's foreign policy affect the Cold War? | Conclusion: What was the long-term impact of the conservative turn? | ☑ LearningCurve Check what you know. bedfordstmartins.com /roarkunderstanding |

911

Iran hostage crisis

▶ Crisis that began in 1979 after the deposed shah of Iran was allowed into the United States following the Iranian revolution. Iranians broke into the U.S. Embassy in Teheran and took sixty-six Americans hostage. The hostage crisis contributed to President Carter's defeat in the 1980 presidential election.

more militaristic foreign policy. Opposition to Soviet-American détente, combined with the Soviet invasion of Afghanistan, nullified the thaw in superpower relations that had begun in the 1960s. The Iran hostage crisis dominated the news during the 1980 presidential campaign and contributed to Carter's defeat. Iran freed the hostages the day he left office, but relations with the United States remained tense.

> **QUICK REVIEW**

How did Carter implement his commitment to human rights, and why did human rights give way to other priorities?

CHAPTER LOCATOR | How did the Nixon presidency reflect the rise of postwar conservatism? | Why did the "outsider" presidency of Jimmy Carter fail to gain broad support?

CHAPTER 30
912 THE CONSERVATIVE TURN

What conservative goals were realized in the Reagan administration?

Reagan's victory in 1980 helped to reshape the Republican Party by attracting millions of evangelical Christians. In his 1983 address to the National Association of Evangelicals, Reagan called the Soviet Union an "evil empire" and appealed to religious conservatives with strong words about abortion and prayer in the schools, rejoicing that "America is in the midst of a spiritual awakening and a moral renewal." Ronald Reagan Presidential Library.

THE ELECTION OF RONALD REAGAN in 1980 marked the most important turning point in politics since Franklin D. Roosevelt's election in 1932. Reagan's victory established conservatism's dominance in the Republican Party, while Democrats searched for voter support by moving toward the right. The United States was not alone in this political shift. Conservatives rose to power in Britain, West Germany, Canada, and Sweden, while socialist and social democratic governments elsewhere trimmed their welfare states.

The Reagan administration embraced the conservative Christian values of the New Right, but it left its most important mark on the economy: victory over inflation, deregulation of industry, enormous tax cuts, and a staggering federal budget deficit. Popular culture celebrated financial success and displaying wealth, but poverty increased and economic inequality grew. Although the Reagan era did not see a policy revolution comparable to that of the New Deal, it dealt a sharp blow to the liberalism that had informed American politics since the 1930s.

What conservative goals were realized in the Reagan administration?

What strategies did liberals use to fight the conservative turn?

How did Ronald Reagan's foreign policy affect the Cold War?

Conclusion: What was the long-term impact of the conservative turn?

☑ LearningCurve
Check what you know.
bedfordstmartins.com
/roarkunderstanding

New (Christian) Right
▶ Politically active religious conservatives who became particularly vocal in the 1980s. The New Right criticized feminism, opposed abortion and homosexuality, and promoted "family values" and military preparedness.

Appealing to the New Right and Beyond

Sixty-nine-year-old Ronald Reagan was the oldest candidate ever nominated for the presidency. Coming first to national attention as a movie actor, he initially shared the politics of his staunchly Democratic father but moved to the right in the 1940s and 1950s. He campaigned for Barry Goldwater in 1964.

Reagan's political career took off when he was elected governor of California in 1966. He ran as a conservative, but in office he displayed flexibility, approving a major tax increase, a strong water pollution bill, and a liberal abortion law. Displaying similar agility in the 1980 presidential campaign, he softened earlier attacks on programs such as Social Security and chose the moderate George H. W. Bush as his running mate.

Reagan's campaign capitalized on the economic recession and the international challenges symbolized by the Americans held hostage in Iran. Repeatedly, Reagan asked voters, "Are you better off now than you were four years ago?" He promised to "take government off the backs of the people" and to restore Americans' morale and other nations' respect. Reagan won the election, while Republicans took control of the Senate for the first time since the 1950s.

While the economy and the Iran hostage crisis sealed Reagan's victory, he also benefited from the burgeoning grassroots conservative movements. Reagan's support from religious conservatives, predominantly Protestants, constituted a relatively new phenomenon in politics known as the **New Right** or **New Christian Right**.

> The Reagan Coalition

- Free-market advocates
- Militant anti-Communists
- Fundamentalist Christians
- White southerners
- Reagan Democrats: white working-class Democrats who were disenchanted with the policies of the Democratic Party

During the 1970s, evangelical and fundamentalist Christianity claimed thousands of new adherents. Evangelical ministers such as Pat Robertson preached to huge television audiences, attacking feminism, abortion, and homosexuality. They called for the restoration of old-fashioned "family values." A considerable number of Catholics shared the fundamentalists' goal of a return to "Christian values."

Conservatives created political organizations such as the Moral Majority, founded by the Reverend Jerry Falwell in 1979, to fight "left-wing, social welfare bills, . . . pornography, homosexuality, [and] the advocacy of immorality in school textbooks." Dr. James Dobson, a clinical psychologist with a popular Christian talk show, founded the Family Research Council in 1983 to lobby Congress for measures to curb abortion, divorce, homosexuality, and single motherhood. The publications and think tanks of more traditional conservatives, who stressed limited government at home and militant anticommunism abroad, likewise flourished, while the monthly *Phyllis Schlafly Report* merged the sentiments of the old and new right.

CHAPTER LOCATOR | How did the Nixon presidency reflect the rise of postwar conservatism? | Why did the "outsider" presidency of Jimmy Carter fail to gain broad support?

CHAPTER 30
914 THE CONSERVATIVE TURN

Reagan spoke for the New Right on such issues as abortion and school prayer, but he did not push hard for so-called moral or social policies. Instead, his major achievements fulfilled goals of the older right—strengthening the nation's anti-Communist posture as well as reducing taxes and government restraints on free enterprise. "In the present crisis," Reagan declared, "government is not the solution to our problem, government is the problem."

Reagan was extraordinarily popular, appealing even to Americans who opposed his policies but warmed to his optimism, confidence, and easygoing humor. Ignoring the darker moments of the American past, he presented a version of history that Americans could feel good about.

Unleashing Free Enterprise

Reagan's first domestic objective was a massive tax cut. To justify tax cuts in the face of a large budget deficit, Reagan relied on a new theory called **supply-side economics**, which held that cutting taxes would actually increase revenue by enabling businesses to expand, encouraging individuals to work harder because they could keep more of their earnings (especially the wealthy who enjoyed the greatest tax savings), and increasing the production of goods and services—the supply—which in turn would boost demand. Reagan promised that the economy would grow so much that the government would recoup the lost taxes, but instead it incurred a galloping deficit.

In the summer of 1981, Congress passed the **Economic Recovery Tax Act**, the largest tax reduction in U.S. history. Rates were cut from 14 percent to 11 percent for the lowest-income individuals and from 70 percent to 50 percent for the wealthiest, who also benefited from reduced levies on corporations, capital gains, gifts, and inheritances. A second measure, the Tax Reform Act of 1986, cut taxes still further. Although the 1986 law narrowed loopholes used primarily by the wealthy, affluent Americans saved far more on their tax bills than did average tax-payers, and the distribution of wealth tipped further in favor of the rich. Carter had confined deregulation to particular industries, such as air transportation and banking, while increasing health, safety, and environmental regulations. The Reagan administration, by contrast, pursued across-the-board deregulation. It declined to enforce the Sherman Antitrust Act (see chapter 18), which limited monopolies, against an unprecedented number of business mergers and takeovers. Reagan also loosened regulations protecting employee health and safety, and he weakened labor unions. When members of the Professional Air Traffic Controllers Organization—one of the few unions to support him in 1980—struck in 1981, Reagan fired them, destroying the union and intimidating organized labor.

Reagan blamed environmental laws for the nation's sluggish economic growth and targeted them for deregulation. His first secretary of the interior, James Watt, declared, "We will mine more, drill more, cut more timber," and released federal lands to private exploitation. Meanwhile, the head of the Environmental Protection Agency relaxed enforcement of air and water pollution standards. Of environmentalists, Reagan wisecracked, "I don't think they'll be happy until the White House looks like a bird's nest," but their numbers grew in opposition to his policies. Popular support for environmental protection forced several officials to resign and blocked full realization of Reagan's deregulatory goals.

supply-side economics
▶ Economic theory claiming that tax cuts for individuals (especially the wealthy) and businesses encourage investment and production (supply) and stimulate consumption (demand) because individuals can keep more of their earnings. Despite promises to the contrary, under President Reagan supply-side economics created a massive federal budget deficit.

Economic Recovery Tax Act
▶ Legislation passed by Congress in 1981 that authorized the largest reduction in taxes in the nation's history. The tax cuts disproportionately benefited affluent Americans and widened the distribution of wealth in favor of the rich.

| What conservative goals were realized in the Reagan administration? | What strategies did liberals use to fight the conservative turn? | How did Ronald Reagan's foreign policy affect the Cold War? | Conclusion: What was the long-term impact of the conservative turn? | ✓ LearningCurve Check what you know. bedfordstmartins.com /roarkunderstanding |

915

Deregulation of the banking industry, begun under Carter with bipartisan support, created a crisis in the savings and loan industry. Some of the newly deregulated savings and loan institutions (S&Ls) extended enormous loans to real estate developers and invested in other high-yield but risky ventures. S&L owners reaped lavish profits, and their depositors enjoyed high interest rates. When real estate values began to plunge, hundreds of S&Ls went bankrupt. After Congress voted to bail out the S&L industry in 1989, American taxpayers bore the burden of the largest financial scandal in U.S. history, estimated at more than $100 billion.

The S&L crisis deepened the federal deficit. Reagan cut funds for food stamps, job training, student aid, and other social welfare programs, and hundreds of thousands of people lost benefits. Yet increases in defense spending far exceeded the budget cuts, the deficit soared, and the nation's debt tripled to $2.3 trillion, consuming one-seventh of all federal expenditures. Despite Reagan's antigovernment rhetoric, the number of federal employees increased from 2.9 million to 3.1 million during his presidency.

It took the severest recession since the 1930s to squeeze inflation out of the U.S. economy. Unemployment approached 11 percent late in 1982, and record numbers of banks and businesses closed. The threat of unemployment further undermined organized labor, forcing unions to make concessions that management insisted were necessary for industry's survival. In 1983, the economy recovered and entered a period of unprecedented growth.

That economic upswing and Reagan's own popularity posed a formidable challenge to the Democrats in the 1984 election. They nominated Carter's vice president, Walter F. Mondale, to head the ticket, but even his precedent-breaking move in choosing a woman as his running mate—New York representative Geraldine A. Ferraro—did not save the Democrats from a humiliating defeat. Reagan charged his opponents with concentrating on America's failures, while he emphasized success and possibility. Democrats, he claimed, "see an America where every day is April 15th [the deadline for income tax returns] . . . we see an America where every day is the Fourth of July." Reagan was reelected in a landslide victory, winning 59 percent of the popular vote and every state but Mondale's Minnesota.

Winners and Losers in a Flourishing Economy

After the economy took off in 1983, some Americans won great fortunes. Popular culture celebrated making money and displaying wealth. Books by business wizards topped best seller lists, the press described lavish million-dollar parties, and a new television show, *Lifestyles of the Rich and Famous,* drew large audiences. College students listed making money as their primary ambition.

Many of the newly wealthy got rich from moving assets around rather than from producing goods, making money by manipulating debt and restructuring corporations through mergers and takeovers. Notable exceptions included Steve Jobs, who invented the Apple computer in his garage; Bill Gates, who transformed the software industry; and Liz Claiborne, who created a billion-dollar fashion enterprise. Most financial wizards operated within the law, but greed sometimes led to criminal convictions.

Older industries faced increasing international pressures, as German and Japanese corporations overtook U.S. manufacturing in steel, automobiles, and

CHAPTER LOCATOR | How did the Nixon presidency reflect the rise of postwar conservatism? | Why did the "outsider" presidency of Jimmy Carter fail to gain broad support?

CHAPTER 30
916   THE CONSERVATIVE TURN

electronics. International competition forced the collapse of some older companies, while others moved factories and jobs abroad to be closer to foreign markets or to benefit from the low wages in countries such as Mexico and Korea. Service industries expanded and created new jobs at home, but at substantially lower wages.

The weakening of organized labor combined with the decline in manufacturing to erode the position of blue-collar workers. Chicago steelworker Ike Mazo, who contemplated the $6-an-hour jobs available to him, fumed, "It's an attack on the living standards of workers." Increasingly, a second income was needed to stave off economic decline. By 1990, nearly 60 percent of married women with young children worked outside the home. Yet even with two incomes, families struggled. Speaking of her children, Mazo's wife confessed, "I worry about their future every day. Will we be able to put them through college?"

In keeping with conservative philosophy, Reagan adhered to trickle-down economics, insisting that a booming economy would benefit everyone. Average personal income did rise during his tenure, but the trend toward greater economic inequality that had begun in the 1970s intensified in the 1980s, encouraged in part by his tax policies.

> Economic Inequality in the 1980s

- The number of full-time workers earning wages below the poverty level rose from 12 percent to 18 percent of all workers.
- The average $10,000 gap between men's and women's annual earnings made survival harder for the nearly 20 percent of families headed by women.
- The percentage of Americans living in poverty increased from 11.7 to 13.5, the highest poverty rate in the industrialized world.
- The economic boom bypassed racial minorities, female-headed families, and children.
- One in five children lived in poverty.

QUICK REVIEW <

Why did economic inequality increase during the Reagan administration?

| What conservative goals were realized in the Reagan administration? | What strategies did liberals use to fight the conservative turn? | How did Ronald Reagan's foreign policy affect the Cold War? | Conclusion: What was the long-term impact of the conservative turn? | ☑ LearningCurve Check what you know. bedfordstmartins.com /roarkunderstanding |

What strategies did liberals use to fight the conservative turn?

The Abortion Debate After the *Roe v. Wade* decision in 1973, several states enacted restrictions on abortion. In 1989, the Supreme Court upheld a Missouri law prohibiting public employees from performing abortions except to save a woman's life. The law also banned abortions in public buildings and required physicians to perform viability tests on the fetus after twenty weeks. Here, activists on both sides rally before the Supreme Court. AP Images/Ron Edmonds.

THE RISE OF CONSERVATISM put liberal social movements on the defensive, as the government moved away from the national commitment to equal opportunity undertaken in the 1960s and the president's federal court appointments reflected that shift. Feminists and minority groups fought to keep protections they had recently won, and the gay and lesbian rights movement grew.

Battles in the Courts and Congress

Ronald Reagan agreed with conservatives that the nation had moved too far in guaranteeing rights to minority groups. Crying "reverse discrimination," conservatives maintained that affirmative action unfairly hurt whites. Instead, they called for "color-blind" policies, ignoring statistics showing that minorities and white women still lagged far behind white men in opportunities and income.

Intense mobilization by civil rights groups, educational leaders, labor, and even corporate America prevented the administration from abandoning affirmative action, and the Supreme Court upheld important antidiscrimination policies. Moreover, against Reagan's wishes, Congress extended the Voting Rights Act with veto-proof majorities. The administration did, however, limit civil rights enforcement by appointing conservatives to the Justice Department, the Civil Rights Commission, and other agencies as well as by slashing their budgets.

CHAPTER LOCATOR | How did the Nixon presidency reflect the rise of postwar conservatism? | Why did the "outsider" presidency of Jimmy Carter fail to gain broad support?

918 CHAPTER 30
THE CONSERVATIVE TURN

Congress stepped in to defend antidiscrimination programs after the Justice Department, in the case of *Grove City v. Bell* (1984), persuaded the Supreme Court to severely weaken Title IX of the Education Amendments Act of 1972, a key law promoting equal opportunity in education. In 1988, Congress passed the Civil Rights Restoration Act over Reagan's veto, reversing the administration's victory in *Grove City* and banning government funding of any organization that practiced discrimination on the basis of race, color, national origin, sex, disability, or age.

The *Grove City* decision reflected a rightward movement in the federal judiciary, on which liberals had counted as a powerful ally. With the opportunity to appoint half of the 761 federal court judges and three new Supreme Court justices, President Reagan encouraged this trend by carefully selecting conservative candidates. The full impact of these appointments became clear after Reagan left office, as the Court allowed states to impose restrictions that weakened access to abortion for poor and rural women, reduced protections against employment discrimination, and whittled down legal safeguards against the death penalty.

Feminism on the Defensive

A signal achievement of the New Right was capturing the Republican Party's position on women's rights. For the first time in its history, the party took an explicitly antifeminist tone, opposing both the **Equal Rights Amendment (ERA)** and abortion rights, key goals of women's rights activists. When the time limit for ratification of the ERA ran out in 1982, feminists suffered defeat on a central objective (see chapter 28).

Cast on the defensive, feminists focused more on women's economic and family problems, where they found some common ground with the Reagan administration. The Child Support Enforcement Amendments Act helped single and divorced mothers collect court-ordered child support payments from absent fathers. The Retirement Equity Act of 1984 benefited divorced and older women by strengthening their claims to their husbands' pensions and enabling women to qualify more easily for private retirement pensions.

The Reagan administration had its own concerns about women, specifically about the gender gap in voting—women's tendency to support liberal and Democratic candidates in larger numbers than men did. Reagan appointed three women to cabinet posts and, in 1981, selected the first woman, Sandra Day O'Connor, a moderate conservative, for the Supreme Court, despite the Christian Right's objection to her support of abortion. But these actions accompanied a general decline in the number of women and minorities in high-level government positions. And with higher poverty rates than men, women suffered most from Reagan's cuts in social programs.

Although Supreme Court decisions placed restrictions on women's ability to obtain abortions, feminists fought successfully to retain the basic principles of *Roe v. Wade*. Moreover, they won a key decision from the Supreme

> CHRONOLOGY

1981
- Researchers discover AIDS virus.
- Sandra Day O'Connor becomes first woman Supreme Court justice.

1984
- Retirement Equity Act is passed.

1988
- Civil Rights Restoration Act is passed over Reagan's veto.

Equal Rights Amendment (ERA)

▶ Constitutional amendment passed by Congress in 1972 that would require equal treatment of men and women under federal and state law. Facing fierce opposition from the New Right and the Republican Party, the ERA was defeated as time ran out for state ratification in 1982.

Ratified the ERA

Did not ratify the ERA

Ratified and then voted to rescind ratification

The Fight for the Equal Rights Amendment

What conservative goals were realized in the Reagan administration?

What strategies did liberals use to fight the conservative turn?

How did Ronald Reagan's foreign policy affect the Cold War?

Conclusion: What was the long-term impact of the conservative turn?

✓ LearningCurve
Check what you know.
bedfordstmartins.com /roarkunderstanding

919

Since June 1970, when gays and lesbians marched in New York City on the first anniversary of Stonewall (see chapter 28), annual gay pride parades have taken place throughout the United States. According to history professor Robert Dawidoff, the parades are not about "flaunting private things in public," as some people have charged, but a way for gay men and lesbians to express "pride . . . in having survived the thousand petty harassments and reminders of a special status we neither seek nor merit." Friends and families of homosexuals participate in the parades, as this sign from a parade in Los Angeles indicates. © Bettmann/Corbis.

Court ruling that sexual harassment in the workplace constituted sex discrimination. Feminists also made some gains at the state level in such areas as pay equity, rape, and domestic violence.

The Gay and Lesbian Rights Movement

In contrast to feminism and other social movements, gay and lesbian rights activism grew during the 1980s, galvanized in part by the discovery in 1981 of a devastating disease, acquired immune deficiency syndrome (AIDS). Because initially the disease disproportionately affected male homosexuals in the United States, activists mobilized to promote public funding for AIDS education, prevention, and treatment.

The gay and lesbian rights movement helped closeted homosexuals "come out," and their visibility increased awareness, if not always acceptance, of homosexuality among the larger population. Beginning with the election of Elaine Noble to the Massachusetts legislature in 1974, several openly gay politicians won offices ranging from mayor to member of Congress, and the Democrats began to include gay rights in their party platforms. Activists organized gay rights marches throughout the country.

Popular attitudes about homosexuality moved toward greater tolerance but remained complex, leading to uneven changes in policies. Dozens of cities banned job discrimination against homosexuals, and beginning with Wisconsin in 1982, eleven states made sexual orientation a protected category under civil rights laws. Local governments and large corporations began to offer health insurance and other benefits to same-sex domestic partners.

Yet a strong countermovement challenged the drive for gay rights. The Christian Right targeted gays and lesbians as symbols of national immorality, and they succeeded in overturning some homosexual rights measures. Many states removed antisodomy laws from the books, but in 1986 the Supreme Court upheld the constitutionality of such laws. Until the Court reversed that opinion in 2003, more than a dozen states retained statutes that left homosexuals vulnerable to criminal charges for private consensual behavior.

> **QUICK REVIEW**

What gains and setbacks did minorities, feminists, and gays and lesbians experience during the Reagan years?

CHAPTER LOCATOR | How did the Nixon presidency reflect the rise of postwar conservatism? | Why did the "outsider" presidency of Jimmy Carter fail to gain broad support?

CHAPTER 30
920 THE CONSERVATIVE TURN

How did Ronald Reagan's foreign policy affect the Cold War?

The Fireside Summit This photograph captures the warmth that developed between President Ronald Reagan and Soviet leader Mikhail Gorbachev at their first meeting in Geneva in November 1985. Although the meeting did not produce any key agreements, the two men began to appreciate each other's concerns and to build trust, launching a relationship that would lead to nuclear arms reductions and the end of the Cold War. Ronald Reagan Presidential Library.

RONALD REAGAN ACCELERATED Jimmy Carter's arms buildup and harshly censured the Soviet Union, calling it "an evil empire." Yet despite the new aggressiveness—or, as some argued, because of it—Reagan presided over the most impressive thaw in superpower conflict since the Cold War had begun. On the periphery of the Cold War, however, Reagan practiced militant anticommunism, assisting antileftist movements in Asia, Africa, and Central America. He also dispatched troops to the Middle East and the Caribbean.

Militarization and Interventions Abroad

Reagan expanded the military with new bombers and missiles, an enhanced nuclear force in Europe, a larger navy, and a rapid-deployment force. Throughout Reagan's presidency, defense spending averaged $216 billion a year, up from $158 billion in the Carter years and higher even than in the Vietnam era.

Reagan startled many of his own advisers in March 1983 by announcing plans for research on the **Strategic Defense Initiative (SDI)**. Immediately dubbed "Star

Strategic Defense Initiative (SDI)

▶ Project launched by President Reagan to deploy lasers in space that would destroy enemy missiles before they could reach their targets. The Soviets protested that it violated the 1972 Antiballistic Missile Treaty. The project cost billions of dollars without producing a working system.

What conservative goals were realized in the Reagan administration?

What strategies did liberals use to fight the conservative turn?

How did Ronald Reagan's foreign policy affect the Cold War?

Conclusion: What was the long-term impact of the conservative turn?

✓ LearningCurve
Check what you know.
bedfordstmartins.com /roarkunderstanding

921

Wars" by critics who doubted its feasibility, the project would deploy lasers in space to destroy enemy missiles before they could reach their targets. Such a defense would allow the United States to strike first and not fear retaliation. The Soviets reacted angrily because SDI violated the 1972 Antiballistic Missile Treaty and because they would have to make huge investments to develop their own Star Wars technology. Subsequent administrations continued to spend billions on SDI research without producing a working system.

Reagan justified the military buildup and SDI as a means to negotiate with the Soviets from a position of strength, but he provoked an outburst of pleas to halt the arms race. In 1982, a rally demanding a freeze on additional nuclear weapons drew 700,000 people in New York City. That same year, the National Conference of Catholic Bishops issued a strong call for nuclear disarmament. Hundreds of thousands demonstrated across Europe, stimulated by fears of new U.S. missiles scheduled for deployment there in 1983.

The U.S. military buildup was impotent before the growing threat of terrorism by non-state organizations that sought political objectives by attacking civilian populations. Terrorism had a long history throughout the world, but in the 1970s and 1980s Americans saw it escalate in the Middle East, used by Palestinians after the Israeli occupation of the West Bank and by other groups hostile to Western policies. The terrorist organization Hezbollah, composed of Shiite Muslims and backed by Iran and Syria, arose in Lebanon in 1982 after Israeli forces invaded that country to stop the Palestine Liberation Organization from using sanctuaries in Lebanon to launch attacks on Israel.

Reagan's effort to stabilize Lebanon by sending 2,000 Marines to join an international peacekeeping mission failed. In April 1983, a suicide attack on the U.S. Embassy in Beirut killed 63 people, and in October a Hezbollah fighter drove a bomb-filled truck into a U.S. barracks there, killing 241 Marines. The attack prompted the withdrawal of U.S. troops, and Lebanon remained in chaos, while incidents of murder, kidnapping, and hijacking by various Middle Eastern extremist groups continued.

Following a Cold War pattern begun under Eisenhower, the Reagan administration sought to contain leftist movements across the globe. In October 1983, 5,000 U.S. troops invaded Grenada, a small Caribbean nation where Marxists had staged a successful coup. In Asia, the United States quietly aided the Afghan rebels' war against Afghanistan's Soviet-backed government. In the African nation of Angola, the United States armed

Attack on the Marine Barracks in Beirut

On October 23, 1983, members of Islamic Jihad, an anti-Israel, anti-Western, Iran-sponsored terrorist group, attacked U.S. troops stationed in Lebanon by exploding a car bomb outside the Marine compound near the Beirut airport. The Reagan administration withdrew from Lebanon, called "a thousand-year-old hornet's nest" by one official. Here military personnel search for and remove bodies of their 241 dead comrades. © Bettmann/Corbis.

CHAPTER LOCATOR | How did the Nixon presidency reflect the rise of postwar conservatism? | Why did the "outsider" presidency of Jimmy Carter fail to gain broad support?

922 CHAPTER 30
THE CONSERVATIVE TURN

rebel forces against the government supported by the Soviet Union and Cuba. Reagan also sided with the South African government, which was brutally suppressing black protest against apartheid, forcing Congress to override his veto in order to impose economic sanctions against South Africa.

Administration officials were most fearful of left-wing movements in Central America, which Reagan claimed could "destabilize the entire region from the Panama Canal to Mexico." When a leftist uprising occurred in El Salvador in 1981, the United States sent money and military advisers to prop up the authoritarian government. In neighboring Nicaragua, the administration secretly aided the Contras, an armed coalition seeking to unseat the left-wing Sandinistas, who had toppled a long-standing dictatorship.

El Salvador and Nicaragua

The Iran-Contra Scandal

Fearing another Vietnam, many Americans opposed aligning the United States with reactionary forces not supported by the majority of Nicaraguans. Congress repeatedly instructed the president to stop aiding the Contras, but the administration continued to secretly provide them with weapons and training. The Reagan administration also helped wreck the Nicaraguan economy. With support for his government undermined, Nicaragua's president, Daniel Ortega, agreed to a political settlement, and when he was defeated by a coalition of all the opposition groups, he stepped aside.

Secret aid to the Contras was part of a larger project that came to be known as the **Iran-Contra scandal**. It began in 1985 when officials of the National Security Council and CIA covertly arranged to sell arms to Iran, then in the midst of an eight-year war with neighboring Iraq, even while the United States openly supplied Iraq with funds and weapons. The purpose was to get Iran to pressure Hezbollah to release American hostages being held in Lebanon. Funds from the arms sales were then channeled through Swiss bank accounts to aid the Nicaraguan Contras. Over the objections of his secretary of state and secretary of defense, Reagan approved the arms sales, but the three subsequently denied knowing that the proceeds were diverted to the Contras.

When news of the affair surfaced in November 1986, the Reagan administration faced serious charges. The president's aides had defied Congress's express ban on military aid for the Contras. Investigations by an independent prosecutor appointed by Reagan led to a trial in which seven individuals pleaded guilty or were convicted of lying to Congress and destroying evidence. One felony conviction was later overturned on a technicality, and President George H. W. Bush pardoned the other six officials in December 1992. The independent prosecutor's final report found no evidence that Reagan had broken the law, but it concluded that he had known about the diversion of funds to the Contras and had "knowingly participated or at least acquiesced" in covering up the scandal.

Iran-Contra scandal

▶ Reagan administration scandal that involved the sale of arms to Iran, in exchange for Iran's efforts to secure the release of hostages held in Lebanon, and the redirection of the proceeds of those sales to the Nicaraguan Contras.

A Thaw in Soviet-American Relations

A momentous reduction in Cold War tensions soon overshadowed the Iran-Contra scandal. The new Soviet-American accord depended both on Reagan's flexibility

| What conservative goals were realized in the Reagan administration? | What strategies did liberals use to fight the conservative turn? | **How did Ronald Reagan's foreign policy affect the Cold War?** | Conclusion: What was the long-term impact of the conservative turn? | ✓ LearningCurve Check what you know. bedfordstmartins.com /roarkunderstanding |

923

and profound desire to end the possibility of nuclear war and on an innovative Soviet head of state who recognized that his country's domestic problems demanded an easing of Cold War antagonism. Mikhail Gorbachev assumed power in 1985 determined to revitalize the Soviet economy, which was incapable of delivering basic consumer goods. Hoping to stimulate production and streamline distribution, Gorbachev introduced some elements of free enterprise and proclaimed a new era of *glasnost* (greater freedom of expression), eventually allowing contested elections and challenges to Communist rule.

Concerns about immense defense budgets moved both Reagan and Gorbachev to the negotiating table. Enormous military expenditures stood between the Soviet premier and his goal of economic revival. With growing popular support for arms reductions, Reagan made disarmament a major goal in his last years in office and readily responded when Gorbachev took the initiative. The two leaders met four times between 1985 and 1988. Although Reagan's insistence on proceeding with SDI nearly killed the talks, by December 1987 the superpowers had completed an **intermediate-range nuclear forces (INF) agreement**. It eliminated all short- and medium-range missiles from Europe and provided for on-site inspection for the first time. This was also the first time that either nation had agreed to eliminate weapons already in place.

In 1988, Gorbachev further reduced tensions by announcing a gradual withdrawal from Afghanistan, which had become the Soviet equivalent of America's Vietnam. In addition, the Soviet Union, the United States, and Cuba agreed on a political settlement of the civil war in Angola. In the Middle East, both superpowers supported a cease-fire and peace talks in the eight-year war between Iran and Iraq. Within three years, the Cold War that had defined the world for nearly half a century would be history.

intermediate-range nuclear forces (INF) agreement

▶ Nuclear disarmament agreement reached between the United States and the Soviet Union in 1987, signifying a major thaw in the Cold War. The treaty eliminated all short- and medium-range missiles from Europe and provided for on-site inspection for the first time.

> **QUICK REVIEW**

How did anticommunism shape Reagan's foreign policy?

CHAPTER LOCATOR | How did the Nixon presidency reflect the rise of postwar conservatism? | Why did the "outsider" presidency of Jimmy Carter fail to gain broad support?

"OURS WAS THE FIRST REVOLUTION in the history of mankind that truly reversed the course of government," boasted Ronald Reagan in his farewell address in 1989. The word *revolution* exaggerated the change, but his administration did mark the slowdown or reversal of expanding federal budgets for domestic programs and regulations that had taken off in the 1930s. Although he did not deliver on the social or moral issues dear to the heart of the New Right, Reagan used his skills as "the Great Communicator" to cultivate antigovernment sentiment and undermine the liberal assumptions of the New Deal.

Antigovernment sentiment grew along with the backlash against the reforms of the 1960s and the conduct of the Vietnam War. Watergate and other lawbreaking by Nixon administration officials further disillusioned Americans. Presidents Ford and Carter restored morality to the White House, but neither could solve the gravest economic problems since the Great Depression—slow economic growth, stagflation, and an increasing trade deficit. Even the Democrat Carter gave higher priority to fiscal austerity than to social reform, and he began the government's retreat from regulation of key industries.

A new conservative movement helped Reagan win the presidency and flourished during his administration. Reagan's tax cuts, combined with hefty increases in defense spending, created a federal deficit crisis that justified cuts in social welfare spending, made new federal initiatives unthinkable, and burdened the country for years to come. These policies also contributed to a widening income gap between the rich and the poor, weighing especially heavily on minorities, female-headed families, and children. Many Americans continued to support specific federal programs—especially those, such as Social Security and Medicare, that reached beyond the poor—but public sentiment about the government in general had taken a U-turn from the Roosevelt era. Instead of seeing the government as a helpful and problem-solving institution, many believed that not only was it ineffective at solving national problems but it also often made things worse. As Reagan appointed new justices, the Supreme Court retreated from liberalism, curbing the government's authority to protect individual rights and regulate the economy.

With the economic recovery that set in after 1982 and his optimistic rhetoric, Reagan lifted the confidence of Americans about their nation and its promise—confidence that had eroded with the economic and foreign policy blows of the 1970s. Beginning his presidency with harsh rhetoric against the Soviet Union and a huge military buildup, he left office having helped move the two superpowers to the highest level of cooperation since the Cold War began. Although that accord was not welcomed by strong anti-Communist conservatives, it signaled developments that would transform American-Soviet relations—and the world—in the next decade.

| What conservative goals were realized in the Reagan administration? | What strategies did liberals use to fight the conservative turn? | How did Ronald Reagan's foreign policy affect the Cold War? | Conclusion: What was the long-term impact of the conservative turn? | ✓ LearningCurve Check what you know. bedfordstmartins.com /roarkunderstanding |

CHAPTER 30 STUDY GUIDE

STEP 1 **GET STARTED ONLINE**

✓ **LearningCurve** ■ bedfordstmartins.com/roarkunderstanding
Now that you've read the chapter, make it stick by completing the LearningCurve activity.

STEP 2 **EXPLAIN WHY IT MATTERS**

Put your reading into practice. Identify each term below, and then explain why it matters in U.S. history.

TERM	WHO OR WHAT & WHEN	WHY IT MATTERS
Watergate (p. 901)		
National Energy Act of 1978 (p. 907)		
Panama Canal treaty (p. 910)		
Camp David accords (p. 911)		
Iran hostage crisis (p. 912)		
New (Christian) Right (p. 914)		
supply-side economics (p. 915)		
Economic Recovery Tax Act (p. 915)		
Equal Rights Amendment (ERA) (p. 919)		
Strategic Defense Initiative (SDI) (p. 921)		
Iran-Contra scandal (p. 923)		
intermediate-range nuclear forces (INF) agreement (p. 924)		

STEP 3 **MOVE BEYOND THE BASICS**

To demonstrate a more advanced understanding, describe the key conservative strategies and policies of the 1970s and 1980s. Whom did they benefit? What was the ultimate result of their implementation?

Conservative strategy/policy	Who benefited?	Results
Nixon's "southern strategy"		
Supply-side economics		
Reagan's tax and environmental policies		
Strategic Defense Initiative (SDI)		

THE RISE OF CONSERVATISM

▶ What aspects of Nixon's domestic policy appealed to the conservative movement and why?

▶ What specific conservative goals were fulfilled during the presidency of Ronald Reagan?

LIBERALISM

▶ Should Jimmy Carter be considered a liberal? Why or why not?

▶ What tactics did liberal groups use to resist the conservative turn? How successful were they?

U.S. FOREIGN POLICY

▶ What were the major currents of Jimmy Carter's foreign policy agenda?

▶ How and why did U.S. foreign policy change during Reagan's presidency?

LOOKING BACKWARD, LOOKING AHEAD

▶ How did U.S. foreign policy evolve from the 1950s through the 1980s?

▶ In what way does the domestic legacy of the 1970s and 1980s continue to shape contemporary American society?

> **IN YOUR OWN WORDS**

Imagine that you must give an oral report to the class answering the following question: **What were the effects of America's move to the political right on American society and on U.S. foreign policy?** What would be the most important points to include and why?

 Do it online at the Student Site ▪ bedfordstmartins.com/roarkunderstanding

31

FACING THE PROMISES AND CHALLENGES OF GLOBALIZATION

SINCE 1989

> How have globalization and international terrorism changed the focus of U.S. domestic and foreign policy since the end of the Cold War? Chapter 31 explores the changing nature of American politics and foreign policy from 1989 to the present. It examines the end of the Cold War during the presidency of George H. W. Bush; the domestic and foreign policies of the Clinton administration; the George W. Bush administration's departures from previous U.S. policy in the wake of the September 11, 2001, terrorist attacks; and the first term of Barack Obama.

LearningCurve
bedfordstmartins.com/roarkunderstanding
After reading the chapter, use LearningCurve to
retain what you've read.

Nike store, Chongqing, China. A man walks past a Nike factory store in Chongqing, China, in January 2011. Imagine China via AP Images.

How did the United States respond to the end of the Cold War and tensions in the Middle East?

The Gulf War This soldier arriving in Saudi Arabia in September 1990 was part of the massive military buildup in the Persian Gulf area before the U.S.-led coalition drove Iraqi forces out of Kuwait. For the first time, women served in combat-support positions. More than 33,000 women were stationed throughout the area; eleven died, and two were held as prisoners. Among their duties were piloting planes and helicopters, directing artillery, and fighting fires. © Bettmann/Corbis.

VICE PRESIDENT GEORGE H. W. BUSH announced his bid for the presidency in 1988, declaring, "We don't need radical new directions." As president, Bush proposed few domestic initiatives, but he signed key environmental and disability rights legislation.

More dramatic changes swept through the world, and Bush confronted situations that did not fit the free-world-versus-communism framework of the Cold War years. Most Americans approved of Bush's handling of the disintegration of the Soviet Union and its hold over Eastern Europe as well as his response to Iraq's invasion of neighboring Kuwait. But voters' concern over a sluggish economy limited him to one term as president.

Gridlock in Government

The son of a wealthy New England senator, George Herbert Walker Bush fought in World War II, served in Congress during the 1960s, and headed the CIA during the Nixon and Ford years. When Ronald Reagan tapped him for second place on

CHAPTER LOCATOR | **How did the United States respond to the end of the Cold War and tensions in the Middle East?** | How did President Clinton seek a middle ground in American politics?

CHAPTER 31

930 FACING THE PROMISES AND CHALLENGES OF GLOBALIZATION

the Republican ticket in 1980, Bush adjusted his more moderate positions to fit Reagan's conservative agenda. At the end of Reagan's second term, Republicans rewarded Bush with the presidential nomination.

Several candidates competed for the Democratic nomination in 1988. The Reverend Jesse Jackson—a civil rights leader whose Rainbow Coalition campaign centered on the needs of minorities, women, the working class, and the poor—made an impressive bid, winning several primaries and seven million votes. But the centrist candidate, Massachusetts governor Michael Dukakis, won the nomination. On election day, Bush won 54 percent of the vote, but the Democrats gained seats in Congress.

President Bush promised "a kinder, gentler nation" and was more inclined than Reagan to approve government activity in the private sphere. For example, Bush approved the **Clean Air Act of 1990**, the strongest, most comprehensive environmental law in history.

Some forty million Americans benefited when Bush signed another regulatory measure in 1990, the **Americans with Disabilities Act**, banning discrimination and requiring that private businesses and public facilities be accessible to people with disabilities. Disability advocate Cynthia Jones, feeling a breeze stirring over the White House lawn at the signing ceremony, said, "It was kind of like a new breath of air was sweeping across America. . . . People knew they had rights. That was wonderful." Yet Bush also needed to satisfy party conservatives to whom he had pledged, "Read my lips: No new taxes." Bush vetoed thirty-six bills, including those extending unemployment benefits, raising taxes, and mandating family and medical leave for workers. Press reports increasingly used the words *stalemate*, *gridlock*, and *divided government*.

Continuing a trend begun during the Reagan years, some states compensated for this paralysis with their own innovations. States passed bills to establish parental leave policies, improve food labeling, and protect the environment. Dozens of cities passed ordinances requiring businesses receiving tax abatements or other city benefits to pay wages well above the federal minimum wage. And in 1999, California passed a much tougher gun control bill than reformers had been able to get through Congress.

Clean Air Act of 1990

▶ Environmental legislation signed by President George H. W. Bush. The legislation was the strongest and most comprehensive environmental law in the nation's history.

Americans with Disabilities Act

▶ Legislation signed by President George H. W. Bush in 1990 that banned discrimination against the disabled. The law also required handicapped accessibility in public facilities and private businesses.

Bush and Taxes

Running for president in 1988, George H. W. Bush appealed to conservatives, avowing, "Read my lips: No new taxes." Yet when the federal budget deficit he inherited grew even larger, Bush agreed to both budget cuts and tax increases, outraging many Republicans. Here, conservative cartoonist Scott Stantis likens Bush to Pinocchio, whose nose grew when he lied. Scott Stantis/Copley News Service.

| How did President Clinton respond to the challenges of globalization? | How did President George W. Bush change American politics and foreign policy? | What obstacles stood in the way of President Obama's reform agenda? | Conclusion: How have Americans debated the role of the government? | ✓ LearningCurve Check what you know. bedfordstmartins.com /roarkunderstanding |

The huge federal budget deficit inherited from the Reagan administration impelled Bush in 1990 to abandon his "no new taxes" pledge, outraging conservatives. The new law modestly raised taxes on high-income Americans and increased levies on gasoline, cigarettes, alcohol, and luxury items, while leaving intact most of Reagan's massive tax reductions. Neither the new revenues nor controls on spending curbed the deficit, which was boosted by rising costs for Social Security, Medicare, Medicaid, and natural disasters.

Like Reagan, Bush created a more conservative Supreme Court. His first nominee was a moderate, but in 1991, when the only African American on the Court, Justice Thurgood Marshall, retired, Bush set off a national controversy by nominating Clarence Thomas, a conservative black appeals court judge who had opposed affirmative action as head of the Equal Employment Opportunity Commission (EEOC) under Reagan. Charging that Thomas would not protect minority rights, civil rights groups and other liberal organizations fought the nomination. Then Anita Hill, a black law professor and former EEOC employee, accused Thomas of sexual harassment. Thomas angrily denied the charges, and Hill's testimony failed to sway the Senate, which voted narrowly to confirm Thomas. The hearings angered many women, who noted that only two women sat in the Senate. They denounced the male senators for not taking sexual harassment seriously.

Going to War in Central America and the Persian Gulf

President Bush won greater support for his actions abroad. In Central America, the United States had depended on Panamanian dictator Manuel Noriega for helping the Contras in Nicaragua and providing the CIA with information about Communist activities in the region. But in 1989, after an American grand jury indicted Noriega for drug trafficking and after his troops killed an American Marine, Bush ordered 25,000 military personnel into Panama. In Operation Just Cause, U.S. forces quickly overcame Noriega's troops, sustaining 23 deaths, while hundreds of Panamanians, including many civilians, died. General Colin Powell noted that "our euphoria over our victory in Just Cause was not universal." Both the United Nations and the Organization of American States censured the unilateral action taken by the United States.

By contrast, Bush's second military engagement rested solidly on international approval. Viewing Iran as America's major enemy in the Middle East, U.S. officials had quietly assisted the Iraqi dictator Saddam Hussein in the Iran-Iraq war, which began in 1980 and ended inconclusively in 1988. In August 1990, Hussein sent troops into the small, oil-rich country of Kuwait (**Map 31.1**), and the invasion soon neared the Saudi Arabian border, threatening the world's largest oil reserves. President Bush quickly ordered a massive mobilization of American forces and assembled an international coalition to stand up to Iraq. He invoked principles of national self-determination and international law, but long-standing interests in Middle Eastern oil also drove the U.S. response.

Reflecting the easing of Cold War tensions, the Soviet Union voted for a UN embargo on Iraqi oil and authorization for using force if Iraq did not withdraw

CHAPTER LOCATOR | How did the United States respond to the end of the Cold War and tensions in the Middle East? | How did President Clinton seek a middle ground in American politics?

CHAPTER 31
932 FACING THE PROMISES AND CHALLENGES OF GLOBALIZATION

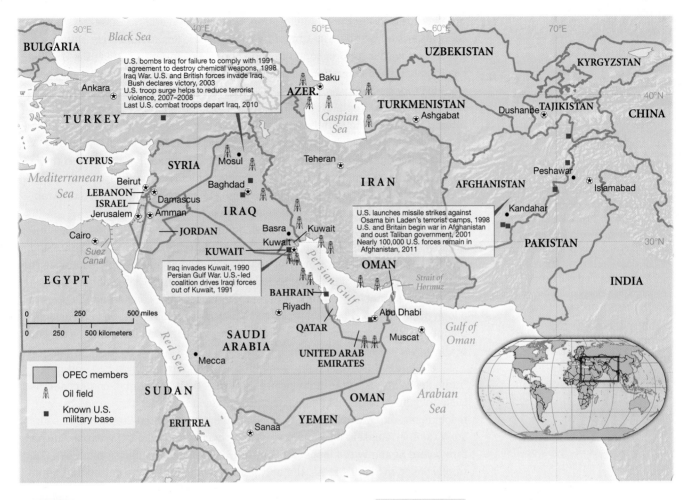

Labels within map:

30°E 40°E 50°E 60°E 70°E

BULGARIA

Black Sea

Ankara ⊛

TURKEY

CYPRUS

Mediterranean Sea

SYRIA Mosul •

Beirut
LEBANON ⊛ Damascus
ISRAEL
Jerusalem ⊛ ⊛ Amman

Baghdad ■

IRAQ

JORDAN

Cairo ⊛

Suez Canal

EGYPT

Basra • ⊛ Kuwait
Kuwait ⊛

KUWAIT

U.S. bombs Iraq for failure to comply with 1991 agreement to destroy chemical weapons, 1998 Iraq War. U.S. and British forces invade Iraq. Bush declares victory, 2003 U.S. troop surge helps to reduce terrorist violence, 2007–2008 Last U.S. combat troops depart Iraq, 2010

AZER. ⊛ Baku

Caspian Sea

TURKMENISTAN Ashgabat

Teheran ⊛

IRAN

UZBEKISTAN

KYRGYZSTAN

Dushanbe ⊛ TAJIKISTAN

CHINA

40°N

AFGHANISTAN

Peshawar •
Islamabad •

Kandahar •

PAKISTAN

INDIA

30°N

U.S. launches missile strikes against Osama bin Laden's terrorist camps, 1998 U.S. and Britain begin war in Afghanistan and oust Taliban government, 2001 Nearly 100,000 U.S. forces remain in Afghanistan, 2011

Iraq invades Kuwait, 1990 Persian Gulf War. U.S.-led coalition drives Iraqi forces out of Kuwait, 1991

Persian Gulf

BAHRAIN
Riyadh •

Abu Dhabi •

QATAR

OMAN

Strait of Hormuz

Muscat •

Gulf of Oman

0   250   500 miles
0   250   500 kilometers

SAUDI ARABIA

Mecca •

Red Sea

OPEC members
⅄ Oil field
■ Known U.S. military base

SUDAN

ERITREA

UNITED ARAB EMIRATES

OMAN

Sanaa ⊛ YEMEN

Arabian Sea

MAP 31.1 ■ Events in the Middle East, 1989–2011

During the Persian Gulf War of 1991, the twenty-two-member Arab League supported the war to liberate Kuwait, and after September 11, 2001, it also approved of U.S. military operations in Afghanistan. Yet, except for the countries where the United States had military bases — Bahrain, Kuwait, Qatar, and Saudi Arabia — no Arab country supported the American invasion and occupation of Iraq in 2003. Arab hostility toward the United States also reflected the deterioration of Israeli-Palestinian relations after 1999, as Arabs charged that the United States allowed Israel to deny Palestinians land and liberty.

> **MAP ACTIVITY**

READING THE MAP: In what countries are the sources of oil located? In what countries does the United States have military bases?

CONNECTIONS: What conditions prompted the U.S. military interventions in Iraq and Afghanistan in 1991, 2001, and 2003? What were the U.S. goals in each of these interventions? To what extent were those goals realized?

from Kuwait by January 15, 1991. By then, the United States had deployed more than 400,000 soldiers to Saudi Arabia, joined by 265,000 troops from two dozen other nations, including several Arab states. "The community of nations has resolutely gathered to condemn and repel lawless aggression," Bush announced. "With few exceptions, the world now stands as one."

With Iraqi forces still in Kuwait, in January 1991 Bush asked Congress to approve war. Considerable sentiment favored waiting to see if the embargo and other means would force Hussein to back down, a position that Colin Powell

How did President Clinton respond to the challenges of globalization?

How did President George W. Bush change American politics and foreign policy?

What obstacles stood in the way of President Obama's reform agenda?

Conclusion: How have Americans debated the role of the government?

✓ LearningCurve
Check what you know.
bedfordstmartins.com /roarkunderstanding

933

quietly urged within the administration. Congress debated for three days and then authorized war by a margin of five votes in the Senate and sixty-seven in the House, with most Democrats in opposition. On January 17, 1991, the U.S.-led coalition launched Operation Desert Storm, a forty-day bombing campaign against Iraqi military targets, power plants, oil refineries, and transportation networks. Having severely crippled Iraq by air, the coalition then stormed into Kuwait, forcing Iraqi troops to withdraw (see Map 31.1).

"By God, we've kicked the Vietnam syndrome once and for all," President Bush exulted on March 1. Most Americans found no moral ambiguity in the **Persian Gulf War** and took pride in the display of military prowess. The United States stood at the apex of global leadership, steering a coalition in which Arab nations fought beside their former colonial rulers.

Some Americans criticized the Bush administration for ending the war without deposing Saddam Hussein. But Bush pointed to the limited UN mandate and to Middle Eastern leaders' concerns that an invasion of Iraq would destabilize the region. His secretary of defense, Richard Cheney, doubted that coalition forces could secure a stable government to replace Hussein and considered the price of a long occupation too high. Instead, administration officials counted on Hussein's pledges not to rearm or develop weapons of mass destruction, secured by a system of UN inspections to contain him.

Yet Middle Eastern stability remained elusive. Israel, which had endured Iraqi missile attacks, was more secure, but the Israeli-Palestinian conflict seethed. Despite military losses, Saddam Hussein remained in power and turned his war machine on Iraqi Kurds and Shiite Muslims whom the United States had encouraged to rebel. Hussein also found ways to conceal arms from UN weapons inspectors before he threw the inspectors out in 1998. Finally, the decision to keep U.S. troops based in Saudi Arabia, the holy land of Islam, fueled the hatred and determination of Muslim extremists like Osama bin Laden.

The Cold War Ends

Soviet support in the Persian Gulf War marked a momentous change in superpower relations. The progressive forces that Mikhail Gorbachev had encouraged in the Communist world (see chapter 30) swept through Eastern Europe in 1989, where popular uprisings demanded an end to state repression and inefficient economic bureaucracies. Communist governments toppled like dominoes (**Map 31.2**), virtually without bloodshed, because Gorbachev refused to prop them up with Soviet armies. East Germany opened its border with West Germany, and in November 1989 ecstatic Germans danced on the Berlin Wall.

Unification of East and West Germany sped to completion in 1990. Soon Poland, Hungary, and other former iron curtain countries lined up to join NATO. Although U.S. military forces remained in Europe as part of NATO, Europe no longer depended on the United States for its security. Its economic clout also grew as Western Europe formed a common economic market in 1992. Inspired by the liberation of Eastern Europe, republics within the Soviet Union soon sought their own independence. In December 1991, Boris Yeltsin, president of the Russian Republic, announced that Russia and eleven other republics had formed a new entity, the Commonwealth of Independent States, and other former Soviet states declared

Persian Gulf War

▶ 1991 war between Iraq and a U.S.-led international coalition. The war was sparked by the 1990 Iraqi invasion of Kuwait. A forty-day bombing campaign against Iraq, followed by coalition troops storming into Kuwait, brought a quick coalition victory.

CHAPTER LOCATOR | **How did the United States respond to the end of the Cold War and tensions in the Middle East?** | How did President Clinton seek a middle ground in American politics?

CHAPTER 31
934 FACING THE PROMISES AND CHALLENGES OF GLOBALIZATION

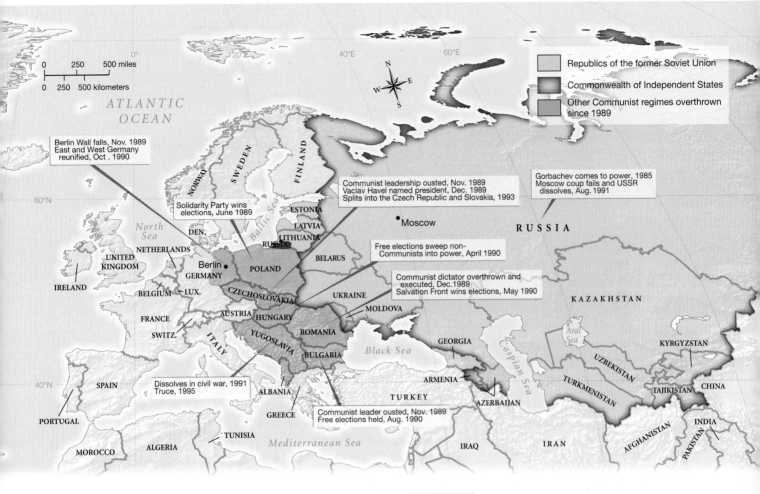

MAP 31.2 ■ Events in Eastern Europe, 1989–1995

The overthrow of Communist governments throughout Eastern Europe and the splintering of the Soviet Union into more than a dozen separate nations were the most momentous changes in world history since World War II.

> MAP ACTIVITY

READING THE MAP: Which country was the first to overthrow its Communist government? Which was the last? In which nations did elections usher in a change in government?

CONNECTIONS: What problems did Mikhail Gorbachev try to solve, and how did he try to solve them? What policy launched by Ronald Reagan contributed to Soviet dilemmas (see chapter 30)? Did this policy create any problems in the United States?

their independence. With nothing left to govern, Gorbachev resigned. The Soviet Union had dissolved, and with it the Cold War conflict that had defined U.S. foreign policy for decades.

Colin Powell joked that he was "running out of villains. I'm down to Castro and Kim Il Sung," the North Korean dictator who, along with China's leaders, resisted the liberalizing tides sweeping the world. In 1989, Chinese soldiers killed hundreds of pro-democracy demonstrators in Beijing, and the Communist government arrested some ten thousand reformers. North Korea remained a Communist dictatorship, committed to developing nuclear weapons.

| How did President Clinton respond to the challenges of globalization? | How did President George W. Bush change American politics and foreign policy? | What obstacles stood in the way of President Obama's reform agenda? | Conclusion: How have Americans debated the role of the government? | ✓ **LearningCurve** Check what you know. bedfordstmartins.com /roarkunderstanding |

Fall of the Berlin Wall

After 1961, the Berlin Wall stood as the prime symbol of the Cold War and the iron grip of communism over Eastern Europe and the Soviet Union. More than four hundred Eastern Europeans were killed trying to flee to the West. After Communist authorities opened the wall on November 9, 1989, permitting free travel between East and West Germany, Berliners from both sides gathered at the wall to celebrate. Eric Bouvet/Gamma Press Images.

> **> VISUAL ACTIVITY**
>
> **READING THE IMAGE:** What does the image tell you about the revolutions in Eastern Europe in 1989?
>
> **CONNECTIONS:** What were the major factors that made possible the dismantling of the Berlin Wall?

"The post–Cold War world is decidedly not post-nuclear," declared one U.S. official. In 1990, the United States and the Soviet Union signed the Strategic Arms Reduction Talks treaty, which cut about 30 percent of each superpower's nuclear arsenal. And in 1996, the UN General Assembly overwhelmingly approved a total nuclear test ban treaty. Yet India and Pakistan, hostile neighbors, refused to sign the treaty, and both exploded atomic devices in 1998. Moreover, the Republican-controlled U.S. Senate defeated ratification of the treaty. The potential for rogue nations and terrorist groups to develop nuclear weapons posed an ongoing threat.

The 1992 Election

In March 1991, Bush's chances for reelection in 1992 looked golden. The Gulf War victory catapulted his approval rating to 88 percent, causing the most prominent Democrats to opt out of the presidential race. But that did not deter William Jefferson "Bill" Clinton, who at age forty-five had served as governor of Arkansas for twelve years. Like Carter in 1976, Clinton and his running mate, Tennessee

CHAPTER LOCATOR | How did the United States respond to the end of the Cold War and tensions in the Middle East? | How did President Clinton seek a middle ground in American politics?

CHAPTER 31
936 FACING THE PROMISES AND CHALLENGES OF GLOBALIZATION

senator Albert Gore Jr., presented themselves as "New Democrats" and sought to rid the party of its liberal image.

Clinton promised to work for the "forgotten middle class," who "do the work, pay the taxes, raise the kids, and play by the rules." He promised a tax cut for the middle class, pledged to reinvigorate government and the economy, and vowed "to put an end to welfare as we know it." Bush was vulnerable to an unemployment rate of 7 percent and to a challenge from self-made Texas billionaire H. Ross Perot, whose third-party organization revealed Americans' frustrations with government and the major parties. Clinton won 43 percent of the popular vote, Bush 38 percent, and Perot 19 percent—the strongest third-party finish in eighty years. By casting nearly two-thirds of their votes against Bush, voters suggested a mandate for change but not the direction that change should take.

QUICK REVIEW

How did George H. W. Bush respond to threats to U.S. interests as the Cold War came to an end?

How did President Clinton respond to the challenges of globalization?

How did President George W. Bush change American politics and foreign policy?

What obstacles stood in the way of President Obama's reform agenda?

Conclusion: How have Americans debated the role of the government?

How did President Clinton seek a middle ground in American politics?

Clinton's Appointments

President Clinton broke new ground by appointing women to offices traditionally considered to be male territory. Janet Reno served as attorney general, Laura Tyson as chair of the President's Council of Economic Advisers, Sheila Widnall as secretary of the air force, and Madeleine Albright as secretary of state. Here, Albright (left) and Reno (second from right) applaud Clinton's 1999 State of the Union address. AP Images/Doug Mills.

BILL CLINTON'S ASSERTION that "the era of big government is over" reflected the Democratic Party's move to the right that had begun with Jimmy Carter. Clinton did not completely abandon liberal principles. He extended benefits for the working poor; delivered incremental reforms to feminists, environmentalists, and other groups; and spoke out in favor of affirmative action and gay rights. Yet his administration restricted welfare benefits and attended more to the concerns of middle-class Americans than to the needs of the disadvantaged.

Clinton's eight-year presidency witnessed the longest economic boom in history and ended with a budget surplus. Although various factors generated the prosperity, many Americans identified Clinton with the buoyant economy, elected him to a second term, and supported him even when his reckless sexual behavior led to impeachment. Clinton was not convicted, but the scandal crippled his leadership in his last years in office.

Clinton's Reforms

Clinton wanted to restore confidence in government as a force for good while not alienating antigovernment voters. The huge budget deficit that he inherited — $4.4 trillion in 1993 — precluded substantial federal initiatives. Moreover, Clinton

CHAPTER LOCATOR | How did the United States respond to the end of the Cold War and tensions in the Middle East? | **How did President Clinton seek a middle ground in American politics?**

938 CHAPTER 31 FACING THE PROMISES AND CHALLENGES OF GLOBALIZATION failed to win a majority of the popular vote in both 1992 and 1996, and the Republicans controlled Congress after 1994. Throughout his presidency, Clinton was burdened by investigations into past financial activities and private indiscretions.

Despite these obstacles, Clinton achieved a number of incremental reforms. He issued executive orders easing restrictions on abortion and signed several bills that Republicans had previously blocked. Most significantly, Clinton pushed through a substantial increase in the **Earned Income Tax Credit (EITC)** for low-wage earners. Begun in 1975, the EITC gave tax breaks to people who worked full-time at meager wages or, if they owed no taxes, a subsidy to lift their family income above the poverty line. By 2003, some fifteen million low-income families were benefiting from the EITC, almost half of them minorities. One expert called it "the largest antipoverty program since the Great Society."

> **Liberal Reforms under President Clinton**

- Family and Medical Leave Act of 1993
- Violence against Women Act of 1994
- Stricter air pollution controls and greater protection for national forests and parks
- A minimum-wage increase
- Expansion of aid for college students
- Expansion of the Earned Income Tax Credit

Shortly before Clinton took office, the economy had begun to rebound. Economic expansion, along with spending cuts, tax increases, and declining unemployment, produced in 1998 the first budget surplus since 1969. Despite a substantial tax cut in 1997 that reduced levies on estates and capital gains and that provided tax credits for families with children and for higher education, the surplus grew. Clinton failed, however, to provide universal health insurance and to curb skyrocketing medical costs. Under the direction of First Lady Hillary Rodham Clinton and with little congressional consultation, the administration proposed a complicated plan that drew criticism from all sides. Liberals wanted a single-payer plan similar to Medicare, while conservatives charged that the proposal would increase taxes and government interference in medical decisions. Congress enacted smaller reforms, such as underwriting health care for 5 million uninsured children, yet 40 million Americans remained uninsured.

Pledging to change the face of government to one that "looked like America," Clinton built on the gradual progress women and minorities had made since the 1960s. For example, African Americans and women had become mayors in major cities from New York to San Francisco. Virginia had elected the first black governor since Reconstruction, and Florida the first Latino. Clinton's cabinet appointments included six women, three African Americans, two Latinos, and an Asian American. Clinton's judicial appointments had a similar cast, and in 1993 he named the second woman to the Supreme Court, Ruth Bader Ginsburg, whose arguments as an attorney had won key women's rights rulings from that Court.

Earned Income Tax Credit (EITC)
▶ Federal antipoverty program initiated in 1975 that assisted the working poor by giving tax breaks to low-income, full-time workers or a subsidy to those who owed no taxes. President Bill Clinton pushed through a significant increase in the program in 1993.

> **CHRONOLOGY**

1993
– President Clinton institutes a "don't ask, don't tell" policy for gays in the military.

1995
– Bombing of federal building in Oklahoma City.

1996
– Personal Responsibility and Work Opportunity Reconciliation Act.
– President Clinton is reelected.

1999
– Senate trial fails to approve impeachment of Clinton.

How did President Clinton respond to the challenges of globalization?

How did President George W. Bush change American politics and foreign policy?

What obstacles stood in the way of President Obama's reform agenda?

Conclusion: How have Americans debated the role of the government?

☑ LearningCurve
Check what you know.
bedfordstmartins.com /roarkunderstanding

939

Accommodating the Right

The 1994 midterm elections swept away the Democratic majorities in Congress and helped push Clinton to the right. Led by Representative Newt Gingrich of Georgia, Republicans claimed the 1994 election as a mandate for their "contract with America," a conservative platform to end "government that is too big, too intrusive, and too easy with the public's money" and to elect "a Congress that respects the values and shares the faith of the American family."

The most extreme antigovernment sentiment developed far from Washington in the form of grassroots armed militias that stockpiled weapons, celebrated white Christian supremacy, and reflected conservatives' hostility to such diverse institutions as taxes and the United Nations. The militia movement grew after passage of new gun control legislation and after government agents stormed the headquarters of an armed religious cult in Waco, Texas, in April 1993, killing more than 80. On the second anniversary of that event, militia sympathizers bombed a federal building in Oklahoma City, taking 169 lives in the worst terrorist attack in the nation's history up to that point.

"don't ask, don't tell" policy

▶ Military policy announced by President Clinton in 1993 that barred officials from inquiring into the sexual orientation of military personnel but permitted the dismissal of personnel who admitted to being gay or engaged in homosexual behavior.

Clinton bowed to conservative views on gay and lesbian rights, backing away from his promise to lift the ban on gays in the military. Although many other nations welcomed homosexual soldiers, U.S. military leaders and key legislators objected to the proposal, and Clinton reverted to a **"don't ask, don't tell" policy** in 1993. Officials could not ask military personnel about their sexuality, but soldiers who said they were gay or who engaged in homosexual behavior could be dismissed. In 1996, Clinton signed the Defense of Marriage Act, prohibiting the federal government from recognizing state-licensed marriages between same-sex couples.

Nonetheless, attitudes and practices relating to homosexuality became more tolerant. By 2006, a majority of the five hundred largest companies provided health benefits to same-sex domestic partners and included sexual orientation in their nondiscrimination policies. A majority of states banned discrimination in public employment, and many of those laws extended to private employment, housing, and education. By 2012, gay marriage was legal in nine states and the District of Columbia. Several more states recognized civil unions and domestic partnerships, extending to same-sex couples rights available to married couples in such areas as inheritance, taxation, and medical decisions.

Clinton's efforts to dissociate his party from liberalism were apparent in his handling of the New Deal program Aid to Families with Dependent Children (AFDC), popularly called welfare. Public sentiment about poverty had shifted. Instead of blaming poverty on external circumstances, such as lack of adequate jobs, more people blamed the poor themselves and welfare programs that trapped the poor in cycles of dependency. Many questioned why they should subsidize poor mothers when so many women worked outside the home. Defenders of AFDC doubted that the economy could provide sufficient jobs at decent wages.

Personal Responsibility and Work Opportunity Reconciliation Act

▶ Legislation signed by President Clinton in 1996 that replaced Aid to Families with Dependent Children with Temporary Assistance for Needy Families, which provided grants to the states to assist the poor and limited welfare payments to two years, with a lifetime maximum of five years.

After vetoing two welfare bills, Clinton signed a less punitive measure as the 1996 election approached. The **Personal Responsibility and Work Opportunity Reconciliation Act** replaced AFDC with Temporary Assistance for Needy Families, which provided grants to the states to assist the poor. It limited welfare payments to two years, with a lifetime maximum of five years.

CHAPTER LOCATOR | How did the United States respond to the end of the Cold War and tensions in the Middle East? | **How did President Clinton seek a middle ground in American politics?**

CHAPTER 31

940   FACING THE PROMISES AND CHALLENGES OF GLOBALIZATION

Clinton's signature on the new law denied Republicans a partisan issue in the 1996 presidential campaign. The Republican Party also moved to the center, nominating Kansan Robert Dole, a World War II hero and former Senate majority leader. Clinton won 49 percent of the votes; 41 percent went to Dole and 9 percent to third-party candidate Ross Perot. Voters sent a Republican majority back to Congress.

In 1999, Clinton and Congress further deregulated the financial industry by repealing key aspects of the Glass-Steagall Act, passed during the New Deal to avoid another Great Depression. The Financial Services Modernization Act ended the separation between banking, securities, and insurance services, allowing financial institutions to engage in all three, practices that leading economists would link to the severe financial meltdown of 2008.

Impeaching the President

Clinton's magnetism, his ability to capture the middle ground, and the nation's economic resurgence enabled him to survive scandals and impeachment. Early in his presidency, charges related to firings of White House staff, political use of FBI records, and "Whitewater"—the nickname for real estate investments that the Clintons had made in Arkansas—led to an official investigation by an independent prosecutor.

In January 1998, the independent prosecutor, Kenneth Starr, began to investigate a charge that Clinton had had sexual relations with a twenty-one-year-old White House intern and then lied about it to a federal grand jury. After vehemently denying the charge, Clinton subsequently bowed to the mounting evidence against

How did President Clinton respond to the challenges of globalization? | How did President George W. Bush change American politics and foreign policy? | What obstacles stood in the way of President Obama's reform agenda? | Conclusion: How have Americans debated the role of the government? | ✓ LearningCurve Check what you know. bedfordstmartins.com /roarkunderstanding

941

him. Starr prepared a case for the House of Representatives, which in December 1998 voted to impeach the president for perjury and obstruction of justice. Clinton became the second president (after Andrew Johnson, in 1868) to be impeached by the House and tried by the Senate.

The Senate trial took place in early 1999. Most Americans condemned the president's behavior but approved of the job he was doing and opposed his removal from office. Some saw Starr as a fanatic invading individuals' privacy. One man said, "Let him get a divorce from his wife. Don't take him out of office and disrupt the country." Those favoring removal insisted that the president must set a high moral standard and that lying to a grand jury, even over a private matter, was a serious offense. With a two-thirds majority needed for conviction, the Senate voted 45 to 55 on the perjury count and 50 to 50 on the obstruction of justice count. A majority, including some Republicans, seemed to agree with a Clinton supporter that the president's behavior, though "indefensible, outrageous, unforgivable, shameless," did not warrant his removal from office. The investigation that led up to impeachment ended in 2000 when the independent prosecutor reported insufficient evidence of illegalities related to the Whitewater land deals.

The Booming Economy of the 1990s

Clinton's ability to weather impeachment owed much to the prosperous economy, which in 1991 began a period of tremendous expansion. Clinton's policies also contributed to the boom. He made deficit reduction a priority, and in exchange the Federal Reserve Board and bond market traders encouraged economic expansion by lowering interest rates. Businesses also prospered because they had lowered their costs through restructuring and laying off workers. Economic problems in Europe and Asia helped American firms become more competitive in the international market. And the computer revolution and the application of information technology boosted productivity.

> The Booming Economy of the 1990s

- Gross domestic product grew by more than one-third.
- Thirteen million new jobs were created.
- Inflation remained in check.
- Unemployment dropped to 4 percent.
- The stock market soared.

People at all income levels benefited from the economic boom, but income inequality, rising since the 1970s, endured (Figure 31.1). The growing use of computer technology increased demand for highly skilled workers, while the movement of manufacturing jobs abroad diminished opportunities and wages for the less skilled. Moreover, deregulation and the continuing decline of unions hurt lower-skilled workers, tax cuts favored the better-off, and the minimum wage failed to keep up with inflation.

CHAPTER LOCATOR | How did the United States respond to the end of the Cold War and tensions in the Middle East? | How did President Clinton seek a middle ground in American politics?

CHAPTER 31
942   FACING THE PROMISES AND CHALLENGES OF GLOBALIZATION

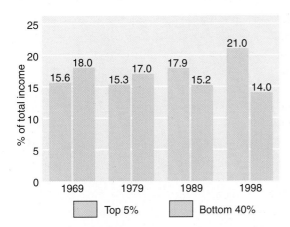

FIGURE 31.1 ■ The Growth of Inequality: Changes in Family Income, 1969–1998

For most of the post–World War II period, income increased for all groups on the economic ladder. But after 1979, the income of the poorest families actually declined, while the income of the richest 20 percent of the population grew substantially. Adapted from the *New York Times*, 1989.

Although more minorities than ever attained middle-class status, people of color overall remained lowest on the economic ladder. For instance, in 1999 the median income for white households surpassed $45,000, but it stood at only $29,423 and $33,676 for African American and Latino households, respectively. In 2000, poverty afflicted more than 20 percent of African Americans and Latinos, in contrast to 7.5 percent of whites.

QUICK REVIEW

What policies of the Clinton administration moved the Democratic Party to the right?

How did President Clinton respond to the challenges of globalization?

How did President George W. Bush change American politics and foreign policy?

What obstacles stood in the way of President Obama's reform agenda?

Conclusion: How have Americans debated the role of the government?

✓ LearningCurve
Check what you know.
bedfordstmartins.com
/roarkunderstanding

How did President Clinton respond to the challenges of globalization?

U.S. Troops in Kosovo

In 1999, American troops joined a NATO peacekeeping unit in the former Yugoslav province of Kosovo after a U.S.-led NATO bombing campaign forced the Serbian army to withdraw. The NATO soldiers were dispatched to monitor the departure of Serbian troops, assist the return of ethnic Albanians who had fled the Serbian army, and reestablish civil governments. Here, an ethnic Albanian boy walks beside Specialist Brent Baldwin from Jonesville, Michigan, as he patrols the town of Gnjilane in southeast Kosovo in May 2000. Wide World Photos, Inc.

AMERICA'S ECONOMIC SUCCESS in the 1990s was linked to its dominance in the world economy, which was undergoing tremendous transformations in a process called globalization—the growing integration and interdependence of national citizens and economies. President Clinton lowered a number of trade barriers, despite critics who emphasized the economic deprivation and environmental devastation that often resulted. Debates likewise arose over the large numbers of immigrants entering the United States.

Clinton agreed with George H. W. Bush that the United States must retain its supreme position in the world. He took military action in Somalia, Haiti, the Middle East, and eastern Europe, and he pushed hard to ease the conflict between Israel and the Palestinians. Clinton also strove to safeguard American interests from terrorist attacks around the world, a challenge in many ways more difficult than combating communism.

CHAPTER LOCATOR | How did the United States respond to the end of the Cold War and tensions in the Middle East? | How did President Clinton seek a middle ground in American politics?

Defining America's Place in a New World Order

In 1991, President George H. W. Bush declared a "new world order" emerging from the ashes of the Cold War. As the sole superpower, the United States was determined to let no nation challenge its military superiority or global leadership, spending five times more on defense than did its nearest competitor, China. Yet policymakers struggled to define guiding principles for deciding when and how to use the nation's military and diplomatic power in a post–Cold War world.

Africa, where civil wars and extreme human suffering rarely evoked a strong American response, was a case in point. In 1992, guided largely by humanitarianism, President Bush had attached U.S. forces to a UN operation in the northern African country of Somalia, where famine and civil war raged. In 1993, President Clinton allowed that humanitarian mission to turn into "nation building"—an effort to establish a stable government—and eighteen U.S. soldiers were killed. After Americans saw film of a soldier's corpse dragged through the streets, the outcry suggested that most citizens were unwilling to sacrifice lives when no vital interest seemed threatened. Indeed, both the United States and the United Nations stood by in 1994 when more than half a million people were massacred in a brutal civil war in Rwanda.

As always, the United States was more inclined to use force nearer its borders. In 1994, after a military coup overthrew Jean-Bertrand Aristide, Haiti's democratically elected president, Clinton persuaded the United Nations to impose economic sanctions on Haiti and to authorize military intervention. Hours before U.S. forces were to invade, Haitian military leaders promised to step down. U.S. forces landed peacefully, and Aristide was restored to power, but Haiti continued to face grave economic challenges and political instability.

In eastern Europe, the collapse of communism ignited a severe crisis. During the Cold War, the Communist government of Yugoslavia had held together a federation of six republics. After the Communists were swept out in 1989, ruthless leaders exploited ethnic differences to bolster their power. Yugoslavia splintered into separate states and fell into civil war.

The Serbian aggression under President Slobodan Milosevic against Bosnian Muslims, which included rape, torture, and mass killings, in particular, horrified much of the world, but European and U.S. leaders hesitated to use military force. Finally, in 1995, Clinton ordered U.S. fliers to join NATO forces in intensive bombing of Serbian military concentrations. That effort and successful offensives by the Croatian and Bosnian armies forced Milosevic to the bargaining table, where representatives from Serbia, Croatia, and Bosnia hammered out a peace treaty.

In 1998, new fighting broke out in the southern Serbian province of Kosovo, where ethnic Albanians, who constituted 90 percent of the population, demanded independence. The Serbian army retaliated, driving out one-third of Kosovo's 1.8 million Albanian Muslims. In 1999, NATO launched a U.S.-led bombing

> CHRONOLOGY

1993
– Israel and Palestine Liberation Organization (PLO) sign peace accords.
– North American Free Trade Agreement (NAFTA).

1994
– United States sends troops to Haiti.
– General Agreement on Tariffs and Trade establishes World Trade Organization.

1995
– United States, with NATO, bombs Serbia.

1998
– United States bombs terrorist sites in Afghanistan and Sudan.

1998–2000
– United States bombs Iraq.

Breakup of Yugoslavia

| How did President Clinton respond to the challenges of globalization? | How did President George W. Bush change American politics and foreign policy? | What obstacles stood in the way of President Obama's reform agenda? | Conclusion: How have Americans debated the role of the government? | ✔ LearningCurve Check what you know. bedfordstmartins.com /roarkunderstanding |

Events in Israel since 1989

Map labels:
LEBANON
Beirut
Mediterranean Sea
Damascus
GOLAN HEIGHTS
SYRIA
Tel Aviv
WEST BANK
Amman
Jerusalem
GAZA STRIP
ISRAEL
Suez Canal
EGYPT
JORDAN
Sinai
Gulf of Suez

Israel and PLO sign accords, 1993
Israel and Jordan sign peace treaty, 1994
Progress of Israeli-Palestinian negotiations halts and violence escalates, 2000
Israel withdraws from Gaza, 2005
Israel at war with Hezbollah in Lebanon, 2006
Israel invades Gaza, 2008

attack on Serbian military and government targets that, after three months, forced Milosevic to agree to a settlement. Serbians voted Milosevic out of office in October 2000, and he died in 2006 while on trial for genocide by a UN war crimes tribunal.

Elsewhere, Clinton deployed U.S. power when he could send missiles rather than soldiers, and he was prepared to act without international support or UN sanction. In August 1998, bombings at the U.S. embassies in Kenya and Tanzania killed 12 Americans and more than 250 Africans. Clinton retaliated with missile attacks on terrorist training camps in Afghanistan and facilities in Sudan controlled by Osama bin Laden, a Saudi-born millionaire who financed the Islamic-extremist terrorist network linked to the embassy attacks. Clinton also launched air strikes against Iraq in 1993 when a plot to assassinate former president Bush was uncovered, in 1996 after Saddam Hussein attacked the Kurds in northern Iraq, and repeatedly between 1998 and 2000 after Hussein expelled UN weapons inspectors. Whereas Bush had acted in the Gulf War with the support of an international force that included Arab states, Clinton acted unilaterally and in the face of Arab opposition.

To defuse the Israeli-Palestinian conflict, Clinton used diplomatic rather than military power. In 1993, Norwegian diplomats had brokered an agreement between Yasir Arafat, head of the Palestine Liberation Organization (PLO), and Yitzhak Rabin, Israeli prime minister, to recognize the existence of each other's states. Israel agreed to withdraw from the Gaza Strip and Jericho, allowing for Palestinian self-government there. In July 1994, Clinton presided over another turning point as Rabin and King Hussein of Jordan signed a declaration of peace. Yet difficult issues remained, especially control of Jerusalem and the presence of more than 200,000 Israeli settlers in the West Bank, the land seized by Israel in 1967, where 3 million Palestinians were determined to establish their own state. Continuing violence between Israelis and Palestinians strengthened anti-American sentiment among Arabs, who saw the United States as Israel's ally.

Debates over Globalization

North American Free Trade Agreement (NAFTA)

▶ 1993 treaty that eliminated all tariffs and trade barriers among the United States, Canada, and Mexico. NAFTA was supported by President Clinton, a minority of Democrats, and a majority of Republicans.

World Trade Organization

▶ International economic body established in 1994 through the General Agreement in Tariffs and Trade to enforce substantial tariff and import quota reductions. Many corporations welcomed these trade barrier reductions, but critics linked them to job loss and the weakening of unions.

Building on efforts by Reagan and Bush, Clinton sought to speed up the growth of a "global marketplace" with new measures to ease restrictions on international commerce. Although the process of globalization was centuries old, new communications technologies such as the Internet and cell phones connected nations, corporations, and individuals at much greater speed and much less cost than ever before. To advance globalization, in 1993 Clinton won congressional approval of the **North American Free Trade Agreement (NAFTA)**, which eliminated all tariffs and trade barriers among the United States, Canada, and Mexico, in the face of opposition from organized labor and others fearing loss of jobs and industries to Mexico. A majority of Democrats opposed NAFTA, but Republican support ensured approval. In 1994, the Senate ratified the General Agreement on Tariffs and Trade, establishing the **World Trade Organization** to enforce substantial tariff and import quota reductions among some 135 member nations. And in 2005, Clinton's successor, George W. Bush, lowered more trade barriers with the passage of the Central American–Dominican Republic Free Trade Agreement.

CHAPTER LOCATOR | How did the United States respond to the end of the Cold War and tensions in the Middle East? | How did President Clinton seek a middle ground in American politics?

CHAPTER 31
946 FACING THE PROMISES AND CHALLENGES OF GLOBALIZATION

The free trade issue was intensely contested. Much of corporate America welcomed the elimination of trade barriers. "Ideally, you'd have every plant you own on a barge," remarked Jack Welch, CEO of General Electric. Critics linked globalization to the loss of jobs, the weakening of unions, and the growing gap between rich and poor. Demanding "fair trade" rather than simply free trade, critics wanted treaties to require decent wage and labor standards. Environmentalists wanted countries seeking increased commerce with the United States to reduce pollution and prevent the destruction of endangered species.

Globalization controversies often centered on relationships between the United States, which dominated the world's industrial core, and developing nations on the periphery, whose cheap labor and lax environmental standards caught investors' eyes. United Students against Sweatshops, for example, attacked the international conglomerate Nike, which paid Chinese workers $1.50 to produce a pair of shoes selling for more than $100 in the United States. Yet leaders of developing nations actively sought foreign investment, because wages deemed pitiful by Americans often provided their impoverished people a much better living than they could otherwise obtain. At the same time, developing countries often pointed to American hypocrisy in advocating free trade in industry while heavily subsidizing the U.S. agricultural sector. "When countries like America, Britain and France subsidize their farmers," complained a grower in Uganda, "we get hurt."

Whereas globalization's cheerleaders pointed to the cheap consumer goods available to Americans and argued that everyone would benefit in the long run, critics focused on the short-term victims. American businessman George Soros conceded that international trade and investments generated wealth, "but they cannot take care of other social needs, such as the preservation of peace, alleviation of poverty, protection of the environment, labor conditions, or human rights." In 2000, President Clinton responded to such criticism by ordering an environmental impact review before the signing of any trade agreement. Beyond the United States, officials from the World Bank and the International Monetary Fund, along with representatives from wealthy economies, promised to provide poor nations more debt relief and a greater voice in decisions about loans and grants. According to World Bank president James D. Wolfensohn, "Our challenge is to make globalization an instrument of opportunity and inclusion—not fear."

The Internationalization of the United States

The United States experienced the dynamic forces of globalization within its own borders. Already in the 1980s, Japanese, European, and Middle Eastern investors had purchased U.S. stocks and bonds, real estate, and corporations. Local communities welcomed foreign capital, and states competed to recruit foreign automobile plants. By 2002, the paychecks of nearly four million American workers came from foreign-owned companies, such as Honda and BMW.

Globalization was also transforming American society, as the United States experienced a tremendous surge of immigration, part of a worldwide trend that counted some 214 million immigrants across the globe in 2010. The promise of economic opportunity, as always, lured immigrants to America, and the Immigration and Nationality Act of 1965 enabled them to come. The law allowed close relatives of U.S. citizens to enter above the annual ceiling of 270,000 immigrants, thus creating

| How did President Clinton respond to the challenges of globalization? | How did President George W. Bush change American politics and foreign policy? | What obstacles stood in the way of President Obama's reform agenda? | Conclusion: How have Americans debated the role of the government? | ✔ LearningCurve Check what you know. bedfordstmartins.com /roarkunderstanding |

947

family migration chains. Moreover, during the Cold War, U.S. immigration policy was generous to refugees from communism, welcoming more than 800,000 Cubans and more than 600,000 Vietnamese, Laotians, and Cambodians.

> Globalization and American Demography

- By 2006, the 35.7 million immigrants in the United States constituted 12.4 percent of the population.
- By the 1980s, the vast majority of immigrants came from Asia, Latin America, and the Caribbean.
- By 2004, 41 million Latinos constituted — at 14 percent — the largest minority group in the nation.

The racial composition of the new immigration heightened the long-standing wariness of native-born Americans toward newcomers. Pressure for more restrictive policies stemmed from beliefs that immigrants took jobs from the native-born, suppressed wages by accepting low pay, strained the capability of social services, or eroded the dominant culture and language. Americans expressed particular hostility toward immigrants who were in the country illegally—an estimated 12 million in 2008—even though the economy depended on their cheap labor.

The new immigration was once again making America an international, interracial society. The largest numbers of immigrants flocked to California, New York, Texas, Florida, New Jersey, and Illinois, but new immigrants dispersed

Immigrant Labor Large commercial farms depended on Latino workers, who constituted more than 45 percent of agricultural labor in 2002. The dependence of agriculture and service industries on immigrant labor helped block movements for greater immigration restrictions. The workers here are harvesting strawberries near Carlsbad, California. In 2002, the median weekly pay for migrant farmworkers was $300. Sandy Huffaker/Getty Images.

CHAPTER LOCATOR | How did the United States respond to the end of the Cold War and tensions in the Middle East? | How did President Clinton seek a middle ground in American politics?

CHAPTER 31
948 FACING THE PROMISES AND CHALLENGES OF GLOBALIZATION

throughout the country. Taquerias, sushi bars, and Vietnamese restaurants appeared in southeastern and midwestern towns; cable TV companies added Spanish-language stations; and the international sport of soccer soared in popularity. Mixed marriages displayed the growing fusion of cultures, recognized in 2000 on Census Bureau forms, where Americans could check more than one racial category. Like their predecessors, the majority of post-1965 immigrants were unskilled and poor. They took the lowest-paying jobs, constituting nearly half of all farmworkers and housekeepers. They also performed other work that employers maintained native-born Americans would not do. Yet a significant number of immigrants were highly skilled workers, sought after by burgeoning high-tech industries. By 2006, nearly one-third of all software developers were foreign-born, as were 28 percent of all physicians.

QUICK REVIEW

What key issues surrounding globalization did the United States face in the 1990s?

| How did President Clinton respond to the challenges of globalization? | How did President George W. Bush change American politics and foreign policy? | What obstacles stood in the way of President Obama's reform agenda? | Conclusion: How have Americans debated the role of the government? | ✔ LearningCurve Check what you know. bedfordstmartins.com /roarkunderstanding |

> How did President George W. Bush change American politics and foreign policy?

9/11

The magnitude of the destruction and loss of lives in the 9/11 attacks made Americans feel more vulnerable than they had since the Cold War ended. The attacks also affected people around the world, who streamed to U.S. embassies or expressed their shock and sympathy in other ways. Steve Ludlum/The New York Times/Redux.

ALTHOUGH FAILING TO CAPTURE a plurality of the popular vote in 2000, George W. Bush made his mark in domestic policy with key legislation to improve public school education, subsidize prescription drugs for elderly citizens, and greatly reduce taxes for the wealthy. The tax cuts, along with spending on new international and domestic crises, turned the substantial budget surplus that Bush had inherited into the largest deficit in the nation's history, and a financial crisis near the end of his presidency sent the economy into a recession.

As Islamist terrorism replaced communism as the primary threat to U.S. security, the Bush administration launched a war in Afghanistan in 2001 and adopted a policy of unilateralism and preemption by going to war against Iraq in 2003. Bush won reelection in 2004, but stability in Iraq and Afghanistan remained elusive, and he confronted serious foreign and domestic crises in his second term. Democrats capitalized on widespread dissatisfaction with his administration to gain control of Congress in 2006 and the White House in 2008.

The Disputed Election of 2000

George W. Bush won the Republican nomination after a series of richly funded, hard-fought primaries. The oldest son of former president George H. W. Bush, he had served as governor of Texas since 1994. Inexperienced in national and international affairs, Bush chose for his running mate a seasoned official, Richard B. Cheney, who had served in three previous Republican administrations. Many observers predicted that the thriving economy would give the Democratic contender, Vice President Al Gore, the edge, and he did surpass Bush by more than half a million votes. Once the polls closed, however, it became clear that Florida's 25 electoral college votes would decide the presidency. Bush's tiny margin in Florida prompted an automatic recount of the votes, which eventually gave him an edge of 537 votes in that state.

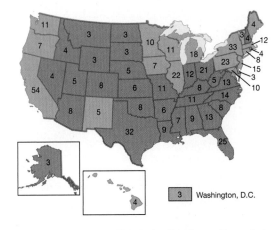

Candidate	Electoral Vote	Popular Vote	Percent of Popular Vote
George W. Bush (Republican)	271	50,456,062	47.8
Al Gore (Democrat)	267	50,996,862	48.4
Ralph Nader (Green Party)	0	2,858,843	2.7
Patrick J. Buchanan (Reform Party)	0	438,760	0.4

MAP 31.3 ■ The Election of 2000

Meanwhile, the Democrats asked for hand-counting of Florida ballots in several heavily Democratic counties where machine errors and confusing ballots may have left thousands of Gore votes unrecorded. The Republicans, in turn, went to court to try to stop the hand-counts. The outcome of the 2000 election hung in the balance for weeks as cases went all the way to the Supreme Court. Finally, a bitterly divided Court ruled five to four against further recounts. While critics charged partisanship, noting that the conservative justices had abandoned their custom of favoring state over federal authority, Gore conceded the presidency to Bush. For the first time since 1888, a president who failed to win the popular vote took office (**Map 31.3**). Despite the lack of a popular mandate, the Bush administration set out to make dramatic policy changes.

The Domestic Policies of a "Compassionate Conservative"

Bush had promised to govern as a "compassionate conservative." A devout born-again Christian, he immediately established the White House Office of Faith-Based and Community Initiatives to encourage religious groups to participate in government programs aimed at prison inmates, the unemployed, and others. The religious right praised the initiatives, but others charged that they violated the constitutional separation of church and state. Federal courts ruled in several dozen cases that faith ministries were using government funds to indoctrinate the people they served.

Bush's fiscal policies were more compassionate toward the rich than toward average Americans. In 2001, he signed a bill reducing taxes over the next ten years

How did President Clinton respond to the challenges of globalization?

How did President George W. Bush change American politics and foreign policy?

What obstacles stood in the way of President Obama's reform agenda?

Conclusion: How have Americans debated the role of the government?

✔ LearningCurve
Check what you know.
bedfordstmartins.com /roarkunderstanding

951

No Child Left Behind Act
▶ 2002 legislation championed by President George W. Bush that expanded the role of the federal government in public education. The law required every school to meet annual testing standards, penalized failing schools, and allowed parents to transfer their children out of such schools.

by $1.35 trillion. A 2003 tax law slashed another $320 billion. The laws heavily favored the rich by reducing income taxes, phasing out estate taxes, and cutting tax rates on capital gains and dividends. They also provided benefits for married couples and families with children and offered tax deductions for college expenses.

The tax cuts contributed to a mushrooming federal deficit—the highest in U.S. history. In 2009, the deficit surpassed $1 trillion as the government struggled to combat a recession. By then, the national debt had risen to $9.6 trillion, making the United States increasingly dependent on China and other foreign investors, who held more than half of the debt.

Bush used executive powers to weaken environmental protection as part of his larger goals of reducing government regulation, promoting economic growth, and increasing energy production. The administration opened millions of wilderness acres to mining, oil, and timber industries and relaxed standards under the Clean Air and Clean Water Acts. To worldwide dismay, the administration withdrew from the Kyoto Protocol on global warming, signed in 1997 by 178 nations to reduce greenhouse gas emissions.

Conservatives hailed Bush's two appointments to the Supreme Court. In 2005, John Roberts, who had served in the Reagan and George H. W. Bush administrations, was named chief justice. Bush then replaced the moderate Sandra Day O'Connor with Samuel A. Alito, a staunch conservative who won confirmation by a narrow margin. While the Court stood up to the administration in rulings on the rights of accused terrorists, it tilted right on cases concerning abortion, gun control, sex discrimination in employment, campaign financing, and regulation of business.

In contrast to the partisan conflict over judicial appointments and tax and environmental policy, Bush won bipartisan support for the **No Child Left Behind Act** of 2002, marking the first substantial expansion of the federal government in public education since the 1960s. Promising to end, in Bush's words, "the story of children being just shuffled through the system," the law required every school to meet annual testing standards, penalized failing schools, and allowed parents to transfer their children out of such schools. As states struggled to finance the new standards, school officials began to criticize the one-size-fits-all approach, and they pointed to family and community impoverishment as sources of student deficiencies.

The Bush administration's second effort to co-opt Democratic Party issues constituted what the president hailed as "the greatest advance in health care coverage for America's seniors" since Medicare became law in 1965. In 2003, Bush signed a bill authorizing prescription drug benefits for the elderly and also expanding the role of private insurers in the Medicare system. Most Democrats opposed the legislation, charging that it subsidized private insurers with federal funds, banned imports of low-priced drugs, and prohibited the government from negotiating with drug companies to reduce prices. The law was a boon to the elderly, but medical costs overall continued to soar, and the number of uninsured Americans surpassed forty million in 2008.

One domestic undertaking of the Bush administration found little approval anywhere: its handling of Hurricane Katrina, which in August 2005 devastated the coasts of Alabama, Louisiana, and Mississippi and ultimately resulted in some fifteen hundred deaths. The catastrophe that ensued when the levees in

CHAPTER LOCATOR | How did the United States respond to the end of the Cold War and tensions in the Middle East? | How did President Clinton seek a middle ground in American politics?

CHAPTER 31
952 FACING THE PROMISES AND CHALLENGES OF GLOBALIZATION

Residents of the poverty-stricken Lower Ninth Ward of
New Orleans cry for help after floods submerged 80
percent of the city in the wake of Hurricane Katrina in
August 2005. The boat was useless to these people
because it had lost its motor. Some residents waited as
long as five days to be rescued. A historian of the disaster
wrote, "Americans were not used to seeing their country
in ruins, their people in want." Wide World Photos, Inc.

New Orleans broke, flooding 80 percent of the city, shook a deeply rooted
assumption held by Americans: that government owed its citizens protection
from natural disasters. New Orleans residents who were too old, too poor, or too
sick to flee the flooding spent anguished days waiting on rooftops for help; wad-
ing in filthy, toxic water; and enduring the heat, disorder, and lack of basic
necessities at the convention center and Superdome, where they had been told
to go for safety and protection. "How can we save the world if we can't save our
own people?" wondered one Louisianan. Thousands of volunteers rushed to
help, and millions more opened their pocketbooks to aid the victims. Yet the
immense private generosity and the superb response of a few groups, such as
the U.S. Coast Guard and the Louisiana Department of Wildlife and Fisheries,
could not make up for the feeling that the nation had failed some of its citizens
when they needed it most. Since so many of Katrina's hardest-hit victims were
poor and black, the disaster also highlighted the injustices and deprivations
remaining in American society.

How did President
Clinton respond to
the challenges of
globalization?

**How did President
George W. Bush change
American politics and
foreign policy?**

What obstacles stood
in the way of President
Obama's reform agenda?

Conclusion: How have
Americans debated the
role of the government?

✓ LearningCurve
Check what you know.
bedfordstmartins.com
/roarkunderstanding

953

The Globalization of Terrorism

The response to Hurricane Katrina contrasted sharply with the government's decisive reaction to the horror that had unfolded four years earlier on the morning of September 11, 2001. Nineteen terrorists hijacked four planes and flew two of them into the twin towers of New York City's World Trade Center and one into the Pentagon near Washington, D.C.; the fourth crashed in a field in Pennsylvania. The attacks took nearly 2,800 lives, including U.S. citizens and people from ninety countries.

The hijackers belonged to Osama bin Laden's Al Qaeda international terrorist network. Organized from Afghanistan, where the radical Muslim Taliban government harbored Al Qaeda, the attacks reflected Islamic extremists' rage at the spread of Western culture and values into the Muslim world. The attacks also demonstrated their opposition to the 1991 Persian Gulf War against Iraq and the stationing of American troops in Saudi Arabia. Bin Laden sought to rid the Middle East of Western influence and install puritanical Muslim control.

The 9/11 terrorists and others who came after them ranged from poor to middle-class; some lived in Middle Eastern homelands governed by undemocratic and corrupt governments, others in Western cities where they felt alienated and despised. All saw the West, especially the United States, as the evil source of their humiliation and the supporter of Israel's oppression of Palestinian Muslims.

In the wake of the September 11 attacks, President Bush sought a global alliance against terrorism and won at least verbal support from most governments. On October 11, the United States and Britain began bombing Afghanistan, and American special forces aided the Northern Alliance, the Taliban government's main opposition. By December, the Taliban government was destroyed, but bin Laden eluded capture, continuing to direct Al Qaeda forces throughout the world, until U.S. special forces killed him in Pakistan in 2011. Afghans elected a new national government, but the Taliban remained strong in large parts of the country, continued to challenge U.S. and NATO troops, and contributed to economic instability and insecurity.

After the September 11 attacks, anti-immigrant sentiment revived throughout the United States, and anyone appearing to be Middle Eastern or practicing Islam often aroused suspicion. Authorities arrested more than a thousand Arabs and Muslims, and a Justice Department study later reported that many people with no connection to terrorism spent months in jail, denied their rights. "I think America overreacted . . . by singling out Arab-named men like myself," said Shanaz Mohammed, who was jailed for eight months for an immigration violation.

In October 2001, Congress passed the **USA Patriot Act**, which gave the government new powers to monitor suspected terrorists and their associates, including the ability to access personal information. It soon provoked calls for revision from both conservatives and liberals. Kathleen MacKenzie, a councilwoman in Ann Arbor, Michigan, explained why the

USA Patriot Act

▶ 2001 law that gave the government new powers to monitor suspected terrorists and their associates, including the ability to access personal information. Critics charged that it represented an unwarranted abridgment of civil rights.

Afghanistan

CHAPTER LOCATOR | How did the United States respond to the end of the Cold War and tensions in the Middle East? | How did President Clinton seek a middle ground in American politics?

CHAPTER 31

954 FACING THE PROMISES AND CHALLENGES OF GLOBALIZATION

council opposed the Patriot Act: "As concerned as we were about national safety, we felt that giving up [rights] was too high a price to pay." A security official countered, "If you don't violate someone's human rights some of the time, you probably aren't doing your job."

Insisting that presidential powers were virtually limitless in times of national crisis, Bush stretched his authority as commander in chief until he met resistance from the courts and Congress. The United States detained more than seven hundred prisoners captured in Afghanistan and taken to the U.S. military base at Guantánamo, Cuba, where, until the courts acted, they had no rights and some were tortured. Although President Barack Obama promised to close the detention camp, more than one hundred prisoners remained there in 2012. The government also sought to protect Americans from future terrorist attacks through the greatest reorganization of the executive branch since 1948. In November 2002, Congress authorized the new Department of Homeland Security, combining 170,000 federal employees from twenty-two agencies responsible for various aspects of domestic security. Chief among the department's duties were intelligence analysis; immigration and border security; chemical, biological, and nuclear countermeasures; and emergency preparedness and response.

Unilateralism, Preemption, and the Iraq War

The Bush administration sought collective action against the Taliban, but on most other international issues it adopted a go-it-alone approach. In addition to withdrawing from the Kyoto Protocol on global warming and violating international rules about the treatment of military prisoners, it scrapped the 1972 Antiballistic Missile Treaty in order to develop the space-based Strategic Defense Initiative first proposed by Ronald Reagan. Bush also withdrew the United States from the United Nations' International Criminal Court, and he rejected an agreement to enforce bans on biological weapons—an agreement signed by all of America's European allies.

Nowhere was the policy of unilateralism more striking than in a new war against Iraq, a war endorsed by Vice President Dick Cheney and Secretary of Defense Donald H. Rumsfeld, but not by Colin Powell, who was then secretary of state. Addressing West Point graduates in June 2002, President Bush proclaimed a new security strategy based not on containment but on preemption: "Traditional concepts of deterrence will not work against a terrorist enemy whose avowed tactics are wanton destruction and the targeting of innocents; whose so-called soldiers seek martyrdom in death and whose most potent protection is statelessness." Because nuclear, chemical, and biological weapons enabled "even weak states and small groups [to] attain a catastrophic power to strike great nations," the United States had to "be ready for preemptive action." The president's claim that the United States had the right to start a war was at odds with international law and with many Americans' understanding of their nation's ideals. It distressed most of America's great-power allies.

Nonetheless, the Bush administration soon applied the doctrine of preemption to Iraq, whose dictator, Saddam Hussein, appeared to be violating UN resolutions from the 1991 Gulf War restricting Iraqi development of nuclear, chemical, and biological weapons. In November 2002, the United States persuaded the UN

How did President Clinton respond to the challenges of globalization?

How did President George W. Bush change American politics and foreign policy?

What obstacles stood in the way of President Obama's reform agenda?

Conclusion: How have Americans debated the role of the government?

✓ LearningCurve
Check what you know.
bedfordstmartins.com
/roarkunderstanding

955

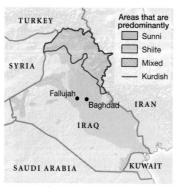

Iraq

Security Council to pass a resolution demanding that Iraq disarm or face "serious consequences." When Iraq failed to comply fully with new UN inspections, the Bush administration decided on war. Making claims (subsequently refuted) that Hussein had links to Al Qaeda and harbored terrorists and that Iraq possessed weapons of mass destruction, the president insisted that the threat was immediate and great enough to justify preemptive action. Despite opposition from the Arab world and most major nations—including France, Germany, China, and Russia—the United States and Britain invaded Iraq on March 19, 2003, supported by some thirty nations (see Map 31.1). Coalition forces won an easy victory, and Bush declared the end of the **Iraq War** on May 1. Saddam Hussein remained at large until December 2003.

Chaos followed the quick victory. Damage from U.S. bombing and widespread looting resulting from the failure of U.S. troops to secure order and provide basic necessities left Iraqis wondering how much they had gained. "With Saddam there was tyranny, but at least you had a salary to put food on your family's table," said a young father. A Baghdad hospital worker complained, "They can take our oil, but at least they should let us have electricity and water." Five years after the invasion, continuing violence had caused 2 million to flee their country and displaced 1.9 million within Iraq.

The administration had not planned adequately for the occupation and failed to send sufficient troops to Iraq. The 140,000 American forces there came under attack almost daily from remnants of the former Hussein regime, religious extremists, and hundreds of foreign terrorists now entering the chaotic country. Seeking to divide Iraqis and undermine the occupation, terrorists launched deadly assaults resulting in the death of tens of thousands of Iraqis. By the end of the Iraq War, nearly 4,500 U.S. soldiers had lost their lives, and many returned home grievously wounded.

The war became an issue in the presidential campaign of 2004. Massachusetts senator John Kerry, the Democratic nominee, criticized Bush's unilateralist foreign policy and the administration's conduct of the war. A slim majority of voters, however, indicated their belief that Bush would better protect American security than Kerry. The president eked out a 286 to 252 victory in the electoral college, winning 50.7 percent of the popular and carrying Republican majorities into Congress.

In June 2004, the United States transferred sovereignty to an interim Iraqi government, and in January 2005 Iraqis elected a national assembly, which then had to organize a government satisfactory to Iraq's three major groups—Sunnis, Shiites, and Kurds. Violence escalated against government officials, Iraqi civilians, and occupation forces. A nineteen-year-old Iraqi confined to his house by his parents, who feared their son could be killed or lured into terrorist activities, said, "If I'm killed, it doesn't even matter because I'm dead right now." In 2006, a majority of Americans told pollsters that the Iraq War was a mistake.

By 2006, Bush's conduct of the war faced criticism that crossed party lines and included military leaders. Critics acknowledged that the United States had felled a brutal dictator, but coalition forces were not large enough or adequately

Iraq War

▶ War launched by the United States, Britain, and several smaller countries in March 2003 against the government of Iraqi dictator Saddam Hussein. The decision to go to war was based on claims (subsequently refuted) that Hussein's government had links to Al Qaeda, harbored terrorists, and possessed weapons of mass destruction.

CHAPTER LOCATOR | How did the United States respond to the end of the Cold War and tensions in the Middle East? | How did President Clinton seek a middle ground in American politics?

CHAPTER 31

956 FACING THE PROMISES AND CHALLENGES OF GLOBALIZATION

prepared for the turmoil that followed. Nor did they find the weapons of mass destruction or links to Osama bin Laden that administration officials had insisted made the war necessary. Rather, in the chaos brought on by the invasion, more than a thousand terrorists entered Iraq—the place, according to one expert, "for fundamentalists to go . . . to stick it to the West."

The war and occupation exacted a steep price in American and Iraqi lives, dollars, U.S. relations with other great powers, and the nation's reputation in the world, especially among Arab nations. Revelations of prisoner abuse in the Abu Ghraib prison in Iraq and in the Guantánamo detention camp housing captives from the war in Afghanistan further tarnished the image of the United States. Anti-Americanism around the world rose to its highest point in history. The budget deficit swelled, and resources were diverted to Iraq from other national security challenges, including the stabilization of Afghanistan, the elimination of bin Laden and Al Qaeda, and the threats posed by North Korea's and Iran's pursuit of nuclear weapons.

Voters registered their dissatisfaction in 2006, when Democrats captured both houses of Congress for the first time since 1994. The Bush administration displayed more willingness to work with other nations in dealing with Iraq, Iran, and North Korea. In 2007, it began a troop surge in Iraq, increasing U.S. forces there to 160,000. The surge, along with actions by Iraqi leaders, contributed to a significant reduction in violence, and the administration began planning for the withdrawal of U.S. forces, which was completed at the end of 2011.

QUICK REVIEW <

What impact did the terrorist attacks on September 11, 2001, have on U.S. foreign and domestic policy?

How did President Clinton respond to the challenges of globalization?

How did President George W. Bush change American politics and foreign policy?

What obstacles stood in the way of President Obama's reform agenda?

Conclusion: How have Americans debated the role of the government?

☑ LearningCurve Check what you know. bedfordstmartins.com /roarkunderstanding

957

> What obstacles stood in the way of President Obama's reform agenda?

Health Care Reform In March 2010, President Obama signed the Patient Protection and Affordable Care Act, sometimes called "Obamacare," as congressional leaders and others look on. At the signing were Marcelas Owens (left), whose mother died after she lost her job and her health insurance, and former Michigan congressman John Dingell (right, seated), who first introduced national health insurance in the 1940s. The Supreme Court upheld the controversial measure in June 2012. AP/Wide World Photos

DESPITE THE IMPROVING SITUATION IN IRAQ, President Bush's approval ratings sank on the eve of the 2008 elections. The Republicans nominated Senator John McCain of Arizona, a Vietnam War hero, who chose as his running mate Alaska governor Sarah Palin, the second woman to run for vice president on a major party ticket. Even more historic changes occurred in the Democratic Party when, for the first time, an African American and a woman were the top two contenders. In hard-fought primary battles, Illinois senator Barack Obama edged out New York senator and former First Lady Hillary Rodham Clinton for the nomination.

Born to a white mother and a Kenyan father and raised in Hawai'i and Indonesia, Obama served in the Illinois senate and won election to the U.S. Senate in 2004. At the age of forty-seven, he won the Democratic nomination with brilliant grassroots and Internet organizing and by appealing to deep-seated longings for a new kind of politics and racial reconciliation. He won 53 percent of the popular vote and defeated McCain 365 to 173 in the electoral college to become the first African American president, while Democrats increased their majorities in the House and Senate.

Obama hoped to work across party lines as he pursued reforms in health care, education, the environment, and immigration policy, but he confronted a severe economic crisis. A recession had struck in late 2007, fueled by a breakdown in financial institutions that had accumulated trillions of dollars of bad debt, much of

CHAPTER LOCATOR | How did the United States respond to the end of the Cold War and tensions in the Middle East? | How did President Clinton seek a middle ground in American politics?

958 CHAPTER 31
FACING THE PROMISES AND CHALLENGES OF GLOBALIZATION

it from risky home mortgages. As the recession spread to other parts of the world, home mortgage foreclosures skyrocketed, major companies went bankrupt, and unemployment rose to 9.8 percent in late 2010, the highest rate in more than twenty-five years.

The crisis was so severe that Congress passed the Bush administration's $700 billion Troubled Asset Relief Program in 2008 to inject credit into the economy and shore up banks as well as other businesses. Obama followed with the American Recovery and Reinvestment Act of 2009, $787 billion worth of spending and tax cuts to stimulate the economy and relieve unemployment. He also arranged a federal bailout of General Motors and Chrysler, saving an estimated one million jobs related to the automobile industry. Finally, to address the conditions that triggered the financial crisis, Congress expanded governmental regulation with the Wall Street Reform and Consumer Protection Act in 2010.

Obama's judicial appointments increased the number of women on the Supreme Court to three, including the first ever Latina justice. His greatest domestic achievement was passage of a health care reform bill, the **Patient Protection and Affordable Care Act** of 2010, which represented the largest expansion of government since the Great Society.

> ### > The Patient Protection and Affordable Care Act of 2010

- Required nearly all Americans to carry health insurance and provided subsidies to those in need
- Encouraged businesses to offer coverage to employees
- Imposed new regulations on insurance companies to protect their customers
- Contained provisions to limit health care costs

Republicans had previously endorsed key elements of the measure, but not a single one voted for it. In the face of widespread opposition to what critics called "Obamacare," the Supreme Court upheld its constitutionality by a five-to-four vote, as the United States became the last of the industrialized democracies to underwrite health care for all its citizens.

In foreign affairs, Obama reached out to Muslim nations, recommitted the United States to multilateralism, and worked to contain the proliferation of nuclear weapons. He continued the Bush administration's plan to withdraw from Iraq, and the last troops departed in 2011, although Iraq continued to endure terrorist violence. Even though corruption permeated Afghanistan's government and a majority of Americans opposed the war there, which by 2011 had taken more than 2,000 American lives, Obama dispatched 50,000 more military personnel, promising that the United States would fully withdraw by 2014. In May 2011, U.S. special forces killed Osama bin Laden, who was hiding in Pakistan.

Voters were more concerned with domestic issues when they issued a sharp rebuke to Obama in the 2010 midterm elections, turning over the House to the Republicans and cutting into the Democratic majority in the Senate. Although the stock market had rebounded, nearly 10 percent of American workers were unemployed, the federal deficit that Obama had inherited from the Bush administration soared to $1.4 trillion, and a vocal minority of mostly older and white voters expressed their fury at what they considered an overreaching government by

> CHRONOLOGY

2008
- Worst financial crisis since the Great Depression.
- Barack Obama is elected president.

2009
- American Recovery and Reinvestment Act.

2010
- Patient Protection and Affordable Care Act.
- Wall Street Reform and Consumer Protection Act.
- United States ends combat operations in Iraq and increases troops in Afghanistan.

2011
- Osama bin Laden is killed.

Patient Protection and Affordable Care Act

▶ Sweeping 2010 health care reform bill that established nearly universal health insurance by providing subsidies and compelling larger business to offer coverage to employees. Championed by President Barack Obama, the act also imposed new regulations on insurance companies and contained provisions to limit health care costs.

How did President Clinton respond to the challenges of globalization?

How did President George W. Bush change American politics and foreign policy?

What obstacles stood in the way of President Obama's reform agenda?

Conclusion: How have Americans debated the role of the government?

✓ LearningCurve
Check what you know.
bedfordstmartins.com
/roarkunderstanding

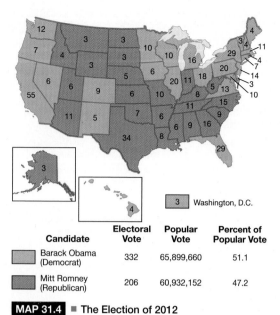

Candidate	Electoral Vote	Popular Vote	Percent of Popular Vote
Barack Obama (Democrat)	332	65,899,660	51.1
Mitt Romney (Republican)	206	60,932,152	47.2

MAP 31.4 ■ The Election of 2012

joining grassroots movements that took the name the Tea Party revolt. As one Tea Party supporter put it, "The government is taking over everything—I want my freedom back."

The intensely polarized political environment complicated Obama's efforts to reduce unemployment and cut the enormous federal debt. It also thwarted his efforts to reform environmental and immigration policy. With Congress blocking him at every turn, Obama used his executive authority to stiffen requirements on motor vehicle emissions, to temporarily protect young illegal immigrants from deportation, and to end discrimination against gays in the military.

Obama carried the burden of a nearly 8 percent unemployment rate into the 2012 election, in which he faced Republican Mitt Romney, former governor of Massachusetts and the first Mormon to be nominated for the presidency. With the electorate deeply divided over the role of the federal government, Obama won easily in the electoral college, with 332 votes to Romney's 206, and he captured 51 percent of the popular vote to Romney's 47 percent (**Map 31.4**). The Democrats made small gains in Congress, but Republicans still controlled the House, and government remained divided as the nation continued to struggle to reduce unemployment and deal with a staggering national deficit and debt. Abroad, Obama faced nuclear ambitions in Iran and North Korea, along with intensified instability in the Middle East, where U.S. support of democratic revolutions also risked strengthening Muslim extremists.

> QUICK REVIEW

What were the successes and failures of President Obama's first term as president?

Conclusion: How have Americans debated the role of the government?

COLIN POWELL REFERRED to the unfinished nature of the American promise when he declared that the question of America's role in the world "isn't answered yet." The end of the Cold War, the rise of international terrorism, and the George W. Bush administration's doctrines of preemption and unilateralism sparked new debates over the long-standing question of U.S. actions beyond its borders.

Americans had also debated for more than two centuries what responsibilities the government should shoulder and what was best left to private enterprise, families, churches, and other voluntary institutions. Far more than most industrialized democracies, the United States had relied on individual or private rather than collective or public solutions. In the twentieth century, Americans significantly enlarged the federal government's powers, but since the 1960s fewer people trusted in government's ability to improve people's lives, even as a poverty rate of 20 percent among children continued and a growing gap between rich and poor intensified.

The see-sawing of control of the government between Republicans and Democrats from 1989 to 2010 reflected ongoing debate over government's role in domestic affairs. The first Bush administration's civil rights measure for people with disabilities and Bill Clinton's incremental reforms both built on a tradition that sought to realize the American promise of justice and well-being. Those who mobilized against the ravages of globalization worked internationally for what earlier reformers had sought for the domestic population: protection of individual rights, curbs on capitalism and assistance for its victims, and fiscal policies that placed greater responsibility on those best able to pay. Even the second Bush administration, which sought to limit government's reach, supported the No Child Left Behind Act, the Medicare prescription drug program, and a gigantic bail-out of failing businesses when the financial crisis hit the economy in 2008. The controversy over Obama's efforts to stimulate the economy and to reform health care and the financial industry replayed America's long-standing debate about the government's appropriate role.

The United States became more embedded in the global economy as products, information, and people crossed borders with amazing speed and frequency. New waves of immigration altered the face of the American population. Globalization also contributed to the threat of deadly terrorism within America's own borders. In response to those dangers, the second Bush administration launched wars in Afghanistan and Iraq. Obama ended the Iraq War in 2011, but he pursued terrorists aggressively and continued the war in Afghanistan. Both administrations sought to maintain U.S. preeminence in the world, but debate continued about how best to use that power.

How did President Clinton respond to the challenges of globalization?

How did President George W. Bush change American politics and foreign policy?

What obstacles stood in the way of President Obama's reform agenda?

Conclusion: How have Americans debated the role of the government?

☑ LearningCurve
Check what you know.
bedfordstmartins.com
/roarkunderstanding

CHAPTER 31 STUDY GUIDE

STEP 1 — GET STARTED ONLINE

 LearningCurve ■ bedfordstmartins.com/roarkunderstanding
Now that you've read the chapter, make it stick by completing the LearningCurve activity.

STEP 2 — EXPLAIN WHY IT MATTERS

Put your reading into practice. Identify each term below, and then explain why it matters in U.S. history.

TERM	WHO OR WHAT & WHEN	WHY IT MATTERS
Clean Air Act of 1990 (p. 931)		
Americans with Disabilities Act (p. 931)		
Persian Gulf War (p. 934)		
Earned Income Tax Credit (EITC) (p. 939)		
"don't ask, don't tell" policy (p. 940)		
Personal Responsibility and Work Opportunity Reconciliation Act (p. 940)		
North American Free Trade Agreement (NAFTA) (p. 946)		
World Trade Organization (p. 946)		
No Child Left Behind Act (p. 952)		
USA Patriot Act (p. 954)		
Iraq War (p. 956)		
Patient Protection and Affordable Care Act (p. 959)		

STEP 3 — MOVE BEYOND THE BASICS

To demonstrate a more advanced understanding, analyze the impact of some of the key events and developments of the 1990s and 2000s on the United States and the global community. Which events or developments are still having an impact today? In what way?

Event/development	Impact
End of the Cold War	
Booming economy of the 1990s	
Free trade and globalization	
Attacks of September 11, 2001	
Iraq War	

STEP 4

PUT IT ALL TOGETHER

Now, take a step back and try to explain the big picture. Remember to use specific examples from the chapter in your answers.

THE END OF THE COLD WAR

► How did U.S. foreign policy change after the fall of communism in Eastern Europe and the Soviet Union?

► How did U.S. economic policy change after 1992?

DOMESTIC REFORM

► How did domestic reforms of the Clinton administration affect lower-income people in the United States?

► Why have the reforms of the Obama administration created intense disagreement among lawmakers and U.S. citizens?

THE POST-9/11 WORLD

► How were international relations between the United States and other nations affected by the events of September 11, 2001?

► How did 9/11 affect Americans in the decade that followed?

LOOKING BACKWARD, LOOKING AHEAD

► Compare and contrast the place of the United States in the world in 1900 and in 2013.

► Defend or refute the following statement: In fifty years' time, the United States will still be the most powerful nation in the world.

> ## IN YOUR OWN WORDS

Imagine that you must give an oral report to the class answering the following question: **How have globalization and international terrorism changed the focus of U.S. domestic and foreign policy since the end of the Cold War?** What would be the most important points to include and why?

APPENDIX I

DOCUMENTS

THE DECLARATION OF INDEPENDENCE

In Congress, July 4, 1776,

THE UNANIMOUS DECLARATION OF THE THIRTEEN UNITED STATES OF AMERICA

When in the course of human events, it becomes necessary for one people to dissolve the political bands which have connected them with another, and to assume, among the powers of the earth, the separate and equal station to which the laws of nature and of nature's God entitle them, a decent respect to the opinions of mankind requires that they should declare the causes which impel them to the separation.

We hold these truths to be self-evident, that all men are created equal; that they are endowed by their Creator with certain unalienable rights; that among these, are life, liberty, and the pursuit of happiness. That, to secure these rights, governments are instituted among men, deriving their just powers from the consent of the governed; that, whenever any form of government becomes destructive of these ends, it is the right of the people to alter or to abolish it, and to institute a new government, laying its foundation on such principles, and organizing its powers in such form, as to them shall seem most likely to effect their safety and happiness. Prudence, indeed, will dictate that governments long established, should not be changed for light and transient causes; and, accordingly, all experience hath shown, that mankind are more disposed to suffer, while evils are sufferable, than to right themselves by abolishing the forms to which they are accustomed. But, when a long train of abuses and usurpations, pursuing invariably the same object, evinces a design to reduce them under absolute despotism, it is their right, it is their duty, to throw off such government and to provide new guards for their future security. Such has been the patient sufferance of these colonies, and such is now the necessity which constrains them to alter their former systems of government. The history of the present King of Great Britain is a history of repeated injuries and usurpations, all having, in direct object, the establishment of an absolute tyranny over these States. To prove this, let facts be submitted to a candid world: He has refused his assent to laws the most wholesome and necessary for the public good.

He has forbidden his governors to pass laws of immediate and pressing importance, unless suspended in their operation till his assent should be obtained; and, when so suspended, he has utterly neglected to attend to them.

He has refused to pass other laws for the accommodation of large districts of people, unless those people would relinquish the right of representation in the legislature; a right inestimable to them, and formidable to tyrants only.

He has called together legislative bodies at places unusual, uncomfortable, and distant from the depository of their public records, for the sole purpose of fatiguing them into compliance with his measures.

He has dissolved representative houses repeatedly for opposing, with manly firmness, his invasions on the rights of the people.

He has refused, for a long time after such dissolutions, to cause others to be elected; whereby the legislative powers, incapable of annihilation, have returned to the people at large for their exercise; the state remaining in the mean-time exposed to all the danger of invasion from without, and convulsions within.

He has endeavoured to prevent the population of these States; for that purpose, obstructing the laws for naturalization of foreigners, refusing to pass others to encourage their migration hither, and raising the conditions of new appropriations of lands.

He has obstructed the administration of justice, by refusing his assent to laws for establishing judiciary powers.

He has made judges dependent on his will alone, for the tenure of their offices, and the amount and payment of their salaries.

He has erected a multitude of new offices, and sent hither swarms of officers to harass our people, and eat out their substance.

He has kept among us, in times of peace, standing armies, without the consent of our legislature.

He has affected to render the military independent of, and superior to, the civil power.

He has combined, with others, to subject us to a jurisdiction foreign to our Constitution, and unacknowledged by our laws; giving his assent to their acts of pretended legislation:

For quartering large bodies of armed troops among us:

For protecting them by a mock trial, from punishment, for any murders which they should commit on the inhabitants of these States:

For cutting off our trade with all parts of the world:

For imposing taxes on us without our consent:

For depriving us, in many cases, of the benefit of trial by jury:

For transporting us beyond seas to be tried for pretended offences:

For abolishing the free system of English laws in a neighboring province, establishing therein an arbitrary government, and enlarging its boundaries, so as to render it at once an example and fit instrument for introducing the same absolute rule into these colonies:

For taking away our charters, abolishing our most valuable laws, and altering, fundamentally, the powers of our governments:

For suspending our own legislatures, and declaring themselves invested with power to legislate for us in all cases whatsoever.

He has abdicated government here, by declaring us out of his protection, and waging war against us.

He has plundered our seas, ravaged our coasts, burnt our towns, and destroyed the lives of our people.

He is, at this time, transporting large armies of foreign mercenaries to complete the works of death, desolation, and tyranny, already begun, with circumstances of cruelty and perfidy scarcely paralleled in the most barbarous ages, and totally unworthy the head of a civilized nation.

He has constrained our fellow citizens, taken captive on the high seas, to bear arms against their country, to become the executioners of their friends, and brethren, or to fall themselves by their hands.

He has excited domestic insurrections amongst us, and has endeavored to bring on the inhabitants of our frontiers, the merciless Indian savages, whose known rule of warfare is an undistinguished destruction of all ages, sexes, and conditions.

In every stage of these oppressions, we have petitioned for redress; in the most humble terms; our repeated petitions have been answered only by repeated injury. A prince, whose character is thus marked by every act which may define a tyrant, is unfit to be the ruler of a free people.

Nor have we been wanting in attention to our British brethren. We have warned them, from time to time, of attempts made by their legislature to extend an unwarrantable jurisdiction over us. We have reminded them of the circumstances of our emigration and settlement here. We have appealed to their native justice and magnanimity, and we have conjured them, by the ties of our common kindred, to disavow these usurpations, which would inevitably interrupt our connections and correspondence. They, too, have been deaf to the voice of justice and consanguinity. We must, therefore, acquiesce in the necessity which denounces our separation, and hold them as we hold the rest of mankind, enemies in war, in peace, friends.

We, therefore, the representatives of the United States of America, in general Congress assembled, appealing to the Supreme Judge of the world for the rectitude of our intentions, do, in the name, and by authority of the good people of these colonies, solemnly publish and declare, that these united colonies are, and of right ought to be, free and independent states: that they are absolved from all allegiance to the British Crown, and that all political connection between them and the state of Great Britain is, and ought to be, totally dissolved; and that, as free and independent states, they have full power to levy war, conclude peace, contract alliances, establish commerce, and to do all other acts and things which independent states may of right do. And, for the support of this declaration, with a firm reliance on the protection of Divine Providence, we mutually pledge to each other our lives, our fortunes, and our sacred honor.

The foregoing Declaration was, by order of Congress, engrossed, and signed by the following members:

JOHN HANCOCK

New Hampshire
Josiah Bartlett
William Whipple
Matthew Thornton

Massachusetts Bay
Samuel Adams
John Adams
Robert Treat Paine
Elbridge Gerry

Rhode Island
Stephen Hopkins
William Ellery

Connecticut
Roger Sherman
Samuel Huntington
William Williams
Oliver Wolcott

New York
William Floyd
Phillip Livingston
Francis Lewis
Lewis Morris

New Jersey
Richard Stockton
John Witherspoon
Francis Hopkinson
John Hart
Abraham Clark

Pennsylvania
Robert Morris
Benjamin Rush
Benjamin Franklin
John Morton
George Clymer
James Smith

George Taylor
James Wilson
George Ross

Delaware
Caesar Rodney
George Read
Thomas M'Kean

Maryland
Samuel Chase
William Paca
Thomas Stone
Charles Carroll, of
   Carrollton

North Carolina
William Hooper
Joseph Hewes
John Penn

South Carolina
Edward Rutledge
Thomas Heyward, Jr.
Thomas Lynch, Jr.
Arthur Middleton

Virginia
George Wythe
Richard Henry Lee
Thomas Jefferson
Benjamin Harrison
Thomas Nelson, Jr.
Francis Lightfoot Lee
Carter Braxton

Georgia
Button Gwinnett
Lyman Hall
George Walton

Resolved, That copies of the Declaration be sent to the several assemblies, conventions, and committees, or councils of safety, and to the several commanding officers of the continental troops; that it be proclaimed in each of the United States, at the head of the army.

THE CONSTITUTION OF THE UNITED STATES*

Agreed to by Philadelphia Convention, September 17, 1787. Implemented March 4, 1789.

Preamble

We the people of the United States, in order to form a more perfect union, establish justice, insure domestic tranquility, provide for the common defense, promote the general welfare, and secure the blessings of liberty to ourselves and our posterity, do ordain and establish this Constitution for the United States of America.

Article I

Section 1 All legislative powers herein granted shall be vested in a Congress of the United States, which shall consist of a Senate and a House of Representatives.

Section 2 The House of Representatives shall be composed of members chosen every second year by the people of the several States, and the electors in each State shall have the qualifications requisite for electors of the most numerous branch of the State Legislature.

No person shall be a Representative who shall not have attained to the age of twenty-five years, and been seven years a citizen of the United States, and who shall not, when elected, be an inhabitant of that State in which he shall be chosen.

Representatives and direct taxes shall be apportioned among the several States which may be included within this Union, according to their respective numbers, *which shall be determined by adding to the whole number of free persons, including those bound to service for a term of years and excluding Indians not taxed, three-fifths of all other persons.* The actual enumeration shall be made within three years after the first meeting of the Congress of the United States, and within every subsequent term of ten years, in such manner as they shall by law direct. The number of Representatives shall not exceed one for every thirty thousand, but each State shall have at least one Representative; *and until such enumeration shall be made, the State of New Hampshire shall be entitled to choose three, Massachusetts eight, Rhode Island and Providence Plantations one, Connecticut five, New York six, New Jersey four, Pennsylvania eight, Delaware one, Maryland six, Virginia ten, North Carolina five, South Carolina five, and Georgia three.*

Passages no longer in effect are in italic type.

When vacancies happen in the representation from any State, the Executive authority thereof shall issue writs of election to fill such vacancies.

The House of Representatives shall choose their Speaker and other officers; and shall have the sole power of impeachment.

Section 3 The Senate of the United States shall be composed of two Senators from each State, *chosen by the legislature thereof,* for six years; and each Senator shall have one vote.

Immediately after they shall be assembled in consequence of the first election, they shall be divided as equally as may be into three classes. The seats of the Senators of the first class shall be vacated at the expiration of the second year, of the second class at the expiration of the fourth year, and of the third class at the expiration of the sixth year, so that one-third may be chosen every second year; and if vacancies happen by resignation or otherwise, during the recess of the legislature of any State, the Executive thereof may make temporary appointments until the next meeting of the legislature, which shall then fill such vacancies.

No person shall be a Senator who shall not have attained to the age of thirty years, and been nine years a citizen of the United States, and who shall not, when elected, be an inhabitant of that State for which he shall be chosen.

The Vice-President of the United States shall be President of the Senate, but shall have no vote, unless they be equally divided.

The Senate shall choose their other officers, and also a President *pro tempore,* in the absence of the Vice-President, or when he shall exercise the office of President of the United States.

The Senate shall have the sole power to try all impeachments. When sitting for that purpose, they shall be on oath or affirmation. When the President of the United States is tried, the Chief Justice shall preside: and no person shall be convicted without the concurrence of two-thirds of the members present.

Judgment in cases of impeachment shall not extend further than to removal from the office, and disqualification to hold and enjoy any office of honor, trust or profit under the United States: but the party convicted shall nevertheless be liable and subject to indictment, trial, judgment and punishment, according to law.

Section 4 The times, places and manner of holding elections for Senators and Representatives shall be prescribed in each State by the legislature thereof; but the Congress may at any time by law make or alter such regulations, except as to the places of choosing Senators.

The Congress shall assemble at least once in every year, and such meeting *shall be on the first Monday in December, unless they shall by law appoint a different day.*

Section 5 Each house shall be the judge of the elections, returns and qualifications of its own members, and a majority of each shall constitute a quorum to do business; but a smaller number may adjourn from day to day, and may be authorized to compel the attendance of absent members, in such manner, and under such penalties, as each house may provide.

Each house may determine the rules of its proceedings, punish its members for disorderly behavior, and with the concurrence of two-thirds, expel a member.

Each house shall keep a journal of its proceedings, and from time to time publish the same, excepting such parts as may in their judgment require secrecy; and the yeas and nays of the members of either house on any question shall, at the desire of one-fifth of those present, be entered on the journal.

Neither house, during the session of Congress, shall, without the consent of the other, adjourn for more than three days, nor to any other place than that in which the two houses shall be sitting.

Section 6 The Senators and Representatives shall receive a compensation for their services, to be ascertained by law and paid out of the treasury of the United States. They shall in all cases except treason, felony and breach of the peace, be privileged from arrest during their attendance at the session of their respective houses, and in going to and returning from the same; and for any speech or debate in either house, they shall not be questioned in any other place.

No Senator or Representative shall, during the time for which he was elected, be appointed to any civil office under the authority of the United States, which shall have been created, or the emoluments whereof shall have been increased, during such time; and no person holding any office under the United States shall be a member of either house during his continuance in office.

Section 7 All bills for raising revenue shall originate in the House of Representatives; but the Senate may propose or concur with amendments as on other bills.

Every bill which shall have passed the House of Representatives and the Senate, shall, before it become a law, be presented to the President of the United States; if he approve he shall sign it, but if not he shall return it with objections to that house in which it shall have originated, who shall enter the objections at large on their journal, and proceed to reconsider it. If after such reconsideration two-thirds of that house shall agree to pass the bill, it shall be sent, together with the objections, to the other house, by which it shall likewise be reconsidered, and, if approved by two-thirds of that house, it shall become a law. But in all such cases the votes of both houses shall be determined by yeas and nays, and the names of the persons voting for and against the bill shall be entered on the journal of each house respectively. If any bill shall not be returned by the President within ten days (Sundays excepted) after it shall have been presented to him, the same shall be a law, in like manner as if he had signed it, unless the Congress by their adjournment prevent its return, in which case it shall not be a law.

Every order, resolution, or vote to which the concurrence of the Senate and House of Representatives may be necessary (except on a question of adjournment) shall be presented to the President of the United States; and before the same shall take effect, shall be approved by him, or being disapproved by him, shall be repassed by two-thirds of the Senate and House of Representatives, according to the rules and limitations prescribed in the case of a bill.

Section 8 The Congress shall have power

To lay and collect taxes, duties, imposts, and excises, to pay the debts and provide for the common defense and general welfare of the United States; but all duties, imposts and excises shall be uniform throughout the United States;

To borrow money on the credit of the United States;

To regulate commerce with foreign nations, and among the several States, and with the Indian tribes;

To establish an uniform rule of naturalization, and uniform laws on the subject of bankruptcies throughout the United States;

To coin money, regulate the value thereof, and of foreign coin, and fix the standard of weights and measures;

To provide for the punishment of counterfeiting the securities and current coin of the United States;

To establish post offices and post roads;

To promote the progress of science and useful arts by securing for limited times to authors and inventors the exclusive right to their respective writings and discoveries;

To constitute tribunals inferior to the Supreme Court;

To define and punish piracies and felonies committed on the high seas and offences against the law of nations;

To declare war, grant letters of marque and reprisal, and make rules concerning captures on land and water;

To raise and support armies, but no appropriation of money to that use shall be for a longer term than two years;

To provide and maintain a navy;

To make rules for the government and regulation of the land and naval forces;

To provide for calling forth the militia to execute the laws of the Union, suppress insurrections and repel invasions;

To provide for organizing, arming, and disciplining the militia, and for governing such part of them as may be employed in the service of the United States, reserving to the States respectively the appointment of the officers, and the authority of training the militia according to the discipline prescribed by Congress;

To exercise exclusive legislation in all cases whatsoever, over such district (not exceeding ten miles square) as may, by cession of particular States, and the acceptance of Congress, become the seat of the government of the United States, and to exercise like authority over all places purchased by the consent of the legislature of the State, in which the same shall be, for erection of forts, magazines, arsenals, dock-yards, and other needful buildings;—and

To make all laws which shall be necessary and proper for carrying into execution the foregoing powers, and all other powers vested by this Constitution in the government of the United States, or in any department or officer thereof.

Section 9 *The migration or importation of such persons as any of the States now existing shall think proper to admit shall not be prohibited by the Congress prior to the year one thousand eight hundred and eight; but a tax or duty may be imposed on such importation, not exceeding ten dollars for each person.*

The privilege of the writ of habeas corpus shall not be suspended, unless when in cases of rebellion or invasion the public safety may require it.

No bill of attainder or ex post facto law shall be passed.

No capitation, or other direct, tax shall be laid, unless in proportion to the census or enumeration herein before directed to be taken.

No tax or duty shall be laid on articles exported from any State.

No preference shall be given by any regulation of commerce or revenue to the ports of one State over those of another; nor shall vessels bound to, or from, one State be obliged to enter, clear, or pay duties in another.

No money shall be drawn from the treasury, but in consequence of appropriations made by law; and a regular statement and account of the receipts and expenditures of all public money shall be published from time to time.

No title of nobility shall be granted by the United States: and no person holding any office of profit or trust under them, shall, without the consent of the Congress, accept of any present, emolument, office, or title, of any kind whatever, from any king, prince, or foreign state.

Section 10 No State shall enter into any treaty, alliance, or confederation; grant letters of marque and reprisal; coin money; emit bills of credit; make anything but gold and silver coin a tender in payment of debts; pass any bill of attainder, ex post facto law, or law impairing the obligation of contracts, or grant any title of nobility.

No State shall, without the consent of Congress, lay any imposts or duties on imports or exports, except what may be absolutely necessary for executing its inspection laws: and the net produce of all duties and imposts, laid by any State on imports or exports, shall be for the use of the treasury of the United States; and all such laws shall be subject to the revision and control of the Congress.

No State shall, without the consent of Congress, lay any duty of tonnage, keep troops, or ships of war in time of peace, enter into any agreement or compact with another State, or with a foreign power, or engage in war, unless actually invaded, or in such imminent danger as will not admit of delay.

Article II

Section 1 The executive power shall be vested in a President of the United States of America. He shall hold his office during the term of four years, and, together with the Vice-President, chosen for the same term, be elected as follows:

Each State shall appoint, in such manner as the legislature thereof may direct, a number of electors, equal to the whole number of Senators and Representatives to which the State may be entitled in the Congress; but no Senator or Representative, or person holding an office of trust or profit under the United States, shall be appointed an elector.

The electors shall meet in their respective States, and vote by ballot for two persons, of whom one at least shall not be an inhabitant of the same State with themselves. And they shall make a list of all the persons voted for, and of the number of votes for each; which list they shall sign and certify, and transmit sealed to the seat of government of the United States, directed to the President of the Senate. The President of the Senate shall, in the presence of the Senate and House of Representatives, open all the certificates, and the votes shall then be counted. The person having the greatest number of votes shall be the President, if such number be a majority of the whole number of electors appointed; and if there be more than one who have such majority, and have an equal number of votes, then the House of Representatives shall immediately choose by ballot one of them for President; and if no person have a majority, then from the five highest on the list said house shall in like manner choose the President. But in choosing the President the votes shall be taken by States, the representation from each State having one vote; a quorum for this purpose shall consist of a member or members from two-thirds of the States, and a majority of all the States shall be necessary to a choice. In every case, after the choice of the President, the person having the greatest number of votes of the electors shall be the Vice-President. But if there should remain two or more who have equal votes, the Senate shall choose from them by ballot the Vice-President.

The Congress may determine the time of choosing the electors, and the day on which they shall give their votes; which day shall be the same throughout the United States.

No person except a natural-born citizen, *or a citizen of the United States at the time of the adoption of this Constitution,* shall be eligible to the office of President; neither shall any person be eligible to that office who shall not have attained to the age of thirty-five years, and been fourteen years a resident within the United States.

In cases of the removal of the President from office or of his death, resignation, or inability to discharge the powers and duties of the said office, the same shall devolve on the Vice-President, and the Congress may by law provide for the case of removal, death, resignation, or inability, both of the President and Vice-President, declaring what officer shall then act as President, and such officer shall act accordingly, until the disability be removed, or a President shall be elected.

The President shall, at stated times, receive for his services a compensation, which shall neither be increased nor diminished during the period for which he shall have been elected, and he shall not receive within that period any other emolument from the United States, or any of them.

Before he enter on the execution of his office, he shall take the following oath or affirmation: — "I do solemnly swear (or affirm) that I will faithfully execute the office of the President of the United States, and will to the best of my ability preserve, protect and defend the Constitution of the United States."

Section 2 The President shall be commander in chief of the army and navy of the United States, and of the militia of the several States, when called into the actual service of the United States; he may require the opinion, in writing, of the principal officer in each of the executive departments, upon any subject relating to the duties of their respective offices, and he shall have power to grant reprieves and pardons for offenses against the United States, except in cases of impeachment.

He shall have power, by and with the advice and consent of the Senate, to make treaties, provided two-thirds of the Senators present concur; and he shall nominate, and by and with the advice and consent of the Senate, shall appoint ambassadors, other public ministers and consuls, judges of the Supreme Court, and all other officers of the United States, whose appointments are not herein otherwise provided for, and which shall be established by law: but Congress may by law vest the appointment of such inferior officers, as they think proper, in the President alone, in the courts of law, or in the heads of departments.

The President shall have power to fill up all vacancies that may happen during the recess of the Senate, by granting commissions which shall expire at the end of their next session.

Section 3 He shall from time to time give to the Congress information of the state of the Union, and recommend to their consideration such measures as he shall judge necessary and expedient; he may, on extraordinary occasions, convene both houses, or either of them, and in case of disagreement between them, with respect to the time of adjournment, he may adjourn them to such time as he shall think proper; he shall receive ambassadors and other public ministers; he shall take care that the laws be faithfully executed, and shall commission all the officers of the United States.

Section 4 The President, Vice-President and all civil officers of the United States shall be removed from office on impeachment for, and on conviction of, treason, bribery, or other high crimes and misdemeanors.

Article III

Section 1 The judicial power of the United States shall be vested in one Supreme Court, and in such inferior courts as the Congress may from time to time ordain and establish. The judges, both of the Supreme and inferior courts, shall hold their offices during good behavior, and shall, at stated times, receive for their services a compensation which shall not be diminished during their continuance in office.

Section 2 The judicial power shall extend to all cases, in law and equity, arising under this Constitution, the laws of the United States, and treaties made, or which shall be made, under their authority; — to all cases affecting ambassadors, other public ministers and consuls; — to all cases of admiralty and maritime jurisdiction; — to controversies to which the United States shall be a party; — to controversies between two or more States; — between a State and citizens of another State; — *between citizens of different States*; — between citizens of the same State claiming lands under grants of different States, and between a State, or the citizens thereof, and foreign states, citizens or subjects.

In all cases affecting ambassadors, other public ministers and consuls, and those in which a State shall be party, the Supreme Court shall have original jurisdiction. In all the other cases before mentioned, the Supreme Court shall have appellate jurisdiction, both as to law and fact, with such exceptions, and under such regulations, as the Congress shall make.

The trial of all crimes, except in cases of impeachment, shall be by jury; and such trial shall be held in the State where said crimes shall have been committed; but when not committed within any State, the trial shall be at such place or places as the Congress may by Law have directed.

Section 3 Treason against the United States shall consist only in levying war against them, or in adhering to their enemies, giving them aid and comfort. No person shall be convicted of treason unless on the testimony of two witnesses to the same overt act, or on confession in open court.

The Congress shall have power to declare the punishment of treason, but no attainder of treason shall work corruption of blood, or forfeiture except during the life of the person attainted.

Article IV

Section 1 Full faith and credit shall be given in each State to the public acts, records, and judicial proceedings of every other State. And the Congress may by general laws prescribe the manner in which such acts, records, and proceedings shall be proved, and the effect thereof.

Section 2 The citizens of each State shall be entitled to all privileges and immunities of citizens in the several States.

A person charged in any State with treason, felony, or other crime, who shall flee from justice, and be found in another State, shall on demand of the executive authority of the State from which he fled, be delivered up, to be removed to the State having jurisdiction of the crime.

No Person held to service or labor in one State, under the laws thereof, escaping into another, shall, in consequence of any law or regulation therein, be discharged from such service or labor, but shall be delivered up on claim of the party to whom such service or labor may be due.

Section 3 New States may be admitted by the Congress into this Union; but no new State shall be formed or erected within the jurisdiction of any other State; nor any State be formed by the junction of two or more States, or parts of States, without the consent of the legislatures of the States concerned as well as of the Congress.

The Congress shall have power to dispose of and make all needful rules and regulations respecting the territory or other property belonging to the United States; and nothing in this Constitution shall be so construed as to prejudice any claims of the United States, or of any particular State.

Section 4 The United States shall guarantee to every State in this Union a republican form of government, and shall protect each of them against invasion; and on application of the legislature, or of the executive (when the legislature cannot be convened), against domestic violence.

Article V

The Congress, whenever two-thirds of both houses shall deem it necessary, shall propose amendments to this Constitution, or, on the application of the legislatures of two-thirds of the several States, shall call a convention for proposing amendments, which, in either case, shall be valid to all intents and purposes, as part of this Constitution, when ratified by the legislatures of three-fourths of the several States, or by conventions in three-fourths thereof, as the one or the other mode of ratification may be proposed by the Congress; provided *that no amendments which may be made prior to the year one thousand eight hundred and eight shall in any manner affect the first and fourth clauses in the ninth section of the first article; and that no State, without its consent, shall be deprived of its equal suffrage in the Senate.*

Article VI

All debts contracted and engagements entered into, before the adoption of this Constitution, shall be as valid against the United States under this Constitution, as under the Confederation.

This Constitution, and the laws of the United States which shall be made in pursuance thereof; and all treaties made, or which shall be made, under the authority of the United States, shall be the supreme law of the land; and the judges in every State shall be bound thereby, anything in the Constitution or laws of any State to the contrary notwithstanding.

The Senators and Representatives before mentioned, and the members of the several State legislatures, and all executive and judicial officers, both of the United States and of the several States, shall be bound by oath or affirmation to support this Constitution; but no religious test shall ever be required as a qualification to any office or public trust under the United States.

Article VII

The ratification of the conventions of nine States shall be sufficient for the establishment of this Constitution between the States so ratifying the same.

Done in convention by the unanimous consent of the States present, the seventeenth day of September in the year of our Lord one thousand seven hundred and eighty-seven and of the Independence of the United States of America the twelfth. In witness whereof we have hereunto subscribed our names.

GEORGE WASHINGTON
PRESIDENT AND DEPUTY FROM VIRGINIA

New Hampshire
John Langdon
Nicholas Gilman

Massachusetts
Nathaniel Gorham
Rufus King

Connecticut
William Samuel Johnson
Roger Sherman

New York
Alexander Hamilton

New Jersey
William Livingston
David Brearley

William Paterson
Jonathan Dayton

Pennsylvania
Benjamin Franklin
Thomas Mifflin
Robert Morris
George Clymer
Thomas FitzSimons
Jared Ingersoll
James Wilson
Gouverneur Morris

Delaware
George Read
Gunning Bedford, Jr.
John Dickinson

Richard Bassett
Jacob Broom

Maryland
James McHenry
Daniel of St. Thomas
   Jenifer
Daniel Carroll

Virginia
John Blair
James Madison, Jr.

North Carolina
William Blount
Richard Dobbs Spaight
Hugh Williamson

South Carolina
John Rutledge
Charles Cotesworth
   Pinckney
Charles Pinckney
Pierce Butler

Georgia
William Few
Abraham Baldwin

AMENDMENTS TO THE CONSTITUTION WITH ANNOTATIONS
(including the six unratified amendments)

Amendment I

Congress shall make no law respecting an establishment of religion, or prohibiting the free exercise thereof; or abridging the freedom of speech, or of the press; or the right of the people peaceably to assemble, and to petition the government for a redress of grievances.

Amendment II

A well-regulated militia being necessary to the security of a free State, the right of the people to keep and bear arms shall not be infringed.

Amendment III

No soldier shall, in time of peace, be quartered in any house without the consent of the owner, nor in time of war, but in a manner to be prescribed by law.

Amendment IV

The right of the people to be secure in their persons, houses, papers, and effects, against unreasonable searches and seizures, shall not be violated, and no warrants shall issue but upon probable cause, supported by oath or affirmation, and particularly describing the place to be searched, and the persons or things to be seized.

Amendment V

No person shall be held to answer for a capital, or otherwise infamous crime, unless on a presentment or indictment of a grand jury, except in cases arising in the land or naval forces, or in the militia, when in actual service in time of war or public danger; nor shall any person be subject for the same offence to be twice put in jeopardy of life or limb; nor shall be compelled in any criminal case to be a witness against himself, nor be deprived of life, liberty, or property, without due process of law; nor shall private property be taken for public use without just compensation.

Amendment VI

In all criminal prosecutions, the accused shall enjoy the right to a speedy and public trial, by an impartial jury of the State and district wherein the crime shall have been committed, which district shall have been previously ascertained by law, and to be informed of the nature and cause of the accusation; to be confronted with the witnesses against him; to have compulsory process for obtaining witnesses in his favor, and to have the assistance of counsel for his defence.

Amendment VII

In suits at common law, where the value in controversy shall exceed twenty dollars, the right of trial by jury shall be preserved, and no fact tried by a jury shall be otherwise reexamined in any court of the United States, than according to the rules of the common law.

Amendment VIII

Excessive bail shall not be required, nor excessive fines imposed, nor cruel and unusual punishments inflicted.

Amendment IX

The enumeration in the Constitution, of certain rights, shall not be construed to deny or disparage others retained by the people.

Amendment X

The powers not delegated to the United States by the Constitution, nor prohibited by it to the States, are reserved to the States respectively, or to the people.

Unratified Amendment

Reapportionment Amendment (proposed by Congress September 25, 1789, along with the Bill of Rights)

After the first enumeration required by the first article of the Constitution, there shall be one Representative for every thirty thousand, until the number shall amount to one hundred, after which the proportion shall be so regulated by Congress, that there shall be not less than one hundred Representatives, nor less than one Representative for every forty thousand persons, until the number of Representatives shall amount to two hundred; after which the proportion shall be so regulated by Congress, that there shall not be less than two hundred Representatives, nor more than one Representative for every fifty thousand persons.

Amendment XI

[Adopted 1798]

The judicial power of the United States shall not be construed to extend to any suit in law or equity, commenced or prosecuted against one of the United States by citizens of another State, or by citizens or subjects of any foreign state.

Amendment XII

[Adopted 1804]

The electors shall meet in their respective States, and vote by ballot for President and Vice-President, one of whom, at least, shall not be an inhabitant of the same State with them-selves; they shall name in their ballots the person voted for as President, and in distinct ballots the person voted for as Vice-President, and they shall make distinct lists of all persons voted for as President, and of all persons voted for as Vice-President, and of the number of votes for each, which lists they shall sign and certify, and transmit sealed to the seat of government of the United States, directed to the President of the Senate;—the President of the Senate shall, in the presence of the Senate and House of Represen-tatives, open all the certificates and the votes shall then be counted;—the person having the greatest number of votes for President shall be the President, if such number be a majority of the whole number of electors appointed; and if no person have such majority, then from the persons hav-ing the highest numbers not exceeding three on the list of those voted for as President, the House of Representatives shall choose immediately, by ballot, the President. But in choosing the President, the votes shall be taken by States, the representation from each State having one vote; a quo-rum for this purpose shall consist of a member or members from two-thirds of the States, and a majority of all the States shall be necessary to a choice. And if the House of Repre-sentatives shall not choose a President whenever the right of choice shall devolve upon them, *before the fourth day of March* next following, then the Vice-President shall act as President, as in the case of the death or other constitutional disability of the President.

The person having the greatest number of votes as Vice-President shall be the Vice-President, if such number be a majority of the whole number of electors appointed; and if no person have a majority, then from the two highest numbers on the list the Senate shall choose the Vice-President; a quorum for the purpose shall consist of two-thirds of the whole number of Senators, and a majority of the whole number shall be nec-essary to a choice. But no person constitutionally ineligible to the office of President shall be eligible to that of Vice-President of the United States.

Unratified Amendment

Titles of Nobility Amendment (proposed by Congress May 1, 1810)

If any citizen of the United States shall accept, claim, receive or retain any title of nobility or honor or shall, without the con-sent of Congress, accept and retain any present, pension, of-fice or emolument of any kind whatever, from any emperor, king, prince or foreign power, such person shall cease to be a citizen of the United States, and shall be incapable of holding any office of trust or profit under them or either of them.

Unratified Amendment

Corwin Amendment (proposed by Congress March 2, 1861)

No amendment shall be made to the Constitution which will authorize or give to Congress the power to abolish or inter-fere, within any State, with the domestic institutions thereof,

including that of persons held to labor or service by the laws of said State.

Amendment XIII

[Adopted 1865]

Section 1 Neither slavery nor involuntary servitude, except as a punishment for crime whereof the party shall have been duly convicted, shall exist within the United States, or any place subject to their jurisdiction.

Section 2 Congress shall have power to enforce this article by appropriate legislation.

Amendment XIV

[Adopted 1868]

Section 1 All persons born or naturalized in the United States, and subject to the jurisdiction thereof, are citizens of the Unit-ed States and of the State wherein they reside. No State shall make or enforce any law which shall abridge the privileges or immunities of citizens of the United States; nor shall any State deprive any person of life, liberty, or property, without due pro-cess of law; nor deny to any person within its jurisdiction the equal protection of the laws.

Section 2 Representatives shall be appointed among the several States according to their respective numbers, count-ing the whole number of persons in each State, excluding In-dians not taxed. But when the right to vote at any election for the choice of Electors for President and Vice-President of the United States, Representatives in Congress, the executive and judicial officers of a State, or the members of the legisla-ture thereof, is denied to any of the male inhabitants of such State, being twenty-one years of age and citizens of the Unit-ed States, or in any way abridged, except for participation in rebellion, or other crime, the basis of representation therein shall be reduced in the proportion which the number of such male citizens shall bear to the whole number of male citizens twenty-one years of age in such State.

Section 3 No person shall be a Senator or Representative in Congress, or Elector of President and Vice-President, or hold any office, civil or military, under the United States, or under any State, who, having previously taken an oath, as a member of Congress, or as an officer of the United States, or as a member of any State legislature, or as an executive or judicial officer of any State, to support the Constitution of the United States, shall have engaged in insurrection or rebellion against the same, or given aid or comfort to the enemies thereof. Congress may, by a vote of two-thirds of each house, remove such disability.

Section 4 The validity of the public debt of the United States, authorized by law, including debts incurred for payment of pensions and bounties for services in suppressing insurrection or rebellion, shall not be questioned. But neither the United States nor any State shall assume or pay any debt or obligation incurred in aid of insurrection or rebellion against the United States, or any claim for the loss or emancipation of any slave;

but all such debts, obligations, and claims shall be held illegal and void.

Section 5 The Congress shall have power to enforce, by appropriate legislation, the provisions of this article.

Amendment XV

[Adopted 1870]

Section 1 The right of citizens of the United States to vote shall not be denied or abridged by the United States or by any State on account of race, color, or previous condition of servitude.

Section 2 The Congress shall have power to enforce this article by appropriate legislation.

Amendment XVI

[Adopted 1913]

The Congress shall have power to lay and collect taxes on incomes, from whatever source derived, without apportionment among the several States, and without regard to any census or enumeration.

Amendment XVII

[Adopted 1913]

Section 1 The Senate of the United States shall be composed of two Senators from each State, elected by the people thereof, for six years; and each Senator shall have one vote. The electors in each State shall have the qualifications requisite for electors of [voters for] the most numerous branch of the State legislatures.

Section 2 When vacancies happen in the representation of any State in the Senate, the executive authority of such State shall issue writs of election to fill such vacancies: Provided, that the Legislature of any State may empower the executive thereof to make temporary appointments until the people fill the vacancies by election as the Legislature may direct.

Section 3 This amendment shall not be so construed as to affect the election or term of any Senator chosen before it becomes valid as part of the Constitution.

Amendment XVIII

[Adopted 1919; repealed 1933 by Amendment XXI]

Section 1 After one year from the ratification of this article the manufacture, sale, or transportation of intoxicating liquors within, the importation thereof into, or the exportation thereof from the United States and all territory subject to the jurisdiction thereof, for beverage purposes, is hereby prohibited.

Section 2 The Congress and the several States shall have concurrent power to enforce this article by appropriate legislation.

Section 3 This article shall be inoperative unless it shall have been ratified as an amendment to the Constitution by the legislatures of the several States, as provided by the Constitution, within seven years from the date of the submission thereof to the States by the Congress.

Amendment XIX

[Adopted 1920]

Section 1 The right of citizens of the United States to vote shall not be denied or abridged by the United States or by any State on account of sex.

Section 2 Congress shall have the power to enforce this article by appropriate legislation.

Unratified Amendment

Child Labor Amendment (proposed by Congress June 2, 1924)

Section 1 The Congress shall have power to limit, regulate, and prohibit the labor of persons under eighteen years of age.

Section 2 The power of the several States is unimpaired by this article except that the operation of State laws shall be suspended to the extent necessary to give effect to legislation enacted by Congress.

Amendment XX

[Adopted 1933]

Section 1 The terms of the President and Vice-President shall end at noon on the 20th day of January, and the terms of Senators and Representatives at noon on the 3rd day of January, of the years in which such terms would have ended if this article had not been ratified; and the terms of their successors shall then begin.

Section 2 The Congress shall assemble at least once in every year, and such meeting shall begin at noon on the 3rd day of January, unless they shall by law appoint a different day.

Section 3 If, at the time fixed for the beginning of the term of the President, the President-elect shall have died, the Vice-President-elect shall become President. If a President shall not have been chosen before the time fixed for the beginning of his term, or if the President-elect shall have failed to qualify, then the Vice-President-elect shall act as President until a President shall have qualified; and the Congress may by law provide for the case wherein neither a President-elect nor a Vice-President-elect shall have qualified, declaring who shall then act as President, or the manner in which one who is to act shall be selected, and such person shall act accordingly until a President or Vice-President shall have qualified.

Section 4 The Congress may by law provide for the case of the death of any of the persons from whom the House of Representatives may choose a President whenever the right of choice shall have devolved upon them, and for the case of the death of any of the persons from whom the Senate may choose a Vice-President whenever the right of choice shall have devolved upon them.

Section 5 Sections 1 and 2 shall take effect on the 15th day of October following the ratification of this article.

Section 6 This article shall be inoperative unless it shall have been ratified as an amendment to the Constitution by the Legislatures of three-fourths of the several States within seven years from the date of its submission.

Amendment XXI

[Adopted 1933]

Section 1 The eighteenth article of amendment to the Constitution of the United States is hereby repealed.

Section 2 The transportation or importation into any State, Territory, or Possession of the United States for delivery or use therein of intoxicating liquors, in violation of the laws thereof, is hereby prohibited.

Section 3 This article shall be inoperative unless it shall have been ratified as an amendment to the Constitution by conventions in the several States, as provided in the Constitution, within seven years from the date of the submission thereof to the States by the Congress.

Amendment XXII

[Adopted 1951]

Section 1 No person shall be elected to the office of the President more than twice, and no person who has held the office of President, or acted as President, for more than two years of a term to which some other person was elected President shall be elected to the office of President more than once. But this article shall not apply to any person holding the office of President when this Article was proposed by the Congress, and shall not prevent any person who may be holding the office of President, or acting as President, during the term within which this Article becomes operative from holding the office of President or acting as President during the remainder of such term.

Section 2 This article shall be inoperative unless it shall have been ratified as an amendment to the Constitution by the legislatures of three-fourths of the several States within seven years from the date of its submission to the States by the Congress.

Amendment XXIII

[Adopted 1961]

Section 1 The District constituting the seat of Government of the United States shall appoint in such manner as the Congress may direct: A number of electors of President and Vice-President equal to the whole number of Senators and Representatives in Congress to which the District would be entitled if it were a State, but in no event more than the least populous State; they shall be in addition to those appointed by the States, but they shall be considered for the purposes of the election of President and Vice-President, to be electors appointed by a State; and they shall meet in the District

and perform such duties as provided by the twelfth article of amendment.

Section 2 The Congress shall have the power to enforce this article by appropriate legislation.

Amendment XXIV

[Adopted 1964]

Section 1 The right of citizens of the United States to vote in any primary or other election for President or Vice-President, for electors for President or Vice-President, or for Senator or Representative in Congress, shall not be denied or abridged by the United States or any State by reason of failure to pay any poll tax or other tax.

Amendment XXV

[Adopted 1967]

Section 1 In case of the removal of the President from office or of his death or resignation, the Vice-President shall become President.

Section 2 Whenever there is a vacancy in the office of the Vice-President, the President shall nominate a Vice-President who shall take office upon confirmation by a majority vote of both Houses of Congress.

Section 3 Whenever the President transmits to the President pro tempore of the Senate and the Speaker of the House of Representatives his written declaration that he is unable to discharge the powers and duties of his office, and until he transmits to them a written declaration to the contrary, such powers and duties shall be discharged by the Vice-President as Acting President.

Section 4 Whenever the Vice-President and a majority of either the principal officers of the executive departments or of such other body as Congress may by law provide, transmit to the President pro tempore of the Senate and the Speaker of the House of Representatives their written declaration that the President is unable to discharge the powers and duties of his office, the Vice-President shall immediately assume the powers and duties of the office as Acting President.

Thereafter, when the President transmits to the President pro tempore of the Senate and the Speaker of the House of Representatives his written declaration that no inability exists, he shall resume the powers and duties of his office unless the Vice-President and a majority of either the principal officers of the executive department[s] or of such other body as Congress may by law provide, transmit within four days to the President pro tempore of the Senate and the Speaker of the House of Representatives their written declaration that the President is unable to discharge the powers and duties of his office. Thereupon Congress shall decide the issue, assembling within forty-eight hours for that purpose if not in session. If the Congress, within twenty-one days after receipt of the latter written declaration, or, if Congress is not in session, within twenty-one days after

Congress is required to assemble, determines by two-thirds vote of both Houses that the President is unable to discharge the powers and duties of his office, the Vice-President shall continue to discharge the same as Acting President; otherwise, the President shall resume the powers and duties of his office.

Amendment XXVI

[Adopted 1971]

Section 1 The right of citizens of the United States, who are eighteen years of age or older, to vote shall not be denied or abridged by the United States or by any State on account of age.

Section 2 The Congress shall have power to enforce this article by appropriate legislation.

Unratified Amendment

Equal Rights Amendment (proposed by Congress March 22, 1972; seven-year deadline for ratification extended to June 30, 1982)

Section 1 Equality of rights under the law shall not be denied or abridged by the United States or by any State on account of sex.

Section 2 The Congress shall have the power to enforce, by appropriate legislation, the provisions of this article.

Section 3 This amendment shall take effect two years after the date of ratification.

Unratified Amendment

D.C. Statehood Amendment (proposed by Congress August 22, 1978)

Section 1 For purposes of representation in the Congress, election of the President and Vice-President, and article V of this Constitution, the District constituting the seat of government of the United States shall be treated as though it were a State.

Section 2 The exercise of the rights and powers conferred under this article shall be by the people of the District constituting the seat of government, and as shall be provided by Congress.

Section 3 The twenty-third article of amendment to the Constitution of the United States is hereby repealed.

Section 4 This article shall be inoperative, unless it shall have been ratified as an amendment to the Constitution by the legislatures of three-fourths of the several states within seven years from the date of its submission.

Amendment XXVII

[Adopted 1992]

No law, varying the compensation for the services of the Senators and Representatives, shall take effect, until an election of Representatives shall have intervened.

U.S. POLITICS AND GOVERNMENT

PRESIDENTIAL ELECTIONS

Year	Candidates	Parties	Popular Vote	Percentage of Popular Vote	Electoral Vote	Percentage of Voter Participation
1789	GEORGE WASHINGTON (Va.)*				69	
	John Adams				34	
	Others				35	
1792	GEORGE WASHINGTON (Va.)				132	
	John Adams				77	
	George Clinton				50	
	Others				5	
1796	JOHN ADAMS (Mass.)	Federalist			71	
	Thomas Jefferson	Democratic-Republican			68	
	Thomas Pinckney	Federalist			59	
	Aaron Burr	Dem.-Rep.			30	
	Others	—			48	
1800	THOMAS JEFFERSON (Va.)	Dem.-Rep.			73	
	Aaron Burr	Dem.-Rep.			73	
	John Adams	Federalist			65	
	C. C. Pinckney	Federalist			64	
	John Jay	Federalist			1	
1804	THOMAS JEFFERSON (Va.)	Dem.-Rep.			162	
	C. C. Pinckney	Federalist			14	
1808	JAMES MADISON (Va.)	Dem.-Rep.			122	
	C. C. Pinckney	Federalist			47	
	George Clinton	Dem.-Rep.			6	
1812	JAMES MADISON (Va.)	Dem.-Rep.			128	
	De Witt Clinton	Federalist			89	
1816	JAMES MONROE (Va.)	Dem.-Rep.			183	
	Rufus King	Federalist			34	
1820	JAMES MONROE (Va.)	Dem.-Rep.			231	
	John Quincy Adams	Dem.-Rep.			1	

*State of residence when elected president.

Year	Candidates	Parties	Popular Vote	Percentage of Popular Vote	Electoral Vote	Percentage of Voter Participation
1824	JOHN Q. ADAMS (Mass.)	Dem.-Rep.	108,740	30.5	84	26.9
	Andrew Jackson	Dem.-Rep.	153,544	43.1	99	
	William H. Crawford	Dem.-Rep.	46,618	13.1	41	
	Henry Clay	Dem.-Rep.	47,136	13.2	37	
1828	ANDREW JACKSON (Tenn.)	Democratic	647,286	56.0	178	57.6
	John Quincy Adams	National Republican	508,064	44.0	83	
1832	ANDREW JACKSON (Tenn.)	Democratic	687,502	55.0	219	55.4
	Henry Clay	National Republican	530,189	42.4	49	
	John Floyd	Independent			11	
	William Wirt	Anti-Mason	33,108	2.6	7	
1836	MARTIN VAN BUREN (N.Y.)	Democratic	765,483	50.9	170	57.8
	W. H. Harrison	Whig			73	
	Hugh L. White	Whig	739,795	49.1	26	
	Daniel Webster	Whig			14	
	W. P. Mangum	Independent			11	
1840	WILLIAM H. HARRISON (Ohio)	Whig	1,274,624	53.1	234	78.0
	Martin Van Buren	Democratic	1,127,781	46.9	60	
	J. G. Birney	Liberty	7,069		—	
1844	JAMES K. POLK (Tenn.)	Democratic	1,338,464	49.6	170	78.9
	Henry Clay	Whig	1,300,097	48.1	105	
	J. G. Birney	Liberty	62,300	2.3	—	
1848	ZACHARY TAYLOR (La.)	Whig	1,360,099	47.4	163	72.7
	Lewis Cass	Democratic	1,220,544	42.5	127	
	Martin Van Buren	Free-Soil	291,263	10.1	—	
1852	FRANKLIN PIERCE (N.H.)	Democratic	1,601,117	50.9	254	69.6
	Winfield Scott	Whig	1,385,453	44.1	42	
	John P. Hale	Free-Soil	155,825	5.0	—	
1856	JAMES BUCHANAN (Pa.)	Democratic	1,832,995	45.3	174	78.9
	John C. Frémont	Republican	1,339,932	33.1	114	
	Millard Fillmore	American	871,731	21.6	8	
1860	ABRAHAM LINCOLN (Ill.)	Republican	1,866,452	39.8	180	81.2
	Stephen A. Douglas	Democratic	1,375,157	29.4	12	
	John C. Breckinridge	Democratic	847,953	18.1	72	
	John Bell	Union	590,631	12.6	39	
1864	ABRAHAM LINCOLN (Ill.)	Republican	2,213,665	55.1	212	73.8
	George B. McClellan	Democratic	1,805,237	44.9	21	
1868	ULYSSES S. GRANT (Ill.)	Republican	3,012,833	52.7	214	78.1
	Horatio Seymour	Democratic	2,703,249	47.3	80	

Year	Candidates	Parties	Popular Vote	Percentage of Popular Vote	Electoral Vote	Percentage of Voter Participation
1872	ULYSSES S. GRANT (Ill.)	Republican	3,597,132	55.6	286	71.3
	Horace Greeley	Democratic; Liberal Republican	2,834,125	43.9	66	
1876	RUTHERFORD B. HAYES (Ohio)	Republican	4,036,298	48.0	185	81.8
	Samuel J. Tilden	Democratic	4,288,590	51.0	184	
1880	JAMES A. GARFIELD (Ohio)	Republican	4,454,416	48.5	214	79.4
	Winfield S. Hancock	Democratic	4,444,952	48.1	155	
1884	GROVER CLEVELAND (N.Y.)	Democratic	4,874,986	48.5	219	77.5
	James G. Blaine	Republican	4,851,981	48.3	182	
1888	BENJAMIN HARRISON (Ind.)	Republican	5,439,853	47.9	233	79.3
	Grover Cleveland	Democratic	5,540,309	48.6	168	
1892	GROVER CLEVELAND (N.Y.)	Democratic	5,555,426	46.1	277	74.7
	Benjamin Harrison	Republican	5,182,690	43.0	145	
	James B. Weaver	People's	1,029,846	8.5	22	
1896	WILLIAM McKINLEY (Ohio)	Republican	7,104,779	51.1	271	79.3
	William J. Bryan	Democratic-People's	6,502,925	47.7	176	
1900	WILLIAM McKINLEY (Ohio)	Republican	7,207,923	51.7	292	73.2
	William J. Bryan	Dem.-Populist	6,358,133	45.5	155	
1904	THEODORE ROOSEVELT (N.Y.)	Republican	7,623,486	57.9	336	65.2
	Alton B. Parker	Democratic	5,077,911	37.6	140	
	Eugene V. Debs	Socialist	402,283	3.0	—	
1908	WILLIAM H. TAFT (Ohio)	Republican	7,678,908	51.6	321	65.4
	William J. Bryan	Democratic	6,409,104	43.1	162	
	Eugene V. Debs	Socialist	420,793	2.8	—	
1912	WOODROW WILSON (N.J.)	Democratic	6,293,454	41.9	435	58.8
	Theodore Roosevelt	Progressive	4,119,538	27.4	88	
	William H. Taft	Republican	3,484,980	23.2	8	
	Eugene V. Debs	Socialist	900,672	6.1	—	
1916	WOODROW WILSON (N.J.)	Democratic	9,129,606	49.4	277	61.6
	Charles E. Hughes	Republican	8,538,221	46.2	254	
	A. L. Benson	Socialist	585,113	3.2	—	
1920	WARREN G. HARDING (Ohio)	Republican	16,143,407	60.5	404	49.2
	James M. Cox	Democratic	9,130,328	34.2	127	
	Eugene V. Debs	Socialist	919,799	3.4	—	
1924	CALVIN COOLIDGE (Mass.)	Republican	15,725,016	54.0	382	48.9
	John W. Davis	Democratic	8,386,503	28.8	136	
	Robert M. La Follette	Progressive	4,822,856	16.6	13	

Year	Candidates	Parties	Popular Vote	Percentage of Popular Vote	Electoral Vote	Percentage of Voter Participation
1928	HERBERT HOOVER (Calif.)	Republican	21,391,381	57.4	444	56.9
	Alfred E. Smith	Democratic	15,016,443	40.3	87	
	Norman Thomas	Socialist	881,951	2.3	—	
	William Z. Foster	Communist	102,991	0.3	—	
1932	FRANKLIN D. ROOSEVELT (N.Y.)	Democratic	22,821,857	57.4	472	56.9
	Herbert Hoover	Republican	15,761,841	39.7	59	
	Norman Thomas	Socialist	881,951	2.2	—	
1936	FRANKLIN D. ROOSEVELT (N.Y.)	Democratic	27,751,597	60.8	523	61.0
	Alfred M. Landon	Republican	16,679,583	36.5	8	
	William Lemke	Union	882,479	1.9	—	
1940	FRANKLIN D. ROOSEVELT (N.Y.)	Democratic	27,244,160	54.8	449	62.5
	Wendell Willkie	Republican	22,305,198	44.8	82	
1944	FRANKLIN D. ROOSEVELT (N.Y.)	Democratic	25,602,504	53.5	432	55.9
	Thomas E. Dewey	Republican	22,006,285	46.0	99	
1948	HARRY S. TRUMAN (Mo.)	Democratic	24,105,695	49.5	303	53.0
	Thomas E. Dewey	Republican	21,969,170	45.1	189	
	J. Strom Thurmond	States'-Rights Democratic	1,169,021	2.4	38	
	Henry A. Wallace	Progressive	1,156,103	2.4	—	
1952	DWIGHT D. EISENHOWER (N.Y.)	Republican	33,936,252	55.1	442	63.3
	Adlai Stevenson	Democratic	27,314,992	44.4	89	
1956	DWIGHT D. EISENHOWER (N.Y.)	Republican	35,575,420	57.6	457	60.6
	Adlai Stevenson	Democratic	26,033,066	42.1	73	
	Other	—	—		1	
1960	JOHN F. KENNEDY (Mass.)	Democratic	34,227,096	49.9	303	62.8
	Richard M. Nixon	Republican	34,108,546	49.6	219	
	Other	—	—		15	
1964	LYNDON B. JOHNSON (Tex.)	Democratic	43,126,506	61.1	486	61.7
	Barry M. Goldwater	Republican	27,176,799	38.5	52	
1968	RICHARD M. NIXON (N.Y.)	Republican	31,770,237	43.4	301	60.9
	Hubert H. Humphrey	Democratic	31,270,533	42.7	191	
	George Wallace	American Indep.	9,906,141	13.5	46	
1972	RICHARD M. NIXON (N.Y.)	Republican	47,169,911	60.7	520	55.2
	George S. McGovern	Democratic	29,170,383	37.5	17	
	Other	—	—		1	
1976	JIMMY CARTER (Ga.)	Democratic	40,830,763	50.0	297	53.5
	Gerald R. Ford	Republican	39,147,793	48.0	240	
	Other	—	1,575,459	2.1	—	

Year	Candidates	Parties	Popular Vote	Percentage of Popular Vote	Electoral Vote	Percentage of Voter Participation
1980	RONALD REAGAN (Calif.)	Republican	43,901,812	51.0	489	54.0
	Jimmy Carter	Democratic	35,483,820	41.0	49	
	John B. Anderson	Independent	5,719,722	7.0	—	
	Ed Clark	Libertarian	921,188	1.1	—	
1984	RONALD REAGAN (Calif.)	Republican	54,455,075	59.0	525	53.1
	Walter Mondale	Democratic	37,577,185	41.0	13	
1988	GEORGE H. W. BUSH (Tex.)	Republican	47,946,422	54.0	426	50.2
	Michael S. Dukakis	Democratic	41,016,429	46.0	112	
1992	WILLIAM J. CLINTON (Ark.)	Democratic	44,908,254	43.0	370	55.9
	George H. W. Bush	Republican	39,102,282	38.0	168	
	H. Ross Perot	Independent	19,721,433	19.0	—	
1996	WILLIAM J. CLINTON (Ark.)	Democratic	47,401,185	49.2	379	49.0
	Robert Dole	Republican	39,197,469	40.7	159	
	H. Ross Perot	Independent	8,085,294	8.4	—	
2000	GEORGE W. BUSH (Tex.)	Republican	50,456,062	47.8	271	51.2
	Al Gore	Democratic	50,996,862	48.4	267	
	Ralph Nader	Green Party	2,858,843	2.7	—	
	Patrick J. Buchanan	—	438,760	0.4	—	
2004	GEORGE W. BUSH (Tex.)	Republican	61,872,711	50.7	286	60.3
	John F. Kerry	Democratic	58,894,584	48.3	252	
	Other	—	1,582,185	1.3	—	
2008	BARACK OBAMA (Ill.)	Democratic	69,456,897	52.9	365	56.8
	John McCain	Republican	59,934,314	45.7	173	
2012	BARACK OBAMA (Ill.)	Democratic	65,909,451	51.02	332	58
	Willard Mitt Romney	Republican	60,932,176	47.16	152	
	Other	—	2,350,895	1.82	—	

ADMISSION OF STATES TO THE UNION

State	Date of Admission	State	Date of Admission
Delaware	December 7, 1787	Virginia	June 25, 1788
Pennsylvania	December 12, 1787	New York	July 26, 1788
New Jersey	December 18, 1787	North Carolina	November 21, 1789
Georgia	January 2, 1788	Rhode Island	May 29, 1790
Connecticut	January 9, 1788	Vermont	March 4, 1791
Massachusetts	February 6, 1788	Kentucky	June 1, 1792
Maryland	April 28, 1788	Tennessee	June 1, 1796
South Carolina	May 23, 1788	Ohio	March 1, 1803
New Hampshire	June 21, 1788	Louisiana	April 30, 1812

State	Date of Admission	State	Date of Admission
Indiana	December 11, 1816	West Virginia	June 19, 1863
Mississippi	December 10, 1817	Nevada	October 31, 1864
Illinois	December 3, 1818	Nebraska	March 1, 1867
Alabama	December 14, 1819	Colorado	August 1, 1876
Maine	March 15, 1820	North Dakota	November 2, 1889
Missouri	August 10, 1821	South Dakota	November 2, 1889
Arkansas	June 15, 1836	Montana	November 8, 1889
Michigan	January 16, 1837	Washington	November 11, 1889
Florida	March 3, 1845	Idaho	July 3, 1890
Texas	December 29, 1845	Wyoming	July 10, 1890
Iowa	December 28, 1846	Utah	January 4, 1896
Wisconsin	May 29, 1848	Oklahoma	November 16, 1907
California	September 9, 1850	New Mexico	January 6, 1912
Minnesota	May 11, 1858	Arizona	February 14, 1912
Oregon	February 14, 1859	Alaska	January 3, 1959
Kansas	January 29, 1861	Hawaii	August 21, 1959

INDEX

Hurston, Zora Neale, 690
Hussein (Jordan), 946
Hussein, Saddam, 932, 933–934, 955–956
Hydroelectricity, New Deal programs for, 720

ICBMs. *See* Intercontinental ballistic
    missiles
Idaho
    mining in, 500, 501(m)
    voting rights for women in, 592(i)
"I have a dream" speech (King), 845
Illegal immigrants, 820–821, 948
Illinois, Ku Klux Klan in, 694
Illness. *See* Disease
Illustrated Weekly, 586(i)
Immigrants and immigration. *See also*
    Migration
    in American Communist Party, 725
    anti-immigrant sentiment and, 502,
        693–694, 696
    Asian, 502, 504–505, 505(i), 553
    cities and, 548–552, 548(i), 692
    as domestic servants, 567
    education for, 570
    European, 548, 550–552, 550(m), 551(f),
        553–554
    globalization and, 947
    global migration, urbanization, and,
        548–552, 549(m)
    Hispanic, 733
    McCarran-Walter Act and, 795
    Mexican, 671–672, 671(i)
    mining and, 502
    old and new immigration, 552
    progressive social work and, 611(i)
    quotas on, 693–694, 695, 795
    racial composition of, 948–949
    racism and, 552–554
    restrictions on, 504–505, 554, 692,
        693–694, 695
    sentiment against, 954
    travel by, 551
    voting and, 687
Immigration and Nationality Act (1965),
    840, 947–948
Impeachment
    of Clinton, 938, 941–942
    of Johnson, A., 468–469, 942
    of Nixon, 902
Imperialism, 488
    cultural, 494–496, 495(i)
    debate over, 604–606, 605(m)
    First World War and, 648, 665
    Indians and, 488–489, 494–496, 495(i)
    in West, 488–496, 495(i)
Imperial presidency, 902
Imports, tariffs and, 599, 599(f)
Inauguration
    of Eisenhower, 811
    of Hoover, 679
    of Kennedy, 837, 870–871
    of Reagan, 897(i)
    of Roosevelt, T., 498
Incandescent light bulb, 525
Income. *See also* Wages
    in 1920s, 683, 684, 698–699
    in 1950s, 822
    of African Americans, 764, 943
    agricultural, 703(f)

of Latinos, 943
    manufacturing, 703(f)
    national, 702
    redistribution of, 841
    rise in per capita, 683
    Social Security as, 731
    of whites, 943
Income tax, 731
    Sixteenth Amendment and, 630
    state, 618
Independent magazine, 557, 563
India
    atomic bomb and, 936
    England and, 787
    railroads in, 520(f)
    in Second World War, 753
Indian(s). *See* Native Americans
Indiana
    Ku Klux Klan in, 694
    prohibition in, 686
Indian Citizen Day (1892), 495(i)
Indian Citizenship Act (1924), 694
Indian Claims Commission (1946), 809
Indian country. *See* Indian Territory;
    Oklahoma; West
Indian policy. *See also* Native Americans
    allotment as, 494, 496
    assimilation as, 494–496, 495(i)
    removal of, 488–490
    reservations and, 488–490, 497
Indian Relocation Program (1948), 809
Indian Reorganization Act (1934), 733
Indian Rights Association, 496
Indian Territory, 489(i), 490–493, 496–499
Indian wars, in West, 489, 491–493
Indies. *See* East Indies
Indigenous people. *See* Native Americans
Individualism
    limits on, 700–701
    Nixon on, 898
Indochina, 800. *See also* Cambodia; Laos;
    Vietnam
Indonesia. *See* East Indies
Industrial core (global economic region),
    549, 549(m)
Industrial cowboys, 511–512
Industrialism
    bison herds and, 491
    urban, 500
    western commercial farming and,
        510–512, 511(f), 512(i)
    women activists and, 591
Industrial Workers of the World (IWW),
    637, 668, 669
Industry
    bison slaughter and, 491
    in First World War, 657–658, 657(f)
    in Gilded Age, 518–524, 518(i), 522(f),
        538–540, 543
    globalization and, 947
    Great Depression and, 700–701
    heavy, 818
    New Deal and, 721–722
    production by, 818
    in Second World War, 762–763
    service, 917
    technology and, 818
Inequality. *See also* Equality
    social Darwinism and, 527–528
    wealth and, 698–699

Infant Welfare Society, 611(i)
Inflation. *See also* Economy; Stagflation
    in 1990s, 942
    Carter and, 906
    after First World War, 668
    Nixon and, 862
    in Second World War, 763
    after Second World War, 790
Influenza. *See* Spanish influenza epidemic
Inheritance, tax on, 731, 915
In His Steps (Sheldon), 614
Initiative, 618, 619
Installment buying, 684, 823
Insurance, national health, 906, 952
Integration. *See also* Segregation
    Freedom Rides and, 845(m)
    in Little Rock, 828
    of public schools, 828, 829(i), 900
    after Second World War, 792
Intellectual thought. *See* Education;
    Literature; specific individuals
Intelligence agencies, 786(i), 903–904. *See
    also* Central Intelligence Agency;
    Federal Bureau of Investigation
Intercontinental ballistic missiles (ICBMs),
    815
Interlocking directorates, 634
*Intermediate-range nuclear forces (INF)
    agreement, 924*
International Criminal Court (UN), 955
Internationalism
    of Roosevelt, F. D., 745
    after Second World War, 770
    of Wilson, 680
Internationalization, of United States,
    947–949
International Ladies' Garment Workers
    Union (ILGWU), 615
International Monetary Fund, 947
Internment camps, for Japanese
    Americans, *756,* 756(m)
*Interstate Commerce Commission (ICC),
    540,* 622–623
*Interstate Highway and Defense System
    Act* (1956), *807*–808, 807(m), 819. *See
    also* Roads and highways
Intervention and interventionism
    in Afghanistan, 959
    in Beirut, 922(i)
    by CIA, 787
    in Grenada, 922
    in Haiti, 944, 945
    in Latin America, 813–814, 872, 876,
        932
    in Second World War, 748
Inventions and inventors. *See also*
    Electricity; specific inventors and
    inventions
    from 1865–1899, 524(f)
Investment
    foreign, in United States, 947
    after Second World War, 781
    in United States by China, 952
Iran. *See also* Iran hostage crisis
    CIA and, 814
    Hezbollah and, 922
    Nixon administration and, 888
    nuclear weapons and, 957
    revolution in (1979), 907, 907(i), 911
    Soviet Union and, 781

About the Authors

James L. Roark (Ph.D., Stanford University) is Samuel Candler Dobbs Professor of American History at Emory University. In 1993, he received the Emory Williams Distinguished Teaching Award, and in 2001–2002 he was Pitt Professor of American Institutions at Cambridge University. He has written *Masters without Slaves: Southern Planters in the Civil War and Reconstruction* and coauthored *Black Masters: A Free Family of Color in the Old South* with Michael P. Johnson.

Michael P. Johnson (Ph.D., Stanford University) is professor of history at Johns Hopkins University. His publications include *Toward a Patriarchal Republic: The Secession of Georgia*; *Abraham Lincoln, Slavery, and the Civil War: Selected Speeches and Writings*; and *Reading the American Past: Selected Historical Documents*, the documents reader for *The American Promise*. He has also coedited *No Chariot Let Down: Charleston's Free People of Color on the Eve of the Civil War* with James L. Roark.

Patricia Cline Cohen (Ph.D., University of California, Berkeley) is professor of history at the University of California, Santa Barbara, where she received the Distinguished Teaching Award in 2005–2006. She has written *A Calculating People: The Spread of Numeracy in Early America* and *The Murder of Helen Jewett: The Life and Death of a Prostitute in Nineteenth-Century New York*, and she has coauthored *The Flash Press: Sporting Male Weeklies in 1840s New York*.

Sarah Stage (Ph.D., Yale University) has taught U.S. history at Williams College and the University of California, Riverside, and she was visiting professor at Beijing University and Szechuan University. Currently she is professor of Women's Studies at Arizona State University. Her books include *Female Complaints: Lydia Pinkham and the Business of Women's Medicine* and *Rethinking Home Economics: Women and the History of a Profession*.

Susan M. Hartmann (Ph.D., University of Missouri) is Arts and Humanities Distinguished Professor of History at Ohio State University. In 1995 she won the university's Exemplary Faculty Award in the College of Humanities. Her publications include *Truman and the 80th Congress*; *The Home Front and Beyond: American Women in the 1940s*; *From Margin to Mainstream: American Women and Politics since 1960*; and *The Other Feminists: Activists in the Liberal Establishment*.